The King of Inventors

By the same author

Thackeray's Universe

The King of Inventors

A Life of Wilkie Collins

CATHERINE PETERS

Princeton University Press
Princeton, New Jersey

Originally published by Secker and Warburg, Limited;
first published in the United States of America,
with corrections,
by Princeton University Press, 41 William Street,
Princeton, New Jersey 08540

Library of Congress Cataloging-in-Publication Data
Peters, Catherine.
The king of inventors: a life of Wilkie Collins / Catherine Peters.
p. cm.
Originally published: London: Secker & Warburg, ©1991. With new appendix.
Includes bibliographical references (p.) and index.
ISBN 0-691-03392-7 (alk. paper)
1. Collins, Wilkie, 1824–1889—Biography. 2. Novelists, English—19th century—Biography. I. Title.
PR4496.P48 1993
823'.8—dc20
[B] 93-15824

Princeton University Press books are printed on acid-free paper and meet the guidelines for permanence and durability of the Committee on Production Guidelines for Book Longevity of the Council on Library Resources

3 5 7 9 10 8 6 4 2

Printed in the United States of America

To
Matthew, Robert and William
and in memory of Thomas

CONTENTS

ILLUSTRATIONS

ACKNOWLEDGEMENTS

This book could never have been completed without the help of many institutions and individuals. I am particularly grateful for travel grants from the British Academy and the Leverhulme Trust, which enabled me to carry out preliminary research in American libraries, and for two terms' leave from teaching and a research grant from Somerville College, Oxford.

I am greatly indebted to the copyright owners who have given me permission to publish unpublished material. Mrs Faith Clarke (née Dawson), the great-granddaughter of Wilkie Collins and Martha Rudd, has allowed me to quote copiously from his unpublished letters, and to reproduce photographs in her possession. Timothy Iredale, the great-grandson of Harriet Bartley, has kindly given permission for quotations from her letters; Sir Ralph Millais, permission to quote from a partly unpublished letter by Sir John Everett Millais; and the editors of the Pilgrim edition of the letters of Charles Dickens, permission to quote from Dickens' unpublished letters.

For permission to quote from material in their collections I am indebted to the following individuals and institutions: the Armstrong Browning Library, Baylor University, Waco, Texas; the British Library, Manuscript Library; the Dickens House Museum; the Fales Library, New York University; the Folger Shakespeare Library, Washington, DC; Andrew Gasson; Glasgow City Council Libraries Department; the Houghton Library, Harvard University; Harry Ransom Humanities Research Center, University of Texas at Austin; Henry E. Huntington Library, San Marino, California; University of Illinois at Urbana, Rare Book Room; University of Iowa Libraries; New York Public Library, Berg and Arents

Collections; Professor Norman Page; Pierpont Morgan Library, New York; Princeton University Libraries; the Board of Trustees of the Victoria & Albert Museum.

I have received unstinting help from the librarians and staff of the above institutions, and also from those of the Bodleian Library, Oxford; the British Library Newspaper Library; Eastbourne Public Library; Kent County Libraries; the National Library of Scotland; the Public Record Office, London; the Scottish Record Office, Edinburgh; the Society of Genealogists; Georgetown University, Washington, DC; State Library of Victoria, New South Wales, Australia; City of Dunedin Public Library, New Zealand.

Many other people have helped with the book, through their own writings, published and unpublished, and in correspondence and personal discussions which have often thrown an entirely new light on a problem. I should particularly like to mention Professor John Batchelor; Kirk Beetz, founder and president of the Wilkie Collins Society, and editor of its *Journal*; Mark Haworth Booth; Peter Caracciolo; William M. Clarke and Faith Clarke, who have been unfailingly generous and encouraging; Dr Ruth Deech; Andrew Gasson, secretary of the Wilkie Collins Society, whose unrivalled bibliographical knowledge helped solve many problems; Christina Hardyment; Professor Francis Haskell; Sara Hodson at the Huntington Library, who dealt enthusiastically with my graphological and other queries; Claire Hudson of the Theatre Museum, Covent Garden; Winifred Hughes; Diana Holman Hunt; Sir John Lawrence; the late John Lehmann; Dr Roger Lonsdale; Dr Irvine Loudon, whose knowledge of nineteenth-century medicine proved invaluable, and to whom I am indebted for the footnote on p. 327; Dr David Parker and Andrew Bean of the Dickens House Museum; John Pym; Eric Quayle; Graham Storey; Reg and Judith Terry, who organized a stimulating Wilkie Collins Centenary Conference at the University of Victoria, British Columbia; Claire Tomalin; and Alexander Wainwright. Anthony Storr read the manuscript and made valuable suggestions, and, as always, provided support and reassurance. My editor Dan Franklin has been both helpful and rigorous, and Vicki Harris has gone through the text in scrupulous detail. Douglas Matthews of the London Library compiled the index with skill and care. The help of others, who prefer not to be named, is also remembered with gratitude.

Much of the research for the book was completed before the publication of William M. Clarke's *The Secret Life of Wilkie Collins*. It was fascinating to see how we had, often by slightly different routes, come to similar conclusions. I had, for example, already traced the background of Caroline Graves and Martha Rudd. In the many instances where I am indebted to his book (for example in his references to Wilkie Collins' bank account, or the later history of Martha and her children), specific acknowledgements are made in the References.

Oxford, 1991

ONE

Families

(1788–1822)

All his life, Wilkie Collins was haunted by a second self. When he was a young man he told Percy Fitzgerald, on their first meeting, 'how he was subject to a curious ghostly influence, having often the idea that "someone was standing behind him" and that he was tempted to look round constantly'.[1] In old age, suffering from painful illnesses and addicted to opium, this experience became not merely uncanny, but terrifying. When he worked late into the night, another Wilkie Collins appeared: '. . . the second Wilkie Collins sat at the same table with him and tried to monopolise the writing pad. Then there was a struggle . . . when the true Wilkie awoke, the inkstand had been upset and the ink was running over the writing table. After that Wilkie Collins gave up writing of nights.'[2]

A laudanum fantasy? No doubt. But, as De Quincey wrote, 'If a man "whose talk is of oxen," should become an Opium-eater, the probability is, that (if he is not too dull to dream at all) – he will dream about oxen'.[3] If a man who is preoccupied in his writing and his life with double identity becomes an opium eater, his dreams will be of a double. This was a late appearance – one of many – of the double in Wilkie Collins' life and work.

There is a question of identity at the heart of every one of his novels, from *Antonina*, which he started to write when he was twenty-two, to *Blind Love*, left unfinished at his death. The form of this question varies from book to book, but it recurs so insistently as to suggest that their author was troubled as well as intrigued by it. Doubles are often, though not always, involved. Sometimes a character has her identity forcibly taken from her, and one 'the same but different' substituted, as happens to Laura Fairlie in *The Woman in White*. Something similar happens to Magdalen Vanstone, when she discovers that she has 'No Name' in the eyes of the law. She then deliberately jumps into other skins, to serve her own interests. Characters in other novels deliberately conceal their true identities, or assume the identities of others. Sometimes identity is put in question by the loss of a physical sense: sight, or hearing, or speech. Sometimes physical deformity threatens a character's identity in the eyes of others. Madness, drugs and dreams permanently or temporarily interfere with the full possession of the self, and bring hidden personalities to the surface. However the question comes up, it is insistent and powerful. Who am I? How can I cling to this fragile sense of self that is always under threat of extinction or usurpation? The theme of the second self in the novels of Wilkie Collins forms a link between the better-known doubles of the Romantics and the writers of the *fin de siècle*.*

It may be supposed that a man obsessed with the need to search out and repeatedly exorcize such powerful *doppelgängers* himself felt some uncertainty about his identity. Who was Wilkie Collins?

To anyone more than a mere acquaintance, man or woman, adult or child, he was always Wilkie. Not 'Mr Collins', not 'Collins'. What has become normal practice was then so unusual that the reminiscences of his friends make a point of it. They knew him as a witty and amusing companion, but before all as a simple and unpretentious one: 'the least *posé* public man I ever met'.[4] There is an undercurrent of amusement, often tender, occasionally contemptuous, in accounts of him. He prompted the accepting shrug, the patronizing aside about being his own worst enemy. He was known, for example, for his susceptibility

* '[The second self] is the self that has been left behind, or overlooked, or unrealized, or otherwise excluded from the first self's self-conception; he is the self that must be come to terms with.' (C. F. Keppler, *The Literature of the Second Self*, p. 11)

to women, and his amorous life was not a subject for conversation in mixed company. But his male friends thought him gullible, an easy prey for unscrupulous harpies. If he was a Don Juan, it was on the model of his much-loved Byron, not that of Molina and Mozart. Women were more shocked – or pretended to be – but loved him none the less. 'And Wilkie?' wrote the septuagenarian Mrs Procter to her friend Nina Lehmann, with whom she had a comic rivalry for his favours. 'No, I will not speak to you of him, because you will then revenge yourself by writing about some wretched woman.'[5]

To the public at large, Wilkie Collins was the author of a series of dark, intense, shocking, but highly entertaining novels, guaranteed to bring a blush to the cheek of the Young Person. 'I wonder why he puts so little fun in his books, seeing there is so much fun in his conversation', wrote one naïve acquaintance, bewildered by the contrast.[6] He dealt in the hidden secrets of Victorian society, the emotional and physical violence of family lives riven by cruelty and crime. He protested indignantly at legal and social injustice, and championed servants and prostitutes. His style might be easy and readable, distinctive if not distinguished, accessible to the literate as well as the literary. But though he could create a comic character or write a comic scene, there was nothing in the least comic about the writer Wilkie Collins.

He came from a background that does not immediately suggest any reason for the determined unconventionality that his friends knew, or for the sensational content of his writing. He was born on Thursday, 8 January 1824, a few months before Byron's death. It was a time when Romanticism was fast being overtaken by respectability. He was the first child of a happy and financially secure marriage. His parents held comfortably orthodox religious and political views. They had a wide circle of friends, among whom were some of the foremost writers and painters of the time. They also had a clear desire to make their children happy as well as good. Yet their favoured son was to reject the statutory form of marriage altogether, replacing it with a double relationship that created two happy families. He was to work in an organized and businesslike way at writing wild and sensational fiction. Combining popularity with subversion, he provided the reading public with what it wanted, while it raised prudish objections even as it read. In his work and his life he was to retain the bourgeois virtues of hard work and family responsibility, while straying very far from the blameless orthodoxy of his parents.

Perhaps no blameless life is ever achieved without struggle, or is quite as open to scrutiny as it looks. The Collins family already had its secrets. Though the early lives of his mother and his father differed in many ways, they had both experienced poverty and insecurity. They both worked hard to overcome their disadvantages and, by the time their first son was born, they had succeeded. But their early difficulties left a residue of anxiety which never wholly disappeared, and it shadowed their children's otherwise happy childhood.

In 1853, six years after her husband's death, Wilkie Collins' mother Harriet wrote an account of her childhood and youth to the time of her marriage, until now never identified or discussed by her son's biographers.[7] This substantial autobiographical manuscript gives a very different picture of her background and early life from the publicly accepted one, rapidly sketched in Wilkie Collins' life of his father, and repeated by his own biographers. While William Collins could be applauded for his enterprise and hard work as a young man, Harriet, as a respectable young woman, was supposed to wait until called for. By her own account, she did not.

Harriet Collins' story is superficially disguised as fiction, though little is altered except names of people and places, and those only erratically and inconsistently. Though naïve and disorganized, it is a lively, amusing narrative. It throws considerable light on the characters of her parents and siblings, and on the personalities of Harriet herself and her future husband William Collins.

She was the eldest daughter of an army officer, Alexander William Reynolds Geddes, of Scottish descent, but brought up in London. His mother died when he was a child. He claimed he was related to the renegade Catholic priest Dr Alexander Geddes; more certain is a relationship with the Scottish painter Andrew Geddes, probably his nephew. The Geddes clan was widely dispersed: Wilkie Collins was pestered by another clerical Alexander Geddes, of Lincolnshire, in 1867. 'The Revd. gentleman thinks of adding to his income by literature, and came to ask my advice. He described himself as rather a pretty hand with the pen – but as not exactly knowing what to write about!'[8]

Alexander William Reynolds Geddes joined the army in 1780 at the age of sixteen, with the rank of Ensign, and served for several years in Canada. His promotion to Lieutenant was purchased for him in 1783.[9] By 1789 he had returned to England with his regiment, and, while on recruitment duty in Salisbury, he met and married Harriet Easton, daughter of Alderman James Easton, of Salisbury.

It was a well-known local family: another James Easton was a printer and bookseller with a shop in the High Street.[10] But the alderman was not prosperous: he could give his daughter no marriage portion. Lieutenant Geddes' father had by now died, leaving his son a very small inheritance. The young couple were dependent on this, the lieutenant's pay and the Micawberish hope of something more when a lawsuit should be settled. But it was a highly respectable marriage, listed in the *Gentleman's Magazine* with other 'Marriages of Considerable Persons'.[11]

Their eldest daughter, Harriet, was born at Hagley, Worcestershire, on 27 July 1790, and baptized at St Thomas' Church in Salisbury. In her narrative she reverses her birth and that of her sister Margaret. This masks the fact that her sister, who was to become a successful and distinguished portrait painter, and who married first, five years before Harriet, was the younger of the two. It also blurs Harriet's age when she met her future husband. She was then twenty-four, no longer a young girl. When she did finally get married, she was thirty-two, well on the way to being an old maid. She was not the only woman in Wilkie Collins' life to conceal her true age.

After a couple of years in which the family followed the regiment in quarters in Birmingham and Wolverhampton, Lieutenant Geddes sold his commission and left the army, at his wife's insistence. The family settled in a cottage belonging to Lord Radnor at Alderbury, a village three miles south of Salisbury. Five more children were born after Harriet, all but one of them girls. Except when he was unsuccessfully searching for government employment in London,

Alexander Geddes and his wife spent the rest of their lives in Alderbury. Wilkie Collins often stayed there as a child.

Harriet's narrative portrays her early life in a country village in terms which recall the world of Jane Austen's novels, indeed that of the young Jane Austen herself, playing games with the boys and acting impromptu plays in the barn. Mrs Geddes, obsessed with the problem of marrying five portionless daughters, is acidly drawn by her eldest child as a pretentious fantasist, the Mrs Bennet of Alderbury, 'very prone to extremes'. She nagged her good-natured, ineffectual husband and encouraged her daughter's wildest romantic flights, while ignoring the realities of life on a tiny income in a rented cottage with six children, one maid of all work, and a husband incapable of earning his own living. The children grew up haphazardly: 'as to Education we took that very easy . . .'. The girls' schooling, such as it was, came from their father, and though Harriet read Hume's *History of England* to please him, her preferred reading was *Gil Blas, Don Quixote* and (stolen from an aunt and read secretly in her bedroom) Anne Radcliffe's *The Italian* and *The Mysteries of Udolpho* – tastes eventually handed on to her eldest son.

By her early teens a romantic fascination with dances and handsome officers had replaced earlier tomboy amusements. This was vigorously encouraged by her mother, who was prepared to keep the household short of food in order that the two eldest daughters might be properly dressed, have dancing lessons and be paraded round the local balls and assemblies, to catch husbands as soon as possible. Harriet, despite her criticisms of her mother, gives a cheerful and enthusiastic account of these worldly pleasures, unaffected by any reflections from her later religious conversion. She describes, in often tedious detail, the ways she and her friends chased the smart officers, and lists her amorous conquests, with zest and a certain amount of humour. The excitements of Salisbury society – meeting the local MP's brother, the militia being quartered in the town – were small-scale but sufficient, and there is little sense of the wider world in her account of her early life. She casts herself in the role of 'beauty', with her sister as her plain attendant. By the time she was married, in her thirties, David Wilkie described her as 'a nice woman, not particularly handsome, but accomplished and intelligent', but early portraits of her suggest she was pretty, if not classically beautiful.[12] Harriet had inherited her father's 'easy hopeful disposition', and in early youth she possessed the blessings of good health, good temper and boundless energy. She reveals herself at this period of her life as also having the candour and vulgarity of Lydia Bennet. She admits to an almost complete lack of 'accomplishments'. She couldn't draw, couldn't play an instrument, and remained invincibly ignorant. Acting, for which Harriet had a passion, was not an acceptable activity in polite provincial society, but it was the only talent by which she could hope to match her younger sister's achievements.

Margaret Geddes began, while still very young, to gain the entrée to the houses of the county families, where she painted portraits in return for 'presents' which helped out the family finances. Lord and Lady Radnor, who had a famous collection of paintings at Longford Castle, were among her first patrons, and later subsidized her move to London, so that she might be properly taught. When their father lost almost all his money – his income was reduced to £50 a year through the machinations of a 'family friend' whom he trusted with his capital – Margaret's courage and initiative helped to keep them all. By the time she was twenty-one she had established herself as a successful portrait painter, living independently in London at a time when few respectable single women left the shelter of their parents' homes. In 1816 she began to exhibit at the Royal Academy. The following year she married William Carpenter, an unsuccessful book and print seller, and it was as Margaret Carpenter that she made her name, and an adequate income for herself, her husband and their children.

William Carpenter was made Keeper of Prints and Drawings at the British Museum in 1845, which eased their problems, but his wife continued her professional career, becoming one of the foremost portraitists of her day. Between 1818 and 1866 – she was then seventy-four – she exhibited 147 paintings at the Royal Academy, fifty at the British Institution and nineteen at the Society of British Artists. There are portraits by her in the National Portrait Gallery, and six of her paintings are in the Sheepshanks Collection of British Artists in the Victoria & Albert Museum. Three of her children, her sons

Percy and William and her youngest daughter Henrietta, also became painters. Her exceptional independence and success in a largely masculine world have only recently been adequately acknowledged. Women at that time were not eligible to become Academicians; there was an unsuccessful movement within the Royal Academy to alter this rule in Margaret Carpenter's favour. Her nephew was to portray many ambitious and independent-minded women in his fiction; but in his life of his father he accords his aunt only half a sentence.

Harriet, faced with her father's ultimatum that the girls still living at home at the time of his financial collapse would have to go into 'service' if they did not find husbands, or at best go out to work as governesses, decided to rival Margaret's achievements, put her fantasies to good use, and take to the stage. The play that appealed to her most for her début was, as might have been expected, *She Stoops to Conquer.* Her ambitions were encouraged by her mother, who, though she accused her daughter of 'giving herself airs' in rejecting more humdrum occupations, fantasized that the life of an actress would lead to a brilliant marriage. Matters went as far as an invitation from the manager of the Theatre Royal Bath, a famous theatre with a good resident company, for her to appear in the following season.

Harriet was on the brink of dropping through the fragile net of respectability, at a time when actresses were still widely thought of as little better than prostitutes. At the last minute she was rescued by the earnest endeavours of an evangelical clergyman and his wife. They converted her, enlightened her on the moral dangers of the theatrical world, and then gave her two years' free tuition to fit her to be a governess.[13] Her mother's characteristic reaction was to imagine that she would find a job with a nobleman's family and marry the eldest son. In January 1814 Harriet instead discovered the reality of life for a teacher, when she took a job in a school near Portman Square, London, not far from her sister's lodgings with a dressmaker in Maddox Street.

It might be said to be the end of the Austen phase of her life, and the beginning of the Brontë one, though she kicked a good deal at first, and never ceased to relish good food, good clothes and the company of amusing young men. When she wrote her narrative in her fifties, she still had total recall of the clothes she wore as a girl: '. . . my smart cerise muslin dress, trimmed with white bugles, crimson roses and white beads in my hair'; 'Green silk bodices laced in front, showing the white muslin under, and a bunch of Hyacinths in our hair'. But evangelical earnestness was rapidly spreading through society, and it is doubtful whether giddy Harriet Geddes would have ever become Mrs William Collins without her apprenticeship to seriousness and suffering. Jane Austen herself wrote to her favourite niece in 1814, the year Harriet became a teacher: 'I am by no means convinced that we ought not all to be Evangelicals, & am at least persuaded that they who are so from Reason and Feeling, must be happiest and safest.'[14]

Harriet was, as she candidly admits, hardly well qualified as a schoolmistress. But the Frenchwoman who ran the school was unaware of her failings, or glad enough, perhaps, to get anyone at a salary of £20 a year, who was prepared to share a bedroom and even a bed with her pupils, to be badly fed and suffer in unheated rooms through the winter. Her meagre salary was never paid after the first quarter, and nine months later the proprietress went bankrupt. Harriet was forced into the semi-menial life of a resident governess. However, it was at this bleak period of her life that she went to an artists' ball with her sister, and met the rising young painter William Collins.

At first she thought him too pale and austere, and not tall enough to be really good-looking. But she soon found that he was, though properly serious about religion, an amusing and urbane companion, capable of 'a happy flow of spirits', even of practical joking of a slightly macabre kind, dressing up his lay-figure as a ghost to frighten a sleeping apprentice. A dinner at his house turned out to be a delightfully Bohemian experience. They ate in a room so small that the maid could not wait on them, but 'leant with her back to the wall and a dirty apron turned back to hide the worst of it, laughing at all the good jokes . . . and seeming quite put out if required to do anything else'.[15]

Though Harriet and William were immediately attracted to one another, William already had family responsibilities, and was in no position to marry a portionless teacher. Harriet was worried to discover that 'a degree of pride . . . was mixed with his opinions on the pursuits and callings of women. I found he did not think it fit they should be working for their bread in any way.'[16]

There was a Collins family history of imprudent marriages and financial disasters, which increased his caution. William's grandfather, a native of County Wicklow, had made such a match, 'bringing with it the usual train of domestic privations and disappointments',[17] and his son, William Collins' father, had done the same, marrying a young Scotswoman with no money of her own. William Collins Senior settled in London, hoping like many another clever young Irishman of the time to make his fortune in the literary and artistic worlds of the metropolis. He wanted to be a poet, like his namesake (there was a family tradition, impossible to substantiate, that they were related to the more famous William Collins). But the need to make a living forced him to set up as a picture dealer and restorer, with a shop in Bolsover Street, St Marylebone. It proved a disastrous choice. Like Wilkie Collins' maternal grandfather, he was gullible and hopelessly unbusinesslike, seeing the shop as a reasonably gentleman-like way of scraping a living whilst devoting his real energies to writing. His grandson gives a tongue-in-cheek account of his frantic scrabble for recognition:

> Articles in the public journals, songs, fugitive pieces . . . flowed plentifully from Mr. Collins' pen . . . no literary occupations were too various for the thoroughly Irish universality of his capacity. He wrote sermons for a cathedral dignitary, who was possessed of more spiritual grace than intellectual power . . . composed a political pamphlet to further the views of a friend; which procured that fortunate individual a Government situation of four hundred a year, but left the builder of his fortunes in the same condition of pecuniary embarrassment . . . in which, to the last day of his life, he was fated to remain.[18]

Amongst his unsuccessful productions was a poem on the slave trade, which inspired a painting by his friend George Morland. He had trouble getting it published, and his preface strikes a typically querulous note:

> The ignorant malevolence of arrogant dulness, the unsuccessful exertions of the friends to humanity, and a combination of other troublesome circumstances, have hitherto retarded the publication of this little Offering at the Shrine of Justice.[19]

The 'Offering' is in fact unreadably pedestrian; but the same note of complaint is heard in his preface to his one full-length book, *Memoirs of a Picture*. This very strange three-volume work so intrigued Wilkie Collins that he interrupted the narrative of his life of his father to devote nine pages to unravelling the complicated plot of a book which he compared, not absurdly, to Smollett, Sterne and even Fielding. It is a picaresque story, containing a rogue's gallery of thieves and forgers, which hinges, appropriately enough for the work of a picture dealer, on the question of authenticity and forgery. Narrative is subverted by authorial interjections and asides; one set of characters is dropped for chapters at a time to pursue others; secondary narratives, with little or no connection with the main one, are introduced. The style is an extraordinary mixture of orotund circumlocution and comic bathos, intermittently entertaining, but with little artistic control of its method. The longest and strangest interruption of all comes in the second volume, which is entirely devoted to a life of George Morland, a refreshingly frank appraisal and vivid portrait of an eighteenth-century Gulley Jimson. Morland was always in debt, often living 'within the rules of the bench'; more often drunk than not; not above making copies of the pictures of the famous Dutch painters and having them passed off as originals. There is a racy pen-portrait of Morland on the run from his creditors, holed up in the Cavendish Square Coffee House, and sending for Collins to rescue him.

> There, in a little back parlour, his friend found him, with a bason of rum and milk, a large pointer by his side, a Guinea pig in his handkerchief, and a beautiful American squirrel he had just bought for his wife. He said matters were pretty well settled, but as yet he was rather shy, and directed his friend how to proceed down the sly way, which was through a mews; the manner in which he was to open the stable door, and secure it after him, taking especial care none of the bums nosed him.[20]

Problems of authenticity, identity and substitution; cheerfully disreputable rogues; complications of plot and multiple narratives; all these elements, hopelessly tangled and incoherent in *Memoirs of a Picture*, are meticulously worked out in the novels of William Collins Senior's grandson, and the book provided a direct inspiration for Wilkie Collins' lively novella of 1856, *A Rogue's Life*. Even the preface may have some connection with Wilkie Collins' defensive claims, in the prefaces he insisted on attaching to his novels, of their foundation in fact. His grandfather, too, stressed, though most unconvincingly, the importance of truth in his unlikely narrative:

> As to the arrangement of the several anecdotes and adventures contained in the following volumes, dates and often names, have been frequently disguised, and sometimes wholly dispensed with. But the most scrupulous attention hath always been paid to their authenticity, and the justice of their application.[21]

The impecunious Irish picture dealer and his wife had two surviving children: William, born 18 September 1788 in Great Titchfield Street, and his younger brother Francis. William was slow at school, often in trouble for not doing his lessons well enough, but he showed artistic promise when still very young. His father arranged for Morland to teach him. This amounted to little more than watching the painter at work, and the boy, already serious-minded, was shocked by Morland's dissipation. But he reverenced Morland as a painter, and adopted much of the subject matter of his paintings.

The younger William was very different in character from his ebullient father, whose spirit does not ever seem to have been wholly quenched; though, as his son wrote, 'His life was one scene of narrow poverty'.[22] William was no infant genius, but he decided that with industry and perseverance his artistic ability could become the salvation of the family. He worked with single-minded determination to develop his one talent, carrying a sketch-book wherever he went, anxious to take every opportunity to improve. His father was proud of the boy, and warmly supportive, hoping to live long enough 'to see poor Bill an R.A.'.[23]

Many of the anecdotes in Wilkie Collins' life of his father stress his obsessional anxiety about his art, and his concern for accuracy of detail. His friend David Wilkie later warned him against 'a want of breadth' in painting, and 'a constant disturbing and torturing of everything . . . by a niggling touch'.[24] Against this must be set William Collins' 'often expressed conviction . . . that "the study of the Art was in itself so delightful, that it balanced almost all the evils of life . . . that an artist with tolerable success had no right to complain of anything" '.[25] This double view of artistic creation, as both a delight and an anxiety, had an effect on the lives and work of both his sons. So did the emphasis on 'minute particulars', rather than any larger conception of the artistic process.

William Collins was admitted to the Royal Academy Schools in 1807, and in the same year had two landscape paintings hung in the Academy Summer Exhibition. The laborious methods of the Academy schools, involving much drawing from casts of antique sculpture and copying from Old Masters, seem to have suited his conscientious and orderly character. The chief instructor at that date was Henry Fuseli, creator of nightmare fantasies; an eccentric who still wore an eighteenth-century pigtail, he was capable of swearing at his pupils, whom he called 'wild beasts', in nine languages. A group of pupils invited to his house to see his newly completed 'Witch of Endor' were greeted by their master wearing his wife's work-basket on his head. Yet he was a strict and orthodox tutor, refusing to allow any creative deviation from accurate representation in his pupils. He cannot have found much to complain of in William Collins' steady progress, which earned him a silver medal in 1809.

William's timidity was partly governed by the need to earn money. His father's affairs became ever more hopelessly tangled, and the younger son Francis, who had gone into the picture business with him, was too young and inexperienced to be much help. Everything fell on 'poor Bill'. Early in 1812, when he had begun to sell some of his paintings for reasonable sums, his father died bankrupt.

Letters of administration were granted to the chief creditor. The lease on their house in Great Portland Street had some time to run, but the furniture had to be sold, and a family friend found them eating supper off an old box. The catastrophe is reflected in the paintings William Collins exhibited and sold the following year: 'The Burial-place of a Favourite Bird' and 'The Sale of the Pet Lamb', the picture which first made his name. Both were scenes of cottage life of the kind which he made his speciality, and which became immensely popular. Idealized, charming and undemanding, they feature children whose innocence and vulnerability mirror the unexpressed fragility of the rural idyll in the face of industrialization. The pet lamb was a favourite symbol of childhood innocence – Gainsborough used it in this way[26] – and Collins' painting expressed the rape of innocence and the end of childhood; the children and their pet are, inevitably, betrayed by the parents for money.

William Collins steadily consolidated his reputation in the ten years following the death of his father, but his income still fluctuated considerably, and it would be a long while before he was in a position to consider marriage. In 1815 he moved, with his mother and brother, to a larger house, 11 New Cavendish Street. The slump which followed the end of the Napoleonic War made pictures difficult to sell. Though they let half the house, he was forced to apply to one of his patrons, Sir Thomas Heathcote, for an advance on an unfinished painting, to avoid bankruptcy. This humiliation, so reminiscent of his father's financial disasters, increased his habitual anxiety, self-doubt and determination.

He kept a record of all the paintings he sold from 1808, when he was twenty, to 1846, the year before his death. In a beautiful copperplate hand, which only deteriorates near the end, he listed where each painting was exhibited, the name of the purchaser and the price received.[27] This reveals that as early as 1811 he sold a painting, 'May Day', for 150 guineas. In 1818 he only sold three pictures, for a total of £399, but this year proved the turning point. The Prince Regent bought a painting for 150 guineas; the Duke of Newcastle had him to stay; he also stayed with Sir George Beaumont at Keswick. There he met the Wordsworths and their circle of friends. He went for a long walk with Wordsworth, who became very attached to him, and read his poetry aloud to him through a wet morning. It was on this visit that William Collins painted a portrait of Coleridge's daughter Sara as 'The Highland Girl', which caused a sensation when it was exhibited in London the following year. De Quincey described Sara at this time as 'the most perfect of all pensive, nun-like, intellectual beauties that I have seen', and was enthusiastic about her portrait by 'that admirable man William Collins'.[28] Collins' portrait captured her spiritual quality, and enchanted her father, who had not seen her since she was a child.

William Collins was elected an Associate of the Royal Academy in 1814, and became a full Academician in 1820. According to John Linnell, who never achieved this, Collins was delighted that he was entitled to call himself 'Esquire', and he thereafter looked down on other painters who were not so honoured. Linnell thought him amiable but weak-minded, 'oppressed by the twin bugbears propriety and respectability'.[29] Though Collins and Linnell were close friends all their lives, as their fathers had been before them, and near neighbours for several years, their relationship was punctuated by quarrels. Linnell, who was a Unitarian who refused on principle to go to church, claimed that Collins called him a 'Sabbath breaker' for tying up his peach and nectarine trees on a Sunday afternoon, and even threatened him with prosecution for not attending a place of worship.

The accusations of snobbery, by others besides Linnell, were well founded; but there was a hard financial necessity behind the tuft-hunting, comic though it may sound when he confides it to his diary: '. . . as it is impossible to rise in the world, without connection – connection I must have. Therefore, I will paint some high personage for the next Exhibition. (Why not the Princess Charlotte?)'[30] His son came to hate snobbery and pretentiousness, wherever it manifested itself. Though he would not admit it, he was to benefit from his father's anxious cultivation of the right people. As a young man he could take his place in literary and artistic circles as a matter of course, and his path to becoming a writer was easily cleared by the connection with a well-known and respected painter. Though he deplored his father's snobbery, he understood its origins very well. His life of him makes clear, without overt comment, that William Collins' depressive character, and his uncertainty about his own abilities, made him eager to please, and not only for snobbish reasons. He was the exemplification of his friend Coleridge's attack on the Regency period:

> an age of *anxiety* from the crown to the hovel, from the cradle to the coffin; all is an anxious straining to maintain life, or appearance – *to rise*, as the only condition of not falling.[31]

In England in the first quarter of the century, a painter was expected to know his place. He was dependent on private patrons for his livelihood: either the traditional aristocrat, or a member of the rapidly rising (and often richer) merchant class. Wilkie Collins pointed out the debt owed by English painters to the industrialists, who preferred domestic to religious or historical subjects.[32] Only the greatest artists, Blake, Constable and Turner, dared to ignore or break the rules. William Collins, constitutionally insecure and self-critical, was not one of them. Though he could be kind and warm to the failure Benjamin Haydon, there is a famous anecdote of his meeting Blake in the Strand, carrying a pot of porter for his dinner, and cutting him. William Macready, himself one of the first actors to be considered a gentleman, was shocked, when he met Collins at an evening party in 1841, at 'the submissive *menial*-like tone he assumed – not supposing "I should (I think) *condescend* to recollect him"!'[33]

In spite of this inner insecurity, which he never entirely overcame, William Collins' material prospects steadily improved after 1818, and he was at last able to consider marrying. When he met Harriet Geddes again at her sister's house in Brook Street in 1822, she was delighted to find that his feelings for her had not changed. They had seen each other in 1816, and again in 1818, but only briefly. When the London school closed, Harriet had taken several posts as a governess, most of them in the country. One had taken her to Scotland for two years, as governess to the downtrodden and half-starved daughter of a high-handed Scotswoman. Harriet's romantic notions of Scottish life and scenery, derived from reading Scott, were considerably dampened by the climate and by her employer's behaviour.

On her return from Scotland she was more fortunate. She took a post as governess to the two daughters of a family with a London house in Montagu Square, and a country property in Hampshire. It was a happy, disorganized household, in which she was treated entirely as a member of the family, and could feel herself to be of real use.[34]

She had a generous salary of £70 a year, which enabled her to subsidize her parents. The one drawback (which initially made her hesitate to take the job) was, as she candidly admitted in her narrative, that the country house was too close to Salisbury, and to her parents. 'I should be again likely to meet those I had known in my gay days, of balls, plays and parties. I should be stared at, and talked about, by the gossips'.[35] She was obliged to visit Alderbury, see her father in a state of perpetual depression, and listen to her mother's complaints. But her employers moved permanently to London, to a larger house in Great Cumberland Street, and she began to meet William Collins regularly once more.

Their courtship proceeded steadily, with cheerful and touching innocence. They made a good couple. He steadied his 'dear little fidget', as he called her tenderly in an early letter; she livened him. She taught him to dance quadrilles at a party at his house in New Cavendish Street; on another evening they all played round games before supper. They spent happy days walking in the fields at Hendon, where William had wandered with his sketch-book as a boy. William took her to see the 'monopolyloge' Charles Mathews, later an inspiration to Dickens, performing his one-man show. When William held her hand in the theatre Harriet was sure he was about to propose. She was right.

He was determined to marry her. His letters to her are those of a man deeply in love and impatient of delays. However, there were confessions to be exchanged, 'not of a cheering nature'. She felt she must write telling him without equivocation of her family's disastrous financial affairs, but, following the family tradition, he brushed this aside: 'You hardly do me justice in supposing the knowledge of the circumstances you mention . . . would in the least alter my determination . . .'[36] He in his turn had to confess his mother's implacable opposition to his marriage to a governess with no dowry and no prospects. Harriet rather courageously agreed to live with William's mother and brother after marriage, to save expense, and he decided not to tell his mother until they were safely married.

This was not the end of their difficulties. In July the opportunity arose for William to go to Scotland, to be present at George IV's official visit to Edinburgh. This was an important occasion, the first time a monarch had visited the Scottish capital since the Union, and painters followed the royal progress as press photographers do now; even the unpredictable Turner arrived unexpectedly in Edinburgh, and produced the best record of the occasion – a wonderfully satiric painting of the King attending divine service in St Giles' Cathedral.[37] There were to be a number of public ceremonials (with 'ancient' pageantry invented for the occasion by Sir Walter Scott). David Wilkie had been bidden by the King to attend. William Collins, travelling with Wilkie and the Scottish painter Andrew Geddes (related to Harriet), would have the opportunity of making himself a quasi-official painter, and of meeting Scott and other Scottish notables.

The marriage, originally planned for August, would have to be postponed. But Harriet had given up her job, and had nowhere to live; William was impatient of further delay. 'They had been sighing for years, till they could sigh no longer', David Wilkie explained in a letter to his sister.[38] Finally a solution was privately agreed on, though no one but Harriet's parents knew. Harriet would join him in Edinburgh, and they would be married there.

Harriet travelled by steamer to Leith, and joined William in Edinburgh. It was no Gretna Green elopement: they were respectably married on 16 September 1822, in the English Episcopal Chapel. The minister, Dr Archibald Alison, famous as the author of *Essay on the Nature and Principles of Taste*, rose to the occasion by refusing to take a fee from anyone connected with the arts who bore the same name as the poet. Old Mrs Collins' reaction to the news, which she was told only when it was too late for her to interfere, is not recorded. She accepted the inevitable, and when the married couple returned to London after a brief honeymoon on the Fife coast, they joined her and her younger son Francis in the house in New Cavendish Street.

TWO

A Happy Family

(1823–1835)

William and Harriet Collins had both been brought up in households in which an easygoing, unassertive man had been dominated by his more forceful wife. They tried not to repeat the pattern. Though Harriet had more natural energy and enthusiasm than William, there was no question that he was the man of the house. He had asserted himself against his mother's wishes, perhaps for the first time, when he got married; he was to remain the pivot of the household, though at some cost to his tranquillity, until he died.

He and Harriet escaped by themselves to Hampstead for the summer of 1823, renting a cottage at North End, where they were close neighbours of John Linnell. According to David Wilkie, marriage and the peace of Hampstead had a good effect on William's painting: 'I . . . rejoiced to see the dark-brown, vigorous shadows, with the fat surface you have got upon them. This augurs well . . .'[1] Harriet was expecting their first child, and they returned to New Cavendish Street for the winter. Except for some years in childhood, Wilkie Collins was to live until his death in various houses in the same small area of north-west London, a rhomboid defined by Oxford Street to the south, Regent's Park to the north, with Edgware Road to the west and Great Portland Street to the east.

His birth may have been a difficult one, for he was marked by a permanent deformation of his head with a noticeable bulge on the right side of his forehead. He was a small child, with light hair and rather prominent grey eyes. He was extremely short-sighted, and as an adult always wore glasses. In a letter William Collins wrote to his sons in 1832, when Wilkie was eight and his younger brother four, there is what may be a joking reference to his small size: 'A pretty long letter, methinks, for two such short fellows . . .'[2] He grew eventually to five feet six: not tall, but not freakishly short for a man of his era. However as an adult he was oddly disproportioned, with a bulging forehead, head too large for his body, short arms and legs and 'pretty little hands and feet, very like a woman's'.[3] He continued to be self-conscious about his appearance, often calling attention to the swelling on the right side of his forehead:

> saying that Nature in his case had been a 'bad artist' who had depicted his forehead 'all out of drawing.' He also found fault with 'Nature' in having given him high shoulders, with a short and somewhat broad figure, which, as he himself observed, was 'quite out of all proportion' to his remarkably large and intellectual head.[4]

A cancelled passage in the manuscript of *The Woman in White*, deleted at proof stage, underlines his sensitivity about his physical disproportion. The symmetry of the diminutive Professor Pesca – modelled on Gabriele Rossetti – is insisted upon, in much greater detail than in the published version:

> Unlike most men of little stature he was, however, perfectly well-proportioned from head to foot. His hands, feet, and face were all in complete harmony with each other. His delicate diminutive features were admirably regular . . . Except in the matter of height, my little friend had no cause to complain of Nature. She had done her best to make him a miniature model of a handsome man, and, before sending him into the world, had fondly and carefully finished him off down to the last detail.[5]

The beard Wilkie Collins grew in his thirties helped to balance his face, compensating for the bulging forehead and disguising a slight weakness about the chin. There was nothing to be done about his tiny hands and feet: he learnt to accept them. Once, when he was in Paris as a middle-aged man, he bought his mother two pairs of boots, making sure they would fit her by trying them on himself, quite unembarrassed by their high heels.[6] On another occasion, when he got his feet wet on the way to visit his friend and doctor Frank Beard, no one in the house, not even one of the children, had a pair of shoes small enough to fit him. Eventually an old aunt produced a pair of slippers, 'checked black and white, and with steel buckles . . . worn a little loose, it is true, but which were the nearest approach to a fit that could be found'.[7] Even these fell off during dinner, to everyone's amusement.

He was christened William Wilkie. The second name was never used during his childhood, but it was the name he chose for himself as a young man, even before he became a published writer. It was a happy chance that the substitution of one consonant in the abbreviation 'Willie', his childhood name, eliminated its childishness, yet still reflected the charm and approachability which were so striking to all who knew him. 'Wilkie' was also distinctive enough to bring him out from under the shadow of his famous father, and avoid the anonymity of being one of hundreds of William Collinses.

His adoption of his second name also signalled a more fundamental escape from his childhood. Willie, the docile and promising child of conventional parents, was rapidly ousted by Wilkie, the non-conformist. He had only to identify a conventional attitude to want instantly to outrage it; to hear a platitude and contradict it; to have an expectation held of him and disappoint it. Rejecting his father's rigid attitudes towards his acquaintances, Wilkie became the original flexible friend, the gold card good for endless credit in the business of personal relations. There was a price to be paid in the end, of course; there always is. But even the few hostile accounts of him stress his amiability. They are far outnumbered by the enthusiasm of those who remembered him as a true friend, the best friend anyone ever had, the free giver of 'steady friendship . . . always the same, always kind, always earnest, always interested, always true, always loving and faithful'.[8] It was not so easy to see the *alter ego* in the background, that upright, single-minded, rigid moralist that he might have been if he had been 'a good boy'. He could never be entirely ousted. Someone – a William – stood behind Wilkie always, tempting him to look round.

Wilkie Collins was fortunate in the godfather who provided the name that freed him from the carapace of William Collins. David Wilkie, one of the most popular and successful artists of his day, was a gentle, unassuming eccentric, who decided his prices by the unorthodox though sensible method of fixing a notional salary for himself of a thousand pounds a year, and charging for a picture according to the length of time it had taken to paint. But in spite of his success he was shy and withdrawn, and suffered several periods of severe depressive illness, when he was unable to paint at all. His friends thought that marriage might help him, but though William Collins did his best to interest him in 'eligible young ladies', and he and Harriet sent him a 'certificate' of wedded bliss at the end of a year's marriage, he 'continued all his life, to hover irresolute at a discreet distance from Hymen's permanent grasp'.[9] His godson, in most ways very different, was to follow his example in this at least.

David Wilkie had a bachelor's uncertainty about child development: peering at his godson at the christening, he was reported to have said, in great surprise, 'He *sees*'; and writing from Geneva in August 1827, when his godson was three and a half, he supposed 'he will be able to speak to me when I return'.[10] But his godson had warm memories of his kindness and patience; he recounts how Wilkie would take him on his knees and draw cats, dogs and horses 'with a readiness and zeal which spoke eloquently for his warmth of heart and gentleness of disposition'.[11]

William and Harriet Collins spent the summer of 1825 in the village of Hendon, where they had walked together in the fields before their marriage. It was a year of crises in the City, and William found 'some advantage in being too poor to keep a banker', though he was in fact earning a respectable amount from his painting.[12] His chronic anxiety about money may have encouraged this escape from the expenses of London. He also found that living in a country village enabled him 'to keep down . . . that natural tendency to excitement, which I have always found so difficult a task' – suggesting he suffered moods of agitation, even elation, as well as depression.[13] In the following year they moved out of the New Cavendish Street house altogether, and set up a home of their own in Hampstead Green, Pond Street, very near Hampstead Heath. Nearly forty years later, Wilkie Collins remembered it clearly:

'The house was on the right hand, as you descend the hill – the second house (on the way down the hill) in a row of small houses which still remains.'[14] The site is now covered by the unlovely bulk of the Royal Free Hospital.

They spent three years in this small house, and it was there that their second son, Charles Allston Collins, 'a blue-eyed red-haired bonny bairn', was born on 25 January 1828, ending Willie's four-year reign as the only child.[15] Another painter friend, the American Washington Allston, was godfather, by proxy. He never saw his godson, but had an indirect influence on his development which did him no good at all. William Collins always said that he owed to Allston, whom he met in 1814, 'the explanation of many religious difficulties . . . and the firm settlement of [his] religious principles . . .'.[16] Charles, who inherited his father's depressive temperament, also developed an exaggerated version of his religious tendencies.

The village of Hampstead was near enough to London for William Collins to keep in touch with Academy business, but rural enough to provide the scenery he needed for his paintings. It was a favourite spot for painters, and the little Collins boys were familiar from infancy with the artists who came to visit. The habit of viewing the world in painterly terms is obvious in Wilkie Collins' writing, and metaphors of painting came naturally to him. 'I have done! (except my *varnishing days* in respect of proof sheets . . .)', he wrote to a painter friend on finishing *The Woman in White*.[17] Holman Hunt envied Charles Collins his artistic head start in having this easy acquaintance with great painters, and for having been, as he said, dandled on Turner's knee as a baby.[18] Constable was a near neighbour, at Lower Terrace and then at Well Walk. William Collins spoke warmly of him after his death to his biographer Charles Leslie, but they were not always on good terms. Constable, whose personal relationships were often stormy, disliked Collins and despised his pictures. He described his entries for the Academy Exhibition one year as 'a coast scene with fish, as usual, and a landscape like a large cow-turd . . .'.[19]

There were literary friends, too. Coleridge, living at Highgate, was glad to know the man who had painted his beautiful daughter; he visited the Collinses in Hampstead, and Crabb Robinson met

William Collins at one of Coleridge's 'Attic Nights', on 10 June 1824. Coleridge, who had introduced William to the poetry of George Herbert, was enthusiastically grateful for his more mundane recommendation of mustard seed as a remedy for 'dysenteric diarrhoea' and constipation. William, chronically anxious about his own health and that of his family, seems to have collected nostrums as other men collect *objets d'art*. Coleridge took a liking to Harriet, and talked to her in his characteristically incomprehensible fashion, deluging this unintellectual woman with metaphysical speculation by the half-hour. On another occasion he was in great distress at being unable to break his opium addiction:

> His grief was excessive. He even shed tears. At last my mother addressed him, saying, 'Mr. Coleridge, do not cry; if the opium really does you any good, and you *must* have it, why do you not go and get it?' At this the poet ceased to weep, recovered his composure, and . . . said, with an air of much relief and deep conviction: 'Collins, your wife is an exceedingly sensible woman!'[20]

Telling the story many years later, Wilkie Collins said that the incident 'made a strong impression on my mind, and I could not forget it'. His mother's common-sense attitude to the drug undoubtedly influenced his own. As the Collins family left Hampstead in 1830, and Coleridge died in 1834, the boy was certainly no more than ten, and probably no more than six years old, when this incident occurred.

In the autumn of 1829, the family moved to a larger house, in Hampstead Square, and William's mother came to live with them. The house in New Cavendish Street was finally given up, and Frank Collins moved into lodgings. Old Mrs Collins, once so dominating a figure in her sons' lives that one never married and the other only managed to do so by subterfuge, was now both physically decrepit and senile. Her son Frank made an unofficial will, dated 22 January 1828, in which he explained that, finding that his mother would be the beneficiary if he died intestate, and 'well knowing that she is utterly incapable of managing her own affairs', he was leaving everything 'to my dear Brother William for had it not been for him I should never have had anything to leave'.[21] 'Mother much as usual' is the recurrent phrase used in letters between William and Harriet, with an addition in a letter of 1833 (the year of her death): 'perhaps rather more troublesome'.[22] The added burden was shouldered without complaint, but for the next four years the erratic and irrational presence of their grandmother must have had an impact on the children, and given Willie his first opportunity to observe bizarre behaviour at close quarters.

For William Collins, there was the added frustration of not being able to leave his mother and undertake the long journey to Italy that David Wilkie had been urging on him. According to Linnell, Collins was devoted to the Dutch school of painting, and scornful of the great Italians. His friends felt that this prejudice narrowed and hampered his art. But he was not willing to spend a year or more apart from his adored wife and children, nor to take them with him and leave his mother to the care of strangers. The postponement was a fortunate chance for his elder son. When they finally got away in 1836, he was old enough to take full advantage of an experience he considered a turning point in his development.

The family did go abroad for six weeks in the summer of 1829, to Boulogne, taking old Mrs Collins with them in the forlorn hope that a 'change of air' might be beneficial. William sketched the seashore and the fishermen and their wives and children, and Willie, at five and a half, took in and remembered much of what he saw and heard. A tale of heroism by one of the fishermen, no doubt used as a moral lesson by his parents, made a lasting impression. After a shipwreck, a moribund Negro seaman, the sole survivor, was refused admittance to any house because of the quarantine laws. One of the fishermen

> in defiance of all danger and objection, carried the poor wretch to a straw-hut on the beach; and, taking off his own clothes, laid [*sic*] down by him the whole night long, endeavouring to restore the dying negro by the vital warmth of his own body. (*Memoirs of the Life of William Collins*, Vol. 1, p. 329)

The brotherhood of man could hardly have been more vividly demonstrated. The dark *alter ego* who so often haunts Wilkie Collins' characters perhaps had his first embodiment on the beach at Boulogne.

They were at the seaside again in September, this time at Ramsgate. William found 'nothing worth a straw' for artistic purposes; but it was to be the first of many visits to this increasingly popular Kent resort throughout Wilkie Collins' life. A painting by their father exhibited in 1831, 'The Morning Bath', commemorated the children's experiences. A naked baby is shown being handed back to his mother by the bathing woman, while an older child is being dressed again. 'Willy behaved nobly in the sea', his mother reported proudly.[23]

The Hampstead Square house, not large enough to provide a proper painting-room, had never been intended as a permanent home. William had hoped to buy land and build in Hampstead; but in 1830 they moved back to the outskirts of London, to 30 Porchester Terrace, Bayswater. John Linnell lived in the same street, a few doors away. At that time Bayswater was still surrounded by fields, and sheep grazed at the end of Porchester Terrace. It was from this house, near the demonstrators' rallying ground in Hyde Park, that Wilkie Collins remembered seeing the mass demonstrations at the time of the First Reform Bill.

> In the year 1832 when I was eight years old, my poor father was informed that he would have his windows broken if he failed to illuminate* in honour of the passing of the First Reform Bill. He was a 'high Tory' and a sincerely religious man – he looked on the Reform Bill and the cholera (then prevalent) as similar judgements of an offended Deity punishing social and political 'backsliding'. And he had to illuminate – and, worse still, he had to see his two boys mad with delight at being allowed to set up the illumination. Before we were sent to bed, the tramp of the people was heard in the street. They were marching six abreast (the people were in earnest in those days) provided with stones . . . They broke every pane of glass in an unilluminated house, nearly opposite our house, in less than a minute. I ran out to see the fun, and when the sovereign people cheered for the Reform Bill, I cheered too.[24]

High Toryism, strict religious observance and careful adherence to conventional social codes fenced in the safety zone of family life for William Collins. Children, the heart of the family, often featured in his idealized rural paintings. His most famous picture, 'Happy as a King', which has a Hampstead setting, was painted in 1836, when

* I.e. place lights in all the windows of the house.

his own children were twelve and eight, and shows a boy delighting in swinging on a gate. It reveals an understanding of children that is lively and tender, without being sentimental.

The nineteenth-century ideal of a happy home life as a refuge from the outside world was particularly important for William Collins, who had to be parent and provider to his mother and brother, and probably to some extent to his wife's family, as well as to his wife and children. If this later induced claustrophobia in his elder son, it also provided him with a secure background in early childhood. The children were always with one or other of their parents. The writer who was to be accused of an unhealthy interest in the lives of servants was never left to their care during his childhood. For the first four years of his life Willie often had his mother to himself, sometimes sleeping with her when his father was away.* On a rare occasion when Harriet was away from home without the children, having treatment in Brighton for 'nerves', William stayed at home and cared for them, writing that they were missing her, but behaving 'exceedingly well'.[25]

More often the children were with their mother, while William continued to spend part of each year travelling, working on commissioned paintings of his patrons' families and properties, or visiting new landscapes. His loving letters to his wife often contain, as well as chat about the titled and famous people he is mixing with, reference to a good sermon, or a pious exhortation not to forget the blessings of the Almighty.

Though William Collins adored his children as much as he did his wife, his messages to them seem to the modern reader heavy-handed in their guilt-inducing emphasis on kind and responsible behaviour. The four-year-old Willie is told, 'I hope to hear when I return that he will make his poor pappy happy by the account he will be able to give of his kindness and readiness to do everything his Mama tells him to do.' Charley, at seven and a half, is expected to look up references in the Bible on the duty of children to their parents.[26]

* In a letter dated September 1827 to Harriet (five months into her second pregnancy), William suggests that she should let one of the servants take Willie at night 'that you might get that rest which is so necessary to your health after the anxieties you have suffered'. (Morgan Library)

Fortunately Charley was not yet overwhelmed by these expectations. His first extant letter to his father, written at the same age, is lively and uninhibited. He wishes he had a pony, like the butcher's boy. 'Just now punch came by and they did not shew it to me', he complains; and he wants his father to come home and play battledore and shuttlecock with him.[27] He clearly didn't see his father as a heavy-handed tyrant, and indeed loving messages and little presents reached the boys from their father as often as pious exhortations. He took trouble to think of things to interest them and stimulate their imaginations and intellectual development, and was always interested in their lives and activities. At Ventnor, Isle of Wight, in 1827, he picked up 'two nice little scuttle fish bones' for Willie.[28] He made a drawing of a horse for Charley: not just any horse but 'a large grey horse which was brought to me from the plough . . . evidently of the Flanders breed and I know Charley always likes to see horses of that class. I think I shall have it framed and make a present of it to my own Charley'.[29] When the boys were at Ramsgate with their mother, William asked if Willie had his book about ships with him: 'he might learn a good deal while at the sea about vessels'.[30] This interest in the sea and ships stayed with Wilkie Collins for the rest of his life.

The overwhelming impression of William Collins from his letters and journals corroborates his son's account of him as a deeply pious but also kindly, warmly affectionate, simple man, though not one lacking in common sense. Asked in 1824, when he had just become a father, for advice on the education of a child who showed artistic talent, he wrote stressing that early promise did not mean that the boy would have the constitution and temperament needed for a painter. He added:

> Let our little friend go on drawing, without being much encouraged or depressed; not allowing him to give up such other schoolboy employments as will be necessary and advantageous to him, whatever his future destination may be; and if, after a couple of years, his preference for drawing continue, and his works should improve, something may be determined upon.[31]

His children were never neglected or harshly treated, and there is no evidence that corporal punishment was ever used by either parent;

the only reference to beating is a joking one, in a letter from William Collins to his wife, telling her to give Charley, aged thirteen, 'a good thrashing' for not drawing portraits of 'his kind friends'.[32] When Willie, aged thirteen, 'offended his father' he was punished by not being allowed to ride.[33] Willie was once playing with the Linnell children in the garden of their Porchester Terrace house when their behaviour made their father angry. 'Said young Wilkie when the passing storm was over: "I should not like your father to be mine. Your father is a bull; mine is a cow."'[34] The moo of anxious complaint was more familiar to the child than the bellow of anger.

Though church-going was an established part of the household routine – often twice on Sundays and also on days of religious observance such as Ash Wednesday and Good Friday – Harriet would often stay away from church if one of the children were ill. But Sunday did cast a blight over the week. Wilkie Collins recalled the endless sermons of his childhood in *Hide and Seek*, his third novel. The little boy Zack, similarly tortured, is defended by his grandfather:

> 'You've no business to take Zack to church at all, till he's some years older than he is now. I don't deny that there may be a few children, here and there, at six years old, who are so very patient . . . and so very precocious that they will sit quiet in the same place for two hours; making believe . . . that they understand every word of the service . . . But Zack isn't one of that sort . . . *You* keep on cramming church down his throat; and *he* keeps on puking at it as if it was physic . . . Is that the way to make him take kindly to religious teaching? . . . he roared like a young Turk at the sermon. And pray what was the subject of the sermon? Justification by Faith. Do you mean to tell me that he, or any other child at his time of life, could understand anything of such a subject as that; or get an atom of good out of it?' (*Hide and Seek*, Book I Chap. 1, p. 6)

Zack's verdict, 'I say, grandpapa, I hate Sunday!', was Wilkie's own: in the character of Zack's grandfather he was perhaps paying tribute to the good sense of the easygoing Alexander Geddes.

Both parents were more concerned about the children's moral welfare and physical condition than about their early education, given by their mother. They seem to have been reasonably healthy in early childhood, though Charley in particular suffered from colds and coughs, and was more severely ill than his brother when they both had measles in 1835. Their father's obsessional, pernickety care for their physical as well as their spiritual welfare recurs constantly in his letters. Though marriage and fatherhood was a source of great happiness to him, he seems to have felt, and to have impressed on his sons, that it was also a great, an almost overwhelming, responsibility. In his son's biography of him there is a phrase, significant for its relationship to Wilkie's later attitudes, which also sounds as though it echoes William Collins' own rather heavy-handed sense of humour. Writing of his father's forthcoming marriage, Wilkie Collins described it as 'the most momentous risk in which any man can engage – the speculation of marriage'.[35]

This sense of the momentous invades the most humdrum details of his father's letters. Writing from Brighton in 1830 to urge Harriet to join him there with the boys, he tells her in elaborate detail how to arrange the journey for herself and the children. She must be sure to take them INSIDE places, and 'Bring plenty of warm clothing for yourself and the chicks . . .' In 1832 he wants to know 'how the dear boys are in health as well as in behaviour to their dear Mama'. When Harriet is at Ramsgate with the children in 1833 she is given detailed instructions: she must stop using camphor for her teeth; she may take tepid sea-water baths twice or three times a week ('dip in the sea but by no means *remain long* in the water'); and she must 'take care of the Cliff when the children go that way'. His anxieties did not diminish as the boys grew up. When Harriet was at her parents' house in Alderbury in 1841, where one of the delights was the river that ran along the end of the garden, he warns, 'pray take care Charlie does not run into danger about the river, I know his love for fishing which I regret'. In the same year poor Charley, who passionately loved horses, was frustrated again. 'I am not satisfied that either Willy or Charley shd. ride the Mare . . . I hope to be in time to give my opinion before the Mare is ridden again.'[36] The boys were then seventeen and thirteen years old.

However, both parents took care to provide fun as well as protection and religious instruction. The boys had seaside holidays and visits to their grandparents; their mother's nieces and nephews, the Geddes, Gray and Carpenter cousins, came to stay. They also played with the numerous Linnell children, and had other friends of their own. Harriet's journal for 1835 – the only one to survive, apart from one she kept during the journey to Italy in 1836–37 – records a busy, humdrum, unintellectual life which must have been typical of Wilkie Collins' early childhood. Though Wilkie Collins described his mother as a 'woman of remarkable mental culture' from whom he inherited 'whatever of poetry and imagination there may be in my composition',[37] her diaries hardly ever mention books, and pictures only when they were in Italy, and she was making notes for her husband's use. She occupied her time in caring for and teaching the children, supervising the servant girl, making clothes for herself and her sons, and paying visits. She was, all her life, an extremely sociable person, whose ability to get on with everyone she met was of the greatest help to her less confident husband. It was a gift she was to pass on to her eldest son. She seems to have renounced all personal ambition during her marriage, and subsumed her own earlier longing for fame in promoting her husband's career; later she gave encouragement and practical support to her sons. But there are hints that she had a secret resentment of women who did achieve careers in their own right. She scolded the painter Henrietta Ward for continuing her career when she was a wife and mother, and her attempt to play down her sister's achievements in her reminiscences suggests a degree of understandable envy.

Harriet organized the unpretentious household economically and efficiently; her husband's fussing was clearly unnecessary. With her experience as a governess, it was natural that she also taught the children their early lessons. William provided artistic stimulus and instruction: his sons had mixed feelings about that. Wilkie remembered that 'an excursion with him in the country was a privilege . . . He possessed the peculiar faculty of divesting his profession of all its mysteries and technicalities, and of enabling the most uneducated in his Art to look at Nature with *his* eyes, and enjoy Nature with *his* zest.'[38] But Charley, four years younger, vividly recalled the tedium of trailing round art galleries: 'Why was that poor little girl brought here? She changes the leg she is standing on continually . . . and when they ask her "Are you tired dear?" says resignedly, "A little." The sight of that child's torments reminded the Eye-witness of some that he had himself gone through in early years, in galleries full of pictures by the old masters.'[39]

Wilkie Collins' reading began with the traditional childhood favourites: *Robin Hood*, which he was given at eight years old; *Don Quixote*; the novels of Marryat; *The Vicar of Wakefield*; *The Arabian Nights' Entertainment*. All these were still among his books at his death. Like so many Victorian writers, he adored Scott, calling him 'King, Emperor, President and God Almighty of novelists'.[40] Dickens always came after Scott. He also revelled in his mother's collection of Ann Radcliffe's Gothic romances.[41] He read poetry too: Shakespeare, Pope, Scott, Shelley and Byron remained among his favourite authors. He seems to have been a bright child, though not exceptionally precocious, and not at this stage showing promise in any particular direction.

In the summer of 1833 William Collins at last felt secure financially, and he had enough spare cash that year to invest £150 in government stock.[42] He wrote to his wife in his usual affectionate terms – he was staying with Sir Thomas Baring – telling her that though no longer a young man, he was much happier than he used to be. At the beginning of September, Harriet and Francis Collins took the boys to Ramsgate, and William joined them there. But the usual tranquillity of their lives was to be suddenly broken.

Francis Collins became ill at Ramsgate and, though he was well enough to return to London as planned when William arrived to replace him, he rapidly worsened. He had typhus. He was nursed at Porchester Terrace, where he became delirious, thinking he was in a strange house, 'under an impression that a vast time had elapsed, and that all things had undergone great revolutions'.[43] He broke a window in an attempt to escape from his room, and it took two men to restrain him. The family doctor, William Thomson, sent misleadingly optimistic reports – on 23 September he wrote that Mr Green (a surgeon and friend of Coleridge who had been called in) thought there was no danger 'at present . . . a common continued fever, with a disposition to become low, but decidedly not a low fever'; but a fierce letter from John Linnell of the same date, emphasizing the severity of Frank's illness and the necessity of William's presence ('you can have no idea of the difficulties which your servants and friends are placed in owing to the continued delirium . . . poor Lucy [the maid] is almost exhausted'), hurried William back to London.[44] Harriet and the children stayed at Ramsgate, out of the way of infection. When they did return, Harriet, sensibly leaving the children with friends, arrived at Porchester Terrace on 5 October to find that Frank had just died.

William was shattered by his younger brother's death. Frank was a sweet-natured, gentle man, quite without ambition, though knowledgeable about everything to do with art and the lives of painters. He was devoted to his brother and his family, and a great favourite with his nephews. He was the perfect uncle, a model for both Willie and Charley in their later relationships with children. William, who acknowledged 'a sort of fatherly care for him, as well as a brotherly love',[45] went into a state of severe depression: six weeks later he was still unable to paint. 'A dreary blank, with much mental and nervous suffering', he recorded in his diary.[46] Frank's death was quickly followed by that of his mother, on 29 December, leaving William Collins with 'no relative now, either on my mother's or my father's side, that I ever saw'. His depression was still marked in the following summer: 'the society of the world depresses me greatly. I am sadly low in mind at times, and in body weak – apt to be vexed, very impatient, not bearing my afflictions with that patience, which afflictions were sent to teach.'[47]

But the death of his mother did at last free William Collins to consider the long-postponed trip to Italy. As a kind of dress rehearsal, the family spent four months touring Wales, from June to September 1834. Beginning in the south with Chepstow, Raglan and Tintern, all places endowed with romantic and sketchable ruins, they moved gradually north to the seashore scenery of Aberystwyth, and then to the mountains of north Wales. It was a fairly thorough test of their ability to endure the necessary discomforts of stage-coaches and remote country inns with two small children, the younger only six. For William it provided new subjects for paintings, and for the children it must have seemed an exciting adventure. Harriet, though, suffered a series of anxieties, as she wrote to Mrs Linnell from Llanberis:

> I wish you could see our present place of residence – surrounded by such mountains and rocks – but I have not lost my cat-like propensity of loving home. There are troubles and difficulties everywhere. Lucy has been very ill since we have been here, and no servant is kept by our landlady, who has a young child and a shop to mind . . .
>
> It is quite a foreign country; no-one understands us, nor can we comprehend their jargon. Milk is scarce – eggs the same; bread is very doubtful to get, unless you send seven miles to Carnarvon . . . no fruit; good potatoes – but no other vegetable . . .[48]

From Llanberis they moved on to Beddgelert, Barmouth and Dolgelly, before making their way home slowly, staying with Harriet's parents before returning to London.

William began preparing paintings for the next Academy Exhibition from his Welsh sketches, and Willie enjoyed his last autumn of freedom with Charley and the Linnell children, who never went to school – their father was said to be too mean to pay the fees. On his eleventh birthday, Harriet recorded in her journal, 'two young Mannings to dine and spend day play and fun'.[49] Five days later he started attending a day school off the Edgware Road, the Maida Hill Academy, run by a Mr Gall. He began promisingly, pleasing his schoolmaster by working hard, and winning first prize (two volumes of Southey's *Essays*) at the end of his first year. This may have led to his first experience of the dangers of good behaviour, for as he later wrote, probably with journalistic exaggeration: 'The idle boys deserted him as a traitor, the workers regarded him as a rival; and the previous winner gave him a thrashing . . . from that time his life at school became a perpetual burden to him.'[50] Sessions with a drill sergeant were arranged by his parents. These may also have been a burden to one who was, and remained all his life, clumsy and not over-keen on physical activity. But his fond mother kept him at home from school if he had a cold, or even if the day was very wet.

In the school holidays the children were kept occupied by their devoted mother. In one typical fortnight in July 1835, they were taken to the 'Panorama of Jerusalem'; to play in Kensington Gardens; had a large party of children visiting them; sailed their toy boat on the pond in Kensington Gardens; went to the Zoological Gardens; stayed the night with a friend; and finally (Charley only, Willie being back at school) visited the Diorama in Regent's Park. Their parents' life, too, left little time for the Devil's work. William and Harriet attended meetings of the Reformation Society and the Servants' Charitable Bible Society, and went to the Great Protestant Meeting (to combat the threat of Roman Catholicism) at Exeter Hall on 11 July.[51] The following year changed all that. They were at last ready for the Italian adventure that William had so long been planning.

THREE

Educations

(1836–1840)

Wilkie Collins always believed that the journey to Italy was crucial for his development as a writer. He was inclined to exaggerate its length: many of his acquaintances thought he had been educated almost entirely abroad. In 1862, looking back twenty-five years, he wrote that he learnt more in Italy 'which has since been of use to me, among the pictures, the scenery and the people, than I ever learnt at school'.[1] As well as an education in art and languages, he learnt that the age of anxiety was not a universal phenomenon, and that a life went on in the streets with very different values from those of the tight family unit. He learnt that food consisted of more than joints and boiled puddings, and could be delicious. He discovered there was a value in conversation that was amusing rather than edifying. Life, in fact, could be fun in ways outside his father's comprehension. The attitudes formed then were kept to the end of his life; in later years he insisted that 'everything English was badly done, from politics to cookery'.[2] Continental habits in social life, continental views on morality and religion, were in vivid contrast with William Collins' neophobia and his anxious pursuit of virtue. They were a revelation to his son.

The family left London on Monday, 19 September 1836. The journey was to take them away from home for nearly two years. Though Italy, Rome in particular, was their goal, there was much to see on the way, and the slow, uncomfortable methods of travel at that time encouraged a leisurely pace. They spent nearly a fortnight in Paris, where William and Harriet were shocked by scenes of dissipation that were even worse on Sundays than during the rest of the week. There was some comfort to be had at the English church. They thought the morning sermon, from worldly Bishop Luscombe (who had married Isabella Shawe to William Thackeray the month before), was not very edifying. However, an evening one, on the power of the Devil, was much more satisfactory. In Paris as elsewhere they were careful to make up for continental laxity in religious observance by increased strictness: wherever there was an English church the children were taken to both morning and evening service on Sundays, as well as having to recite the catechism to their mother. If there was no suitable church, they held a private service in their lodgings.

The showiness of the Catholic religion on the Continent aroused scorn, perhaps concealing some alarm, in William and Harriet. They despised the candle-lit churches with their exotic music and incense, the stiffly clothed and jewelled statues, the embroidered vestments. 'Frippery and idolatry', 'ridiculous', 'absurd' are the expressions that pepper Harriet's journal. In the 1840s they joined the fashionable congregation of the spellbinding Tractarian William Dodsworth at Christ Church, Albany Street, and Dodsworth became a close enough friend to be made an executor of William's will. But William would have been shocked to know that Dodsworth, like others in the Oxford Movement, eventually crossed the great divide in 1850, resigning his living over the Gorham case, and 'going over' to Rome. Wilkie Collins in later life associated Roman Catholicism with political repression, and expressed the usual English prejudices in his novel *The Black Robe*. But his parents' religiosity became irksome to him as a young man; and throughout his life he expressed impatience with the outward forms of religion, feeling they were a perversion of Christ's teaching. The discovery that the Church of England did not have a monopoly on claims to truth may have begun this process.

The children's spiritual welfare, in these new and exciting surroundings, was more of a worry to their parents than their intellectual development. Lessons from their mother or from visiting tutors were desultory and frequently interrupted, for the family were conscientious tourists. They saw all the major sights and museums of Paris, while grumbling, as most English travellers then did, at anything French: '. . . not at all reconciled to Paris noise and smells insufferable not at all answering my expectations streets most wretched for walking no shops at all to compare to Regent Street', Harriet complained, with her habitual lack of punctuation.[3] They continued to find French hotels dirty and uncomfortable, with the luxurious exception of the Meurice in Paris, which their son was to return to more than once. The fancy French food was not at all to their taste: 'tough mutton but glad of anything plain', Harriet recorded of a dinner served 'à l'anglais' in their own room.

Willie, at twelve and a half, was quite old enough to form his own opinions, whether or not he voiced them. As soon as he was let off the leash and able to travel without his parents, it was Paris he made for, and in Paris he spent some of the most enjoyable times of his adult life. But he gives no hint of his first impressions of the city in the *Memoirs* of his father, and for the moment we can only see him through Harriet's eyes. He is a good child, playing with the French children in the Tuileries gardens; 'delighted' with Punch; gazing at the orang-utan 'of remarkable size' in the Jardin des Plantes; walking home from Père Lachaise cemetery with his father, while Harriet and Charley, exhausted by the outing, rode home in that new form of public transport, the 'omni' (bus).[4]

From Paris they moved gradually south, suffering all the usual difficulties of continental travel before railways. Forced by the driver of a *diligence* to get out and finish the journey in a cart, they took to hiring carriages when they could, and, where possible, went by boat. Though the mutton chops at Auxerre had 'quite an English flavour', the towns were still a disappointment. Harriet dismissed Lyons as a typical French town: 'dirt smoking spitting gaming the men herding together at the cafés chattering like monkeys'. The shops in Marseilles were shut on Sunday – a good sign after the 'awful scene' of a Parisian Sunday – but they found it, too, smelly and dirty. At Cannes Charley picked up shells on the beach while William and Willie went off together sketching. But Charley, always the more delicate, became ill, and Harriet was 'miserable and anxious' about him.

They reached Nice at the beginning of November. The news from Italy was unpromising. There was widespread cholera, and quarantine restrictions were being imposed on travellers. Harriet was now unwell ('stomach in utter rebellion'), and she almost decided to stay put with the children and let William go on to Italy alone. They settled in an apartment in Nice for six weeks, waiting for further news. A young Jew was engaged to tutor Willie, and impressed Harriet, when he was given a biscuit, by standing up, putting on his hat, and saying a blessing on the food before eating it. William and Harriet, so prejudiced against other forms of Christianity than their own, had a liberal attitude to Judaism: they had visited the synagogue at Ramsgate, though probably only as curious tourists, when they were staying there in 1829.[5] There was an English church at Nice, and the children's own religious observances continued to be strictly enforced: they were taken to Wednesday Scripture meetings every week, as well as to the two Sunday services.

By the beginning of December the news from Italy was better, and they decided to go on. As they crossed the Alps everything improved: the rain stopped, the road wound through precipitous and magnificent scenery. The euphoria so often felt by English travellers at the first sight of Italy heartened the whole family; William in particular was nearly driven mad by having to pass by so many splendid landscapes with no time to sketch them. At Genoa, where they spent six nights, the splendour of the palaces and their contents for once receives as much notice in Harriet's journal as discomfort and tiredness.

By the time they reached Florence on Christmas Eve, the weather had become exceptionally severe: the snow was knee-deep in the streets. The English church was so cold on Christmas Day that Harriet had to take Charley out; he became ill again. William and his elder son diligently visited churches and galleries, in spite of the weather. At one church Harriet noted a macabre display of wax dolls representing dead babies, all magnificently dressed. But the cold indoors and out was too much for them to bear, and after ten days they decided to continue to Rome.

The journey, now a matter of a few hours, took them six days. Harriet was ill at Siena, with symptoms that were frighteningly like cholera, but a morphia lozenge improved her, and in spite of a relapse three days later they pressed on, arriving in Rome the day before Willie's thirteenth birthday.

Rome was full of British artists. Some, like Joseph Severn, who came with Keats in 1821 and nursed him through his last days, were permanent residents; others were visitors who stayed for weeks or months. The Severns befriended the Collins family, helping them to find comfortable lodgings near the Pincian Hill and introducing them to many of the British colony. Severn lent William Collins his studio to paint in. The family settled down happily to a busy life of work and sightseeing. Italian lessons were arranged for Willie, and he is more likely than the rest of the family to have had some communication with the world of the Roman streets. Rome remained his favourite city, and whenever he returned he was delighted to find it unchanged. In 1866 he celebrated 'the magnificent Roman women of the people . . . gossiping and nursing their children' in the streets still, as they had always done.[6]

This love for Rome was intensified by love for a woman: no idealizing schoolboy crush, but a Byronic encounter. There are two accounts of the boy's infatuation with a married woman whom he met in Rome. One is given by the German critic Ernst von Wolzogen, who published a short life and critical appreciation of Wilkie Collins in 1885, based on information from Collins himself. The other was told by Dickens. In a letter from Rome when he and Collins were in Italy together in 1853, he wrote:

> He gave us . . . in a carriage one day, a full account of his first love adventure. It was at Rome it seemed, and proceeded, if I may be allowed the expression, to the utmost extremities – he came out quite a pagan Jupiter in the business.[7]

To play the role of 'a pagan Jupiter' Wilkie must have been – or thought himself to be – the seducer, not the seduced, even forcing his attentions on the woman. Wolzogen's version, written for publication, is rather different. He gives no hint of a sexual initiation, and sees the episode as 'comic'; but writes that Collins, having fallen in love with a woman at least three times his age, was so furiously jealous of her husband that he could not bear to be in the same room with him.[8] This strongly suggests that his feelings for this unknown woman were not platonic. Dickens, who had been a very different kind of adolescent, probably thought Collins was boasting about his sexual precocity, and he may have underestimated his age in telling the story. Both Wolzogen and Dickens give it as twelve, rather than thirteen, his age at the time of his first stay in Rome, or fourteen, as he was when the family returned there on the homeward journey. Even if he were fourteen, it would have been an unusual experience for most boys of that age in the 1830s.[9] Still a child, taken for walks with his mother and playing games with the children of the English colony, he was, in secret, playing at being a man. The episode, whether entirely experienced or partly a fantasy, remained important enough for him to think it worth telling to his German biographer half a century later, and the description of the housekeeper, Mrs Lecount, in *No Name* may give a hint of the mysterious woman's appearance:

> Not a wrinkle appeared on her smooth white forehead, or her plump white cheeks . . . Her large black eyes might have looked fierce if they had been set in the face of another woman: they were mild and melting in the face of Mrs. Lecount . . . The comely plumpness of her face was matched by the comely plumpness of her figure: it glided smoothly over the ground; it flowed in sedate undulations when she walked. There are not many men who could have observed Mrs. Lecount entirely from the Platonic point of view – lads in their teens would have found her irresistible –[10]

Whatever their son was secretly up to, William and Harriet made little attempt to make friends with the Romans, or to adapt to an Italian way of life. Harriet's journal is full of the names of the visitors who came to call and to spend evenings with them (Harriet recorded 'seven gents. to tea' on 24 February), but they are all British, and mostly artists. Among them were the sculptors John Gibson and Matthew Wyatt; Penry Williams; Linnell's future son-in-law Samuel Palmer; the young John Leech; and E. M. Ward. Ward, who was, with his brother Charles, to become a lifelong friend of Wilkie Collins, was the twenty-one-year-old son of a manager at Coutts Bank, studying art in Italy. He was grateful for William Collins' praise of his paintings, 'as I know him to be a very sincere kind of man'. He and William Collins went on a 'grand expedition' on donkeys, with all the artists of Rome, to the cave of Cefalara. It was a jolly occasion, in spite of torrential rain: Ward wrote that he laughed more that day than he had ever done in his life.[11]

The earnest tone the Collins family was accustomed to at home was resumed with some of these visitors: 'A great deal of discussion in the evg. on the question of faith and works.'[12] Wordsworth was in Rome with Crabb Robinson; he breakfasted with the Collins family and dutifully went to morning and evening service at the English church with them. Crabb Robinson recorded that William Collins was a great favourite of Wordsworth's. Robinson, as a Unitarian, was conscious of his prejudices, and more wary.[13]

Willie and Charley were confined as much as possible to home routine, doing a few lessons, playing with children of the British community, and going for walks on the Pincio. They were also shown the splendours of Rome. They saw the Colosseum by moonlight, St Peter's and the Sistine Chapel, the Villa Borghese. They were in Rome for Easter, and were spectators at the great ceremonial services in St Peter's. William took them to a horse race, and the whole family went with the Severns to a performance at the opera which included a 'Comic Ballet' and two acts of a Bellini opera, almost certainly Willie's first experience of secular music on a grand scale. A spectacular firework display on Easter Monday included an imitation of Vesuvius erupting, and the Castel' St Angelo was magically transformed into a diamond palace. When the English Cardinal Weld died, they went, as did most of the British community, to see his lying-in-state; Edward Ward, who had given away his ticket, went disguised as a priest. A less dignified occasion was a service at the church of St Antony, when the priest blessed pigs, horses and other domestic animals, baptizing them with a brush full of holy water – 'most ridiculous and disgusting ceremony', Harriet commented, though William seized the opportunity to make a sketch, and the boys no doubt enjoyed it.

They visited the studios of other artists. A painting by one of the German Nazarite school, perhaps Overbeck, a landscape that had taken four years to paint, every leaf painstakingly laboured over, may have had an early influence on Charley Collins, later to be an associate of the Pre-Raphaelites. Harriet thought it 'very tame'. Picturesque models came to be painted by William: a boy bagpiper from the Abruzzi mountains, in his sheepskins, and a dazzlingly beautiful boy of twelve, used whenever a painter needed an angel or cupid, 'in private life a gambler, a thief, and a stiletto wearer'. William used him as a model for the boy Christ in the Temple: the contrast between his role and his way of life were a revelation to the sheltered English boy, a little older than he. The Severns' Italian nurse came to sit for William several times while Harriet took her charge out for walks with her own children; perhaps she was also the model for Mrs Lecount.

One occasion at the Colosseum is described in the *Memoirs*:

> It was evening; the friars had retired, after singing before the little chapels placed round the interior of the mighty ruin; darkness was approaching. Beneath the tall crucifix in the middle of the arena, knelt a peasant woman, prostrate in adoration, and a Carmelite monk beating his breast . . . At some distance from them stood a penitent – his face covered with a hood pierced with two apertures for the eyes – looking spectral, as his veiled, motionless form half disappeared in the gathering gloom.[14]

'It impressed the painter with emotions not easily forgotten', his son wrote; clearly it was not forgotten by the boy either. The scene seems a direct link with Wilkie Collins' first novel, *Antonina*, which explores different types of religious faith and fanaticism.

Throughout his travels in Italy, William Collins showed an uncharacteristic recklessness in facing the threat of cholera. He had been warned before they left England that the disease was raging: in Turin in 1836 it had been so bad that the whole English Legation took refuge at the top of Mount Cenis.[15] Wordsworth, who had planned to go to Naples from Rome, instead left Italy when he heard that there was an outbreak there, and urged William Collins to do the same. Wilkie remembered being 'quite astonished' at his earnestness.[16] William Collins, normally hypochondriacal and cautious, seems on this journey to have felt that it was worth risking not only his own health, even his life, but also those of his family, in order to visit the places and see the paintings he had come so far to study. In spite of the rumours, they left Rome for Naples on 2 May.

At first sight, Naples seemed promising. They made the usual tourist expeditions, up Vesuvius, to the Sibyl's cave and to Capri. They settled in to their expatriate routine, by now familiar, of church twice on Sundays and a visiting tutor for Willie. Willie, already addicted to the solitary vice of reading, was grateful to a tall, lugubrious American who lent him his only two 'amusing' books, *The Sorrows of Werther* and *A Sentimental Journey*. 'I took them home and read them and told him what I thought of them much more freely than I would now', Wilkie remembered.[17] But by the end of the month there were signs of trouble:

> Strange-looking yellow sedan chairs, with closed windows, had for some days been observed passing through the street before the painter's house . . . it was ascertained that their occupants were sick people, being conveyed to the hospital; and, on further investigation, these sick people were discovered to be cholera patients.[18]

The family got out quickly, before quarantine restrictions on movement were imposed. They decided on Sorrento, which proved a great success with everyone. William painted indefatigably, refusing to waste time by taking a siesta in the midday heat. There were sea- and landscapes all around, and picturesque models easily available. For the boys it was almost all holiday. They bathed and explored, and the tutor engaged for Willie, Mr Hills, took time off from Latin verbs to help Charley make a kite which the boys flew together.

There were plenty of other summer visitors to Sorrento, and a lively social life, with only minor shadows over the first six weeks. William and Harriet went to an elegant dinner party and found, to their horror, that they were expected to play cards – for money. Not liking to refuse, they did so, and lost. 'Very stupid if not worse,' Harriet acknowledged in her journal. Then Willie made a nuisance of himself for a whole day and his father had to punish him at dinner-time. 'Made us all very miserable', his mother commented, making clear that this was an exception to their general harmony. Willie got his own back the next day: when his mother was on the roof by herself watching the sunset, he 'thoughtlessly' locked her out.[19] (It did not occur to her that he might have done it on purpose.)

Such hard-working blameless lives: William and Harriet might have hoped that the Almighty would grant a respite from trouble. But at the end of July William became ill, with symptoms that had plagued his father, and were to become all too familiar to his son. He had rheumatic pains in his back and chest, his left knee and ankle, and terrible inflammation in the eyes. The English doctor was called in, and tried one remedy after another, many of them crude purges; clearly he was at a loss to know what might help. The unfortunate William was treated with every current nostrum. Leeches were applied, and blisters behind the ears; he was dosed with James' powder and nitre, colchicum, rhubarb and ginger, blue pill, camphor and castor oil; he was given fomentations of camomile flowers and sea-water baths. They even moved to lodgings on higher ground. After a month of these desperate measures he was no better, and finally the doctor sent him to Ischia, to try the sulphur baths. He was now so ill that he had to be carried to the boat.

Whether the baths worked the cure, or whether it was enough for him to be out of reach of Dr Strange and his potions, William did gradually improve on Ischia. Perhaps the illness had run its course. After a few days he managed to get about on a donkey, and he began sketching again.

Poor Harriet not only had the anxiety of caring for an invalid husband, but also that of controlling and disciplining two children, one of whom became, not surprisingly, increasingly restive and troublesome during his father's illness. 'William much worried with the boys'; 'Willy offended his father' are typical entries in her journal at this time. She gives no indication of the nature of Willie's offences; to judge from the irreverent tone of his letters a few years later, he may well have begun to show his impatience with his parents' anxious religiosity and earnestness. In a way familiar to parents of sons in early adolescence, he was becoming the problem child of the family.

They returned to Naples, now free from cholera, at the beginning of November. But poor William had more illness to cope with. First Willie came out in an itching rash, from which he rapidly recovered, and then his father suffered an eruption of the head and face, almost certainly caught from his son, which caused him great pain. Then, on the last day of 1837, Charley was pushed off a wall by one of a group of boys with whom they were playing, and broke his arm. It was the last straw for Harriet. She assumed a guilty responsibility for the accident: it happened on a Sunday evening, when the boys should, if she had not been over-indulgent, have been in church with her. They had of course been to church in the morning, but clearly once a day was not enough to avert divine displeasure. (The Collins parents believed firmly in personal intervention by the Lord: when William's face was badly cut some years before by a dropped pruning knife, he considered it a mercy directly attributable to the Almighty that it missed his eye.) Charley's arm was set, his bed was moved into his parents' bedroom, and his screams of pain kept them awake all night. 'The chastisement I pray may yield the fruits the Lord has sent it to produce', Harriet exclaimed, winding up her journal with a self-accusatory peroration:

> Many times my patience has failed me many times my heart has been oppressed with heaviness by reason of sin a spirit of discord & misery seemed to press upon me that never existed before . . . The climate of Italy is not favourable to the bodily or mental temperament of my husband . . . The chief drawback to the enjoyment of the beauties and advantages of Italy is the dreadful and debasing idolatry they call the Christian religion . . .[20]

She had, in other words, had enough of living abroad. But William, in spite of his sufferings, was still doggedly determined to go on. They had to spend another month at Naples while Charley's arm healed, and William briefly took over the job of journal-keeping, his entries showing a marked interest in any anecdotes denigratory of the Catholic Church. Tales of priests found guilty of financial and sexual misconduct, and of murder, particularly enthralled him. A visit to Pompeii aroused mixed feelings. 'Divine justice' was of course right in destroying 'this profligate city'; but he cannot help admitting the impression made by the amphitheatre.

> As an instance of . . . the grand, wholly without reference to the moral degradation of the entertainments prepared for the people . . . one can conceive nothing more striking than the vast assemblies that once congregated in this spot, which is worthy of an assemblage of Christians meeting for purposes of worship –[21]

They left Naples for Rome in early February. This time William went to the expense of renting a studio of his own, and in spite of continued physical weakness, went back to work, as a much younger painter, George Richmond, recalled, 'with fervour and youthful energy . . . It was a great lesson to the young men about him, to see with what simple earnestness he followed the chosen employment of his life, making all other engagements subservient or tributary to this one object.'[22] William himself wrote to David Wilkie from Rome that he no longer suffered from 'the excessive anxiety I always experienced about my pictures during their progress, [which] invariably made them the worse'.[23] Though he too longed to be done with the 'rambling, unsettled life' they had led for over a year, he determined to make the most of Italy by revisiting Florence, in better weather, and also spending time in Venice.

They stayed in Rome until the end of April. After nine days in Florence they made a rapid tour of Bologna, Modena, Parma and Mantua, ending in Venice, where they took lodgings opposite Titian's house near the Gesuiti Church. William sketched indefatigably, on one occasion halting his gondola in the middle of the Grand Canal on market day for over an hour – the equivalent, as his son put it, of drawing up a cab 'across the Strand at noonday, to paint a portrait of the lion on Northumberland-house' – while the accommodating boats on their way to market 'sloped quietly off on either side'.[24] Other pleasures of Venice were provided by a former cook of Byron's, known as 'Beppo', who not only cooked for the family during their month's stay, but acted as guide to the lesser-known corners of the city. He complained of Byron's lack of interest in food; Harriet and William's preference for plain English cooking cannot have appealed to his artistic approach. Probably Wilkie's later un-British love of sauces and garlic owed something to Beppo's efforts.

The return journey through Austria and Germany to Holland is only briefly described in the *Memoirs*, as being of less importance to the painter's development than his time in Italy. The family reached England again on 15 August 1838, and had immediately to find somewhere to live, as Captain Washington, the temporary tenant of 30 Porchester Terrace, had now taken over the lease permanently. They found an apparently suitable house near Regent's Park, 20 Avenue Road, quiet, convenient and in the part of the London suburbs which they liked best. Willie, now fourteen and a half, was quickly dispatched to school, this time a boarding school in the north London suburb of Highbury.

His experience of Mr Cole's school at 39 Highbury Place, after the roving life of the past two years, proved traumatic. The boy was highly intelligent, but his education had been unorthodox and fragmented. He had been to school for only eighteen months before going abroad, and he was soon under attack from his schoolmaster, accused of laziness and inattention. He was cast in the role of 'bad boy' by the master, who used him as a moral example for the model scholars. '"If it had been Collins I should not have felt shocked and surprised. Nobody expects anything of *him*. But *You*!" &c. &c'.[25] His one academic accomplishment – fluent French and Italian – was seen by his fellow-pupils as showing off.[26]

Wilkie's Italian experiences made him in many ways more sophisticated than his contemporaries, and he completely bypassed the crypto-homosexual culture of middle-class Englishmen. Though he was to have many good friendships with his own sex, there is never any hint of the passionate, obsessive involvement that was substituted for relationships with women by many young men of his time. He was already aware of his sexual orientation. At almost fifteen, small for his age, contemptuous of the society he had been thrown into, missing the supportive if restrictive atmosphere of home, he was a natural target for bullies. His sufferings at the hands of a 'great fellow of eighteen' in his dormitory provided the one useful lesson he learnt at school.

> He was as fond of hearing stories, in bed, as the oriental Despot to whose literary tastes we are indebted for The Arabian Nights . . . On the first night, my capacity for telling stories was tested at a preliminary examination – vanity urged me to do my best – and I paid the penalty

> . . . I was the unhappy boy appointed to amuse the captain from that time forth. It was useless to ask for mercy, and beg leave to go to sleep. 'You will go to sleep Collins, when you have told me a story.' . . . If I rebelled, the captain possessed an improved cat o' nine tails invented by himself. He roused his satraps among the other boys, and ordered me to be brought before him in words which I have never forgotten: 'Bring Collins out to be thrashed.' When I was obstinate, I took my thrashing. When my better sense prevailed, I learnt, in the presence of the instrument of correction to make those calls on my invention which have been pretty often repeated in later years. Like some other despots, the Captain had his intervals of generosity. The most unwholesome things that I have ever eaten were gifts which rewarded me for telling a good story. In after years I never had the opportunity of reminding him that I had served my apprenticeship to fiction under his superintendence. He went to India with good prospects, and died, poor fellow, a few years after he had left school.[27]

The good-humoured forgivingness of the last sentence was characteristic of Wilkie, whatever his feelings may have been at the time. Telling the story on another occasion, he added:

> I owe him a debt of gratitude . . . it was this brute who first awakened in me, his poor litle victim, a power, of which but for him I might never have been aware. Certainly no-one in my own home credited me with it; and when I left school I still continued story-telling for my own pleasure . . .[28]

Wilkie's powers as an oral story teller continued to be remarkable throughout his life. 'I have always to think twice before being sure that I have not read the one which made "Monk" Lewis's reputation, simply from hearing it narrated by him, with all its force and supernatural terror condensed into about ten minutes,' the son of one of his friends remembered, and there are many other accounts of his skill and fluency.[29] This practice in the oral tradition taught him the importance of capturing and holding his readers in the same way. 'I think so much of sound', he once told an interviewer, 'that, when I do not like the look of a sentence, I read it aloud, and alter it till I can read it easier. I think this test infallible.'[30]

Mr Cole's school, though far from cheap, was not even a good one. Wilkie often confessed his ignorance of English grammar: he told his friend Nina Lehmann that though the school had cost his father £90 a year, he had never learnt when to use 'I' or 'me'.[31] He also continued to share his mother's confusion over the active and passive forms 'lay' and 'laid'; habitually used superlatives for comparatives (the 'eldest' of two sisters, for example); and never learnt the use of the subjunctive. Nor does the classical syllabus, then the basis of schooling for boys, seem to have been well taught. One of his letters from school – a task rather than a letter, meant as an indication of progress – is a 'theme' on a subject from Homer, 'the government of many is not good'.[32] This anti-democratic piece is a stilted, dull piece of work, in sharp contrast with the liveliness of other, unsupervised letters home. It bears all the marks of a badly taught pupil, not encouraged to express his own ideas in his own language. Wilkie Collins later claimed that his father had sent him to the school, not because the education was good, but in the hope that he would make useful connections. William Collins' mixture of snobbery and unworldliness served him badly. The 'connections' might well have been more easily made at one of the recognized public schools. In a passage in *A Rogue's Life*, Wilkie sardonically recalled his father's hopes:

> 'You are the son of a gentleman' said my father, at parting, 'and you are going to be educated among gentlemen, where you will make aristocratic connections that will be of the greatest use to you in after life.' There is a remarkable observance of form in the talking of arrant nonsense. Wisdom utters itself in varying phrases and tones; but folly has its set forms of expression, which seem to suit alike all the talkers of a whole generation . . . [I have heard] the same solemn assurance of expression, and the same bland contentment of tone, which I remember as characteristic of the Doctor, when he and I parted at the school door: 'Make aristocratic connections!' (*A Rogue's Life*, *Household Words* XIII (1856), p. 158)

One, at least, of Willie's companions was memorable, though not for aristocratic birth. For a fee of a penny, he would swallow a live spider. 'If the spider was a particularly large one the price of places was higher.' This weird accomplishment 'really was worth a penny', he considered.[33]

His letters from school are fairly stoical, concentrating more on home matters than on complaints about school, but he also mentions schoolboy pleasures such as sliding on the ice in winter. There are signs that he is beginning to take pleasure in the use of words: a cake sent by his mother is '*delectably luscious*'. Two of the letters are in Italian, an attempt to keep up his knowledge of the language that suggests how important he already felt the past two years' experience to have been. He also tried to keep up his drawing and painting. There are frequent requests for news of the family, and increasing anxiety for them all. His father was never really well again after his illnesses in Italy. A recurrence of the rheumatic illness, with severe inflammation of the eyes, seriously affected his ability to paint towards the end of 1839. Willie's concern for his mother, in a letter written in December 1839 when Charley had been suffering from earache, begins to echo his father's anxious tones: 'between them both I really wonder how you keep as well as you do'. But this adult attitude is undercut by affectionate but superior teasing of his younger brother, reminding him of his 'agonized yells' when he broke his arm at Naples, 'when your vocal (I will not say *musical* powers) were exercised . . . but I am what the boys here would call *bullying* you . . .'.[34] The brothers were good friends, and though Wilkie was too short-sighted ever to be good at games and Charley was always timid, they enjoyed making and sailing model boats, flying kites and skating. 'The whole secret of skating consists in not being afraid of perpetual sprawling at full length,' Wilkie advised Holman Hunt, on learning he had taken it up. 'When Charley and I learnt, as lads, we . . . stripped after a morning's practise – and anointed each other's bruises by the fireside. Thirty tumbles a-piece was one morning's average, in learning the "outside edge" and "the three".'[35]

In the summer of 1840 the family moved house again. William Collins became convinced that his continued ill-health was due to the situation of the Avenue Road house, built on clay soil. Whether places were intrinsically 'healthy' or 'unhealthy' continued to be an obsession for the Collins family: Wilkie Collins worried about situation and climate throughout his life. The family moved back to Bayswater, to 85 Oxford Terrace (now Sussex Gardens), a fairly substantial house on three floors, with a double drawing-room thirty feet in length.[36] The rural character of the area which they had enjoyed when they first lived at Porchester Terrace had now disappeared under the new suburban streets of Bayswater and Tyburnia, but William Collins claimed that his health did improve with the move.

William was appointed Librarian of the Royal Academy at this time, an office which entailed responsibility for the Academy's art collection, as well as the library. He gave up the post a couple of years later, because of ill-health; but he had reached an assured position in his profession, and his anxieties were henceforth for his children, rather than for himself.

By the early 1840s it was becoming apparent that Charley's artistic talent was greater than his brother's, and his father began to feel that he might even possess genius. He does not seem to have considered that Willie might become a painter, and what he was to do in life was becoming a problem. At this time the boys were apparently repeating the pattern of their mother and aunt, the younger progressing steadily towards artistic recognition; the elder amusing, extravert, but uncertain of his aims, a continuing worry to his parents. It became obvious that school – or at any rate Mr Cole's school – was not proving a success. Willie was removed, probably much to his relief, around the time of his seventeenth birthday.

FOUR

The Prison at the Strand

(1841–1847)

Wilkie was hustled into a tea importer's office in the Strand – more to keep him busy than as a permanent solution for his future. The job was probably found for him by his father's friend and banker Charles Ward, who worked at Coutts Bank, for Wilkie's employer, Edward E. Antrobus, was a relation of one of the directors of Coutts. He was reassuringly public-spirited and serious: in the late 1840s and 1850s he wrote books on social problems. He became a friend of Wilkie's parents: in 1842 William Collins painted a group portrait of his three children, for which he received the decent sum of two hundred guineas. Mr Antrobus' young employee, to judge from the freedom he had to take liberal holidays, and his behaviour while at his desk, was probably an unpaid apprentice, rather than a salaried clerk; certainly he was being subsidized by his father.

In May 1842, when Wilkie had endured the office for about eighteen months without settling into commercial life, William Collins, now suffering from the heart disease that eventually killed him, as well as recurrent 'rheumatic gout', made another attempt to arrange his son's future. He asked his old patron Sir Robert Peel, now First Lord of the Treasury, for help in getting him into the Civil Service. His request was framed with a characteristic mixture of grovelling humility, anxiety and family affection:

> My great desire is to see him placed in the Treasury, or in some other government office where, should he be found worthy, he might have the prospect, however distant, of rising to eminence. – I have ventured to mention the Treasury, because I believe in that department there would be no necessity for leaving England, for I know I could not part with him altogether.[1]

Peel's reply was designed to be discouraging: he had received more than a hundred similar requests, and there was not likely to be more than one vacancy a year. The following summer William asked Charles Ward about the possibility of a vacancy in the Admiralty, but this too came to nothing.[2] Wilkie seemed doomed, after all, to a life in commerce.

After he had begun to succeed as a writer, Wilkie Collins took care to give the impression that his early career had followed a smoother and more predictable course. An account he gave in 1870 follows education at a 'well-reputed private school' with the question of Oxford or Cambridge, or the Church (in fact the one would have preceded, rather than been an alternative to the other), but stated that he so disliked both prospects that he decided to go into commerce.[3] A clergyman son may well have been William Collins' private fantasy, but it is clear from the family papers that Wilkie's opposition to university was in agreement with his father's wishes at the relevant time. Staying in Oxford in 1844, with the President of Corpus Christi, William showed him some of Wilkie's stories – by then he was beginning to get them published – and reported to Harriet: 'Dr. Norris . . . thinks he ought to do great things, he wishes he had been sent to College, of course – it is now however too late [Wilkie was now twenty], and after all I see of a College life I know not what I shd. do had he been young enough to become a student.'[4] Wilkie later echoed his father's sentiments in his attack on university athletes and rowdies in his 1870 novel *Man and Wife*, but he might have found university a tolerable alternative to the tea business. He was to spend over five years in the Strand office; at his age it must have seemed a life sentence. No doubt he felt much like Zack Thorpe in *Hide and Seek*:

> here I have been, for the last three weeks, at a Tea Broker's office . . . They all say it's a good opening for me, and talk about the respectability of

> commercial pursuits. I don't want to be respectable and I hate commercial pursuits. What is the good of forcing me into a merchant's office, when I can't say my Multiplication table? Ask my mother about that: *she'll* tell you! (*Hide and Seek*, p. 31)

He was less openly rebellious than Zack, whose fondness for athletics and longing for an open-air life were not modelled on his own habits. But Zack's habit of creeping out late at night after the family had gone to bed 'with the noiseless dexterity of a practised burglar' suggests that Wilkie, too, was 'haunting night-houses at two in the morning, while his father believed him to be safe in bed'.[5] Wilkie managed to have his night-time adventures, get through the work assigned to him in the office and still find time to scribble epic poems, tragedies, comedies, 'the usual literary rubbish', in office hours. The 'habits of business' he was supposed to be acquiring were brushed aside. The copperplate handwriting of his early schooldays changed to a highly individual but not easily read hand, not at all that of a docile clerk. It tended, at this time, to have an optimistic upward slope. Even his parents seem to have accepted that the office work was not being taken seriously. William Collins complained at not hearing from his sons, adding that Willie 'must know I shd. like to hear from him and at the office he has much spare time'.[6]

On at least one occasion Wilkie responded, with a teasing account of his enthusiasm for the lighter aspects of literature, and his abilities as a story teller, which reveals how little he was in awe of his father. He told of taking tea at the house of his aunt, Catherine Gray.

> I sat . . . freezing my horrified auditors by a varied recital of the most terrible portions of the Monk and Frankenstein – every sentence that fell from my lips, was followed in rapid succession by – 'Lor!' – 'Oh!' 'Ah!' . . . none of our country relations I am sure ever encountered in their whole lives before such a hash of diablerie, demonology & massacre, with their souchong and bread and butter – I intend to give them another course, comprising The Ancient Mariner, Jack the Giant Killer, The Mysteries of Udolpho, and an enquiry into the life and actions (when they were little girls) of the witches in Macbeth.[7]

William Collins continued to be a gentle and concerned, if sometimes bewildered father to his children. He found it difficult to realize how rapidly they were growing up, writing to assure Harriet that 'Willy [aged seventeen and a half] has been a very good boy'.[8] But his interest in his son and his concern to provide amusement for him are also very evident. 'I wish I could show you Willy's poem,' he wrote to Harriet, who, taking Charley with her, spent two months away from home in the summer of 1841. 'Don't say a word to him however about it, I should never be allowed to see another'. He listed the arrangements he had made for his son's entertainment, and the fun they had giving an informal dinner party – not unlike the one he asked her to when they first met:

> if Missis had left the key of the plate chest we shd. not have been obliged to help the peas with dessert spoons nor have been under the necessity of wiping our forks so often however we had plenty of fun and as dinners are very stupid things in general it was a feature –[9]

In the summer of 1842 he took the eighteen-year-old Wilkie with him on a trip to Scotland, going by sea to Edinburgh. It was the first time he had returned there since his marriage in 1822. His son was enthusiastic about the Old Town, but '*tremendously disgusted* with the melancholy, grass-grown, ill-paved, covered-all-over-with-large-squares' New Town. They did the sights with their usual thoroughness. 'I've seen Rizzio's blood, Queen Mary's work basket, the Calton Hill, dirty children, filthy fishwives, slovenly men, dropsical women, Salisbury Crags, ill managed drains, Grassmarket . . .'[10]

They went on by steamer to Wick in the far north of Scotland. They stayed on the coast at Thurso, and visited John o' Groat's (thirty-six miles on horseback, William boasted) before going on to Lerwick, in Shetland. William had been asked to provide the illustrations for Scott's novel *The Pirate*, set in Orkney and Shetland, for the Abbotsford Edition. Though now a seriously sick man, William was still indefatigable when making sketches for paintings: in Shetland they rode thirty to forty miles a day (the only way of getting about), often in drenching rain.

Wilkie made consciously literary use of the journey, first in his letters to his mother, and then, five years later, in his life of his father. The memory of the wild and romantic scenery of the highlands and islands stayed with him all his life. About twenty miles west of Thurso the coastal hamlet of Armadale, with its fine beach enclosed by rugged arms of rock, gave him the title, over twenty years later, of one of his most popular novels.

At Lerwick they stayed in an inn 'admirably removed from the usual conventionalities' of southern hotels, where all the guests sat together in one sitting-room and all the bedrooms opened out of each other. 'The characters of the company, who met for eating, and drinking, and talking purposes . . . would have furnished famous material to any novelist.' As well as an all-purpose sitting-room, there was an all-purpose servant, 'a slatternly, good-natured wench, who took extraordinary care of her master's guests, plying them with little dishes of sweetmeats of her own composing, as if they had been a large nursery-full of children . . .'. They made expeditions in search of scenery: the experience of riding across the boggy moors, made doubly treacherous by sudden mist, was recalled in one of Wilkie's late novels, *The Two Destinies*. They also visited a fleet of Dutch herring-boats, 'regularly ranged side by side, like volumes of Hume and Smollett on a school-room bookshelf', where they had a ludicrous encounter with the skipper, 'a man of vast breeches and cloudy physiognomy', and his crew, who entirely failed to understand that William wanted to sketch them and their boat:

> the captain pulled from a shelf a bottle of 'schnapps', three glasses, and a map of Europe . . . he spread forth the map on a locker, slowly placed his thumb on that part of it occupied by England, nodded his head solemnly at his guests, and drank off his dram . . . He then pushed the map to the painter and his companion, who, finding it necessary to act their parts in this pantomime of international amity, put their thumbs on Holland, nodded their heads, and emptied their glasses . . .[11]

The encounter left William Collins 'inarticulate with laughter'; he and Wilkie seem to have enjoyed each other's company uninhibitedly and thoroughly on this journey. It was perhaps the only time they were to be so intimate.

During the summer of 1843 the family moved again, round the corner from Oxford Terrace to the last house in which they were all to be together, 1 Devonport Street, Hyde Park Gardens. Here, for the first time in William Collins' life, he had a well-equipped, suitable place in which to paint, a real studio rather than a painting-room. He seems, in his final years, to have completely overcome the depression and anxiety that had so oppressed him for most of his life. He was unrealistically optimistic about his health – though it was clear to others that it was deteriorating – co-operating with the numerous doctors he consulted in their suggestions about diet and medicines, and looking forward to years of productive work in the new studio. Wilkie Collins describes this room in his life of his father, and again, in loving detail, in *Hide and Seek*. Its controlled chaos of artist's clutter and *trompe-l'œil* joke, with his father's schoolboy enjoyment of it, are used in his account of Valentine Blyth's painting-room.

> There was a painting-stand with quantities of shallow little drawers, some too full to open, others, again, too full to shut . . . portfolios, dog's-eared sheets of drawing paper, tin pots, scattered brushes, palette-knives, rags variously defiled by paint and oil, pencils, chalks, port-crayons – the whole smelling powerfully at all points of turpentine . . . All the surplus small articles which shelves, tables, and chairs were unable to accommodate, reposed in comfortable confusion on the floor . . . And worse than all his own disorderly habits – Mr. Blyth had jocosely desecrated his art, by making it imitate litter where . . . there was real litter enough already. Just in the way of anybody entering the room he had painted, on the bare floor, exact representations of a new quill pen and a very expensive-looking sable brush . . . Fresh visitors constantly attested the skilfulness of these imitations by involuntarily stooping to pick up the illusive pen and brush; Mr. Blyth always enjoying the discomfiture and astonishment of every new victim, as thoroughly as if the practical joke had been a perfectly new one on each successive occasion. (*Hide and Seek*, Chap. 2, p. 29)

1843 was a good year for William Collins' sons. In August Wilkie (the name by which he was now known to everyone outside the family circle) had a story, signed W. Wilkie Collins, published in *The Illuminated Magazine*. 'The Last Stage Coachman' is a brief fantasy on the fashionable theme of the replacement of coaches by rail, the grass-grown, silent highways, the deserted roadside inns. The description of the phantom stage-coach develops his fascination with the macabre: '. . . a railway director strapped fast to each wheel, and a stoker between the teeth of each of the four horses . . . [the coachman] clothed in a coat of engineers' skin, with gloves of the hide of railway police . . .'. It was his first signed publication; though other articles and stories were beginning to 'find their way modestly into the small periodicals', they did so anonymously.[12] But his increasing success began to be taken seriously by his father. He began a new journal in 1844 with the note – or instruction:

> As I think it quite possible that my dear son, William Wilkie Collins, may be tempted, should it please God to spare his life beyond that of his father, to furnish the world with a memoir of my life, I purpose occasionally noting down some circumstances as leading points, which may be useful.[13]

The fifteen-year-old Charley became, to his father's delight, a student at the Royal Academy Schools. He was, unlike his brother, a good-looking boy: well-proportioned, with bright blue eyes and flaming red hair. But he was already too serious; like his father anxious and prone to depression, he was to remain close to, and dependent on, his mother. 'Charlie is dreadfully Mother sick, and very desperate', his father wrote in 1840, when she was staying with her parents at Alderbury.[14] Four years later, just before Charley's sixteenth birthday, his father reported, 'I could not have stayed away another day from Charley . . . poor chick, he cannot go on without one of *us* at least.'[15] The twenty-year-old Wilkie's bouncy self-confidence and ability to enjoy himself was in striking contrast. 'The *parties* have knocked me up', he informed his mother.

> I've made two *speeches* at supper and drunk so much of the juice of the grape that (to use the impassioned language of Elihu the Buzzite a *comforter* of Job –) 'my belly is as wine'. We got home after one of the festive scenes at 10 minutes past 4 *A.M.* Charlie was so horrified at hearing the cock crow that he showed a disposition to whimper and said that people out so late as we were not in a *fit state to die* . . .
>
> William Collins Esqre R.A. . . . will eat no pudding and swears that everything is poison but mutton and bread. He says he laid my case before the *Galens* of Southampton [their doctor friends, the Bullars].

> If they are to be believed – by the time you return I shall have no stomach at all. Vive la Gastronomie! 'which being interpreted' means Damn Digestion![16]

It comes as something of a relief to know that Charley loved dancing, and two years later Wilkie, for once playing the elder brother, considered that he 'seems to have more chance of becoming a member of the Royal Academy of Dancing at Paris, than of the Royal Academy of Art at London'.[17]

In the summer of 1844 Wilkie and Charley, now twenty and sixteen, were at last considered old enough to be left at home for more than a few days without either parent, and Harriet spent four months with her sick husband in the country. Their sons took it in turns to write. 'Charlie is a *Scribe* and I am a *Pharisee*', Wilkie wrote apologetically, 'for he pays you real attention, while I only talk about it.' He made amends in a long and amusing letter, practising his talent for comic verse in a tale of a mislaid key and a maidservant roused from her bed to account for it:

> 'I've not got it' says she – 'Pon my life'
> Says I, 'You're o'erdoing the spree!
> You may cheat the man out of his wife
> But damn it Ma'am! Give him his key.
> You'll find him, I think, in the hall,
> I leave you my blessing and candle,
> Ere you seek him just put on a shawl
> Or I swear I won't answer for scandal.'

He couldn't resist teasing his mother gently about their reception of a pious visitor: 'Currant pie, drawing room sofa and captains biscuit awaited her – moral conversation soothed her – Bed and washing-stand refreshed her – Breakfast settled her –' But affection and reassurance are uppermost in his mind: he promises her they are managing the house well, get up early, don't drink, and are 'on tremendously affable terms' with the servants.[18] Earlier in the letter he had been lordly about the stupidities and muddles the servants had got themselves into, but, however strongly he resisted his parents' pietistic outlook, their emphasis on treating servants as human beings, integrated into the household rather than isolated in their own quarters, was one of the positive values Wilkie Collins absorbed from them. Harriet Collins, who had known the difficulties and uncertain social status of a governess, taught her sons not to despise the work that ensured their comfort.

Another letter from this period betrays a bewildered but unusually detailed concern, for a young man of the time, for the intimate needs of female guests. Three are expected, and Wilkie has asked a girl cousin to 'help me put them to bed, and "let down their back hair" and tuck them up . . . What in the devil's name am I to do with this seraglio of women? (*six*, including the servants) . . . I suppose I have done right in asking Marian Gray to come . . . I intended to have asked one of Charley's "*sluts*"* . . . Good God, suppose they should want a change of chemises!'[19]

At the end of August Wilkie went abroad for five weeks, the first time without his parents. He travelled to Paris with Charles Ward, the elder son of William's friend and E. M. Ward's elder brother. Charles, who was about ten years older than Wilkie, was already courting Wilkie's cousin, the eighteen-year-old Jane Carpenter. 'I've only seen Romeo Ward once the last fortnight', Wilkie wrote to his mother in July. 'He's so taken up with Juliet Chips that he's as impossible to be seen as a picture in the Octagon Room.'†[20] Charles Ward had followed his father into Coutts Bank, and was to work there all his life.

Wilkie, objecting violently to taking the family carpet-bag with him, 'the most disagreeable machine to pack – the most troublesome to unpack – the most impracticable to carry that human science ever invented', managed to borrow a box from 'the "confederate"' Charles Ward as a substitute.[21] If William and Harriet thought Ward a suitably staid and mature companion for their wayward son, they were swiftly disillusioned: Wilkie took the lead, as he continued to do throughout their lifelong friendship.

The two young men planned to follow in the footsteps of Sterne's *A Sentimental Journey*: 'London to Calais – Calais to Montreuil &c.

* Presumably artists' models.

† The Octagon Room at the Royal Academy was considered the 'den' – the worst place to have a picture hung in the annual Exhibition.

&c.' Wilkie's letters from France fizzed with excitement. The sense of liberation is palpable: as if to underline it he signs a letter to his mother 'Wilkie Collins', jettisoning 'William' entirely. He alternately teases and reassures: they are 'dissipating fearfully' – but the dissipations are listed as 'Jardins, theatres, and Cafés'; and he includes descriptions of the pictures he has seen on visits to the Louvre and Versailles, including Géricault's 'The Raft of the Medusa', for his father's benefit. He made the visit to the Morgue which seems to have been almost obligatory for English tourists, and described a dead soldier laid out naked 'like an unsaleable cod fish', 'a glorious subject for Charlie'. As always, music meant less to him than painting and he found the music of Rossini's popular opera *Otello* 'monotonously dismal'. At the theatre his tastes were for the less respectable forms of French drama, rather than Racine. But French food delighted him; he relished 'Déjeuner à la fourchette – oysters and chablis, omlettes and radishes – much better than that infernal charity-boy-cum-servant-maid-compound commonly called bread-and-butter'. He promises, not very convincingly, to 'repent upon leg of mutton and rice-pudding when I get home'. There were weddings in all the churches, he reported, commenting loftily: 'Don't take much interest in matrimony – so can't tell you anything more about the ceremony than that the bridegrooms looked foolish and wore ill-cut coats and that the Priests looked sulky . . .'[22]

His easily alarmed father reacted predictably to his effervescence: 'I do not like his flippant companion they seem to think of nothing but doing absurd things – he seems to think he may stay 'till the 3rd of Octr has he heard from Mr. Antrobus himself?'[23] Wilkie tested his employer's patience to the uttermost, but he returned to the office before annoyance turned to outrage.

Once back there he spent his working hours writing a novel, set in Tahiti before its discovery by Europeans, which was submitted to Longmans by his father in January 1845.* Wilkie later recalled the story as being something of a shocker – a Gothic romance transferred to the South Seas. 'My youthful imagination ran riot among the noble savages in scenes which caused the respectable British publisher to

* See Appendix C.

declare that it was impossible to put his name on the title page . . .'[24] Early western accounts of Tahiti stressed the shocking promiscuity of the women before they learnt Christian ideas of marriage – a theme that would have appealed to Wilkie, and might well have scared off publishers. In fact one publisher, probably Longmans, kept the manuscript for two months, originally suggesting to William Collins that it could be published if he would bear part of the expense, and finally rejecting it (after it had been approved by their reader) on financial grounds alone. They would have gone ahead if Wilkie's father had undertaken to bear the entire cost; William, proud parent though he was, was too cautious for that.[25] Wilkie, as usual making a dull truth into a good story, claimed that the reader had considered it 'hopelessly bad, and that in his opinion the writer had . . . no possible prospect of succeeding in a literary career' and that they had finally met and laughed about it after the publication of *The Woman in White*.[26] The book was later submitted to Chapman and Hall, who also rejected it. His path out of commerce seemed to be blocked once more. Wilkie kept the manuscript, however, and thirty years later he reused the Polynesian setting, and some of the material, in a short story, 'The Captain's Last Love', in which an Englishman falls in love with a priest's daughter isolated on an island with her father, like Miranda with Prospero.[27]

Wilkie did not immediately begin another full-length book, and in September he took a second Paris expedition, this time by himself: Charles Ward had married Jane Carpenter in February.[28] It became clear that it was not Charles' example that had led him into trouble on his previous visit. Wilkie was now twenty-one, and impatient of restraint; only his financial dependence on his father kept him under control.

He boasted that he was one of only three people able to eat dinner during the crossing to Rouen. He was to have a lifelong immunity from seasickness, and to continue to pride himself on it. He went on:

> As (like 'Marlow') 'I generally make my father's son welcome wherever he goes' I made acquaintance with every soul in the ship, from a good-natured *negro* who told me he was a student in *philosophy*! to a man with a blood-spotted nose, who knew all the works, of all the artists, ancient and modern, all over the world.[29]

Perhaps he identified himself further with Goldsmith's character in *She Stoops to Conquer*, who is attracted by a supposed barmaid, but stutters to a halt in the presence of a lady. Marlow cannot face the 'terrors of a formal courtship' and believes that 'this stammer in my address, and this aukward prepossessing visage of mine, can never permit me to soar above the reach of a milliner's prentice, or one of the dutchesses of Drury Lane'.[30] Arriving at the Hôtel de Tuileries in Paris, Wilkie discovered that his unpretentious friendliness, or Marlovian advances, had made an unexpected impression the year before on one of the humblest of the hotel servants.

> '*Virginia*, desires her kindest remembrances to you, Monsieur' said she – and then the kitchen maid put down the boiling ingredient and wiped a 'black' off her nose with the end of her apron . . . I discovered that Virginia was *last year's* kitchen maid. Fancy the astonishment of a thoroughbred Englishman at learning that a kitchen maid named Virginia (!) whom he scarcely recollected and whom he never feed with money, had sent him her kindest remembrances.[31]

He conscientiously sweated through the Louvre, with a family met on the boat, who asked him to go to Nice with them. He was still hoping to get the South Seas novel published, for he asked his mother if she could not send him £100 'on the strength of my manuscript and Chapman and Hall', to pay for the journey south. His ideas became more and more expansive.

> Or could you not make up your minds to take the journey yourselves and stay at Nice (think of the Protestant Church and the 'resident English'!) while I conveyed the younger branches of 'my family' to – what Plummer the portly calls – 'Cara Italia'? Life is short – we should enjoy it. I am your affectionate son W. Wilkie Collins – you should humour me![32]

But his parents, staying with Mr Antrobus at Torquay (did Harriet show him the letter?), were not prepared to humour him, and wrote sternly. Wilkie, quite unashamed, responded with a disrespectful message to his father: 'Considering he is a lamb of Mr. Dodsworth's flock, Mr. Collins evinces a most unchurchmanlike disposition to scandalise other people', wickedly turning evangelical doctrine on its head.

> 'The Evil One' (whom you mention with somewhat unladylike want of courtesy at the close of your letter) is such an exceedingly gentlemanlike dog in this city, with his theatres and his kitchens, that I find it rather difficult to 'cut his connection'. I have bought an Opera Glass, so I must, of necessity, go to the Play to use it. I have got a box of Soda Powders, so I must, in common justice, deliver myself to Gastronomy . . . 'I sticks' to the 'Pomps and vanities' – ne'er an Evangelical of the lot of 'em can accuse me of being 'a spiritual rebel.'[33]

He discovered that he thoroughly enjoyed being alone: 'the privilege of being able to consult my own tastes and inclinations without the slightest reference to any one else' was a novel delight, and had the additional advantage that he improved his French by speaking nothing else.[34] He was beginning to read the French novelists, Balzac in particular, who were to be an important influence on his own writing. He also made a return visit to the Morgue, and reported, in the terms of compassionate indignation that were to fuel his novels:

> A body of a young girl had just been fished out of the river. As her bosom was 'black and blue' I suppose she had been beaten into a state of insensibility and then flung into the Seine. The spectators of this wretched sight were, for the most part, *women and children*.[35]

However, Paris seemed to have the edge over London in many respects: 'the *start* of a new man in Literature or Art is a matter of intense moment to every educated individual in this city', and he was told – and believed – that dramatists in France earned 70–80,000 francs year. But he also had to confess, by the end of three weeks, that he was penniless. As well as the opera glass he had bought 'some loves of boots in the newest Paris fashion . . . *toes* broader than any other part'. He had opened a subscription with Galignani, been to all the theatres, eaten and drunk until the waistband of his trousers was perceptibly tightening. Now he had no money to pay his hotel bill, or his passage home. Accurately judging how far to go in horrifying his parents, he pretended to be indifferent to the prospect of imprisonment for debt: 'the actual difference between imprisonment at Paris and imprisonment at the Strand being too inconsequential to be worth ascertaining'.

After this threat, a wheedling request for £10 was meant to seem a small price to pay to get the prodigal home. 'You said you hoped I should make my cheque last for my *trip*', he reminded them, adding jesuitically, 'It *has* lasted for my *trip*, but not for my *return*.'[36] A further cheque arrived, but Wilkie, far from rushing home in penitence, stayed on to the last possible moment, explaining, 'the Italian Opera has begun, and Patés de Foies Gras are daily expected at the principal restaurants'.[37]

He returned to the prison at the Strand. But his distaste for commerce was clearly not to be overcome, and when he had suffered through a further six months, his father agreed to release him. William Collins was failing fast. His son, watching him still at work in the autumn and winter of 1845, was deeply impressed by his courage and his suffering.

> His heart was . . . fearfully deranged in its action, appearing not to beat, but to heave with a rushing, irregular, watery sound. His breathing was oppressed, as in the last stages of asthma . . . His cough assailed him with paroxysms so violent and so constantly recurring, as to create apprehension that he might rupture a blood-vessel . . . in spite of this combination of maladies . . . he disposed himself to labour . . . Sometimes the brush dropped from his hand from sheer weakness; sometimes it was laid down while he gasped for breath . . . the strong mind bent the reluctant body triumphantly to its will, in every part of the pictures on which, already a dying man, he now worked.[38]

Knowing he could not live much longer, William made one more attempt to settle his son. Wilkie was admitted as a student of Lincoln's Inn on 17 May 1846. It was a respectable cover for his real ambitions. 'I had sadly disappointed my father by choosing the Law as my profession, in preference to the Church', says the narrator of one of Wilkie's late stories. 'At that time, to own the truth, I had no serious intention of following any special vocation. I simply wanted an excuse for enjoying the pleasures of a London life.'[39] Wilkie was more ambitious than his character. With his father and his aunt both making good incomes as painters, he had grown up in a milieu which took the practice of one of the arts for granted as a reasonable way of making a living. Indeed his parents seem to have been relieved when they discovered that their good-for-nothing son had a talent for something. Though the intricacies and inconsistencies of the law interested him – he could have made a good lawyer – he soon closed the law books he was supposed to be studying. His fees were paid, and he kept terms and 'ate dinners', then the only requirements for qualifying as a barrister. But Lincoln's Inn was chiefly memorable for some good friends he made there, a joke played on an earnest candidate for the Bar who was persuaded to take seriously the purely nominal legal exercise necessary to qualify, and the small, idiosyncratic museum recently opened in Lincoln's Inn Fields, which housed, as it still does, Sir John Soane's collection of pictures and antiquities. He referred to it affectionately in a late novel as 'a nice little easy museum in a private house, and all sorts of pretty things to see'.[40]

He had already begun his second novel, *Antonina*, before he entered Lincoln's Inn.[41] He chose to write it in the night-time quiet of his father's untidy painting-room. Tidiness was never a virtue he admired, or practised. Hard work was; and Wilkie was ambitious. His letters from Paris showed the unmistakable influence of Byron: he acquired Moore's *Life, Letters and Journals of Lord Byron* in 1843, and thought the letters 'the best English I know of – perfectly simple and clear, bright and strong'.[42] But a serious historical novel seemed, at that date, to be the proper way to begin a literary career, and he took Scott, and Bulwer-Lytton's *The Last Days of Pompeii*, as his models.

Antonina is certainly no more unreadable than Bulwer-Lytton's once-popular work. Wilkie set his novel in Rome, the city where his childhood had ended, and set about researching the historical background. *Antonina* – perhaps the only 'Gothic novel' to include Goths in its cast – was based on the account in Gibbon of the conquest of Rome by Alaric in AD 410, augmented from other sources, such as Sismondi's *Histoire de la Chute de l'Empire Romain* of 1835. The subject gave its twenty-two-year-old author the chance to reconstruct imaginatively the Roman scenes, still vividly remembered, that had fired his imagination as a boy.

The manuscript shows that he began writing hesitantly, choosing each word with care, and very consciously writing for publication: there are notes suggesting the length, in pages, of each episode.[43] From the beginning Wilkie knew that writing was a craft, as well as an art: he had absorbed his father's meticulous attitude to his profession. Later he was able to assure printers that manuscript pages in his handwriting were always the same length. The many insertions and deletions in the manuscript of *Antonina* tend to make (or try to make) the story more vivid by sensory descriptions; the descriptive passages are more successful than the narrative and dialogue. The future master of plot flounders badly in shifting from one set of characters to another, and in his attempts to draw together the different strands of his narrative. The style, a combination of the antithetical Gibbonian sentence with flowery decorative flourishes taken from Bulwer-Lytton, is quite unlike anything else Wilkie Collins wrote. But though *Antonina* appears superficially very different from the contemporary liveliness and unpretentious style he was later to develop, the way in which the sensational and the uncanny are combined with explorations of individual psychology and attacks on social abuses will be familiar to readers of his other novels.

The central theme is the destructive force of religious fanaticism, exemplified in two brothers, one a Christian, the other a pagan. The brothers are separated in childhood, and grow up in ignorance of their relationship. As adults each hates and fears everything the other stands for. Yet their experiences are parallel, and the flight to extremism in each case is seen as having its origins in psychological disturbance, rather than being the result of conscious and rational thought. The fanatic Numerian, turned, by his wife's infidelity, from passionate love of her to an equal passion for primitive Christianity, 'flew to religion as the suicide flies to the knife – in despair'.

> In the stoical practice and ungenial theory of the ancient believers, he found a system which sympathised with his new convictions. Day after day he searched anxiously among the records left by the most austere of the primitive fathers, until the constant perusal of their pitiless doctrines led him at length to believe that the very existence within him of the social emotions was in itself a sin. (*Antonina*, first edition, Vol. 1, p. 146 (omitted from later editions))

The pagan Ulpius, later to be revealed as Numerian's brother, is equally fanatical in the practice of his religion, fast disappearing before the rising power of Christianity:

> His gradual initiation into the mysteries of his religion, created a strange, voluptuous sensation of fear and interest in his mind. He heard the oracles, and he trembled; he attended the sacrifices and the auguries, and he wondered. All the poetry of the bold and beautiful superstition to which he was devoted, flowed overwhelmingly into his young heart, absorbing the service of his fresh imagination, and transporting him incessantly from the vital realities of the outer world to the shadowy regions of aspirations and thought. (*Antonina*, Vol. 1, p. 191)

In his case, the early loss of his mother, followed by that of the uncle to whom Ulpius transfers his affection and loyalty, are the traumata which lead him to extremism. Having lost his first identity, he creates a new one based on his religious faith.

Wilkie's emphasis on the harm done to the heroine (Numerian's daughter) by her father's virtual imprisonment of her, and his doctrinaire refusal of the most innocent pleasure – her delight in music – would have met with William Collins' agreement. But the expression of Wilkie's forthright, and more controversial views on Christian dogma was not inhibited by any fear of his father's disapproval. The modern parallels to the beliefs of Numerian and Ulpius, clearly intended, are the evangelical wing of the Church of England, and the Roman Catholicism of France and Italy which he had encountered as a boy. The charms of the pagan religion, compared with Numerian's gloomy code, are made as obvious as its dangers: Wilkie seems more whole-hearted in his condemnation of puritanism, and more susceptible to the aesthetic appeal of Catholicism, than his father might have thought proper.

All forms of extremism are under attack in *Antonina*, the sybaritic luxury of the effete aristocracy and the violent cruelty of the Goths as much as the excesses of religion. Even Antonina's overriding passion for music is seen as unbalanced sensibility, potentially dangerous. Attempts, crude and intermittent, are made to give each a convincing cause, in the personal background and psychology of the main characters as well as in general, social terms.

There are other foreshadowings of Wilkie's future novels. The intelligent, forceful woman with a grudge against society is first encountered in *Antonina* in the character of the Goth Goisvintha, whose children have been murdered by the Romans. She is a broodingly destructive presence, owing much to the character of Norna in Scott's *The Pirate*. But she is seen from the outside: the reader is never encouraged to identify with her feelings, or even to feel much pity for her. The description of the malicious dwarf Reburrus, whose outward deformities might later have been the subject of compassion and identification, is more characteristic of early Dickens than of Wilkie Collins. Here the physical appearance mirrors inward distortion, in conformity with the physiognomic theories of character then current.

> This man was humpbacked; his gaunt, bony features were repulsively disproportioned in size to his puny frame, which looked doubly contemptible, enveloped as it was in an ample tawdry robe. Sprung from the lowest ranks of the populace, he had gradually forced himself into the favour of his superiors by his skill in coarse mimicry, and his readiness in ministering to the worst vices of all who would employ him. (*Antonina*, Vol. 2, p. 86)

The liveliest scenes in the novel – for example 'The Banquet of Famine', from which this description is taken – are relished with the pleasure in Gothic horror that Wilkie had shown in his 1842 letter to his father. There are hints of cannibalism, and the 'banquet' is presided over by a hunger-bitten corpse which turns out to be that of the dwarf's mother. A brass dragon in a pagan temple is an engine of destruction that swallows sacrificial victims. Wilkie had, for the sections of the book he most enjoyed, absorbed 'Monk' Lewis to more purpose than Edward Gibbon. He was careful, though, to give scholarly backing for his horrors: the first edition of *Antonina* has notes and appendices giving his sources. The most extreme passages in the novel occur in the part written after his father's death; but this seems more to do with the usual problem faced by the writer of shockers – that the horrors have to be increased throughout the book in order to maintain tension – than to the removal of a moderating influence.

Work on the novel was interrupted briefly by the now yearly visit to the Continent. This time Wilkie, with Charles Ward, went to Belgium, in a July heatwave. The extravagant Wilkie persuaded the thrifty Ward to go first-class on the train, but couldn't get him to stay away longer than a week. Ward, now a father, 'tells me I am a profligate'; after looking at pictures at Antwerp and Bruges, Charles returned to his family, and Wilkie to his novel.[44]

He had written rather more than half of it when his father, who had taken to his bed in October, finally died on 17 February 1847, after much suffering, relieved only by an opiate, 'Battley's Drops'. He died peacefully, with his family around him. He was buried with his mother and brother in the churchyard of St Mary's, Paddington.

By the terms of his will, small legacies were left (in a codicil added just before his death) to Harriet's four sisters. There was an annuity to a cousin, Mrs Elizabeth Jones, of the interest on a sum of £700, a provision which was to become a recurrent irritation to Wilkie. The rest of his estate was left in trust to Harriet for her lifetime, and after her death to his two sons equally, the capital still in trust for any children they might have.[45] It was a typically cautious arrangement, which left Wilkie and Charles, during their mother's lifetime, dependent on her good will for any money they did not earn.

Wilkie was twenty-three, Charley just nineteen. Neither was earning a living. Wilkie's tenuous connection with his legal studies was confirmed by his next step in establishing himself in the world. He abandoned work on *Antonina*, marking on the manuscript the place he had reached on the night William Collins died, and turned, not to the study of the law, but to the promised life of his father.

FIVE

Publication

(1847–1851)

In a story written three years before his death, Wilkie Collins pondered the relationship of parents and children – no doubt considering his own equivocal role as a father of illegitimate children as well as his experiences as a son – and summed up his own feelings on the distinction to be drawn between love for a mother, and for a father:

> Our mothers have the most sacred of all claims on our gratitude and our love. They have nourished us with their blood; they have risked their lives in bringing us into the world; they have preserved and guided our helpless infancy with divine patience and love. What claim equally strong and equally tender does the other parent establish on his offspring? What motive does the instinct of his young children find for preferring their father before any other person who may be a familiar object in their daily lives? They love him – naturally and rightly love him – because he lives in their remembrance (if he is a good man) as the first, the best, the dearest of their friends. (*The Guilty River*, *Arrowsmith's Christmas Annual*, 1886, p. 3)

Wilkie Collins' life of his father is his account of such a good man. By this act of respect to a parent by no means always respectfully treated while he was alive, Wilkie attempted to conclude and exorcize his relationship with him. He did this with humility and remarkable maturity. He also took the opportunity to examine the life and character of a creative artist: to consider what motivated him; how he went about preparing himself for his lifetime's task; and how he balanced up the mundane business of making a living for himself and his dependants with the creative urge for self-expression and self-fulfilment. Often he seems to be making notes for his own consideration, while ostensibly describing his father:

> It is a peculiar quality in the mental composition of those enthusiastically devoted to an intellectual aim, that they make – often unconsciously – their very pleasures and relaxations minister to the continued study of their pursuit.

And again:

> It is to the absence of habits of reading – of frequent intercourse with the intellects of others, in a sister pursuit, that the inaptitude to originality, the perverse reiteration, by some modern artists . . . is . . . due. The originality of the conception is more thoroughly dependent on the novelty of the subject, than is generally imagined.[1]

The *Memoirs* also have another significance, as his first published book. He dropped *Antonina* in order to write them as an act of filial duty; but the hard-headed author of later years is also emerging. Wilkie saw that a biography of a popular and notable painter was a respectable enterprise which might prepare the way for an unknown novelist. His first attempt at fiction had been rejected; it might be better to offer publishers a biography with an assured, if limited sale, than to risk another rejection. The project was helped by his mother's willingness to back it financially, but she ran no great risk in doing so. Wilkie was later to learn much from Dickens about marketing his work, but he already had the makings of the shrewd business sense that was to bring him into conflict with more than one publisher.

The *Memoirs* took him a surprisingly short time to complete. By the end of May 1847 he had got as far as 1815.[2] The biography was ready for publication by May 1848, and (as he noted on the manuscript of the novel) he resumed work on *Antonina* on 25 July 1847.[3] He gave the biography his whole attention for less than six months: he already had a mature capacity for concentrated work, when the task was of his own choosing. Some of his materials were easily available: his father's careful record of every picture he had ever sold, with the price received for it; exhibition catalogues; William and Harriet's journals; and the family and other letters. Wilkie also wrote to his father's friends and fellow-artists at home and in Italy asking for their reminiscences. Several of William Collins' closest friends were already dead, David Wilkie and Washington Allston among them. Most of those who were still alive contributed with enthusiasm. One who is notably absent is Linnell, though his portrait of William Collins was engraved for the frontispiece. Linnell had been asked for anecdotes of Collins in 1835 by Alaric Watts, and responded generously, emphasizing his modesty and goodness, and not mentioning the snobbery and prejudice that had sometimes divided them.[4] But the relationship had been plagued by quarrels, and Wilkie may have been uncertain of the notoriously bad-tempered Linnell's feelings. He remained in touch with Linnell, however, asking his advice on the reproduction of the illustrations for his travel book *Rambles Beyond Railways*, in 1850.

The *Memoirs* were modelled on other contemporary lives of painters, notably on Allan Cunningham's biography of David Wilkie, and Charles Leslie's of Constable. Wilkie did not attempt to follow his grandfather's livelier and more eccentric life of Morland. A reviewer of the *Life of Sir David Wilkie* complained of its length (three volumes): 'All that was necessary to be written of Wilkie . . . might have been contained in a plump duodecimo'.[5] Though the *Memoirs* are in two, not especially plump volumes, they follow the organization of Cunningham's book closely, even to the provision of an appendix listing the painter's works and their whereabouts. The extended passages of description of the paintings William Collins produced, year by year, are, to modern readers, unnecessarily lengthy, though a useful exercise in developing descriptive and atmospheric writing: they, too, are modelled on Cunningham. For anyone interested in early-nineteenth-century painting and its social background, the book is extremely readable: remarkable, for so inexperienced a writer, in its portrayal of a personality, and the control, organization and shaping of material into narrative. Wilkie took considerable trouble over the arrangement of his manuscript, delaying publication to do so.[6] A long and appreciative letter from the aged Maria Edgeworth praises the 'style so clear and unaffected' and the 'judiciously affectionate' portrait, 'not a eulogy upon his father but making every reader of sense taste or feeling appreciate his merits fully both as an artist and as a man'.[7] It remains to this day the only life of William Collins.

Wilkie asked permission to dedicate the book to Sir Robert Peel, who not only agreed, but invited him to his country house, where two of William Collins' paintings that Wilkie had never seen were hung in the gallery. The book was finally published by Longmans in November 1848. In that year of political upheaval Wilkie became uncertain whether the book would find any readers 'amid the vital and varied interests of home politics and foreign revolutions'.[8] But William Collins was, by the time of his death, an establishment figure, whose paintings continued to fetch considerable sums. In a Christie's sale in June 1866, Constable's 'The haywain' made 1,300 guineas, and William Collins' 'The Skittle Players', originally sold, with some difficulty, for four hundred guineas, made 1,200. The same picture fetched 2,400 guineas when it was sold again in 1875; but by 1888 it had fallen back to £1,585.

Wilkie took trouble to promote the book, writing personal letters to accompany prospectuses of it to a long list of possible subscribers in the worlds of art and literature, and receiving only one frosty answer, from the irascible John Wilson Croker, who couldn't see why he was being asked to subscribe to a book that was already written.[9] It was bought by art lovers and William Collins' friends, and received excellent reviews. The *Observer* critic was especially enthusiastic about the subject and the author: '. . . no better work upon art and artists has been given to the world within the last half century . . . The general reader, as well as the artistic aspirant, is . . . strongly recommended to its perusal.'[10] Six weeks after publication more than half the edition of 750 copies had been sold, and the costs of publication covered; by the end of the year Wilkie had even made a respectable profit.[11]

Wilkie Collins was a year younger, when his father died, than William Collins had been when he was left the sole support of his mother and younger brother. Wilkie was more fortunate. He may later have exaggerated the amount his father left. A biographical notice, probably first drafted in 1857, claims 'Mr. Collins is independent of literature, and may therefore write what he will without suffering much from a failure', but he did not have to help his mother financially; Harriet, who also inherited some money from an aunt, Mrs Davis, continued to live comfortably. Until 1860, when he had other family obligations, Wilkie did not trouble to open a bank account of his own, instead using Harriet's, both to deposit his earnings and to draw on when he needed cash, making the necessary arrangements with Charles Ward.

Wilkie made his yearly journey to the Continent in August 1847, and as usual ran out of money. Harriet made another attempt – her last – to control him by withholding funds. The plan was that he and Charles Ward, both of them amateur painters, should stay in Normandy sketching the French countryside. Wilkie took an elaborate new painting box with him, 'stocked with a wonderfully complete assortment of colours, brushes, mill-boards, palette-knives, palettes, oil-bottles, gallipots and rags. Being of the inferior, or embryo order of artists, I, of course, required a perfect paraphernalia of materials to work with . . .'[13] Some accomplished sketches survive, to confirm his assurance that he had the intention, at least, of sketching 'furiously at all points'.[14] As before, Wilkie was the leader, persuading the more timid and conventional Ward to return from a disastrous expedition in a huckster's cart, though Ward was too proud to drive up to the hotel in 'our excellent but humble and uneasy vehicle'. But Rouen was depressing; a fête they attended was a 'funereal Saturnalia' where the women varied in ugliness 'from the simply plain to the utterly repulsive'. Wilkie's next letter (written on the same day) bore the exultant heading 'Paris!!!!'. 'Are you not disgusted? Would you not give up a week's walking in Kensington Gardens to be able to express to me, viva voce, the feelings aroused by the date of this letter?'[15] A five-pound note was needed. Boots (two pairs) were again among the more mentionable delights of Paris that proved his undoing. Boots and gloves for his diminutive feet and hands were better and cheaper there than in London – as always, Wilkie finds an ingenious and rational explanation for his financial problems.

Ward left for home alone. Wilkie, confident that his mother would supply him, stayed on. A week later he had heard nothing, and wrote desperately to Ward, asking him to intercede, and teasing his mother, through his intermediary, with threats of dissolute behaviour: if she won't supply £10 (the demand had doubled) 'it will then be time to pawn my watch and coat . . . and try my fortune . . . at a table of Rouge et Noir (Horror! Horror!!)'; 'I have been very ill-used by the Devonport Street dynasty', he complained, suggesting that his more virtuous younger brother took their mother's side over Wilkie's aberrations.[16] After this ultimatum, he got home safely.

The following year he was involved in a more dangerous enterprise, this time on behalf of Edward Ward. The Ward brothers were both attracted to very much younger women, and Ned had fallen in love with a girl who became his pupil when she was a child of ten or eleven. Henrietta Ward (she was no relation to her lover) was the daughter and granddaughter of painters and engravers, and a great-niece of Morland: a link from the past with the Collins family. By the time she was fourteen she and Ned were engaged. Her parents, naturally alarmed by her youth and the difference in age, at first agreed that the marriage could take place when she became sixteen, but then retracted. Wilkie, impatient of such restrictions, and already fascinated by marital intrigue, consulted his law books, and a plan of campaign was settled in the obscurity of the Octagon Room. Charles Collins and Jane Ward were also involved in the plot. Henrietta Ward remembered that 'Wilkie Collins . . . impressed great caution and secrecy, as he planned out the whole affair with zest and enjoyment'.[17] Wilkie knew that anyone under twenty-one required a declaration that the consent of the parents had been obtained; but by one of those quirks of law that always intrigued him, a marriage obtained by a false declaration was valid, though not legal. However, as the hero and sixteen-year-old heroine of *Armadale* discover on consulting *Blackstone*, there could have been a penalty of up to seven years' imprisonment for Edward Ward. Henrietta was not quite sixteen, Ned nearly thirty-three. They took the risk, and were married by licence at All Souls, Langham Place, on 4 May 1848. Wilkie gave the bride away, and he and his cousin Jane Ward were the witnesses.[18] Henrietta spent the afternoon playing with Jane's little girls, and then returned to her unsuspecting parents. Ned could have been found guilty of abduction of a minor if they lived together before she was sixteen – this point is raised in Wilkie's novella *Miss or Mrs?* of 1871.

Three months later Henrietta finally ran away with her husband, to a honeymoon at Iver – Wilkie found the rooms for them. Their eldest child, Alice, born the following year, was the first of his many godchildren. She howled throughout the christening; her godfather behaved impeccably. Wilkie was not, as claimed in a much reprinted apocryphal story, drunk at the ceremony. It was at a party at the Wards, when their second child Leslie was brought downstairs, that Wilkie, having dined well, admonished the crying baby: 'You bad boy! you ought to be downright ashamed of yourself for getting drunk on such an occasion as this!'[19]

Wilkie made fictional use of the Ward marriage several times. In his first novel with a contemporary setting, *Basil*, the affair ends disastrously; in a short story, 'The Biter Bit', and in *Miss or Mrs?* it is treated more light-heartedly. Though irregular and unusual marriages were always staple intrigues in the Victorian novel, even before the fashion for them in the 'sensation' novels of the 1860s, Wilkie does also seem to have had experience of them in his own circle: the Wards' was the first of several.

During the summer of 1848 Harriet and her sons moved from Devonport Street to a smaller house, 38 Blandford Square: a return to St Marylebone. Blandford Square was an unpretentious late-Georgian London square similar to many others; one side of it still exists. Here Harriet's character underwent a startling transformation. Her natural capacity for enjoyment burst out: the family relaxed.* Wilkie and Charley went on one occasion to a 'Fancy Ball', Charley as a rake of the time of Charles II, Wilkie as '*somebody* . . . in the reign of Louis the 16th . . . I am obliged to shave off my whiskers to be in costume!'[20] The house became a meeting place for young men: painters, journalists, law students. Many of the painters were students at the Academy schools with Charley, among them the young prodigy John Millais, a favourite of Harriet's. Some, such as Augustus Egg, W. P. Frith and Edward Ward, were rather older.

* Books with Harriet's signature in them in Wilkie Collins' library at his death include several works of religion and piety; but all date from before her husband's death.

Harriet provided an easygoing atmosphere – smoking was allowed, and meals were always informal. There was serious talk about painting, and reminiscences of the painters of the previous generation. She seems to have been unconventional and, to young men, entirely unalarming: Millais paid comic court to her, and joked that he would ask her to 'fix the day'. She had a similar flirtatious relationship with Holman Hunt which went on to the end of her life.[21] There is no question that her sons adored her. Charley addressed her as 'my darling' in his letters, and Wilkie more than once referred to her death, at the age of seventy-seven, as the greatest sorrow of his life. To see such devotion as perverse, rather than as a tribute to her capacity for friendship with her grown-up sons, would itself have seemed perverse to her sons and to their contemporaries.

Harriet was less open-hearted in her welcome to other women, particularly young women. She terrified Henrietta Ward into becoming, briefly, a full-time wife and mother, until the young painter found that not only she, but her husband and children too, were far happier when she went back to her career. Harriet's daughter-in-law Kate, Dickens' younger daughter, described her husband's mother, many years later, as 'a woman of great wit and humour – but a devil!', adding hastily that she was an unselfish mother to her sons.[22] Certainly, at this stage of their lives, she helped to launch both of them on their chosen careers by entertaining the coming men in literature and art, and by enthusiastic appreciation of their achievements. When *Antonina* was published, Wilkie wrote to his publisher Richard Bentley asking for a complimentary copy for 'my mother (who *of course* thinks that I have written the most remarkable novel that ever was produced!)'.[23]

The young people got up theatricals in the new house, in the 'Theatre Royal, Back Drawing Room'. For one of these productions, Goldsmith's *The Good-Natur'd Man*, Wilkie was producer, actor and author of the prologue, an eighteenth-century pastiche replacing the original by Johnson:

As coward schoolboys, longing for a slide,
Stand doubtful by the frozen water's side,
And dread a ducking, till they urge at length
One valiant boy to try the ice's strength;

So all our troupe of embryo actors dread
Boldly to try the stage they fain would tread;
And madly obstinate to know the worst
Have forced me here to test your tempers first –[24]

The embryo actors in the performance on 19 June 1849 included, besides Wilkie and Charley, Edward Ward, who designed the costumes and played the part of the misanthropic Croaker; Frith; and Millais. It is not recorded whether Harriet was in the cast, but with her passion for acting she would have found the excellent part of the gossipy, scandalmongering Mrs Croaker, 'always in such spirits', hard to resist. Henrietta Ward was not among the actors; she gave birth to her first child Alice on the same night.

There was friction between the male and female leads in *The Good-Natur'd Man*, which Wilkie as producer handled tactfully. Though he complained at the time, 'The disappointments we have met with in getting up the Play would fill a three volume novel', he was to remember these first efforts with enormous pleasure.[25] 'I have been engaged in far more elaborate private theatrical work, since that time – but the real enjoyment was at the T.R. Blandford Square', he wrote to Edward Ward in 1862. His novel of that year, *No Name*, features an amateur production of *The Rivals*, another of the plays staged at Blandford Square.[26]

The Blandford Square productions encouraged Wilkie to think of the possibility of writing plays himself. His first attempt was an adaptation from the French, a melodramatic piece by 'Monsieur Lockroy' (Joseph Philippe Simon) and Edmond Badon, set at the French court of 1726, which Wilkie translated as *A Court Duel*.[27] He was following established practice: it has been calculated that in the first half of the nineteenth century, at least half the plays performed on the London stage were adaptations or translations from the French. Wilkie's friend Charles Reade began his lifelong habit of plagiarism with an unauthorized translation and adaptation of a play by Scribe and Legouvé, *La Bataille des Dames*, produced at the Olympic Theatre in 1851.

Foreign authors were quite unable to protect their work from piracy in England. Wilkie was to claim in 1856, 'I never have worked, and never intend to work, with any other than my own materials and tools . . . My prejudices on this subject are indeed so inveterately strong that even if I were to write a play for the English stage, I think I should be eccentric enough *not* to take it from the French.'[28] He toned down this statement before publishing it, presumably remembering the one instance when he had lifted other men's work without acknowledgement or payment. By then he shared Dickens' passionate advocacy of international copyright laws. He wrote to Kate Field (the American actress, Trollope's friend) in 1877 warning her not to perform a French play without the author's permission. 'The original author's permission and share for him in the profits are "articles of religion" with me', he insisted.[29]

A Court Duel was staged at Miss Kelly's Theatre, Dean Street, on 26 February 1850, two days before the publication of *Antonina.* The handsome Charley played the lead, and Wilkie the minor part of a comic courtier. It was a charity performance – Miss Kelly's little theatre was often used by amateurs for such purposes – in aid of the Female Emigration Fund, founded in 1849 by Sydney Herbert's wife, to help poor but honest seamstresses start a better life in the colonies. The only woman's part, that of a doomed adulteress, was played by a professional actress, Jane Mordaunt.* In the farce that followed, James Kenney's famous piece *Raising the Wind*, Wilkie played the lead, Jeremy Diddler, an appropriately short-sighted sponger. Wilkie was never in Dickens' class as an actor; but he was establishing himself as a competent amateur, capable of appearing in public before a more critical audience than that of Blandford Square.

Wilkie was not only acting and writing during this year. For the first (and as it turned out the only) time, one of his paintings was accepted for the Royal Academy Exhibition of 1849.† It was

* The beautiful Miss Mordaunt had come down in the world: her father was an army officer who had run through his fortune and been forced to allow his daughters to go on the stage. One of them later made a great success at Drury Lane. (Edward Stirling, *Old Drury Lane*, 1881, Vol. 2, p. 165)

† 'The Smuggler's Retreat'. Usually described as a landscape, though it is listed in Algernon Graves' *Dictionary of Artists*, London 1895, as a figure painting.

'skyed' in the Octagon Room, and nobody bought it; but it was a satisfying achievement none the less. He had already given up the idea of an artistic career, perhaps after the frustrations of the Normandy sketching trip of 1847. At the beginning of 1849 he had described himself as 'only painting at leisure moments, in humble *amateur-fashion* for my own amusement'.[30] In later years Wilkie's painting hung in his dining-room, and he used to joke that he had retired from painting only out of compassion for other, lesser painters. Painting would be left to Charley, who had been exhibiting in a variety of styles since 1847, and was now closely associated with the Pre-Raphaelite Brotherhood begun by his friends Hunt and Millais.

1849 opened with the excellent reviews of the *Memoirs*, and closed with the acceptance for publication of *Antonina*. It had been turned down by George Smith of Smith, Elder, who did not want a historical novel. On 30 August Wilkie wrote to Richard Bentley, offering the nearly completed novel to him. He was prepared, if it was turned down again, to publish it himself.[31] But Bentley responded encouragingly to the first two volumes, and Wilkie, after taking time off for his customary fortnight in France with Charles Ward, sent the final portion on 12 November. Bentley replied asking how much he wanted for the book. Wilkie wrote modestly, but firmly: £200 was his figure. This would not compensate him for his time and trouble, but, though he was already businesslike enough to point out that he was not a novice author, and that the *Memoirs* had made a profit, he felt it best to ask less than the going rate, rather than more.[32] Bentley agreed, and gave Wilkie £100 on publication, and another £100 when five hundred copies had been sold.

Richard Bentley, originally in partnership with Henry Colburn, had been in business on his own account since 1832, and had offices in New Burlington Street. In 1845 he was joined by his son George. Bentley was still one of the most important London publishers; many of the popular writers of the day, including Dickens and Isaac and Benjamin Disraeli, had been published by him. Dickens fell out with Bentley in 1840, moved his books to Chapman and Hall, and continued to refer to Bentley as 'the Burlington Street Brigand'. But the firm's list of 'Standard Novels', published at 6s., was famous, and *Bentley's Miscellany* was popular and influential. The association with Bentley, though it caused frequent minor irritations, was to be on the whole of great benefit to Wilkie over the next five years in helping to establish him as a writer.

Wilkie discovered at the last minute that 'The only *Antonina* of any celebrity, was, I am sorry to say, what we should call "by no means a respectable woman" – the infamous wife of Belisarius'. He suggested changing the title to *The Mount of Gardens*, and the heroine's name to 'Serapha'.[33] But Bentley was not prepared to allow a new author such literary fidgets, and the novel came out on 28 February 1850 with the original title. It was dedicated to Lady Chantrey. Wilkie was not above making use of his father's connections again, as he had done with the *Memoirs*. Bentley, to Wilkie's annoyance, rather spoilt the effect by announcing the novel as by the 'Author of the Life of *Samuel* Collins, R.A.'.[34]

Antonina had a preface, an unusual feature for a novel, and a precedent which Wilkie was to follow, often against the advice of his friends, for most of his full-length stories. He felt the need to explain the principles behind the writing of each book, to educate his public in the way he was to be read, which seems unnecessarily heavy-handed: his friends thought he would have done better to let the books speak for themselves. For *Antonina* there is perhaps more excuse: Wilkie uses the preface to explain why he has only introduced historical persons as minor characters and why the chapter lengths vary: 'the author thought it best to let the plot divide itself; to end each chapter only when a pause naturally occurred in the events that it related . . . By this plan it was thought that the different passages . . . might be most forcibly contrasted . . . that, in the painter's phrase, the "effects" might thus be best "massed," and the "lights and shadows" most harmoniously "balanced" and "discriminated".'[35] His father's influence on the writing of the book is clearly at work here. Later, the demands of serial publication, with the need for episodes shaped to uniform lengths, were to supersede these painterly considerations.

The reviews were almost all excellent; none of the reviewers picked up the unfortunate significance of the heroine's name. Wilkie was even compared to Shakespeare, and placed 'in the very first rank of English novelists': claims which suggest reviewers were desperate to discover some heir to Scott and Bulwer-Lytton.[36] He was to say in the introduction to the reprint of 1861 that he had never had such a chorus of praise sung over him since, and though this was something of an exaggeration, he certainly achieved a critical success with the book which opened doors for him. He was wryly amused, though, to be confused with Charley at a reception, taken for a 'P-R. B.', and asked whether the author of *Antonia* was present.[37] The novel went into a second edition at the end of May, for which Wilkie made many minor revisions, improving the style and shortening some of the long speeches. Though he could not, under the terms of his agreement, make much money from the book, its success finally convinced him that he could make a career as a writer.

In the summer of 1850 Wilkie, instead of taking his usual trip to the Continent with Charles Ward, went to Cornwall with another old friend, the artist Henry Brandling, one of Charley's contemporaries at the Academy schools. They wanted to explore, on foot, a still remote part of the British Isles, soon to be reached by the railways. This time the sketching would be left to Brandling, and Wilkie armed himself only with a notebook and pencil, hoping to make a book of the tour.

Cornwall was a good choice, for they had found a gap in the increasingly popular genre of chatty travel books. The two young men on foot, carrying their luggage on their backs, aroused the friendly curiosity and helpfulness of the inhabitants, who thought them odd, but liked them for not being 'effeminate dandies'. At Looe a fat landlady and fat chambermaid 'coddled us in comfortable beds, and fuddled us with comfortable ale, and stuffed us to bursting with good pies and puddings and sweet cakes, and then sent us into the garden . . . to keep us out of mischief, like children'.[38] At Penzance, where they found another fat landlady, Brandling, who shared Wilkie's interest in food, made an omelette: 'six eggs, a teacupfull of clotted cream, new milk, an onion, and chopped parsley . . . We gave the fat landlady a bit.'[39] Wilkie tried, without success, to persuade Charles Ward to join them. He was bursting with enthusiasm over Cornish scenery and Cornish food. 'I know France, from Boulogne to Marseilles,' he claimed, with the hyperbole of youth:

> there is no scenery in the country worth a d—n compared to Cornish scenery – And as for eating, "stap my vitals", if I have eaten chop or steak more than once, since I have been here! *Here*, sir, we live on Ducks, Geese, Chickens, tongue, pickled pilchards, curried Lobster – Clotted cream – jam tarts, fruit tarts – custards – cakes – *red mullet*, conger eels – salmon trout . . . I have almost forgotten the taste of joints – we have nothing to do with them.
>
> I have seen such rocks! Rocks like pyramids – rocks like crouching lions . . . rocks pierced with mighty and measureless caverns – rocks covered with the most exquisite natural mosaic-work . . . rocks crowned by mist at one hour, and brightened by sunshine at another . . .[40]

It was an unusually energetic journey for Wilkie, better adapted to eating and play-going in Paris than to walking ten to fifteen miles a day with a knapsack on his back, in the uncertain climate of Cornwall. But he thoroughly enjoyed it, and found plenty to write about. He produced an attractive short book, a mixture of history, legend, statistics and social commentary. He still had enough energy left at the end of the day to write long letters. Though he described those to his mother as 'about as fit for print as your washerwoman's bills', they augmented his notes, and contain passages later incorporated into the book almost verbatim. There is a hilarious account, for example, of a mass vaccination in an inn parlour at the Lizard. 'Perhaps, as a mother yourself, you can imagine the noise these babies made – I can't describe it', he told Harriet.[41] Wilkie records crawling, serpent-like, through caves, and scaling and descending cliffs in the teeth of the wind. Another chapter describes a descent into the copper mine at Botallack. Wilkie is funny at his own expense, and evocative in his description of the industry, then already in decline. Wilkie and Brandling were instructed to put on miners' clothes to save their own.

> The same mysterious dispensation of fate, which always awards tall wives to short men, decreed that a suit of the big miner's should be reserved for me. He stood six feet two inches – I stand five feet six inches. I put on his flannel shirt – it fell down to my toes, like a bedgown; his

> drawers – and they flowed in Turkish luxuriance over my feet. At his trousers I helplessly stopped short, lost in the voluminous recesses of each leg . . . He put the pocket button through the waist buttonhole, to keep the trousers up in the first instance; then, he pulled steadily at the braces until my waistband was under my armpits . . . The cuffs of the jacket were next turned up to my elbows – the white nightcap was dragged over my ears – the round hat was jammed down over my eyes. When I add to all this, that I am so near-sighted as to be obliged to wear spectacles, and that I finished my toilet by putting my spectacles on . . . nobody, I think, will be astonished to hear that my companion seized his sketch-book, and caricatured me on the spot; and that the grave miner, polite as he was, shook with internal laughter, when I took up my tallow candles and reported myself ready for a descent into the mine. (*Rambles Beyond Railways*, Chap. 9, pp. 104–5)

A vivid account of the mine follows. In the subaqueous galleries they heard the sound of the surf twenty feet above, as 'a long, low, mysterious moaning, which never changes, which is *felt* on the ear as well as *heard* by it . . . so ghostly and impressive when listened to in the subterranean recesses of the earth, that we continue instinctively to hold our peace, as if enchanted by it'.

Charles Collins also spent the summer out of London, sketching with Millais at Botley, near Oxford. Wilkie wrote to his mother that he had heard Charley was painting 'a fly's eye, with lashes to match'.[42] Charley's uncertainty about his own ability always laid him open to new influences. Now he was following Millais' lead, and Wilkie was not impressed by the Pre-Raphaelite obsession with detail. Millais' portrait of Charles Collins, drawn this summer, shows an almost girlish face, anxious and immature.[43] Though he joined in the pleasures of an Oxford summer, 'moist fishing expeditions', masked balls and an attempt to mesmerize young ladies, he was, if Millais is to be believed, drinking heavily. 'Collins cannot go half an hour without a swig at pure brandy', Millais reported.[44] But his father's belief in his talent was being fulfilled: while he and Millais were staying with Thomas Combe of the Oxford University Press, a generous patron to the Pre-Raphaelite painters and one of their few early supporters, he painted one of his best pictures: an excellent portrait of Mrs Combe's ancient uncle Mr Bennett.[45]

While her sons were both away, Harriet Collins moved house. There were thoughts of moving to Fitzroy Square, near the Brandlings. Wilkie, playing the part of man of the house, urged his mother to have the drains thoroughly checked (there had been a serious outbreak of cholera the year before). But in the end, rather to his dismay, she decided to lease 17 Hanover Terrace, a large and handsome house in Regent's Park. The jerry-built Nash terraces were showing their age: Thackeray, in 1846, described the 'plaster patching off the house walls', and Wilkie feared the house would be ruinously expensive.[46] Apart from rent and dilapidations, there would be 'something *considerable* to pay annually for keeping up the *inclosure* in the Park', he pointed out.[47] But he was no match for his determined mother. 'I resign myself to Hanover Terrace (and the Queen's Bench afterwards)', he wrote from Cornwall, offering to come home to help her move. Harriet was perfectly capable of managing by herself – thankful, perhaps, to have her fussy sons out of the way. 'For Heaven's sake take care of my unfortunate *papers*', Wilkie begged.[48] For all his attempts to intervene in the negotiations, she didn't even trouble to tell him the number of the new house; he had to write to her asking for it.

Number 17 Hanover Terrace, where they were to live happily for the next six years, looks much the same today externally, though it has been radically altered inside. When the Collins family lived in it there was a beautiful upstairs drawing-room facing Regent's Park.* There was room for Wilkie to have a study, and Charles a painting-room. They gave dinner parties, and on one occasion in 1852 a dance for seventy people. Millais sent an enthusiastic account to Thomas Combe:

> I truly wish you had been there. It was a delightful evening. Charlie never got beyond a very solemn quadrille, though he is an excellent waltzer and polka dancer. Poor Mrs. Collins was totally dumb from a violent

* Edmund Gosse described the view from the room as it was in the 1920s when he lived in the house. 'As you entered, you obtained a lovely vista, green and watery, of pool and weeping willow and stretches of grass, and distant depths of shadow between the taller, further trees.' (Quoted by Ann Thwaite in *Edmund Gosse: A Literary Landscape*, London 1984)

> influenza she unfortunately caught that very afternoon. She received all her guests in a whisper and a round face of welcome. There were many lions – amongst other the famous Dickens who came for about half an hour and officiated as principal carver at supper.[49]

Their friends were frequently invited to stay, on a casual, *ad hoc* basis. Millais and Holman Hunt, whom Harriet called her 'third and fourth' sons, were particularly welcome, and Millais lived there for over two months in 1854, when his parents left the family house in Gower Street.

Wilkie spent the autumn at Hanover Terrace, writing *Rambles Beyond Railways*. By November he was negotiating with Bentley for its publication. Determined to make some money this time, he had a profit-sharing agreement: all profits to be equally divided between author and publisher after costs had been paid, plus a ten per cent allowance to the publisher. Bentley seems to have considered the illustrations an unimportant extra, though they add greatly to the attractiveness of the book. An addition to the printed contract allows for a payment of £37. 16s. 0d. to Henry Brandling, and a further payment of £25 for the copyright of his drawings, after the sales had reached eleven hundred copies. There were some delays over publication: six weeks after signing the contract Wilkie complained that the book did not seem to have '*rambled into print*', as he had not been sent proofs. Brandling's care in preparing the lithographs from his drawings was partly the problem, but at last the book appeared, on 20 January 1851. It was handsomely produced, as Wilkie acknowledged, but it came too late for the Christmas market. Though it did modestly well – Bentley published a second edition two years later, and a new edition in 1861 – Wilkie was to have continuing trouble over the years winkling the small sums due to him out of the publishers.

The association with Bentley was helping his career in another way. The well-established journal *Bentley's Miscellany*, whose first editor had been Charles Dickens, provided a regular outlet for his stories, reviews and articles throughout the next two years. His first piece for *Bentley's Miscellany*, a short story called 'The Twin Sisters', appeared on 1 March 1851. A slight and clumsily written piece, which he never reprinted, it combines two themes important in his fiction: love at first sight and the double. A young man falls in love with a girl he sees in a balcony, and does not rest until he has met and become engaged to her. The theme of the irrational and overwhelming emotion of 'love at first sight' was to be handled better, and at much greater length, in the novel he wrote the following year; but the story, like the novel, conveys vividly the pain and obsession.

In 'The Twin Sisters', the girl the young man first saw is not the girl he meets and becomes engaged to. They are identical twins. He is uneasily aware that something is wrong, and when he discovers his mistake he breaks off the engagement. The 'wrong' girl is heart-broken, but nobly gives him up. He eventually marries the 'right' girl. She, in an unexpected twist, is a very much more commonplace person than her sister. His feeling of a mysterious affinity is an illusion.

Wilkie had twin cousins, William and Percy Carpenter. In the 1850s he also got to know twin sisters, Eliza and Janet Chambers, who played the usual substitution tricks that identical twins delight in; Janet was to die young, leaving her sisters haunted by her loss. But this story precedes his friendship with the Chambers family. Wilkie's fascination with the Romantic idea of the double is here given its first literary expression.

The double has an obvious function as a plot device for the writer of mystery and sensation, but for Wilkie Collins, as for Robert Louis Stevenson after him, the fascination of the theme seems often to have prompted the ingenuity of the plot. Both used the double in investigations of the shadow-self: the underside of a personality which compensates for inadequacies in the external persona, or, suppressed or denied full expression, takes revenge in unexpected ways. By the late 1860s, in large part because of the popularity of Wilkie's fiction, the double had become a stock property of the sensation novel. Mary Braddon, asked for a new story, promised to do her best with the old bits of rubbish.

> There they all are – the young lady who has married a burglar, and who does not want to introduce him to her friends . . . the two brothers who are perpetually taken for one another; the twin sisters ditto, ditto; the high-bred and conscientious banker, who has made away with

> everybody's title-deeds. Any novel combination of the well-known figures is completely at your service, workmanship careful, delivery prompt.[50]

Nevertheless, the double remained, and remains to this day, a theme endlessly explored yet never exhausted; one that Wilkie Collins made peculiarly his own.

A relationship more lasting and more important to Wilkie than the professional one with Bentley began in the month 'The Twin Sisters' appeared. It was initiated casually enough, when Augustus Egg arrived at Blandford Square with an invitation Wilkie had been hoping, indeed angling, for. Charles Dickens, casting a new production for his troupe of amateur actors, wrote to Egg, who had acted both with him and with Wilkie: 'I think *you* told *me* that Mr. Wilkie Collins would be glad to play any part in Bulwer's Comedy; and I think *I* told *you* that I considered him a very desirable recruit.'[51] Now there was a part available, and Wilkie leapt at it.

SIX

'The Fire of Artistic Ambition'

(1851–1852)

It was surprising that Charles Dickens and Wilkie Collins had not met before. As Dickens wrote to Egg, 'I knew his father very well, and should be very glad to know him'.[1] Augustus Egg, their go-between, had acted with Dickens' theatrical company since 1848, but he had known Wilkie even longer: he was a friend of the Collins family when Wilkie was a boy. At the Royal Academy he had been part of 'The Clique', a group of friends who met regularly to discuss and criticize each others' work. Other members were W. P. Frith, Wilkie's close friend E. M. Ward and Richard Dadd. Dadd became more and more eccentric: he was obsessed with eggs, and lived on nothing else. Frith and Egg tried to watch him, but immediately after they had left for a trip to the Continent in 1843, Dadd went spectacularly mad and cut his father's throat. When his studio was searched, drawings of his friends, including Frith, Egg and Ward, were found with a red slash painted across the throat of each. There was to be an uncanny sequel. Ward committed suicide in 1879, by cutting his throat.

Dickens had met William Collins in the 1830s. In April 1839, elated by the success of the early numbers of *Nicholas Nickleby*, he had commissioned 'a sea shore with figures' from this establishment painter. They discussed the picture on at least one occasion, and in 1841 Dickens took delivery of 'Ischia Bay of Naples', for which he paid £100.[2]

Dickens met the painter's son for the first time on 12 March 1851, when Wilkie dined with him and was present at a reading of the play, *Not So Bad As We Seem*, at the house of Dickens' old friend John Forster. This eighteenth-century pastiche, in which the troubles of Grub Street writers were related, by implication, to those of their Victorian successors, had been written by Bulwer-Lytton, and was to be performed in aid of the newly established Guild of Literature and Art. Dickens was to star in the play; Wilkie was offered the part of his valet, Smart: '. . . a small part – but, what there is of it, decidedly good – he opens the play . . . in which he would have an opportunity of dressing your humble servant, frothing some chocolate with an obsolete milling-machine . . . and dispatching other similar "business," dear to actors'.[3]

The part had first been offered to W. H. Wills, Dickens' assistant editor on *Household Words*, who turned it down on the reasonable plea that someone should be left to mind the shop. To play the part of Dickens' servant in public may have seemed too much for even the equable Wills to stomach. For Wilkie, on the edge of a literary career, the omens seemed excellent.

The Guild, dreamt up by Dickens and Bulwer-Lytton, was intended as a form of assurance society for writers and artists, to provide them with pensions and sickness payments when they were unable to work. Dickens saw it as a way of enhancing the status of writers, putting them on a footing with other professionals. Others disagreed: Macaulay wrote with distaste, 'I utterly abominate it'; and Thackeray called the refuge for indigent authors planned for the grounds of Knebworth 'a literary soup kitchen'.[4] It was, in the end, one of Dickens' least successful projects. Nobody wanted to live in the three cottages eventually built at Knebworth; and very few grants were ever made from the Guild's funds. Dickens took very little interest in it after 1856, and it was quietly wound up after his death in 1870. But in the 1850s, swept along by his energy, the distinguished amateurs acted and scene-painted with enthusiasm, with an edge of danger added to the first performance by Bulwer-Lytton's estranged wife, who threatened to gatecrash the antics of what she referred to as the 'Guilt' of Literature and Art, selling oranges *à la* Nell Gwyn and a scandalous life of her husband. Dickens posted sentries to keep her out. When *The Woman in White* was published, she was to complain to Wilkie Collins that Count Fosco was a very poor sort of villain, offering to supply him with details of a far more satisfactory one – her husband.

At first only one or two performances were proposed, at Devonshire House. The Duke of Devonshire's library became the stage and green-room, the audience were to sit in the gallery. The presence of the Queen and other members of the royal family, vital for the success of the fund-raising effort, was promised for the first performance, originally intended for 30 April. As the plans took shape, and Dickens drilled his company two nights a week, five hours at a time, further performances were arranged, in the more public setting of the Hanover Square Rooms.

Amateur dramatics brought out the best and worst in Dickens. As actor-manager and director he was relentless. By 28 March the company were rehearsing three nights a week until far into the morning, and growing 'quite pale with the slow agonies of incessant drill'.[5] Dickens' letters to Bulwer-Lytton about the progress of the play are full of complaints about his actors: Forster was too loud and violent, Lemon too farcical, Stone a 'millstone', Horne 'the very worst actor the world ever saw'.[6] Dickens was silent about Wilkie, who must have performed adequately, if not with distinction.

The obsessional, perfectionist side of Dickens bullied his actors, demanding more and more of their time and attention. But his enormous capacity for enjoyment made the whole enterprise an exciting adventure. Exhausting and lengthy rehearsals would be followed by jolly gargantuan suppers; while a Dickens production was under way life became a series of impromptu parties. The mixture of concentrated work, licensed exhibitionism and riotous fun was all very much to Wilkie's taste. He was not at first aware that in the middle of all this activity Dickens was seriously troubled. His marriage was increasingly unsatisfying, and Catherine Dickens, taking a 'cure' at Malvern, was in a nervous, near-hysterical state. The death of Dickens' father, after a horrifying and painful operation, was closely followed by that of his baby daughter Dora.

Forster and Wills, both loyal friends, had become involved in these serious and tragic elements in Dickens' life. Now he needed a different kind of companion. The rehearsals and performances served as a forcing ground for friendship, and he soon realized that Wilkie could be valuable to him in other ways. Dickens was well known for his kindness to young writers; but the young man who now penetrated the charmed circle was unusual. He had many of the habits common to the young Bohemians who clustered round Dickens, but there was one difference which Dickens quickly appreciated: Wilkie was already a professional. G. A. Sala, who started writing for *Household Words* in 1851, wrote of himself and his friends at that time:

> most of us were about the idlest young dogs that squandered away their time on the pavements of Paris or London. *We would not work* . . . from the year 1852 to the year 1856, both inclusive, the average number of hours per week which I devoted to literary production did not exceed four . . . I usually wrote one article a week for Household Words; and I very rarely contributed to any other publication.[7]

Wilkie, however, was a prolific and reliable journalist, prepared, like Dickens, to take infinite pains over the slightest article. Though his incorrigible untidiness in private life infuriated Dickens whenever they lived and travelled together, in professional matters he was meticulous. A man who worked hard and then played uninhibitedly was exactly the person Dickens was looking for. When he wrote to Wilkie at the end of 1852, congratulating him on his novel *Basil*, he made clear his appreciation of both aspects of Wilkie's character:

> It is delightful to find throughout that you have taken great pains with it besides, and have 'gone at it' with a perfect knowledge of the jolter-headedness of the conceited idiots who suppose that volumes are to be tossed off like pancakes, and that any writing can be done without the utmost application, the greatest patience, and the steadiest energy of which the writer is capable . . .
>
> P.S. – I am open to any proposal to go anywhere any day or days this week . . . If I could only find an idle man (this is a general observation) he would find the warmest recognition in this direction.[8]

Wilkie was now Dickens' preferred companion on his 'nightly wanderings into strange places'.[9] During the mid-1850s he largely supplanted earlier cronies such as Daniel Maclise. Together Dickens and Wilkie prowled the Haymarket and Regent Street, notorious for rowdiness, the number of 'night houses' and the open transactions of the prostitutes. Sometimes they penetrated the slums of Soho or the East End.

It was Dickens' favourite way of seeking out subjects for investigative journalism, but there is no reason to suppose that this was their only purpose. There are many hints in Dickens' letters to Wilkie that he took courage from his younger companion's relaxed attitude to sexual adventures. In 1858, protesting, obviously in reply to a tease from Wilkie about his involvement with the actress Ellen Ternan, that he has been 'as chaste as Diana' on a reading tour, Dickens clearly indicates this had not always been so. He also hints that he had, like the Caliph of Baghdad, taken care to preserve his incognito during their earlier excursions:

> But the mysterious addresses, O misconstructive one, merely refer to places where Arthur Smith did not know aforehand the names of the best hotels. As to that furtive and Don Giovanni purpose at which you hint, that may be all very well for *your* violent vigor, or that of the companions with whom you may have travelled continentally, or the Caliphs Haroon alrashid – with whom you have unbent metropolitanlly; but anchorites who read themselves red-hot every night are chaste as Diana (I suppose *she* was, by the bye, but I find I don't quite believe it when I write her name).[10]

If Wilkie's letters to him had survived Dickens' bonfires, the question might have been settled. Forster's deliberate avoidance, in his life of Dickens, of any discussion of Wilkie's friendship with him may have had as much to do with this side of their relationship as with his jealousy of Wilkie. Dickens did not, in any event, need Wilkie to initiate him into the sexual underworld.* But Wilkie was unique in his ability to be both a relaxed and uncensorious companion and a literary ally and collaborator who could understand Dickens' aims, working with concentration and skill on their joint fiction and journalism for *Household Words*.

* In 1841, ten years before he met Wilkie, Dickens wrote to Maclise, trying to tempt him into a trip to Margate, '. . . there are conveniences of *all kinds* at Margate (do you take me?) and I know where they live'. (Sotheby's Sale Catalogue, 23/24 July 1987)

Wilkie also looked different from other young men. Though his engaging personality quickly overcame the slight shock, his odd appearance was the first thing people noticed. His small hands and feet and the disproportion of his head and shoulders to the rest of his body were often to be caricatured. In 1862, when he was eleven, Edward and Henrietta Ward's son Leslie, who later became famous as the cartoonist 'Spy', made a drawing of Wilkie. Leslie thought Wilkie had a cast in one eye, which made the child uneasy, because Wilkie appeared to be addressing him, while talking to his father.[11] Edmund Yates, another of Dickens' 'young men' and an early admirer of Wilkie Collins' writing, remembered him as already having, in the 1850s, 'something weird and odd in his appearance, something which removed him widely from the ordinary crowd of young men of his age'.[12] This oddity is captured in Millais' portrait of him, painted at this time, though it is considerably softened in the portrait by Charles Collins of 1855.[13] Wilkie was conscious that, in the words of Walter Hartright's description of Professor Pesca (in *The Woman in White*), his 'singular personal appearance made a marked man of him'.[14] He had, too, strange tics and fidgets: he would sit with his hands between his knees and his legs dangling, rocking to and fro. This restlessness, which seems to have been a family trait, became known jokingly as being 'in a Collinsian state'. Later in his life his fidgeting seemed to be not only a nervous habit, but related to the state of his health. His doctor's son remembered that 'when one of his bad gouty attacks was threatening, he would be depressed and nervous, and we all knew, by the horrible shaking of the room, produced by his "fidgetting" with one foot upon the floor, when "Wilkie was out of order."'[15]

Wilkie also had an idiosyncratic taste in dress. He shared his mother's passion for clothes and her indifference to convention. Harriet wore her elastic-sided kid boots on the correct feet first, then changed them over when they wore down; as an old lady she wore huge caps, and decorated them with what her daughter-in-law described as 'cauliflowers'.[16] Wilkie favoured bright colours, shirts with checks or wide stripes. He had a fixed aversion to evening dress: his invitations to dinner always insisted on no dressing or formality of any kind. 'He would sit down to dinner in a light camel hair or tweed suit, with a broad pink or blue striped shirt, and perhaps a red tie, quite as often as he would in a dark suit or regulation evening dress'.[17] His appearance signalled that the charm of his conversation, his approachability and kindness, were not to be bound within social expectations. His flamboyant appearance, eccentric rather than dandyish, acted as a flag of defiance, probably originally raised against his father's stultifying correctness, but kept flying for the rest of his life.

Wilkie had made a more or less conscious decision to be not quite a gentleman. Dickens, who had created himself, was secretly anxious about his status (as Wilkie's father had all too transparently been). He found Wilkie's lack of concern about such matters an enormous relief. Though he sometimes laughed at his friend's idiosyncrasies, he appreciated someone so different from the Podsnappian John Forster. Dickens was now the self-styled 'Inimitable', the most famous living writer in England, and one of the best-known in the world. He relished his status and the power it gave him. But he was also imprisoned by it. His most recent enterprise, *Household Words*, dear as it was to him, created constant conflict for him, as editor, between the demands of decency and openness. 'Beware of writing things for the eyes of everybody, which you would feel the smallest delicacy in saying anywhere', he felt constrained to warn a contributor. 'Mrs. Scutfidge may have stripped in public – I have no doubt she did – but I should be sorry to have to tell young ladies so in the nineteenth century, for all that.'[18] He felt obliged to tone Wilkie's articles down from time to time, to make sure there was nothing 'unnecessarily offensive to the middle class'.[19] But Wilkie, who refused to wear what everyone wore, eat what everyone ate, say and not say what everyone said and kept silent about, also acted as a safety valve, and his openness about sexual behaviour gradually helped to free Dickens from the prison of his status as a Victorian household icon, to an extent which Wilkie himself can hardly have anticipated. There was, too, an element of hero-worship on Wilkie's part in the early years, to which Dickens responded with constructive criticism and generous praise of his writing and his acting abilities.

The Guild play occupied a large part of Wilkie's time for over a year. The Devonshire House performances in May were followed by four at the Hanover Square Rooms in the summer. There was a series of tours starting in November which continued to the following autumn. It was all exciting but disruptive: Wilkie had no time to start a new novel in 1851, but he worked hard at miscellaneous journalism, in an effort to make an independent living. For *Bentley's Miscellany* he concentrated, after 'The Twin Sisters', on pieces connected one way and another with the visual arts. His only other signed contribution to *Bentley's Miscellany*, 'A Pictorial Tour to St. George Bosherville', shows his gift for comic writing. An account of the episode in his Normandy holiday of 1847 with Charles Ward, it is a reminiscence, both vivid and funny, of a disastrous painting expedition on a hot day. Ward is cast as the earnest amateur painter 'Mr. Scumble' and Wilkie as the lazy dilettante, burdened by his pretentious paintbox and sceptical of high artistic purpose. '. . . What are critics and writers on painting about? What are Academies and Lecturers about? . . . [Why don't they tell beginners] how to get gnats, for instance, off a wet picture; or how to paint them into the picture, and make it look like "fine execution" . . .?' Finally, in a gesture of despair, he buries his ruined picture in a shallow grave.[20]

The rest of his pieces for *Bentley's Miscellany* in 1851 were more topical, and more serious. A review of the Royal Academy Summer Exhibition, in which Millais, Holman Hunt and Charles Collins all exhibited Pre-Raphaelite paintings, was published on 1 June. The critics, Dickens among them, had violently attacked the Pre-Raphaelites the previous year; Harriet Collins had managed to make peace between Millais and Dickens by inviting them to dinner together. Now the press attacked the three young painters again, accusing them of offensiveness, absurdity and perversity. They were slightly – very slightly – less venomous to Charles Collins than to Millais and Hunt. Ruskin came to the defence in reasoned letters to *The Times*.[21] Wilkie might have been expected to counter-attack more fiercely, but his article is cautious and judicious, very similar in tone to Ruskin's.

He took a broad view, emphasizing the importance of that year's exhibition for British painters because of the vast influx of foreigners coming to the Great Exhibition. Before considering the Pre-Raphaelites, he praised historical paintings by other friends, Frith, Egg, Maclise and E. M. Ward. These were uncontroversial, acceptable to the taste of the day, which Wilkie clearly shared. It is not hard to see that he was less in sympathy with the Pre-Raphaelites:

> The characteristics of this style . . . may . . . be pretty correctly described as follows: – an almost painful minuteness of finish and detail; a disregard of the ordinary rules of composition and colour; and an evident intention of not appealing to any popular predilections on the subject of grace or beauty . . .
>
> Mr. Collins's picture, in the middle room, is entitled 'Convent Thoughts'; and represents a novice standing in a convent garden . . . the various flowers and the water-plants in the foreground are painted with the most astonishing minuteness and fidelity of nature – we have all the fibres in a leaf, all the faintest varieties of bloom in a flower . . . The sentiment conveyed by the figure of the novice is hinted at, rather than developed, with deep poetic feeling . . . this picture is one which appeals, in its purpose and conception, only to the more refined order of minds – the general spectator will probably discover little more in it, than dexterity of manipulation. Mr. Millais aims less high, and will therefore be more readily understood . . .
>
> . . . We should say that Mr. Collins was the superior in refinement, Mr. Millais in brilliancy, and Mr. Hunt in dramatic power. The faults . . . are common to all three. Their strict attention to detail precludes, at present, any attainment of harmony and singleness of effect. They must be admired bit by bit, as we have reviewed them, or not admired at all . . . they appear . . . to be wanting in one great desideratum of all art – judgement in selection . . . we admire sincerely their earnestness of purpose, their originality of thought, their close and reverent study of nature. But we cannot . . . fail to perceive that they are . . . at the critical turning point of their career; and that, on the course they are now to take; on their renunciation of certain false principles in their present practice, depends our chance of gladly welcoming them, one day, as masters of their art . . .[22]

Wilkie seems to have kept his authorship of this piece a secret, not wanting to hurt his friends and his morbidly sensitive brother: Holman Hunt believed that his intention of writing an article on Pre-Raphaelitism was never carried out.[23] Wilkie was always fiercely loyal to his brother; but the Pre-Raphaelite break with the tradition in which his father had painted, which he had been taught to understand and admire, baffled him, and he disliked it, in secret, as much as Dickens did. Why did Charley's convent garden consist of straight lines and formal shapes, without any of 'the accidental sinuosities of nature'? Why must Millais' 'Woodman's Daughter' look like a 'sharp-featured little work-house drudge', rather than one of the charming cottage children in his father's canvases?

Hunt's later account of Charles Collins at this time gives good grounds for Wilkie's secrecy. Hunt, Millais and Collins spent the summer of 1852 together, painting at Worcester Park Farm, near Cheam. Hunt described Charles Collins' timidity, irresolution and lack of confidence. He felt his artistic upbringing to be a burden, as though a painter's career had been thrust on him by his father's expectations, rather than having been chosen freely, as it had been by Millais, or in the teeth of opposition, like Hunt. Charley was cut to the quick by his rejection as a full member of the Brotherhood: the sculptor Thomas Woolner was particularly insistent that he was not suitable. The shadow of his father hung over him from beyond the grave: he was thought to be 'very much of a conventional man who would be out of his element with us'.[24] He had also changed his painting style several times as he came under different influences: he had, said Hunt, 'a nature which yielded itself to the sway of the current'.[25] In 1851 and 1852 Charles Collins was considered by the critics one of the three leaders of the new movement: the *Athenaeum* reviewer called him 'the most prominent among this band', yet he is barely mentioned in most accounts of the Brotherhood. To add to his problems, he was unhappily in love, either with a girl he met at Oxford, or, by some accounts, with Christina and Dante Gabriele Rossetti's elder sister Maria, who later became a nun in an Anglican community.

The Collins brothers seem to have shared a family temperament which encouraged creativity in one and destroyed it in the other. Both had a gentle charm, and an endearing way with children. Leslie Ward remembered all his life Charley's magic snuff-box: '. . . at a word of command a little bird appeared on it, which disappeared in the same wonderful manner. But what was even more wonderful, Mr. Collins persuaded me that the bird flew all round the room singing until it returned to the box . . .'[26] But what emerged in Wilkie as nervous energy, versatility and a highly professional attitude to his writing became, in his brother, agitation, hopeless vacillation and an inability ever to be satisfied with a piece of work. Charles Collins inherited many of his father's more distressing traits in extreme forms: depression, religious gloom, an oppressive sense of artistic destiny; even William's snobbery. He was nervous, and physically timid: after a skating accident on the Round Pond in 1845, when he nearly drowned, he was terrified of water. According to Millais, 'one could not induce him to commit his body (for fear of drowning) within a coffin bath of hot water'.[27] He had become painfully religious, and had taken to High Church practices as obnoxious to Wilkie as they were to Ruskin. He was damaging his already fragile health by fasting, and though his refusal of blackberry pudding for the good of his soul might seem comic to his friends, and his paralysing fear of being out alone in the dark contemptible, his brother found his state of mind and body (he became excessively thin through fasting) worrying. Wilkie begged Hunt and Millais not to encourage him by taking too much notice of his fancies.

In another anonymous piece in *Bentley's Miscellany* in the following year, Wilkie took a less serious view of his brother's predicament, in a further comic attack on the high seriousness about art in which they had been brought up. 'A Passage in the Life of Mr. Perugino Potts', which appeared in February 1852, is a spoof version of *Memoirs of the Life of William Collins Esquire, R.A.*, a joke at the expense of his brother's artistic vacillations, and a send-up of every variant of the current 'schools' of painting. Within its brief compass it has more than a touch of the ebullience of Wilkie's grandfather. It begins with a parody of William Collins' journal entry of 1844.*

> I may be wrong, but my impression is that, as an Historical Painter, my biography will be written some of these days: personal particulars of me will then be wanted. I have great faith in the affectionate remembrance

* See p. 61.

> of my surviving friends . . . but, upon the whole, I would rather provide these particulars myself . . . I paint my own pictures; why should I not paint my own character?
>
> I was destined to be an artist from my cradle; my father . . . told me with his last breath to be Potts RA or perish in the attempt . . .

Potts paints in every conceivable genre in his attempt to have a picture accepted for the Academy Exhibition, but without success.

> The third year I changed to the sentimental and pathetic; it was Sterne's 'Maria' this time, with her goat; Maria was crying, the goat was crying, Sterne himself (in the background) was crying, with his face buried in a white cambric pocket-handkerchief, wet through with tears . . . The fourth year I fell back on the domestic and familiar: a young Housemaid in the kitchen, plighting her troth, at midnight, to a private in the Grenadier Guards, while the policeman of the neighbourhood, a prey to jealousy and despair, flashed his 'bulls-eye' on them through the window . . .

Wilkie includes a satiric dig at himself:

> Personally (when I have my high-heeled boots on) I stand five feet, three inches high . . . I am, outwardly, what is termed a little man. I have nothing great about me but my mustachios and my intellect . . . The fire of artistic ambition that burns within me, shoots upwards with a lambent glow – in a word, I am a good-humoured man of genius.[28]

Potts' misadventures in Italy – encounters with swindling models, and a predatory mother and daughter who try to hook him as a husband – conclude this high-spirited foolery, written at a time when Wilkie was gestating *Basil*, his passionate and gloomy 'story of modern life'.

Another outlet for journalism was provided by Wilkie's active and reasonably lucrative association with *The Leader*, the radical newspaper founded by George Lewes and Thornton Leigh Hunt.[29] Wilkie began to write for the paper in 1851, through his friendship with Edward Pigott, a fellow-student of Lincoln's Inn. Pigott was to become Examiner of Plays in the Lord Chamberlain's office in 1874. He became notorious for his narrow-mindedness, and was attacked by Bernard Shaw as 'a walking compendium of vulgar insular prejudice'.[30] But in the 1850s he was a liberal-minded young man with a wide circle of friends. Pigott's relationship to his law studies was as tangential as Wilkie's: his real interests were literary and political, and after spending some time living in Paris he became a deputy editor, and later the proprietor, of *The Leader*.

Wilkie took a lively interest in the management of the paper, and wrote Pigott long letters of advice on its organization and content. He sympathized with *The Leader*'s radical outlook, and suggested how it might be made more emphatic.

> As to Socialism – I would suggest being still more explicit; for the sake of that large portion of the intelligent public who don't know *exactly* what Socialists want. I should like to see Socialism reduced to '*articles*' or 'points' – to a practical statement in the plainest and fewest words, of what Socialism wants to achieve – unaccompanied by reflections, comparisons, or vindications of any kind – I think an article of this sort might do good, as a plain straightforward avowal of truth – confined to such narrow limits, as to insure the readers' attention to the end. *Long* articles and serial letters won't do at first with the people you want to reach.[31]

Wilkie had a wide range of suggestions for the improvement of the paper, everything from articles on legal abuses and the matter of Law Reform to practical suggestions for improving finances: 'Notices of new prints, for instance, might bring print-sellers advertisements'. Having seen Dickens and Wills at work at *Household Words*, just up the street from *The Leader*, the mechanics of magazine management had begun to fascinate him.

From 1852 to 1855 Wilkie regularly reviewed books, art exhibitions, plays and operas for *The Leader*; these are mostly short anonymous pieces. His first contribution signed with his initials was more characteristic. 'A Plea for Sunday Reform' updates Dickens' pseudonymously published 'Sunday under Three Heads' of 1836; the atmosphere of joylessness spread over the British working classes' only free day had not altered in fifteen years. Wilkie's solutions followed those of Dickens: shorter church services, and the opening of museums and other places of innocent amusement, to compete with the attractions of the pub and the street. Though the piece was not particularly original, it came from the heart: Wilkie's hatred of the English Sunday went deep.

It is thus all the more surprising that a serious difference of opinion with the editors of *The Leader* over religion led to Wilkie refusing to have his contributions to the 'Portfolio' section of the paper signed after April 1852. Though he was never a church-goer, disapproved of many of the religious institutions of his time and had no belief in an afterlife – he once wrote that he could not see how heaven was possible unless spirits could be folded up like clothes in a portmanteau – a couple of long private letters to Pigott show that it is misleading to think of him as a lifelong atheist. Like many free-thinkers of the time, he took the life of Jesus to be the model for social behaviour. The message of the Gospels, the emphasis on forgiveness, tolerance and the reintegration of outcasts into society, was one he repeatedly referred to in his fiction. It was the forms of established religion that he objected to, rather than private belief.

> Nothing will ever persuade me that a system which permits the introduction of the private religions, or irreligions, or heterodoxical opinions of contributors to a newspaper into the articles on politics or general views which they write for it, is a wise or good system . . . It is for this reason *only* that I don't desire to be 'one of you' – simply because a common respect for my own religious convictions prevents me from wishing to —— but *writing* on this subject is no use. I hate controversies on paper, almost more than I hate controversies in talk –

Nevertheless he continued the argument in his next letter, emphasizing, 'It is not your freedom of religious thought that I wish to object to; but your license of religious expression – a license which is, to *me*, utterly abhorrent . . . Surely there is some difference between the "*orthodoxy*" which would keep you within the limit of this or that particular creed . . . and the "orthodoxy" which simply believes Our Saviour's name to be something too sacred for introduction into articles on the political squabbles and difficulties of the day.' He concludes this long and impassioned letter by insisting, 'The course I have taken is *my own course* – no one has prompted me to it . . . I act under the dictates of my own opinion – only my own.'[32] His concern to underline his independence from family pressures perhaps sounds over-emphatic. There is no hint in his later correspondence of religious belief in the customary sense in which his parents and brother would have understood it. It was at Charley's insistence that he took Jeremy Taylor's *Holy Living and Holy Dying* to Italy with him in 1853. He found it heavy-going.

In spite of this difference, Wilkie and Edward Pigott remained the closest of friends for the rest of Wilkie's life, and Wilkie continued to write for *The Leader* until Pigott ceased to be the proprietor. They shared a passion for sailing, and the easygoing Pigott was a perfect holiday companion. He seems to have had much in common with Wilkie, to judge from Margaret Oliphant's description of him:

> a man to whom everybody's heart went out . . . he was always interested, always kind – a sort of atmosphere of humanity and warm feeling and sympathy about him, his little round form and round head radiating warmth and kindliness. He is the only man I have ever met, I think, from whom I never heard an unkind word of anyone . . . he was never dull, though always kind.[33]

Wilkie also wrote for *The Leader* a series of letters on the fashionable subject of experiments in hypnotism and clairvoyance, 'Magnetic Evenings at Home', which appeared from January to April 1852. (Hypnotism was then thought to be a form of 'electricity' passing between the 'magnetizer' and 'magnetized'.) The letters, on a subject that Wilkie, like Dickens, took seriously, were addressed to Lewes, who did not: they show that Wilkie's lifelong fascination with the uncanny was not simply assumed to intrigue his readers.[34] Yet he showed a degree of ambivalence: he explained to Pigott that he would have wanted these articles to be anonymous in any event, quite apart from his disagreements on the religious issue. When Richard Bentley's son George approached him for an article on 'spirit-rapping' for *Bentley's Miscellany* in the following year, Wilkie replied evasively that he knew nothing of the subject. 'I should be very glad to assist in exposing it . . . but I have never attended a "Seance" or exhibition of this last new Spirit of the Age'.[35] Yet the *Leader* articles show that Wilkie, recuperating from overwork at Weston-super-Mare duing Christmas and New Year 1851/2, had been an enthusiastic witness of related experiments in hypnotism and telepathy carried out at neighbouring country houses. The Pigott family, who lived at Brockley Hall, near Weston, were probably involved in these.

The articles are accounts of standard hypnotic demonstrations, but with occasional passages which display his developing descriptive powers:

> It was now evening – a still, cold, clear winter evening. Dim shadows were gathering over the room; contrasted on one side by the ruddy firelight, on the other by the last rays of the setting sun, floating through the window. The positions of the spectators, as they anxiously watched the progress of the new experiment; the strange, wild contrasts of light and shade falling on every figure; the beauty and variety of the attitudes into which the children and the young girls accidentally fell, as they sat, reclined, or stood together; the natural harmony and grace in the formation of the different groups, made the room a perfect school for painters . . .[36]

Another experiment was in clairvoyance. The clairvoyant gave an accurate description of Charles Collins, whom she had never seen. Use was made of a mirror of polished coal: Wilkie later used this as an image of imagination and memory in an article for *Household Words*.[37] He may have recalled the experiment when he came to write the passage in *The Moonstone* where the boy clairvoyant looks into a pool of ink.

Wilkie and Edward Pigott were called to the Bar together, on 21 November 1852.[38] Though they had not worked for or passed exams, they saw no reason why they should not celebrate the occasion, and they shared a 'call party'. 'What a night! What chicken! What songs! I carried away much clarets, and am rather a seedy barrister this morning – I think it must have been the *oaths* that disagreed with me!' he confessed to Pigott the next morning.[39] While his attitude to law was casual, he was working hard as a writer. The latest of his literary experiments was an attempt to tap the lucrative market for Christmas books created by Dickens. Rather late in the year he had an idea for one, and wrote to Bentley suggesting that it might be illustrated by Millais, Holman Hunt and Charles Collins, a friendly attempt to associate the controversial painters with a popular genre and perhaps help them to be accepted by the general public.

Charley was at a particularly low ebb that winter, according to Millais: 'I am tremendously dull here . . . and I have positively no person except Charles Collins (who is frightfully chilling) to associate with . . . I run off to Hanover Terrace merely because it is an object, jest with the old lady, say about a dozen words to her lay figure son, and tumble out into the freezing night miserable . . .'[40] Charley may have been too depressed to draw an illustration for *Mr. Wray's Cash Box*, which appeared with a frontispiece by Millais, but no other illustrations, just in time for Christmas.[41] It had some favourable reviews, but did not sell. Ruskin's opinion that it was a 'gross imitation of Dickens . . . not merely imitated – but stolen . . . a mere stew of old cooked meats – Jeremiah's cast clouts'[42] is unnecessarily harsh. The book, which hinges on the legality or otherwise of reproducing the bust of Shakespeare in Stratford Church, was perhaps inspired by the Soane Museum 'Shakespeare Recess', which contains a copy of the bust. It is an uncharacteristic piece; yet even in this very slight story there is an interest in unusual states of mind.

Wilkie's annoyance with Bentley's continued inefficiency increased: having realized that his preface to the story gave the plot away, he told Bentley to omit it, but the book still appeared with it, and was advertised as 'Mr. Wray's Cash Book', illustrated by 'Willais', by the author of 'Antonini'. 'Make it a Cash-*Box* (on the ear) to the miserable printer,' he complained to George Bentley.[43]

Wilkie had been casting around for an idea for a novel for some months, considering, and rejecting, another historical subject.[44] At the beginning of 1852 he started a 'story of modern life', but was soon interrupted by the tour of *Not So Bad As We Seem* to Manchester and Liverpool, for which he had to 'get up' the larger part of Shadowly Softhead, taken over when Douglas Jerrold, 'who never in his life was true to anything' according to Dickens, deserted the company.[45] Wilkie's success confirmed a severe case of inherited stage-fever that stayed with him for the rest of his life. In Manchester:

> Two thousand, seven hundred people . . . never missed a single 'point' in the play – and applauded incessantly. *My* part, you will be glad to hear, was played without a single mistake – and . . . so as to produce some very warm congratulations from my Manager . . . The dress and wig made me (everybody said) look about *sixteen* . . . I did not feel in the slightest degree nervous, and was not 'thrown off my balance' by

> a round of applause which greeted my first appearance . . . When the curtain fell on Dickens and your dutiful son at the end of the first act, the audience were all rolling about like a great sea, and roaring with laughter at the tops of their voices.[46]

By March Wilkie was home again, revising the first volume of the new novel, and in April his short horror story 'A Terribly Strange Bed' was published in *Household Words*. It has become a classic, and may have been the inspiration for Joseph Conrad's very similar 'The Inn of the Two Witches', though Conrad denied it.* Dickens had reason to be proud of his protégé.

Household Words was only one among many magazines Wilkie contributed to, often anonymously. For *Bentley's Miscellany* he wrote one more piece in 1852: 'Nine O'Clock!', a story with a French Revolution setting. This tale of precognition and an out-of-body experience may have been inspired by the 'magnetic evenings' and the discussions they provoked. It also explores again the idea of the double. In 'The Twin Sisters' this was handled in a straightforward way, simply as a case of mistaken identity; 'Nine O'Clock!' treats the uncanny aspect. A young man, standing beside his brother, sees the brother's projection or shadow-self simultaneously walking in the garden with their father. The father, though sympathetically presented, cannot tell the shadow from the real son: a fleeting but effective image of parental obtuseness.

There was a final, triumphantly successful tour of *Not So Bad As We Seem* in August and September, in the Midlands and north of England. At Newcastle Wilkie stayed with the Brandling family, and was much taken with his friend's eldest sister: 'the cleverest and the most agreeable woman I think I ever met with – all the elegance and vivacity of a Frenchwoman – and all the sincerity and warm-heartedness of an Englishwoman. How it is, she has never been married, is beyond all imagination', he wrote to Harriet, who must have wondered if she were to be presented with a daughter-in-law.[47] The beautiful Brandling sisters affected both the Collins brothers:

* Wilkie acknowledged that the facts on which he based this story, and another, 'The Yellow Mask', came from a friend, the painter W. S. Herrick. His story and Conrad's may have had a common origin.

Charley was later rumoured to be hopelessly in love with Emma Brandling.

After the tour, Wilkie stayed for the first time with Dickens and his family. They were spending the summer at Camden Crescent, Dover, while the move from Devonshire Terrace to Tavistock House was completed. Catherine Horne, meeting Wilkie there, thought him 'a nice funny little fellow but much too fond of eating and snuff'.[48] Dickens' orderly and self-disciplined routine, combined with his apparently inexhaustible energy, set an example Wilkie tried to live up to. 'Our life here is as healthy and happy as life can be – work in the morning – long walks – sea-bathing – early hours – famous meals – merry evenings – make up the various fuel with which we feed the fire of life.'[49] But he found 'The sea air acts on me as if it was all distilled from laudanum', and after one of Dickens' famous fifteen-mile walks he was too sleepy even to write a letter. Still, 'If good ideas are as infectious as bad, the end of the novel, written in *this* house, ought to be the best part of it.'[50] (It is not.) Dickens was writing *Bleak House*, and reading the latest chapters to the household before they were published, 'speaking the dialogue . . . as dramatically as if he was acting . . . and making his audience laugh and cry with equal fervour and equal sincerity'.[51] Wilkie, fired by his example, finished his novel on 15 September, and on 1 October he delivered the corrected manuscript to Richard Bentley.

SEVEN

The Sorcerer and the Apprentice

(1852–1853)

Bentley liked *Basil*, though he took fright at some too-explicit passages. In Wilkie's first version, the hero followed his wife and her seducer to a house in a lonely street, and the door was opened to him by a girl: 'I had intended to ask her who lived in the house, but the . . . sight of her made the question needless.'[1] In the published version this obvious reference to a brothel or house of assignation was omitted. The house becomes a hotel, and the prostitute a waiter: '. . . you will see that I have only mentioned "the Hotel" as a "deserted, dreary-looking building" ', Wilkie assured Bentley.[2] On his side, Wilkie, instructed by Dickens, issued an 'ultimatum' on terms: an unconditional payment of £350 for the copyright. *Basil* was published on 16 November, with a dedication to Charles Ward.

Wilkie was deeply serious about his novel. In a long preface – deplored by Dickens, and much shortened in later editions – he attempted a defensive, somewhat confused manifesto of his intentions. He made a bid at once for popularity, aiming at 'the largest number of readers, by writing a story of our own times'. Like his father, he had no interest in appealing to a minority taste: his was to be a democratic art that would speak to his readers by recalling their own experiences. 'I founded the main event out of which this story springs, on a fact in real life which had come within my own knowledge: and in afterwards shaping the course of the narrative thus suggested, guided it as often as I could where

I knew by my own experiences, and by the experiences incidentally related to me by others, that it would touch on something real and true, in its progress.' But he also made large claims for his art, dismissing

> the mob of ladies and gentlemen who play at writing . . . who coolly select as an amusement 'to kill time,' an occupation which can only be pursued, even creditably, by the patient, uncompromising, reverent devotion of every moral and intellectual faculty, more or less, which a human being has to give . . . To escape classification with the off-hand professors of this sort of off-hand authorship, by the homely but honourable distinction of being workers and not players at their task, has really become an object of importance . . . for those who follow Literature as a study and respect it as a Science.

Wilkie's preface has always teased readers. Was the suggestion that this story, of a young man who falls in love with a girl he meets in an omnibus and marries her secretly, only to be betrayed by her, founded on 'a fact in real life' from Wilkie's own experience? It is possible. The only biographical study of him written during his lifetime, based in part on information from Wilkie himself, and never contradicted by him, speaks of his deep sadness about an unfortunate love.[3] If Wilkie did ever have a disastrous love affair of this kind, he carefully removed all traces of it from his personal papers. In the last years of his life he burnt a mass of letters when he moved house.

The 'real' in the situation of *Basil* is as likely to be a creative reworking of fragments of experiences, his own and those of his friends. The secret marriage of Ned and Henrietta Ward, with its delayed consummation, obviously suggested one element of the plot. More important, and possibly the 'fact in real life', was the involvement of Holman Hunt with his model Annie Miller. Hunt met Annie, an illiterate working girl with red-gold hair and astonishing sexual magnetism, in 1850, when she was fifteen. He saw her in the street and followed her home, and for the next thirteen years they had a stormy relationship. Hunt made earnest efforts to have her educated and made fit to be his wife, while she, against his wishes, modelled for several of his friends, and deceived him with some of them. According to Millais, who knew him better than anyone at this time, Hunt and Annie never went to bed together. On 27 April 1856

Ford Madox Brown walked with Millais to the Royal Academy, 'he conversing much about babies and the advantages of marriage, the disgustingness of stale virginities etc., in relation to Hunt'.[4] Annie certainly had an affair with Rossetti, and was the cause of a permanent rift between him and Hunt. She seems to have found Rossetti a good deal more entertaining. She was kept for a while by the notorious rake Lord Ranelagh, a fact known to everyone but Hunt. She very possibly augmented her earnings as a model by prostitution. Though many of these events were still in the future when Wilkie wrote *Basil*, it was soon clear to most of Hunt's friends that in spite of his frantic efforts to turn her into marriageable material, Annie was not likely to prove a chaste and reliable companion. She was the model for the girl in Hunt's painting 'The Awakening Conscience' of 1854 (he later altered the face). According to Edward Lear, the conscientious Hunt rented a room in a *maison de convenance* to get the setting right; it might be an illustration for the passage in *Basil* describing the Sherwins' sitting-room:

> Everything was oppressively new. The brilliantly-varnished door cracked with a report like a pistol when it was opened; the paper on the walls, with its gaudy pattern of birds, trellis-work, and flowers, in gold, red and green on a white ground, looked hardly dry yet; the showy window-curtains of white and sky-blue, and the still showier carpet of red and yellow, seemed as if they had come out of the shop yesterday; the round rosewood table was in a painfully high state of polish; the morocco-bound picture books that lay on it, looked as if they had never been moved or opened since they had been bought; not one leaf even of the music on the piano was dogs-eared or worn. (*Basil*, Part 1, X, p. 61)[5]

Wherever the facts behind *Basil* came from, Wilkie's repeated insistence on the literal truth of his fictions starts early. 'The Twin Sisters' has the sub-heading 'A True Story'; *Mr. Wray's Cash Box* starts 'from a curious *fact*'.[6] This defensiveness suggests Wilkie may have suffered from disapproval of his childish 'tall stories'. Behind the lengthy preface to *Basil* one senses, in spite of its large claims, the child desperate to convince an increasingly sceptical adult audience. It had the opposite effect. A predominantly friendly notice in *The Leader* pointed out, 'however true as a matter of fact the main incident may be, it is not truly presented in this story; an air of unreality pervades the book which makes even commonplace incidents look "improbable" ... The question never is, "Did you have a living model?" The question always is, "Have you created a living figure?" '[7]

Wilkie, fascinated by his acting experiences, and thinking of writing plays, further weakened his own claim to realism by twinning the novel with the drama.

> Believing that the Novel and the Play are twin-sisters in the family of Fiction; that the one is a drama narrated, as the other is a drama acted; and that all the strong and deep emotions which the Play-writer is privileged to excite, the Novel-writer is privileged to excite also, I have not thought it either politic or necessary, while adhering to realities, to adhere to common-place, everyday realities only.[8]

This doubling-back leaves the author in effect free to move from naturalism to artifice and back again. *Basil* is a powerful, larger-than-life, tragic tale attached, sometimes rather uncertainly, to naturalistic descriptions of contemporary life. *Basil*, rather than *The Woman in White*, has a strong claim to be considered the first sensation novel. The enthusiastic reviewer in *Bentley's Miscellany* summed it up thus:

> The *intense* everywhere predominates ... The fatality of the Greek tragedians broods over it. There is a Nemesis not to be escaped. The hero of the tale sees a pretty girl in an omnibus; and he – goes to his doom ...[9]

The plot is simple, even banal: an aristocrat's son; a tradesman's daughter; a secret marriage; a villain seeking revenge on the son of the man who killed his father. The ingredients are those of a thousand pot-boilers. But, as the reviewer in *Bentley's Miscellany* spotted, 'There is a startling antagonism between the intensity of the passion, the violent spasmodic action of the piece, and its smooth, commonplace environments ... this very discrepancy enhances the terror of the drama; and there is something artist-like even in this apparent want of art.'

The settings are deliberately chosen to show the shadow side of the commonplace. The omnibus, for example, provides a meeting place where encounters between the sexes and classes are to a limited extent licensed. In *My Secret Life*, 'Walter' records several sexual intrigues which resulted from such encounters.[10] The omnibus, dimly lit, on the move, neither indoor nor open-air, is an ambiguous area, mysterious and yet banal: the key to Basil's later relationship with Margaret. The suburb in which Margaret lives, raw new villas and squares 'intermingled with wretched patches of waste land, half built over', is a metaphor for the lives that are lived there. The fascinated horror that Dickens felt for all forms of decay, in architectural terms the decay of the inner city, Wilkie Collins reserved for the abortive, half-formed villa-dom that was ringing London during his lifetime. In novel after novel the scaffolding of the half-built replaces the ruined castle or the tumbledown tenement to become the haunt of modern evil.

The powerfully physical nature of Basil's attraction to Margaret, irrational and overwhelming, is stressed by the descriptions of her. The Pre-Raphaelites encouraged their women to abandon crinolines and corsets, and Wilkie had a fascination with the uncorseted female figure, amounting almost to an obsession, which may have begun in his teens. William Collins, for all his conventionality, saw nothing wrong in introducing his young sons to the nude, as long as it was framed or set on a pedestal. Wilkie and Charley were trailed round the art galleries of Italy, and in Naples the young Wilkie found an image that haunted him for life. In a late letter he confessed, 'My beau ideal is the "Venus Callipyge" – holding up her robe, and looking over her shoulder at her own divine back view. From the small of her back to the end of her thighs she has escaped the detestable restorers – and my life has been passed in trying to find a living woman who is like her – and in never succeeding.'[11] Basil's first glimpse of Margaret is of a clothed Venus:

> She put down her veil again immediately . . . Still there was enough left to see – enough to charm. There was the little rim of delicate white lace, encircling the lovely, dusky throat; there was the figure visible, where the shawl had fallen open, slender, but already well developed in its slenderness, and exquisitely supple; there was the waist, naturally low, and left to its natural place and natural size . . . There was all this to behold, all this to dwell on, in spite of the veil. The veil! how little of the woman does it hide, when the man really loves her! (*Basil*, Part I, VII, p. 31)

This emphasis on a woman's body and its coverings (Wilkie always had a keen eye for women's clothes), rather than her face, serves in *Basil* to emphasize physical at the expense of spiritual love, the cause of Basil's downfall. In later novels the same kind of description is used more equivocally.

As the novel develops, the relationship of Margaret and Basil becomes less significant than that of Basil and the villain Mannion: obsessional love gives way to obsessional hate. Mannion is not only Basil's pursuer but his double, Hyde to his Jekyll. The revenge plot is supported at a psychological and mythic level as Basil and Mannion repeatedly change places during the course of the story, alternating the roles of avenger and victim, substance and shadow. Both are outcasts and wanderers, both are obsessed by the same woman. Basil at first hopes to educate Margaret, usurping Mannion's role as her tutor. Like Holman Hunt with Annie Miller, he struggles in vain to fill her beautiful, empty head with artistic and literary understanding: 'Sometimes, when I was away from her, I might think of leading her girlish curiosity to higher things; but when we met again, the thought vanished; and it became delight enough for me simply to hear her speak, without once caring or considering what she spoke of.'[12] It is Mannion who teaches her the demonic lessons of carnal knowledge that Basil has agreed to defer. These culminate in her deflowering. Like some eighteenth-century seigneur, Mannion anticipates by one night the consummation of her marriage to Basil, while Basil, concealed in the room next door, listens to the sounds of their coupling. Basil's attack on his shadow-self, who has done what he could only dream about, follows. It leave Mannion literally faceless, deprived of his identity. It is fully as horrific as Mannion's deliberate pursuit of Basil.

Read for surface realism, *Basil* is as preposterous as most Gothic or sensation novels. Seen as a modern myth, in which archetypal figures act out the underlying preoccupations of the Victorian age with sexuality, possession and usurpation, it still has a powerful impact. The characterization, however, alternates between the naturalistic and the archetypal, with intermittent success. Basil's father, the remote and chilly aristocrat whose children can never behave naturally in his presence, is nothing like a portrait of the anxious and loving William Collins. *Basil* is not, as has sometimes been suggested, a blow aimed at William Collins, so much as an attack on the causes of his anxieties and snobberies. Basil is given some biographical details based on Wilkie's own experience (he is reading for the Bar and writing a historical novel). But the more naturalistically drawn character of Basil's elder brother Ralph is closer to the face Wilkie Collins showed to the world. Ralph is a cheerful hedonist living with his mistress, 'the morganatic Mrs. Ralph', who takes a common-sense approach to Basil's predicament. He was picked out by Collins' friend Edmund Yates as the best character in the book. Whether the Sherwins, in their gimcrack north London nest, have real-life counterparts or not, they and their setting are drawn with an exemplary naturalism. But Basil, his innocent and loving sister Clara, placed as the light angel to whom Margaret is the opposed dark temptress (in a Dickens novel Clara would have been a sisterly second wife, rather than a wifely sister), and the demonic Mannion seem relics from an earlier tradition.

The novel made the reviewers uneasy, though there is no suggestion that any of them considered it autobiographical. The *Athenaeum* deplored its 'vicious atmosphere' and warned the author against enrolling in the 'unwholesome literary school' of Maturin and Eugene Sue.[13] Another reviewer, while praising his 'imaginative excellence' and 'distinguished, eloquent and graceful' writing, warned that the taste of the age demanded fiction which would 'elevate and purify . . . unless the writer keeps this object constantly before him, he can never hope to win a lasting popularity'.[14] Most reviewers seem to have been impressed by the quality of the writing, and, almost against their wills, by the power of the narration. Dickens praised the 'admirable writing' and 'delicate discrimination of character', while pointing out that Wilkie should take more care with the probabilities. It was *Basil* that confirmed Dickens' opinion of Wilkie as a serious artist.

Though Wilkie was enchanted and flattered by Dickens' praise and attention, he still belonged to a number of overlapping circles of London artistic life, and moved easily from one to another, rather than becoming a satellite revolving round Dickens' fixed star. Wilkie continued to have many friends who were painters, both among the Pre-Raphaelites, with whom he shared a fine disregard for conventional behaviour, even if he did not care for their painting, and the Academy painters Ward, Frith and Egg, whose work he secretly preferred.

To Edward Pigott he could freely express heresies he might have hesitated to reveal to Dickens: 'My appreciation is all wrong on no end of literary subjects . . . Excepting Falstaff and Dogberry, I think Molière a greater humourist than Shakespeare, and one of the most tedious books (to me) that I ever read in my life was *Tom Jones*.'[15] Through his work for *The Leader* he got to know G. H. Lewes and, somewhat later, George Eliot. Catherine Horne saw 'little Wilkie Collins' at the house of Robert Bell, the journalist and editor whose edition of Chaucer he reviewed for *The Leader*: 'He is become a great pet of Mrs. B's.'[16] At Richard Bentley's literary dinner parties and the regular Wednesday-evening gatherings at George Bentley's house, he may have met for the first time another Bentley author, Frances Dickinson, who was to become a close friend. He introduced Pigott, Frances Dickinson and the novelist Charles Reade to the Dickens circle. Through W. H. Wills and his wife, he met Mrs Wills' nieces, Nina Chambers, who married Frederick Lehmann; her sisters the twins Eliza and Jenny; and Amelia, or 'Tucky', who married Frederick Lehmann's brother Rudolf, to become her own sister's sister-in-law.

Though he was far from conventionally attractive, Wilkie had the ability to charm and amuse women of all ages. He wooed them with his story-telling, with comic verse and intimate, affectionate letters. To sit next to Wilkie at dinner was to have 'a brilliant time of it'.[17] Many of the most respectable wives and mothers kept an affectionate regard for him through all the scandals that hung about him in his later life.

Though Wilkie was not in the least interested in female emancipation, he liked women who were intelligent and gifted and spoke their minds, like Nina Lehmann. Nina, who became one of his dearest friends, was an accomplished pianist. At the time of her marriage she lamented that her father Robert Chambers, the author of the pre-Darwinian *Vestiges of Creation*, 'does not admire women with minds . . . He would have us all . . . mild unoffending creatures . . . writing a small delicate female hand, and expressing little thoughts in the most strictly proper and polite terms. Why am I not like this? . . . Why am I born with reason, and with power to comprehend readily and to argue?'[18] It could be Marian Halcombe speaking.

From 1853 Wilkie was also part of the *Household Words* group, becoming as familiar a face at the magazine's unpretentious offices in the bow-windowed house in Wellington Street as he was at Tavistock House. In the 1850s Dickens enjoyed a blend of popularity and respect, unique then, and never since equalled in the English-speaking world. Yet his hunger for acceptance was unappeasable. *Household Words*, started in 1850, became, among other things, a kind of house magazine for the Dickens myth: contributions were anonymous, but as the paper carried the running heading, on every double page, 'Conducted by . . . Charles Dickens', the subliminal message was clear. *Household Words* gave him an opportunity to keep in touch, week by week, with his huge audience – regulating opinion, enlivening the imaginative capacity, alternately disturbing and reassuring – in a way more direct and immediate than could be achieved even through the monthly numbers of the novels.

Even Dickens' extraordinary energy could not power the magazine without help. His assistant editor W. H. Wills took on much of the day-to-day business of the paper, as well as being a regular contributor. Wills, kindly and pedantic, provided ballast, though Dickens thought him too concerned with niggling detail, 'decidedly of the Nutmeg-grater or Fancy-Bread Rasper-School'.[19] 'Keep Household Words imaginative!' Dickens admonished Wills from Italy in 1853. In addition to irregular contributions from outsiders, there was a 'stable' of regular contributors, many of them young, who included R. H. Horne, Dudley Costello, Elizabeth Gaskell, W. B. Jerrold, Henry Morley and G. A. Sala. John Forster, until then one of the people closest to Dickens, contributed very little.[20]

Several of Dickens' 'young men' wrote happy reminiscences of those years. They remembered the office dinners (baked leg of mutton with veal-and-oyster stuffing sent in from Rules in Maiden

Lane; Dickens' own gin-punch). They joined the investigative trips to the slums. They went to the famous haunted house at Cheshunt, to inspect the ghost; and to Broadmoor, to inspect the criminal lunatics, Richard Dadd among them. Wilkie's name often appears in these recollections. All of them stress his modesty and good humour, but also emphasize his brilliance as a conversationalist and his conviviality. At this stage of his life he was the most sociable of men. Though he still kept house with his mother and brother at Hanover Terrace, where his friends were often entertained and always welcome, he led an independent life with few, if any, restrictions. He had the advantages of a home, without the responsibilities of a wife and family. Wilkie went regularly to his clubs – he belonged to the Garrick, the Reform and the Athenaeum, as well as other minor ones – and made many friends; but he was never primarily a clubman. As a reviewer for *The Leader* he received free theatre tickets, and he was becoming familiar with the green-rooms, sharing with Dickens a fascination with backstage life. He also went with Dickens to music halls and the East End entertainments of the poor. He travelled on the Continent, with no questions asked at home. Harriet had long ceased to attempt any control over her son, and he felt so little sense of restriction that he did not even trouble to open a bank account of his own, still paying the cheques for his literary earnings into her account at Coutts and calling on her for cash when he needed it, as he had always done.

It was a way of life with many advantages for him, and the impetus to change it came originally from his mother. Harriet was sixty-three, and she began to long to give up London housekeeping and retire to the country. From the winter of 1853 onwards, various plans were mooted. 'I highly approve of Miss Otter's plan for pitching her tent near my mother's', Wilkie wrote to Charles. 'To begin in the country with a good neighbour in the shape of an old friend, seems as promising an entrance into a state of rural existence as could well be desired. But where are they to go? We must discuss that question when I get home'.[21]

The prospect of losing the family home did not worry Wilkie. Nor did he consider marriage as an alternative. At this stage of his life he was a confirmed Malthusian: 'Leigh Hunt's son's wife has been at it again', he told his mother in 1844.* 'Charlie commiserated and that *was all* . . . If that great man Malthus had been attended to we should have had no beggars by this time.'[22] Bachelor jokes at the expense of newly married men and the fathers of families continued to punctuate his correspondence. He teased the Ward brothers about their existing and forthcoming children, telling Charles to stop complaining about his family troubles: '. . . you are a British Father! (my respects to your Social Title); and you *have* begotten, and *are* begetting and *will* beget many British Babies (smack their bottoms in *my* name, and for *my* sake!) What are measles, and tumblings out of bed compared to such blessed privileges as these?' He added with complacent insincerity, 'I wish I was married, and had a family and a respectable pot belly, and a position in the country as a householder and ratepayer – but this is not to be. By all the napkins of all the babies of England, I begin to fear that I am a little better than a vagabond.'[23] He noted that 'married men look as though their feelings were hurt when you flatter them about their large families', and when Edward Pigott's brother George married in February 1853 Wilkie joked rather heavy-handedly, 'Nothing ought to pass his lips on Wednesday but *oysters*, and the strongest port wine.'[24]

When Millais married the still-virgin Mrs Ruskin in 1855, the reactions of the two Collins brothers were characteristically different. Charles, who had acted as go-between for Ruskin and Millais and knew of Millais' misgivings, was pious, earnest and anxious, writing sympathetically of Effie as having 'passed through what seems to me about as terrible an ordeal as any human being can', and adding, 'It is an awful step, this of marriage . . . your prayers will not be wanting that whatever is best for *both* of them may be the issue of this strange affair.'[25] Millais had written to Charles Collins about the forthcoming marriage, 'There are some startling accomplishments, my boy, like the glimpse of the dentists instruments – My poor brain and soul is fatigued with dwelling on unpleasant probabilities . . .'[26] Charles could identify with his friend's fears of sexual inadequacy.

* Thornton Leigh Hunt had ten children by his wife Catherine, and four by Agnes Lewes.

But Wilkie, after ribaldly hoping that this time Effie's marriage would be successfully consummated, put it rather differently. 'I can't resist *Priapian* jesting on the marriage of my friends. It is such a dreadfully serious thing afterwards, that one ought to joke about it as long as one can.'[27] With Effie's encouragement Millais came through the marital ordeal triumphantly. 'By George, Charlie, I am truly a favoured man,' he wrote to Charles Collins after the wedding night. 'It is such a delight to feel a woman always about one part of oneself.'[28] It was not a delight Wilkie yet felt in need of.

Wilkie was still fully involved in journalism for *The Leader*. This was not always of the most interesting kind: he complained to Pigott that a novel he had been sent for review was 'only fit for the water-closet'. Pigott made amends by sending him Trollope's *The Warden*. Wilkie admired it, but he criticized Trollope's authorial intrusions:

> It is always the reader's business, never the author's, to apostrophize characters. The 'illusion of the scene' is invariably perilled, or lost altogether, when the writer harangues in his own person on the behaviour of his characters, or gives us, with an intrusive 'I', his own experiences of the houses in which he describes those characters as living.[29]

He is here anticipating, by nearly thirty years, Henry James' well-known complaint of Trollope's 'betrayal of a sacred office'.

Wilkie's contributions to *Household Words* were sparse at first. For an ambitious young writer to become one of Dickens' 'young men' and be put through an apprenticeship to *Household Words* could be educative and stimulating; it could also be frustrating. The magazine had a distinct 'house style' based on Dickens' own. Often an article would be written in collaboration with Dickens. That could mean that the editor would take the piece and entirely rewrite it, until the supposed author could hardly recognize his or her original conception. Elizabeth Gaskell, an early contributor (her story 'Lizzie Leigh' was serialized in the first three numbers of *Household Words*), became increasingly incensed at Dickens' well-meant interference with her fiction. To get the most from an association with Dickens – not necessarily the same as being a successful writer for *Household Words* – a young author needed an unusual combination of self-confidence and humility; a capacity for taking pains equivalent to Dickens' own; and a childlike ability to switch, on the instant, from concentrated work to uninhibited play. All these Wilkie had. Yet after the publication of 'A Terribly Strange Bed' he submitted nothing until the beginning of 1853. The story he offered then, 'Mad Monkton', was rejected. It is a powerful tale about a man haunted by the ghost of his unburied uncle, whose body must be found, reclaimed and returned to the family vault. As Monkton's madness is hereditary, Dickens was alarmed that the story might upset his readers. He wrote to Wills that it would be best to accept Wilkie's offer of a different story. But he added:

> I think there are many things, both in the inventive and descriptive way, that he could do for us . . . And I particularly wish him to understand this, and to have every possible assurance conveyed to him that I think so, and that I should particularly like to have his aid.[30]

Wilkie's alternative, 'Gabriel's Marriage', a hotchpotch of crime and the uncanny, set in France at the time of the Revolution, was published in *Household Words* in April 1853. 'Mad Monkton' went instead to *Fraser's Magazine*.

Wilkie was later to write, in an appreciation of Douglas Jerrold, 'A contributor who can strike out new ideas from the original resources of his own mind, is one man, and a contributor who can be depended on for the small work-a-day emergencies which are felt one week and forgotten the next, is generally another. Jerrold united these two characters in himself'.[31] So did Wilkie, as Dickens was already aware. But Wilkie also learnt much from *Household Words*. The magazine carried many excellent investigative articles on matters of social concern, on the kind of topics Wilkie later used in his novels. A piece by W. H. Wills and Dickens on 'Idiots', which appeared on 4 June 1853, seems a likely inspiration for the character of Hans Grimm in Wilkie's play *The Red Vial* of 1858. An article on 'Neapolitan State Prisoners' may have suggested aspects of the political background of Pesca and Fosco in *The Woman in White*.[32] Another article, on the status of married women, foreshadows many of Wilkie's indignant protests on their behalf – the situation of Laura Glyde in *The Woman in White*, and of the persecuted Hester Dethridge in *Man and Wife*, are two examples.

> When she marries, she dies; being handed over to be buried in her husband's arms, or pounded and pummelled into the grave *with* his arms . . . a wife – like a convict – cannot have or hold one iota of anything that has value. (W. H. Wills, 'A Legal Fiction', *Household Words*, 21 July 1855)

In the same month that 'Gabriel's Marriage' was published, Wilkie began work on a new novel, *Hide and Seek*.[33] He had a chameleon-like ability to turn from one kind of writing to another, and, though his novel has some frightening moments, it is essentially a small-scale, domestic mystery story. Wilkie, writing to George Bentley refusing a 'half-profit' contract similar to that for *Rambles Beyond Railways*, promised him: 'I am piping quite a new tune this time, and expect to make the readers of Antonina and Basil prick up their ears, and at least allow that I have given them some fresh variations which they did not expect from me.'[34]

Dickens, who was spending the summer with his family at Boulogne, encouraged Wilkie, now one of the companions most essential to him, to join them in June, promising him 'a Pavilion room in the garden, with a delicious view, where you may write no end of Basils'.[35] But Wilkie was seriously ill throughout May and June, perhaps the first attack of the inherited 'rheumatic gout' that was to plague him for the rest of his life. He wrote to Pigott at the end of June that he was 'not yet strong enough yet to do more than "toddle" out for half an hour at a time with a stick . . . My illness and long confinement have muddled my brains dreadfully'.[36] He was frightened into making efforts to reform his habits for a while. Convalescing at Maidenhead in early July, he wrote assuring his mother that for the first time in his life he was dressed and ready for breakfast at ten to nine. He also thought it worth remark that he was drinking no more than three glasses of wine, and no beer. Set up by this rigorous regime, he went off to Boulogne, armed with the partly written *Hide and Seek*, at the end of July.

Dickens had rented the Villa des Moulineaux, an eccentrically constructed house with various follies in the grounds. Among them was a Swiss cottage, a rustic chapel, 'a miniature château (de Tom Pouce)' and the Pavilion, in which Augustus Egg had the lower room and Wilkie the upper, away from the distractions and childish noise of the house. As usual Dickens managed to combine conviviality with hard work. 'I am hardly less industrious in my smaller way', Wilkie reported; though he was once seen at the Casino breakfasting off paté de foie gras, having missed the breakfast hour in the strictly regulated Dickens household.[37] He managed to write several chapters of the second volume of *Hide and Seek* while he was there, in spite of the great festivities to celebrate the completion of *Bleak House*. But the enchantments of the sorcerer were once again to come between the apprentice and his work: Wilkie was to spend a third of 1853 in close companionship with Dickens. The summer in Boulogne deepened the friendship, and Dickens, exhausted by the writing of *Bleak House*, had been discussing a trip to Switzerland and Italy. He wanted to travel fast and extensively, without his family: he asked Wilkie and Augustus Egg to go with him in the autumn. Wilkie, for whom Italy was always the land of lost delight, needed little urging.

EIGHT

In the Sorcerer's Footsteps

(1853–1854)

Augustus Egg, the third member of the travelling 'triumvirate', as Dickens called them, was the son of a successful gunsmith. Egg was, according to Frith (himself the son of servants), 'a tolerably well-educated man, but, either from a defective ear or from Cockney surroundings . . . he had some peculiarities in his pronunciation which were embarrassing and sometimes ludicrous'.[1] He had a private income, which he used generously to help his friends, buying their paintings and finding them rich patrons. Egg is known now for his paintings of contemporary life, and his much-reproduced triptych of 1858, 'Past and Present', showing the fate of a faithless wife, has come to typify mid-Victorian painting, but it was an unusual subject for him, and was not popular. His paintings of scenes from history and literature, now forgotten, were far more successful during his lifetime.

Egg was small, gentle and invincibly modest. 'His readiness to be convinced that he was wrong on any question . . . his misgivings about the value of his own labours; the continual researches he made in his art after new secrets – all showed, to the day of his death, a diffidence in his own nature such as few men after success great as that he had achieved . . . would entertain.'[2] He was a severe asthmatic. When he was acting in Wilkie's play *The Frozen Deep* in 1857, he gave the character he played, a comic cook, the asthmatic wheezings he suffered from in reality, which his friends would have found painful 'had he not at the same time made himself so thoroughly the character that the player was forgotten'.[3] Acting a charity boy in the farce *Mr. Nightingale's Diary*, he painted a skeleton-like face over his own. Richard Hengist Horne found 'the thing was too real; it was more painful than amusing'.[4] A sketch of him by Frith catches the sensitivity and vulnerability that he exposed to his friends.

Egg was a foil to the talkative Wilkie, who loved him dearly, and to the manically energetic Dickens. He conscientiously kept a diary of their travels, 'concerning the materials of which he remembers nothing, but is perpetually asking Collins . . . about the names of places where we have been, signs of hotels we have put up at, and so forth'.[5] Dickens, outpacing his two companions physically and, he felt, intellectually, was dismissive of Egg's intelligence, though he thought him 'an excellent fellow' and appreciated, as did all his friends, his sweet and gentle nature. Egg had proposed to Dickens' sister-in-law Georgina Hogarth a year or two earlier, but to Dickens' great relief the mainstay of his household turned Egg down, though they remained good friends.

The three travellers left London on 10 October 1853. A journey with the star of English letters was an impressive experience, almost, at times, a royal progress. Dickens had introductions everywhere, and old friends to see; at Lausanne his arrival created a 'prodigious sensation' in the English colony. On their way back the train from Dover to London was delayed expressly for him. But journeying round Europe in the 1850s provided marked contrasts of modern convenience and primitive, if picturesque, squalor and difficulty. Dickens complained that Egg, in particular, was not always ready to allow for this. Sometimes they travelled by comfortable trains and modern steamers, sometimes in 'the most extraordinary vehicles – like swings, like boats, like Noah's arks, like barges and enormous bedsteads'.[6] One country, even one district, differed sharply from another, especially where, as in Switzerland, the difficulties of access were extreme.

Being part of Dickens' entourage had other disadvantages, less immediately obvious. He was restless, footloose, bored by staying more than a few days anywhere. He complained, only half humorously, 'I find my companions so unused to the notion of never going to bed, except in large towns, that Sicily is already erased from the trip, and Naples substituted for its utmost limit'.[7] He preened himself on his superior stamina, superior knowledge of Europe, greater linguistic ability and more tactful handling of foreigners, especially officials and servants. His companions were less experienced. Wilkie was considerably younger, and Egg, though near to Dickens in age, had travelled very little. Though both were born, as Dickens was not, into a financially secure middle class that ought to be able to manage such matters, it was, according to Dickens, always he who had to act as mentor and man of the world. He had chosen the other members of his triumvirate well, for neither seems to have resented his leadership or rebelled against his authority. Dickens was a stimulating and amusing companion as long as he was in charge. For the moment both Wilkie and Egg were content to travel in the great man's shadow, aided by a German private courier who at first seemed excellent, but was later to let them down by his ignorance of Italian.

They went first to Paris, altered out of recognition by Haussmann's rebuilding and overflowing with English visitors. There they dined with Miss Coutts in grand company: a prince (unidentified) warned them that it was impossible to enter Italy from Switzerland because of Austrian suspicion of that refuge for political exiles. It was advice which proved quite untrue. They went by rail to Strasbourg, where Wilkie saw the sights: the cathedral clock, with its biblical puppet show, which he later made use of in *Armadale*, and the embalmed bodies, two hundred years old, of a count and his daughter, perfect except for her face 'falling slowly away into dust'.[8] After Basle the railway was replaced by a carriage; it took three days to reach Lausanne, where they stayed with Dickens' friend Chauncy Hare Townsend. Townsend, who had taken holy orders, was a wealthy man who, perhaps fortunately, never practised his profession: he would have made a most eccentric clergyman. He was an excruciatingly bad poet whose poems Dickens published in *Household Words* from time to time, a collector of jewellery and *objets d'art*, one of the first connoisseurs of photography as an art form and a severe hypochondriac. He was also unfailingly hospitable and kind, insisting the travellers should stay several days with him.

From Lausanne they went to Geneva by boat, and then had a hair-raising journey to Chamonix, starting at four in the morning. Wilkie intended to subsidize the holiday by writing a series of articles about the journey, for publication in *Bentley's Miscellany*. He wrote consciously literary letters to family and friends, to be handed round, carefully preserved, and then worked up for publication. Each letter seems to have been aimed at the particular interests of the recipient, so as to cover a different aspect of the journey. He wrote to Charles Ward mainly about the paintings he saw; to Edward Pigott about the adventures and misadventures of travelling by boat; to his mother and brother not only about art but also general descriptions of scenery and reminiscences of the people and places they had visited together sixteen years before. A letter to his mother gives a typical description of the perils of Swiss travel:

> Rather more than halfway to Chamounix, we had to leave the carriage, and get into a vehicle called a 'char' . . . [which] looked exactly like a rotten sedan chair on wheels . . . When we were not up to our axle trees in mud, we were jolting over the dry bed of a torrent . . . Imagine a thousand feet of almost perpendicular precipice and pine forest on either side of you, with the gloom of night settling grandly on *miles* of weird rock and gloomy foliage – imagine a torrent beneath you sprawling, crashing and leaping over a chaos of split stone – imagine a wild mule track winding about and heaving up and down before you whenever the tossed up ground will allow it a few feet of tenable space to continue its course – imagine, lastly, right in front the eternal snows of Mont Blanc, ghastly and awful in the deepening twilight rising and rising even into the night sky, till the great clouds themselves looked earthly by comparison with it –[9]

They crossed into Italy by the Simplon Pass, thankful to leave the Swiss valleys behind. Switzerland was not then the highly developed and sanitary country it has since become, and they were horrified by the cretinism and goitre endemic in the population. Wilkie described goitre with horrified fascination: '. . . a bag of flesh growing from the throat, generally as large as a hat, often the size of a carpet bag . . .

Some of [the women] walk with the goitre actually slung over their shoulders, and we heard of a boy (but I am glad to say did not see him) who trundles his goitre before him in a wheelbarrow'.[10]

Italy was a contrast with these grim scenes, as stimulating to the imagination as it had been when he crossed from France with his family seventeen years earlier. The warm, sunny shores of Lake Maggiore, where they crossed a river on a ferry and listened to a blind fiddler singing patriotic songs 'harshly, but with a certain earnestness of spirit', almost moved Wilkie to tears as the music reminded him of that journey. Italy had been then a door opening on a world of imagination and delight. He was determined it would not fail him now.

Their journey to Milan in a 'carriage of the period of Louis the 14th' was enlivened by the imaginative suggestion of a postmaster, notable for being 'extremely attentive and drunk', that their luggage would only be safe from thieves if they tied one end of a string to each trunk and held the other end in their hands. 'We held our three impromptu bell-ropes all the way to Milan. It was like being in a shower-bath and waiting to pull the string – or rather like fishing in the sea, where one waits to feel a bite by a tug at the line round one's finger . . .'[11]

At Milan Wilkie began to recall the artistic education his father had given him on the earlier journey, commenting on many of the paintings, and deploring the ruinous restoration of Leonardo's 'Last Supper'. His assumption of superior knowledge of everything to do with art, and his constant references to his earlier Italian experiences, in a man-of-the-world tone that suggested he had been a hard-drinking Byronic roué rather than a schoolboy of thirteen, irritated Dickens. Dickens' letters are full of complaints of Egg's and Wilkie's appearance and personal habits; neither of them shared Dickens' obsession with cleanliness and tidiness. Egg was slow, Wilkie mean over trifles. He was driven mad by Wilkie's inability to sing or whistle in tune: 'I was obliged to ask him, the day before yesterday, to leave off whistling the overture to William Tell. "For by Heaven," said I, "there's something the matter with your ear – I think it must be the cotton – which plays the Devil with the commonest tune." '[12] But the grumbles are followed by assertions that they are all getting on very well together. He made fun of Egg's determined but hopeless struggle with the Italian language: 'Our great joke is, at all times and on all occasions, to ask him what is the Italian for slippery – a word which he never can by any means get out.'[13] He objected to the embryo moustaches both were growing, and reported to his wife, 'Collins's moustache is gradually developing. You remember how the corners of his mouth go down, and how he looks through his spectacles and manages his legs. I don't know how it is, but the moustache is a horrible aggravation of all this.'[14] But he thought Wilkie a good travelling companion: 'He takes things easily and is not put out by small matters'; 'Collins eats and drinks everything. Gets on very well everywhere, and is always in good spirits.'[15] Wilkie and Egg responded with calm obstinacy to Dickens' criticisms: when he shaved off his beard as an encouragement to them to get rid of the moustaches, they merely commented, 'It looks better so.'[16]

Wilkie's letters have no hint of any reservation about Dickens. He complains in a thoroughly modern way of the crowds of tourists everywhere: 'the travelling part of the human race wants thinning'. But there is nothing but admiration and affection for both his companions. Wilkie's letters from the Italian trip are travel writing; Dickens' those of a novelist, who cannot resist seeing even his close friends and companions through his own comic distorting lens.

On the appalling journey in an overcrowded boat from Genoa to Naples, described in great detail by both Dickens and Wilkie, they spent the first night on deck in the rain rather than suffering in the saloon 'a nautical Pandemonium, sulphery [*sic*] with the fumes of past dinner and and present human breath'. Dickens took the situation in hand at dinner the next day: '[he] let off an incessant fire of jokes at the Captain (with a pretty pointed meaning in them)'. After this fusillade Dickens ended up in the steward's cabin. Egg and Collins slept good-humouredly on the dressers in the store-room, together with the dispossessed steward, an old gentleman and the ship's cat, among drums of figs, bunches of grapes and canisters of onions: 'and we all "pigged together" as the vulgar saying is, in the most amicable and comfortable manner imaginable. I never slept better in my life.'[17] It was Dickens who added the detail that the steward 'all night long fell head foremost, once in every five minutes, on Egg'.[18]

Dickens had innumerable calls to make at every place they visited, and Wilkie and Egg often struck off on their own. At Naples they went without Dickens to 'the Baiae side of the Bay':

> got on men's backs in the Sibyl's cave, and so splashed through much subterranean water by torchlight – wandered about temples and amphitheatres, and saw the wretched dog tortured at the Grotto del Cane (I roared fiercely to the man to let him go before he became insensible, being unable to bear the howling of the poor brute as the mephitic air acted on him . . .)[19]

An experience both comic and sad was a visit to Mr Iggulden, an English banker the Collins family had known in 1838. Wilkie wrote to his brother:

> He was extremely depressed and gloomy, and surrounded by wretched pictures, on which he had been lending money, I suspect. He expressed himself as quite amazed that Dickens should still be a 'lively man' with nine children – and grievously desired to know whether I was still going on 'writing books' and whether I ever meant to practise my profession . . . [He] introduced me to a tall young gentleman with a ghastly face, immense whiskers, and an expression of the profoundest melancholy . . . Do you remember little '*Lorenzo*' who was the lively young 'Pickle' of the family? . . . He asked me whether I had not broken my arm when I was last in Naples. I told him *you* had. He rejoined gloomily 'Galway's dead'* – and then waited for me to say something.

Wilkie discovered that Charles Iggulden, 'the pattern good boy' of the family, who had always been held up as an example to him, had gone to the bad, married a pretty girl without his parents' approval and been packed off to Australia. 'I was rather glad to hear this, as I don't like "well-conducted" young men. I know it is wrong – but I always feel relieved and happy when I hear that they have got into a scrape.'[20] Not an entirely tactful comment in a letter to his brother, another 'pattern good boy'. They heard another unconventional love story at Naples which would have had a particular appeal to Wilkie, though

* Galway was the boy who broke Charles Collins' arm in 1837.

Dickens' account is determinedly unromantic. Brinsley Norton, the son of the gifted feminist writer Caroline Norton, had married 'a bare-footed girl off the Beach, with whom he had previously fulfilled all matrimonial conditions except the ceremony . . . Mrs. Brinsley has no idea of a hair brush and is said to be extremely dirty – which her young husband particularly admires, observing that it is "not conventional".'[21]

Rome seemed so much the same that Wilkie felt as though he had gone to sleep at the age of fourteen and woken up at twenty-nine. They stayed only briefly in Rome – probably too briefly for Wilkie, wrapped in nostalgia, and eager to see more of the great painting and sculpture. Many of the British artists he had met with his father were still there. He and Egg visited their studios, Dickens keeping away 'when pictures are in question'. Dickens, increasingly restless and irritable, resented Wilkie's artistic knowledge, or, as he saw it, pretension. 'To hear Collins learnedly holding forth to Egg (who has as little of that gammon as an artist *can* have) about reds, and greens, and things "coming well" with other things, and lines being wrong, and lines being right, is far beyond the bounds of all caricature.' He also claimed to object to Wilkie's 'code of morals taken from modern French novels, which I instantly and with becoming gravity smash'.[22] Most ridiculous of all, in Dickens' eyes, was Wilkie's account of his boyhood sexual experience with a married woman.

They managed to attend vespers at St Peter's during their short stay in Rome, Wilkie, unpunctual as ever, arriving late:

> And for once in a way the procrastinating man was the lucky man of the party . . . two dragoons dashed past me, clearing the road at full gallop, two carriages came after with cardinals inside – and next came a state coach with the Pope himself . . . The Pope (I suppose seeing me the only erect figure out of a group of 30 or 40 people) looked straight at me as he passed . . . He looked careworn, old, anxious and miserable – I just saw his head sunk sadly on his breast as the carriage dashed by me.[23]

Venice, where they arrived at the end of November, was again full of memories for Wilkie. The contrast between the modern age of steam

– the railway link with the rest of Italy was a recent one – and the city still seemingly sunk in the Middle Ages enchanted him. It was possible for the visitor to lead a life not much different from that of Byron half a century before, with 'turbanned Turks and petticoated Greeks by dozens' on the Mole. The triumvirate lived in high style, and hired their own gondola, with two *gondolieri*. Wilkie, with his usual indifference to convention, bought one of the warm capote greatcoats worn by off-duty gondoliers: 'an immense long garment . . . made of some hair cloth, thickly lined and renowned for its resistance to wind and weather. A monk's hood is attached to the collar . . . the whole is sold for sixteen English shillings.' He found the Venetians 'the most *original* race of painters'. He especially admired Tintoretto, finding his 'Paradise' in the Ducal Palace 'beyond compare, the more you look the *less* confused it seems'. He gave a delighted account of a visit to the opera to hear *Nabucco*. It was 'very fairly and pleasantly done', and seats were unbelievably cheap. An entire box cost, at 7s. 6d., the same as a place in the pit in London. They arrived in state, 'one of the rowers going before us . . . to light us upstairs into our box by means of a huge ship's lanthorn . . . which the gondoliers persisted in bringing as a proper assertion of our own magnificence'.[24] Wilkie's pleasure was not marred by any awareness of Dickens' rising irritation with his companions.

> Imagine the procession – led by Collins with incipient moustache, spectacles, slender legs, and extremely dirty dress gloves – Egg second, in a white hat, and a straggly mean little black beard – Inimitable bringing up the rear, in full dress and big sleeved greatcoat, rather considerably ashamed.[25]

They returned to England in early December. Wilkie, who had spent more than he intended – his share of the expenses came to £126. 16s. 8d. for the two-month trip and he had twice been forced to borrow small sums in cash from Dickens – set about organizing his travel material. He sent a first instalment to George Bentley on 14 January, confidently requesting space in six numbers of the *Miscellany*, and announcing that he wanted to reserve the copyright.[26] The second instalment, he promised, 'lets out some rather *un*conventional opinions on the subject of art', and the last number would contain a true love story – perhaps that of Brinsley Norton and his tousle-headed fisher-girl, or of the banished Charles Iggulden.

Bentley responded with a flat rejection, perhaps because *Bentley's Miscellany* had just published a series on similar lines. Wilkie kept himself afloat with hack reviewing for *The Leader*; articles for *Punch*, placed through his connection with Mark Lemon; and an attempt to squeeze money due for *Mr. Wray's Cash Box* out of George Bentley. Unable to place his own articles on Italy, he generously took the trouble to introduce the work of his friend Frances Dickinson to the editor of the *Art Journal*, Samuel Carter Hall. In May 1854 he wrote to Hall, sending an article 'written by a friend of mine now resident in Rome . . . sent to me to be offered for publication in England. At it treats of a subject of some Art-interest, I take the liberty of sending it to the Editor of the *Art Journal*'.[27] The *Art Journal* published this article and six others by Frances Dickinson on the art and artists of Rome under the pseudonym 'Florentia', which she also used for her many contributions to the *New Monthly Magazine*.[28] The Collins and Dickinson families were by now close friends. When old Mrs Dickinson, Frances' widowed mother, called at Hanover Terrace to ask Harriet Collins to dinner, Wilkie got a lift in her carriage to a party at Miss Coutts'.[29] The shade of William Collins would have been proud of his son.

Wilkie took up the neglected *Hide and Seek* once more, promising Bentley that by early April it would be 'not quite done, but done *enough* to be judged by, and negotiated about'. He was a little optimistic, but the contract, much haggled over and not finally drawn up until after the book was delivered, was signed on 17 May. Bentley acquired the copyright for a period of eighteen months only: Wilkie was now wary of losing his rights in his work for ever. There was a first edition of five hundred copies, for which Wilkie received £150. Bentley also had the right to publish a second edition of 250 copies within eighteen months, for £75, and any further editions on the same terms, within the eighteen-month period.[30]

Hide and Seek, dedicated to Dickens 'as a token of admiration and affection', was published in three volumes on 5 June. Though the library subscription was poor, Wilkie was confident. 'The booksellers and librarians are a parcel of asses, and the public voice is the stick that cudgels them into activity.'[31] Nearly half of the first edition was sold before any reviews had appeared. 'Not so bad in War times', Wilkie considered.[32] This edition sold out, but there were no more until a revised edition was published by Sampson Low. It was the last book by Wilkie Collins to be published by Bentley until 1871.

Hide and Seek was, as Wilkie had promised Bentley, an entirely new venture. His aim had been, he states in the preface, to keep a balance between 'interest of story and development of characters'. He also drew attention to the character of the painter Valentine Blyth as 'a homely study from nature, done by a student who has had more opportunities than most men, out of the profession, of observing what the varieties of artist-life, and the eccentricities of artist-character, are really like . . . I have ventured on the startling novelty . . . of trying to make an artist interesting, without representing him as friendless, consumptive, and penniless . . .' The character of the cheerful Blyth is a development of Perugino Potts: a profoundly untalented painter determined, against all the odds, to persevere with his art. He is given the family background of Holman Hunt, whose father, like Blyth's, 'was seriously disappointed and amazed at the strange direction taken by the boy's inclinations'.[33] The incorrigible young hero Zack Thorpe, virtually adopted by the painter, is to some extent a self-portrait of the adolescent Wilkie, in personality as well as his experiences in a tea importer's office. But the tyrannical and hypocritical Mr Thorpe is no more a study of William Collins than is the cheerful Valentine Blyth. Though Zack's childhood experiences of the evangelical English Sunday, already attacked by Wilkie in *The Leader*, have the ring of personal experience, the novel also mounts a more generalized attack on the dreary lives of the English middle classes. The Thorpes live in 'Baregrove Square':

> It was just that sort of place where the thoughtful man looking about him mournfully at the locality, and physiologically observing the inhabitants, would be prone to stop suddenly, and ask himself one plain, but terrible question: 'Do these people ever manage to get any real enjoyment out of their lives, from one year's end to another?' (*Hide and Seek*, Book I, Chap. 1, p. 18)

Hide and Seek was the first of Wilkie's novels to explore the ways in which severe handicaps may be accepted, compensated for and overcome. The sympathetic account of the profound deafness of the young girl Mary, or 'Madonna', Grice, was carefully researched: Wilkie based his description on the first-hand account by John Kitto of his loss of hearing after falling from a ladder.[34] But perhaps Wilkie's fascination with physical disabilities and their effect on the psyche, repeatedly used until it became a hallmark of his fiction, was originally triggered by his own physique. Short sight, small stature, disproportion of limbs and hands and feet and the protrusion on his forehead did not amount to disability. Yet his own awareness of the oddity of his appearance must have had an effect on him, especially as a young man. The terrifying scene in which the girl is left deprived of the sense of sight on which she relies, when her candle is deliberately blown out, gains its impact from the author's imaginative identification with her handicap, carefully built up throughout the book, and not from a wilful desire to shock. Her terror is mediated through the consciousness of a *listener*, which has the effect of emphasizing the absence of normal expectations in her silent world. The listener, who turns out to be her uncle, is, though she does not know this, sympathetic towards her, and upset at having caused her distress.

> He knew not how long it was before the dumb moaning seemed to grow fainter; to be less fearfully close to him; to change into what sounded, at one moment, like a shivering of her whole body; at another, like a rustling of her garments; at a third, like a slow scraping of her hands over the table on the other side of her, and of her feet over the floor. She had summoned courage enough at last to move, and to grope her way out – he knew it as he listened. He heard her touch the edge of the half-opened door; he heard the still sound of her first footfall on the stone passage outside; then the noise of her hand drawn along the wall; then the lessening gasps of her affrighted breathing as she gained the stairs . . . she was gone, and the change and comfort of silence and solitude stole over him . . . (*Hide and Seek*, Book II, Chap. 12, p. 280)

Hide and Seek is a novel about familial relationships – about blood ties, and also those bonds of affection which can be stronger and more significant: the emphasis throughout is on love and reconciliation. 'Madonna' is fostered twice: first by the poor woman who charitably suckles her when her mother is dying, and then by Valentine Blyth, who is also a substitute father to Zack Thorpe. Zack and Madonna turn out to be blood brother and sister as well, for Madonna is the illegitimate daughter of Zack's grim father, the one good thing remaining of his spontaneous and affectionate youth.

The novel was enthusiastically reviewed, and generally considered to be a great advance on *Basil*. The reviewer in *The Leader* (possibly George Eliot) praised it for economy of narration, style and 'complicated clearness' of plot; but criticized the characterization for relying on description rather than revelation, a failing Wilkie was to be accused of more than once.[35] A review in the *Athenaeum*, by Geraldine Jewsbury, fastened with relief on the different atmosphere of the new novel:

> Over [*Antonina* and *Basil*] there hung a close, stifling, unwholesome odour: if fascinating, they were not wholesome; if powerful, they were not pleasant . . . he has ceased walking the moral hospital to which he has hitherto confined his excursions. Here we have health and strength together . . . Mr. Collins has a genuine healthy sense of fun . . . the root from which the story grows is a deep and most pitiful tragedy . . . but it is almost free from exaggeration and false sentiment.

'. . . A work which everyone should read,' Miss Jewsbury concluded.[36]

Dickens was even more enthusiastic: 'I think it far away the cleverest novel I have ever seen written by a new hand', he told Georgina Hogarth. 'It is much beyond Mrs. Gaskell, and is in some respects masterly . . . Nor do I really recognize much imitation of myself . . . I . . . have been very much surprised by its great merit . . .'[37]

It was now an accepted pattern for Wilkie to spend a long summer holiday with Dickens and his family. On 12 July Dickens wrote from Boulogne to say that he would be briefly in London, and suggesting Wilkie should return to France with him. 'The interval I propose to pass in a career of amiable dissipation and unbounded license in the metropolis. If you will come and breakfast with me about midnight – anywhere – any day, and go to bed no more until we fly to these pastoral retreats, I shall be delighted to have so vicious an associate.' The teasing, suggestive tone is a new development, to become familiar in the correspondence, though it was not until

1857 that Dickens habitually addressed him as 'Wilkie' rather than 'Collins'. Wilkie seems always to have addressed Dickens by his surname, at least when writing to him, or writing or speaking of him to others; intimacy with Dickens was always on his terms.

They travelled to France together on 25 July, and Wilkie stayed for six weeks, in a 'state of Elysian laziness', at the Villa du Camp de Droite, a larger house than the Villa des Moulineaux, though in its way just as eccentric, 'all doors, cupboards and windows'. He played rounders and trap and ball with the children, 'matches in which there is very little science and a great deal of fun', and flew a mighty kite with Dickens. A nearby military camp with forty thousand well-behaved soldiers in it added to their enjoyment. On one occasion a regiment was drawn up in the market place, attended by an unusual example of the working women who always interested Wilkie:

> a real live *Vivandière* serving out drams to the men in the most operatic manner possible . . . She had on a short glazed hat, stuck very much on one side – a tight blue jacket that fitted her without a wrinkle – an ample scarlet petticoat – ample as to breadth – that came to her knees, and scarlet trowsers. Her hair was dressed in the regular feminine way – plain bands, with a knot, or lump, or bunch, or whatever you call it, behind . . . She was a very passably pretty woman – was evidently treated by the men with great distinction . . .[39]

The holiday was not all idleness. Wilkie wrote to Charles Ward, who was already acting as his unofficial agent with the newspapers and magazines, confiding that he had been thinking of branching out in a new direction:

> I have plenty of hard work in prospect – some of it, too, work of a new kind and of much uncertainty as to results. I mean the dramatic experiments which I have been thinking of, and which you must keep a profound secret from everybody, in case I fail with them. This will be an anxious winter for me. If I were not constitutionally reckless about my future prospects, I should feel rather nervous just now . . .[40]

Wilkie was anxious about the effect of the Crimean War on the sales of fiction. Richard Bentley, in severe financial trouble, offered to sell him the copyrights of *Antonina* and *Basil* for £200. Wilkie wrote in July explaining that he could not afford them.

> I cannot disguise from myself that if this war continues, the prospects of Fiction are likely to be very uncertain . . . I may find myself obliged to turn my pen in other directions . . .[41]

Dickens, as yet unaware of the 'dramatic experiments', invited Wilkie for the first time to contribute to the Christmas extra number of *Household Words*. Wilkie provided the fourth tale in *The Seven Poor Travellers*. 'The Lawyer's story of A Stolen Letter' was perhaps suggested by Poe's story 'The Purloined Letter'. The stories have similar titles, and both have a self-satisfied narrator, an obvious hiding place and a clever boy. Wilkie also took material from closer to home: 'A Stolen Letter' refers in passing to Harriet Collins' early experiences. The young man in the story, whose father objects to his marrying a governess, must retrieve a letter which implicates her father in a forgery. 'The great mistake of her father's life was his selling out of the army and taking to the wine trade. He had no talent for the business; things went wrong with him from the first. His clerk, it was strongly suspected, cheated him'. There is also an expression of Wilkie's anti-corset obsession: 'She was one of my sort, was that governess . . . good lissome figure, that looked as if it had never been boxed up in a pair of stays.'[42]

Wilkie was also invited to act in the Tavistock House Twelfth Night children's entertainment. 'Here is a part in Fortunio – dozen words – but great Pantomime opportunities – which requires a first-rate old stager to devour Property Loaves . . . There is an eligible opportunity of making up dreadfully greedy.'[43] Wilkie, perhaps in a Dickensian dig at his Italian pretensions, was billed as 'Wilkini Collini', and threw himself into the part of Gobbler. It was a light-hearted start to a year in which Wilkie and Dickens were to collaborate in a more ambitious dramatic adventure.

NINE

The Setting-up of a Balloon

(1855–1856)

As Dickens grew more dissatisfied with his domestic life, his need to have Wilkie with him grew more urgent. Wilkie's failings, so irritating during the Italian trip, were all forgotten. Now, instead of being pretentious about painting, Wilkie 'has a good eye for pictures'.[1] It is to Wilkie that Dickens makes fun of others, Forster, Townsend, Wills; with Wilkie alone that he wants to prowl the streets of Paris and London. They were often seen together. One not entirely accurate eye witness described them 'in the neighbourhood of Covent Garden and the Strand; Collins, short and rather thickset, with bold forehead, long black beard, large bright-blue eyes, and gold spectacles, forming a decided contrast with the airiness and "sailorlike aspect" of his great friend'. A special table was always reserved for them at Verrey's restaurant in Regent Street.[2] 'You know I am not in the habit of making professions,' Dickens wrote in a typical letter from Dover,

> but I have so strong an interest in you and so true a regard for you that nothing can come amiss in the way of information as to your well-doing.
>
> How I wish you were well now! For I am in two of the most charming rooms (a third, a bedroom you could have occupied, close by), overlooking the sea in the gayest way . . . and here we might have been, drinking confusion to Baronetcies, and resolving never to pluck

a leaf from the Toady Tree, till this very small world shall have rolled us off![3]

There were disadvantages to being absorbed in this way. It was difficult not to be monopolized, and all Wilkie's good-humoured stubbornness was needed to keep his own style and literary integrity, to remain something more than one of Dickens' 'young men'. It may have been partly because he was so caught up in the Dickensian whirlwind that there was a three-year gap between *Hide and Seek* and his next novel, *The Dead Secret.* To be so much in Dickens' company cost Wilkie money as well as time, and the quick returns of journalism were needed to finance their English and French excursions. Dickens was hospitable, but not spendthrift: the man who reduced the allowance of his only successful son by the amount of his Cambridge scholarship expected even his favourite companions to pay their way.

Early in February 1855, Dickens wrote to his friend Régnier of the Comédie Française, 'I am coming to Paris for a week with my friend Collins – son of the English painter . . . as we are coming to Paris expressly to be always looking about us . . . what we want to find is a good apartment, where we can have our breakfast but where we shall never dine . . . I want it to be pleasant and gay, and to throw myself *en garçon* on the festive *diableries de Paris*.'[4]

Their nine days in Paris were spent in great comfort in an apartment at the Hôtel Meurice, where Wilkie had briefly stayed with his parents in 1836. But the holiday was bedevilled by an illness of Wilkie's, rather than beguiled by the *diableries* Dickens had hoped for. He became ill almost at once. 'Collins continues in a queer state', Dickens reported to Georgina Hogarth five days after they arrived. 'We breakfast at ten, read and write till two, and then I go out walking all over Paris, while the invalid sits by the fire or is deposited in a cafe . . . I live in peace, like an elderly gentleman, and regard myself as in a negative state of virtue and respectability.'[5] They managed to dine in a different restaurant every night, though doctor's orders deprived Wilkie of wine. They went to the theatre, sometimes to two or three, nightly. But Wilkie was not well enough to get on with writing his story 'Sister Rose' for *Household Words* as fast as he would have liked.

Wilkie, not usually one to suffer in silence, does not mention the illness in the two letters he wrote to his mother from Paris. Instead he tells her of the gaieties of Paris. There was to be a masked ball at the Opéra, to which they intend to go. The exhibition building for the Paris World Fair was nearly completed, the restaurants and theatres were full. Everything went on in spite of the Siberian weather, which filled the cafés with shivering Frenchmen, huddled round the stoves. There were many more notices in English in the shops and 'the once rare class who speak English' were all practising their few words: results of the Anglo-French Alliance, though the war in the Crimea, they found, was only occasionally spoken of.[6]

The illness, about which Dickens was mysterious and jocular, was not easily cleared up when they returned to London. 'I hope you will soon begin to see land beyond the Hunterian Ocean',* Dickens wrote on 4 March, proposing to 'come up [to Hanover Terrace] . . . with a cigar in my pocket and inspect the Hospital'. Harriet was in bed with influenza; Millais, who was staying with them, was also ill; and Charley 'goes on slowly – slowly – with his picture. – We are all sick and sorry together', Wilkie told Ned Ward.[7] Wilkie was well enough to struggle to Ashford to hear Dickens reading *A Christmas Carol* on 27 March, but on 4 April he was still 'an amiable, corroded hermit' and Dickens jokes, 'I hope the medical authorities will not – as I may say – cut your nose off to be revenged on your face. You might want it at some future time. It is but natural that the Doctor should be irritated by so much opposition – still, isn't the offending feature in some sort a man and a brother?' Not until 15 April is Wilkie congratulated on being 'once more in a Normal state'.[8]

In a letter to Ned Ward about the difficulty of protecting paintings and literature from piracy, Wilkie referred incidentally to his illness, still confining him to the house on 20 March, calling it 'a long story which I will not bother you with now'.[9] Whatever the illness was, it seems not to have been an episode of his usual arthritic problems. Dickens' nudging references raise the possibility that some of the later manifestations of his 'rheumatic gout', in particular the 'gout

* The anatomist and surgeon John Hunter, FRS (1728–93) wrote *A Treatise on the Venereal Disease*, 1786.

in the eyes', which caused him so much pain and made his eyes 'veritable bags of blood' as one observer described, may have been Reiter's disease, triggered by a venereal infection caught at this time. Reiter's disease is far more common in those, such as Wilkie Collins, who have a genetic predisposition to arthritis.

'Sister Rose', another French Revolution story, appeared in *Household Words* in four episodes throughout April 1855: the first episode was given the dignity of the lead position. Dickens thought it 'An excellent story, charmingly written, and showing everywhere an amount of pains and study in respect of the art of doing such things that I see mighty seldom.'[10] It may have given him the first hint for his 1859 novel *A Tale of Two Cities*. The French Revolution setting, and the character of a villain who acts heroically and self-sacrificingly because of his love for the heroine (a theme expanded on in Wilkie's 1857 play *The Frozen Deep*), are common to both. 'Sister Rose' suffers from compression: it contains enough incidents in its hundred pages to provide material for a full-length novel. Wilkie, overflowing with ideas, still had a young man's prodigality with them. He was pleased to be paid £40 for the story.

In May, Wilkie revealed the secret of the 'dramatic experiments' to Dickens, sending him the two-act play, *The Lighthouse*. This was based on his story 'Gabriel's Marriage', much altered and adapted. Dickens, gestating *Little Dorrit*, was restless. 'I feel as if nothing would do me the least good but the setting-up of a Balloon', he told Wilkie.[11] He seized on this 'old-style melodrama' and appropriated it. He would play the part of Aaron Gurnock, a lighthouse keeper haunted by remorse for his part in a murder. The other main parts would be taken by Wilkie, Egg and Lemon, with Mary Dickens playing young Martin Gurnock's sweetheart, and Georgina Hogarth as a mysterious lady from the sea. Dickens tinkered with the dialogue, and wrote a song for Mary to sing. The children's theatre in the schoolroom at Tavistock House was radically reorganized and the stage much enlarged, and his old friend the painter Clarkson Stanfield was roped in to design the set and act-drop.

Dickens was so much in the public eye that the four performances given at Tavistock House in May were oversubscribed many times.

However, it was not the professional production Wilkie had hoped might launch him as a dramatist, and when Benjamin Webster of the Adelphi Theatre was approached by Mark Lemon on Wilkie's behalf at the end of June, offering the rights in the play for twelve months, Webster wouldn't bite. Dickens was asked to perform the play for charity, and one performance was given at Camden House, Kensington, where there was a private theatre with a larger auditorium, on 10 July. From Janet Wills, one of those who attended the dress rehearsal, came a description of Harriet Collins' reactions, and Wilkie's failure in the part of Mary's ardent young lover:

> Mrs. Collins sat next to me and got every now and then so excited applauding her son Wilkie that I thought the respectable, comely old woman would explode, he all the time looking and acting most muffishly. Nothing could be better than the drama as drama, but oh, he makes a most unloving and unlovable actor. Dickens and Mark [Lemon] do *not* act, it is the perfection of *real* nature.[12]

Dickens invited the newspapers to send reporters. Henry Morley admired both the construction and the acting: 'None of the leading incidents are shown actually, but their workings on the minds of the three lighthouse-men . . . contribute interest enough to sustain an earnest attention throughout . . . rarely has acting on a public stage better rewarded scrutiny.'[13] Alfred Wigan, the proprietor of the Olympic Theatre, expressed interest, but was unable to cast the play. Wilkie made the best of it: 'Dickens thinks I have had a lucky escape . . . The principal part really requires a first rate serious actor – and where is he to be found Anno Domini 1855 in . . . England?'[14] Macready might have done it before he retired; the best hope now was to show it to Régnier for translation and performance in Paris.

For the time being, his bread and butter continued to come from journalism. 'The Yellow Mask', an effective Browningesque shocker set in eighteenth-century Italy, was published in *Household Words* in four instalments in July. The characteristic device of a mask concealing a face which is in fact another mask, behind which lurks the face of the wrong woman, has the suggestive quality of layered deceit which intrigued him, and which was to be more fully developed in the novels he wrote in the 1860s.

His earnings from *Household Words* amounted to just over £100 during 1855, and he also continued to draw a modest but regular income from his contributions to *The Leader*. With his mother still acting as his banker, Wilkie always had something to fall back on, though the arrangement was sometimes awkward. Writing to ask Pigott for a cheque for £10 owed to him, he explained that 'as *my* money is always put to my mother's account at Coutts's, I can't draw any of it without a cheque from her. She is . . . staying at Southsea – or I could get my "supplies" from Hanover Terrace easily enough.'[15] He seems, at least after his early Paris indiscretions, to have been remarkably level-headed about money, taking after his father to an extent that might have surprised that anxious parent. His extravagances were mostly connected with his expeditions with the far wealthier Dickens.

The Dickens family were at Folkestone in the summer of 1855, where Wilkie spent his usual six weeks with them. Folkestone was crowded. 'Troops of hideous women stagger about in the fresh breezes under hats as wide as umbrellas and as ugly as inverted washhand basins. The older, uglier and fatter they are, the bigger hats they put on and the more execrably they dress themselves.'[16] The Dickens household, too, was crowded with its usual influx of visitors. Thackeray and Kinglake dined, 'Thackeray pleasanter and quainter than I ever saw him before'; Pigott, now a friend of Dickens as well as Wilkie, stayed a night; Mark Lemon was there with his daughter. Wilkie saw George Smith, who was to publish his next book, nearly every day.

The Queen and Prince Albert came to Folkestone to review the Foreign Legion, and were received by the local population with stolid indifference. Wilkie was never a monarchist, and with his enthusiasm for France at a high level he compared the British troops, 'the filthiest, clumsiest, drunkenest, ugliest set of unmitigated louts', unfavourably with the 'picturesquely martial look' of the French camp across the Channel at Boulogne, where the Dickens household went for a short visit. At Folkestone he was lured into taking 'prodigious walks and climbing inaccessible places'. Dickens' latest passion was for climbing the sea cliffs, a form of exercise Wilkie had last taken in Cornwall six years before. But he was, also, 'beginning a new speculation', a collection of his short stories framed and linked by a narrative suggested by the painter's-household setting of *Hide and Seek*. This time 'the joys and sorrows of a poor travelling portrait-painter – represented from his wife's point of view' provided an artificial but just about adequate matrix for the stories, all but one already published in *Household Words*.[17]

Wilkie was also attempting to edit his mother's manuscript account of her life before marriage, begun two years earlier, which Harriet hoped might be publishable. He wrote to her explaining how he was getting on.

> I began work again on your MS three weeks ago. After I had done fifty pages, leaving out many things, and transferring others, but keeping as close as I could to the simplicity of your narrative, I began to have my doubts whether it would not be necessary (with the public) to make a story to hang your characters and incidents on . . . Strangers could not know that the thing was real – and novel readers seeing my name on the title page would expect a story. So I am going to throw a little dramatic interest into what I have done – keeping the thing still simple, of course, and using all the best of your materials.[18]

Harriet's manuscript, which has suggestions for cuts and rearrangement in her son's handwriting on the first sixty-eight pages, was never published. Wilkie seems to have given up the idea of more radical alterations, and the framing device of *After Dark*, 'Leah's Diary', makes no use of her autobiography. Harriet was eagerly bombarding Wilkie with material. 'Your story about the lady and the dentist is very good', he told her in the letter which refers to her manuscript, 'but useless for book purposes, because the public would not believe it. There would be the old cry of exaggeration – nevertheless it is very amusing.' The framework of *After Dark*, which does relate rather loosely to some aspects of his parents' lives together, may have originated in an attempt to soothe and please her.

In late September Wilkie and Edward Pigott went on a cruise down the Bristol Channel to the Scilly Isles. Wilkie, never seasick on the roughest Channel crossing, and fascinated from childhood by small boats, caught Pigott's passion for sailing. It was to remain his favourite outdoor occupation for the rest of his life. But he had no intention of roughing it more than was strictly necessary, seeing a yacht as having all the advantages of home without the drawbacks, as he wrote in a *Household Words* article:

> We can stop when we like, see what we like, and always come back to our favourite corner on the sofa, always carry on our favourite occupations and amusements, and still be travelling, still be getting forward to new scenes all the time . . . The bores we dread, the letters we don't want to answer, cannot follow and annoy us. We are the freest travellers under Heaven.[19]

He insisted, therefore, on preliminary planning. The size of the boat, the number of people going on the trip, the expense per person, the supplies (Wilkie suggested they should come from Fortnums) and above all the timing, were anxiously enquired into in his letters to Pigott. 'Everything very jolly, *except* the tremendous consideration of the *Equinox*. I find by my Almanack that it begins on the 23rd September. Surely we shall not have time for the Scilly Islands, starting only on the 18th or 19th? And as for returning in an Equinoctal gale in a boat of 8 tons, is that not rather "tempting Providence" by making a toil of a pleasure?'[20] Wilkie's niggles seem to have been brushed aside by the more experienced Pigott. The trip, with a professional crew of three brothers, took place successfully in spite of the equinox, and included a visit to the Scilly Isles. Wilkie, pressured by Dickens, wrote it up engagingly as 'The Cruise of the Tomtit' for *Household Words*.[21] 'Got Wilkie into the Xmas number by sledge hammer force', Dickens reported to Pigott. 'He has written a charming paper . . . nothing can be more pleasant, easy, gay and unaffected . . .'[22]

'The Cruise of the Tomtit' was the first of Wilkie's many non-fiction pieces for *Household Words*. It is typical of the energetic, humorous work of his early years, unsparing in its account of comic misadventures, detailed in its account of eating and drinking: the genre that Jerome K. Jerome was to make famous in *Three Men in a Boat*, published the year Wilkie Collins died. But it is individual in its emphasis on the complete democracy of shipboard life, and it is clear that this freedom from the stifling conventional hierarchies of

Victorian society was one of the things Wilkie valued most about his sailing trips:

> . . . we have solved the difficult problem of a pure republic in our modest little craft. No man in particular among us is master – no man in particular is servant. The man who can do at the right time, and in the best way, the thing that is most wanted, is always the hero of the situation among us . . . We have no breakfast hour, no dinner hour, no time for rising or going to bed. We have no particular eatables at particular meals. We don't know the day of the month, or the day of the week; and never look at our watches, except when we wind them up . . . We wear each other's coats, smoke each other's pipes, poach on each other's victuals. We are a happy, dawdling, undisciplined, slovenly lot. We have no principles, no respectability, no business, no stake in the country, no knowledge of Mrs. Grundy. We are a parcel of Lotos-Eaters; and we know nothing, except that we are poking our way along anyhow to the Scilly Isles in the Tomtit. ('The Cruise of the Tomtit', pp. 182–83)

Wilkie was again one of the contributors to the *Household Words* Christmas number. His story 'The Ostler' in *The Holly Tree Inn*, later expanded and renamed 'The Dream Woman', takes up one of the themes of *Basil*: the disastrous consequences of infatuation with, and hasty marriage to, an unknown and evil woman. The ostler, Isaac Scatcherd, is an ineffectual middle-aged man, living at home with his mother, who has a prophetic dream of a murderous woman, but fails to recognize her – only his mother does – in the woman by whom he becomes enslaved. The story is effectively open-ended, and quite the best contribution to *The Holly Tree Inn*, not excepting those of Dickens himself. It might suggest some restlessness at the writer's continuing filial dependence, balanced by a barely suppressed anxiety about the dangers of marriage.

Wilkie was back in London at the beginning of October, but the settled family life at Hanover Terrace was beginning to dissolve. Though Harriet had not found a house in the country, she had spent the summer visiting friends, an arrangement which suited Wilkie. 'Why not stop away until the end of October, when it does you so much good? I should be at home all that month – and you know how well I can keep house.'[23] The lease of 17 Hanover Terrace was due to run out the following year, and it was arranged that the house should be sublet to Ned and Henrietta Ward. Wilkie and Charley would go into lodgings, Harriet would visit friends, until another house could be found.

Dickens, who was planning to transplant his family to Paris for six months, was eager for Wilkie to join them, in his double capacity as companion and co-writer. 'It strikes me that a good deal might be done for Household Words on that side of the water.'[24] It was a suggestion Wilkie was glad to take up. It came at a convenient moment, and in Paris, always one of his favourite places, he was beginning to be recognized as a writer who appealed to French literary tastes. In November a long appraisal of his art, by the French critic and translator Émile Forgues, appeared in the *Revue des Deux Mondes*.[25] In his thirty-four-page article Forgues discussed all Wilkie Collins' major work in considerable detail, though at that time it had not been translated into French. He also briefly considered the unpublished play *The Lighthouse* – Wilkie had sent him a copy, which Forgues translated – and the short story 'Mad Monkton', which was then appearing in French in the *Revue Britannique*. The article, in a series on British novelists, was a sign that Wilkie's literary reputation was rising rapidly: an article on Dickens in the same series, by Hippolyte Taine, appeared the following February. Forgues saw Wilkie Collins as a serious literary figure at a turning point, with the freedom to choose to continue in the tradition of English fiction, or to attempt something radical and new.

Forgues began his essay indirectly, with a comparison of the art of William Collins with that of David Wilkie, pointing out that where Wilkie's figures were at the heart of his pictures, for Collins they were adjuncts to a landscape. With this deliberate reference to Wilkie Collins' antecedents, he prepared the ground for an assessment of his writing, its potential and its shortcomings.

In his discussion of Wilkie Collins' first novel, which he took seriously while acknowledging its faults, he saw the protagonist of *Antonina* not as the typical damsel in distress of a Gothic romance, but as the artist in revolt against subjection to the conventional: '*Tous les instincts qui font l'artiste éminent vivent en cette jeune fille, et se révoltent contre la volonté absolue qui la condamne à s'anéantir dans une longue* *prière.*'* But he felt that Collins had chosen the right path in turning away from historical fiction, and he much admired *Basil*, which he, unlike English critics, preferred to *Hide and Seek*. Though he warned that the ending of *Basil* retreated into second-rate melodrama, he praised the author for his freedom, in the earlier part of the novel, from English prejudice:

> *. . . ses opinions sont vraiment libérales, hostiles à l'hypocrisie, aux préjugés orgueilleux, aux tendances mercenaires qui sont les vices caractéristiques de l'Angleterre actuelle. Il haït, on le voit, le* cant *nasillard et les prescriptions minutieuses du faux puritanisme.*†

By contrast, Forgues found *Hide and Seek* too cosy, too deliberately charming. Though he does not call it Dickensian, as some English critics, intending praise, had done, the implication is clear. Forgues warns, later in his article, that it is not enough for Collins to call on the sympathies of the readership of *The Caxtons* (by Bulwer-Lytton), *David Copperfield* and *Vanity Fair*. Obliquely comparing him with his father by using images taken from painting, Forgues suggests that Wilkie Collins' characters, in this novel, are subordinated to setting, artistically posed but carelessly drawn, not exploiting the new extension of depth and limits that is now possible for the novel. However, Forgues paid Collins the compliment of comparing his writing with that of Balzac, and even preferring him for the qualities of charm and kindliness that the French writer entirely lacked. He saw Collins as having, more than any other English writer of the time, the potential to expand English fiction from its provincialism and prudery, importing the adult values of French writing into the English tradition. He was writing a year before the publication of *Madame Bovary* in the *Revue de Paris*; but his advice to Collins suggests not only that he should develop his capacity to write penetrating psychological studies, but also seems to urge a Flaubertian rigour and objectivity. It is also an encouragement to press against the limits of censorship.

* 'All the instincts which form the distinguished artist exist in this girl, and rise against the despotic will which sentences her to humble herself in prayer.'

† '. . . his opinions are truly liberal, hostile to the hypocrisy, arrogant prejudices and venal propensities which are the characteristic English vices of the day. It is clear that he hates the snuffling "cant" and fussy limitations of false puritanism'.

Wilkie took the article seriously, and it undoubtedly affected the direction of his fiction. He never again wrote so Dickensian a novel as *Hide and Seek*, and his great novels of the 1860s are a demonstration of his ability to strike out his own line, as Forgues had urged. The article initiated a friendship and professional association that he was to value greatly. When he dedicated his collection of short stories *The Queen of Hearts* to Forgues in 1859, he acknowledged his debt. 'I read that article at the time of its appearance', he wrote, 'with sincere pleasure and sincere gratitude, and I have honestly done my best to profit by it ever since.'

While Wilkie's career was developing steadily, his brother Charles was suffering severe doubts about his. Wilkie shared with his brother the family habit of obsessional tinkering. His manuscripts, from *Antonina* to his last, unfinished, novel, are covered in multiple overscorings and substitutions. He altered his stories, not always for the better, and not always as much as he claimed, whenever they were republished. Dickens vividly described his own manuscripts as 'inky fishing nets'; Wilkie's are the same, or worse. The overscoring and interlining must have been a nightmare for the compositors. But like his father, and unlike his brother, he felt that the practice of his art was 'the pride and the pleasure of my life'.[26] He worked through severe illness and through unhappiness and emotional upheaval. Though he hated the process of serial publication, particularly in weekly numbers, he prided himself on keeping deadlines.

Charley, by contrast, seems to have been thrown into turmoil by any kind of competition. He was already, at twenty-seven, convinced he was incapable of matching his father's success as a painter, and the comparison with 'Lucky Jack' Millais, who still carried the confident aura of the child prodigy, underlined Charley's painful lack of self-esteem. Wilkie, concerned and protective towards his younger brother as their father had been towards Francis Collins, couldn't help feeling, and occasionally expressing, impatience with his brother's slow progress: 'Is Charley's new painting ever to be in the drawing room?'[27] In 1855 Charley had confided in Holman Hunt, confessing 'the extreme suffering and anxiety which painting causes me'. He reacted like Browning's Pictor Ignotus, 'Shrinking, as from the soldiery a nun', to the news that one of his paintings was to be auctioned by its purchaser. 'This is terrible news to me. Fancy a picture carried round by two porters while the dealers sit looking on and looking it over . . .'[28] He now began to find the anxiety unbearable.

Charley was surrounded on his deathbed by half-finished paintings; one, of a wife anxiously awaiting news of her husband via the Electric Telegraph, 'the best subject I shall ever get', caused him particular anguish. He wrote a long document in April 1856, while he was temporarily living in lodgings and perhaps more depressed than usual, which he sent to Holman Hunt. In it he accused himself, quite unreasonably, of unintentionally plagiarizing Millais in the painting. Effie Millais had sat for the central figure of the woman, and Millais had suggested some alterations to her pose, which Charley agreed much improved the picture. He revealed to Hunt that he had worried over the legitimacy of the painting for two years: 'a very painful part of my life more painful than anyone would believe'. 'Such causes at last after months of struggling . . . seemed to strike the brushes out of my hand. And at last it was almost a relief to find that the year had advanced so far that the thing could not be done in time for the exhibition.'[29]

Charley's emotional troubles found physical expression in recurrent stomach pains which became worse whenever he tried to paint. He had an ulcer, severe enough to turn him, while still a young man, into a chronic invalid. In 1857 he decided to give up painting. He tried, instead, to make a living as a writer. He became the art critic of the *Echo*, and contributed whimsical, gentle pieces to *Household Words*. But his agonized conscience over his envy of Millais was replaced by a submerged envy of his successful, womanizing, socially adept brother. He loved Wilkie dearly, but in 1860, when *The Woman in White* was appearing in *All the Year Round*, and just before his marriage to Kate Dickens, he wrote to Hunt: 'I have known all sorts of remarkable men. I don't think I ever knew one who was not injured by success. As a completely unsuccessful man myself it is useless for me to say that there are times when I actually rejoice that I am so.'[30] He went further in print, cheering himself up by claiming that 'the life of a successful man is generally less interesting than that of the individual whose career has been on the whole a failure'.[31]

Wilkie finished work on *After Dark* early in 1856, and made the break from Richard Bentley that he had been contemplating for some time. The book was published by Smith, Elder, and was an immediate and enduring success. It was at once published by Tauchnitz for circulation on the Continent.

Dickens, who had settled his family in the Avenue Champs-Élysées and was shuttling backwards and forwards across the Channel, was bored in Paris without male company, and expected Wilkie to join him in early February, when *After Dark* was ready for the printer. He was full of plans for work and pleasure. 'I find that the guillotine can be got set up in private, like Punch's show. What do you think of *that* for an article?'[32] But Wilkie postponed the journey for several weeks, apparently without at first telling Harriet, away in the country, that he was going to do so. He was ill – though perhaps, a letter from Dickens suggests, not so ill as he claimed: 'I told them at home that you had a touch of your "old complaint" and had turned back to consult your Doctor. I thought it best, in case of any contre temps hereafter with your mother on one hand or my people on the other.'[33] Perhaps Wilkie was using illness as a convenient excuse to stay in London on his own. However, when he did arrive in Paris at the end of February, nearly missing the boat train after troubles with a 'lame, sickly and miserable cabman' and his 'still more miserable horse', he immediately became ill in truth.

He stayed six weeks. Dickens, always attracted by miniatures, had found lodgings for him in another little pavilion, like a 'cottage in a ballet'.[34] Wilkie was enchanted with it.

> I expect . . . to see Clown grinning at the door, and Harlequin jumping through the window, to the accompaniment of lively music of the most agreeably unclassical kind . . . the drawing room . . . is about the size of a large packing-case . . .

Smallest of all was the kitchen:

> When my spirits are low I look into it, and call up imaginatively the figure of a restless gesticulating French cook, composing made-dishes excitably,

with my kitchen range roasting his stomach, my coal-cellar forcing itself between his legs, and my cistern scrubbing his shoulder.[35]

Though he wrote to his mother that he was already better, he was soon suffering 'rheumatic pains and aguish shivering'. 'My arms, legs, back, head, neck and teeth were all rheumatic by turns.'[36] He recorded with gratitude the kindness not only of Dickens, but of his overworked landlady and her family, and acutely analysed the self-absorption of the sick, whose world becomes narrowed down to an awareness of their symptoms and a self-pitying demand for sympathy. He noticed, from his window, only those incidents and people bearing some relation to his own condition, in particular a nursemaid,

> neither young nor pretty, very clean and neat in her dress, with an awful bloodless paleness in her face, and a hopeless consumptive languor in her movements. She has only one child to take care of – a robust little girl of cruelly active habits. There is a stone bench opposite my window; and on this the wan and weakly nursemaid often sits, not bumping down on it with the heavy thump of honest exhaustion, but sinking on it listlessly, as if in changing from walking to sitting she were only passing from one form of weariness to another.[37]

The weeks in Paris were not all consumed by illness. Wilkie cured himself, or so he thought, by sweating in vapour baths, and managed to finish *A Rogue's Life*, then appearing in *Household Words*, and to work out the plot of his next novel, *The Dead Secret*. Dickens was excited and surprised by it, and couldn't guess the ending. 'He prophesies that I shall get more money and more success with it than I have got by anything else I have done. Keep this a profound secret from everybody but Charley – because people would be sure to say all the good things in it come from Dickens.'[38] Dickens was also delighted with *A Rogue's Life*, and told Wills to pay £50 for it, as Wilkie was 'a careful and good writer on whom we can depend' and one, furthermore, who was now getting good offers for stories elsewhere.[39]

A Rogue's Life owes more to Thackeray – the early Thackeray of *Barry Lyndon* and *A Shabby-Genteel Story* – than it does to Dickens. Wilkie, buoyed up by Forgues' appraisal and distanced from English propriety, cocks a snook at English sensibilities in a free and witty first-person narrative which adapts the picaresque hero of his grandfather's *Memoirs of a Picture* to the middle-class early-Victorian milieu of his parents. 'The critical reader may possibly notice a tone of almost boisterous gaiety in certain parts of these imaginary Confessions', Wilkie wrote in the introduction to the revised edition of 1879. 'I can only plead, in defence, that the story offers the faithful reflection of a very happy time in my past life. It was written at Paris, when I had Charles Dickens for a near neighbour and a daily companion, and when my leisure hours were joyously passed with many other friends, all associated with literature and art'.

A Rogue's Life satirizes the inveterate preference of the English for the sham over the real. The Rogue, rendered incapable of earning an honest living by his bogus, snobbish education, tries his hand first at caricature, then portrait-painting, then forgery. Wilkie took the opportunity, in a long parenthetical passage, to launch an attack on British taste in the early nineteenth century, which always, so he claimed, preferred a bad old painting to a good new one. His attack still holds good.

> The consequence was, that some of the most famous artists of the English school, whose pictures are now bought at auction sales for fabulous sums, were then hardly able to make an income ... They sat resignedly in their lonely studios, surrounded by unsold pictures which have since been covered again and again with gold and bank-notes by eager buyers at auctions and show-rooms, whose money has gone into other than the painter's pockets ... Year after year, these martyrs of the brush stood, palette in hand, fighting the old battle of individual merit against contemporary dullness ... (*A Rogue's Life*, Chap. 5, p. 30)

The Rogue makes a modest living for a while, concocting Rembrandts:

> Three parts of my picture consisted entirely of different shades of dirty brown and black; the fourth being composed of a ray of yellow light falling upon the wrinkled face of a treacle-coloured old man. A dim glimpse of a hand, and a faint suggestion of something like a brass wash-hand basin, completed the job ... I got five pounds for it. I suppose Mr. Pickup [the dealer] got one-ninety-five. (*A Rogue's Life*, Chap. 6, p. 35)

When this becomes too dangerous, the Rogue exploits another form of phoneyness, becoming the secretary of a provincial Literary and

Scientific Institution, and trying in vain to liven it up. Wilkie trots out another of his hobby-horses:

> My unhappy countrymen! (and thrice unhappy they of the poorer sort) – any man can preach to them, lecture to them, and form them into classes – but where is the man who can get them to amuse themselves? Anybody may cram their poor heads; but who will brighten their grave faces? Don't read story-books, don't go to plays, don't dance! Finish your long day's work and then intoxicate your minds with solid history, revel in the too-attractive luxury of the lecture room, sink under the soft temptation of classes for mutual instruction! . . . What if a bold man spring up one day, crying aloud in our social wilderness, 'Play, for Heaven's sake . . . Shake a loose leg to a lively fiddle! Women of England! drag the lecturer off the rostrum, and the male mutual instructor out of the class, and ease their poor addled heads of evenings by making them dance and sing with you.' (*A Rogue's Life*, Chap. 6, p. 43)

When the Rogue falls in love, he is inveigled into the most dangerous form of forgery: coining, at that time a capital offence. But all ends happily, with his transportation to Australia, where, in a parodic version of the Victorian solution of emigration, he makes good and becomes respectable. 'Look attentively at the 4th and 5th Chapters', Wilkie wrote to his mother from Paris, 'I am rather proud of them.'[40]

Through Dickens, Wilkie met members of the French literary establishment, and was gratified to find himself spoken of by the playwright Scribe, among others, as a coming literary man. He enjoyed, too, the recent architectural splendours of Paris, with the Rue de Rivoli perpetually illuminated by gas, 'as brilliant as Vauxhall in its best days. The square of the Louvre is all but completed – the matchless new street is in great part inhabited . . . a new Boulevard the next thing to be made.'[41] It was a contrast with the mean brick boxes of the London suburbs; his appreciation shows that it was not the new, as such, that he objected to.

There were the usual outings with the acutely restless Dickens, whose domestic skeleton, he wrote to Forster, 'is becoming a pretty big one'.[42] Appropriately enough, he and Wilkie visited the catacombs. They made the rounds of the galleries, and paid their usual visits to the theatres. They saw Frédérick Lemaître in *Thirty Years of a Gambler's*

Life, which they both considered the theatrical experience of a lifetime. Wilkie remembered it many years later as the greatest acting he ever saw: '. . . at the end of one of the acts we were so utterly overcome that we both sat for a time perfectly silent!'[43] They were critical of an over-ambitious effort to dramatize the Old Testament at the Théatre Ambigu. 'All the supernatural personages are alarmingly natural . . . Which has occasioned Collins and myself to institute a perquisition whether the French ever have shown any kind of idea of the supernatural, and to decide this rather in the negative.' They were impressed, however, by some stage machinery for the scene of the Flood: 'When the rain ceased . . . as the mists cleared and the sun broke out, numbers of bodies drifted up and down. These were all real men and boys, each separate, on a new kind of horizontal float. They looked horrible and real.'[44]

They also explored less respectable places. 'On Saturday night I paid three francs at the door of that place where we saw the wrestling,' Dickens wrote to Wilkie after he had left Paris,

> and went in, at 11 o'clock, to a Ball . . . Some pretty faces, but all of two classes – wicked and coldly calculating, or haggard and wretched in their worn beauty. Among the latter was a woman of thirty or so, in an Indian shawl, who never stirred from a seat in a corner all the time I was there. Handsome, regardless, brooding, and yet with some nobler qualities in her forehead. I mean to walk about tonight and look for her. I didn't speak to her there, but I have a fancy that I should like to know more about her. Never shall, I suppose.[45]

It was during this fruitful visit to Paris that Wilkie made one of his greatest finds. He picked up on a bookstall 'some dilapidated volumes of records of French crimes, a sort of French *Newgate Calendar*', and immediately spotted their potential as source material, much as Browning discovered the old yellow book in Florence which gave him the plot of *The Ring and the Book*. The early-nineteenth-century *Recueil des Causes Célèbres*, by Maurice Méjan, gave him, he told an interviewer, the basis of some of his best plots. That of *The Woman in White* was among them.

TEN

The Frozen Deep

(1856–1858)

Wilkie returned to London on 12 April, crossing the Channel in a half-gale and arriving, ill once more, with nowhere to live. While he was in Paris his mother had taken a lease on a cheaper house, 2 (later 11) Harley Place, a terraced house between Harley Street and Devonshire Place, on the south side of the New Road. The house needed renovating, and was not yet habitable. There were disputes with the landlord; Wilkie approved the situation, but wrote that he did not want them to be committed to a 'a long twelve years lease'.[1] Clearly, he did not want to be tied down for too long, though there is no suggestion that he was intending to set up house on his own.

When he got back to London his mother was staying with the Combes in Oxford; Charley was in lodgings in Percy Street, off the Tottenham Court Road. Wilkie could have gone to recuperate in the country – he had offers from both Pigott and Frances Dickinson – but after one night in a hotel took lodgings at 22 Howland Street, Fitzroy Square. He was ill again, and by his own account took the first place he saw that was near his doctor and friends.[2] It was near Charley, and the Brandlings had a house in Fitzroy Square.

Wilkie stayed at Howland Street a little more than three weeks, miserably ill. 'I have been quite taken aback by your account of your alarming seizure', Dickens wrote on 22 April.[3] The article for *Household Words* in which he describes the squalor of the neighbourhood,

'Smeary Street', is a powerful and melancholy piece, contrasting his lodgings with those he had in Paris.[4] It could hardly be further in tone from *A Rogue's Life*. He was particularly appalled by his monstrous landlady, and her treatment of the succession of miserable maids of all work. 'Mrs Glutch screams at them all indiscriminately by the name of Mary, just as she would scream at a succession of cats by the name of Puss.' His lifelong concern for the status and welfare of servants is at its sharpest here. For the maid of all work:

> Life means dirty work, small wages, hard words, no holidays, no social station, no future . . . no human being ever was created for this. No state of society which composedly accepts this, in the cases of thousands, as one of the necessary conditions of its selfish comforts, can pass itself off as civilised except under the most audacious of false pretences. These thoughts rise in me often, when I ring the bell, and the maid of all work answers it wearily. I cannot communicate them to her: I can only do my best to encourage her to peep over the cruel social barrier which separates her unmerited comfortlessness from my undeserved luxury, and encourage her to talk to me now and then on something like equal terms.

There was nothing he could do for this poor girl, except have 'a decent anxiety to spare her all useless trouble in waiting on me', but the experiences of his short time in Howland Street 'have taught me to feel for my poor and forlorn fellow-creatures as I do not think I ever felt for them before'. The experience, short though it was, also gave him a sharp reminder of what life could be like for an invalid without a wife or mother to care for him.

Harriet Collins moved into Harley Place in July, after protracted problems over the lease.[5] But Wilkie, once recovered, was in no hurry to join her. His whereabouts in the spring are not known, but in late June he went sailing with Pigott and Pigott's brother, who turned out to be 'the kind of man one becomes familiarly friendly with directly'.[6] They hired a boat of the Royal Yacht Squadron, the *Coquette*. It was a sybaritic trip: 'Dublin was given up, and Cherbourg . . . substituted . . . principally because Champagne and Sauterne are wanted in the Cabin Cellar.'[7] At Cherbourg they spent a delightful evening with the family of a tailor: 'The young man showed us his library and gave us coffee and pipes in his bedroom. The old people walked a mile into the country to gather us nosegays and gave us such noyau and claret, as I have seldom found equalled anywhere. There was no interested gratitude for much money spent, in all this. It was simply politeness and hospitality'.[8]

August was spent with Dickens at the Villa des Moulineaux working on Wilkie's new play, *The Frozen Deep*. 'Drop a line to the servants at Harley Place (I don't know their names),' he wrote to Harriet from Boulogne in September, 'telling them that I am coming back'. 'You are not to think of hurrying back from your visit at Maidenhead on my account', he insisted. 'If you come back before the right time, I shall take you to the railway and return you forcibly to the Langtons! . . . you know I can keep house as well as anybody.'[9] His concern for the due length of her holiday was not, perhaps, entirely disinterested.

Before Wilkie arrived in Boulogne Dickens had written enthusiastically to him about his story 'The Diary of Anne Rodway', a first-person account of a poor working girl who turns detective to hunt down the killer of her friend. Dickens praised its 'genuine force and beauty' and 'the admirable personation of the girl's identity and point of view . . . I think it excellent, feel a personal pride and pleasure in it which is a delightful sensation, and know no one else who could have done it.'[10] The story is not in itself remarkable; but its identification with the life of a working woman, and its successful impersonation of her simple narration, were significant. They were to be developed further in the years ahead.

In September Dickens took a further step to strengthen the literary and personal bond, writing to Wills to suggest that Wilkie should be made a member of the regular staff of *Household Words*, at a salary of £5 a week. 'He is very suggestive, and exceedingly quick to take my notions. Being industrious and reliable besides, I don't think we should be at an additional expense of £20 in the year . . .'[11] Dickens felt that the disadvantages of the anonymity of *Household Words*, for a young writer 'fighting to get on', would be compensated for by '*a certain engagement*'. Wilkie was not so sure. He was unwilling to be tied down to writing too many short, anonymous pieces in the 'house style' imposed by Dickens, and would only agree to the arrangement if his next novel were serialized in the magazine under his own name. Dickens, keeping out of the negotiations 'because I think it right that he should consider and decide without any personal influence on my part', would have preferred to confine Wilkie to the journalism he was so adept at; 'as to a long story itself, I doubt its value to us, and I feel perfectly convinced that it is not one quarter so useful to us as detached papers, or short stories in four parts'.[12] But he was anxious not to lose Wilkie, and told Wills to agree.

For the rest of the year they were closely involved in collaboration on *The Frozen Deep*, much discussed and rewritten, and the Christmas story, *The Wreck of the Golden Mary*, written by Dickens and Wilkie in roughly equal portions. 'I am the Captain of the Golden Mary, Mr. Collins is the Mate', Dickens told Miss Coutts.[13] Both *The Wreck of the Golden Mary* (perhaps suggested by the representation of the Flood at the Ambigu) and *The Frozen Deep* are stories of the limits of physical endurance, and explore the behaviour of men in extreme conditions. It was no coincidence that they were being written at the same time.* Wilkie was, during these months, writing as a willing instrument and extension of Dickens. Story and play are strongly marked by Dickens' personal turmoil, which found expression in the theme of man pitted against the elements and in conflict with his own soul.

The Frozen Deep, and above all Dickens' performance in it, became famous. It was this production that gave him the impetus to begin the famous readings which took up much of his time, and added enormously to his income, from 1858 until his death. 1857, more generally marked as the year of the Indian mutiny and the Matrimonial Causes Act, was for Dickens and Wilkie Collins pre-eminently the year of *The Frozen Deep*. A year later Dickens' marriage was collapsing irretrievably, the final break precipitated by the very success of the play.

The idea for the *The Frozen Deep* sprang from the report of Dr John Rae, published in 1854, on the fate of Sir John Franklin's expedition to discover the North West Passage, lost with all hands

* A dramatic version of *The Wreck of the Golden Mary* was licensed by the Lord Chamberlain in 1857, but was never, it seems, produced. It was probably a piracy.

in 1845. Rae's report uncovered evidence that Franklin's men had, *in extremis*, resorted to cannibalism. This was vehemently rejected by Dickens in two articles he wrote for *Household Words* in 1854: no English gentleman could have been capable of such conduct. He was haunted by the Arctic explorers' sufferings and deaths, and the initial suggestion for a play on the subject was his. Wilkie wrote the first draft, but during the autumn it was extensively rewritten, with so many contributions from Dickens that the play became a true collaboration. The revision went on during the rehearsal period, turning the play into a vehicle for Dickens, who directed and oversaw every aspect of the production as well as playing the lead. The character of Richard Wardour, a villain who struggles with jealousy and murderous impulses, finally becoming a sacrificial hero, reverses the suggestion that Franklin and his men were heroes who turned into cannibalistic villains. Far from devouring his rival (played by Wilkie), Wardour kills himself in the effort of bringing him back safely from the frozen deep. It was a heroic role that greatly appealed to Dickens' manic-depressive temperament at a moment when he felt himself more than ever 'a misplaced and mismarried man'.

The schoolroom at Tavistock House was torn apart again: 'The sounds in the house are like Chatham Dockyard – or the building of Noah's Ark.'[14] The nautical similes reinforce the feeling that for Dickens the play was a way of floating over chaos. Clarkson Stanfield and William Telbin were commissioned to paint the sets and backdrops; the young composer Francesco Berger, who had written music for *The Lighthouse*, wrote the overture and incidental music. The usual group of friends and relations were enticed into performing and helping behind the scenes. As well as Dickens' family, Mark Lemon, Frederick Evans, Augustus Egg and Edward Pigott were among the actors; Forster spoke the prologue, and Wills was the prompter. Wills' wife Janet, playing a nurse with the gift of second sight, had broad Scots dialogue specially written in for her by Dickens, removed when Wilkie rewrote the play in 1866. After a dress rehearsal on 5 January, attended by the servants and tradespeople, four more performances were given at Tavistock House before audiences of about ninety people on each occasion. Dickens invited the press, and reviews appeared in seven London papers, including *The Times*.

The play, and Dickens' virtuoso performance, were the talk of London. Dickens immersed himself totally in his part: he confessed that he nearly fainted during one performance. The intensity of his emotion infected Wilkie: 'he . . . terrified Aldersley to that degree, by lunging at him to carry him into the cave, that the said Aldersley always shook like a mould of jelly, and muttered, "This is an awful thing!" '[15]

As soon as the last performance, followed by the usual substantial supper and a dance on the stage, was over, Wilkie disappeared to Richmond. (He was spending less and less time at Harley Place.) He needed to catch up on *The Dead Secret*, being serialized in *Household Words*. It was the first time he had produced a full-length work for serialization. Though Wilkie had, as always, thoroughly worked out the plot of the novel in advance, Dickens had assured him that there would be no need to write more than a fraction of the story in advance of publication. But now Wilkie was having to work 'day *and* night',[16] keeping only a fortnight ahead of the printers. The novel was also being serialized in the United States, and instalments had to be written to coincide with the sailings of transatlantic steamers. All this pressure had been intensified by the Tavistock House production of *The Frozen Deep*.

Dickens, within sight of finishing *Little Dorrit*, found it hard to do without the continued stimulus of public appearances. He tried to explain what his interpretation of the character of Wardour meant to him. 'It enables me, as it were, *to write a book in company* . . . and to feel its effect coming freshly back upon me from the reader . . . I could blow off my superfluous fierceness in nothing so curious to me'.[17] When the Tavistock House performances were over he felt 'shipwrecked'. He cajoled Wilkie into a trip to sample the illicit pleasures of Brighton, complaining that he was 'generally in a collinsion [Collinsian] state', and was extravagantly delighted when Wilkie agreed: '*I cannot tell you* what pleasure I had in the receipt of your letter . . . I immediately arose (like the desponding Princes in the Arabian Nights, when the old woman – Procuress evidently, and probably of French extraction – comes to whisper about the Princesses they love) and washed my face and went out; and my face has been shining ever since.'[18] He finished *Little Dorrit* early in May while Wilkie was still struggling with 'a terribly trying chapter' of *The Dead Secret*. Wilkie was not to be tempted from his desk by suggestions of 'a wildly insane response' to 'any mad proposal you please'; though he did join the all-male house-warming picnic at Gad's Hill House when Dickens took possession on 22 May. A few days later Wilkie too had finished, and the last episode appeared on 13 June. 'Hooray!!!' wrote Dickens:

> . . . on Wednesday – if the mind can devise anything sufficiently in the style of sybarite Rome in the days of its culminating voluptuousness, I am your man . . . If you can think of any tremendous way of passing the night . . . I don't care what it is. I give (for that night only) restraint to the Winds![19]

Bradbury & Evans, the publishers of *Household Words*, issued the library edition of the novel at the beginning of June. On Dickens' advice, an agreement was made for a two-volume edition of 750, rather than five hundred copies, priced at a guinea. Wilkie, again prompted by Dickens, suggested that the publishers should take a quarter of the profits, rather than one-third. Dickens also advertised the novel in every number of *Household Words* from 20 June to 7 November: a generous and helpful gesture.

The novel was dedicated to Edward Pigott, and for once there was no preface, though Wilkie added one for the second edition in 1861. The reviews were lukewarm, suggesting that the novel was clever but flatly written, that the action was too slow, the characterization and action thin. 'It is . . . rare to find an author who, without originality, or great powers of any sort, has the gift of seeing how much arrangement and contrivance may do to enhance the value of the little he has to offer,' wrote the anonymous reviewer in the *Saturday Review*.[20]

It is not one of Wilkie Collins' best novels. One of the reviewers suggested that it suffered from the influence of *Household Words*; perhaps it was also affected by the creative energy invested in *The Frozen Deep*. 'I was blamed', Wilkie wrote in 1861,

> for allowing the 'Secret' to glimmer on the reader at an early period of the story . . . If this was a mistake . . . I committed it with both eyes open. After careful consideration, and after trying the experiment both ways, I thought it most desirable to let the effect of the story depend on expectation rather than surprise . . .[21]

He was to use this technique in a number of novels, with varying degrees of success. In *The Dead Secret* the reader's interest depends, as the 1861 preface points out, on the character of the mentally disturbed servant Sarah Leeson, the real mother of an illegitimate child passed off as being her mistress' daughter. 'The idea of tracing, in this character, the influence of a heavy responsibility on a naturally timid woman, whose mind was neither strong enough to bear it, nor bold enough to drop it altogether, was a favourite idea with me, at the time.' The servant is torn between her love for the child, which keeps her silent, and her duty to carry out her mistress' command to tell her husband the truth after her death. She should be a compelling character; but the structure of the book fatally weakens the impact. The facts of the plot are revealed, but the dramatization of them is withheld until near the end, when they are brought to life in second-hand narration. In *Hide and Seek* one of the major characters was deaf; in *The Dead Secret* the young heroine's husband is blind, but the condition is perfunctorily handled. Since he is a peripheral character, it has no structural relationship to the central theme of the novel. It was to be another fifteen years before Wilkie explored the physical and psychological aspects of blindness in any depth.

Nevertheless, *The Dead Secret* had, and still has, its admirers. An article by Edmund Yates which appeared in June thought Wilkie's power of story-telling in his latest novel 'more vigorous and more perfect than ever'. Yates placed him, as a novelist, ahead of all his contemporaries except Dickens, Thackeray and Charlotte Brontë. He even stated boldly that 'as a story-teller he has no equal . . . he possesses the *art de conter* above all living writers'.[22] It is an astonishing claim, which demolishes the common belief that *The Woman in White* burst like a meteor on an unprepared public.

As soon as the novel was published, Wilkie took a week's holiday. But he was unable to go for long without writing, or thinking about writing; and he immediately began to plan articles for *Household Words*.[23] He was not to be left in peace for long. Dickens was unexpectedly given the perfect excuse for reviving *The Frozen Deep* when Douglas Jerrold, an old friend of his and Wilkie's, died unexpectedly. The financial plight of Jerrold's widow and children (not in fact as dire as Dickens chose to believe) would be relieved by benefit performances given by Jerrold's friends. Thackeray was persuaded to give a lecture, and further performances of *The Frozen Deep* were given at the Gallery of Illustration in Regent Street, where the stage and auditorium, though small, were larger and more suitable for public performance than the Tavistock House schoolroom. The amateur cast remained the same, except that a substitute was needed for Mrs Wills, who was lame and unable to play the Scotch nurse Esther. 'You once said you knew a lady who could and would have done it. Is that lady producible?' Dickens asked Wilkie.[24]

The lady was Wilkie's friend Frances Dickinson. Not herself a Scot, she had profited by her miserable married years in Dumbarton to acquire a convincing stage Scotch accent, and she took over the part of Esther for all the performances at the Gallery of Illustration, with great success. It was typically courageous – or foolhardy – of her to expose herself in public. She had been caught up in a ten-year-long matrimonial wrangle, finally decided in her favour on appeal to the House of Lords, of the kind that particularly intrigued and outraged her friend Wilkie. The legal question was over the conflict of Scotch and English law. Frances had left her husband, John Edward Geils, because of his adultery and cruelty, in 1845. He sued for restitution of conjugal rights, but she was granted a divorce *a mensa et toro* (a judicial separation) in the ecclesiastical Court of Arches in 1848, which prevented either party from remarrying during the life of the other. She then tried to get a more complete Scotch divorce *a vinculo matrimonii*. This was at first refused, and it was not until 1855 that she was an entirely free woman. The proceedings were protracted, public, and messy. By her own account, old friends had turned against her when she parted from her husband, though she was the innocent party. In 1859 Wilkie wrote a story for *Household Words*, 'A New Mind', clearly based on her experiences:

> At that time, England stood disgracefully alone as the one civilized country in the world having a divorce-law for the husband which was not also a divorce-law for the wife. The writer in the Times . . . hinted delicately at the unutterable wrongs suffered by Mrs Duncan; and plainly showed that she was indebted to the accident of having been married in Scotland, and to her subsequent right of appeal to the Scotch tribunals, for a full and final release from the tie that bound her to the vilest of husbands which the English law . . . would have mercilessly refused.[25]

His friend's experiences were to recur in his later novels, and to add an edge of personal indignation to his campaigning 'fiction with a purpose'. Meanwhile, Frances Dickinson appeared on stage under the transparent pseudonym of 'Mrs Francis', even braving the royal presence on the first night.

Dickens had refused a request from the Queen to perform the play for the court at Windsor, considering that it would be awkward for his daughters and sisters-in-law, who had not been presented, to appear there as actresses. The Queen agreed instead to attend a private performance at the Gallery of Illustration, on 4 July, restricted to members of the royal family and the Court, and a few specially invited distinguished guests, such as Hans Andersen, then staying with Dickens at Gad's Hill, and Thackeray. The Queen, so her equerry reported to Dickens, was impressed by 'the high moral tone . . . her Majesty particularly wishes that her high approval should be conveyed to Mr. Wilkie Collins'.[26] It was the closest Wilkie ever came to being considered the thoroughly respectable son of William Collins, RA.

Hans Andersen left an account of the evening, singling out Dickens' performance as 'free from all those mannerisms one finds in England and France just in tragic parts . . . the death scene so moving that I burst into tears at it'. Afterwards there was a champagne supper at the *Household Words* office; Harriet attempted to flirt with the lugubrious Andersen: 'Collins' mother gave me a bouquet of parsley which lay on the ham, and Lemon told her she was a coquette, called her the mama of the piece.' But even her high spirits could not relieve his underlying melancholy: the gloomy Dane's diary entry concludes unexpectedly, '(Not at all in good humour really the whole evening.)'[27]

The next day, a Sunday, there was a celebratory dinner party at Gad's Hill; after the following Saturday's performance the whole company spent the afternoon and evening at Albert Smith's house, where they were photographed on the lawn. When they were both staying at Gad's Hill, the ponderously playful Andersen adorned Wilkie's wide-brimmed hat with a garland of daisies. The Dickens boys took Wilkie, so decorated, for a walk through the village. They thought him quite unaware of the reason for the villagers' amusement. It would have been like Wilkie to have known very well what was going on, but to let the boys have their fun; no one ever cared less for appearances. His view of Andersen, probably the most difficult guest ever entertained at Gad's Hill, appeared in a piece he wrote for *All the Year Round* in 1859, 'The Bachelor Bedroom'. Andersen appears transparently disguised as an eccentric German, Herr von Müffe, 'a man naturally destitute of all power of adapting himself to new persons and new circumstances . . . He could not join one of us in any country diversions. He hung about the house and garden in a weak, pottering, aimless manner, always turning up at the wrong moment, and always attaching himself to the wrong person.' Wilkie, with characteristic good nature, confesses to an uneasy conscience at the way he was treated, and includes a skit on himself as the hypochondriacal 'Mr Jeremy'.

> If anyone tumbles up-stairs, or down-stairs, or off a horse, or out of a dog-cart, it is Mr Jeremy. If you want a case of sprained ankle, a case of suppressed gout, a case of complicated earache, toothache, headache, and sore-throat, all in one, a case of liver, a case of chest, a case of nerves, or a case of low fever . . . he will supply you, on demand . . . he has but two sources of consolation to draw on . . . The first is the luxury of twisting his nose on one side, and stopping up his air-passages and Eustachian tubes with inconceivably large quantities of strong snuff. The second is the oleaginous gratification of incessantly anointing his miserable little beard and mustachios with cheap bear's-grease . . .[28]

Dickens, who felt that *The Frozen Deep* could have run successfully for a further twelve months, was delighted to be asked to give two more performances, in the vast Free Trade Hall in Manchester. This was a very different matter from the little theatre at the Gallery of

Illustration, and Dickens realized that the women amateurs would never be able to project their voices adequately. Professional actresses would have to be hired, 'though I have written to our friend Mrs. Dickinson to say that I don't fear her, if she likes to play with them'. Frances Dickinson did not care to risk appearing with professional actresses. The part of nurse Esther was taken over by the experienced actress Mrs Ternan, with her daughters, Maria – in the part of the girl Wardour gives up to his rival Aldersley – and Ellen in Georgina Hogarth's part. Charles Collins substituted for Frederick Evans.

The three performances (an extra one was added by public demand), on 21, 22 and 24 August, were, Wilkie thought, the finest of all. It was not only the amateurs who were overcome by the power of Dickens' performance. Maria Ternan wept uncontrollably, and had to be revived by her mother and sister. Dickens, disastrously in love with the eighteen-year-old Ellen, nevertheless kept his artistic detachment throughout, conceiving new ideas of 'surprising force and brilliancy' for his next novel, *A Tale of Two Cities*, as he lay on the stage at the end of the play. Exhausted by so much emotion, Dickens and the ladies retired to bed, but the male members of the cast sat up after the second performance, singing, drinking and dancing, until the early hours. '. . . Suddenly the dining-room door was tragically opened, and the figure of Charles Dickens appeared in a dressing-gown and carrying a bedroom candlestick . . . with one hand uplifted, and *such* a look! partly of reproof, partly of amusement . . . and partly of horror! . . . we all sneaked off to bed without so much as a "good-night" . . . like naughty schoolboys.'[29]

Wilkie also had a play produced on the professional stage for the first time in August, when *The Lighthouse* was at last performed at the Olympic Theatre, with Frederick Robson in the main part. The first night was a great success. 'The audience so enthralled by the story that they would not even bear the applause at the first entrance of Robson . . . A perfect hurricane of applause at the end of the play – which I had to acknowledge from a private box. Dickens, Thackeray, Mark Lemon publicly appearing in my box. In short an immense success,' he wrote triumphantly to Harriet.[30] Two months later the theatre was still full every night.[31] Wilkie, as was then customary, received a flat fee of £100.

He was making money from translations of his books, and, in spite of many piracies, from publishing both novels and stories in the United States: he was a contributor to *Atlantic Monthly* from its earliest days. *The Dead Secret* was serialized in a Danish magazine during the summer, and he signed a contract on 27 August 1857 with Charles Lahure in Paris for the French translation rights of all his novels to date, which also gave Lahure an option on any published subsequently.[32] The highest price – 750 francs – was paid for *The Dead Secret*, which was translated by Émile Forgues. With his steady income from *Household Words*, Wilkie was now earning a good living by writing. If an international copyright law had been in operation, he would have earned a great deal more. He became increasingly infuriated by the piratical behaviour of unscrupulous foreign publishers, who calmly stole the product of another man's brain, giving him nothing for it. Baron Tauchnitz was a shining exception: he always paid for the right to publish continental English-language editions. The bargain with Charles Lahure was a reasonable one, and the following year he told a correspondent, '. . . there is talk at Boston of a complete American edition of my works, in which the publishers propose to give me a share of the profits'.[33] But there was no guarantee of any payment. For a writer beginning to be as popular abroad as he was in his own country, this exploitation became a constant irritation.

After the *Frozen Deep* performance had ended, Dickens, abruptly cut off from the excitement of performance and the daily association with the Ternans, turned to Wilkie for companionship. Only Forster knew as much about Dickens' feelings at this time, and he was more disapproving than the easygoing and non-judgemental Wilkie. Five days after the last Manchester performance, Dickens wrote:

> Partly in the grim despair and restlessness of this subsidence from excitement, and partly for the sake of Household Words, I want to cast about whether you and I can go anywhere – take any tour – see anything – whereon we could write something together. Have you any

idea tending to any place in the world? Will you rattle your head and see if there is any pebble in it which we would wander away and play at marbles with? We want something for Household Words, and I want to escape from myself. For when I *do* start up and stare myself seedily in the face . . . my blankness is inconceivable – indescribable – my misery amazing.[34]

Wilkie suggested Norfolk. Dickens by now had private reasons for visiting the north of England, and held out for the 'bleak fells of Cumberland'. He settled on a Hogarthian title for the *Household Words* articles: 'The Lazy Tour of Two Idle Apprentices', and they left London for Carlisle on 7 September.

Dickens planned to spend some days in Cumberland, and then to go on to Doncaster, with the excuse of finding *Household Words* copy at the races. Ellen and Maria Ternan were arriving there to act at the Theatre Royal on 14 September. But on 9 September the trip nearly ended disastrously before it had fairly begun. Dickens insisted on climbing Carrick, or Carrock, Fell, a mountain which 'Nobody goes up. Guides have forgotten it.' 'Much better to die, doing', he had written to Forster, and though the weather was appalling, he persuaded the landlord of a local inn to take them. He gave a Jingle-ish account of the adventure to Forster:

Went up, in a tremendous rain. C.D. beat Mr. Porter (name of landlord) in half a mile. Mr. P. done up in no time . . . Rain terrific, black mists, darkness of night. Mr. P. agitated. C.D. confident. C. (a long way down in perspective) submissive. All wet through. No poles. Not so much as a walking stick in the party . . . Darker and darker. Nobody discernible, two yards off, by the other two . . . Proposals from C.D. to go 'slap down'. Seconded by C. Mr. P. objects, on account of precipice called the Black Arches, and terror of the countryside. More wandering. Mr. P. terror-stricken, but game. Watercourse, thundering and roaring, reached . . . Leaps, splashes, and tumbles, for two hours. C. lost. C.D. whoops. Cries for assistance from behind. C.D. returns. C. with horribly sprained ankle, lying in rivulet![35]

Dickens' need to replay the situation of *The Frozen Deep* by pushing himself and Wilkie into absurd and unnecessary danger had painful consequences for Wilkie, whose ankle was already weak from a sprain six weeks earlier. Dickens, in his own accounts, emerges the hero:

'How I enacted Wardour over again in carrying him down, and what a business it was to get him down . . . now I carry him to bed, and into and out of carriages, exactly like Wardour in private life. I don't believe he will stand for a month to come! He has had a Doctor, and can wear neither shoe nor stocking, and has his foot wrapped up in a flannel waistcoat (dirty), and has a breakfast-saucer of liniment and a horrible dabbling of lotion incessantly in progress.'[36] Four days later the ankle was a great deal better: '. . . he can get into new hotels and up the stairs with two thick sticks, like an admiral in a farce . . . he contemplates cheerfully the keeping house at Doncaster . . . Of course he can never walk out, or see anything of any place.'[37] The accident-prone Wilkie, disabled and chronically untidy, annoyed Dickens as he had done in Italy. Allonby was 'the dullest little place I ever entered; and what with the monotony of an idle sea, and . . . the monotony of another sea in the room (occasioned by Collins's perpetually holding his ankle over a pail of sea water, and laving it with a milk jug), I struck yesterday, and came away'. From Doncaster, which they did after all manage to reach on 14 September, Dickens complained, 'I am perpetually tidying the rooms after him, and carrying all sorts of untidy things which belong to him into his bedroom, which is a picture of disorder. You will please to imagine mine, airy and clean . . . perfect arrangement, and exquisite neatness.'[38] All the old gibes were revived: when they were given an especially good meal at Lancaster, 'Collins turned pale, and estimated the dinner at half a guinea each.'[39]

In spite of Wilkie's disability and severe pain for the first few days, which left all the legwork to Dickens, they managed to keep up to date with writing 'The Lazy Tour'. By 17 September Dickens was able to assure Wills that he had received the proofs of his portion of the second instalment. 'Collins is sticking a little with his story, but I hope will come through it tomorrow. He . . . can limp about the room, and has had two Doncaster rides in a carriage. Is to be treated to another tomorrow if he has done.' Wilkie was also treated to a night at the theatre, where he and Dickens were instantly recognized by the audience, becoming 'objects of the most marked attention and conversation'.[40] They parted on 21 September, Dickens returning to London and Wilkie, now able to walk a mile with a stick, going on to

Scarborough to convalesce. But the ankle was slow to heal completely. It was still giving a good deal of trouble in March, and more than a year later he was still using it as an excuse for not accepting an invitation to a dance, though it was well enough 'so far as walking purposes are concerned'.[41]

'The Lazy Tour', the visible result of this disastrous expedition, is a good example of Wilkie's skill at complementing Dickens. The two of them made an amusing series out of scanty material. It is, under the not very opaque cloak of anonymity, candid about both the Idle Apprentices. Francis Goodchild (Dickens) tells Thomas Idle (Collins), '"It's no trouble, Tom, to fall in love" ... "It's trouble enough to fall out of it, once you're in it" retorted Tom. "So I keep out of it altogether. It would be better for you, if you did the same."' But Goodchild 'is always in love with somebody, and not infrequently with several objects at once'. He is also

> laboriously idle, and would take upon himself any amount of pains and labour to assure himself that he was idle; in short, had no better ideal of idleness than that it was useless industry. Thomas Idle ... was an idler of the unmixed Irish or Neapolitan type; a passive idler, a born-and-bred idler.

Idle complains of Goodchild, 'You *can't* play. You don't know what it is. You make work of everything ... To me you are an absolutely terrible fellow. You do nothing like another man. Where another fellow would fall into a footbath of action or emotion, you fall into a mine ... Where another man would stake a sixpence, you stake your existence ... A man who can do nothing by halves appears to me to be a fearful man.'

By playing on this exaggerated contrast of character, and applying it to their reactions to the various situations in which they found themselves, Dickens and Wilkie expertly filled out their five episodes. Dickens mostly contributed scenes of activity: descriptions of railway travel, a lunatic asylum and Doncaster Races; Wilkie, immobilized on the sofa, reminisced about his schooldays and the time when he was reading – or rather not reading – for the Bar. However, Wilkie told his mother, '*All* the mountain part in H.W. is mine.'[42] They also interpolated two stories. Wilkie's, later reprinted as 'The Dead Hand' in *The Queen of Hearts*, is here presented as the life history of the white-faced assistant of the doctor who treated his ankle, whose strange appearance and manner he was to use again for the character of Ezra Jennings in *The Moonstone*.

'The Dead Hand' is an uncanny, compelling story, a fit companion to 'A Terribly Strange Bed'. It treats Wilkie's favourite theme of the double in a way he was to return to in *Armadale*: it is a trial run for the relationship of Allan Armadale and Ozias Midwinter. A young man, 'one of those reckless, rattle-pated, open-hearted, and open-mouthed young gentlemen, who possess the gift of familiarity in its highest perfection', unable to find a room for the night during Doncaster Race Week, finally consents to share with a corpse. But the dead man comes back to life. They prove to be half-brothers, the stranger Mr Lorn as wild, uncanny and depressed as his brother is sanguine and easygoing, as dark as he is fair. '"I have no name and no father. The merciful law of Society tells me I am Nobody's Son!"' They are also in love with the same woman. The ex-corpse gives her up to his legitimate brother, and lives out his life in obscurity as the assistant to the country doctor. Wilkie's relationship to this curious story, and to the two characters who have 'a likeness between them – not in features or complexion, but solely in expression', was not obvious. But it went deep; and the two sides of his character were already known to his closest friends.

Whatever Dickens' irritation with Wilkie's personal habits and physical clumsiness (he wrote to Miss Coutts telling her that 'Mr Collins . . . never goes out with me on any expedition, without receiving some damage or other'), they remained close. Wilkie made allowance, without complaint, for Dickens' extreme irritability; he was aware of Dickens' genuine affection for him. Dickens appreciated his value to *Household Words*, and raised his salary by £50 a year in October. 'I have no doubt of his being devoted to H.W., and doing great service', he assured Wills. Only Wilkie and Forster shared Dickens' birthday dinner at Gravesend with him the following February.

Wilkie's next assignment for *Household Words* was the writing, shared with Dickens, of the Christmas number for 1847, *The Perils of Certain English Prisoners*. This, like the other Christmas stories written with Wilkie as his only collaborator, had a unified plot, rather than being a collection of stories hung on a tenuous thread. Dickens wanted to refer indirectly to the Mutiny; the natives were to be seen as treacherous and cunning, and the English, especially the women, as courageous and noble. The original idea, which transferred the theme to South America and involved silver mines, was Wilkie's; Dickens wrote the first and last chapters, and Wilkie the second. Wilkie drew heavily on a *Household Words* article by Henry Morley, describing the ruins of Copan in Honduras, for his section of the story. This describes the imprisonment of the English in a ruined temple in the jungle, and their escape from it. The story, especially Wilkie's section, is still exciting, though unpleasantly racist, but of little literary interest except for two names. A subsidiary character, barely characterized, is called Captain Carton, and the resourceful and courageous heroine who marries him, Marion Maryon. Wilkie rifled Morley's article again, when he came to write *The Woman in White*, for some of the details of Marian Halcombe's dream.[43]

Preoccupied with the prospect of dramatic success, which seemed to be within his grasp after *The Lighthouse* and *The Frozen Deep*, Wilkie wrote two 'Letters' for *Household Words*. The first, from reader to author, complains of the state of the English theatre, compared with that in France. The second, from author to reader, explains the lack of incentives for British playwrights: '. . . while the remuneration for every other species of literature has enormously increased in the last hundred years, the remuneration for dramatic writing has steadily decreased . . . I could only write a play for the English stage – a successful play, mind – by consenting to what would be . . . a serious pecuniary sacrifice.' Whereas the actors' and managers' incomes had enormously increased, the author of a three-act play received, as a rule, no more than £150. 'The utmost annual income the English stage would, at present prices, pay me . . . would be three hundred pounds!'[44] But in spite of this 'barbarously low' estimate of the author, he remained stage-struck, and finished another play early in 1858.

The Red Vial was a melodrama specifically designed as a vehicle for Frederick Robson, who had asked Wilkie for another play after the success of *The Lighthouse.* Robson, 'a strange little genius . . . said to have resembled Edmund Kean in his bursts of passion',[45] had some physical similarities to Wilkie: 'He was a little nervous man with a large head and a small body; his legs and feet were particularly neat.'[46] Wilkie created the part of Hans Grimm, a simpleton rescued from imprisonment in a madhouse, for Robson. But when it was produced at the Olympic on 11 October, with Mrs Stirling in the part of a melodramatic villainess, it was hooted off the stage. Henry Morley analysed why.

> The author has . . . forgotten that in a drama characters are not less essential than a plot. There is not a character in *The Red Vial* . . . they are all shadows for a tale that should be read in ten minutes, not characters to be offered bodily to our senses, for a two hours' study . . . The fatal defect . . . is that it makes no allowance for the good or bad habit that an English audience has of looking out for something upon which to feed its appetite for the absurd. The orthodox writer of melodrama satisfies that hunger with a comic underplot . . . But Mr. Wilkie Collins has experimented in a drama without a break in the chain of crime and terror, and the audience therefore makes breaks for itself at very inconvenient places . . . The piece is the work of a popular writer, admirably mounted, perfectly acted, with the favourite actor of the day labouring his utmost in what should have been a striking part. Nevertheless it was condemned . . . for a defect arising from misapprehension of the temper of an English audience.[47]

The climax of the melodrama, in which a supposed corpse thrusts a naked arm from behind a curtain, was greeted by the audience with waves of hysterical laughter.

Wilkie was deeply humiliated by the failure of the play. He always believed that the public appreciated his writing, even when the reviewers were critical; this time he had totally misjudged their reactions. He refused to allow *The Red Vial* to be printed, or ever performed again. He salvaged the plot, and used it again for one of his weakest novels, *Jezebel's Daughter.*

Wilkie never lost his admiration for Robson's acting, and the following year he tried to suit the public's love of the ludicrous by writing a one-act farce, adapted from his story 'The Twin Sisters', for Robson and Mrs Stirling.

> It is – though I can hardly believe it myself – actually the product of *my* pen. I have had better ideas for better and more elaborate dramatic works – but they *would* run, in spite of me, into that vein of strong and serious interest which it would be, for the present at least, mere rashness and folly to attempt opening again. A farce to keep the audience roaring with laughter all through, was the piece I was determined to write *this time* – and such as it is, you now have it.[48]

Emden and Robson, joint managers of the Olympic, must have rejected the farce, for no more is heard of it. Wilkie never wrote another.

Though disappointed in his theatrical ambitions, Wilkie was, as Dickens had foreseen, more than earning his salary for *Household Words*. During 1858 he contributed twenty articles (two of them rewritten by Dickens) and also wrote two episodes and, with Dickens, the conclusion, of the 1858 Christmas number, *A House to Let*. The subjects are wide-ranging. There are topical pieces, literary ones, comic sketches of character and narratives from French history. They are written in a variety of styles, and in the guise of many different characters. A shy young man contemplating marriage is answered in the next number by an irascible elderly bachelor. Making use of his own experience of a seaside holiday, Wilkie presents himself as a middle-aged husband. The novelist is clearly at work in many of the pieces, making use of his facility in sketching character and keeping in practice for the next major work. But certain preoccupations recur. When Wilkie writes of the English enjoyment of boredom, or the interruptions suffered by a writer whose friends don't consider what he does is really work, or the dreariness of 'Society'; when he calls 'the business of courting and marrying' 'a system of social persecution against the individual', his own voice is clear. It is particularly evident in 'The Unknown Public', an article on the cheap fiction sold in 'penny journals' with a circulation of millions:

> The known reading public . . . are easily discovered and classified. There is the religious public . . . There is the public which reads for information, and devotes itself to Histories, Biographies, Essays, Treatises, Voyages

> and Travels. There is the public which reads for amusement, and patronises the Circulating Libraries and the railway book-stalls. There is, lastly, the public which reads nothing but newspapers. We all know where to lay our hands on the people who represent these various classes . . . We know, if we are at all conversant with literary matters, even the very districts of London in which certain classes of people live who are to be depended upon beforehand as the picked readers for certain kinds of books. But what do we know of the enormous outlawed majority – of the lost literary tribes – of the prodigious, the overwhelming three millions? Absolutely nothing.[49]

Wilkie's reading of the fiction in these 'penny journals' led him to conclude that there was no wickedness in the stories: they were merely immensely dull, and atrociously badly written. The huge sale was accounted for by the ignorance of their readers: 'The Unknown Public is, in a literary sense, hardly beginning, as yet, to learn to read. The members of it are . . . from no fault of theirs, still ignorant of almost everything which is generally known and understood among readers whom circumstances have placed, socially and intellectually, in the rank above them.' The investigation covers much the same ground as Thackeray's 'Half-a-crown's worth of cheap knowledge' published in *Fraser's Magazine* in 1838, but the conclusion is characteristically Collinsian: 'An immense public has been discovered: the next thing to be done is, in a literary sense, to teach that public how to read . . . it is perhaps hardly too much to say, that the future of English fiction may rest with this Unknown Public . . . A great, an unparalleled prospect awaits, perhaps, the coming generation of English novelists. To the penny journals . . . belongs the credit of having discovered a new public. When that public shall discover its need of a great writer, the great writer will have such an audience as has never yet been known.'

Wilkie's first detective story in the classic mode, best known as 'The Biter Bit', appeared in the newly launched American journal *Atlantic Monthly* in April 1858, as 'Who is the Thief?'. It is a comedy told in letters, mostly by a foolish and self-satisfied new recruit to the Detective Police, intent on solving a theft, who suspects everyone but the true culprit. Wilkie once more recycled the romantic secret wedding of Edward and Henrietta Ward in the story. The young detective is one of Wilkie's spies, boring holes in walls to keep watch, following suspects through the streets, creeping up to overhear their conversations. But he is ludicrous rather than sinister, and the mysteries are relatively innocent ones; the story belongs with *A Rogue's Life*, rather than *Armadale* or *The Moonstone*.

Dickens kept a cautious control over Wilkie's more radical outbursts in *Household Words*. He suggested the topic of one piece, a complaint about actors' children being excluded from private schools, but then warned Wills to look at it carefully, 'and not to leave anything in it that may be sweeping, and unnecessarily offensive to the middle class. He has always a tendency to overdo that – and such a subject gives him a fresh temptation.'[50] He 'toned down' 'The Unknown Public', 'not because I dispute its positions, but because there are some things (true enough) that it would not be generous in me, as a novelist and a periodical editor, to put too prominently forward.'[51] He rewrote Wilkie's attack on the absurdities in Charlotte Yonge's *The Heir of Redclyffe* so thoroughly that the article became a joint venture.[52] But then Dickens had good reason to be cautious in 1858.

ELEVEN

Secret Connections

(1858–1859)

Dickens' marriage had been in difficulties for years, as Wilkie was now well aware. At the time of the public performances of *The Frozen Deep*, and on the 'Idle Apprentices' tour, when he and Dickens went to Doncaster to see Ellen Ternan act, Wilkie, as close to Dickens as he was ever to be, was in the secret of his friend's infatuation with the young actress, which finally brought the marriage to an end. In the last months of 1857 and early part of 1858 a series of incidents, designed, it would seem, to humiliate Catherine Dickens, culminated in an order – which she obeyed – to call on the Ternans, to defuse the rumours flying around. But by now matters had gone too far to avoid the final break.

Was Dickens encouraged by Wilkie's easygoing attitudes to carry through the painful and public relinquishing of his marriage? Or was it perhaps the other way round? Did Wilkie, seeing that Dickens could survive, if precariously, the scandal surrounding the break, decide that it was safe to begin living with the woman he had for some time been keeping? For only a few months after the Dickens separation Wilkie openly acknowledged what had been, until then, a well-kept secret.

The disintegration of Dickens' private life naturally distressed his friends deeply, Wilkie among them. Some, notably Forster, also disapproved of the public readings, now a regular part of his life.

Forster felt that they would cheapen him in the eyes of his public, and that he was exhausting himself. But the two matters were inextricably connected, and not only because of Dickens' increased need for money. He wrote to Wilkie in March, knowing that he at least would try to understand and not criticize, explaining that the readings were an essential guard against despair.

> All day yesterday I was pursuing the Reading idea. Forster seems to me to be extraordinarily irrational about it . . . the domestic unhappiness remains so strong upon me that I can't write, and (waking) can't rest, one minute. I have never known a moment's peace or content, since the last night of the Frozen Deep . . . In this condition though nothing can alter or soften it, I have a turning notion that the mere physical effort and change of the Readings would be good, as another means of bearing it.[1]

By May Dickens and Catherine were separated, and the break had become public knowledge. The scandal was exacerbated by Dickens' attempts at self-justification: he quarrelled with almost everyone who did not fully endorse his position. He even destroyed *Household Words*, breaking away from Bradbury & Evans because they would not publish his self-justificatory letter about his marriage in *Punch*. He replaced his magazine with a new periodical, *All the Year Round*, defiantly proclaiming, on shaky legal ground, that it incorporated *Household Words*.

Wilkie was told, both in person and by letter, Dickens' version of the reasons for the separation.[2] That letter has disappeared, but on 25 May (the date on which he also wrote, to Arthur Smith, the letter later known as the 'violated letter') Dickens showed his appreciation of Wilkie's typical refusal to pass judgement on his friend, promising to explain the details of his quarrel with his wife's family over his relationship with Ellen Ternan.

> A thousand thanks for your kind letter. I always feel your friendship very much, and prize it in proportion to the true affection I have for you.
>
> . . . Can you come round to me in the morning (Wednesday) before 12? I can then tell you all in lieu of writing. It is rather a long story – over, I hope now.[3]

Wilkie continued to visit Catherine Dickens, who had always been kind to him, while still supporting Dickens and remaining on good terms with him. An entry in his diary for 1868 includes her in a list of people to call on, and Kate Dickens remembered that Wilkie visited her mother often at Gloucester Crescent, her home after the separation. Dickens' absolutism, the dictation of an either/or position to his friends and even his children, was quite alien to Wilkie's temperament. He longed always to reconcile opposites, to postpone the existential moment of decision.

That attitude, too, was to create problems, notably in his relationship with Caroline Graves, the woman with whom he began to live openly towards the end of 1858. If Wilkie was involved with other women before her, they vanished without trace. It was not the incorrigible Wilkie who first sullied the name of Collins with a sexual misdemeanour, but, it seems, his high-minded brother.

When the happy years at 17 Hanover Terrace ended in January 1856, Harriet must have felt that her sons, aged thirty-two and twenty-eight, were old enough to cope on their own in lodgings. Wilkie spent three miserable weeks at Howland Street; Charley stayed in Percy Street for six or seven months. The news was soon circulating in Pre-Raphaelite circles that the meek and well-behaved Charley, who had been considered too stuffy to be made a member of the Brotherhood, had been ensnared by a disreputable woman. In January Michael Halliday wrote to Holman Hunt, on his way home from the Middle East, to tell him that Collins was 'shamelessly' living in sin.[4] Later that year Millais, delighted by married love and the recent experience of fatherhood, wrote a long letter to Hunt from Scotland, where he was spending the summer, referring to the predicament of an old friend who had been inveigled into a 'disreputable secret connection' with a woman. Though the name of the friend was discreetly crossed out by Hunt, the evidence, both graphological and circumstantial, points strongly to Charles Collins.* It is clear from Millais' letter that he felt Charley had been preyed upon by a harpy, and needed rescuing. Millais asked Hunt to talk

* See Appendix A.

to Charley: 'You . . . may greatly forward a separation between him and this woman.' Hunt may have succeeded. At all events, Charley ceased to live with his mysterious mistress after six months or so. He returned to live with his mother when she moved into her new house, 2 Harley Place, in July, and he continued to live with Harriet for the next four years.[5] His mother did not fulfil her long-cherished ambition to move to the country until Charley was safely married to Kate Dickens in July 1860.

Wilkie must surely have known what his brother was up to, but there is no reference to the affair in any of his extant letters. Perhaps the business was kept from Harriet: certainly it was, as far as the outside world was concerned, hushed up as successfully as Augustus Egg's marriage, Dickens' arrangement with Ellen Ternan, or Holman Hunt's own long and painful relationship with Annie Miller. There is no way of knowing who the woman was, why she was considered so disreputable, or what became of her. She emerges from the shadows of mid-Victorian London for an instant, only to be swallowed up again for ever; one of the unfortunates who figure with increasing force in Wilkie's later novels. She may have had as much to do with Wilkie's portrayal of 'Magdalens' as his own relationships with women.

Charles Collins contributed an article to *Household Words* in 1858, 'Her Face', which recounts, in the first person, how the narrator saw the photograph of a woman in a photographer's shop window, and was haunted by it. Later he saw the woman herself in the street. After following several false trails, he at last traced her to her home in 'a poorish square', discovered she was the daughter of a dancing-master and married her.[6] Some of this is certainly fiction. Perhaps all of it is.

It is difficult to imagine Wilkie playing the heavy elder brother: he was in no position to do so. His easygoing attitude to irregular sexual relations was well known to all their friends, and it was not to him that Millais turned in his attempt to rescue Charley. It is curious that our only knowledge of Charles Collins' peccadillo should come from a letter written by John Millais, for the best-known and most frequently repeated story about Wilkie

Collins' relationship with Caroline Graves – the woman who lived with him, with one intermission, for the rest of his life – was also reported to come from Millais. It is in marked contrast to Millais' outrage about Charles Collins. According to Millais' son, his father told him how, after he had spent an evening at Hanover Terrace, the Collins brothers walked back with him to his parents' house in Gower Street:

> they were suddenly arrested by a piercing scream coming from the garden of a villa close at hand. It was evidently the cry of a woman in distress; and while pausing to consider what they should do, the iron gate leading to the garden was dashed open, and from it came the figure of a young and very beautiful woman dressed in flowing white robes that shone in the moonlight. She seemed to float rather than run in their direction, and, on coming up to the three young men, she paused for a moment in an attitude of supplication and terror. Then . . . she suddenly moved on and vanished in the shadows cast upon the road.
>
> 'What a lovely woman!' was all Millais could say. 'I must see who she is, and what is the matter,' said Wilkie Collins, as, without a word he dashed off after her. His two companions waited in vain for his return, and next day, when they met again, he seemed indisposed to talk of his adventure. They gathered from him, however, that he had come up with the lovely fugitive and had heard from her own lips the history of her life and cause of her sudden flight. She was a young lady of good birth and position, who had accidentally fallen into the hands of a man living in a villa in Regent's Park. There for many months he kept her prisoner under threats and mesmeric influence of so alarming a character that she dared not attempt to escape, until, in sheer desperation, she fled from the brute, who, with a poker in his hand, threatened to dash her brains out. Her subsequent history, interesting as it is, is not for these pages.[7]

This sensational farrago reads like a parody of Wilkie's own novels. It probably originated as one of his good stories, a piece of foolery designed to cover the less exciting and certainly less acceptable reality. John Guille Millais' memoir of his father is full of errors about Wilkie and Charles Collins, and it was published in 1899 when the three men and one woman involved in this story were all dead. With no one left to contradict it, the story of the woman in distress has been generally accepted. It has been ingeniously connected with a statement by someone who knew Wilkie well, his brother's wife

Kate, the daughter of Dickens, who married Charles Collins in 1860. Kate said that Wilkie Collins had a mistress called Caroline, a lady by birth, who was the original of 'the woman in white' in the novel.[8]

She was a widow, with one young daughter. She was not, during the 1850s, the mesmerically controlled, high-born mistress of a poker-wielding villain – unless the post was a part-time one. She was eking out a precarious existence keeping a marine store, the mid-Victorian equivalent of a junk shop and low-grade pawnbroker, at 5 Charlton Street, Fitzroy Square, under her original name, Mrs Elizabeth Graves.*[9] Howland Street, where Wilkie Collins lodged in the spring of 1856, is one block away. Charlton Street is also on the way from Hanover Terrace to Gower Street, where Millais was living until the autumn of 1855. There would be some basis for the night-time meeting later worked up into melodrama in the Millais account. Perhaps Wilkie did rescue her, from a bully or a pimp rather than a wealthy villain.

Caroline's background was poor but not disreputable. She later went in for thorough-going self-aggrandizement, claiming in official documents that her husband, George Robert Graves, was either 'of independent means' or an army officer, and that she was the daughter of a gentleman, John Courtenay, and was born in Cheltenham. In reality she was the daughter of John Compton, a carpenter, and his wife Sarah, who lived at Toddington, near Cheltenham.[10] Elizabeth Compton moved to Bath, where, on 30 March 1850, she married George Robert Graves, described variously as 'accountant', 'shorthand writer' and 'solicitor's clerk', at Walcot Parish Church.[11] Her husband was probably too delicate to be apprenticed to his father's trade – Lot Graves was a mason – but he might be thought to have taken a step up in the world by joining the shabby-genteel Dickensian company of office clerks.

George Graves had been born in Greenwich, but by the time of his marriage he was living at 11 Cumming Street, Pentonville, and

* It was perhaps Wilkie who christened her 'Caroline'. He always referred to her thus, and she adopted the name, using it in official documents, but one of the books from Wilkie's library sold after his death was signed in pencil 'Lizzie Collins'.

the young couple started their married life there. The household also included George's widowed mother, Mary Ann Graves.[12] Wherever Elizabeth (Caroline) Graves subsequently turns up in the records, Mary Ann is close on her heels.

A daughter, Elizabeth Harriet, was born at Cumming Street on 3 February 1851.[13] The young couple's struggle upwards into the precarious lower reaches of the middle class was short-lived. George Graves was suffering from consumption; before his daughter was a year old, he was dead. They returned to Bath when he became too ill to work, for he died at Moravian Cottage, Weston, Bath, on 30 January 1852.[14] The Moravians had a thriving church and schools in Bath, and though the Graves family were members of the Church of England, they may have been benefiting from Moravian charity at a time when they would otherwise have been destitute. Mary Ann was with them when he died, and registered the death.

The three generations of unprotected women, grandmother, mother and daughter, disappear for a while. Then Elizabeth Graves surfaces in the 1853 London Post Office Directory, keeping her miserable little shop in one sublet room.[15] She was later joined by her mother-in-law, who is listed in the 1855 Trades Directory as keeping a tobacconist's shop in Hertford Street, Fitzroy Square. Elizabeth Graves is also listed in the 1856 and 1857 Directories; Mary Ann is still in the 1858 Directory, but Elizabeth is not. She disappears for good; probably because she had begun to live with Wilkie, and was being kept by him.

Wilkie may have rescued Caroline from another man, or from poverty and illness. In both *The Woman in White* and the novel which followed it, *No Name*, a woman suffering illness and emotional trauma is tenderly nursed back to health, in shabby lodgings, by the man who rescues and finally marries her. Perhaps Wilkie saw Caroline in her shop, or bought tobacco from her mother-in-law. However it began, the relationship with Caroline, as she will henceforth be known, did not become an open one until late in 1858.

This was the time when Wilkie ceased to live even intermittently with his mother and brother. His final departure probably coincided with Harriet Collins' move back to Regent's Park, this time to 2

Clarence Terrace, her last London address. It was a dark, damp, stuccoed house: Charley christened it 'Lumbago Terrace'.[16] The reclaimed Charley, on a visit to Paris, wrote to her there in November: 'Do caution Willie against committing himself to London lodgings before he has tried Paris again,' and '. . . how it is that Willie is not here oftener I cannot understand. Every one of his tastes would be gratified here.'[17] Charley himself was soon disillusioned with Paris, finding, as his father would have done, that French 'equality' was detestable. It would not have been offensive to Wilkie, but he had no intention of removing himself: he had at last made the decision to acknowledge his relationship with Caroline.

On 1 December 1858 Wilkie wrote to his cousin Jane Ward from 2 Clarence Terrace, which he seems to have used as an accommodation address. He was apologizing for a muddle over his Christmas plans.

> I am sincerely sorry that my having carelessly allowed myself to *drift* into an engagement for this Christmas Day, should have caused you even a moment's vexation. I say '*drift*', because the invitation of the friends who now claim me, began conditionally, and grew, I hardly know how, into an actual engagement . . . My own opinion is that I shall, in some small degree, atone for my shortcomings towards you by failing my country friends at the eleventh hour. I am far from well, and sadly in want of another change. My term, at my own house, is up this Christmas – I have no idea where to go to – and I think it quite likely that I may be at Paris, or by the seaside, in search of relief to body and mind, or *in bed* on Christmas Day. I never felt less certain of my future proceedings than I do at this moment . . .[18]

It is not clear where 'my own house' was (he was not referring to Clarence Terrace, where his mother and brother continued to live). In the following month, January 1859, he had drifted to 124 Albany Street, where Caroline Graves was living with her little daughter, and began to address letters from there.[19] He had probably been supporting them both for some time past. Caroline's only occupation for the rest of her life was as his 'housekeeper'. After a few months together in Albany Street they moved, in the spring of 1859, to lodgings at 2a New Cavendish Street, close to the house where Wilkie was born.

No letters from Wilkie to Caroline, or from her to him, have survived. Some were probably burnt on the bonfire he made of his private papers shortly before his death, others destroyed by Caroline or her daughter.* Their relationship can never be fully reconstructed. One can only conjecture that the shady areas where the worlds of respectability and licence overlapped, so often explored in his books, were those Wilkie preferred in his own life. His loathing of dinner parties and evening receptions was well known. Whenever possible he avoided the physical restrictions of dress clothes and crowded rooms, and the mental inhibitions of the obsession with class that his father had allowed to throttle his freedom. An aspect of this bohemianism that went deeper was his interest in women who had never been constricted by middle-class upbringing. A boy who crept out of his father's house when the family were in bed would have had many opportunities to get to know them.

Yet Caroline, even if not entirely respectable, could give a convincing representation of middle-class propriety. One of Wilkie's 1857 contributions to *Household Words*, 'A Journey in Search of Nothing', gave a humorous account of the author's attempt at a rest-cure in the country, on doctor's orders, with his wife. Wilkie used many personae for his *Household Words* pieces, of all ages, both sexes, and varied marital status; but in this article the circumstantial detail sounds convincing. It suggests that even though he was not living exclusively with Caroline, he was spending a considerable amount of time with her, and observing her with affectionate amusement.

> She has got a strip of calico, or something of that sort, punched all over with little holes, and she is sewing round each little hole with her needle and thread. Monotonous, to a masculine mind. Surely the punching of the holes must be the pleasantest part of this sort of work? And that is done at the shop, is it dear? How curious!
>
> Does my wife lace too tight? . . . I have been uncritically contented hitherto, to take her waist for granted. Now I have my doubts about it. I think the wife of my bosom is a little too much like an hour-glass. Does

* In 1898 Harriet Graves wrote to A. P. Watt, 'May I send you a lot of MSs notes & books of our dear Wilkie's, & ask you . . . whether I may destroy them and if they are worth anything. Do you think the letters he wrote to us during his American Tour, would be of any value . . .?' (Berg Collection, NYPL)

> she digest? Good Heavens! In the existing state of her stays, how do I know whether she digests? ('A Journey in Search of Nothing', *Household Words*, 5 September 1857)

One of his earliest contributions to *All the Year Round*, 'A New View of Society', hints at his delight in the double life he was leading. Wilkie tells how, getting ready for an evening party in a heatwave, he suddenly revolted against 'the hideous habilimentary instruments of torture which Society . . . expected me to put on' and the 'refinement of slow torture unknown to the Inquisition and the North American savages . . . the name of it in England is Pleasure'. Instead of going to the party, he put on comfortable clothes and went to stand outside the house where he should have been dining, joining an admiring group of the working class peering in through the uncurtained windows.

> There they were, all oozing away into silence and insensibility together; smothered in their heavy black coats, and strangled in their stiff white cravats!
>
> There is a fourth place vacant . . . *My* place . . . I see my own ghost sitting there: the appearance of that perspiring spectre is too dreadful to be described. I shudder . . . as I survey my own full-dressed Fetch at the dinner-table – I turn away my face in terror, and look for comfort at my street-companions, my worthy fellow-outcasts.

'In the course of a long experience of Society', Wilkie concluded, 'I never enjoyed any party half as much as I have enjoyed this'.[20]

His arrangement with Caroline Graves seems to have been enjoyable in the same way: an escape from the politely perspiring 'Fetch' that middle-class society mistook for Wilkie Collins. If the arrangement closed some 'Society' doors to him, so much the better. He continued to spend long periods staying with Dickens and other friends; he could dine anywhere he wished. With his closest male friends, Dickens, Pigott, Charles and Ned Ward, Frederick Lehmann, Caroline was often present. But she was not included in Wilkie's invitations to Gad's Hill, or to Nina and Frederick Lehmann's house, where Wilkie was treated as a valued and petted bachelor; though Nina, as well as Frederick, was well aware of her existence. Caroline may have resented this, but for the time being she accepted it, allowing Wilkie to continue the easygoing way of life he had enjoyed with his mother. That would probably have ended, even without the complication of his relationship with Caroline. Harriet was now spending much time outside London staying with friends, the Combes at Oxford, the Bullars and Otters in Hampshire. She was still determined to move permanently to the country.

Wilkie's relationship with Caroline gave him, at the lowest estimate, a sexual partner, a housekeeper and a comfortable home to work in. Probably it gave him a great deal more. His hesitant approach to setting up house with Caroline and his refusal to marry her may not seem the actions of a man overcome by passion. But his quiet but steady defiance of family and friends, his lifelong attachment to her and the way in which he took responsibility for her and her daughter do suggest that he was, in his own way, in love. Holman Hunt explained his attitude in cautious and roundabout terms in his memoirs: '. . . Wilkie was entirely without ambition to take a place in the competition of society, and avoided plans of life that necessitated the making up of his mind enough to forecast the future. In this respect he left all to circumstance.'[21]

Wilkie, though he was still living, or partly living, at Harley Place throughout 1858, was out of London for much of the year. He was unwell in the spring, and went to the country on doctor's orders, no doubt with Caroline to look after him. He had a new serial novel to write, originally destined for *Household Words*, 'the plan of which is all drawn out' – the first mention of *The Woman in White.*[22] He spent much of July and August in seaside lodgings at 3 Prospect Place, Broadstairs. Charley was with him; and with Pigott and another old friend, the barrister Henry Bullar, they hired a lugger and sailed across to Dunkirk. There is no mention of Caroline's presence in Wilkie's letters, but a *Household Words* article about the holiday is written as if by a married man, and she and her daughter were surely part of the household. Dickens wrote hoping that he was enjoying himself, 'holding on by your great advance in health – and getting into the condition, physically, of Ben Caunt* – morally of William Shakespeare'.[23] (Was Dickens suggesting that Wilkie might, like

* A famous pugilist who had fought his last big fight the year before.

Shakespeare, find himself reluctantly manoeuvred into marriage?)

Wilkie was never estranged from his family, though the reaction of Walter Hartright's mother and sister to his life in lodgings with Laura Glyde and Marian Halcombe suggests Harriet Collins' attitude to the new arrangement: '[They] believed me to be the dupe of an adventuress and the victim of a fraud . . . the painful necessity which that prejudice imposed on me of concealing my marriage from them till they had learned to do justice to my wife . . . added to my anxieties and embittered my disappointments.'[24] But he called frequently at Clarence Terrace, and used it as an address when he wrote to family friends and slight acquaintances.[25] Business letters, when a prompt answer was important, came from his real address.

Why Wilkie did not marry Caroline Graves, although they lived together quite openly, sometimes passing for man and wife, will remain a mystery. It has been suggested that he may have suffered an unhappy love affair which made him decide never to marry. Thomas Seccombe in the *Directory of National Biography* referred to 'intimacies formed as a young man [which] led to his being harassed, after he became famous, in a manner very prejudicial to his peace of mind'. It has also been supposed that he contracted an early secret marriage, like the one in *Basil*. No record of such a marriage has been discovered.

Wilkie was, it is true, vehemently opposed to marriage. In an article for *Household Words* written at the end of 1856 he gave some of his rational reasons for avoiding the married state, complaining, perhaps with Millais in mind, that new wives often tried to estrange their husbands from their old male friends:

> the general idea of the scope and purpose of the institution of marriage is a miserably narrow one. The same senseless prejudice which leads some people, when driven to extremes, to the practical confession (though it may not be made in plain words) that they would rather see murder committed under their own eyes, than approve of any project for obtaining a law of divorce which shall be equal in its operation on husbands and wives of all ranks who cannot live together, is answerable also for the mischievous error in principle of narrowing the practice of the social virtues, in married people, to themselves and their children . . . The social advantages which [marriage] is fitted to produce ought to extend beyond one man and one woman, to the circle of society amid

> which they move. ('Bold Words by a Bachelor', *Household Words*, 13 December 1856)

Yet he settled down to a domestic existence with Caroline, complete with a much-loved adopted child, which was a marriage in all but name. It was a situation very different from Dickens' carefully guarded secret life with Ellen Ternan. Though Caroline's class and background might have made her unacceptable to Harriet Collins as a daughter-in-law, Harriet, who had herself married against her mother-in-law's wishes, would surely have preferred an unfortunate marriage to an illicit union. Even if Caroline had been forced, either through poverty or by a lover, into prostitution, Wilkie was one of the few Victorians who would not have hesitated to marry a 'fallen woman', as several of his heroes do. Indeed, such a history would probably have added to Caroline's fascination for him. But where his characters made wives of their Magdalens, Wilkie did not.

As Wilkie well knew, there were many other irregular unions in Victorian society, and by no means all of them in bohemian artistic circles. At one time and another during his life his personal friends were involved in clandestine marriages, irregular marriages, bigamous marriages, an annulment, an ecclesiastical and a Scotch divorce. There were illegitimate children, some acknowledged, some not. Highly respectable couples, such as George Eliot and George Lewes, lived openly 'in sin'. M. E. Braddon lived with the publisher John Maxwell and bore him six children, also bringing up the five he already had, writing a string of best-sellers and editing his magazines. Charles Reade, who had an illegitimate son by an earlier liaison, possibly an irregular marriage, lived with the actress Laura Seymour. But Charles Reade did not want to lose his Magdalen Fellowship; John Maxwell had, like Thackeray, a mad wife; and Lewes' condoning of his wife's adultery with Thornton Leigh Hunt had made a divorce impossible to get. Wilkie set his face against the institution of marriage itself.

He was not alone. The long section on prostitutes in the fourth volume of Mayhew's *London Labour and the London Poor*, added in 1862, includes a passage that describes his position exactly:

> It is frequently a matter of surprise amongst the friends of a gentleman of position and connections that he exhibits an invincible distaste

> to marriage. If they were acquainted with his private affairs their astonishment would speedily vanish, for they would find him to all intents and purposes united to one who possesses charms, talents, and accomplishments . . . the prevalence of this custom, and the extent of its ramifications is hardly dreamed of . . . The torch of Hymen burns less brightly than of yore . . . (Henry Mayhew, *London Labour and the London Poor*, Vol. 4, p. 215)

Whatever his reasons for not marrying her, there was certainly something about Caroline that Wilkie found delightful and everyone else deplored. What it was can only be guessed at. It cannot have been her age or her appearance that shocked his friends. She was beautiful. In 1860, when she was nearly thirty, and Wilkie an increasingly invalidish thirty-six, Dickens referred to her jokingly as her daughter's elder sister. She knocked four or five years off her age – the years she preferred to forget, between the death of George Graves and her association with Wilkie – with no difficulty. She gave her age as twenty-six in the 1861 census, and stuck to the revision for the rest of her life.[26] She clearly had a chameleon-like ability to adapt to improved circumstances, even if an innate vulgarity still showed through. Frederick Lehmann's account of an evening he and his brother, the painter Rudolf Lehmann, spent with Wilkie and Caroline in 1866 suggests there was still a flavour of the *demi-monde* about her, a *Dame aux Camélias* performance. Lehmann's tone, in a letter to his wife, is amused rather than censorious:

> Mrs. Graves and Wilkie insisted on Rudolf and me dining at 9 Melcombe Place, which we have just done and a capital dinner she gave us. She had cooked most of it herself I am sure, but you would not have guessed it from her very décolleté white silk gown. She seemed immensely taken with Rudolf. Wilkie was delightful as usual, and sends you no end of love.[27]

It may have been Caroline's capacity for fantasizing, and her refusal to be honest about her past in spite of the evidence, that originally antagonized his friends and intrigued Wilkie. She seems to have had a precarious hold on 'the real' and 'the true', the everyday facts that Wilkie so stoutly insisted on in his prefaces, and so effectively undermined in his novels. The difference between

Caroline's accounts of herself and the reality, evidenced by her adjustments to the public records, suggest a fantasist with the power to invent and reinvent her identity. As a portrait of a lady, she was a beautiful fake.

It is possible that Caroline took on the role of the wicked queen, or spider-woman, in Wilkie's private mythology: the fascinating and beautiful woman who devours the innocent man who marries her. The pattern was already established in his fiction. Margaret in *Basil* and the wife in 'The Dream Woman' are the prototypes; Magdalen Vanstone and Lydia Gwilt were yet to come. Their victims sense the danger, yet they cannot keep away. Caroline may have borne little relationship to such women in reality; but the other self, who haunted the unpretentious, delightful companion that Wilkie's friends saw and loved, both needed and feared an equivalent. But not in marriage. That was the final trap, the oubliette that would swallow up and destroy the imaginative self.

There was probably a row of tremendous proportions with his mother over his new domestic arrangements. Harriet must have said, 'Never mention that woman's name to me!', for Wilkie never alludes to Caroline in his frequent letters to his mother. He writes always 'I' rather than 'we' when he is travelling with Caroline; and there is an unexplained gap, between June 1858 and July 1859, in the sequence of letters to Harriet, possibly due to censorship. Kate Perugini called her former mother-in-law 'a devil'; Caroline's view of Harriet might well have been even more outspoken. But there are, from 1859 onwards, many references to Caroline in Wilkie's letters to friends. Charles Collins often stayed with them, as did many of Wilkie's male friends. She became known to his intimates as an accepted part of his life, who acted as his hostess and housekeeper, made him comfortable and tended him when he was ill; she accompanied him on journeys both in England and on the Continent. Whatever her significance for his imaginative life, she functioned admirably as a common-law wife, rather than a disreputable mistress.

It was during the years that Wilkie was most closely involved with Caroline that he wrote his great novels of the 1860s, *The Woman in White*, *No Name*, *Armadale* and *The Moonstone*. He was already intrigued by questions of identity, substitution and doubling. These novels are developments of trends already mapped out in his fiction, and in line with the fashion for sensation. But to meet in real life someone willing, even eager, to live out his fantasies intensified his imaginative identification. To lead a double life with a woman herself precariously poised between two identities was to defy the critics who called his fiction immoral, or far-fetched. The King of Inventors had discovered, or invented, his queen.

Wilkie's relationship with Caroline's daughter Harriet, who was about five years old when he first met her mother, was the more straightforward one of an affectionate father. His fondness for children, and his childlike capacity to take part in their games and interests, were remembered by many of the children of his friends. The reminiscence of Frederick and Nina Lehmann's son Rudy is typical:

> our dear old Wilkie Collins, the kindest and best friend that boy or man ever had. Wilkie – we never called him by any more formal name, even when we were little fellows – had known my mother before her marriage, and to us boys and to our sister he soon grew to be what he ever afterwards remained: not merely the grown-up and respected friend of our parents, but our own true companion and close associate.[28]

He loved to give children presents and tell them spellbinding stories. He took them to Astley's circus or the pantomime. He even helped them with their homework, once producing an elegant verse translation of an ode by Horace: typically, he undermined authority by showing how satisfactorily this could be done from a crib, not the original Latin. He had a sensitive understanding of their feelings, and took great care not to hurt them, as Nathaniel Beard, the son of Dickens' and Wilkie's doctor Frank Beard, recollected. Nat had been sent to Harley Street by his father, to deliver a note to Wilkie, but found he had forgotten to bring it:

> I was ushered as usual into Wilkie's room, and said to him, 'I've brought you a letter.' Then, fumbling in my pocket, 'Oh, I say, I've left it behind! Never mind. You write the answer while I go back and fetch the letter.' It was exactly characteristic of the man that he never even laughed, but said quite gravely, 'Very well, but it will be rather difficult, perhaps you

had better bring the note round first.' He was too considerate to turn my youthful 'bull' into ridicule to my face . . .[29]

Wilkie, who stood godfather to many of his friends' children, took the secular side of his duties, at least, seriously. Alice Ward was an especial favourite, to whom he wrote letters and sent loving messages. 'I shall be almost afraid to look at my god-daughter. Is she a Young Lady yet? And has she got taller than a certain middle-aged gentleman who answered for her at the baptismal font?'[30] When she became a 'Young Lady', he sent her a pair of earrings to wear at her first ball, 'as some assistance to you in "renouncing the pomps and vanities of this wicked world" '.[31] But he continued to disapprove of some aspects of the youngladyfication of girl children. 'I hope you are not going to take the devil out of that girl,' he objected when Frank Beard's daughter was reproved at the dinner table, and he told Nina Lehmann that her daughter, being 'finished' in Paris, 'must remain like herself'.[32]

It was to Carrie, as Wilkie always called Harriet Graves, that he was the closest of all. He informally adopted her, speaking of her as his adopted daughter; she called him 'godfather'. Writing to her after Wilkie's death, his old friend George Redford, a fellow-contributor to *The Leader*, remembered, 'when you were a wee little thing I witnessed his signing his will'.[33] The implication is that she was even then a beneficiary. He paid for her to be well educated: her mother's longing to be a lady was fulfilled for her daughter. When Wilkie had children of his own Carrie still remained his eldest daughter. She on her side was always fiercely loyal to the man who had brought her up. She seems, at the time Wilkie first knew her, to have been a remarkably stable child, in spite of her early experiences, and plump and cheerful. Dickens, meeting Carrie for the first time at Broadstairs in the summer of 1859, was delighted by her, played card tricks to amuse her, and invented a nickname for her. Carrie seems to have been in an evangelical phase not very acceptable to Wilkie or Caroline, which Dickens found irresistibly comic. 'I am charmed by the Butler. O why was she stopped! Ask her flinty mother from me, why, why, didn't she let her convert somebody! And here the question arises – did she secretly convert the Landlord?'[34]

Whether Carrie converted the landlord or not, she certainly did not convert Wilkie. Instead he converted her: to an easygoing and relaxed way of life that could accommodate the unconventional. He saw to it that she had a happy childhood, as secure as his had been, but also blessedly free from the shadow of religious and social anxiety that his father had hung around him in his youth.

TWELVE

The Woman in White

(1859–1860)

Wilkie was the only friend asked to spend Dickens' birthday with him and 'the girls' in 1859. 'I have not had the heart to make any preparation for it – you know why', Dickens wrote.[1] Wilkie was closely involved with Dickens' personal and business life at this time. When Dickens closed down *Household Words* and launched *All the Year Round* (Forster dissuaded him from calling it, with Inimitable defiance of the scandal, *Household Harmony*), Wills and Wilkie went with him, and it was Wills and Wilkie, not Forster, who witnessed the contract for publishing the magazine in the United States.[2] Wilkie contributed articles to the last number of *Household Words*, and the first of *All the Year Round*, but Dickens now proposed a more important role for him.

Dickens had made the important, and, it turned out, the correct decision that a serial novel by a well-known, named author should always be the first item in the new magazine. He would begin himself, with the story that had come to him as he lay acting the death of Richard Wardour, *A Tale of Two Cities*. Wilkie would follow him with a new novel in the autumn.

Wilkie returned to Broadstairs in the summer to prepare his novel. This time he took a whole house, the isolated and peaceful Church Hill Cottage on the Ramsgate Road, renting it for six weeks, complete with servants. He found it horrifyingly expensive: 'A skinny little chicken is three and sixpence – meat equally dear – vegetables three times the London price – my landlord won't draw me a bucket of water without being paid for it . . .'[3] Wilkie was discovering the expenses that went with family life: the weekly bills made his hair stand on end, he told Charles Ward, asking him to bring down the money due to him from *All The Year Round* – his salary was now six guineas a week – and from other sources. 'I used to disbelieve in Hell. I believe in it now, because I know of no other place, after this life, which will be hot enough to do full justice to the British tradesman.'

Charley was again with them for several weeks, and Charles Ward came to visit: '. . . you and I will go out and hold divine service on the ocean, on Sunday', Wilkie suggested. Dickens spent a few days at a nearby inn, and saw a good deal of Wilkie and his household, but Wilkie's writing always came first. He was hard at work, 'slowly and painfully launching my new serial novel. The story is the longest and most complicated I have ever tried yet – and the difficulties at the beginning of it are all but insuperable'.[4]

Much of the preliminary planning had already been done, and existed in note form, for Wilkie prided himself on never being a hand-to-mouth serial writer.

> Neither 'The Woman in White', nor any other of my serial stories, were completed in manuscript before their periodical publication. I was consequently *obliged* to know every step of my way from beginning to end, before I started on my journey.
>
> . . . When I sat down to write the seventh *weekly part* of 'The Woman in White,' the first weekly part was being published in 'All the Year Round' and in 'Harper's Weekly'. No afterthoughts . . . were possible under these circumstances . . . months before a line of it was written for the press, I ws accumulating . . . a mass of 'notes' which contained a complete outline of the story and the characters. I knew what Sir Percival Glyde was going to do with the marriage register, and how Count Fosco's night at the opera was to be spoiled by the appearance of Professor Pesca, before a line of the book was in the printer's hands.[5]

Wilkie gave several accounts of the genesis and writing of *The Woman in White*, all remarkably consistent, and all uncharacteristically concerned to minimize the sensational. First came the central idea, then the characters, then the incidents, which had to arise naturally from the characters; finally he must 'begin the story at the beginning'.[6] The 'central idea' of *The Woman in White* he identified as 'a conspiracy in private life, in which circumstances are so handled as to rob a woman of her identity by confounding her with another woman, sufficiently like her in personal appearance to answer the wicked purpose'.[7] There is no mention of a meeting with a distraught woman in Regent's Park: the emphasis instead is on the documentary sources of the plot, and the way in which the characters developed naturally out of the needs of the story, and the details of the story from the development of the characters. By his own account, the germ of the plot was extracted from 'some dilapidated volumes of French crimes' picked up on a bookstall in Paris. 'The plot . . . has been called outrageous . . . It was true, and it was from the trial of the villain of the plot – Count Fosco of the novel – I got my story.'[8] The volumes have been identified as *Recueil des Causes Célèbres*, by Maurice Méjan, and the plot of *The Woman in White* as taken from the late-eighteenth-century case of Madame de Douhault, imprisoned in the lunatic asylum of the Salpêtrière by her heirs, and presumed dead. She managed to escape with the help of a friend, but never succeeded in re-establishing her legal identity.[9]

The characters his imagination evolved from this central idea started with the major villain, Count Fosco, and the first victim, Laura Glyde.

> I try to discover the other – and fail. I try what a walk will do for me – and fail. Experience now tells me to take no more trouble about it, and leave that other woman to come of her own accord. The next morning, before I have been awake in my bed for more than ten minutes, my perverse brains set to work without consulting me. Poor Anne Catherick comes into the room and says, 'try me.'[10]

Wilkie emphasized the importance of getting the beginning right, of keeping 'the story always advancing, without paying the smallest attention to the serial division in parts, or to the book publication in volumes', and deciding on the end.

> All this is done, as my father used to paint his skies in his famous sea-pieces, at one heat. As yet I do not enter into details; I merely

> set up my landmarks. In doing this the main situations of the story present themselves; and at the same time I see my characters in all sorts of new aspects. These discoveries lead me nearer and nearer to finding the right end. The end being decided on, I go back again to the beginning, and look at it with a new eye, and fail to be satisfied with it. I have yielded to the worst temptation that besets a novelist – the temptation to begin with a striking incident, without counting the cost in the shape of explanations that must and will follow. These pests of fiction, to reader and writer alike, can only be eradicated in one way . . . to begin at the beginning. In the case of 'The Woman in White' I get back (as I vainly believe) to the true starting point of the story.[11]

It was a false start. The first draft of the novel began in Cumberland, with Mr Fairlie, Laura Glyde and Marian Halcombe all awaiting the arrival of Walter Hartright. Wilkie realized that he must somehow introduce Anne Catherick at the very beginning; for a week he could not see how it was to be done. Then he read a newspaper account, 'a paragraph of a few lines only', of a lunatic escaped from an asylum. 'Instantly the idea comes to me of Walter Hartright's midnight meeting with Anne Catherick . . . The Woman in White begins again'.

The new beginning created one of the most famous fictional episodes ever written: the dramatic appearance of the woman in white on the Hampstead road.

> There, in the middle of the broad, bright high-road – there, as if it had that moment sprung out of the earth or dropped from the heaven – stood the figure of a solitary Woman, dressed from head to foot in white garments; her face bent in grave enquiry on mine, her hand pointing to the dark cloud over London, as I faced her.[12]

Dickens considered it one of the two most dramatic scenes in literature, the other being Carlyle's account of the march of the women to Versailles in *The French Revolution*. Admirers of his own novels might add a third, the sudden appearance of Magwich to Pip at the beginning of *Great Expectations*.

The difficulties of beginning were at last overcome, with a mass of overscoring and rewriting which made it difficult for even the author to decipher what he had written. But the title was still elusive. Wilkie claimed that he did not hit on the title until 'after the story had been finished, and part of it had been set in proof for serial publication. Literally, at the eleventh hour, I thought of "The Woman in White".'[13] But a letter to W. H. Wills of 15 August shows that dramatic licence is at work here:

> I send enclosed (and registered – for I should go distracted if it was lost) my first number. Please let me have duplicate proofs as soon as possible, for I want to see something in connection with the story which is not a mass of confusion. It is an awfully long number – between 8 and 9 pages; but I *must* stagger the public into attention, if possible, at the outset. They shan't drop a number, when I begin, if *I* can help it.
>
> I have hit on a new title, in the course of a night-walk to the North Foreland, which seems to me weird and striking:
>
> THE WOMAN IN WHITE.[14]

Wilkie's account of how the title came to him involves the North Foreland lighthouse: '. . . he apostrophized the building, standing coldly and stiffly in the evening light. "You are ugly and stiff and awkward; you know you are: as stiff and as weird as my white woman. White woman! – woman in white!" '[15] The lighthouse may have brought back memories of his first play. The story 'Gabriel's Marriage', on which *The Lighthouse* was based, contains this melodramatic passage:

> 'The White Women!' he screamed. 'The White Women! the gravediggers of the drowned are out on the sea! . . . You'll see them bright as lightning in the darkness, mighty as the angels in stature, sweeping like the wind over the sea, in their long white garments, with their white hair trailing far behind them!' (*Household Words* 7 (16 April 1855), p. 151)

Wilkie had come a long way since that was written.

'I have not the slightest doubt that The Woman in White is the name of names, and very title of titles', Dickens wrote enthusiastically as soon as Wilkie's first instalment arrived in the office. Others were not so positive. Wilkie remembered that John Forster and everyone else hated it. No matter. With Dickens to back him, and his own growing self-confidence, he pressed on, sticking to his desk from ten until two or three every day. He was, as so often, ill – this time 'suffering torments with a *boil between* my legs', which had to be lanced by the local doctor. The infection took months to clear up: back in London in October Wilkie was still complaining, 'I have had my old torment in the *sac* since I saw you and have never stirred outside the door.'[16] The time at Broadstairs cannot have been the most cheerful of holidays for Caroline, or for the eight-year-old Carrie, whose experiences may have inspired those of Kitty in *The Evil Genius*, the daughter of a divorcée who can't understand why other children are not allowed to come to her party. On top of everything else, Wilkie was 'at mortal enmity with my London landlord, and am resolved to leave him'.[17] Perhaps he was finding there were more complications to his unconventional ménage than he had foreseen.

He was back in London for the publication of a further collection of short stories, *The Queen of Hearts*, in October: Hurst & Blackett in London, and Harper's in New York, now his regular publishers in the United States, brought out simultaneous editions. The stories, all previously published, were strung together on a Scheherazade story in reverse: three old brothers, a clergyman, a doctor and a lawyer, living in an isolated Scottish house, endeavour to entertain a lively young woman and keep her from leaving by telling her stories. She expresses Wilkie's own credo, in suitably forthright terms:

> 'I'm sick to death of novels with an earnest purpose. I'm sick to death of outbursts of eloquence, and large-minded philanthropy, and graphic descriptions, and unsparing anatomy of the human heart, and all that sort of thing . . . isn't it the original intention, or purpose, or whatever you call it, of a work of fiction to set out distinctly by telling a story? . . . what I want is something . . . that keeps me reading, reading, reading, in a breathless state to find out the end.' (*The Queen of Hearts*, Vol. I, pp. 95–96)

The stories are assigned to whichever brother might most plausibly have heard or experienced them. Two, 'The Black Cottage' and 'The Diary of Anne Rodway', are told in the first person by poor working girls. The narrator of 'The Black Cottage' (first published in 1857) is the daughter of a stonemason, the occupation of Caroline's father-in-law. She holds views on the reality of the lives of the poor that, while hardly original, have the ring of experience: 'It is one thing to write fine sentiments in books about uncorruptible honesty, and another thing to put those sentiments in practice, when one day's work is all that a man has to set up in the way of an obstacle between starvation and his own fireside'; 'Timidity is thought rather a graceful attraction among ladies, but among poor women it is something to be laughed at.'[18]

The Queen of Hearts is a highly readable collection of stories, and the formula of the linking narrative, giving unity to the disparate tales, works well. But a grudging critic in the *Saturday Review* complained, 'we cannot agree . . . that this art of setting and solving a puzzle is anything like the ideal of a novelist . . . Mr. Collins constructs his machinery well, but he never rises above machinist. He avoids entirely drawing character.'[19] The novel that was to contradict that kind of criticism was already on its way to the public.

The Woman in White was not an unexpected best-seller by an unknown author: Wilkie Collins had already been described, with some hyperbole, as 'a man of commanding genius, and one destined to occupy a principal place in the republic of letters'.[20] But it did far outstrip his earlier successes, to become one of the best-known novels of the nineteenth century. The successful integration of various levels of significance in the story, as in a myth or folk tale, suggests possible interpretations, not mutually exclusive, which seem almost infinite: '. . . the form of the novel is plainly less dependent on plot than it is usually thought to be; its development is as much by symbolic counterpoint as by linear progression'.[21]

English novelists and their readers seem to have been more than usually intrigued at the end of the 1850s and throughout the 1860s by the questioning of identity which had always fascinated Wilkie Collins. Who am I? was asked indirectly in dozens of novels involving a double, or shadow-self, in which legal and psychological identity was in doubt. The fear of losing complete possession of oneself is a fundamental one; but it often carries with it a secret sense of exhilaration. To be another person, for a while at least, can be liberating as well as terrifying. Both the fear and the exhilaration are used, in differing proportions, in Wilkie Collins' fiction. Few writers have conveyed the terror more effectively than he did in *The Woman in White*.

A Tale of Two Cities, concluded in the 26 November number of *All the Year Round*, used the substitution fantasy for a positive purpose. Sidney Carton, the character Dickens had invented while playing Wilkie's Richard Wardour, can sacrifice himself in place of Charles Darnay because he is his double.* *The Woman in White*, begun in the same number, also turns on a question of identity, this time that of a young woman. But instead of Carton's noble abnegation which saves his soul – his inner identity – and ensures his survival in the hearts of Lucy and Darnay, Laura Fairlie has her identity forcibly stolen from her. Largely because she *is* a woman, and after marriage legally helpless, she becomes a non-person, rather than a different person.

The connection with *A Tale of Two Cities* is probably accidental: *The Woman in White* owes little to Dickens or any other English writer. But it spawned a school of imitators whose productions, labelled 'sensation novels', were grouped into a genre deplored as a new literary and social phenomenon: 'the morbid phenomena of literature – indications of a wide-spread corruption . . . called into existence to supply the cravings of a diseased appetite'.[22] The sensation novel was defined as one in which incident took precedence over character, and criminal activity, particularly violent and sexual crime such as murder or bigamy, took place in a contemporary, domestic, middle-class setting. Whatever the outcome of the novel (and in many of them the good ended as happily and the bad as unhappily as Miss Prism would have thought proper), the assumptions of the Victorian bourgeoisie about the sanctity of home, the purity of woman, the distinction between the respectable and the criminal classes, were at least put in question. It is a potentially subversive genre, and the spokesmen (and women) for respectable society reacted by claiming that the stories were unreal as well as melodramatic, written to meet the coarse taste of an audience of servants in back-kitchens.

The Woman in White lacks one ingredient common to many of its imitators, and used in several of Wilkie Collins' own later novels: the criminal or near-criminal heroine. Margaret Oliphant, herself a

* Fred Kaplan sees Carton and Darnay as 'an antiphonal self-portrait' of Dickens.

novelist, and an influential critic who disliked the genre, saw that *The Woman in White* had more to offer:

> Its power arises from no overstraining of nature: – the artist shows no love of mystery for mystery's sake; he wastes neither wickedness nor passion. His plot is astute and deeply-laid, but never weird or ghastly . . . The more we perceive the perfectly legitimate nature of the means used to produce the sensation, the more striking does that sensation become . . . It is this which gives to his book the qualities of a new beginning in fiction.[23]

The Woman in White still makes its impact as an ingenious crime and mystery novel. Though it gradually becomes clear to the reader that there are several mysteries to be uncovered, and each clarification leads cunningly to a further mystification, the story drives ahead without pausing. There is no sub-plot, no set of subsidiary characters whose antics supply diversion and entertainment: an apparently comic character such as Professor Pesca has a vital role to play. A contemporary suggested, 'It is not the plot or the style which constitutes the fascination of this book. It is the full possession of . . . the power of throwing down . . . a hundred incidents which appear to be perfectly unconnected, and gradually gathering them together to produce the circumstantial or cumulative evidence which removes a veil from a great mystery . . . This is to possess the legal mind in one of its most remarkable qualities, which, after all, is essentially dependent upon the imaginative faculty . . .'[24]

Dickens, though he thought the novel 'a very great advance on all your former writing' and that 'no one else could do it half so well', did not wholly endorse the legal mind at work in it: '. . . the great pains you take express themselves a trifle too much, and you know that I always contest your disposition to give an audience credit for nothing . . . the three people who write the narratives in these proofs have a DISSECTIVE property in common, which is essentially not theirs but yours . . . my own effort would be to strike more of what is got *that way* out of them by collision with one another, and by the working of the story.'[25] This was a counterblast to some criticisms by Wilkie of *A Tale of Two Cities*, which Dickens rejected: 'It would have been overdone in that manner – too elaborately trapped, baited and prepared . . .'.[26] Thackeray, who loved a good story, had no such reservations. He remembered a day's illness made happy by reading it. 'No cares: no remorse about idleness: no visitors: and the Woman in White or the Chevalier D'Artagnan to tell me stories from dawn to night! "Please, ma'am, my master's compliments, and can he have the third volume?" (This message was sent to an astonished friend and neighbour who lent me, volume by volume, the *W. in W.*)'[27]

But *The Woman in White* is more than an exciting mystery. Margaret Oliphant found that 'it was having it thrown in my way a second time which attracted so strongly my technical admiration'.[28] Edward Fitzgerald, who thought of calling a sailing lugger after the 'brave Girl' Marian Halcombe, read it, or had it read to him, at least five times. A mere thriller would hardly bear this constant re-reading. The careful construction and narrative method, the 'experiment' that cost Wilkie Collins so much labour in the early stages, is, as he saw, essential for the book's success. Hartright's authenticity as the primary narrator is supported by the multiple-narrative, 'documentary' formula: his quasi-legal function as the collector and arranger of the narratives of others gives him a status this rather boring and stuffy young man would otherwise lack. 'As the Judge might once have heard it, so the Reader shall hear it now.'[29] The technique achieves both vividness and neutrality. Dickens later thought that Wilkie's repeated use of eye-witness narrative became formulaic and stale. But the absence of authorial moral judgement in *The Woman in White* upholds democratic values against authoritarian and aristocratic ones, and Wilkie's hold on his readers was strengthened by the modesty and lack of pretension of the narrative: the author plays neither advocate nor judge.

The technique recalls the narrative of *Wuthering Heights*; and as in Emily Brontë's novel the personalities of the narrators and the absence of comment naturalize the strange and lurid events described, leading the reader by gradual stages into a more and more bizarre world. In *The Woman in White* as in *Wuthering Heights*, an orderly world is disrupted by an anarchic figure whose disreputable alternative can seem powerfully attractive, as well as dangerous. Fosco is a link between the claustrophobic world of English domestic crime and a wider one of political intrigue and violence that was very much in the mind of the reading public. London was full of Neapolitan political exiles, conspirators and spies in 1859. (The following year Wilkie met one of Garibaldi's sons at Monckton Milnes' house. He found him 'a remarkably stupid boy'.[30]) More threateningly, Fosco is undermining the domestic world from within. He is challenging as well as warning Marian, whom he admires for her courage and unconventionality, when he advises her to stay within acceptable female boundaries:

> 'Exercise your fine natural sense, and remain in retirement. Dear and admirable woman! invite no dangerous publicity. Resignation is sublime – adopt it. The modest repose of home is eternally fresh – enjoy it. The Storms of life pass harmless over the valley of Seclusion – dwell, dear lady in the valley.' (*The Woman in White*, p. 412)

But the 'modest repose of home', the traditional domestic safety zone, has already been shown to be anything but safe, as Henry James saw: 'What are the Apennines to us, or we to the Apennines? Instead of the terrors of *Udolpho,* we were treated to the terrors of the cheerful country-house and the busy London lodgings. And there is no doubt that these were infinitely the more terrible.'[31] The separate worlds of male and female, public and private, good and evil, black and white, are infiltrated and insidiously merged throughout *The Woman in White.*

For this to be convincing, credible characterization was vital, as Wilkie knew. Thanking Edward Pigott for a friendly notice of the first three numbers, he wrote, '. . . it hits the point (in reference to the nonsense talked in certain quarters about my incapacity of character-painting) so cleverly, that I shall take it as the text of what I have to say for myself in the preface . . .'.[32] The characters in *The Woman in White* are a mixture of imagination and portraiture, literature and life. Though Wilkie Collins once said that 'Fosco is not modelled on any one or any half-dozen persons', he also wrote, 'many models, some living, and some dead, have "sat" for Fosco'.[33] Part of the secret of the success of the mountainous, ingenious mouse and canary fancier, with the animal sexual magnetism that alternately attracts and repels his opposite number Marian Halcombe, may lie in Wilkie's identification with him: Fosco holds many of his own beliefs and opinions. As Thackeray put some of his less acceptable ideas about society into the mouth of Becky Sharp, Wilkie acknowledged that he was attacking, through Fosco, 'the vulgar clap-trap that "murder will out"'. He also used Fosco to express some of his own feelings about the relativity of moral standards:

> 'I am a citizen of the world, and I have met, in my time, with so many different sorts of virtue, that I am puzzled, in my old age, to say which is the right sort and which is the wrong. Here, in England, there is one virtue. And there, in China, there is another virtue. And John Englishman says my virtue is the genuine virtue. And John Chinaman says my virtue is the genuine virtue. And I say Yes to one, or No to the other, and am just as much bewildered about it in the case of John with the top-boots as I am in the case of John with the pigtail.' (*The Woman in White*, p. 211)

Fosco claims that 'English society . . . is as often the accomplice, as it is the enemy of crime', and objects to society's masks, '"I say what other people only think; and when all the rest of the world is in a conspiracy to accept the mask for the true face, mine is the rash hand that tears off the plump pasteboard, and shows the bare bones beneath."'[34] Such ideas are close to the opinions of his creator, and readers could have the pleasure of condemning Fosco while admitting that much of what he said made good sense. Fosco has many other resemblances to Wilkie. He is an animal lover. He is greedy, sensual and fond of flamboyant and unconventional clothes. He makes fun of English conventions, insisting on leaving the dinner table with the ladies. He is unfailingly polite, and superficially kind, though ruthlessly determined to get his own way. He is an admirer of clever women, and charms them with his conversation. As Marian confesses, 'Woman can resist a man's love, a man's fame, a man's personal appearance, and a man's money; but they cannot resist a man's tongue, when he knows how to talk to them.'[35] But of course Fosco is no more Wilkie than Becky Sharp is Thackeray: the many models include the villain of the Douhault case in Méjan, Napoleon Bonaparte and Henry VIII. His taste for unusual animals may have been suggested by Edward Pigott, who had acquired, in the summer of 1859, 'a bull-terrier puppy, a parrot, a spaniel, a goldfinch, and a wild black cat'.[36] He has some of the characteristics of Balzac's master-criminal Vautrin, and some, indeed, of Balzac himself. As

Wilkie wrote in his review of a biography of Balzac, one of his favourite authors:

> His personal appearance would have recalled to English minds the popular idea of Friar Tuck . . . But he had the eye of a man of genius, and the tongue of a certain infernal personage . . . The Balzac candlestick might be clumsy enough; but when once the Balzac candle was lit, the moths flew into it, only too readily, from all points of the compass.[37]

Wilkie insisted on a similar multiplicity of sources for Marian Halcombe, who was not an 'abstract personification of my own ideas' but originated in

> my own observation of many women who personally, morally, and mentally resemble her . . . A character in fiction can only be made true to the general experience of human nature, by a principle of selection which is broad enough to embrace many individuals who represent, more or less remarkably, one type. There are many 'Marian Halcombes' among us – and *my* Marian is one of the number.[38]

Hartright's description of Marian Halcombe's appearance recalls Henry James' view of another Marian, George Eliot, who was a friend of Wilkie's by 1858: 'She is magnificently ugly – deliciously hideous', he considered. 'Now in this vast ugliness resides a most powerful beauty, which . . . steals forth and charms the mind.'[39] Wilkie changed the colour of eyes and hair, making Marian dark, as a contrast to Laura and Anne Catherick; but he kept almost everything else that descriptions of George Eliot comment on: the heavy, masculine jaw, the charm of expression, the beautiful speaking voice and the good figure. Bessie Parkes remembered that 'Her height was good, her figure remarkably supple; at moments it had an almost serpentine grace.'[40] Marian Halcombe's unconventionally forthright conversation resembles the letters and journalism of another plain and witty friend, Frances Dickinson, and may also owe something to his friendship with Nina Lehmann, who fiercely proclaimed her inability to conform to feminine stereotypes. The role of the indispensable aunt that Marian insists on choosing at the end of the novel hints at Georgina Hogarth, who refused to marry Augustus Egg and remained a spinster aunt, bringing up the children of a loved brother-in-law.

The portrait of the hypochondriac Frederick Fairlie owes much to one original. He is an imaginative reconstruction, in everything but his heartless selfishness, of Chauncey Hare Townsend. The details of his Swiss valet, his collection of *bibelots*, drawings and jewels, his interest in photography, his hypochondria, even his effeminacy, are all drawn from Townsend, who was a source of private amusement to Dickens and Wilkie. Though Townsend had married, at the age of twenty-six, the marriage did not 'take', and was seldom referred to. 'To pass from the altar to Townsend (which is a long way) . . . [he] is mostly shut up in his beautiful house,' Dickens wrote to a friend in 1859.[41] And a description of Townsend remaining in his carriage on a cross-Channel steamer is even more evocative of Fairlie:

> I could not but mount the Royal Car . . . perforated in every direction with cupboards, containing every description of Physic, old brandy, East India Sherry, sandwiches, oranges, cordial waters, newspapers, pocket handkerchiefs, shawls, flannels, telescopes, compasses, repeaters (for ascertaining the hour in the dark), and finger rings of great value. He . . . asked me the extraordinary question 'how Mrs Williams, the American Actress, kept her wig on?' I then perceived that mankind was to be in a conspiracy to believe that he wears his own hair.[42]

Sir Percival Glyde, adequately but conventionally characterized as a particularly English type of shabby bully, cruel in speech and violent in action (not unlike the master who persecuted Wilkie at school), has the pernickety obsessional tidiness of Dickens himself. 'Sir Percival has already displayed a mania for order and regularity . . . If I take a book from the library and leave it on the table, he follows me, and puts it back again. If I rise from a chair, and let it remain where I have been sitting, he carefully restores it to its proper place against the wall.'[43] The generous, large-hearted Marian Halcombe is, by contrast, as untidy as Wilkie; she suspects someone may have tampered with her desk because her seal is, exceptionally, put away in the right place. Walter Hartright, with his conventional attitudes to God and women and his ponderous style, has a combination of insecurity and complacency reminiscent of William Collins, as well as a similar background. Hartright's mother, hearty and impulsive, younger in behaviour than her own daughter, is obviously based on

Harriet Collins; and the tiny Italian Professor Pesca on Professor Gabriele Rossetti.*

As for the woman in white herself, Anne Catherick's surname was taken from one of the only two Cathericks in the London Post Office Directory, both close to the Fitzroy Square area where Caroline Graves had lived.[44] There is a sense, more complex than the suspect Millais account of Wilkie's first meeting with her suggests, in which Caroline *is* the woman in white. She did acquire the nickname, among Wilkie's friends. In a revealing – perhaps too revealing – passage in the manuscript, deleted before publication, Walter Hartright, describing his love at first sight for Laura Fairlie, confesses:

> Lower her to the rank of her own maid, raise her to the pinnacle of the peerage; disguise the maid as a lady, or the peeress as a servant; and the eyes would still have spoken the same language when they met, and the pen I write with must still have traced the same three words. I loved her.[45]

Here the two women in white are merged, and the possibilities of disguise are raised at an early stage in the novel. The passage may have been deleted for this reason alone – that the plot was being too obviously foreshadowed. Or it may be that the substitution of Caroline Graves, the gentleman's daughter and officer's widow, for Elizabeth Graves, carpenter's daughter, penniless clerk's widow, marine-store keeper, distressed and forlorn, was in the forefront of Wilkie Collins' mind. He said that when he began the novel at Broadstairs, Anne Catherick came into his room in the early morning and said 'try me'. She needed to be more completely hidden. But Wilkie could not resist a hint, perhaps, to the initiated. Fosco plays 'the lively Neapolitan street-song "la mia Carolina", twice over'.[46]

Caroline's two identities, the ladylike self that she was struggling to impose on the world and the lost, perhaps ill-treated woman of

* 'He was a member of the Italian Freemasons in the days when they were an active political force. Throughout his long life he retained an unaffected enthusiasm for any kind of plot . . . Practically every Italian who came to London found himself at some time or other in the Rossetti circle; scholars, organ grinders, refugee aristocrats met in Charlotte Street to lament the state of their country and plot feverishly in four languages'. (Evelyn Waugh, *Rossetti*, pp. 15, 16–17)

doubtful origin, are divided between the half-sisters Laura Fairlie and Anne Catherick. Caroline was not mentally feeble, like Anne Catherick, nor driven to a depressive illness by incarceration and the theft of her identity, as Laura is for a while; but her sense of her own worth and identity may have been fragile. The descriptions of Laura's self-blame and feelings of uselessness in the latter part of the novel ring true. Caroline did suffer from nervous and hysterical symptoms, for which Wilkie's friend and doctor Francis Carr Beard prescribed in 1863.[47] Caroline, however, seems to have been a victim of her own plots, rather than the plots of others; and her deliberately assumed persona was later to become the veiled inspiration for those of Magdalen Vanstone, Lydia Gwilt, Mercy Merrick and the many other women in Wilkie Collins' novels who adopt a false identity with increasing danger to their social standing and cost to their mental health.

But though it is intriguing to speculate on the connections between the novel and Wilkie Collins' own life, it is the mythic and archetypal content of *The Woman in White* which ensures that the novel is as fascinating now as it was 130 years ago. As in *Basil*, contemporary anxieties and preoccupations are combined with timeless ones; but here the myth is integrated into the strong plot and mediated through believable characters. Hardy, influenced in his early writing career by the novels of Wilkie Collins, wrote:

> A 'sensation-novel' is possible in which the sensation is not casualty, but evolution; not physical but psychical . . . whereas in the physical the adventure itself is the subject of interest, the psychical results being passed over as commonplace, in the psychical the casualty or adventure is held to be of no intrinsic interest, but the effect upon the faculties is the important matter to be depicted.[48]

The Woman in White is one of the few sensation novels where the physical and the psychological are inextricably combined. For example, the resemblance between Laura and Anne is vital to the plot, and is finally given a rational explanation, as it might be in the Gothic novels of Mrs Radcliffe. But in its uncanny aspect, in which one girl becomes the *doppelgänger* of the other (an elaboration of 'The Twin Sisters'), it creates deep unease in Hartright, and in the reader.

At his first sight of Laura he falls romantically in love: 'Sympathies that lie too deep for words, too deep almost for thoughts, are touched, at such times, by other charms than those which the senses feel'. But he also has the impression of 'something wanting. At one time it seemed like something wanting in *her*; at another, like something wanting in myself, which hindered me from understanding her as I ought.'[49]

This hint at a failure of erotic communication is later frighteningly identified with the resemblance between the two women, which eventually becomes so strong as to obliterate Laura altogether.

> In those former days, if they had both been seen together, side by side, no person could for a moment have mistaken them one for the other – as has happened often in the instances of twins. I could not say this now. The sorrow and suffering which I had once blamed myself for associating even by a passing thought with the future of Laura Fairlie, *had* set their profaning marks on the youth and beauty of her face; and the fatal resemblance which I had once seen and shuddered at seeing, in idea only, was now a real and living resemblance which asserted itself before my own eyes. Strangers, acquaintances, friends even who could not look at her as we looked, if she had been shown to them in the first days of her rescue from the Asylum, might have doubted if she were the Laura Fairlie they had once seen, and doubted without blame. (*The Woman in White*, pp. 399–400)

Laura's fragile psychological identity, as well as her legal one, is threatened by the existence of Anne Catherick, her ghostly other self. Both have a profound ignorance of sexual desires and relationships: the passion of their parents – Anne's mother and Laura's father – is quite alien to them. When Hartright suggests to Anne that Glyde may have seduced her, she cannot understand what he is hinting at. Marian feels reluctantly obliged to enlighten Laura about the sexual side of marriage, rather than leaving her to experience the shock of the wedding night: 'She has learned her hard, her inevitable lesson. The simple illusions of her girlhood are gone; and my hand has stripped them off. Better mine than his – that is all my consolation – better mine than his.'[50] As it turns out, Marian's instruction may be unnecessary. There are strong hints that Sir Percival, like Ruskin, leaves his bride as virginal as he found her, for he is emphatic that there is no possibility of a child. Marian notes, 'The usual moral transformation which is insensibly wrought in a young, fresh sensitive woman by her marriage, seems never to have taken place in Laura.'[51]

As Margaret Oliphant noticed with approval, 'There is neither murder, nor seduction, nor despair' in *The Woman in White*. Bypassing the age-old fictional situation of virtue in danger, Wilkie Collins suggests instead that virtue contributes to danger: innocence becomes almost culpable, for it lacks survival value. Marian, who tells Walter at their first meeting, 'she is an angel and I am –' (echoing the complacent 'I'm no angel' of Becky Sharp), has a resourcefulness and courage based on knowledge and understanding, which is finally seen as truly angelic rather than devilish: 'Marian was the good angel of our lives – let Marian end our Story.'[52] Laura, in contrast, is increasingly seen as childlike, rather than angelic: 'She spoke as a child might have spoken; she showed me her thoughts as a child might have shown them.'[53] Those who seek to exploit her, and those who love her, equally deny her full status as an adult, as Laura finally complains:

> 'I am so useless – I am such a burden on both of you . . . You work and get money, Walter; and Marian helps you. Why is there nothing I can do? You will end in liking Marian better than you like me – you will, because I am so helpless! Oh, don't, don't, don't treat me like a child!'
>
> I raised her head, and smoothed away the tangled hair that fell over her face, and kissed her – my poor, faded flower! my lost, afflicted sister! 'You shall help us, Laura,' I said; 'you shall begin, my darling, to-day.' (*The Woman in White*, p. 441)

Walter, whose ineffable smugness does not reflect his author's attitude, continues to treat Laura as a child, creating a pretence of occupation for her, as a mother might allow a child to 'help'. The triangular relationship, in which Walter and Marian become her parents, is heavy with ambiguities, as Laura herself perceives.

Sexuality, or lack of it, in the characters in *The Woman in White* is a complex undercurrent, strong, but frequently devious. Marian's love for her half-sister Laura is a powerful emotion with an acknowledged element of jealousy: 'Before another month is over our heads, she will be *his* Laura instead of mine!'[54] This, with her appearance, which sends out conflicting sexual signals; her attraction to Fosco; and her intimate, quasi-matrimonial friendship for

Hartright, give her a sexual aura to which Fosco eagerly responds. Something transsexual is hinted at in both Marian and Fosco: Marian, with her moustache and her 'horrid, heavy, man's umbrella, that you always would walk out with when it rained', is 'masculine' in speech and appearance, and Fosco, whose face, Marian notes, 'is smoother and freer from all marks and wrinkles than mine', is insinuatingly and intuitively 'feminine'.[55] Sexual identity is questionable, too, in other characters. 'Don't shrink under it like a woman . . . trample it under foot like a man', Marian exhorts Hartright, who achieves manhood off-stage, in the South American jungle: 'I had gone out to fly from my own future. I came back to face it, as a man should.'[56] Frederick Fairlie is presented as an effeminate homosexual: '. . . he had a frail, languidly-fretful, over-refined look – something singularly and unpleasantly delicate in its association with a man, and, at the same time, something which could by no possibility have looked natural and appropriate if it had been transferred to the personal appearance of a woman'.[57] Countess Fosco, before her marriage a feminist who 'advocated the Rights of Women', is tamed by her sexual infatuation with her sinister husband in a way that seems to Marian dangerous.

> How far she is really reformed or deteriorated in her secret self, is another question. I have once or twice seen sudden changes of expression on her pinched lips, and heard sudden inflexions of tone in her calm voice, which have led me to suspect that her present state of suppression may have sealed up something dangerous in her nature, which used to evaporate harmlessly in the freedom of her former life. (*The Woman in White*, p. 195)

In spite of Marian's sexuality and Laura and Anne's asexuality, there is a link between the three. They are in fact sisters: Laura and Anne Catherick have a father in common, Laura and Marian a mother. But they are also 'sisters' in their experience of exploitation. The pathetic, blanked-out figure of Anne Catherick, the victim of male manipulation; the strong, intelligent, witty and natural Marian Halcombe, whom Victorian convention and her own desire for freedom of action condemn to celibate spinsterhood; the gentle, pretty Laura Fairlie, the ideal innocent girl of Victorian male fantasy, are presented to Walter Hartright, and to the reader, in that order. The spectrum of ideas about women that they present to the reader is gradually shown to be the refraction of a single ray of white light, a searchlight into the murky corners of society that is more penetrating than in more obvious 'sensation' fiction. Laura, the Victorian ideal, is shown to have so fragile a sense of self that her identity can be broken down in the course of a few weeks. By dutifully sacrificing her own feelings to her dead father's wishes, and by accepting that marriage with Walter is impossible because of the difference in social station, Laura herself takes the first step towards the annihilation of her personality. Margaret Oliphant saw Laura's compliance rationally, as 'Bad morals under any explanation; but when no real reason exists, absolute folly as well, and an ineffaceable blot upon a character meant to be everything that is womanly and tender and pure.'[58] But by using the feeble-minded Anne Catherick, Laura's shadow, as a logical extension of the typical Victorian angel of whom Laura is an example, the attractions of the type are deliberately undermined.

Marian appears to stand out in splendid contrast. The instant popularity of the character – a number of male readers even wrote asking for her address, so that they might propose marriage – showed that her feminist attack reflected a contemporary mood:

> 'No man under Heaven deserves these sacrifices from us women. Men! they are the enemies of our innocence and our peace – they drag us away from our parents' love and our sisters' friendship – they take us body and soul to themselves, and fasten our helpless lives to theirs as they chain up a dog to his kennel. And what does the best of them give us in return?' (*The Woman in White*, p. 162)

'Any woman who is sure of her own wits', she writes later, 'is a match, at any time, for a man who is not sure of his own temper.' But even she is temporarily weakened by Fosco's charm, and the illness that makes her ineffective at a vital moment is caused by catching cold, unprotected by the voluminous female skirts she has slipped out of to undertake her unladylike spying. Her identity can be suspended, though not permanently lost, as she is spirited away to the Gothic wing of Blackwater Park. Though Marian takes the first step to rescue Laura, without Hartright's male freedom of action, earning-ability and knowledge of the world, she cannot conclude her sister's rehabilitation. Even the strongest, most masculine of women is often at the mercy of men.

When Mary Braddon, one of the most talented of the women writers of sensation novels, came to write *Lady Audley's Secret* the following year, she borrowed the idea of substituted identity. But her heroine, the bigamous, murderous and extremely effective Lady Audley, uses substitution for her own ends, taking on the identity of a dead girl in order to escape from her own. Braddon's character was, in her turn, influential in shaping the sensation heroine, 'the fair-haired demon of modern fiction' in Margaret Oliphant's disapproving phrase, who put the passive role of the heroine of the 1850s into reverse. Wilkie's next two novels showed that he had taken note. Readers of both sexes not only preferred the stout-hearted Marian to the helpless Laura, but liked their heroines with at least a dash of wickedness.

THIRTEEN

The Top of the Tree

(1860–1862)

By Christmas the success of *The Woman in White* was certain. Dickens' strategy of serializing full-length fiction had paid off, and Wilkie's novel did much to secure the enormous circulation of *All the Year Round*, three times that of *Household Words* at its best. Queues of eager readers formed outside the offices on press days; the story became the theme of dinner-table gossip. It inspired songs and dances: there was a Woman in White Waltz and a Fosco Galop. The cartoonists used it. Other writers produced women in various shades; even *All the Year Round* published a Bluebeard story by Elizabeth Gaskell, 'The Grey Woman', in 1861, which draws heavily on Wilkie's novel.

The publisher George Smith, usually astute, was one of the few people unconscious of this success. When Wilkie invited him to make an offer for the book-publication rights in January, Smith offered only £500. Wilkie immediately asked Sampson Low to make an offer, on terms by which he kept the copyright and Low had a three-year licence to publish a three-volume edition at the usual price of one and a half guineas.[1] Low leapt at the opportunity. Smith discovered too late, from his neighbour at a dinner party, that the novel had become the talk of London. 'If my offer had been multiplied tenfold, I should have made a large sum by the transaction', he remembered ruefully.

In the spring of 1860 Wilkie and Caroline parted with their disobliging landlord, moving round the corner to 12 Harley Street.

Wilkie was still struggling with the complicated narrative of *The Woman in White*, and the usual nightmare of house-moving couldn't have come at a worse time. It may have been this disruption of his steady working habits that caused an error in chronology, occurring in the parts appearing in May, probably written in March. Though the planning of the novel was all done in advance, this was the kind of detail that might easily go astray. Anyone who has tried to cope simultaneously with builders and deadlines will sympathize with the problems he described in a letter he wrote that month:

> I have been moving, since I saw you last, into new rooms . . . at No 12 Harley Street. I carry about with me an infinite quantity of 'litter' and have been and am still (except that I have found my note paper) in a state of confusion which has, I think, definitely upset my 'mental balance'. Did you find when you last moved that you could *not* get rid of the carpenter? *I* can't. He has been working with me ever since last week. *He* was putting up curtain poles at one end of the room today, and *I* was writing a strong effect of suspended interest at the other. He is coming tomorrow, to saw something off, and he will look in, the day after, to put something on. He is a tall mild deliberate man, with a sympathetic smile – and I don't at all see my way to the end of our connection, unless any friends of mine . . . will be so very kind as to give him a job, and keep him at it for a good long time. *I can strongly recommend him.*[2]

The mistake was not spotted until the *Times* reviewer of the book edition pointed it out in October, two months after publication: '. . . Lady Glyde could not have left Blackwater Park before the 9th or 10th of August', rather than 26 July. The novel was already a runaway success, and Wilkie was not too cast down. 'Shakespeare has made worse mistakes – that is one comfort. And readers are not critics, who test an emotional book by the base rules of arithmetic . . . Nevertheless we will set the mistake right at the first opportunity'.[3] He revised the chronology for the one-volume edition of 1861, and all subsequent editions published in his lifetime used this revised text. He was so annoyed by his own carelessness that when he dramatized the novel in 1871 he held up the action of the play in order to prove, at undue length, the discrepancy between the dates of Laura's departure and Anne's death.

Wilkie clearly intended to make Harley Street his home. As well as undertaking alterations, he ordered writing paper engraved with the address. He employed two servants, though one of them, 'a hybrid white-haired young person', didn't last long. 'The hybrid and Mary don't agree. I am sorry to lose the hybrid. She sees me into the water-closet and out of it *regularly* – and tries the door every time I make water. I have reason to believe that the hybrid must have seen *My Person*!'[4] For once he capitulated to Mrs Grundy: Caroline was known as 'Mrs Collins' while they lived there, perhaps to avoid causing embarrassment to the landlord, a dentist, with whom they shared the house.

The Collins brothers were at last prising themselves away from their mother. Charley had taken to heart the advice of his friends Hunt and Millais; Wilkie said he was 'trying hard to talk himself into believing that he ought to be married'.[5] He became officially engaged to Dickens' younger daughter Kate in May, and they were married at Gad's Hill on 17 July.

The wedding was an odd affair. The bride's mother was conspicuously absent, the bridegroom's mother as conspicuously present, flirting outrageously, according to her new daughter-in-law. Wilkie of course went as a bachelor, taking a day off work. 'Except the day of the wedding (when I was tied to my sister-in-law's petticoat string) I have been tied to The Woman in White's petticoat string, like a dog to his kennel.'[6] The sun shone and the villagers erected floral arches, but Dickens would not allow any speeches, and bride and groom crept away from the reception after an hour, Kate, much to Harriet Collins' annoyance, wearing black. Wilkie, still obstinately anti-marriage, reported with satisfaction 'only the most modest allowance of tears', but after it was all over Dickens was discovered by his elder daughter sobbing into Kate's wedding dress. 'But for me, Katey would not have left home,' he told Mamie when he was able to speak.[7]

The new familial relationship could hardly have brought Wilkie and Dickens closer than they were already. Eventually it had the opposite effect. Dickens, though he did not attempt to prevent the marriage, was not in favour of it. He was convinced that the twenty-year-old

Kate, his much-loved 'Lucifer Box', the closest of his children to him in appearance, personality and ability, was only marrying Charley out of desperation, because of her distress at the break-up of her parents' marriage. Kate confirmed this in old age, saying that she had been in love with the married Edmund Yates, and that she later wanted to get a separation from Charley 'as she could have done', but that her father would not hear of it.[8] Dickens may have felt that another marital scandal in the family would be too much to weather. A few years after the marriage Frederick Lehmann thought that Kate was intensely eager to find other lovers, and that Charley had been 'guilty of an infamy' in marrying: '. . . these two girls [Kate and Mamie] are going to the devil as fast as can be. From what I hear from third parties who don't know how intimate we are with them, society is beginning to fight very shy of them, especially of Kitty C. . . .'[9]

Yet Kate's letters in the early days of her marriage make it clear that she had great affection for Charley, and she was grateful to him later for his insistence that she should visit her mother regularly, as the Collins family all did. Though Dickens thought Charley 'a gentleman, accomplished and amiable', he saw that his prospects largely depended on the good will of his successful father-in-law.[10] Dickens, who complained he had 'never had anything left to me but relations', not unnaturally felt aggrieved at acquiring another useless one. Eight months after the wedding, he was rejoicing that there were 'no "Great Expectations" of prospective Collinses', and was irritable about the whole family. 'Old Mrs Collins dined here . . . and contradicted everybody upon every subject for five hours and a half . . . so I was very glad when she tied her head in a bundle and took it home.'[11]

As for Wilkie's arrangements, Dickens deplored them. He visited Wilkie's 'very handsome and comfortable' Harley Street rooms, but avoided discussing his relationship with Caroline. 'We never speak of the (female) skeleton in that house and I therefore have not the least idea of the state of his mind on that subject. I hope it does not run in any matrimonial groove. I *cannot* imagine any good coming of such an end in this instance.'[12]

Charley's health was already poor, and was to deteriorate further during the thirteen years of his marriage; his ability to earn a living as a writer – he had completely abandoned painting – was very uncertain. He and Kate at first considered living in France, still much cheaper than London: '*There* we are paupers – abroad we are rich.' They hatched a scheme which made even Wilkie, always loyal to his brother, think, 'he and Katie are labouring under temporary insanity'. They became middle-class gypsies, travelling around France in a second-hand cabriolet, Charley writing up their experiences as a travel book. 'Have you heard that Charley has bought another horse, and that he is going to drive himself to Lausanne? . . . *Across the Alps* in a one horse chaise. They have to harness bullocks to pull *four* horses up those passes'.[13] Charley's book, *A Cruise Upon Wheels*, achieved a modest success when it was published in 1863. It constituted a challenge of a muted kind to Wilkie, with his delight in sea cruises: his *Rambles Beyond Railways* was republished in 1861 with 'The Cruise of the Tomtit' added as a postscript.

Kate and Charley were abroad six months, spending much of the winter living in stark simplicity in Paris, without a servant, Charley lighting the fires and frying the bacon. Harriet was enjoined not to tell Kate's mother anything about their 'shifts'. Kate was good-humoured and resilient, but it was all in sharp contrast to Wilkie's increasing fame and prosperity. 'How is my illustrious and gifted brother-in-law?' Kate asked Harriet. 'We have heard of his riches and his growing magnificence and plumpness from all quarters.'[14] Charles Collins' novel *At the Bar* had an account of the struggles of a young married couple 'exposed to privations and troubles of the most harassing and miserable kind . . . which their bringing-up and earlier habits had in no sort fitted them to undergo'.[15] It seems to be based on his and Kate's experiences.

Wilkie finished *The Woman in White* on 26 July. It was a moment for celebration and congratulations. 'Wilkie has finished his White Woman (if he had done with his flesh-colored one, I should mention that too), and is in great force', Dickens told Frances Dickinson.[16] But he was exhausted, worn out by 'winning the battle against the infernal periodical system'. He gave an all-male dinner for old friends at Harley Street on 9 August, in celebration. Holman Hunt, Augustus Egg and

Edward Ward were among those present. As usual, Wilkie insisted, 'No dressing – or ceremony of any kind'. He hired a Genoese cook for the occasion, who '*really did wonders*. I never eat a more perfect dinner in Paris.'[17] The novel was published that month in England, Germany, the United States and Canada, and in Tauchnitz's English-language continental edition.

The Woman in White was chosen, because of its immense popularity, as a test case by the libraries, to break Mudie's monopoly. The other circulating libraries refused, at first, to buy copies, except on the absurdly low terms that Mudie managed to extort from the publishers. Low stood firm: he and Wilkie both trusted the public to force the libraries to buy, and such was the fashion for the book that they succeeded. Wilkie left London for a series of visits: to Dickens at Gad's Hill; to Monckton Milnes' palatial house Fryston, in Yorkshire; to Shanklin to stay with the Lehmanns. (Caroline would not have been acceptable in any of these places.) He yelped with anguish at being confronted with a furniture bill for £103 on his return from the Isle of Wight, but he could well afford it. The first printing of a thousand copies had sold out on publication day, and 1,350 copies were sold during the following week. Three weeks later there was 'All sorts of good news'. The novel 'is soothing the dying moments of a *young* lady – it is helping (by homeopathic doses of a chapter at a time) to keep an *old* one out of the grave – and it is the first literary performance which has succeeded in fixing the attention of a deranged gentleman in his lucid intervals'.

Wilkie was at last earning serious money. Less than a month after publication he had made £1,400, with the copyright 'and the disposal of all editions under the extravagant guinea and a half price, in my hands. Cock-a-doodle-doo! The critics may go to the devil – they are at the book still, as I hear, but I see no reviews.' This lofty disclaimer is contradicted in the same letter, when he tells Harriet he is sending her *The Spectator*, with a review answering the hostile one in the *Saturday Review*.[18] The expensive edition was still selling well, and nothing had been fixed about cheaper ones.

The success brought a rush of proposals for the republication of his earlier novels. Wilkie agreed a sale to Sampson Low of a six-year lease of the copyrights of those available. With all this, he could take life easily: in September he went cruising in the Bristol Channel with Pigott and his friend and solicitor Charles Benham. In October he admitted to Charles Ward, who had called at Harley Street in the middle of the morning, 'Yes – I was in bed – but I was *thinking* of getting up, which makes the offence comparatively venial.'[19]

Also in October, Wilkie took Caroline to Paris, just missing Kate and Charley, off on their equine adventures. Wilkie travelled in style, 'first class all the way, with my own sitting-room at the best hotel when I get there – and every other luxury that the Capital of the civilised world can afford. No horseflesh for *me* – unless in the form of cookery . . . with a satisfactory sauce . . .'[20] He tried to persuade Charles Ward to come with them: '*Sell a child* – terms, £10 – down! Slawkenbergius* would fetch more, if disposed *by weight* – but I think him too amiable to be parted with. Try the baby – and let us devour the proceeds at the *Trois Frères*.'[21] The Tauchnitz edition was already sold out in Paris: 'not a copy . . . to be had there for a week for love or money'.[22]

It was almost certainly the first time Caroline had been out of England. She lacked Wilkie's immunity to seasickness, but coped bravely with a rough Channel crossing. Dickens, whatever he might say about her to his other correspondents, was genial about her in letters to Wilkie, and sent her a friendly message. 'In consequence of her gallant conduct on the Ocean, I . . . hail the Butler's elder sister, as Albania Nelsonia. I beg to send her my kind regards. I hope that she will be able to report to me that you came up to the Parisian scratch like a man, in respect of Pears in the Neapolitan manner, hard by the Bourse, and Truffles at the Provincial Brothers.'†[23]

Wilkie returned to find that an unauthorized dramatization of the novel was about to be staged at the Surrey Theatre, south of the Thames. He said he would certainly go and hiss, if he could not manage to get it stopped. From this time onwards he was repeatedly plagued by the law, or lack of it, of dramatic copyright. Any novel or story that had not been dramatized and printed by the author himself, and produced or at least given a semi-public

* In Sterne's *Tristram Shandy* Slawkenbergius is the author of a treatise on noses.
† Trois Frères Provençaux.

reading to establish copyright, might be freely dramatized by anyone. This time the manager of the Surrey Theatre caved in.

A week later Wilkie teamed up again with Dickens for a brief trip to Devon to find background material for the Christmas number of *All the Year Round.* Wilkie's former delight in West Country cooking was to receive a sharp check at an inn in Bideford. In the picturesque old town within easy reach of the sea, and on a magnificent estuary, there was only 'stinking fish for dinner' and nothing to drink. Otherwise, for once, 'No adventures whatever. Nothing has happened to Wilkie'.[24] They chose the tourist village of Clovelly, one of the places Wilkie and Pigott had sailed to in October, as the setting for the story; Wilkie used it again many years later in his novel *The Black Robe.* He found it difficult to settle to writing again, and fell back on the familiar formula for his section of *A Message from the Sea* which Dickens immediately objected to: '. . . is it not a most extraordinary thing that it began: "I have undertaken to take pen in hand to set down in writing &c &c," like the W in W narratives? Of course I at once pointed out the necessity of cancelling that'.[25] The cancellation, essential to maintain the essentially oral narration of the story, caused temporary writer's block. Wilkie got behind hand, 'and has been getting up spasmodically all day, and looking, in high-shouldered desperation out at window'.[26] With Dickens' urging, the story was finished in time for the printer's deadline at the end of November. It is forgettable, and forgotten: Wilkie's section is memorable chiefly for a melodramatic portrait of an alcoholic, perhaps prompted by news that an acquaintance had cut his throat at Melbourne, the result of delirium tremens. Sensational incidents were not far to seek, whatever the reviewers might say.

Wilkie was beginning to be almost tired of 'that eternal *Woman in White*'. When the cheap edition came out in April, he told Charles Ward, 'It promises to beat everything we have done yet. We *start* with 10,000 copies and Low expects to sell 50,000 before we have done!'[27] Priced at 6s., it was a bargain compared with the one-and-a-half-guinea first edition in three volumes.

The cheap edition has a photograph of him pasted into every copy. These vary slightly from one impression to another; Wilkie explained, 'I have had to sit again, for the photographs can't keep up with us.'[28]

As an associate of Dickens, Wilkie was fast learning the value of personal publicity. In May he presided for the first time at a public meeting, substituting at the last minute for Dickens in the chair at the Newsvendors Benevolent Institution. To his own and everyone else's surprise, he was as successful a public speaker as he was a private conversationalist. Dickens was delighted: 'it is of immense importance to a public man in our way to have his wits at his tongue's end'.[29] Wilkie fully realized the importance of 'this newly discovered knack of mine' for promoting his books 'by occasionally bringing me before the public, in the speechifying capacity which Englishmen are so unaccountably fond of admiring'.[30]

Encouraged by his new wealth and literary notoriety, Wilkie began to erect the scaffolding of a new book for serialization in *All the Year Round*. By July the outline was in place, and tried out on Dickens, who was enthusiastic and 'gave such an account of it to Wills, in my absence, that the said Wills's eyes rolled in his head with astonishment when he and I next met at the office'.[31] Wilkie was determined to write a book utterly unlike *The Woman in White*, and such reactions suggested that he had succeeded. Clinching evidence, if any were needed, of his ability to make a good living as a writer without the support of the Dickens framework soon came in a spectacular offer from George Smith.

Smith, chagrined at his failure to understand the potential of *The Woman in White*, was determined to capture the best-selling author of the day for his new magazine, *The Cornhill*, edited by Thackeray. He was already too late for Wilkie's next novel; but he was prepared to wait, and he was prepared to pay generously:

> Go out on the lawn, and take a good gasp of fresh air before you turn this page – Endeavour to consider me (if life and health last) in the light of a wealthy novelist – are you ready . . .? Smith and Elder have *bought* me away from All the Year Round under circumstances which *in Dickens's opinion* amply justify me in leaving . . . [they] offer me . . . for a work of fiction a little longer than *The Woman in White* . . . to follow the story I am now going away to write for 'All the Year Round' – the sum of —
>
> Five Thousand Pounds
>
> !!!!!!
>
> Ha! ha! ha!

> Five thousand pounds for nine months or at most a year's work – nobody but Dickens has made as much . . . So I now stand committed (if I can manage it) to a work of fiction, to be published (after appearing in All the Year Round) as a book in 1862, and to another work of fiction to be published as a separate serial story, in 1863 or 4 – So that, if I live & keep my brains in good working order, I shall have got to the top of the tree, after all, before forty.[32]

The 'top of the tree' was not only financial. The monthly *Cornhill* was deliberately designed to attract a more discriminating readership than Dickens' weeklies. For Wilkie, growing impatient with the sensation label now firmly attached to his work, it seemed a vindication of his kind of fiction, whatever the reviewers might say. Smith, Elder behaved 'like princes', not haggling over terms or times of delivery: the £5,000 was to be paid in monthly instalments, 'no bills at long dates, and no difficulties'. They were also prepared to match any price offered by other publishers for the novel he was currently writing. 'So here I am "let" (if I live) for the next three years', he wrote to his mother, urging her to get a comfortable home in the country.

Harriet, at last free of obligations to her sons, was ready to leave London. For a while she tried Southsea, where her friends the Otters lived, only fifty miles or so from her childhood home at Alderbury: Wilkie feared his gregarious mother was 'a little *too* secluded'. Finally she settled on Tunbridge Wells, taking lodgings in various houses in and near the town. She was to live in the area, when she was not away visiting friends, until her death. With their mother out of London, and with households of their own to maintain, Wilkie and Charles finally took responsibility for their own financial affairs and opened separate bank accounts: Charles just before his marriage, Wilkie in August 1860.[33]

Wilkie's life seemed set fair in 1861. He had taken willingly to domestic comfort, now as important to him as freedom, not objecting to many of the same constraints as the married friends whose uxoriousness he had so often mocked. Like any married man, he took out life insurance.[34] He no longer joked about his friends' experience of childish ailments: he had himself to cancel a visit to

Edward and Henrietta Ward because 'I have a child spending the holiday here – and, as she had never had the measles, I am prohibited from coming to see you'.[35] He was also beginning to discover, like his father before him, that there were some advantages in being taken up by the great. As he joined the round of grand dinners and country-house visits, he noted with detached amusement the 'luxuries and magnificences of wealthy country life, including a valet to wait on me of twice my height and ten times my dignity', but he didn't refuse the opportunity to experience them.[36]

He was now confident of making his way on his own merits. He could make a living, and a good living, at the work he liked best. Sampson Low published the titles he had bought, *Antonina*, *Basil*, *Hide and Seek*, *The Dead Secret* and *The Queen of Hearts*, in a 'Cheap and Uniform Edition' at 5s. each.[37] Bentley republished *Rambles Beyond Railways*; publishers were competing with each other for his unwritten books; Richard Bentley repeatedly tried to woo him back. Wilkie was now worth more to *All the Year Round*, as writer and adviser, than the magazine connection, with its relatively modest salary, was worth to him. Apart from contributions to the Christmas number he wrote only three short pieces for the paper in 1861, two of them skilful but unoriginal retellings of cases from French criminal records, always a journalistic standby when he was pressed for time.

In the midst of his success he was still plagued by recurrent illness. He went to the Suffolk coast in the spring, seeking that Victorian panacea, change of air, as well as background for the novel. In July he took Caroline and Carrie to Broadstairs to convalesce from an attack of 'liver'. The place was full of familiar figures: middle-aged ladies 'placidly unconscious of their . . . disclosure of lean old legs through the fine exhibiting medium of crinoline', children digging in the sand, fat-faced young ladies reading cheap novels. The following month he tried Whitby on the Yorkshire coast.

Wilkie and Caroline were at first delighted by the place. The approach by train across the moors, the first view of the distant sea and the ruins of Whitby Abbey promised well. The little fishing port with its magnificent harbour, busy with boats laden with herring, was romantically different from the southern resorts. The fine air was especially good for Caroline, who had not been well. They had splendid rooms, overlooking the bay, at the Royal Hotel. Wilkie began the first weekly part of his new story, finding it slow work after so long an interval. But he complained of noise from the children playing under the windows: '. . . among the British matrons . . . in the Hotel is a Rabbit with *fourteen* young ones'.[38] There was also a brass band hired by the proprietor to play '*regularly* four hours a day for the benefit of his visitors'.[39] They cut the holiday short, and travelled to York, for some backgrounds for the book, and the Suffolk town of Aldeburgh, where Wilkie set the seaside scenes of *No Name*. Wilkie admired Crabbe's poetry, and he reminded his readers that Aldeburgh was the poet's birthplace. His descriptions of the town, gradually being reclaimed by the sea, and the surrounding country are deliberately modelled on Crabbe's evocative backgrounds to his tales of rural violence and poverty.

The autumn and winter were spent in the usual struggle with the early stages of a new book. In December, frustrated by the state of his heavily overscored and rewritten manuscript, he had the work he had done so far set in type, so that he could view it more clearly. He was writing carefully and slowly, but he broke off to provide his annual contribution to the Christmas number of *All the Year Round*, *Tom Tiddler's Ground*. Wilkie's section, 'Picking Up Waifs at Sea', made him laugh while he was writing it, 'which is what my own fun seldom does'.[40] The fun involved two babies born simultaneously at sea, one to first-class passengers, one to a humble family in steerage, who are mixed up in the cradle. Wilkie demolishes the sentimental idea that 'the Voice of Nature' will identify which is which (each mother is equally content with either baby), and points out in conclusion that it is only by the accident of birth that one remains poor all his life and the other is rich. The story was later republished as 'The Fatal Cradle'.[41]

The Woman in White continued to sell, and to bring him letters from all over the world. In December the French translation brought 'very civil' reactions from the critics and readers. 'You like a title, don't you?' he teased his mother. 'What do [you] think of a French *Duke* writing to me in raptures?'[42] Asked for an autobiographical sketch for the *Revue Contemporaine*, he produced a cautious and laundered account of his early life, and discouraged any speculation on his present arrangements. 'Apart from my books – my life presents no events which have any claim on the public interest or on your attention.' But he revealed that his fascination with the theatre had not been cured by the failure of *The Red Vial*: 'If I had been a Frenchman – with such a public to write for, such rewards to win, and such actors to interpret me, as the French stage presents, all the stories I have written from "Antonina" to "The Woman in White" would have been told in the dramatic form . . . if I know anything of my faculty it is a *dramatic* one.'[43]

It was a persistent fallacy. Wilkie borrowed from the theatre, with great success, the dramatic presentation of character. To dialogue he added the documentary evidence of diaries, letters, legal papers and so on. *No Name*, concerned with the impersonations of a born actress, uses a theatrical metaphor for its divisions: there are eight 'Scenes' rather than 'Books', and the documents are given 'Between the Scenes'. The author is hidden behind the voices of his characters, as a playwright is. This technique, which became habitual, added immediacy, authenticity and excitement; in this sense his faculty is 'a dramatic one'. But attempts, by the veteran playwright Bayle Bernard and by Wilkie himself, to dramatize *No Name* ended in failure. Wilkie deplored the standard of acting on the English stage compared with that in Paris, and did not trust enough to the artistry of the actors to reveal the inner reality of his characters, achieved in the novels by their thoughts and writings. His stage dialogue is melodramatic and artificial.

Yet he knew, in theory, how a play ought to be constructed. A letter he wrote in 1859 to an unidentified woman who had sent him her dramatization of a novel for his comments gives excellent advice on its technical defects, and warns, 'If you rewrite "The Foster Brothers", try to forget that such a novel as "The Collegians" ever existed. When you have taken the *idea* of the story, you have taken all that the novel can give to the play.'[44]

In January 1862 Wilkie finally made the decision, in the air since the success of *The Woman in White*, to leave the staff of *All the*

Year Round. He had outgrown the apprentice's overalls, and they were becoming a straitjacket. His 'quality of taking pains, united to a natural quickness' had made him very valuable to Dickens as a partner at *All the Year Round*, and his natural judgement could be trusted implicitly, whereas Wills, according to Dickens, had a 'commonplace' literary taste, only useful for gauging the reaction of the ordinary public. Wilkie continued to be associated with the magazine as a contributor, and Dickens appreciated his reasons for going, and was friendly and concerned.

Wilkie gave his health as one excuse. The 'rheumatic gout' which now regularly afflicted him was not being kept in check by medicine, diet, or other regimes. Francis Carr Beard, who had become the Dickens family doctor in 1859, was now also treating Wilkie. Although Wilkie had almost certainly been an occasional opium user for years, since the drug was an ingredient of most popular remedies for gout and rheumatism, it seems clear that it was at this time that Beard prescribed laudanum regularly as a palliative. 'Don't be satisfied with Frank Beard's patching you, now that you have leisure,' Dickens urged, 'but be set up afresh.'[45] In order to keep up with his work Wilkie was started on a dependency that he never afterwards shook off. Laudanum, a tincture of opium in alcohol that was obtainable over the counter at any pharmacy and many back-street corner shops, cost threepence an ounce. Half an ounce was enough to poison a horse. It is an unusually conscientious chemist in *No Name* who asks for Magdalen Vanstone's name and address, and warns her of the dangers of laudanum, before handing over the bottle. Though attitudes to the medical use of opium were changing, and a series of Select Committees suggested that restrictions on its sale were needed, none were imposed until the Pharmacy Act of 1868, and then they were largely ineffective.

Wilkie showed the early numbers of the new novel, still untitled, to Dickens in January. Dickens was encouraging, but did not find the story quite Dickensian enough, objecting to the heroine in the scene where she 'checks off the items of the position one by one' (The First Scene, Chapter XV) as 'too business-like and clerkly'. Dickens considered that 'the more severely and persistently he tells

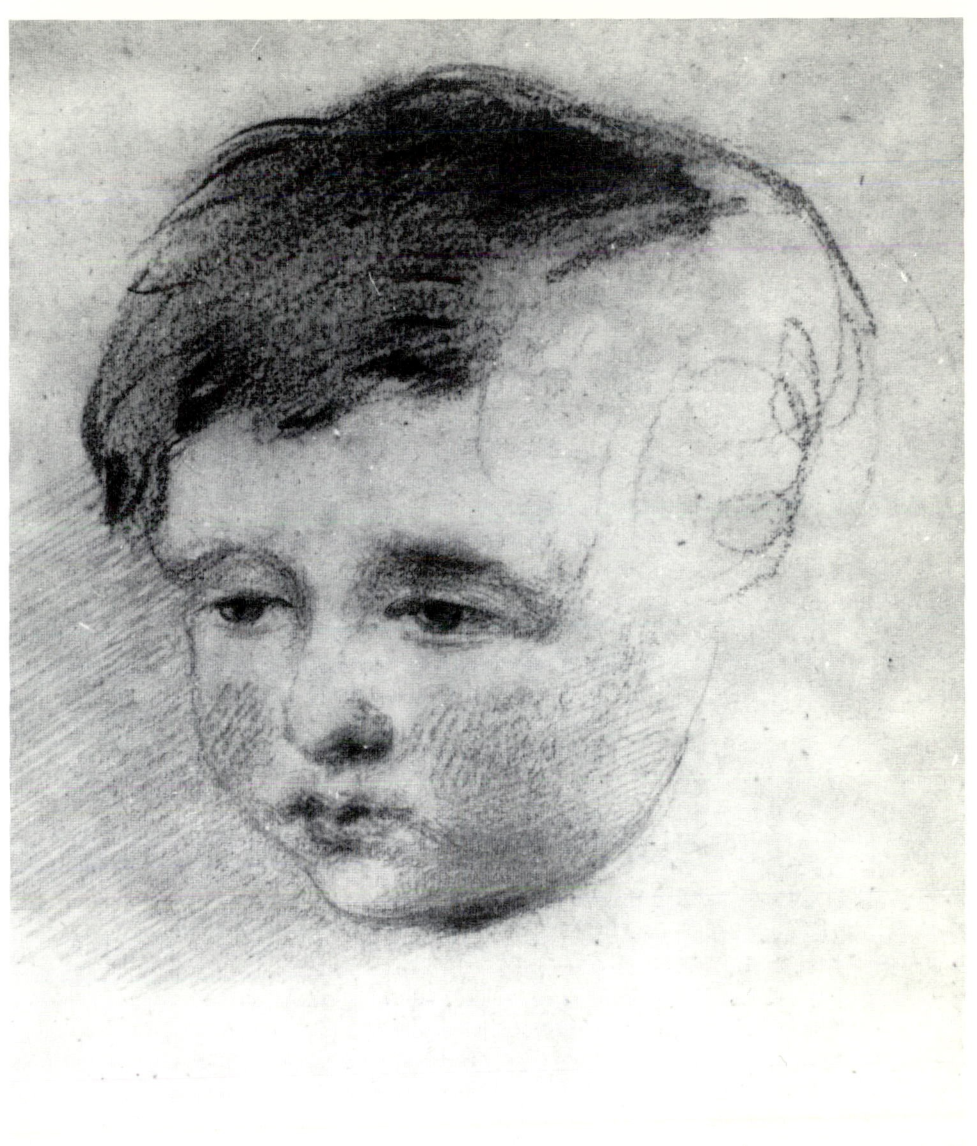

1. Wilkie Collins as a small boy, showing the protuberance on his forehead. Drawing probably by his father.

2. Harriet Collins by John Linnell, painted when they were neighbours in Porchester Terrace, Bayswater.

3. William Collins drawn by his son Charles in 1846, the year before his death.

4. Pond Street, Hampstead,
at the time the Collins family were living there.

5. Wilkie and Charley Collins aged nine and five.
This is probably a painting by their mother's brother Alex Geddes.

6. Landscape drawing by Wilkie Collins, aged seventeen, 1841.

7. Wilkie Collins in 1855, aged thirty-one. From a portrait by Charles Allston Collins.

8. William Holman Hunt in 1853, drawn by John Everett Millais.

9. Charles Dickens in 1852.

10. Augustus Egg in his studio.

11. Charles Allston Collins, probably in the 1860s.

12. The Gallery of Illustration cast of *The Frozen Deep*, 1857. Wilkie Collins, leaning forward, is in front of Frances Dickinson (in bonnet). Next to her, in the centre, Edward Pigott. Augustus Egg (in profile) is to the right of the picture, next to Mark Lemon. Dickens in the foreground, in front of Kate Dickens, Georgina Hogarth, Mamie Dickens and Helen Hogarth.

13. The poster advertising the stage version of *The Woman in White.*

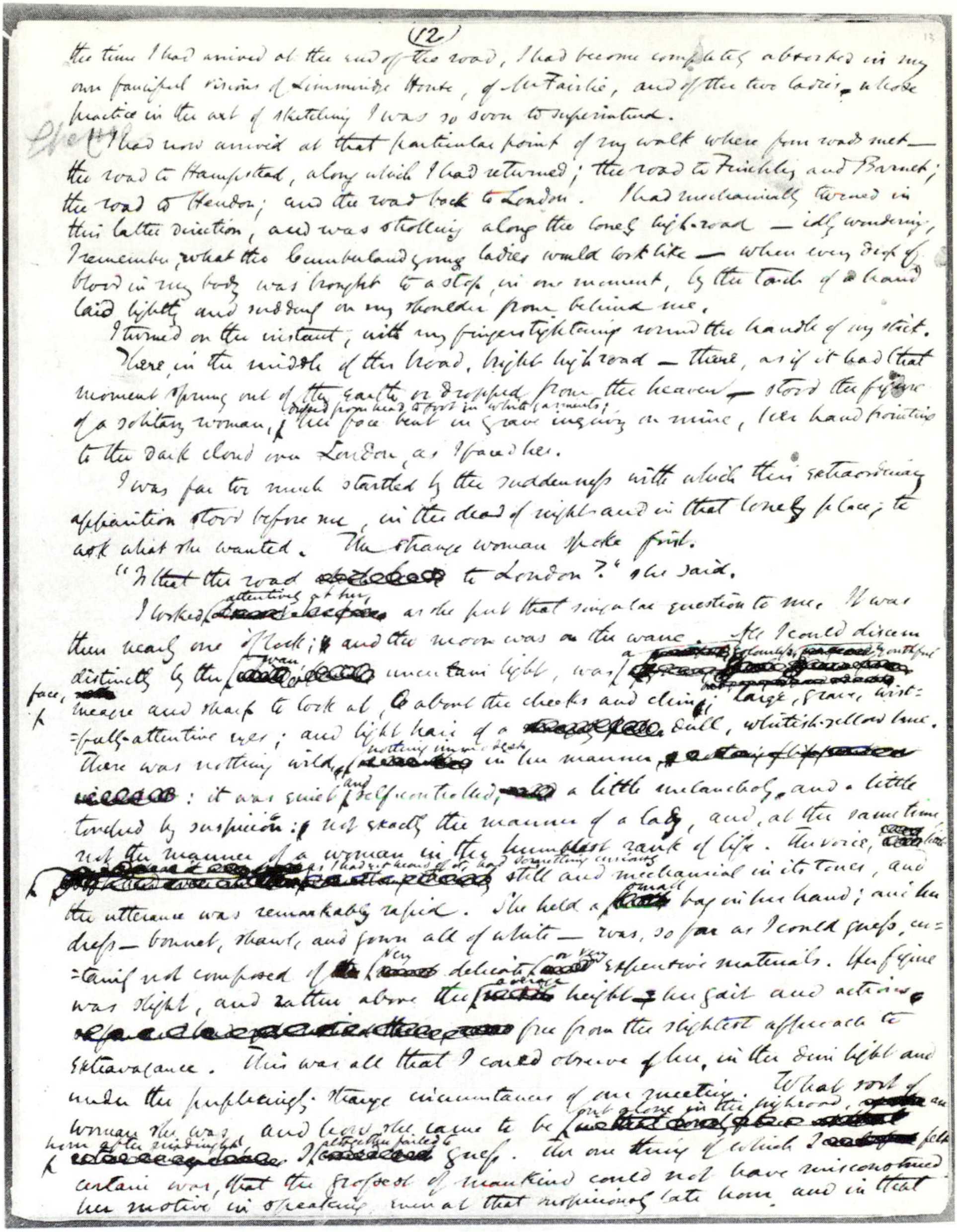
(12)

the time I had arrived at the end of the road, I had become completely absorbed in my own fanciful visions of Limmeridge House, of Mr Fairlie, and of the two ladies, whose practice in the art of sketching I was so soon to superintend.

I had now arrived at that particular point of my walk where four roads met — the road to Hampstead, along which I had returned; the road to Finchley and Barnet; the road to Hendon; and the road back to London. I had mechanically turned in this latter direction, and was strolling along the lonely high-road — idly wondering, I remember, what the Cumberland young ladies would look like — when every drop of blood in my body was brought to a stop, in one moment, by the touch of a hand laid lightly and suddenly on my shoulder from behind me.

I turned on the instant, with my fingers tightening round the handle of my stick.

There, in the middle of the broad, bright high-road — there, as if it had that moment sprung out of the earth or dropped from the heaven — stood the figure of a solitary woman, dressed from head to foot in white garments, her face bent in grave inquiry on mine, her hand pointing to the dark cloud over London, as I faced her.

I was far too much startled by the suddenness with which this extraordinary apparition stood before me, in the dead of night and in that lonely place, to ask what she wanted. The strange woman spoke first.

"Is that the road to London?" she said.

I looked attentively at her, as she put that singular question to me. It was then nearly one o'clock; and the moon was on the wane. All I could discern distinctly by the wan, uncertain light, was a colourless, youthful face, meagre and sharp to look at, about the cheeks and chin; large, grave, wistfully-attentive eyes; and light hair of a dull, whitish-yellow hue. There was nothing wild, nothing immodest in her manner: it was quiet and self-controlled, a little melancholy and a little touched by suspicion: not exactly the manner of a lady, and, at the same time, not the manner of a woman in the humblest rank of life. The voice, little as I had yet heard of it, had something curiously still and mechanical in its tones, and the utterance was remarkably rapid. She held a small bag in her hand; and her dress — bonnet, shawl, and gown all of white — was, so far as I could guess, certainly not composed of very delicate or very expensive materials. Her figure was slight, and rather above the average height — her gait and actions free from the slightest approach to extravagance. This was all that I could observe of her, in the dim light and under the perplexingly strange circumstances of our meeting. What sort of woman she was, and how she came to be out alone in the high-road, an hour after midnight, I altogether failed to guess. The one thing of which I felt certain was, that the grossest of mankind could not have misconstrued her motive in speaking, even at that suspiciously late hour and in that

14. Manuscript of *The Woman in White*, in Wilkie Collins' handwriting. The page includes Walter Hartright's first encounter with the woman in white.

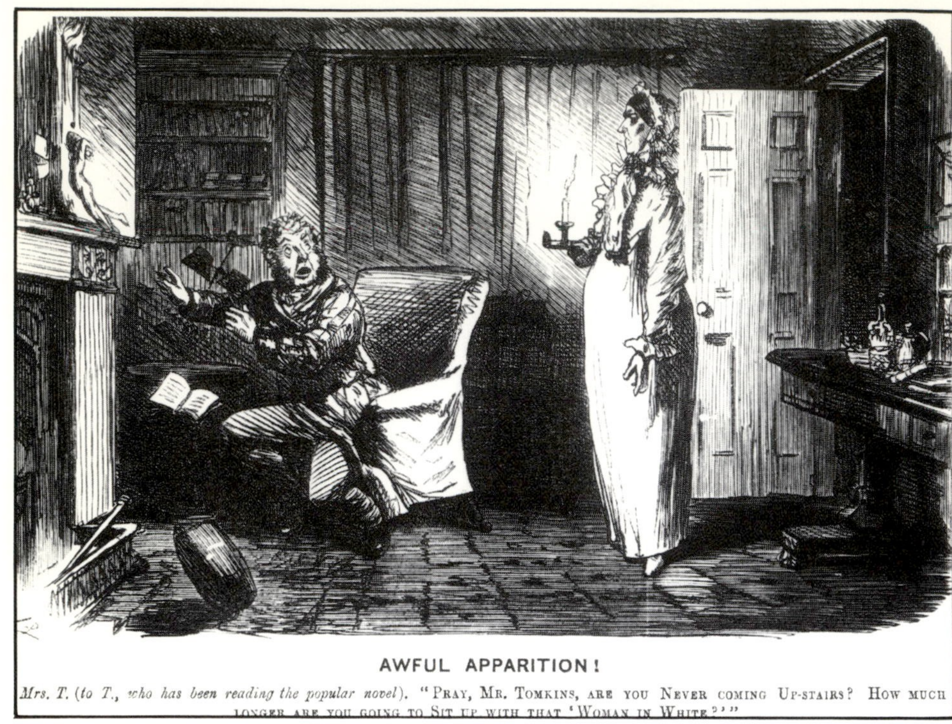

15. *Punch* cartoon by Wilkie Collins' friend John Leech, 6 April 1861.

16. 'Wilkey Collins' by his eleven-year-old friend Leslie Ward, later the cartoonist 'Spy'.

17. Wilkie Collins in the 1860s.

18. A photograph that shows the physical oddities of Wilkie's face and head.

19. Caroline Graves.

20. Wilkie Collins and Martha Rudd.

21. Harriet Collins in old age. She described this photograph when she sent it to William Holman Hunt: 'I look like an old monthly nurse who has had a snug glass of hot and strong gin & water'.

22. Charles Fechter.

23. Ramsgate Harbour.

Wishing You
A Happy
Christmas

Hide and Seek, 'neath the mistletoe
played for a kiss-
I hope you may try it to-night-
I mention No Name, a Dead Secret is this,
With some beautiful
Woman in White.

Wilkie Collins

Frederick Langbridge.

24. 'The season of cant and Christmas'.

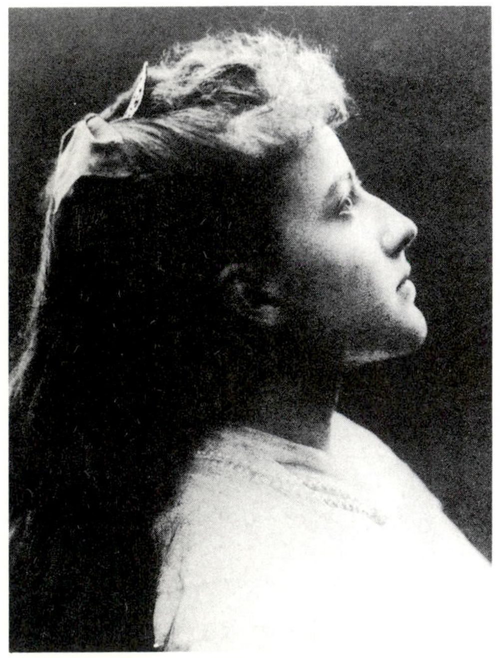

25. 'Dear and admirable Mrs. Collins'. Nannie Wynne at the time Wilkie Collins knew her.

26. Wilkie Collins in the 1880s. 'There is some damnable perversity in me that won't *feel* old'.

the story, unrelieved by whimsical playing about it, the more he will detract from the steadiness and inflexibility of purpose of the girl. Contrast in that wise is most essential.'[46] Wilkie conceded something to Dickens' criticism, appropriating it in the preface as his own idea to contrast other, humorous characters as relief to the central figure of the heroine: '. . . not only because I believed myself to be justified in doing so by the laws of Art – but because experience has taught me . . . that there is no such moral phenomenon as unmixed tragedy to be found in the world around us'. But Magdalen Vanstone's interrogation of the lawyer was left intact: Wilkie's severe, intelligent and ruthless heroine remained most un-Dickensian. Nor did he accept any of the twenty-six rather banal titles Dickens suggested for the novel.[47] He was grateful, however, for the meticulous care with which Dickens attended to the details of the later sections of the story, involving complicated legal points, and adopted almost all his amendments. It was the last time Dickens was to be so closely involved with a Collins novel.

The title came to Wilkie at the last possible moment. Less than six weeks before publication, the title was still not fixed on. *Under a Cloud*, a title Wilkie favoured, had already been used the previous year by Frederick Greenwood.[48] On 4 February, Wilkie asked his mother for her opinion on a short-list of eight, which includes *Man and Wife*, a title he used nine years later, but not *No Name*. 'It *must* be settled tomorrow', Wilkie told Harriet, warning his indiscreet mother not to let his letter out of her possession, and not to say anything about the titles. 'My five thousand pound job for Smith & Elder is known, right and left everywhere', he complained.[49] The serialization, in *Harper's Weekly* in New York as well as in *All the Year Round*, began on 15 March. At Easter Wilkie went to Broadstairs to look for a house where he could spend the summer and get on with writing the book. He rented the Fort House,* the eccentric and imposing building on a headland which Dickens had taken in 1850 and 1851. It was far enough from the town to discourage the brass bands. Wilkie's occupation of the house for four months, from July to October 1862, was a reflection of the changed relationship: if not

* It is now called 'Bleak House'.

Dickens' equal, Wilkie could begin to feel himself in the same league. The spare rooms were an encouragement to visitors; though the house was far too big for his little family, Wilkie went some way towards reconstructing the old style of Dickens' family seaside holidays.

Since they were to stay for four months, Wilkie and Caroline set up house rather grandly at Broadstairs: there was 'a domestic revolution of furniture and luggage. The goods train took *ten* packages today – and we take more with us tomorrow', Wilkie told Frank Beard, urging him to come 'as soon as you can and as often as you can', and warmly thanking him for 'the manner in which you have "brought me up to the scratch" in the slashing battle (still undecided) of Collins against the printer'.[50] Essential conveniences included Dickens' recipe for cider-cup, and a refrigerator.*

Visitors provided diversion and entertainment throughout the summer. Dickens, staying at Dover, discussed plans to meet: 'Would you and yours (Butler of course included) come over in a fly from Broadstairs, and dine with me at the Warden, and then we would all go back to Broadstairs together?'[51] Charles Ward stayed several times, and a sailing lugger was hired for the benefit of Wilkie's old sailing companions Edward Pigott and Henry Bullar. Augustus Egg arrived looking alarmingly ill: Frank Beard's professional eye feared the worst. Wilkie wrote to Millais, asking him, too, to stay. 'I have fled the metropolis to shut myself up and work at my story – which story is a Teazer, and threatens to be longer than "The Woman in White".'[52] Millais was to draw a frontispiece for *No Name*, showing Magdalen gazing from her window, gambling for her life on the number of the passing ships.

Throughout the writing of *No Name* Wilkie pestered Charles Ward, now his general adviser and dogsbody as well as his friend and banker, for information on all sorts of matters for his plot. What day of the week was 4 March 1846 (a Saturday or Sunday wouldn't do)? When would a letter written on 17 March reach Shanghai? And when would the answer be received? How often does the mail go to China? How

* The refrigerator would have been a portable, insulated ice-box more likely to have contained drink than food. Some were shown at the Great Exhibition of 1851.

many days' warning must be given of a marriage by licence? Do you have to leave the licence at the vestry? Must you live in the district where the licence is issued – or in the district of the church? How long does a ship take to go from London to Hong Kong, load up there, and return? 'A letter is posted in Dumfries (N.B.) on the 3rd of November *1847*, in time for that day's post to London. Does the letter reach London, and is it delivered, the morning of the next day (the 4th) – as would be the case now?'[53] The answers to all these and other questions can be found in the novel. Wilkie knew that reviewers and readers, having caught him out on the timing of events in *The Woman in White*, would be on the alert for such mistakes.

Charles Ward was not the only friend to have such demands made on him. Wilkie increasingly made use of – some might say exploited – his other male friends. Though they were all busy professional men, none seems to have resented the way he expected they would drop everything else to discover the answer to a legal or technical point, to arrange for a translation of a letter in a foreign language he didn't know, even to take dictation when he had 'gout in the eyes' and could not write himself. It says much for his charm, and the quality of the accepting, non-judgemental friendship that he gave and expected, that they seem to have been flattered by this involvement in the creative process, rather than irritated. Clearly he gave, in other ways, as much as he took. He was known to everybody as a witty companion and story teller. His close friends could be sure of a welcome, an impromptu meal and a sympathetic ear in Harley Street at any time, a loan when one was needed, and an acceptance of every failing but hypocrisy.

In spite of the visitors, and persistent ill-health, Wilkie wrote steadily while he was at Broadstairs. In August, Low outbid Smith and everyone else for the book-publication rights, offering £3,000, 'the most liberal price that has ever been given for the *re*printing of a work already published periodically'.[54] With the money from *All the Year Round* and *Harper's*, he would have made £4,600. In September Dickens was reading the second volume, going through it at a sitting, and found it 'wonderfully fine'. His earlier reservations were all swept away.

> It goes on with an ever-rising power and force in it that fills me with admiration . . . I cannot tell you with what a strange dash of pride as well as pleasure I read the great results of your hard work. Because, as you know, I was certain from the Basil days that you were the writer who would come ahead of all the Field – being the only one who combined invention and power, both humorous and pathetic, with that invincible determination to work, and that profound conviction that nothing of worth is to be done without work, of which triflers and feigners have no conception . . .[55]

Dickens tactfully pointed out one of Wilkie's persistent grammatical errors: 'There is one slight slip, occurring more than once . . . Magdalen "laid down" and I think someone else "laid down." It is clear that she must either lay herself down, or lie down. To lay is a verb active.' (Wilkie made the alteration.)

Wilkie was delighted with Dickens' praise: 'If I was the vainest man alive, I could not have written of the book, or thought of the book, what *he* has written and thought of it'.[56] But the pressure on him was becoming unbearable. The printing of the book was to begin at once: Low wanted to publish in December, to catch the Christmas market, and at the beginning of October Wilkie sent an account of his symptoms to Frank Beard which suggests that his underlying rheumatic problem was now being complicated by the laudanum he was taking to ease it, or by withdrawal symptoms when he stopped taking it:

> my stomach and nerves are terribly out of order again. Yesterday at 1 o'clock I had to give up work with a deadly 'all-overish' faintness which sent me to the brandy-bottle. No confusion in my brains – but a sickness, faintness, and universal trembling – startled by the slightest noise – more nervous twittering last night – little sleep . . . I seem to digest after dinner pretty well – but at night, or towards the small hours, wake as if I had got drunk . . . my nerves want *soothing* and *fortifying* at the same time.[57]

Alarmed, he cut short his holiday, returning to London to be near Beard. He still had six weeks' work to do on the novel. With the conscientiousness Dickens so much valued, Wilkie felt 'the *possibility* of my breaking down . . . is not only a prospect of miserable loss to *me*, but to others whose money is embarked in *No Name*, in England and out of it'.[58]

Dickens, concerned primarily for his friend, but also for the continuation of the serial in *All the Year Round*, offered his help.

> Write to me at Paris at any moment, and say you are unequal to your work, and want me, and I will come to London straight, and do your work. I am quite confident that, with your notes, and a few words of explanation, I could take it up at any time and do it. Absurdly unnecessary to say that it would be a makeshift! But I could do it, at a pinch, so like you as that no one should find out the difference. Don't make much of this offer in your mind; it is nothing except to ease it. If you should want help, I am as safe as the bank. The trouble will be nothing to me, and the triumph of overcoming a difficulty great . . . You won't want me. You will be well (and thankless) in no time. But there I am; and I hope that the knowledge may be a comfort to you. Call me and I come.[59]

Wilkie didn't want him. He was touched by the generosity of the offer, but also, perhaps, spurred on by it to complete his own novel in his own way. He struggled on, often writing in bed, with Beard in constant attendance, even at times taking down the final instalments from Wilkie's dictation. Wilkie complained that he was doing nothing but write all day and mark proofs all night. But he was near the end at last, and he wrote cheerfully enough to Harriet, to whom he always tried, now, to make light of his illnesses. 'And what I shall do then – whether I shall go mad with the sudden emptiness of head, caused by having nothing to think of, or whether I shall go to Paris and forget myself and my book in that city of dissipation . . .' He added, with an amusement that his mother may not have shared, 'Nothing stirs the stagnation of London but Bishop Colenso. A bishop who doesn't believe in Moses and who writes a book to say so, is an Episcopal portent which makes clergy and laity stare alike.'[60] By 13 November he could tell Nina Lehmann that he had got downstairs 'very, very weak, but decidedly I hope on the road to recovery'.[61] He finished at last on Christmas Eve, at two o'clock in the morning, and he and Caroline celebrated Christmas Day with a dinner at Verrey's, with the bachelor Edward Pigott. Wilkie was always glad to avoid traditional Christmas festivities. 'I suppose you dine at home?' he wrote to Beard. 'As you are a "family man", I dare not say "come too."'[62]

FOURTEEN

No Name

(1862–1864)

No Name was published in three volumes on 31 December 1862, dedicated to Beard in gratitude for his help. The first printing of four thousand copies was almost sold out on the day of publication; but once the reviews began to appear sales fell off sharply. Reviewers were shocked that the novel contained sympathetic characters who outraged the standards of English society and got away with it. The story of the elder Vanstones, who lived in happy and apparently guilt-free domestic harmony for many years though unmarried, was bad enough. Still worse was that of their daughter Magdalen, whose devious and near-criminal acts are finally rewarded by a happy marriage to a loving and protective older man. These affronts to the convention that demanded prompt fictional punishment for social deviation were thought too blatant. A review in the *Athenaeum* by Henry Chorley, a friend of Dickens and of Wilkie, complained that Magdalen was made too attractive a character to be credible: '. . . there must surely be coarseness, as well as meanness, in one capable of such actions and expedients as these'.[1] Margaret Oliphant similarly objected to Magdalen's 'career of vulgar and aimless trickery and wickedness . . . from all the pollutions of which he intends us to believe that she emerges, at the cheap cost of a fever, as pure, as high-minded, and as spotless as the most dazzling white of heroines'.[2] Another reviewer, Alexander Smith, objecting that Wilkie Collins' characters are 'preternaturally acute', found the book clever but repulsive, and complained of its theatricality. 'There never was a young lady like Magdalen, there never was a scoundrel like Wragge, a fool like Vanstone . . . Such people have no representatives in the living world. Their proper place is in the glare of blue lights on a stage sacred to the sensation drama.'[3]

Yet for most of the novel, Wilkie was careful to play down the sensational. His notes on a true story told him by an acquaintance soon after the publication of *The Woman in White* (clearly elicited by the incarceration of Anne Catherick in an asylum) show that, however much he objected to censorship from Mudie and the publishers, he was always careful of the prejudices of his readers. The anecdote concerned a noblewoman who revealed that she had been seduced before marriage and become completely promiscuous, going out at night into the streets of London in the company of a prostitute. Her husband, believing her mad, shut her up in an asylum. All her claims proved true. Her family first suppressed the facts in order to marry her off, then insisted she was deluded and preferred to have her locked up rather than admit the truth. She was let out of the asylum, perfectly sane and completely unrepentant. Wilkie never used this. He considered it would only be possible to do so by adapting it, either 'without the shocking sexual irregularities' or by changing the character's sex 'and making him confess some terrible crime to his wife, who hopes as well as believes the confession to be a delusion – and then finds it true'.[4]

He pointed out in the preface to *No Name* that the theme of the novel was the struggle between good and evil, personified in the 'pathetic' character of Magdalen: 'I have tried hard to attain this result . . . by a resolute adherence, throughout, to the truth as it is in Nature.' He also emphasized that he was not, this time, writing a mystery novel: 'The only Secret contained in this book, is revealed midway in the first volume. From that point, all the main events of the story are purposely foreshadowed, before they take place'. He had turned from the supercharged *Basil* to write the domestic, Dickensian *Hide and Seek*. Now he abandoned the mythic world of *The Woman in White*. *No Name* is, apart from forty pages of highly effective Gothic sensation, a realist investigation of individual psychology that was closer to the fiction of George Eliot than anything else he had written.

> Does there exist in every human being, beneath that outward and visible character which is shaped into form by the social influence surrounding us, an inward, invisible disposition, which is part of ourselves; which education may indirectly modify, but can never hope to change? . . . Are there, infinitely varying with each individual, inbred forces of Good and Evil in all of us, deep down below the reach of mortal encouragement, and mortal repression – hidden Good and hidden Evil, both alike at the mercy of the liberating opportunity and the sufficient temptation? . . . is earthly circumstance ever the key; and can no human vigilance warn us beforehand of the forces imprisoned in ourselves which that key *may* unlock? (*No Name*, The First Scene, Chap. 14, p. 103)

This was to be echoed by the creator of Gwendolen Harleth,* a character who has much in common with Magdalen Vanstone:

> Goodness is a large, often a prospective word; like harvest, which at one stage when we talk of it lies all underground, with an indeterminate future: is the germ prospering in the darkness? . . . Each stage has its peculiar blight, and may have the healthy life choked out of it by a particular action of the foul land which rears or neighbours it, or by damage brought from foulness afar. (*Daniel Deronda*, Book I, Chap. 7)

To explore these questions Wilkie made use of his mother's experiences. He told a correspondent many years later that the plot of *No Name* was entirely imaginary. But some situations, characters and background details do correspond with her autobiographical manuscript, which he probably still had in his possession. The Vanstone family, in their West Country village, their quiet existence interspersed with the gaieties of the local town, have their origin in Harriet's memories of the Geddeses of Alderbury. The cheerful, easygoing Andrew Vanstone, with his background of army service in Canada, is closely modelled on Wilkie's grandfather, Alexander Geddes. The Geddes family had no fortune to lose: for his fictional purposes Wilkie heightened their descent from genteel poverty into

* George Eliot and G. H. Lewes read *No Name* aloud to each other as it came out. '[It] gets rather dreary', Lewes wrote to his son. (*The George Eliot Letters*, Vol. 4, p. 32)

near-indigence, making his heroine and her sister suffer a violent peripeteia from affluence and respectability to penniless illegitimacy. The description of the eighteen-year-old Magdalen, before the family disasters, is very similar to Harriet's self-portrait of a giddy girl, witty, lively and attractive, her father's favourite. Harriet Geddes, like Magdalen Vanstone, was mad about acting. Faced with family catastrophe and the need to earn her own living, she proposed to become an actress. She was persuaded, with great reluctance, to become a governess instead. 'Why must I give up the stage? for which I felt sure I was fit, to be a governess for which I knew I was so totally unfit? . . . surely I thought I need not be wicked because I go on the stage, could I not be religious as an actress?'[5] What if she had carried out her fantasy of retrieving the family fortunes by going on the stage? What if she had become a Magdalen, rather than a docile Norah? Would that 'inward, invisible disposition, which is part of ourselves' have shown itself in some entirely unexpected way?

Wilkie may also have intended a gentle, indirect reproach to his mother in making use of her circumstances and potentialities in this way. Harriet Geddes matured into a governess who, like Harriet Garth in the novel, was treated with respect and affection by the families for whom she worked. 'This was evidently not one of the forlorn, persecuted, pitiably dependent order of governesses. Here was a woman who lived on ascertainable and honourable terms with her employers – a woman who looked capable of sending any parents in England to the right-about, if they failed to rate her at her proper value.'[6] But the upright, honourable and generous Miss Garth has to learn to abandon her rigid principles, and her confidence in her own judgement of character. She discovers that the Vanstones, the happy, loving couple who 'never let me remember that I was their governess . . . only let me know myself as their companion and their friend', had kept from her for twelve years the secret that they were not married.[7] She has to revise her judgement of the girls she had known since they were children, learning to value Norah and to distrust her faith in Magdalen. She has to examine her own hidden motivations. ' "Oh!" she thought bitterly, "how long I have lived in the world, and how little I have known of my own weakness and wickedness until today!" '[8]

Harriet Collins' uncompromising attitude to Wilkie's relationship with Caroline, her refusal even to acknowledge Caroline's existence, are matched, in the novel, by Harriet Garth's temporary abandonment of Magdalen. 'What do good women like you, know of miserable sinners like me? All you know is that you pray for us at church,' Magdalen writes bitterly to her former governess.[9]

The originals of Captain Wragge, the small-time villain who finds himself outclassed by his pupil, and of his huge, pathetic, retarded wife, can also be found in Harriet's manuscript. Her description of the 'family friend Mr. Bartlet', a stockbroker who cheated her father out of the small remains of his inheritance, gave Wilkie the hint on which he constructed his comic confidence-man and wife:

> Mr. and Mrs. Bartlet arrived I at once took a prejudice against him, but as all the rest of the family seemed charmed with him, I held my tongue, and kept out of his way as much as I could, for he had a bold leering expression, when he looked or spoke to me, that gave me a feeling of displeasure I could scarcely define. I found the surest way to avoid him was to stick close to his wife, who he openly derided and neglected. She was a fat goodnatured rather silly person, and evidently very much in awe of him, for after his departure she was left with us a few weeks and seemed to enjoy it as a child home for holidays from a very strict school. Before he went away he made such warm protestations of the interest and attachment he felt for us all, and at the same time more than hinting he could make our fortune, that I began to be ashamed of my dislike . . .[10]

The 'Bartlets' lived in Lambeth, and Margaret Geddes stayed with them for a while when she first went to London. It is to that district that Magdalen, in the novel, takes Mrs Wragge as a cover for her first attempt to deceive Noel Vanstone.

> Mrs. Wragge was seated at the table, absorbed in the arrangement of a series of smart circulars and tempting price-lists . . . 'I've often heard tell of light reading,' said Mrs. Wragge, restlessly shifting the position of the circulars, as a child restlessly shifts the position of a new set of toys. 'Here's light reading, printed in pretty colours. Here's all the Things I'm going to buy when I'm out shopping to-morrow . . .' She looked up at Magdalen, chuckled joyfully over her own altered circumstances, and beat her great hands on the table in irrepressible

delight. 'No cookery-book!' cried Mrs. Wragge. 'No Buzzing in my head! No captain to shave tomorrow! I'm all down at heel; my cap's on one side; and nobody bawls at me. My heart alive, here *is* a holiday and no mistake!' (*No Name*, The Third Scene, Chap. 1, p. 190)

Harriet Collins' naïve account, and the development of it into the complex comic characterization of Captain Wragge and his wife that emerged in the novel, give an instructive glimpse of the novelist's imagination at work. Wragge, the shameless 'moral agriculturalist' who looks like 'a clergyman in difficulties', is one of Wilkie's most convincing rogues. To follow the successful portrait of the Italian Fosco by the essentially English criminal Wragge was a triumph. The complexities of Fosco's ambiguous duel with Marian Halcombe are replaced by Wragge's relationship with Magdalen, one of mutual exploitation which turns into something close to affection. To the hints given by his mother's account, Wilkie added the compulsive neatness and the urge to keep written records that he often gave to his villains. Though their written testimony is essential to his plots, because of his method of construction, he manages to make many of them seem convincing as born writers. The grotesque parody of domestic life in the relationship of the outsize, accident-prone Mrs Wragge, weeping over the incomprehensible instructions in the cookery book, and her fierce little husband carries an irresistible suggestion of Wilkie's observations of a certain great writer and the overweight wife whose bracelets tended to slide into the soup. Whether or not this was intended, Mrs Wragge was acknowledged by Lewis Carroll as the inspiration for that other great literary creation, the White Queen.

'Put your cap straight!' shouted her husband. 'I beg ten thousand pardons,' he resumed, again addressing himself to Magdalen. 'The sad truth is, I am a martyr to my own sense of order. All untidiness, all want of system and regularity, causes me the acutest irritation. My attention is distracted, my composure is upset; I can't rest till things are set straight again. Externally speaking, Mrs. Wragge is, to my infinite regret, the crookedest woman I ever met with. More to the right!' shouted the captain, as Mrs. Wragge, like a well-trained child, presented herself with her revised head-dress for her husband's inspection. (*No Name*, The Second Scene, p. 147)

Some of the comedy in the minor characters seems to have been formed by exaggeration and extension of the traits of Wilkie's friends. Mr Clare's attitude to his sons, 'three human superfluities in dirty jackets and noisy boots', and his determination to pack off his 'lout' Frank to the ends of the earth, echo Dickens' own grumbling about the noise made by his sons, and his sons' boots, in his letters to Wilkie and others. 'I shall pack Frank off tomorrow. In course of time, he'll come back again on our hands like a bad shilling,' says Mr Clare. Frank is dispatched to China; but his father's prediction comes true. Dickens wrote a series of letters to the Lehmanns about getting his seventeen-year-old son Alfred a business post abroad, *after* the publication of *No Name*, which chillingly recall Wilkie's character: 'I still hanker after India, or some such distant field, for the reasons I suggested to you when I last saw you. Those reasons are very strong with me, simply because I have formed them on observation at home.' Dickens found a firm which would employ Alfred first in Manchester, and then send him to China to learn the silk trade, just like Frank Clare. Frank is told that 'If he made a fair use of his opportunities in China, he would come back, while still a young man, fit for a position of trust and emolument'.[11] Dickens was assured that 'There was not the slightest doubt of the young man's getting on in China and making money if he would only be steady and industrious.' However, two years later he was still trying to settle the unfortunate Alfred. 'I have written to [Sir Charles Nicholson] asking him if he can help me to dispose of this boy of mine in Australia. Of course I told him the exact truth without any softening . . . I will give you a Patriarchal piece of advice – Don't have any more children. If the childless Kings and Queens in the stories had only known what they were about, they would never have bothered the Fairies to give them families.'[12]

But of course Wilkie, in Charlotte Brontë's phrase, only suffered reality 'to *suggest*, never to *dictate*'. His mother's experiences were augmented by those of Mary Braddon, who had kept herself and her mother for three years by going on the stage, and by the early history of Laura Seymour, the actress who lived with Charles Reade. Mrs Seymour, left a penniless orphan at fourteen, kept herself and her younger sister by going on the stage, understudying Fanny Kemble, acting for a while with Macready's company in Dublin and marrying, without love, a middle-aged man who had been kind to her. Such experiences provided the jumping-off point for his plot and his central character.

She also has, like all heroes and heroines, something of her creator in her. Magdalen Vanstone is a spoilt child who finds, for the first time in her life, something to fix her attention and exercise her intelligence, when she has the chance to use her histrionic ability. Her 'one-woman' performances are suggested to Captain Wragge by the 'At Homes' of Charles Mathews.* She steals the characteristics of her friends and relations to base her characters on. In the same way the novelist uses certain traits of experiences of *his* friends and relations, and tries out different skins to jump into.

Magdalen soon gives up public performance: 'It was innocent enough, God knows,' she writes bitterly to Miss Garth. Instead she outpaces Captain Wragge, realizing that she has more to gain by using her acting ability secretly, to win the big prizes – revenge, respectability and money – that can only be hers in the conventional way, through marriage. ' "Thousands of women marry for money," she said. "Why shouldn't I?" ' The horror of marrying a man who makes her flesh creep is not glossed over. Sickly as Noel Vanstone is, there is no suggestion in the novel – though there is in the dramatization made from it – that the brief marriage is not consummated. An anonymous reviewer in the *Reader* thought that Wilkie Collins failed to reach 'sensational grandeur' because, as an English novelist, he could not 'dwell upon seductions, intrigues, infidelities and illegitimate connections . . . without sacrificing the sympathy of an ordinary English reader . . . Unfortunately it was essential that Magdalen should not commit the one unpardonable sin of our English code, and the necessity of preserving her respectability to the end has sadly trammelled Mr. Collins's powers of invention.'[13] This missed Wilkie's point that a loveless marriage, cold-bloodedly undertaken, is infinitely more reprehensible than any number of 'illegitimate connections', as Magdalen very well knows: 'I have made the general sense of

* William Collins first showed his love for Harriet Geddes at one of these. See p. 17.

propriety my accomplice this time . . . I am a respectable married woman, accountable for my actions to nobody under heaven but my husband. I have got a place in the world, and a name in the world, at last . . . [my wickedness] has made Nobody's Child, Somebody's Wife.'[14]

No Name is filled with questions about the position of women. They are implicit in Magdalen's story, explicit in her bitter questioning of the legal system which deprives her of her status and inheritance, and the social system which sanctions the selling of a woman's body within marriage but not outside it. Why should the exploitation of a governess be respectable, while the profession of acting is not? In a key scene Magdalen persuades her maid Louisa, who has had an illegitimate child, to change places with her, and teach her the duties and behaviour of a servant. '"I should be found out, ma'am," interposed Louisa, trembling at the prospect before her. "I am not a lady." "And I am," said Magdalen, bitterly. "Shall I tell you what a lady is? A lady is a woman who wears a silk gown, and has a sense of her own importance. I shall put the gown on your back, and the sense in your head."'[15]

Magdalen's assumed characters are easily imposed on men: Wilkie suggests that imposing on men is what all women have to do, all their lives, though most of them do not take their stratagems to such lengths as she does. She is less successful in imposing on other women. She is outwitted by Mrs Lecount, and the women servants at St Crux, where she goes as a parlour maid, are jealous and suspicious of her from the beginning. Viewed objectively, the women are right. Magdalen's behaviour is at best devious, at worst criminal. Like Gwendolen Harleth, she desires the death of her husband, while not going so far as to murder him. Mrs Lecount, in contrast, does nothing criminal, and is restrained where she might be exorbitant, taking only her due from Noel Vanstone's fortune. Yet the reader's sympathies are consistently with Magdalen; Norah, who might act as a counterweight in the scales of good and evil, is so insignificant a figure in the book that in a stage version made in 1870 she is turned into a helpless cripple who never appears.[16] Wilkie took the risk of soliciting the reader's identification with a heroine who behaves in a way that ought to land her in gaol and that makes her an outcast from society. He succeeded triumphantly. At the end of the novel Magdalen cleanses herself by a full confession, first to her sister, then, more importantly, to her rescuer, Captain Kirke, and both accept her without question: '. . . he knew the priceless value, the all-enobling virtue, of a woman who speaks the truth'.[17]

The doctrinal aspect of Magdalen's confession, and the Christian duty of forgiveness of sin, are underlined by Kirke's name and that of his ship, *The Deliverance.* Such hints are increasingly important in the last pages of the novel: St Crux, the house where Magdalen makes her final, unsuccessful attempt to regain her inheritance, and Aaron's Buildings, where she is raised from the dead by Kirke's care, are not accidentally named. A novel which has, for most of its length, been a daring and convincing defence of criminal behaviour manages, in the end, to persuade the reader that it is possible to take the black sheep back into the fold with no recriminations. Wilkie, no orthodox believer, had the impudence to take Christ's teaching literally, retelling the parable of the prodigal son, but applying it to a clever and beautiful woman. No wonder the reviewers objected.

Wilkie, no longer simply one of the runners in the Dickens stable, was now seen as the begetter of a different kind of fiction. George Bentley's description of Wilkie as the 'King of Inventors', who first made sensation fashionable, dates from 1863. More woundingly, Wilkie was told scornfully by one of the guests at a dinner party in Frith's house that his novels were read 'in every back-kitchen in England'. The jibe failed to disturb him. He was more anxious about surviving the strain of producing serial novels. Only thirty-nine, he was prematurely aged by illness. His opium habit proved impossible to break, though he made several attempts to do so. He was never thrown off balance by it, or unable to work because of it. On the contrary, he felt it kept him going. 'Who was the man who invented laudanum? I thank him from the bottom of my heart, whoever he was. If all the miserable wretches in pain of body or mind, whose comforter he has been, could meet together to sing his praises, what a chorus it would be!' The words are Lydia Gwilt's, but the sentiment is undoubtedly Wilkie's.[18] However, he needed ever larger doses to keep him stabilized, and to deal with the pain and sleeplessness his illness caused. Turning down an invitation to become a director of a new journal, he gave his commitment to Smith, Elder and *The Cornhill* as one reason, the state of his health as another. 'The necessity of husbanding my energies . . . I have good reason to know is not to be trifled with.'[19]

For many months after the publication of *No Name* he was unable to write. The contract with George Smith, though it relieved him of anxiety about money, was a pressure on so conscientious a journeyman, and the mysterious 'rheumatic gout' seemed, that January, to have turned to true gout in his right foot. Wilkie was barely able to get up or down one flight of stairs. He made light of the pain to his mother, assuring her it was kept in check by 'a simple poultice of cabbage leaves covered with oiled silk', but he admitted the truth to others. Caroline was also ill with some kind of nervous disorder; and during this crisis Frank Beard, bedridden with erysipelas, was unable to look after them. Wilkie consulted John Elliotson, the unorthodox pioneer of medical hypnosis. He was a friend of Dickens, and had saved Thackeray's life in 1849. Wilkie liked Elliotson, respected him as a scientist, and was interested in his ideas about mesmerism. In *The Moonstone* he refers to him as 'one of the greatest of English physiologists', and quotes from his 1840 book *Human Physiology*. But he had little faith in him as a practitioner. Elliotson obviously disapproved of the opium Beard had prescribed, and tried unsuccessfully to wean Wilkie off it. 'He is so kind and good, and so full of sincere sympathy for both of us, that it pains me to say it . . . He *has* done and *can* do nothing for me.' The gout attacked his left foot, while remaining in his right, immobilizing him. Elliotson suggested that Caroline should 'mesmerize' his feet, and 'mesmerize me into sleeping so as to do without the opium!'[20] Wilkie dutifully tried the new regime, and reported to Beard that it had begun well: he managed a night without opium. But the mesmeric sessions had a bad effect on Caroline, who was 'apparently going to have another nervous-hysterical attack. She was up all last night with the "palpitations".'[21] Withdrawal of the opium also contributed to Wilkie's restless nights and 'fidgets'; he was glad when Beard was well enough to see him again.

He was not yet prepared to accept that his illness was incurable. He spent the next two years searching for better treatments, a more suitable climate, new drugs. Finally he realized that the best he could hope for was to contain the condition and alleviate the symptoms. Whenever possible he avoided taking colchicum, an effective drug, but one with the unpleasant side effects of nausea and vomiting. Instead he took quinine and potassium, in addition to the laudanum. He tried various kinds of baths: salt-water, Turkish and Caplin's 'electro-magnetic' baths, which he considered did wonders for him. 'Rating the pores of my skin at only 7 millions – I have had 7 million currents of electricity running through me for 45 minutes. The result is great cheerfulness and great disinclination to pay Inland Revenue.'[22] From time to time, very reluctantly, he went on diets, 'the flavourless-wholesome, mildly mitigated by sherry and water'.[23] His advice to his mother during a heatwave was more characteristic: '. . . if you feel hot, try a bottle of Sauterne . . . four pinches of snuff – and a mild cigar'.[24]

Beard was encouraging about Wilkie's gout, putting forward the dubious theory that the illness had previously been 'suppressed', and that he would be better now that it had come into the open. 'Are there no baths that would drive the rheumatic Devil out of that game leg?' Dickens wanted to know, suggesting that they might take a trip abroad together.[25] But Wilkie was too ill to travel, even when Dickens sent the tempting news from Paris at the end of January that 'Paris is immeasurably more wicked than ever.'[26] Meanwhile work on the new novel was again postponed. Though the first part should have been ready for *The Cornhill* by the beginning of December, Wilkie had not even begun to think about constructing the book.

On 3 April Holman Hunt brought Wilkie the news that Augustus Egg had died at Algiers. Wilkie rocked to and fro in his distress. 'It is a calamity, in every sense of the word, for everyone who knew him.'[27] 'What a large part of a good many years he seems to have taken with him', Dickens wrote. 'How often have I thought, since the news of his death came, of his putting his part in the saucepan (with the cover on) when we rehearsed the Lighthouse; of his falling out of the hammock when we rehearsed The Frozen Deep . . . of his losing my invaluable knife in that beastly stage-coach . . . In my memory of the dear gentle little fellow, he will be . . . eternally posting up that book at the large table in the middle of our Venice sitting-room, incidentally asking the name of an hotel three weeks back!'[28]

Egg's family circumstances were, in some ways, as dubious as Wilkie's. He had finally married, in 1860, but seems never to have introduced his wife to anyone. She was Esther Mary Brown, from Limehouse in the East End of London.[29] He left her £1,000 and an income of £200 a year for her lifetime, in a strictly controlled trust, which she was not to be allowed to anticipate 'in any manner whatsoever'.[30] His friends closed ranks in silence over his marriage. 'It is not now our purpose to ferret out his private life . . . and unbury his private joys and sorrows', Hunt wrote in his memoir, insisting that 'the domestic matter' was 'shut up and sealed sacredly'.[31]

Such intimations of mortality, acutely felt by Dickens, also cast a shadow over Wilkie. Fortunately he had no immediate need of money: his balance at the bank was large enough for him to lend money to Frank Beard.[32] He could afford to follow Dickens' advice, and he decided to take the waters at the spa towns of Aix-la-Chapelle and Wildbad. George Smith was considerate and forbearing, agreeing to postpone the serialization of the novel once more, and in the middle of April Wilkie and Caroline, with a German courier to take care of all travelling arrangements, left London, journeying to Aix by easy stages.

He was cheered by the excellence of the hotels at Aix, and by finding himself as much of a celebrity there as he was in London. He had to sit for his photograph, and sign his name over and over again for autograph hunters: 'German readers, French readers, American readers, all vying in civilities and attention'.[33] At first the sulphurous water, which came out of the earth so hot that it had to be cooled before it could be used, seemed to do him some good. 'I get into the water up to my middle – an amiable elderly German gets in with me – puts the rose of a gigantic watering pot on to the end of a pipe . . . and lets a . . . stream of hot sulpherous [*sic*] water down on my back and legs'.[34] But the treatment was rapidly undermined by the relaxed attitude of the local doctor. Nuellan's Hotel had an excellent cellar, and a Parisian cook whose entrées encouraged Wilkie's gluttony; the doctor, 'a model physician', was a jolly German who allowed '*all* wines provided they are of the best vintages' and any kind of food, including snacks and luncheons. Wilkie, rather than rising early with the other invalids to drink the disgusting water – 'like the worst London egg you ever had for breakfast' – sent his courier for it, and drank it in bed.[35]

An inconclusive month at Aix was followed by a stay at Wildbad. Wilkie was still unable to begin the novel, but the descriptions of the town he sent to his mother appear almost word for word in the first chapter of *Armadale*. He liked Wildbad, set in the beautiful Black Forest. It had a snug little library, full of English and French books, and a local shoemaker who made him a pair of soft slippers 'which fit to a miracle'. He was struck by the contrast of the luxury and entertainment provided for the invalid visitors – 'a Bath House as big as Buckingham Palace, and infinitely superior to it in architectural beauty' – and the human suffering which paid for it. 'Paralysis comes here, and pays the bills . . . Rheumatism puts its aching hand in its pocket with a groan.'[36]

He was intrigued by pseudo-scientific theories about the possibility of 'electric influence' in the clear warm water; but Wildbad did him little good. His condition seemed if anything to deteriorate, though he was persuaded that this was due to 'the severe curative *process*' of the baths. He left after a month. At last, at Strasbourg on the way home, an idea for the book came to him. He longed to be back at work; after ten years of writing, the long break was irksome. But he was wary of attempting too much too soon, and the patient George Smith was still prepared to wait, though the book was now six months overdue.

Wilkie's ideas for *Armadale* also required a visit to the Isle of Man, 'the one inaccessible place left in the world'. He and Pigott hired a yacht at Cowes in July, hoping to sail there up the west coast, but the damp air at sea made Wilkie's rheumatism worse, and the cruise was abandoned after ten days. He finally got to the island at the end of August, taking Caroline and Carrie with him. It was not an experience he cared for. The man who so often used trains in the plots of his novels hated travelling by them, but he was obliged to go by rail to Liverpool, and then take the steamer. The Isle of Man might be difficult of access, but he soon found that didn't stop the tourists going there. 'All Lancashire goes to the Isle of Man, and all Lancashire is capable of improvement in looks and breeding.'[37] The steamer was horribly crowded, and the passengers were disembarked in boats: 'an old lady tumbled into the water, and fished up again by her venerable heels'.[38] Things were no better once they had landed: Douglas was bitterly cold and their hotel was damp, every third shop sold spirits, and every second inhabitant was drunk. Leaving his women behind, Wilkie made the difficult journey to the Calf of Man, the little island at the south end of the Isle of Man. Failing to get there by sea in a dirty little fishing-boat that had to turn back because of the heavy seas, he tried again by land in a jaunting car, and though he was horribly jolted he found the place was 'wild and frightful . . . everything made for my occult literary purposes'. Having seen what he needed he beat a hasty retreat to London.

His next publication was *My Miscellanies*, two volumes of selections from his non-fiction articles in *Household Words* and *All the Year Round*. The collection was dedicated to Henry Bullar, and in the preface Wilkie specifically dissociated himself from the 'Lay Preacher' school of essayists. 'Views of life and society to set us thinking penitently in some cases, or doubting contemptuously in others, were, I thought, quite plentiful enough already. More freshness and novelty of appeal to the much-lectured and much-enduring reader, seemed to lie in views which might put us on easier terms with ourselves and others'.[39] Leaving Charles Ward the task of overseeing publication, Wilkie left for Italy, determined to 'run for it' to a milder climate before the winter set in.

FIFTEEN

Armadale: The Self and the Shadow

(1863–1866)

Wilkie and Caroline took Carrie with them to Italy, on a journey that lasted over four months. Carrie was the age Wilkie had been when he first went there: he could relive, through her eyes, that enchanted experience. They travelled slowly, for Wilkie was still not strong, stopping in Paris before going in stages, by rail, *vetturino* and steamer, to Rome. Fine weather met them at Nice, where everything had changed since Wilkie was there as a boy: now there were immense hotels all along the sea front, and the town had grown to three times the size. Wilkie was enchanted by San Remo and Mentone, the lemons and olives ripening close to the sea under a cloudless sky, the inhabitants sleeping in the sun on the pavements. His health and spirits improved to such an extent that his only serious worry was the nightly attacks of the mosquitoes, which he foiled by inventing 'a small muslin *balloon* which ties under my beard, and encloses my whole head and face'. Caroline sewed up the sleeves of his nightgown with a couple of old pocket handkerchiefs. 'In this extraordinary costume, I can hear the musquitoes humming all round me . . . in the grey of the morning, I see them crawling over my muslin balloon and my cambric mufflers . . . stopping to consider in "indignation meetings" of twos and threes – expressing their sentiments in a sound like a very small wind at a very great distance – and then flying away in disgust.'[1]

But the sirocco set in at Pisa, and 'the pangs of sciatica wrung me in both *hams* at once'. A rough sea-journey from Leghorn to Civita Vecchia didn't trouble Wilkie, but was a night's martyrdom for Caroline and Carrie: 'Caroline Senior was so ill that she could not be moved from the deck all night.'

They lived in Wilkie's usual style at Rome, taking a hotel apartment of five rooms and hiring a carriage. Wilkie employed a cook as well as their courier. Charles Ward dispatched regular letters of credit, £500 at a time, and essential supplies of Wilkie's favourite snuff. Though the unstable political situation made exchange rates problematic ('There is one price for the Pope's gold and another for Victor Emmanuel's, and another for Louis Napoleon's and another for silver'), Wilkie was in a very different situation from that of ten years earlier, when he could barely afford the laundry bills, and had to borrow from Dickens to get by.

The only annoyances in Rome were the weather, now a cause for invalidish concern wherever Wilkie went, and the French garrison. 'Two ferociously-conceited little warriors were marching briskly about the sacred neighbourhood of the Colosseum yesterday, practising bugle-calls . . . enjoying their own noise as only Frenchmen can – and not far off, an awkward squad was actually being drilled under the very arches of the old Temple of Peace. Nothing is serious, to a Frenchman, except soldiering – and nothing astonishes him but the spectacle of his own bravery.'[2]

They moved on to Naples, hoping for better weather in the south, only to find 'furious, drenching, tropical rain'. The King was in Naples, and all sorts of festivities were held in his honour, but Wilkie, unwell and made cautious by his equivocal status as an unmarried man accompanied by a woman and child, kept out of them. He did call on the banker Iggulden and his wife, now old and shrunken. 'Iggulden was (to my astonishment) struck by *my size*, which he appeared to associate in some way with the success of my books.' Mrs Iggulden, deeply depressed, could talk only about her own approaching death. 'I persisted in making bad jokes all through the interview – and I think I did her good.'[3] Naples, except for gas lighting, was much the same as when he was a boy – deformed beggars in the streets, half-naked children, 'all the old stinks' – and seemed unaffected by the political changes. It stimulated Wilkie's imagination, and ideas for the book began to come 'as thick as blackberries'. Some of the episodes in *Armadale* are set in Naples, and topographical details are careful and accurate. But Wilkie's health deteriorated again. Though the weather was now fine, he persisted in believing that the climate was responsible – this time he blamed the mild sea air – and determined to move. He was urged to try Cairo, but, as he said evasively to his mother, there were many reasons why he could not go there – most of them no doubt relating to Caroline and Carrie. They returned to Rome for the winter.

Back in his favourite city, Wilkie instantly felt better. Rome was crowded with English visitors, but Wilkie again kept out of society, legitimately if conveniently pleading ill-health and the demands of his book. It was turning out to be 'a rather extraordinary story . . . entirely different from anything I have done yet'. When he did go out, he preferred the opera to dinners and balls: 'No infernal fuss and expense and evening costume'; instead Verdi's music, an excellent orchestra, and good singing and dancing.

Wilkie at forty, turning grey and suffering almost continuously from rheumatism and gout, had 'all the worst signs of middle-age sprouting out on me', yet he didn't feel old. 'I have no regular habits, no respectable prejudices, no tendency to go to sleep after dinner . . . Surely, there is some mistake? Are you and I really as old as *you* suppose?' he wrote to Harriet on his birthday, telling her, in the indirect terms he used to avoid any mention of Caroline, '[I] manage to lead my own life at Rome in my own way. I leave *you* to whirl in the vortex of society, and to represent your vagabond eldest son among Persons of Quality'.[4] She was seventy-three, and her 'gay doings' alternately pleased and alarmed the anxious Charley. But death was in the air, and in spite of Wilkie's insouciant tone he was affected by it. Egg had gone first, then Janet Chambers, Nina Lehmann's younger sister, who was only twenty-seven. Wilkie had enchanted her six years earlier, setting himself to please her when she was his neighbour at a fish dinner at Greenwich given by Thackeray. Next, just before Christmas, came Thackeray's own death. Charley and Kate were his near neighbours, and were the first people to be called in by the servants. 'I shall never forget the day which we passed at the house', Charley wrote to Wilkie, 'or the horror of seeing him lying there so dreadfully changed.'[5] Though Wilkie had never been intimate with him, as Charley and Kate were, he was saddened by Thackeray's death. At least he had lived long enough 'to do the work of a great writer'. Less than a year later John Leech's death shocked and distressed him more. 'I heartily liked him – and we had many nervous troubles in common.'

Of more immediate concern was the death at Rome in December of his German courier, Nidecker, of 'gastric fever'. Wilkie cared for him as if he had been a relation, and had a grateful letter from his brother. It seems possible that this death gave rise to one of the apocryphal stories about Wilkie, as untrue as the slander that he was drunk at Alice Ward's christening. A manservant was rumoured to have died from experimenting with a dose from Wilkie's bottle of laudanum. Hall Caine, a very unreliable witness, claimed that Wilkie told this story himself, but there is no evidence that there was any basis for it.

Otherwise, his domestic landscape began to look brighter. Caroline's persistent ill-health cleared up at last, and she had some colour in her cheeks, though she began to long for home after three months abroad. 'How like cats women are!' Wilkie commented, consciously or unconsciously echoing his mother.* 'Caroline Junior' had a small digestive upset, easily cured: 'we threw in a little pill and fired off a small explosion of Gregory's powder'. She was then 'in higher spirits than ever, and astonishes the Roman public by the essentially British plumpness of her cheeks and calves'.[6] Wilkie found time to visit some of the sights with them: Carrie must have enjoyed hearing children, some as young as five, preaching on the Feast of the Innocents, the congregation shouting 'Bravo' as each child (male or female) ended, and the next 'popped up into the temporary pulpit like a Jack in the Box'.[7]

When they returned to London in March the groundwork of *Armadale* had been laid, and Wilkie began to write, hesitantly at

* See p. 34.

first, in April, after a year and a half of 'total literary abstinence'. There was still research to do: he needed to visit the east coast of England for the background to some of the key scenes. He consulted Dickens' solicitor Frederick Ouvry about the details of a marriage by special licence: Ouvry obligingly lent him his own marriage licence so that he could get the details exactly right. Wilkie still found it confusing. 'And why (I add, with both hands entangled madly in my hair) do I find (the bridegroom being described as living in one parish), the bride described, in defiance of the laws of time and space, as living in two parishes at once? Never let your good nature tempt you again into helping a literary man . . . You never get rid of him afterwards . . . the more you grant, the more [the] ungrateful wretch asks . . .' Sure enough, the following day he sent Ouvry a letter full of supplementary questions.[8]

He had all sorts of schemes for the future: they might move from noisy Harley Street, where his work suffered from pianos at the back of the house and 'bagpipes, bands and Punches' at the front. He considered the suburbs, or the peace of the Temple. He might buy a yacht – but not until the book was finished. He was determined to avoid too much dining out, but there was one invitation he was delighted to accept: 'The Royal Academy have woke up at last to the knowledge that your eldest son is a literary man – and have asked him to their Grand Dinner this year.'[9]

He managed to deliver the first part of the novel to Smith at the beginning of June. By August he was able to go to Great Yarmouth with Pigott and Charles Ward, to sail and to look at the landscape of the Broads for the next section of the novel. The little town of Aylsham, about fifteen miles inland, has been suggested as the basis for the Thorpe Ambrose of the novel; more certain is the use made of Horsey Mere, which corresponds closely to the Hurle Mere where Lydia Gwilt makes her dramatic appearance in Chapter 9 of the second book. Wilkie used his favourite pastime as an important ingredient of a novel for the first time: Allan Armadale has a passion for sailing, and the sea provides a linking motif for the dramatic and dangerous events that extend over two generations.

Back in Harley Street at the beginning of September, he was making his own flesh creep with writing the episode of the wreck, and Allan Armadale's dream, the clue to the tortuously complicated plot. The descriptions in this part of the book have a haunting, hallucinatory quality, and it may not be coincidental that Wilkie wrote to Pigott in great distress on 24 September:

> knowing your affectionate regard for me, I am afraid I shall disturb you. My illness declared itself on Monday last – the gout has attacked my brain. My mind is perfectly clear – but the nervous misery I suffer is indescribable.
>
> Beard has no fear of the attack proving absolutely dangerous – but he cannot yet decide when I can work again, or what is to be done about the Cornhill. With Smith away, and the first number made up on the 1st of next month, the disaster is complete – unless I take a turn to the better, in the next few days.
>
> For the present, keep all this *a profound secret* . . . If I *can* conceal my condition from my mother, I *must*.[10]

Gout does not attack the brain. Wilkie's nervous misery may have been due simply to stress, but perhaps he had overdosed on laudanum. He had the habit of using ingenious excuses to evade the real reasons for his indispositions. He claimed, a few weeks later, that his digestion was out of order, not because of eating and drinking, but caused by 'the horrible East Wind stopping up my skin, and by so stopping it, collecting my bile'.[11] Fortunately this attack on his brain was brief, and by the middle of October he was staying at Dover with Dickens and Georgina Hogarth, showing them the early instalments of *Armadale* in proof, and cheered by their reactions. 'Miss Hogarth couldn't sleep till she had finished them – and (to quote quite another sort of opinion) . . . the *Printers* are highly interested in the story . . . it is no easy matter to please the printers.'[12]

The serialization, so long postponed, began in the November issue of *The Cornhill*, and a month later in *Harper's Monthly Magazine*. The United States was in the turmoil of the Civil War, and Wilkie feared its effects on the sale of books. In fact the success of the serialization of *Armadale* saved the magazine from closure, cementing his already excellent relationship with Harper.[13]

Wilkie was reasonably advanced with the writing, but he was ill once more, with nervous and giddy symptoms that alarmed him. At Beard's suggestion he consulted Dr Charles Radcliffe, a specialist in nervous diseases, who diagnosed 'gouty irritation', but was confident that there was nothing seriously wrong. Wilkie was put on a light diet, and enjoined to keep regular hours and take exercise, avoiding dinner parties and 'society'. He managed to stick to this abstinence for about two months. Thereafter he relied more on a concoction of Beard's, a 'fortifying compound of . . . Quinine, Acid and Dandelion that has done me infinite good'.[14] His brother thought that 'Collinsian nerves' were more to blame than anything else: 'When you are doing nothing you are pretty well but directly that you begin to work again or ceasing to be moving about have leisure to be anxious and think you suffer . . . All misgiving about your being able to complete your work must be fought against as if it was a crime . . . to think about work at all, especially at moments of compelled inaction, as in bed for instance, is highly dangerous.'[15] This diagnosis seems to relate more to Charley himself than to his brother.

Wilkie had the additional worry of moving house again, just before Christmas. Number 9 Melcombe Place, Dorset Square, on the north side of the Marylebone Road, was intended to be a temporary address, though he and Caroline were to remain there until the short lease ran out nearly three years later. Charley wrote to their mother that he was very glad to hear of the move: 'It is in the right direction, at any rate.'[16] Perhaps Charley thought it was a preliminary to getting rid of Caroline. Certainly at this address the pretence of marriage was dropped, and Caroline resumed her own name; Wilkie still found no evidence for the supposed benefits of marriage. Charley's health continued to be precarious: he suffered almost continuous stomach pains and nausea in spite of Kate's care. Wilkie reported with satisfaction a meeting with his cousin, Henry Gray, who kept a picture dealer's shop in Old Cavendish Street: 'His eyes were rayless – his cheeks were haggard – his beard was mangy – and he chuckled feebly when I congratulated him on being a married man.'[17]

Wilkie took a break from the book at the end of February when he went briefly to Paris with Fred Lehmann, where they went every night to the theatre. But for most of the year he worked steadily, keeping about three months ahead of the monthly publication in *The Cornhill.* He went on short visits only, to Dickens at Gad's Hill and at Dover, to Yarmouth with Pigott. He visited his mother at regular intervals. The restless Harriet had now more or less settled in Kent, and though she shifted between three addresses – Bentham Hill Cottage, near Tunbridge Wells; Elm Lodge, in the town itself; and her final address, Prospect Hill, Southborough – a room was always kept for Wilkie, and he arranged for other essentials to be available. 'Count the cheap claret again, please', he asked her. 'I want to know how many bottles are left.'[18] He enquired anxiously, when she moved to Elm Lodge, whether the house was quiet, so that he could get on with his work. It was on one of his visits to her there that he wrote in response to a query about his construction of *The Woman in White*, explaining his method, and using *Armadale* as an example:

> In the story I am now writing ('Armadale'), the last number is to be published several months hence – and the whole close of the story is still unwritten. But I know at this moment who is to live and who is to die – and I see the main events which are to lead to the end as plainly as I see the pen in my hand . . . *How* I shall lead you from one main event to the other – whether I shall dwell at length on certain details or pass them over rapidly – how I may yet develop my characters and make them clearer to you by new touches and traits – all this, I know no more than you do, till I take the pen in hand. But the characters themselves were all marshalled in their places, before a line of 'Armadale' was written. And I knew the end two years ago in Rome, when I was recovering from a long illness, and was putting the story together.[19]

After resolving some technical difficulties in reconciling 'certain chemical facts with the incidents of the story' (the final drama turns on poisonous gas being secretly released into a bedroom), Wilkie finished writing on 12 April 1866. From conception to completed book, published in two volumes on 18 May, it had taken him nearly three years. In the end he was almost sorry to part from it. Though he had been well paid, and could afford to buy £300 worth of wine (a considerable amount in modern terms) and invest £1,500 in the Funds,* he estimated that he had only saved as much from the book

* Government stock.

'as Marshall & Snelgrove make in a quarter of an hour by the brains and industry of other people'.[20]

Wilkie celebrated his freedom with another short holiday in Paris with Fred Lehmann, delighted to find Sunday observance more lax than ever: 'A grand morning concert . . . Races at the Bois de Boulogne . . . the heavens smile on these anti-Sabbatarian proceedings.'[21] The Lehmanns were now among his closest friends, and were to remain so for the rest of his life; he and they supported each other through illness and emotional crises. Wilkie's affection was deepened when Nina, who was in poor health, was diagnosed as possibly consumptive. For some time the Lehmanns' strenuous social life was curtailed, and Nina, a pianist of concert standard, was forbidden to play. She spent much time in Switzerland with her children, and Wilkie cheered Fred with his company. When Fred was on business trips to the United States he comforted Nina, whom he valued as a friend, sympathized with as an invalid and admired as a pianist. They shared many interests, including a love of animals. 'Oh, I wanted you so at Rome – in the Protestant cemetery', he told her.

> I went to show my friend Pigott the grave of the illustrious Shelley . . . the finest black Tom you ever saw discovered at an incredible distance that a catanthropist had entered the cemetery – rushed up at a gallop, with his tail at right angles to his spine – turned over on his back with his four paws in the air, and said in the language of cats: 'Shelley be hanged! Come and tickle me!' I stooped and tickled him. We were both profoundly affected.[22]

Nina, the recipient of some of his most amusing letters, now ceased to be 'Mrs. Lehmann' and became 'the Padrona'. She valued him equally: '. . . steady friendship that continues for nearly twenty years, always the same, always kind, always earnest, always interested, always true, always loving and faithful – *that* is worth the name of friendship indeed. I value my Wilkie and I love him dearly', she wrote to Fred, sending him Wilkie's letter about Rome.[23]

Armadale was dedicated to John Forster, to whom Wilkie remained loyal: more loyal than Forster's jealousy over Dickens always deserved. He may have been a little disconcerted by the dedication; *Armadale* is defiantly unconcerned to protect the innocence of a young English female. But Forster was, to Wilkie's great pleasure, impressed with one section at least of the novel: the spectacular and sacrificial end of Lydia Gwilt. 'It is a masterpiece of Art which few indeed have equalled to bring even pity and pathos to the end of such a career as hers. You certainly have done this – and the single page in which it is done is the finest thing in the book.'[24]

In the preface, shorter than usual, Wilkie appealed to 'readers in general', the public who actually bought his books, to appreciate that it had not been 'hastily meditated, or idly wrought out'. 'Readers in particular' (i.e. the reviewers) he expected to be disturbed and offended. 'Estimated by the Clap-trap morality of the present day, this may be a very daring book. Judged by the Christian morality which is of all time, it is only a book that is daring enough to speak the truth.'

His 'readers in general' responded well. Mudie was forced, by public pressure, to stock more copies of *Armadale* than he had originally planned, turning Wilkie's dig, in Lydia Gwilt's diary, at 'the commonplace rubbish of the circulating libraries' back on himself. But, as Wilkie had anticipated, the critics, with a few exceptions, were antagonistic. A typical review in *The Spectator* asked indignantly:

> Is . . . the whole truth about the world in which we live that it is peopled by a set of scoundrels qualified by a set of fools, and watched by retributive providence in the shape of attorneys and spies? Is it the object of half the world to cheat the other half, and the object of the other half to put itself in the way of being cheated? Is it true that all women are idiots till they are twenty, intriguers and murderesses till they are forty, and customers of hags who restore decayed beauty till they are eighty? . . . the fact that there are characters such as he has drawn, and actions such as he has described, does not warrant his overstepping the bounds of decency . . . *Armadale* . . . gives us for its heroine a woman fouler than the refuse of the streets, who has lived to the ripe age of thirty-five, and through the horrors of forgery, murder, theft, bigamy, gaol, and attempted suicide, without any trace being left on her beauty.[25]

Only the reviewer in the *Reader*, Wilkie felt, thoroughly understood his intentions. This critic, calling him 'this most tragic of novel-writers', enthusiastically endorsed Wilkie's claim that the book was moral and exemplary, praised the 'extraordinary ability with which he dissects evil minds', and upheld the novel's realism: 'If life itself is full of such underhand evil proceedings we cannot blame him who discloses the fact to us'.[26]

Armadale conforms more closely than either *The Woman in White* or *No Name* to the classic sensation novel that the moralists objected to. It is a fiendishly complicated story, spanning several generations. Incident is heaped on incident; the characters are moved restlessly from one to another of the places Wilkie had visited while planning the novel. Everyone spies on everyone else. The characters, headed by the magnificent red-haired villainess Lydia Gwilt, include private detectives, a dodgy doctor-cum-abortionist turned asylum keeper, a procuress who keeps a beauty parlour and an insanely jealous bedridden wife. Though the main action is set in the early 1850s, partly to disguise Wilkie's use of contemporary events, the story is concerned with the social life and domestic atmosphere of the 1860s. Attitudes were changing. Views on family life and the position of women were being questioned; women were beginning to be seen as more powerful and more dangerous, above all more devious, polluting the sanctity of home and undermining its security. The typical female crimes were thought to be the secretive ones of poisoning and bigamy.

Armadale is full of references to current scandals. Lydia Gwilt, the typical anti-heroine of a sensation novel, who began her career as a lady's maid and forger and progressed to bigamy, governessing and murder, creates such a stir when she appears in the dock that a public outcry leads to her being granted a pardon by the Home Secretary. The description of the effect she had on the public gallery and the press would have recalled the trial of Madeleine Smith in 1857. When she escaped the charge of poisoning her lover, through a Scottish verdict of 'not proven', the decision was greeted with cheers in court.

Lydia's mentor, 'Mother Oldershaw', is even more closely modelled on a real woman, the notorious Madame Rachel Leverson, at the height of her success at the time Wilkie was writing *Armadale*. The *Saturday Review* called the characterization of Mrs Oldershaw 'disagreeably sensational', but the facts about Rachel Leverson were, if anything, toned down in the novel. In 1863 she had opened a shop in New Bond Street, selling cosmetics and useless beauty treatments at outrageous prices. If you wanted the full works, 'The Royal Bridal Toilet Cabinet', it cost a thousand guineas; the ingredients were mostly bran, grease and pump water. The slogan over the door, 'Beautiful for Ever', and the prominent position of the shop acknowledged that women who were neither prostitutes nor actresses were beginning to use cosmetics. In Wilkie's novel of 1875, *The Law and the Lady*, the heroine, depressed and ill but needing to look her best, allows a corrupt chambermaid to make up her face. ' "Ah, what a thing pearl powder is, when one knows how to use it!" ' says the maid to the reluctant Valeria.[27] Madame Leverson, like Mrs Oldershaw, had a back entrance to her shop, round the corner in Maddox Street, where more dubious activities were carried on. Wilkie seems to have had knowledge of these, either through legal or theatrical contacts, even before she was exposed in court in 1867. Sergeant Ballantine's memoirs reveal that she was well known as a procuress, often seen backstage at the Drury Lane Theatre.[28]

The dubious Dr Downward, the 'ladies physician' (or abortionist) who shares her premises, changes his name and sets up an unlicensed asylum on the latest principles of 'moral management', when the law gets too close. The character reflects the scandals surrounding private madhouses, touched on, but not elaborated, in *The Woman in White*. His sanatorium is, like the one Anne Catherick escapes from, in Hampstead: the description of 'Fairweather Vale' is taken from the Vale of Health on Hampstead Heath. This little hamlet was, from 1862 onwards, being enlarged by the building of new suburban villas. Wilkie would have seen this development on his frequent visits to George Smith, who kept open house on Friday evenings at his Hampstead house, Oak Hill Lodge.

> Fairweather Vale proved to be a new neighbourhood, situated below the high ground of Hampstead, on the southern side . . . We approached it by a new road running between trees, which might once have been the park-avenue of a country house. At the end we came upon a wilderness of open ground, with half-finished villas dotted about, and a hideous litter

> of boards, wheelbarrows, and building materials of all sorts scattered in every direction. At one corner of this scene of desolation stood a great overgrown dismal house . . .[29]

Dr Downward claims to use the method of treating the insane pioneered by the famous Dr John Connolly. The elimination of all external stress, worry and noise that the treatment entailed might have appealed to Wilkie, with his complaints about brass bands, piano practice and unwanted visitors when he was working; but he was alert to the power that such isolation of a patient could place in the hands of the physician, and his sinister alienist is shown to be using fashionable theory to evade investigation rather than to help the sick.

The abuse of privacy is a recurrent theme of the novel. Wilkie also turned an indignant eye on the rise of the private detective, increasingly used in divorce cases, 'the vile creature whom the viler need of Society has fashioned for its own use . . . the Confidential Spy of modern times, whose business is steadily enlarging, whose Private Inquiry Offices are steadily on the increase'.[30] It is not only the private detective who spies, however. Letters are steamed open, conversations are overheard, movements watched from behind curtains. It is a nightmare world, in which even thoughts cease to be private, a picture of English society as a claustrophobic prison.

T. S. Eliot, who admired *Armadale*, thought that the novel 'has no merit beyond melodrama, and it has every merit that melodrama can have'.[31] Lydia Gwilt, the intelligent and cynical diarist who effortlessly outwits all attempts to trap her, who reveals herself to the reader while concealing herself from the other characters, is certainly a melodramatic heroine of the highest order. Wilkie sustained the melodrama with his usual narrative ability, and his habitual care with the legal, chemical and medical facts used in the story. But the reader is left with the strong feeling that beneath the melodramatic surface there is another level of meaning, one in which the uncanny predominates. Lydia Gwilt is a shape-changer like Keats' Lamia; her first name is that of the ancient Greek city in his poem, famous for luxury and witchcraft. The two explanations of Allan Armadale's dream, which symbolically encapsulates the plot, interpret it either naturally or supernaturally. This leaves the reader free to choose whether the action was determined by Fate, or the coincidences were random. But the Dream is not simply a tease, or an opportunity for the reader to accept both a rational and an irrational explanation. The three characters in the Dream – the Dreamer, the Shadow of a Man and the Shadow of a Woman – are linked in a psychic bond of love and death.

Who is Allan Armadale? Possession of the name becomes a key question – an epistemological enquiry, as well as a plot device. There is the 'light' Allan Armadale: the fortunate, fair, relentlessly cheerful and talkative *jeune prémier*, with his love of sailing and hatred of blood sports, the legitimate son and heir, so to speak, of Harriet Collins. And there is his shadow, the 'dark' Allan Armadale, going under the uncouth pseudonym of 'Ozias Midwinter', a solitary, given to depression and to sudden manic outbursts, who falls disastrously in love at first sight. He ends the novel an aspirant writer. His emotions are strong and lasting, his behaviour erratic and disturbed. Yet it is the fair Armadale, whose emotions are all on the surface, who has the dream which presents the relationships and events of the novel symbolically. It is the dark Armadale who provides the non-rational interpretation.

In Jungian terms Collins' 'Shadow of a man', identified by Ozias Midwinter as himself, is 'the shadow', the dark part of a personality that is repressed from consciousness, but which must be recognized if self-knowledge is to be acquired. This possesses 'an *emotional* nature, a kind of autonomy, and accordingly an obsessive, or, better, a possessive quality', and is represented in dreams as dark-skinned, alien, or primitive.[32] In *Armadale* the self and the shadow-self are not linked by physical resemblance, as they are in *The Woman in White*, but by physical dissimilarity. No one could for an instant mistake Ozias Midwinter, the tormented, depressed descendant of a slave on one side, of a murderer on the other, for the impulsive, rather foolish Allan Armadale. Yet the plot turns on the attempts by Lydia Gwilt to substitute one for the other, and neither of the two men exists fully without the complementary qualities of his other self. Before the action of the novel begins, there has been a struggle to the death between the fathers of the two Armadales, for power, wealth and a woman. The main story concerns the essentially negative struggles of the shadow-self to break away from a pattern of repetition. He must not compete with his friend for the woman they both love, and not be manoeuvred into being responsible for his death. The novel ends with the elimination of the woman, who is the most intriguing character, in every sense. Wilkie himself thought he had never written such a good end to a book: '. . . at any rate I never was so excited, myself, while finishing a story . . . Miss Gwilt's death quite upset me'.[33] With her death the two Armadales can be joined together once more, and the dark Armadale, saved by her self-sacrifice, can again become a loving shadow of the light Armadale, who is both his usurper and his benefactor. The framework of melodrama and sensation contains, sometimes rather uneasily, a psychomachia and its resolution.

As soon as the novel was finished, Wilkie made a play out of it, to protect his theatrical rights, and twenty-five copies were printed for him by Smith, Elder. He showed it to Dickens, who was enthusiastic about the compactness of the plot and the excellence of the dialogue, 'terse, witty, characteristic and dramatic'. But he warned:

> insuperable and ineradicable from the whole piece is – *Danger* . . . I do not think any English audience would accept the scene in which Miss Gwilt in that Widow's dress renounced Midwinter. And if you get so far, you would never get through the last act in the Sanatorium . . . you could only carry those situations *by the help of interest in some innocent person whom they placed in peril, and that person a young woman.* There is no one to be interested in here . . . There is no relief from the wickedness of the rest; and in exact proportion to the skilful heaping up of it the danger mounts.[34]

Wilkie felt the play needed more work, and another professional eye. A French one might be more sympathetic to the portrayal of attractive wickedness. In the autumn he went to Italy for a holiday with Edward Pigott, and stopped in Paris to show the play to Régnier. Together, over the next year, they reshaped and expanded it, from three acts to five.

From Milan he wrote words of comfort and advice, not to be taken too seriously, to the invalid Nina Lehmann. His fascination with the details of women's clothes had not abated.

> Don't go to the piano (especially as *I* am not within hearing) . . . Purchase becoming (and warm) things for the neck and chest. Rise superior to the devilish delusion which makes women think that their feet cannot possibly look pretty in thick boots. I have studied the subject, and I say they *can*. Men understand these things; Mr. Worth, of Paris, dresses the fine French ladies . . . and regulates the fashions of Europe. He is about to start 'comforters' and hobnail boots for the approaching winter. In two months' time it will be indecent for a woman to show her neck at night, and if you don't make a frightful noise at every step you take on the pavement you abrogate your position as woman, wife and mother in the eyes of all Europe.[35]

In October *The Frozen Deep* was at last given a professional production, by Horace Wigan at the Olympic Theatre, with Henry Neville in the key role of Richard Wardour. Wilkie made some alterations for this production, in particular to the relationship between Clara and Wardour. Their love becomes a more ambiguous, adult passion. He attended some of the early rehearsals before he left for Italy, and Dickens, pressed by Wigan, went to the dress rehearsal in his place. The first night went well; but on the professional stage the ten-year-old play seemed old-fashioned, and it was a financial failure. Wilkie wrote ruefully to Nina Lehmann that he hadn't made sixpence from it:

> the enlightened British Public declares it to be '*slow*.' There isn't an atom of slang or vulgarity in the whole piece . . . no female legs are shown in it; Richard Wardour doesn't get up after dying and sing a comic song; sailors are represented in the Arctic regions, and there is no hornpipe danced, and no sudden arrival of 'the pets of the ballet' to join the dance in the costume of Esquimaux maidens . . . For these reasons, best of women, I have failed. Is my tail put down? No – a thousand times, no! I am at work on the dramatic 'Armadale', and I will take John Bull by the scruff of the neck and force him into the theatre to see it –[36]

The failure brought Wilkie hurrying back from Rome, but there was nothing to be done to save *The Frozen Deep*. He pinned his hopes for the elusive theatrical breakthrough on *Armadale*, travelling backwards and forwards to Paris in the early months of 1867 to work on the play with Régnier, who also wanted to dramatize *The Woman in White*, now 'all the rage' as a play in Berlin. Wilkie was prepared to sacrifice everything else to the great chance of the collaboration with Régnier: 'Successful play-writing means making a fortune, here'. After the long labour of the novel the quick returns of the theatre seemed more attractive than ever.

Of course he also welcomed the excuse to visit Paris, a city enthusiastic about drama, music and food. When a new opera was performed the theatre was packed; 'the intense interest of the whole audience . . . was something quite electrifying'. Greed overcame caution: 'I have breakfasted this morning on eggs and black butter, and pig's feet à la Sainte Ménèhould! Digestion perfect. Ste. Ménèhould lived to extreme old age on nothing but pig's trotters.'[37] But the collaborations came to nothing; it was to be another ten years before the British public was ready for a dramatic version of *Armadale*.*

1867 began badly. Low's six-year lease of Wilkie's copyrights had expired, and Smith, Elder refused to make an offer for them. Wilkie suspected that Low had flooded the market with his editions, and *Armadale* had not proved another *Woman in White*: after the first rush it sold slowly, and there was no great demand for the earlier novels. Wilkie refused to be downcast. He was full of ideas for books and plays: he thought of expanding *A Rogue's Life* to a two-volume novel, adding the Rogue's adventures in Australia, and he planned to open negotiations with 'the penny journals' for the serialization of his novels, beginning with *The Woman in White*. He even proposed, perhaps not entirely seriously, boiling down *The Lighthouse, The Frozen Deep* and *The Red Vial* into one novel, just the thing for the penny journals. 'I have got my name and my brains – and I will make a new start, with a new public!'[38] None of these schemes came to anything.

There were other troubles over which Wilkie had no control.

* The collaborative version of *Armadale* may have been performed in Paris, though it did not make Wilkie's fortune. An adaptation by an American woman was a success in New York, Wilkie told his mother. (ALS, 8 January 1867)

Both Charley and Kate Collins were ill, Kate in a state of 'nervous exhaustion' and Charley with his usual stomach pains. They went to Gad's Hill to be looked after by Georgina Hogarth. Dickens was by now convinced that his son-in-law would never be well, and probably did not have long to live, and the state of Charley's health was a constant worry to Wilkie and Harriet. He generally refused to borrow money from Wilkie, but Harriet regularly subsidized him, and in May Dickens doubled Kate's marriage portion, which was, as Wilkie thought, 'liberal and just'. It was tacitly agreed that Charley was never going to be able to make an adequate living by his own efforts, though Wilkie did his best to help by introducing him to publishers and magazine editors, and Dickens commissioned him to illustrate his last novel, *Edwin Drood*. But after drawing the cover illustration Charley had to give up: the act of sitting down to draw brought back all his worst nervous symptoms.

Wilkie's old friend Charles Reade was also in trouble, violently attacked for the immorality of his novel *Griffith Gaunt*, being serialized in *Argosy*. The story is a sensation novel about bigamy complicated by adultery. It drew howls of protest, and Reade, who considered the novel his masterpiece, rushed into print in his own defence, with an article, 'The Prurient Prude', which echoes Wilkie's preface to *Armadale*. Reade asked Wilkie and Dickens for support. He tried to persuade Dickens, who had published Reade's earlier novel *Hard Cash* in *All the Year Round*, to be a witness in an action for libel. Dickens, with his usual editor's caution, refused, though he liked Reade and admired his writing. 'If I were reminded', he wrote to Wilkie, who had written to him on Reade's behalf, 'that I was the editor of a periodical of large circulation in which the Plaintiff himself had written, and if I had read to me in court those passages about Gaunt's going up to his wife's bed drunk and the last child's being conceived, and was asked whether, as Editor, I would have passed those passages . . . I should be obliged to reply No.'[39]

Wilkie was able to help Reade in other ways during the thirty-odd years that they were friends. Though Reade was the elder by ten years, they had much in common. Both had studied law at Lincoln's Inn, Reade more seriously than Wilkie, though he never practised.

Both wrote successful novels, and plays that were not so successful. Both remained close to powerful mothers. Both upset contemporary morality in their writing and their lives: Reade fathered an illegitimate son whom he called his 'nephew' and made his heir. Both lived with women they were not married to. Reade met the talented actress Laura Seymour in 1854, in a theatrical enterprise in which they were joint managers, and the following year he became her lodger. They lived together until her death. Though Laura Seymour insisted that they were never lovers, only 'friends and comrades', many people refused to believe this.[40] George Smith would not have Reade to his house, because of the irregularity of his life, and also refused to entertain George Eliot. But Wilkie was accepted, probably because he was prepared to leave Caroline at home, while Reade and Eliot insisted on having their partners recognized.

Wilkie and Reade, Caroline and Laura Seymour, were intimate friends in the '60s and '70s. They often visited each other, dined together, exchanged gifts. Laura Seymour, who went on the stage at fourteen, had, like Caroline, known hard times, and had been a great beauty; she was both charming and unconventional. Reade was a depressive: often paranoid, sometimes suicidal. He was a difficult, prickly man, quick to take offence, vain, egotistical and combative; but he was warmly appreciative of Wilkie's qualities.[41]

Reade was an unashamed plagiarist, who adapted plays from the French without acknowledgement, and stole the plots of novels and adapted them as plays without permission.[42] From a writer who was as vociferous as Dickens and Collins in demanding international copyright, his defence – that in the disgraceful state of the law there was nothing to prevent this – seemed disingenuous at best. Reade's emphasis on a factual basis for his sensation was greater even than Wilkie's: he kept huge files of newspaper cuttings, and encouraged Wilkie to do the same.* As Wilkie eased himself away from the Dickensian embrace, he was, to some extent, confirmed in his views

* Two books of newspaper cuttings were in Wilkie Collins' library at his death, one classified under the headings 'Our civilization', 'Hints for scenes and incidents' and 'Hints for character'. (*Pall Mall Gazette*, 20 January 1890) He also kept a tin box full of ideas for plots.

by Reade's emphasis on bringing contemporary scandals out into the open and using fiction to lobby for change: not the change of heart Dickens wanted, but changes in the law. If Wilkie was the 'King of Inventors', Reade was the originator of 'Fiction with a Purpose'. He has sometimes been implicated in the supposed decline of Wilkie Collins' fiction; but it is too simple to suggest that Reade took over from Dickens as Wilkie's mentor. Wilkie had known Reade for almost as long as he had known Dickens, and he gave quite as much to Reade as he got from him, writing careful and detailed criticism of the fiction and plays Reade sent to him for his comments. In 1863 Wilkie acted as go-between with Émile Forgues to arrange French translations of Reade's novels, and in 1869 sent a long, and shrewd, appraisal of his novel *Put Yourself in his Place*, then appearing in *The Cornhill*. Wilkie's suggestions are all in the direction of maintaining the human interest, avoiding polemic, and making the social and legal points through the actions of the characters. 'I was so fortunate as to please him at last', Reade noted on the letter.[43] Wilkie, one of the few people from whom Reade would have been grateful for advice, sent him an equally detailed analysis of his dramatic adaptation of the same novel in 1871.[44]

Reade and Wilkie were also united in the fight for improved copyright laws. 'If you and I could get our brethren to fight without being paid for it – and to agree together – we should have international copyright all over the world. But (except Dickens) who will take the trouble?' Wilkie wrote to Reade in 1869.[45] But Wilkie was more cautious than these fighting words suggest. He agreed to become involved in a test case over the copyright of one of his plays in the United States – probably *Armadale*, produced in New York in March 1867 – but only within strictly defined limits. He refused to enter on any litigation. If Wallack, the manager of the authorized production, wanted to bring actions against other theatres, he must do so in his own name and at his own expense.[46]

Apart from the expense, he had no time to spare for such wrangles. His next novel was to be serialized in *All the Year Round*, and in May Dickens asked him to share the writing of the Christmas number, promising that both their names would appear on it. For the first time, there was an argument over terms – not with Dickens, who tactfully kept out of the financial arrangements, but with Wills. Wilkie asked £400 for writing half the Christmas number; exactly ten times the amount he had thought liberal for 'Sister Rose' in 1855. He finally agreed to £300, because the opportunity to associate himself publicly and privately with Dickens was an arrangement which 'I cannot consent to regulate by any ordinary considerations'.[47] The serial story was another matter. Wills suggested a financial arrangement similar to that for *No Name*. But Wilkie pointed out that when he had been planning that novel, he was still receiving a regular salary of £7. 7s. 0d. a week from *All the Year Round*, and a share in the profits. Agreement was finally reached on £850 for the serial rights. With another £750 for the American serial rights, Wilkie was in a good position, the following year, to drive a tough bargain with a publisher for the book rights to *The Moonstone*, his second big success.

SIXTEEN

'Wild yet domestic': Wilkie's family mysteries

(1867–1868)

In the summer of 1867 Wilkie's work was once more disrupted by the urgent problem of finding somewhere to live. The lease on Melcombe Place ran out at the end of July, and for a while it seemed as though he would be turned out on the street. At the last moment he signed a twenty-year lease with Lord Portman for a house in Gloucester Place, parallel with Baker Street and just north of Portman Square.

Number 90 (now 65) Gloucester Place was a substantial terraced house, five storeys high, with plenty of room for family, visitors and servants. There was a dining-room on the ground floor, and the room behind it was probably used as a family sitting-room, for Wilkie took over the L-shaped double drawing-room on the first floor as his study. He loved the large, airy rooms, though he still found it difficult to avoid the business and noise of daily living, and the intrusion on his working time of thoughtless visitors. But it was a house for a man who had arrived and intended to settle, not for one who was uncertain of his domestic arrangements.

It was also expensive. However, the lease included stables in the mews behind the houses, which Wilkie sublet for £40 a year, a sizeable contribution to the rent of the house. (He was to become extremely irascible about the difficulty of getting his tenant to pay her rent.) Through his solicitors, he raised a loan of £800 to buy the lease, knowing that on his mother's death he and Charley would inherit, in equal shares, the £5,000 left to her by her aunt, even though, under their father's will, the rest of their capital was still tied up.[1]

Twenty years later, when Wilkie was about to move out of Gloucester Place, a visitor described it as dingy and cheerless, with a cold hall and stone staircase. Most of his friends thought it comfortable, even luxurious. Certainly Wilkie and Caroline undertook thorough renovations when they moved in – though Wilkie refused to have gas lighting, which he considered unhealthy. His houses continued to be lit by wax candles. Wilkie complained as usual about the slowness of the British workman, and took refuge first with his mother, then at Woodlands, the Lehmanns' country house at Highgate. In September he reported sceptically, 'The statement now is that they will be done in a week . . . Never mind. A certain necessary place has got the most lovely new pan you ever saw. It's quite a luxury to look into it.'[2]

Wilkie kept three servants at Gloucester Place. Though naturally over the years individuals came and went, there seem usually to have been two women and a man, or boy. He described them in 1882 as a man, a plump parlourmaid and a small girl.[3] During the move his servants were 'models of human excellence' who worked hard and never grumbled: he gave the women a new gown each.

Wilkie also kept a dog. For many years this was his much-loved Scotch terrier Tommy, who featured in a short story, 'My Lady's Money' of 1878, in which he acts as a detective, helping to unravel the mystery. When Tommy died at an advanced age Wilkie wrote to A. P. Watt, 'I should not acknowledge to many people what I have suffered during his last illness and death.'*[4] There was usually a cat as well, and he tended to attract stray animals: '. . . A kitten who has drifted into the house . . . is galloping over my back and shoulder, which makes writing difficult'.[5]

The house was filled with books; the panelled walls were hung with pictures. Wilkie and Charley divided their father's paintings between

* A memorandum in Wilkie Collins' hand, listing family births and deaths, includes the date of Tommy's death, 28 August 1885.

them, and Jane Ward's daughter Margaret gave him the portrait of Harriet as a young girl in a white dress, by Margaret Carpenter. 'Still like you after all these years', Wilkie told his mother. He hung the picture in his study, with a portrait of his father and a painting of Sorrento by William Collins, which hung to the left of the massive writing table which had belonged to his father. Charley's portrait of Wilkie as a young man and the one by Millais were also in this room, and an etching of Dickens. His own Academy painting, 'The Smuggler's Retreat', went in the dining-room.

By the end of October the house was finished, and Wilkie and Caroline gave a house-warming dinner, which was also a private farewell to Dickens, about to leave for a reading tour of America. It was the first of many dinner parties at Gloucester Place. Wilkie took a personal interest in the cooking and preparation of the meals, always preferring French food to the English habit of enormous joints of meat and solid puddings. His experiments were sometimes bizarre, even disastrous. On one occasion, he and Frank Beard descended to the kitchen to concoct a 'Don Pedro pie', so laden with garlic that it made them both ill. Wilkie was said to keep a French cook; but the cook either lived out or was hired only for special occasions, as at Harley Street.[6] Probably, as Frederick Lehmann suspected, Caroline did much of the day-to-day cooking.

Wilkie was also one of the stewards at the enormous farewell banquet for Dickens in November, held at the Freemasons' Hall. This was a well-orchestrated and emotional occasion. Dickens had wavered for months about touring America with his 'Readings'. He finally decided to go, as Wilkie had privately believed all along he would. There were 450 guests, all male, in the body of the hall, and a hundred women in the purdah of the Ladies' Gallery, joined for coffee by the men. Caroline, with Carrie, now nearly seventeen, seems to have been among them. Wilkie wrote to the organizers twice to make sure that his request for two ladies' tickets would be met.[7]

Dickens left him shouldering a number of responsibilities. 'I am finishing the 3rd act of the play – conducting All the Year Round – and correcting The Moonstone for its first appearance in London and New York . . . my very minutes are counted', Wilkie told Harriet at the end of November.[8] The play, *No Thoroughfare*, was adapted from the Christmas number of *All the Year Round* as a vehicle for Charles Fechter and his leading lady Carlotta Leclercq. Wilkie and Dickens had first seen Fechter when he was a successful romantic actor in Paris. He created the part of Armand Duval in *La Dame aux Camélias*, a play then considered too shocking to be licensed in London, and Wilkie saw him in that role. But Fechter had ambitions to be a classical actor. In 1860 he came to London, and began to play Shakespeare, in English. Against all expectations he made a tremendous success as Hamlet, in spite of his corpulence, his French accent and his startling blond wig. He was a naturalistic actor of the French school that Dickens and Wilkie much preferred to the old-fashioned English style. Reporting a circus performance by monkeys, Wilkie considered, 'We shall see them in Shakespeare next – and why not? They can't be worse than the human actors, and they *might* be better.'[9]

In his short career on the London stage – he went to America at the end of 1869 – Fechter probably did more to change the style of English acting than any other single actor at the time. Wilkie's account of Fechter's preparation for *No Thoroughfare* suggests he was a nineteenth-century forerunner of Method acting: 'Fechter at once assumed the character of *Obenreizer* in private life . . . The play was in his hands all day and at his bedside all night.'[10] His Hamlet, Dickens thought, was 'by far the most coherent, consistent, and intelligible' he had ever seen.[11] Another witness described the characterization as 'a living human being . . . Instead of delivering his words as if they had been learned by heart, [he] spoke them like an ordinary individual.'[12] This, though it hardly seems worth remarking on now, was a revolutionary approach at the time. Wilkie gave a vivid impression of Fechter's performance in his novel of 1872, *Poor Miss Finch*. Nugent Dubourg is giving advice to Mr Finch on the reading of the scene where Hamlet first encounters the Ghost:

> 'What is Shakespeare before all things? True to nature; always true to nature. What condition is Hamlet in when he is expecting to see the Ghost: He is nervous, and he feels the cold. Let him show it naturally;

> let him speak as any other man would speak, under the circumstances. Look here! Quick and quiet – like this. "The air bites shrewdly" – there Hamlet stops and shivers – pur-rer-rer! "It is very cold." That's the way to read Shakespeare!' (*Poor Miss Finch*, Vol. 1, Chap. 23, p. 289)

Fechter and Wilkie had much in common. Fechter, like Wilkie, loved good food and good company, but hated formality. He often received guests at his house in St John's Wood in his dressing-gown and slippers. The diners helped themselves, dined in their shirt-sleeves, and went into the kitchen to help the cook when they felt like it. Dogs were welcome; after-dinner entertainment was provided in a delightfully informal way by the guests themselves. But the dinners were prepared by the French cook Annette, who was, in Wilkie's expert opinion, 'one of the finest artists that ever handled a saucepan'. She had to put up with some eccentricity in her employer and his friends. On one occasion they ordered a 'potato dinner' in six courses; on another the eight courses consisted of nothing but eggs.

But this Arcadian idyll fell apart, like everything in Fechter's life. The culinary artist was dismissed in disgrace: 'she has done all sorts of dreadful things', Wilkie told Nina Lehmann, warning her not to employ her. 'I wish I knew of another cook to recommend – but unless you will take *me*, I know of nobody. And . . . my *style* is expensive. I look on meat simply as a material for sauces.'[13] Fechter made friends easily, but invariably quarrelled with all of them, as he did with all his business associates. He was hopeless with money, borrowing from one friend to lend to another, and Wilkie was undoubtedly one of those caught up in Fechter's cycle of debt, giving rather than receiving. Not only did he have a fearful temper, but he was paranoid to the point of madness: '. . . when he once took offence, a lurking devil saturated his whole being with the poison of unjust suspicion and inveterate hatred'.[14] Wilkie seems to have been one of the few people who remained friends with him to the end.

As the villain Obenreizer in *No Thoroughfare*, Fechter was at his best. The story, a hectic tale of mistaken identity, jealousy and murder, worked better on the stage than in print. It is full of stage 'business', more visual than verbal, with Swiss settings that drew on Dickens' and Wilkie's memories of the journey to Italy of 1853. The climax in particular, a 'wintry flight and pursuit across the Alps' in which the hero is pushed over a precipice by Obenreizer but rescued by the heroism of the girl who loves him, recalls the crossing of the Mer de Glace, when Egg was nearly swept away by a block of stone rolling down the mountainside.

The play opened at the Adelphi Theatre on 26 December. Wilkie gave a graphic account of Fechter's first-night nerves, confirmed by others who were present.[15] His stage fright was so acute that he vomited continuously. Wilkie suggested a few drops of laudanum to calm him. 'Unable to speak, Fechter answered by putting out his tongue. The colour of it had turned, under the nervous terror that possessed him, to the metallic blackness of the tongue of a parrot.'[16] His dresser hovered in the wings with a basin, but once the curtain went up it was not needed: the play was a success and Fechter triumphed.

No Thoroughfare ran in London for seven months before going on tour. A copy of the script had been sent to Dickens in America, so that he might arrange a production in New York. He thought the play too long, and (wrongly) doubted its success on the London stage. The complications of securing copyright proved insurmountable, and the pirates were ahead of him, 'producing their own wretched versions in all directions'. Dickens thought that Boucicault had misled Wilkie about the possibilities for dramatists in America and filled his head with golden dreams. He seems to have resented Wilkie's and Fechter's London triumph, achieved against his predictions and without his help, claiming that they had 'missed so many pieces of stage effect' that he might have to go and oversee the Paris production which opened the following summer. The French version was written by Fechter and Dickens and differed from the English play: Wilkie was, he said, too busy to have anything to do with it.[17] Only Dickens' name, prominently displayed on the posters, saved the play from being damned in Paris; the audience were respectful of a production otherwise thought to be crude and melodramatic.[18]

In this flurry of theatrical activity, Wilkie steadily kept up work on *The Moonstone*. It had originally been planned as a shorter book than his last three: 'I am taking it easy this time', he told his mother. Intended to be only twenty-six weekly parts, it inevitably over-ran to thirty-two. Even at this length, tighter plotting than usual was needed, and meticulous attention to detail. The travelling undertaken for *Armadale* had encouraged expansiveness in the plot: this time Wilkie stayed put. He did his historical research in the library of one of his clubs, probably that of the Athenaeum, and called up his memories of the Yorkshire coast for the setting. As well as published sources, he consulted individuals for advice on the Indian background and information on the Hindu and Muslim religions. He was put in touch with John Wyllie, of the Indian Civil Service, who had served in Kathiawar, though he seems largely to have ignored Wyllie's information. The expert was considerably more prejudiced and conventional in his views on Indians and their religions than the novelist. 'There is no part of India . . . so fanatically Hindoo in religion and so startlingly barbarous in primitive ethics', Wyllie pontificated, directing Wilkie to 'a collection of Wheeler's letters or articles in the *Englishman* . . . Eleusinian mysteries are a joke to the abominations there revealed.'[19] Wyllie also doubted whether loss of caste would be taken as seriously as Wilkie's epilogue suggested – reinstatement would be a question of money rather than an endless quest for purification.

By the end of June 1867 he had written the first three numbers, and Dickens was reading them. He objected to the established Collinsian technique of a series of 'Narratives', but he was intrigued by the 'wild yet domestic' story and pleased at Wilkie's avoidance of the clichés of sensation: 'nothing belonging to disguised women, or the like', he noted with relief. He appreciated the care that had gone into it, and predicted a hit.

The novel was safely launched in *All the Year Round* and *Harper's Weekly* on 1 January 1868. Wilkie arranged a celebratory dinner for 18 January, to be followed by a return visit to *No Thoroughfare* at the Adelphi. Charley, Edwin Landseer, Forster and Holman Hunt were invited. At the last minute he had to cancel, called away by telegram to his mother's bedside. She was seriously ill.

Though the immediate crisis passed, Harriet was dying. Wilkie persuaded her to see Frank Beard, who managed to make her more comfortable, and her sons took turns to stay with her, Wilkie struggling all the time to keep up with writing his book. But at the beginning of February, back for a while in London, he was himself struck down with the worst attack of 'rheumatic gout' he had ever had to endure. For the first time 'gout in the eyes', an inflammation so severe and so painful that he could not read or write, was added to the pains in his legs and back. When Harriet finally died on 19 March he was still bedridden. At least he escaped the ordeal of her funeral. He wrote to Holman Hunt, asking him to represent him. 'I am sure it will be a comfort to him [Charles Collins] to see the face of a dear old friend whom my mother loved, and whom we love'.[20]

Harriet was seventy-seven when she died. She had kept her good spirits and enthusiasm for life to the end, and her death affected both her children deeply. Wilkie had had his problems with Harriet over the years, and since she had moved to Kent he had inevitably seen her less often. Yet he repeatedly called her death the greatest sorrow of his life, and there is no reason to suppose this was a conventional piece of sentimentality. She was, for him, all that a mother should be: affectionate, witty and enthusiastic, outspoken but loyal. In the preface to the 1871 edition of *The Moonstone*, Wilkie recalled this time, when he was enduring 'the bitterest affliction of my life and the severest illness from which I have suffered'. Writing a letter of condolence in 1883, he said that though it was fifteen years since his mother had died, 'when I think of her, I still know what the heartache means'.[21]

Wilkie struggled on with his work. The writing of *The Moonstone* was, he wrote later, 'a blessed relief' at a time of illness and bereavement. There were other reasons why writing became now more than ever '"Its own exceeding great reward"'.[22] Harriet's death, such a blow to her sons, may have seemed the opportunity Caroline Graves had been waiting for. At last, one of the main obstacles to marriage – or the excuse Wilkie had given as an obstacle – Harriet Collins' implacable opposition, was removed. Dickens thought that Caroline issued an ultimatum to Wilkie. She soon discovered that Harriet

Collins was not the only barrier to her becoming a respectable woman at last.

The other was a young woman, Martha Rudd. Though she seems to have drifted into Wilkie's life as casually as a stray kitten, her determination and strong character, combined with his idiosyncratic but firm sense of responsibility, absorbed Martha into his daily life, and she remained an important part of it until his death. Martha Rudd's background was as humble as Caroline's; unlike Caroline, she made no attempt to disguise it. She was born in Norfolk, in the bleak seaside hamlet of Winterton, notorious for its dangerous coastline and famous for its tall church-tower, visible for miles across the flat countryside. She was one of the eight children of a shepherd, James Rudd, and his wife Mary.[23] Looking at the row of tiny early-nineteenth-century cottages in Black Street where they lived, one can see that life for a family of ten must have been overcrowded and squalid: the children went out to work as soon as they were able to earn at all. But a National School had been built in the village in 1845, and Martha probably had a little basic education. By the time she was sixteen, she and her two older sisters had left home.

Alice and Martha Rudd had not moved far. The sisters, aged eighteen and sixteen, were in 1861 employed as general servants by an innkeeper, John Bartram. The Bartrams lived in Runham, then a suburb of Great Yarmouth, now a part of the town. The inn was in Vauxhall Gardens, close to the terminus of the Eastern Counties Railway.[24] John Bartram and his wife Phoebe kept two other young servants, a barmaid and an errand boy, and they had two teenage sons. Alice Rudd was the eldest of the six young people; George Bartram and the errand boy Robert Shepherdson, both fifteen, were the youngest.

In the summer of 1864 Wilkie was in Yarmouth, for the sailing and to sketch in the background for *Armadale*. He stayed at the Victoria Hotel. He left Yarmouth on 9 August, for a visit to Monckton Milnes (now Lord Houghton) at Fryston. After 'long and painful study of Bradshaw', Wilkie wrote to his host. 'If the train is punctual (a very serious "if" on the Great Eastern Railway) I shall get to Peterborough in time for the two o'clock train . . . If there is delay, I must get on from Peterborough by the 4.30 train'.[25] Perhaps the train was late, and Wilkie filled in the time at the inn next door. As he had charmed the kitchenmaid Virginia in Paris twenty years before, so, with the advantages of fame and maturity, he now made a lasting impression on a girl not much older than his adopted daughter.

Martha herself was an incarnation of the courageous and independent-minded young working women Wilkie had always found touching and intriguing. In a story about a marriage which cut across class, written in the last years of his life, Wilkie Collins seems to be looking back twenty years or so, and justifying his last important involvement with a woman.

> I had met with a girl, possessed of remarkable personal attractions . . . – a girl at once simple and spirited; unspoilt by the world and the world's ways, and placed in a position of peril due to the power of her own beauty, which added to the interest that she naturally inspired. Estimating these circumstances at their true value, did a state of mind which rendered me insensible to the distinctions that separate the classes in England, stand in any need of explanation? (*The Guilty River*, *Arrowsmith's Christmas Annual*, 1886, p. 73)

It is impossible to trace the development of their relationship in its early stages. Wilkie's sudden change of plan for a brief seaside holiday in 1865, when he first intended to stay in Yarmouth but moved to the Royal Hotel, Lowestoft, might suggest Martha had moved from one town to the other.[26] By 1868 Martha was in London, perhaps in 'a position of peril', and causing, or at least exacerbating, a crisis in Wilkie's relationship with Caroline.

Caroline's reaction to Wilkie's continued refusal to marry her was startling. If he would not, someone else would. Someone else did. On 29 October 1868, Caroline Graves, aged thirty-eight, was married, legally, respectably and openly, by the Rector of St Marylebone, to Joseph Charles Clow, a young man of twenty-seven, the son of a distiller who lived in Avenue Road. She gave a false name for her father, describing him as 'John Courtenay, gentleman', and no doubt related a convincing life history for herself, which by now she probably half believed. Her daughter Carrie, rather fancifully signing herself

'Elisabeth Harriette Graves', and their doctor Francis Beard were the witnesses, and Wilkie was present at the ceremony.[27]

Dickens' interpretation of this curious event seems plausible. On the day of the wedding he wrote to Georgina Hogarth, 'Wilkie's affairs defy all prediction. For anything one knows, the whole matrimonial pretence may be a lie of that woman's, intended to make him marry her, and (contrary to her expectations) breaking down at last.'[28] Wilkie's comment to his sister-in-law suggests more ambivalence, and the possibility that Caroline nearly forced him into marriage after all. He went to see Kate immediately after the wedding. As Kate reported their conversation to Gladys Storey, many years later, Wilkie asked her:

> 'I suppose you could not marry a man who had –'
>
> 'No, I couldn't,' she broke in decisively. 'Poor Wilkie,' Mrs. Perugini continued, 'I liked him, and my father was very fond of him, and enjoyed his company more than that of any other of his friends – Forster was very jealous of their friendship. He had very high spirits and was a splendid companion, but he was as bad as he could be, yet the gentlest and most kind-hearted of men.'[29]

There is no record of where and how Caroline and Joseph Clow lived, or how he made his living, but it is likely he worked in some branch of the wine and spirit trade. On the marriage certificate he designated himself 'gentleman', without giving an occupation. A Leonard Clow, probably a relative, carried on the business of 'ale and stout merchant' at 28 Grafton Street, Fitzroy Square, for many years, including the period when Caroline was keeping a marine store in Charlton Street, in the same district. If Caroline's acquaintance with young Joseph dated from the 1850s, he would have been a boy of fifteen at the time her relationship with Wilkie began.

Though Wilkie was clearly distressed at Caroline's marriage, he was not prepared to abandon Martha Rudd, who became pregnant with his first child around the time of the wedding. In spite of this Carrie stayed with Wilkie, rather than joining her mother. She was becoming indispensable to him. One of the stories he told so well and vividly in later years was an account of the writing of *The Moonstone.* He was in too much pain from gout to write, and had to dictate the greater part of the book: various young men were tried as secretaries, but were unable to bear his groans and cries; finally a young woman was engaged, who wrote on steadily, disregarding his suffering.[30] A letter to Harper's, explaining that parts of two weekly numbers had been dictated because of his illness, and the extant manuscript (not a fair copy but the much rewritten and overscored text used for serial publication) reveal that this is one of Wilkie's embroideries.[31] Five manuscript pages of Miss Clack's narrative are in Carrie's hand. It was the first time she had written from his dictation. She was to continue to be his secretary and copyist until Wilkie's death. One page, following not preceding these, is in an unidentified hand, very neat and clerkly. Then Wilkie resumed, obviously writing in bed, for the next twelve pages are in pencil. From the sixteenth weekly part he seems to have been working at his desk as usual, writing in ink.[32] What is remarkable is his persistence, at a time when he was certainly in great pain, in carrying through his work, almost entirely in his own hand.

Carrie was also running errands for him and organizing the household in her mother's place, like any dutiful Victorian daughter of an abandoned father. Her grandmother, old Mrs Graves, also lived at Gloucester Place from time to time, perhaps to lend respectability to the arrangement.[33] Whatever phases Wilkie's stormy relationship with her mother went through, Carrie's primary loyalty was to him. She owed everything to Wilkie. Now she repaid him. In a situation full of difficulty for a girl of seventeen, she gave him support, affection and practical help. She had come a long way from her childish desire 'to convert somebody' to an acceptance of his failings and an appreciation of his unvarying kindness.

If Wilkie had been writing his life, instead of living it, he would have married Martha Rudd. Her archetype was, after all, the Wronged Maid, rather than the dangerous Dream Woman. But the King of Inventors, who did not hesitate in the didactic fiction of his later years to arrange marriages for prostitutes (one of them to a clergyman), or to match an elderly aristocrat with the mother of a (stillborn) illegitimate baby and a well-born young man with a lively country girl much like Martha, was himself content with a 'morganatic family'. It was his own phrase for Martha and the three children she bore him. He provided her with an alias, Mrs Dawson.* He 'got up' his latest role with some relish: William Dawson, barrister-at-law, husband and father, played to a strictly limited and no doubt sceptical audience of landladies and tradesmen in St Marylebone and Ramsgate. A photograph of him with Martha is the only adult portrait I have ever seen which shows him not wearing spectacles. He could not see very far without them. Martha, in contrast to Wilkie's often expressed preference, is rigidly encased in a corset.

How could Wilkie continue, throughout his association with Martha, to write passionate and polemical *romans à thèse* in which 'fallen women' were reintegrated into society through marriage to great-hearted, unconventional radicals, fighting to break down class barriers? Though he thought the legal forms quite irrelevant, he took care to keep 'readers in general' contented with a conventional happy ending. His own behaviour might be, as his sister-in-law thought, 'as bad as could be', but it was not, as is so often said, 'unconventional'. It followed only too closely the convention that tacitly accepted well-to-do, middle-aged, middle-class married men having two households. His old friend William Frith did so, keeping a mistress, who bore him seven children, a short walk from the house where he lived with his wife, by whom he had a dozen. Wilkie's variation on this pattern, minor to modern eyes but not to those of his contemporaries, was simply that the first woman was not, and now never would be, his wife. In his next novel a husband, about to repudiate his wife of many years, is accused of never taking her into society with him. ' "You have presented your wife to nobody . . . You go out as if you were a single man. I have reason to know you are actually believed to be a single man . . . in more than one quarter." '[34] This is either aimed at himself, a criticism of his past behaviour to Caroline Graves, or crass insensitivity.

According to her family, Martha claimed that she could have

* Martha may have suggested the name. In the 1871 census she gave her birthplace as Martham, the next village to Winterton. There was a William Dawson living in Martham in 1861; there were no Dawsons in Winterton.

married Wilkie any time she had wanted to.[35] Perhaps she refused in the terms of the soiled doves of his later fiction: ' "Must I remind you of what you owe to your high position, your spotless integrity, your famous name? Think of all that you have done for me, and then think of the black ingratitude of it if I ruin you for life by consenting to our marriage – if I selfishly, cruelly, wickedly drag you down to the level of a woman like me?" '[36] Or perhaps not. Martha, a sensible young woman, would have despised that sort of rhetoric, which was inevitably followed by graceful consent (in *The New Magdalen, The Two Destinies, The Fallen Leaves* and *The Guilty River*). But Martha would surely have given in, like Wilkie's heroines, if she had been pressed. Wilkie was not inclined to press her. A redoubling of the double life that had always intrigued him, with Martha installed in lodgings in Bolsover Street, a short walk from Gloucester Place, suited him very well.

The last piece of the puzzle was to fall into place when Caroline returned to Gloucester Place after about two years as Mrs Clow. She was back, at the latest, by April 1871.[37] She probably returned sometime in 1870: a copy of *Man and Wife* is inscribed 'To Mrs. George Graves, Oct. 1870' in Wilkie's hand.[38] There is no way of telling why the marriage ended. Perhaps she was badly treated. At all events, young Clow can hardly have been so amusing a companion as Wilkie, who could also offer the excitements of literary life, continental travel and the comforts of Gloucester Place. Caroline may just have missed Wilkie and Carrie. The marriage had not, for whatever reason, suited her, and her longing for respectability had received an abrupt check. Life with Wilkie, even with the addition of Martha and the children, was preferable to life without him. She returned to her former name, Caroline Graves, and the whole business seems to have been no more than a hiccup in her relationship with Wilkie.*

Caroline was now widely accepted, by his friends as his unofficial wife, by the world at large as his housekeeper. Her daughter was

* Clow may have made a last attempt to regain his wife in 1875. Wilkie wrote to Tindell, on 29 April 1875, 'Look also at the enclosed note received a little while since. "Keates" is a nickname for Caroline (Mrs Graves).

'Is the fellow's brain softening? Of course, no notice has been taken of his letter.' (Mitchell Library, Glasgow) universally considered his adopted child. Now Carrie was a young lady, her mother also became more acceptable. The two of them appeared with Wilkie in public, at the theatre and at art exhibitions. Caroline was included in dinner invitations from his friends, though on one occasion at least she refused, perhaps tactfully.[39] She wrote on her own initiative to Andrew Chatto, sending him some poems she had been asked to place. 'Wilkie Collins would very properly scold me well did he know what I have done.'[40] She sent her compliments, perhaps with a flicker of triumph, to Wilkie's aunt Emily Clunes, the sister of the woman who had always refused to recognize her, and many of Wilkie's letters to his various correspondents contain messages from Caroline.[41] Caroline continued to go abroad with him; the less presentable Martha did not. Caroline also became, without apparent distaste, one of the cast of Wilkie's new private drama. There is no evidence that Martha ever came to Gloucester Place, but Wilkie's children often did, and also had seaside holidays with Wilkie and Caroline. They were evidently lovingly accepted, finding an extra mother in Caroline and an aunt in Carrie.

By now Martha was trapped, even if she had wanted to get away. Her first child, Marian, called after his most popular female character, and perhaps also after Martha's youngest sister Mary Ann, who died at the age of eleven in 1860, was born on 4 July 1869. By the time Caroline returned to Wilkie Martha was pregnant with the second, Harriet Constance, born 14 May 1871. (Neither birth was registered.) Martha could not afford to lose Wilkie's liberal allowance of £20 a month, later raised to £25.[42] The average wage for a London housemaid in 1871, judging from the 'Situations Vacant' in *The Times*, was £16 a year.

Martha was kept firmly in her place. She is seldom mentioned in Wilkie's letters, hardly ever by name, as Caroline so often is. If Caroline had felt excluded from much of Wilkie's life, and showed her resentment by rushing into an unfortunate marriage, Martha, the mother of his children, should have felt even more aggrieved. But she was young, unsophisticated and undemanding. Perhaps her children, the flattering involvement with a famous man, the paper-thin respectability of being 'Mrs. Dawson' and her new financial security seemed enough.

To do Wilkie justice, he never attempted to end the relationship or to evade his commitments. His peculiar sense of honour involved loyalty to both Martha and Caroline; marriage to one would have meant casting off the other. Instead he created two very different kinds of 'marriage', jumping from bed to bed with the consent of all concerned. With one part of him he was the fatherly protector of a young woman who, though he loved her dearly, could have little in common with him intellectually. With the other, he remained the irrepressible Bohemian, openly defying the respectable world and challenging it to accept him on his own terms.

Martha and his children were included in every will he made; so were Caroline and Carrie. When each of the children was born, a codicil was added, naming the child and acknowledging it as his. Martha was not given trips to Paris, but Wilkie spent holidays with her and the children at Ramsgate. He cared deeply for his children. 'Tottie' and 'Hetty' became the inspiration for the lively and closely observed child-characters in the novels written after they were born.[43] He cannot have spent much time with them, but many Victorian children saw their fathers briefly and rarely: Wilkie at least was never a frightening and punitive paterfamilias. He was greatly distressed when Marian broke her leg. 'Domestic misfortunes are the only serious misfortunes,' he wrote to a publisher whose offices had burnt down. 'And I write with some experience of domestic anxieties – (of the irregular kind) – having a small "morganatic" family of three children, and remembering what I suffered when two of them were seriously ill.'[44] He paid for them to be decently and sensibly educated, first by a governess, then at good day schools.[45]

In the early years of their relationship at least, the association with Martha also revived the idealistic radicalism of his youth. The town-bred middle-class author knew something about the lives of servants, and had written about them long before this relationship with one. He had walked the streets of the East End with Dickens, and seen the down-and-outs in Soho cellars. Now he had his eyes opened to another kind of poverty.

> I had no idea . . . of what the life of a farm-labourer really was, in some parts of England . . . Never before had I seen such dire wretchedness

> as I saw in the cottages . . . the martyrs of old could endure, and die. I asked myself if they could endure, and *live* . . . week after week, month after month, year after year on the brink of starvation; live, and see their pining children growing up around them; live, with the poor man's parish-prison to look to as the end, when hunger and labour have done their worst! (*The New Magdalen*, Vol. I, Chapter the Eighth, p. 140)

The 'Radical, Communist, Incendiary' clergyman who makes this discovery describes the place where he had been living as 'a flat, ugly, barren agricultural' district; and these experiences must have been based on those of Martha's family and friends. Wilkie's generosity enabled her to help them; and the conspicuous stone memorial in the Winterton churchyard to her parents, and to a brother and sister who died young, was surely erected by her.

SEVENTEEN

The Moonstone

(1867–1870)

Wilkie's energy throughout this complicated and traumatic time was astonishing, and he was grateful to laudanum for helping to carry him through. One of the good stories he loved to tell about *The Moonstone* was adapted from Scott's experience of writing *The Bride of Lammermuir*: 'I was not only pleased and astonished at the *finale*, but did not recognise it as my own.'[1] Wilkie was no longer taking laudanum only at night, to help him sleep, but in larger and larger doses during the day. But this story would carry more conviction if he had not given such detailed accounts of his working methods for *The Woman in White* and *Armadale*, and if *The Moonstone* were not the most tightly constructed and best worked-out of all his novels. The opium may have wiped out his memory of the original planning, but it did not interfere with his carrying it through to the end. Central to the plot, of course, is the obliteration of the memory of an action performed under the influence of opium, recognized by another character who is an opium addict. Certainly the experiences of Ezra Jennings, his frightful dreams, the effect of being stunned after a larger than usual dose, the relief from intolerable pain, were based on Wilkie's own experiences at this time of severe pain and deep unhappiness.

Like Ezra Jennings, he now needed huge amounts of the drug. On holiday with Fred Lehmann in Switzerland in August, there was a crisis when Wilkie, who needed a tablespoon of laudanum a night –

enough to kill anyone not habituated to it – discovered that the more rigorous Swiss drug-regulations allowed him to buy only a fraction of what he needed. Fred had to go to four different chemists – or in another version, pretend to be a doctor – to make up the amount.[2]

Yet Wilkie, in severe pain and supposedly not in full command of his imagination, did not rely on a familiar formula for his novel. By 1867, after the outcry against the immorality of *Armadale*, Wilkie, and perhaps his more discriminating readers, wanted a change. 'Sensation novels have become a weariness to the flesh,' wrote Leslie Stephen in 1869 in the magazine that had serialized *Armadale*.[3] In preparing *The Moonstone* Wilkie deliberately set out to subvert many of the conventions of the genre he had initiated, and in the process did much to form a new one, the classic detective novel.*

By now the readers of the 1860s had certain expectations. A sensation novel would have a plot involving bigamy, adultery or illegitimacy; domestic murder was likely; and the heroine would be involved in sexual or criminal activities, often both. Disguise, mistaken identity, eavesdropping and the reading of private letters and diaries set the plots ticking and led to their final defusing. In *The Moonstone* the professional detective, the observant and subtle Sergeant Cuff, takes the position of the habituated reader of sensation, reading the events in a way that assumes the guilt of the maidservant and the young lady, working together to 'steal' her own diamond. By using details from the Road murder case of 1860, when a young girl, Constance Kent, was first cleared of the murder of her brother and then confessed to it five years later, Collins heightened the expectation that Cuff, like the real-life Inspector Whicher who first suspected Constance Kent, could be right. But the Moonstone, coming into the house through the wickedness of one man, has in fact been taken by another, and is lost for ever through the criminal greed and hypocrisy of a third. The struggle for ownership of the jewel is a male one, with its origin in the violence of colonial conquest. As Anthea Trodd has pointed out, there is also an emphasis on male teamwork to solve the mystery: another

* Julian Symons makes a convincing case for *The Notting Hill Mystery* by Charles Felix, 1865, as the first English detective novel.

link with the detective story.[4] The women are back on the sidelines. Whether they are gullible and absurd, vindictive and man-hating, or loyal, courageous and intelligent, they are all, rich and poor alike, at the mercy of men's actions and attitudes. Gabriel Betteredge, on the whole a sympathetic character, finds Rosanna Spearman's love for Franklin Blake comic. Only another woman, his daughter Penelope, can take it seriously. He can think of no better way to help a woman in trouble than to take her on his knee, like a crying child.

But if autonomy is firmly replaced in male hands, so is guilt. Rachel and Rosanna are individually, not collusively, guilty, though only of shielding the man they both love. Though the women are innocent of crime, they are culpable, in another way, as Rachel realizes: they protect men, where they should question and expose them. By submitting to the expectations of society that they will provide a safe haven for male egos, women compound men's errors and crimes. Their complicity creates the mystery. Wilkie thought the character of Nancy in Dickens' *Oliver Twist* 'the finest thing he ever did. He never afterwards saw all sides of a woman's character – saw all round her.'[5] The loyalty of Nancy the prostitute to her criminal associates, and her complicity in her own destruction, are echoed in *The Moonstone.* The pair of girls, one with a criminal past, the other the product of a sheltered upbringing that has in no way prepared her for secrecy and deception, could not seem more different. Yet they are linked through their love for a man who is unworthy of it.

Embedded in the novel, an essential part of its complex structure, is Wilkie's most sustained attack on organized Christian religion as an expression of all he most disliked about his society. This is most obvious in the characters of Godfrey Ablewhite and Miss Clack. Ablewhite was originally conceived as a clergyman, but softened into 'the inevitable gentleman who sits at the Ladies' Committees, and helps them through the business'.[6] Since Ablewhite is a whited sepulchre, who keeps a mistress in a house in St John's Wood and must, for the purposes of the plot, be deeply in debt, Wilkie finally fought shy of making him 'the Reverend'. Miss Clack, who secretes evangelical tracts (whose titles are only slightly parodied) in every corner of the houses she visits, is in her way as much a hypocrite as

Ablewhite. Dripping piety and venom in equal measure, she reflects Wilkie's continued irritation with the religion of his childhood.

The anti-evangelical theme is continued less obviously in Betteredge's superstitious use of *Robinson Crusoe* as a secular bible. The pious, in Wilkie's youth, twisted any page of the Good Book, chosen at random, into absurd relevance to their own predicaments. Defoe's novel has been seen as the archetypal bourgeois-capitalist text; its apposition of mundane concerns with pious ejaculation is exactly the atmosphere projected by Miss Clack, between whom and Betteredge there is an implacable dislike. Betteredge is a likeable old buffer, who expresses Wilkie's own opinions of the English Sunday, but he parodies the Bible-thumping classes with his favourite reading, and the divinatory uses he puts it to. Wilkie wrote to Harper's after the first number had been published, pointing out an error in the American illustrations, which showed Gabriel Betteredge wearing livery: 'As head-servant, he would wear plain black clothes and would look, with his white cravat and grey hair, like an old clergyman.'[7] Even Cuff, the professional sceptic, is like many of Wilkie Collins' detectives, tinged with the clerical. 'He might have been a parson, or an undertaker – or anything else you like, except what he really was.'[8]

There is also a criticism of western religion, by implication, in the serious attention given to the religious significance of the Moonstone, and the respectful treatment of the Indians. The Moonstone has two faces: turned to the capitalist west it is an ornament for conspicuous display, an investment which can be turned into cash, or an example of the disruption and divisiveness of wealth. Returned to its eastern origins, it again becomes a symbol of spiritual power, uniting the intellectual and emotional forces inherent in human and divine nature. Its true place is in the forehead of a moon god. Removed from that setting it can only be a force for harm, and the temporary nature of its stay in the west is underlined by the unconvincing contrivance of 'a little bit of silver wire' which turns it into a brooch for one evening. The only reviewer to understand this was Geraldine Jewsbury. She thought the epilogue 'redeems the somewhat sordid detective element, by a strain of solemn and pathetic human interest. Few will read of the final destiny of *The Moonstone* without feeling the tears rise in their eyes as they catch the last glimpse of the three men, who have sacrificed their cast in the service of their God . . . The deepest emotion is certainly reserved to the last.'[9]

The Indians, dark, mysterious outsiders, constitute a threat to the complacency of the ruling nation, which closes ranks against them. They are the instruments which expose the hypocrisy of that society, by the murder of Godfrey Ablewhite. In *Armadale* the relationship of self and shadow was a personal one. In *The Moonstone* the shadow as – in Jung's phrase – 'a moral problem that challenges the whole ego-personality' becomes a challenge to English society as a whole.* The challenge is finally rejected. With the removal of the diamond the disturbing elements vanish from the domestic tranquillity of the 'cheerful country house'.[10] The *status quo ante* is restored. But the reader remembers that the challenge was mounted; and the closure of the novel, in India, not England, reinforces the message.

Though several publishers, including Chapman & Hall, tried to get the rights to *The Moonstone*, Wilkie made the rather surprising choice of William Tinsley. Tinsley had published novels by G. A. Sala and Mary Braddon, and made so much money from *Lady Audley's Secret* that he built himself a mansion called 'Audley Hall'. As Edmund Yates was the first editor of *Tinsley's Magazine*, Wilkie would have known about the firm from several personal connections. George Moore remembered Tinsley as an innocent, 'quite witless and quite *h*-less'; carrying 'a bag containing fish for the family and a manuscript novel' and 'conducting his business as he dressed himself, sloppily . . . from long habit he would make a feeble attempt to drive a bargain, but he was duped generally'.[11] Wilkie found him a more slippery customer.

The contract was negotiated through Wilkie's solicitors, Benham and Tindell, who knew more about copyright law than most. Tinsley remembered the contract as 'a regular corker; it would pretty well cover the gable of an ordinary-sized house'.[12] The contract in fact

* '. . . No one can become conscious of the shadow without considerable moral effort. To become conscious of it involves recognising the dark aspects of the personality as present and real. This act is the essential condition for any kind of self-knowledge, and it therefore . . . meets with considerable resistance.' (*Jung: Selected Writings*, p. 91)

seems brief by modern standards. It is clear from Wilkie's correspondence with Benham and Tindell that it did not bind Tinsley as tightly as Wilkie had hoped.[13]

The first edition of 1,500 copies sold out rapidly. But there followed a disagreement with Tinsley over the terms for a second edition of five hundred copies. 'Is it possible that the agreement allows him to propose his own terms of payment to us?' Wilkie wanted to know. 'I suppose the truth is, that he may or may not – at his own sole discretion – publish a new edition. In this case, he has us at his mercy.'[14] Tinsley had a rather different version. He remembered that he was asked by Wilkie's solicitors to publish another five hundred, with payment in advance rather than after the copies had been sold, and that he refused. According to him an attempt was made to buy the standing type for use by another publisher. Tinsley, who felt he had been ill-used, finally got the original terms reduced by £50.[15]

In the later stages of serialization, crowds of eager readers hung around the Wellington Street offices on publication day, and bets were placed on where the diamond would eventually turn up. Tinsley remembered porters and errand boys reading it with their packs on their backs. Some of the reviews were lukewarm, but Wilkie was, rightly, confident.

> Both you and I might have good reason to feel discouraged, if this list indicated anything more important than the timidity of the Libraries – and possibly the poverty of the Libraries as well . . . we only have to wait a few weeks, until the book has had time to get *talked about*. I don't attach much importance to the Reviews – except as advertisements which are inserted for nothing. But the impression that I produce on the general public of readers is the lever that will move anything . . . If Mr. Mudie is right in believing 500 to be a sufficient supply – then (judging by past experience) three fourths of my readers have deserted me! . . . It is (in the opinion of more than one good judge) the best book I have written. I believe it myself to have a much stronger element of 'popularity' in it than anything I have written since 'The Woman in White'. *That* book, Mr. Mudie, and the Librarians, took in *driblets* – just as the public *forced* them.[16]

The general public's leverage worked, and *The Moonstone* took the place it has never lost, alongside *The Woman in White*. It too was repeatedly cribbed from. Trollope took the theme of a 'stolen' diamond for *The Eustace Diamonds*, reverting to the young-lady criminal of sensation, but developing her into a psychological study. Dickens borrowed heavily from it for his last novel, *Edwin Drood.* Conan Doyle in *The Sign of Four* took the Indian theme, and the idea of a treasure with a curse on it. A parody in the magazine *The Mask*, a month after book publication, picked, quite cleverly, on weak spots in the novel: 'The professor had the house arranged exactly as it had been on the night of the birthday dinner, following the example set in many melodramas and operas, especially the last scene in *L'Étoile du Nord.*'[17]

Even if it is not the first English detective novel, *The Moonstone* was a most influential one. As in all the best examples of the genre, it is fair with clues, but the clues point in the wrong direction. The professional detective makes intelligent but mistaken deductions; the 'criminal' is the least likely suspect; the 'solution' turns out to be a part-solution only; and there is a twist in the tail. There is a staged reconstruction of a crime – theatrical perhaps, but effective, and copied in innumerable detective stories. Unconscious motivation is revealed, as well as conscious, for it is also, like all Wilkie Collins' best novels, operating on several levels at once; and his interest in the workings of the unconscious mind is backed up by quotations from well-known writers on mental processes, W. B. Carpenter and Wilkie's friend John Elliotson, used to justify the opium experiment which leads to the solution.

The Moonstone is perhaps the most entertaining and agreeable of Wilkie's novels. Though it includes a pervasive satire on the Church of England, and especially on evangelical absurdities, it is not disrespectful of religious belief. Indeed it is remarkable for its serious treatment of the Hindu faith, at a time when the violence of the Mutiny was still fresh in British memory. Though Wilkie adapted details of the Road murder, the mystery turns on a theft, not a murder: the blood on Constance Kent's nightgown becomes paint on Franklin Blake's. In spite of his sensation label, Wilkie disliked the personal violence of murder as much as the impersonal violence of war. In his short story 'A Plot in Private Life' (written before the Road murder), blood on a nightgown, taken to be evidence of a murder, turns out to be nothing of the kind. 'A Plot in Private Life' also has a private investigator, Mr Dark, who foreshadows Cuff and looks 'much more like a parson of free and easy habits than a lawyer's clerk'.

There are deaths in *The Moonstone*. There is the satisfying murder of Godfrey Ablewhite, like the death of Fosco not a domestic crime but brought about by impersonal forces of quasi-divine retribution. More importantly, there is the tragically unnecessary death of the servant Rosanna Spearman, who falls hopelessly in love with a 'gentleman'. In the most uncomfortable episode in the book, the unsatisfactory hero Franklin Blake reacts most convincingly to Rosanna Spearman's posthumous confession. The manuscript reveals a change in Wilkie's original plan for this moment of revelation, in Chapter 4 of the Third Narrative of 'The Discovery of the Truth'. Originally Blake is overcome by remorse. A deleted passage reads:

> The dead woman herself [answered] my rash and reckless suspicion of her. I had rushed at the first chance of escape that I could see from the horrible position in which I now stood. I had cast on another – for all I knew as innocent as I was – the unendurable slur that had been cast on *me*. And there was the answer of the woman whose memory I had slandered. 'I love you.'
>
> This – let me say so much for myself – this was the first effect which Rosanna Spearman's confession produced in me. The natural feeling of astonishment came next.[18]

The published version, by omitting this, reduces Blake's insight, making him a harder and less sympathetic character and throwing into relief his astonishment that Rosanna could have felt love for him and jealousy of Rachel Verinder. In the mind of a 'gentleman', a servant, particularly one who is plain and deformed, hardly belongs to the same species. In the end, the most Blake can say of Rosanna Spearman's tragedy is that he cannot revert to it 'without a pang of distress'; his inability to confront the reality of Rosanna's love makes the reader indignant, and is meant to.

Dickens, after his first enthusiasm, turned against the story. Though – or because – *The Moonstone* had made money for him, as well as

Wilkie, bumping up the circulation of *All the Year Round* probably more than any other novel, and even beating the success of *Great Expectations*, he finally reversed his earlier opinion. 'I quite agree with you about the Moonstone', he wrote to Wills. 'The construction is wearisome beyond endurance, and there is a vein of obstinate conceit in it that makes enemies of readers.'[19]

It would be wrong to read too much into this famous misjudgement. Dickens was probably irritated by the new complications of Wilkie's private life, the moral equivalent of his incorrigible untidiness. It was perhaps Wilkie's affairs that were 'wearisome beyond endurance', and 'the vein of obstinate conceit' was not really in the writing but in the man. Dickens had often found Wilkie tiresome in the past, and had got over his annoyance. But this time there were other factors, and the consequences were more serious. Dickens' growing dislike of his son-in-law Charles Collins, and his resentment at the life his daughter was leading with a man so ill and so neurotic that he could never take any decisions, were increasingly obvious. Soon after Dickens' death Fechter told Annie Fields how Dickens used to look at Charley across the dining table 'as if to say, "Astonishing you should be here today, but tomorrow you will be in your chamber never to come out again."'[20] Wilkie, often at the dinner table at Gad's Hill, could not have missed those looks. Wilkie was slow to take offence on his own account, from his friends at least – business associates were another matter – but his protective loyalty to Charley would have taken precedence even over his friendship with Dickens. When Forster's biography of Dickens was published, Charley told Holman Hunt, 'I always felt myself the impossibility of entire intimacy which you describe.'[21] Wilkie, who had perhaps come closer to Dickens than any other man, now realized, after seventeen years of apparent intimacy, that there was a barrier beyond which it was impossible to go.

Yet any uneasiness in his relationship with Dickens did not amount, as Fechter suggested, to an estrangement. Wilkie and Dickens continued to see each other, to write to each other in the warmest terms and to exchange compliments and advice. It was Wilkie who suggested the form of the conclusion to the famous 'reading' of *Oliver Twist*, which Dickens adopted, bringing it from a 'blank state of horror into a fierce and passionate rush for the end'.[22] The much-debated question of 'influence' of one writer on the other – mostly sterile – does seem to have some foundation where *The Moonstone* and *Edwin Drood* are concerned. It is ironic that Wilkie disliked Dickens' last novel as much as Dickens disliked *The Moonstone.*

But Dickens admired *Black and White*, the play Wilkie wrote from an idea of Fechter's in 1869, and told him so. He wrote to Wills with real pleasure that the first night went brilliantly. 'It was more like a fiftieth night than a first . . . There is no doubt that it ought to run, for it has real merit and is most completely and delicately presented.'[23]

Both men were middle-aged and ailing. Both of them were working harder than ever, had new domestic ties, and were concerned to keep their strength for work. The complicity of earlier years, the nocturnal adventures, were over. Dickens, desperate to keep the secret of his relationship with Ellen Ternan, did not think Wilkie, happy to reveal his own unorthodoxy, a reliable confidant. It was the conventional Wills and Forster who were trusted with the knowledge of his whereabouts and movements.

Moreover the estrangement, if there was one, seems to have been more on Wilkie's side than Dickens', as was to become clear after Dickens' death. Dickens' last letter to Wilkie was, at Wilkie's request, a statement in formal terms that the copyrights of everything he had published in *Household Words* and *All the Year Round* were his own property. Dickens added a personal note, objecting to and altering the phraseology of the draft letter drawn up by Tindell – 'May the Spirit of English be merciful to me!' – and concluded:

> I have been truly concerned to hear of your bad attack . . . I don't come to see you because I don't want to bother you. Perhaps you may be glad to see me by-and-bye. Who knows? – Affectionately always.[24]

Though Wilkie lived for another twenty-one years and wrote fourteen more full-length novels, as well as shorter fiction and plays, none of his work, interesting though much of it is, ever reached the standard of his novels of the 1860s. There were a number of reasons. His opium addiction, it has been suggested, coarsened his art, diminished his ability to construct plots and weakened his capacity for self-criticism.[25] There is no sign of this in *The Moonstone*, written when his opium dependence was fully established.* Swinburne's well-known parody of Pope sums up another explanation current at the time Wilkie died:

> What brought good Wilkie's genius nigh perdition?
> Some demon whispered – 'Wilkie! have a mission.'[26]

But only half the novels written in the last twenty years of Wilkie Collins' life are in the strict sense 'novels with a purpose'. The rest are either out-and-out sensation, or the mixture, familiar from his earlier work, of a well-plotted and exciting narrative with some incidental element of social indignation. But the mythic, fairy-tale quality which underpins his best fiction and lifts it above that of his imitators appears only in fitful gleams. Little of his work after *The Moonstone* transcends its era and the limitations of the sensation genre. By comparison with the novels Wilkie Collins wrote in the 1860s, many of the later ones seem flat and dated.

The loss of Dickens as a candid friend and rigorous critic may have affected him. *The Moonstone*, which Dickens had little to do with and which he finally disliked, would seem to contradict this. But it was an *All the Year Round* book. By now the two men knew each other's views so well that it was perhaps the idea of Dickens as critic, acting as an internal censor, which still affected Wilkie to some extent. After *The Moonstone*, he rejected the influence of the man who was not only the greatest novelist of his time, but also one of the great editors and critics. After his death the sorcerer's spells finally lost their power; the richness of the imaginative web he threw over the lives of those who knew him faded. The light of common day and the lurid glow of nightmare became separate and distinct phenomena in Wilkie's novels, half-heartedly linked by mechanical narrative devices.

* There is an intricate plan in existence for a novel he never wrote, 'Miss Warrener's Wedding' or 'Love and Liberty', drawn up in the late 1870s or early '80s, which shows how carefully he continued to construct the 'scaffolding' of a novel. It is a complex and detailed outline of a 'locked-room' mystery. (MS at HRC)

Another change in Wilkie's literary life undoubtedly had a major and deleterious effect on his fiction, as Kenneth Robinson has noted.[27] His plays began to be successful. Once he had made the breakthrough as a playwright, initially with Fechter's help, he began to design novels, from their conception, for conversion into plays. However 'theatrical' his earlier novels sometimes seemed, they were not, as Wilkie very well knew, primarily dramatic. Though both *The Woman in White* and *Armadale* were eventually successful on the stage, they had to be entirely rewritten for the theatre. Now he found he could get by without expending so much energy, by reversing the process.

His next novel was one of those originally planned as a play. It must have seemed ironic to those in the secret of his tangled private life that it was given one of the titles earlier considered for *No Name*, *Man and Wife*. Attacking the unsatisfactory state of the marriage laws was one way of justifying a failure to get married at all. In September 1868 he wrote to his solicitor, Charles Benham: 'I want to find out what "Mrs. Yelverton's" grievance is . . . with a view to making it the starting point in a play. (this between ourselves). Can you tell me, in what point her marriage, was "null and void"?'[28] Benham provided details of the complicated case, which turned on anomalies in the law of marriage in England, Scotland and Ireland, used for the plot of *Man and Wife*.

The play was intended to mix comedy and drama, 'not in alternate slices, but so that they shall be really parts of each other'.[29] But after writing the first act he decided that the subject was of a 'ticklish nature' for stage representation, and by the summer of 1869 he determined it would be best to make a story of it first: 'As a novelist, I can hold my audience, when I have once got them, and lead them (whether they like it or not) to the end. As a dramatist, I am not equally sure of the ground I walk on.'[30] He was soon to change his mind about this.

Meanwhile *Black and White* was staged at the Adelphi, with Fechter and Carlotta Leclercq. Fechter supplied a plot that was at least intelligible, though preposterous; Wilkie added characters and dialogue. The play is set in Trinidad in 1830: the hero, a supposed French count, is discovered to be the son of a plantation owner by his slave.

He is therefore of mixed blood, and himself a slave. This gives the villain, in love with the girl the hero is engaged to, the opportunity to buy him. Finally it is discovered that his mother was freed before his father's death: her son, too, is free. In one of Wilkie's novels, the clashing identities of the hero, white aristocrat and black slave, might have fired his imagination: it could have been the ultimate expression of self and shadow. In the play, nothing but melodrama results from the revelation of the count's true origins.

The play ran into trouble from the beginning. Fechter was ill during rehearsals, and after a successful first night on 29 March receipts were poor. Wilkie thought the public had suffered an overdose of 'Oncle Tommerie' after the success of the many dramatizations of *Uncle Tom's Cabin*. The play was kept on for sixty nights; but it ran to empty houses. The provincial tour was even more disastrous: at Manchester Fechter gave one of his best performances to the worst house ever known at the theatre.[31]

Wilkie seems to have sunk more of his own money than he could well afford into the production. He learnt the folly of being his own 'angel', and of having any kind of financial relationship with the feckless Fechter, whose spell as an English actor-manager ended in 'inextricable difficulties'.[32] However he assured Fred Lehmann, who offered him a loan in April, that his head was still above water; 'the money anxieties are not added to the other anxieties which are attacking me'. He could manage as long as his health did not give way. 'It is necessary to "lay the keel" of something new – after this disaster'.[33]

The 'other anxieties' may have included worry over his laudanum addiction, brought home to him by his experience in Switzerland the previous year. In February he told Fred Lehmann's sister, Elizabeth Benzon, as an excuse for refusing an evening invitation,

> My doctor is trying to break me of the habit of drinking laudanum. I am stabbed every night at ten with a sharp-pointed syringe which injects morphia under my skin – and gets me a night's rest, without any of the drawbacks of taking opium internally. If I only persevere with this, I am told I shall be able, before long, gradually to diminish the quantity of morphia and the number of the nightly stabbings – and so emancipate myself from opium altogether.[34]

By April he might have realized that the supposed cure was worse than useless. He was probably worried, too, about Caroline's unhappiness in her marriage. Should he take her back? Or marry Martha in time to legitimize their unborn child, so casting Caroline off for ever?

The novel version of *Man and Wife*, Wilkie's first full-blown *roman à thèse*, was serialized in *Cassell's Magazine* from January to June 1870, as well as in *Harper's Weekly* in New York. *Cassell's* was a 'family' magazine, geared to the provision of innocuous reading. Wilkie agreed, under protest, to remove a 'damn it', insisting to Cassell's that this was not to create a precedent: 'It is quite possible that your peculiar constituency may take exception to things to come in my story . . . you will find me deaf to all remonstrances'.[35] Wilkie called it 'an *un*popular book which may possibly make a hit, from the mere oddity of a modern writer running full tilt against the popular sentiment'.[36] He was proved right: the serialization increased the circulation of *Cassell's Magazine* to over seventy thousand. *Harper's* were so delighted with the first number that they sent him an unexpected cheque for £500. At the beginning of June Wilkie also managed to stop a piracy in Canada, by arranging separate publication there, with the firm of Hunter, Rose of Toronto.[37] It was the first time this had ever been tried, and it was a great success. 'We have entirely stopped the importation of American copies . . . and we have made money . . . into the bargain – thus opening a new field to English writers and publishers in an English Colony.'[38] The conflict over Canadian and United States publishing territory was to be complicated later by the importation of Canadian copies of his books into the States. This threat to Harper's' market was to be a serious matter to Wilkie, who depended on their generosity; but for the moment all seemed well. Wilkie was so confident of success that when Tinsley made a bid for the book rights that he considered inadequate, he held out for more:

> It may suit Tinsley's purpose to assume that Man & Wife is to be a failure. It suits mine to assume that it is going to beat the Moonstone . . . I won't have the bargaining off the agreement, this time, which took place with the second edition of the Moonstone . . . My head was muddled when you came here. I am as clear as a bell now – and I see through Tinsley to his marrow – if he has got one.[39]

He decided to publish the book with F. S. Ellis, a bookseller and publisher in a small way, on the commission system. Wilkie was responsible for the costs; Ellis was to get ten per cent of the gross receipts.[40]

In the end Wilkie did well from the arrangement; but it involved him in endless minor irritations. His solicitor William Tindell (Benham had ceased to be active in the firm) was acting as his agent, and was not completely familiar with the publishing scene. The printers, Savill & Edwards, turned out to be unbusinesslike and inaccurate. Wringing payment out of Mudie, now seriously in debt to several publishers, was difficult. Ellis had never published a novel before and was inexperienced at publicity and distribution: 'Mr. Ellis is damaging the chances of the book by keeping its publication as profound a secret as he can', Wilkie complained.[41] Struggling to finish the novel, Wilkie planned to visit Gad's Hill as soon as it was done. On the day he wrote the last pages he heard the news of Dickens' death.

EIGHTEEN

After Dickens

(1870–1872)

It was a tremendous shock. Yet there is a curious hardness in Wilkie's reaction that shows the distance he had already put between them. On 8 June, the day Dickens was struck down, Wilkie heard the news from the Beards, and wrote to Catherine, Frank's wife, that he was 'shocked and grieved' and would call later to hear if she had any news.[1] Perhaps he was too stunned to feel emotion at first. But his letters to William Tindell, who was now a friend to whom he confided intimate family matters, speak of Dickens' death with a chilling remoteness. Wilkie had suggested that *Man and Wife* might be advertised by a slip of coloured paper inserted in the July number of *Edwin Drood*: 'Dickens's circulation is large and influential . . . If private influence is wanted here I can exert it.'[2] Tindell was not in favour. On 10 June Wilkie wrote:

> You are quite right. Besides, since you wrote, he is gone. I finished 'Man and Wife' yesterday – fell asleep from sheer fatigue – and was awakened to hear the news of Dickens's death.
>
> The advertising at the Stations is an excellent idea.[3]

He was, of course, one of the small group of friends at Dickens' simple and unadorned funeral, travelling to Westminster Abbey in the last of the three carriages that followed the hearse, with his brother and Dickens' doctor and lawyer, Frank Beard and Frederic Ouvry. Wilkie stood by the open grave with Charles Reade, who laid his head on Wilkie's shoulder and wept openly. Wilkie himself was much moved, and could never recall the occasion without emotion. Yet afterwards he could write to Tindell: 'The day of Dickens's funeral was a lost day to me. I am backward with the proofs of the book – and, as they are not at all intelligently read, they take a long time.'[4]

Wilkie was, it is true, ill, depressed and exhausted, 'utterly worn out, with all I have gone through'.[5] The outbreak of the Franco-Prussian war made him despair of mankind (and fear that sales would drop). Wilkie wrote to his German translator, Frederick Lehmann's brother Dr Emil Lehmann, with uncanny prescience:

> What is to be said of the progress of humanity? Here are the nations still ready to slaughter each other, at the command of one miserable wretch whose interest it is to set them fighting! Are we before the time of Christ – or after? I begin to believe in only one civilising influence – the discovery one of these days of a destructive agent so terrible that War shall mean *annihilation*, and men's fears shall force them to keep the peace.[6]

He showed a more cynical face to Tindell:

> If the infamous 'war' is injuring us – suppose we alter the heading in the advertisements thus: (???)
>
> New Romance of Domestic War. Man and Wife. or The Mitrailleuse of Home. by W.C.
>
> This would instantly sell an edition!!![7]

Man and Wife was a success, largely because of the topicality of the social and legal issues aired in it. Popular and press agitation in the 1860s brought about reform of the Irish marriage laws in 1870, and the first Married Woman's Property Act was passed in the same year. Wilkie added a note to the preface for the 1871 edition: 'Being an Act mainly intended for the benefit of the poor, it was, of course, opposed by the House of Commons at the first reading, and largely altered by the House of Lords . . . it is, so far, better than no law at all.'

He was shooting at several targets, which he saw as related; all particularly affected women. The absurdities and potential dangers of the anomalous marriage laws of England, Scotland and Ireland, and the lack of any right of a married woman to possess her own property and keep her own earnings, were obvious scandals. He also attacked the enthusiasm for sports and athletics, especially at the universities. This, he thought, led to a coarsening of moral sensibilities in young men in favour of physical qualities, which made them brutal in their dealings with women. His villain is programmed to win: he sees the whole of life as a contest. He has no feeling for others, and no capacity for self-sacrifice. He is specifically compared with the working-class 'rough', who collectively became the 'mob' that the middle classes so much feared.

> We have become so shamelessly familiar with violence and outrage, that we recognise them as a necessary ingredient in our social system, and class our savages as a representative part of our population, under the newly invented name of 'Roughs'. Public attention has been directed by hundreds of other writers to the dirty Rough in fustian . . . the present writer . . . is bold enough to direct attention to the washed Rough in broadcloth . . . is no protest needed, in the interests of civilization, against a revival of barbarism among us, which asserts itself to be a revival of manly virtue . . .? (*Man and Wife*, Preface)

Wilkie, whose only physical activities for a good many years had been gentle strolling round city streets, or sailing, with a hired crew to do the active work, might be felt to have a special interest in attacking the cult of strenuous exercise. However, he touched a chord in many who found the muscular Christianity of Charles Kingsley and his followers distasteful. Wilkie wrote to G. A. Sala in 1871 to congratulate him on an article on the same theme, curiously using the imagery of physical combat:

> I am delighted to find you . . . [setting] the muscular mania before the public eye in the proper light . . . I sit on my book, and fetch my breath, and see how the fight goes on in other hands. But *you* can hit them again . . .[8]

Social purpose is not in itself inimical to good fiction. But in *Man and Wife* it is uneasily combined with a sensation plot relying on coincidence and repetition added to bulk out the novel, much of which was removed again in the final dramatization. Still more destructive to the narrative is its original conception as a play. There is an unusually heavy reliance on dialogue, especially in the early chapters converted from the first act of the play. Light-hearted – but heavy-footed – banter alternates with melodramatic speeches. The stage version works well, and undoubtedly influenced Pinero, who manages this kind of contrast even better in *The Second Mrs Tanqueray*. But on the page it is leaden and unconvincing. Dickens might have revised his opinion of Wilkie's multi-narrational structures if he had read *Man and Wife*, for the narrative added to the original play is, for once, in an authorial voice so prescriptive and interventionist as to make the first half of the book tiresome to read, in spite of the excitements of the plot.[9]

Wilkie researched the athletic, legal and medical details carefully. Asking for advice on 'muscular men', he wrote, 'I know their ignorance, their servility to a hero of their own order – and their enthusiasm for rowing fighting and running – as compared with their stolid indifference to everything else. But I don't know their technical phrases . . .'[10] He even went to a running track with Frank Beard to get the right atmosphere for Geoffrey Delamayn's disastrous race.[11] But no amount of research could compensate for the clumsy characterization. His athlete is such a lout, lacking any of the human inconsistencies of Wilkie's earlier villains, that reviewers pointed out it was impossible to believe that the heroine, Anne Silvester, would have been interested in him for a moment, let alone allowed herself to become pregnant by him. Wilkie defended their relationship to Kate Field, who saw the play and objected to its unreality. 'I *am* surprised at your never having met in real life with a woman who fell in love with a man utterly unworthy of her.'[12] But Kate Field was right. The heroine, a flavourless, self-sacrificing victim, is as unbelievable as the villain. Her elderly admirer, the club-footed Sir Patrick, is a boring old fogey whose dislike of everything modern is echoed by the narrative voice. He needs the charm of an experienced actor to make him interesting.

A reversion to 1860s sensation in the second half of the book seems coarse in texture after the tautly written subtleties of *The Moonstone*. But once Wilkie begins elaborating the character of the crazed and psychomatically speechless cook Hester Dethridge, omitted from the play, he is on familiar ground, and the novel stirs, if not to life, at least to a kind of galvanic activity. Hester, a battered wife married to a brutal husband, lacking legal redress and finally driven to murder and madness, becomes a figure of folk tale, rather than a Blue Book illustration. The sense of entrapment, first of Hester in her marriage, then of Anne Silvester in hers, ceases to be simply a social evil. Here Wilkie once more creates the uncanny atmosphere that Edmund Yates described in his fiction: 'the "creepy" effect, as of pounded ice dropped down the back'.[13] Hester's description of the shadow-self who haunts her appearing behind a child in Regent's Park shows that Wilkie's obsession with doubles could still serve him well:

> The Thing stole out, dark and shadowy in the pleasant sunlight. At first I saw only the dim figure of a woman. After a little it began to get plainer, brightening from within outward – brightening, brightening, brightening, till it set before me the vision of MY OWN SELF repeated as if I was standing before a glass – the double of myself, looking at me with my own eyes . . . it said to me, with my own voice, 'Kill him.' (*Man and Wife*, Sixteenth Scene, Chapter the Fiftyfourth, p. 226)

Man and Wife was 'affectionately dedicated' to Fred and Nina Lehmann, who opened their house at Highgate to Wilkie while he was writing it, and supported him through his domestic and financial problems. The anti-athleticism of the book was perhaps a warning aimed at the Lehmanns' sport-mad teenage sons. Rudy, later a Cambridge oarsman and celebrated rowing coach, remembered that 'We were generous, and forgave the erring author for the sake of the unvarying friend'. He recalled Wilkie in the Woodlands days: 'a neat figure of cheerful plumpness . . . a full brown beard, a high and rounded forehead, a small nose not naturally intended to support a pair of large spectacles, behind which his eyes shone with humour and friendship'.[14]

The novel also contains a graceful compliment to Fred and Nina in the characters of the musical Julius Delamayn and his wife.* Julius much prefers playing the violin to canvassing for a seat in Parliament (Fred stood for Parliament on at least two occasions). Mrs Delamayn is 'one of the few players on the piano-forte under whose subtle touch that shallow and soulless instrument becomes inspired with expression

* (De)lamayn = Lehmann?

not its own, and produces music instead of noise'.[15] Wilkie said that Hallé was the best pianist in England *after* Nina Lehmann, and her son wrote of 'the instinctive sympathy with which she gave life and symmetry and charm to any piece she played'.[16] Their houses in Berkeley Square and Highgate were a focus for talented artists in every field, where the great and the gifted could meet each other. Annie Fields, with Bostonian stuffiness, thought the Lehmanns' circle *too* smart: 'This is the kind of life Dickens's children have known too much of since they have grown up – especially K[ate] C[ollins].'[17] But Wilkie was thoroughly at home there. A visitor to Woodlands felt hard done by when she was subjected to a ten-minute monologue by Sir Charles Dilke while the rest of the company were laughing at Wilkie's stories. The same observer watched him listening entranced at a musical evening. Browning was restless with excitement; Charles Reade sat calmly smiling. 'But I was astonished at the capacity for enjoyment that Wilkie Collins seemed to have, for he generally strikes one as being rather apathetic and weary looking except when he is talking. He seemed to absorb the music (I can use no other expression). He told me afterwards that it had made him feel ten years younger.'[18]

Wilkie's musical tastes were highly selective, however. He loved Mozart, always singled out for praise in his books, but was less enthusiastic about Beethoven: '. . . the "Great Kreutzer Sonata" has upset me about classical music,' he told Nina Lehmann. 'I am afraid I don't like classical music after all – I am afraid I am not the Amateur I once thought myself. The whole violin part of "The Great K.S." appeared to me to be the musical expression of a varying and violent stomach-ache, with intervals of hiccups.'[19] He was equally dismissive of Schumann. 'Herr Schuman's music, Madame Schuman's playing, *and* the atmosphere of St. James's Hall, are three such afflictions as I never desire to feel again. I think of sending a card to Érard's: – "Mr. Collins's compliments, and he would be glad to know how the poor piano is?" '[20]

Even before the serialization of *Man and Wife* began, Wilkie was suffering the usual irritations over copyright. Most European countries had now conceded the principle of international copyright, and though the complications of the different rules for establishing copyright in different countries were endless, he received small sums for the translations of his novels into French, German, Italian, Spanish and the Scandinavian languages, among others. But the Dutch still held out, and Belinfaute Brothers, publishers at The Hague, wrote to 'Madame Wilkie Collins' demanding 'her' intervention to secure them the 'clichés' of *Man and Wife* for translation. Wilkie replied, first revealing that he was not 'the charming person whom you suppose me to be':

> I observe with profound surprise and regret that your request . . . is not accompanied by the slightest hint of any intention on your part of paying for that privilege. All that you offer me is a copy of the magazine. What am I to do with a copy of the magazine? I don't understand Dutch. All that I can do is to look at your magazine, and mourn over my own neglected education.
>
> Permit me to suggest that you might acknowledge the receipt of the right to translate 'Man and Wife' in a much better way than by giving me the magazine. It is quite a new idea – you might give me some money.
>
> . . . You may – and probably will – tell me that the profits are miserably small . . . Call the profits, if you like, a shilling a week, and give me the indescribable satisfaction of seeing for thirty or forty weeks to come, this entry in my banker's book: By Messrs. Belinfaute Brothers' Sense of Justice – six-pence.[21]

Belinfaute continued to protest against even the principle of payment, and in a further letter Wilkie wrote more angrily, 'I persist, in the interest of public morality, in asserting my right to regard as my own property the produce of my own brains and my own labour . . . I declare any publisher who takes my book from me . . . without my permission, and without giving me a share in his profits – to be guilty of theft, and to be morally, if not legally, an outlaw and a pest among honest men.' Wilkie published the correspondence in the *Echo* and *Harper's Weekly*, and Belinfaute gave in. Wilkie had the satisfaction of eventually collecting one hundred guilders, £8. 6s. 8d.[22] But the trouble caused by the collection of these sums was hardly worth his time: 'I am strongly disposed to let myself be robbed, as the preferable alternative to letting myself be worried.'[23]

The potential rewards from the theatre were greater, and the production, in both England and America, of garbled pirated stage versions of his novels continued to infuriate him. 'The obstacle against us is the barbarous indifference of the House of Commons . . . If Disraeli's books were dramatic enough to be stolen for the stage, I should recommend (quite seriously!) an immediate adaptation of one of them, without asking his leave. If *he* could be made to move in the matter, something might be done.'[24] His annoyance was not only at the financial loss. *Poor Miss Finch*, unusual among Wilkie's later novels in that it was not designed for conversion into a play, was pirated by 'some obscure idiot in the country . . . It is eminently *un*fit for stage-purposes', he considered. 'What I dare not do with my own work, another man (unknown in Literature) is perfectly free to do, against my will, and . . . to the prejudice of my novel and my reputation.'[25] At least two unauthorized versions of *Man and Wife* were produced in English theatres, and in New York the arrangements with Augustin Daly for a production of Wilkie's dramatization nearly broke down over Daly's cavalier attempt to have the text rewritten by someone else. Again, it was not simply a matter of money: '. . . my reputation is entirely at Mr Daly's mercy', Wilkie complained. 'I don't know what liberties he may not take with my work – what abrupt and absurd ending he may not introduce – and what rough-and-ready changes he may not make, to the confusion of the dialogue and the perversion of the characters.'[26]

It is no wonder that 'infernal pains in the inside' were added to his usual rheumatic troubles. Wilkie was bothered, for some months, with minor literary tasks, writing and publishing the play of *Man and Wife* and dramatizing *No Name.* He went to Ramsgate to recover at the end of September, perhaps with Martha and the fifteen-month-old Marian. Wilkie was pregnant with a new book, Martha with her second child.

He may equally well have been at Ramsgate with Caroline. When Martha's second daughter, Harriet Constance, was born at Bolsover Street on 14 May 1871, Caroline had been back at Gloucester Place for some months. Wilkie's life now settled into a pattern which he was to maintain for the rest of his life, alternating between his two families and also carrying on a social life lived to a great extent without reference to either of them. This double dose of domesticity was to have some effect on his next novel.

Poor Miss Finch, subtitled 'A Domestic Story', began to be serialized in *Cassell's Magazine* in August, immediately following Charles Reade's *A Terrible Temptation. The Times* had thought Reade's novel too dangerous to put into the hands of an unmarried girl, and one reviewer of *Poor Miss Finch* saw the 'sanctifying influence' of *Cassell's*, 'feebly apparent in every chapter'. It was witheringly called 'a sensation novel for Sunday reading'.[27]

Poor Miss Finch is not primarily a didactic novel, but Wilkie did intend to show that 'the conditions of human happiness are independent of bodily affliction . . . it is even possible for bodily affliction itself to take its place among the ingredients of human happiness'.[28] The point is rather too relentlessly hammered home in the last section of the book. He was distressed to discover that the early numbers of *Poor Miss Finch* raised the hopes of the blind that the surgeon, Herr Grosse, was based on a real person who had some miracle cure. 'The vile periodical system . . . is partly to blame', he explained. 'This poor man . . . is one of the very many readers whom the story is intended to console.'[29]

The plot of *Poor Miss Finch* does not (to put it mildly) stand up to assessment by the criteria of realism. A girl, blinded by cataracts at a year old, falls in love with a young man who is an identical twin. He is cured of epileptic fits (caused by a blow on the head) by taking nitrate of silver, which turns him dark blue.* The girl, who has a horror of dark colours, is operated on by a German eye surgeon and regains her sight. The normal-complexioned twin, also in love with her, pretends to be his brother, and she nearly marries him by mistake. She loses her sight again, and is united with the correct, blue twin.

Hidden in this sensation plot there are suggestions of a highly

* As usual, Wilkie did his research. 'The nitrate of silver [as a treatment for epilepsy has] one very serious objection to it . . . it is apt to produce a permanent discoloration of the skin, a frightful lead-colour. There is a footman in a house near Cavendish Square who has been thus blackened: and there is a gentleman of property resident at Brighton . . . [whose] face looks as if it had been thoroughly and carefully pencilled over with plumbago.' (Thomas Wilson, M.D., *Lectures on the Principles and Practice of Physic*, London 1857)

topical shifting of the ground in the relationship between the sexes. Lucilla Finch is, simply because she *is* blind, liberated from many of the social and moral constraints that imprisoned women. '. . . Modesty is essentially the growth of our own consciousness of the eyes of others judging us . . . blindness is never bashful, for . . . blindness cannot see.'[30] Her attraction to her lover comes not though sight, but first through the sound of his voice, and then the more physical and sexually arousing sense of touch: '. . . a delicious tingle runs from his hand into mine, and steals all over me'.[31] Lucilla's straightforward feelings are not improper, but they are extremely suggestive.

In the characters of the identical twins, Oscar and Nugent Dubourg, Wilkie tentatively explored conflicting ideas of masculinity: again, a topical theme. The weak Oscar, despised by Lucilla's companion Mrs Pratolungo, who tells the story, for not facing the world in a 'manly' way, eventually shows himself capable of a different kind of courage. His brother Nugent, initially charming, energetic and effective, fails the tests of generosity and selflessness. The twins change places and take on each other's identity, psychologically and literally. Finally one is absorbed into the other, who takes on both sets of qualities. The empty shell of the now redundant twin is frozen out of the story. He is, in Ruskin's contemptuous phrase, 'found dead with his hands dropped off, in the Arctic regions'.[32] Like Wardour in *The Frozen Deep*, he dies a willing sacrifice to his brother's happiness.

Ultimately, however, the possibilities Wilkie tantalizingly holds out are never fully grasped. When Lucilla gains her sight she cannot at first judge distances or distinguish shapes. Wilkie vividly brings to life the scene in which, struggling with her new sense, she must close her eyes to reach someone on the opposite side of the room, or tell a circle from a square. She also loses her clear perception of truth and falsehood. But the challenge of relating different kinds of vision to one another, of showing the painful learning processs that precedes the inward gaze of Isabel Archer, 'motionlessly *seeing*', is beyond Wilkie's handling of his character. Lucilla regains her insight when she loses her sight again, with no suggestion that she is permanently altered by her experiences.

The shifting balance of dominance and submission, extraversion and introversion, in the 'light' and 'dark' twins also promises more insight into their psychology than is finally delivered. They remain the standard twins of sensation: the betrayal of one by the other lacks a truly tragic dimension. The multiple meanings which gave depth to the equally absurd and far more complicated plot of *Armadale* have no equivalent in *Poor Miss Finch*.

Nevertheless this 'domestic' story, with its fresh and lively narration by the ardently republican Madame Pratolungo, has a charm that recalls Wilkie's early novel about a deaf girl, *Hide and Seek*. The self-important Mr Finch, 'the Pope of Dimchurch', and his over-productive and hopelessly disorganized wife are lively comic satires, if not as satisfyingly integrated with the plot as the Wragges in *No Name*. There is also a detailed interest in children, which is new. The conversation and behaviour of 'Jicks', at three years old a self-possessed and incorrigible wanderer, are authentic and closely observed.

> The child listened – considered with herself gravely – got off the window-seat – and claimed her reward for being good, with that excellent brevity of speech which so eminently distinguished her:
> 'Jicks will go out.'
> With those words, she shouldered her doll; and walked off. The last I saw of her, she was descending the stairs as a workman descends a ladder, on her way to the garden – and from the garden (the first time the gate was opened) to the hills. If I could have gone out with her light heart, I would have joined Jicks. (*Poor Miss Finch*, Vol. 2, Chap. 12, p. 243)

The descriptions of Jicks, and of Mrs Finch eternally breast-feeding an overflowing baby, surely come from Wilkie's recent observation of his own children. Nugent's opinions on the unsuitability of long clothes for babies suggest Wilkie's sympathetic identification with his new baby's infantile frustrations:

> a more senseless dress doesn't exist, than the dress that is put, in this country, on infants of tender years. What are the three main functions which that child . . . performs? He sucks; he sleeps; and he grows . . . what does he want to do? To move his limbs freely in every direction . . . You clothe him in a dress three times as long as himself. He tries to throw his legs up in the air as he throws his arms, and he can't do it. There is his senseless long dress entangling itself in his toes, and

> making an effort of what Nature intended to be a luxury . . . Take my advice – short petticoats, Mrs. Finch. Liberty, glorious liberty, for my young friend's legs! Room, heaps of room, for that infant martyr's toes! (*Poor Miss Finch*, Vol. 1, Chap. 23, pp. 290–91)

For the volume publication of *Poor Miss Finch* Wilkie went back to his first publisher, after an approach from George Bentley. The sale of the first three-volume edition was put in jeopardy for a while, when Smith's Circulating Library, instead of buying Bentley's more expensive edition, waited until the bound volume of *Cassell's Magazine* containing the story was issued, and bought four hundred copies of that. Wilkie immediately offered to make up to Bentley for any loss caused by 'the present insanely absurd system of circulating library publication'.[33] Fortunately Mudie did buy the Bentley edition, and the two thousand copies sold out. But Mudie's price – 484 copies for £48. 19s. 0d. as against the published price of a guinea and a half – left Bentley with a loss, and Wilkie arranged favourable terms for a 6s. edition to compensate, before the book went into Smith's 2s. 'uniform edition'. Partly because of these complications, Wilkie made little money from *Poor Miss Finch*. Bentley made even less. The profit to the author on the first edition was £760. 10s. 9d., that of the publisher £333. 17s. 2d.[34]

The novel was dedicated to his old friend Frances Dickinson, now 'Mrs. Elliot, of the Deanery, Bristol'. 'Perhaps, one of these days,' Wilkie wrote in his dedication, 'I may be able to make use of some of the many interesting stories of events that have really happened, which have been placed in my hands by persons who could speak as witnesses to the truth of the narrative. Thus far I have not ventured to disturb the repose of these manuscripts in the locked drawer allotted to them. The true incidents are so "far-fetched;" and the conduct of the real people is so "grossly improbable!" '[35]

In addressing his public through his dedicatee, he may very well have had Frances Dickinson's life in mind. The marital tangles of Frances Elliot, bedevilled by the conflict of English and Scotch law, were close to those of Wilkie's previous novel *Man and Wife*, and Frances Dickinson's life had taken an even more unconventional turn since the days when, a divorced woman, she had acted in front of the

Queen in *The Frozen Deep*. She was now respectably, but not at all securely, married to the Dean of Bristol, the Very Reverend Gilbert Elliot. After surviving the social death of divorce, more by luck than good management, she continued to risk further scandal. Some time between 1855 and 1863 she went through a form of marriage to a mysterious doctor, name unknown.* On 9 August 1863, Dickens wrote to Wilkie Collins, warning him to be discreet about Frances Dickinson's past:

> she is extremely anxious you should know that profound confidence as to that adventure with the Doctor has become more than ever necessary, by reason of her having established the fact that the marriage (as no doubt he very well knew at the time) is no marriage and is utterly void. My own impression is that she contemplates a real marriage with somebody else, at no distant time.[36]

Dickens' impression was correct. Frances Dickinson married her second (or third) husband, Gilbert Elliot, on 3 November 1863, describing herself on the marriage certificate as 'single'. As the dean gave his occupation as 'clerk', there was some equivocation on both sides. The Dean of Bristol was a remarkably handsome man and a distinguished churchman and preacher. But, at sixty-three, he was twenty years her senior. The marriage was not a success. When Frances Elliot went to stay with Harriet Collins at Southborough in 1865 she took her maid but her husband was kept at home by 'business'. Wilkie and 'the German soubrette' (Harriet Collins' description of the maid) stayed at the hotel opposite and Frances had Wilkie's room in Harriet's little cottage.[37] No doubt he enjoyed the arrangement.

By 1866 Frances was trying to wriggle out of her marriage, while keeping her fortune intact, threatening to reveal the earlier 'marriage', which would implicate the respectable dean in bigamy. It was blackmail that would not have seemed out of place in a Braddon novel. Dickens, who was fond of them both, tried to mediate between the Elliots, and though he finally gave up in despair, some sort of

* This may have taken place abroad. No record has been found of a marriage in England.

compromise was reached. From 1869 Frances was living abroad much of the time, where she continued to write, producing fiction and popular history, very successful in its day. By 1872 her appearances at 'The Deanery, Bristol' were infrequent, as Wilkie very well knew. The public dedication was also a private joke.

NINETEEN

Wilkie and the Theatre

(1871–1874)

With Caroline back at Gloucester Place Wilkie's life was comfortable and well-organized again. Mary Cunliffe, meeting him at Woodlands, noticed that he was, for once, in much better health, 'very bright and pleasant', looking ten years younger and taking an uncharacteristically optimistic view of French politics, arguing with Fred, just back from Paris, that the Commune would be forgotten in three years.[1]

His literary life, too, took a new direction. The most successful phase of his career as a dramatist began, with the production at the Olympic of *The Woman in White*. The part of Count Fosco was taken by George Vining, Mrs Viner played Marian, Ada Dyas doubled Laura and Anne Catherick and a young actor, Wybert Reeve, was cast as Walter Hartright.

Rehearsals were lengthy and extremely tiresome. Wilkie must have remembered Dickens' amateur productions as they dragged on, day after day from ten in the morning until five, and often again from six or seven in the evening until the early hours of the morning. But Vining, managing as well as acting, was no Dickens. He was difficult and indecisive, and when Ada Dyas and Mrs Viner argued interminably about being upstaged, and neither would give way, it was left to Wilkie to smooth things over. 'I marvelled at him, for authors as a rule are . . . the reverse of patient when attending the rehearsals of a piece they have written', Wybert Reeve remembered.[2]

Wilkie also went through every line of Vining's part with him in private.[3]

Wilkie's dramatization of *The Woman in White* entirely rewrote the novel, by now so familiar that there could have been no surprises for an audience. Much was omitted, including the dramatic first meeting of Hartright and Anne Catherick; new scenes were added. In the play the relationship between Laura and Anne is revealed at the start, and the substitution plot is made much more obvious; the tension comes from dramatic irony, rather than mystification.[4]

A striking poster was designed for the play by Wilkie's friend Fred Walker, who had been one of the guests at the celebration dinner for *The Woman in White* in 1860. Walker was also a friend of Charley and Kate Collins, and the preliminary sketch was made at their house in Thurloe Place. It was the first time that a well-known artist had been commissioned to design a theatre poster: Wilkie was delighted with it.

The play opened on 9 October 1871. Though the performance took four hours it was a box-office and critical success; the critics were almost unanimous in their praise of Wilkie's skill: 'He has firmly grasped the rarely appreciated truth, that situations which appear dramatic to a reader, are not necessarily dramatic when brought to the ordeal of the footlights'.[5] At the first night there was a call for the author at the end of the third act. Wilkie, suffering badly from author's nerves, was forced to take it, but found the rival actresses both waiting for him in the wings, each anxious to be taken on with him. He tactfully took the curtain call with both of them. At the end there was another call for him: the audience were wild with enthusiasm. The theatre was full every night, with extra chairs having to be added in the aisles. Wilkie, who was getting a percentage rather than a flat fee, was making real money: £47. 10s. the first week, £59 the second. His lifelong obsession with the theatre was paying off at last.

Wilkie was, however, increasingly doubtful about Vining. He always insisted, 'The play is *all Fosco*. If he does not take the audience by storm, failure is certain'.[6] He would have liked to replace him with Fechter, but Fechter was fully committed in America. Instead, Wybert

Reeve was asked, after the play had been on a fortnight, to understudy Vining, and replaced him for the first time on 11 January, when Vining was ill.

The run at the Olympic ended on 24 February. It had been arranged that Vining should tour with the play, but after a few weeks the tour was losing money. Vining wanted to cut and rewrite the last act of the play, which dragged, as some of the critics had complained. Wilkie refused to allow this. Instead he released Vining from his agreement and transferred all the rights to Reeve, who successfully toured the provinces with *The Woman in White* for over a year. Reeve, more tactful and accommodating than Vining, later persuaded Wilkie to let him condense the later scenes of the play, as Vining had wished, convincing Wilkie that lengthy explanations of the action bored the audience (a criticism made of several of Wilkie's plays). He and Wilkie became close friends.

After the difficulties of the past two years, Wilkie was back in full production. But his health problems were still severe. After the savage attack of 'rheumatic gout' while he was writing *The Moonstone*, Wilkie was, for the last twenty years of his life, either in the middle of an attack, recovering from one, or feeling the premonitions of the next. His eyes were now very often affected. Charles Kent was shocked at his appearance during one attack: Wilkie's eyes, he said, 'were literally *enormous bags of blood*!'.[7] The inflammation was excruciatingly painful, as well as preventing him from reading or writing. Sometimes only one eye would be affected, and by wearing a shade over it he could continue, cautiously, to use the other. Sometimes he could only dictate, to Carrie or one of his friends. He preferred not to do this: he hated to lose control over his own work by not writing the first draft in his own hand. Wilkie described his typical method in later years in an 1887 article:

> The day's writing having been finished, with such corrections of words and such rebalancing of sentences as occur to me at the time, is subjected to a first revision on the next day, and is then handed to my copyist. The copyist's manuscript undergoes a second and a third revision, and is then sent to the printer. The proof passes through a fourth process of correction, and is sent back to have the new alterations embodied in a

revise. When this reaches me, it is looked over once more before it goes back to press. When the serial publication of the novel is reprinted in book-form, the book-proofs undergo a sixth revision.[8]

Increasing illness and pain inevitably deepened his dependence on opium. This may have affected the quality of his work, but it is obvious that it did not induce the creative paralysis that Coleridge and De Quincey suffered from. Wilkie makes many references in his letters to the exhaustion writing caused; a few to the difficulty of resuming after a long break; none, that I have discovered, to 'writer's block'. Nor did his addiction make him careless about the minutiae of composition, though anecdotal evidence (perhaps exaggerated) suggests that his consumption of laudanum increased steadily in his last years. He carried around a silver flask full of it – similar, one imagines, to a sportsman's hip-flask for spirits. He took enough to kill twelve people, according to the surgeon Sir William Fergusson, to whom Wilkie's eye surgeon George Critchett confided his nightly dose.[9] Hall Caine claimed to have seen him swallow a full wineglass. Certainly, in his last illness, the dose was two tablespoonsful.[10] Wilkie himself admitted that it caused hallucinations and nightmares. Apart from the second Wilkie Collins who tried to take over his writing, 'the staircase seemed to him crowded with ghosts trying to push him down' when he went to bed at night. One of his recurrent terrors appeared in slightly different forms, as a green woman with fangs, or a 'shapeless monster, with eyes of fire and big green fangs'.[11] But these night-time terrors did not alter his essentially practical attitude to the drug.

He considered himself, with some justification, an expert in its use. He told an American friend that 'opium sometimes hurts, but also, *sometimes*, it helps. In general, people know nothing about it.'[12] He urged his friends to take it for their various ailments. 'If only you could take opium! – I say no more,' he wrote to Pigott, who had a cough.[13] He wrote to Charles Kent when he was suffering from insomnia, promising him some of his own 'specially prepared' laudanum and a measuring glass, and giving him a note to take to the chemist he used, Messrs Corbyn & Co., 86 New Bond Street. 'Begin cautiously with only twenty "minims" . . . in a tablespoonful of water

. . . then try 25 minims. If *that* fails we must have a consultation.' It did fail, and Wilkie gave his diagnosis:

> Laudanum has a two fold action in the brain and nervous system – a stimulating and a sedative action. It seems but too plain to *me* that *your* nerves are so strongly affected by the stimulating action that they are incapable of feeling the sedative action which ought to follow . . . You are entirely right in dropping the laudanum after such an experience as yours. I am more sorry than I can well say at this bitter destruction of all my hopes for you.[14]

Laudanum was for Wilkie a therapeutic drug, one among many that he took, not an escape from emotional pressures nor an aid to inspiration. He remembered his mother's sensible advice to Coleridge, and acted on it. His relationship to it was closer to the dependence of a diabetic on insulin, or a chronic asthmatic on steroids, than to the romanticism of the 'opium eater' or the degradation of a heroin addict. Though laudanum often features in his fiction, taking it is always a private and personal business for his characters, not a social evil. It was Dickens, not Wilkie Collins, who wrote an opium-den scene, in *Edwin Drood.*

In spite of an attack in the summer of 1871, he wrote a novella, *Miss or Mrs?*, for the Christmas number of the *Graphic Illustrated Newspaper*, and planned a short novel, *The New Magdalen*. Both were written with dramatization in mind, with limited settings, exits, entrances, critical encounters between pairs of characters, and much dialogue. Both suffer from this literary economy. Wilkie's practised ingenuity in handling a complicated story and his impersonations of differing points of view, his great strengths, were jettisoned. Though he told the actor Frank Archer, who played the hero in *The New Magdalen*, that the art of the novelist and the dramatist were absolutely distinct, he increasingly began to neglect this distinction. These stories seem stagy, rather than dramatic.

Miss or Mrs? is a slight piece of work, for which Wilkie made use, yet again, of the Wards' secret marriage. This time the fifteen-year-old heroine is partly black – her mother was a Creole from Martinique – sexually mature and sexually uninhibited. 'She possessed the development of the bosom and limbs, which in England is rarely attained before twenty . . . She moved like a goddess, and she laughed like a child.' She has an extremely physical relationship with her young man, playing footsie with him under the table, showing him her legs and letting him kiss her on the neck. They communicate in code, and he swears in her presence. As Christmas reading it would have been unthinkable in one of Dickens' magazines. It is difficult to imagine that it would have passed the Examiner of Plays, John Bodham Donne, without a good deal of modification, and in fact it was never seen on stage. *The New Magdalen*, on the other hand, was to become one of his most successful plays.

The New Magdalen first appeared as a serial in *Temple Bar*, Bentley's successor to the discontinued *Miscellany*. It was, as a novel, as didactic as *Man and Wife*, and still more old-fashioned and melodramatic. The narrative leans heavily on the reader, never presenting alternative points of view. The secret, as in the dramatized *Woman in White*, is known to the reader from the outset: on the page there is no suspense and no mystery. The dramatic irony by which an audience knows the truth that is concealed from the characters is of course lost on a reader. The characterization, too, is designed for the stage. In Mercy Merrick, the woman fighting to regain a place in society lost through no fault of her own, Wilkie created a vehicle for a clever actress: several triumphed in the part on stage. In the novel the character seems hollow and platitudinous. The potentially interesting character of the elderly Lady Janet, who refuses to accept the truth about the young woman she has come to love, even when it is inescapable, though plausible on stage, is unbelievable to a reader, who has time to think about her reactions.

Wilkie's 'New' Magdalen was in fact far from new. The rehabilitation of 'fallen women' in life and fiction had been a subject of intense interest and controversy for years. A writer in the *Saturday Review* had satirized the obsession as long ago as 1862: 'The fast man makes love to them; the slow man discusses them; the fashionable young lady copies their dress; the Evangelical clergyman gives them tea, toast and touching talks at midnight; and the devout young woman gives herself up to the task of tending them . . . while they are resting between the acts of their exhausting lives.'[15] Some of the novels on the subject, particularly those by women, were considerably more outspoken than

Wilkie's.* Trollope's portrait of a prostitute, Carry Brattle, in his 1870 novel *The Vicar of Bullhampton*, though not particularly daring, at least created a credible and unidealized woman. The scene in which the vicar tries to persuade Carry that she is not an outcast, and realizes that it will not do simply to tell her that the Lord loves her, is a delicate and perceptive piece of writing, far in advance of Wilkie's theatricality.[16]

Wilkie's Magdalen belonged to the jaded fictional tradition of the woman 'fallen' through no fault of her own. Noble, exploited and longing for rehabilitation, she was, in spite of a poverty-stricken background, so well-spoken that she could effortlessly pass for a lady. Her unsullied character and her upper-class accent both reflected the novel's subordination to the drama. What might be read in private could not be acted in public, and a Cockney accent could only have belonged to a comic character on the stage of the 1870s. For a brief moment near the end of the novel – much softened in the play – Wilkie revealed that he still had an appreciation of the realities of street life. Mercy Merrick is brought into contact with a child brutalized by poverty and neglect, a potential woman of the streets: 'the savage and terrible product of a worn-out system of government and of a civilization rotten to the core!'.[17] But the child is quickly dismissed, and Mercy, failing in her bid to be accepted by respectable society, goes off to make good in the Colonies, married to the Christ-like radical Communist clergyman. Since he is given to this kind of outburst: '"Rise, poor wounded heart! Beautiful, purified soul, God's angels rejoice over you! Take your place among the noblest of God's creatures!"', one can only feel that Wilkie was more at home attacking the clergy than supporting them.[18] Theatre audiences loved it.

What is more disturbing in *The New Magdalen*, and makes her 'new' in a sense the author does not seem to have intended, is the heroine's usurpation of another woman's identity. At first this is fairly innocent – she thinks the other girl is dead – but when the real Grace Roseberry comes back to life, the usurper fights like a alley cat to keep her out

* E.g. Felicia Skene, *Hidden Depths*, 1866, which has scenes set in brothels. (John Sutherland, *The Longman Companion to Victorian Fiction*, 1988, p. 295)

of her rightful place. The 'respectable' girl is given no sympathy, in the narrative or by the other characters, and her position is never wholly regained. In Wilkie's earlier novels, his designing women were primarily concerned to revenge themselves on men rather than on innocent members of their own sex. One of the reviewers of the play objected strongly to this: 'The author throughout appears as the uncompromising apologist and partisan of his heroine, and . . . he labours to present the poor woman who is the victim of her guilt in as odious a light as possible . . . if [Mercy's] early misdeeds are to be charged against society, she must be fully credited with her crime in personating Miss Roseberry.'[19] Wilkie's old fascination with, and sympathy for (in Dickens' phrase), 'disguised women or the like' was as strong as ever. The structure of society being as it was, it seemed to him that deception and concealment were their only weapons. It was an idea that was beginning to look increasingly old-fashioned at a time when feminism was entering a new and positive phase.

The New Magdalen was translated into most European languages, including Russian; but Bentley's first edition did not sell even as well as *Poor Miss Finch*. This time the author cleared £295. 0s. 4d., and the publisher only £132. 17s. 9d.[20] Mudie's caution over the subject matter may have been as much to blame as the novel's theatricality. While it was being serialized, Mudie demanded a change of title for the volume edition. Wilkie indignantly refused: 'His proposal would be an impertinence if he was not an old fool . . . this ignorant fanatic holds my circulation in his pious hands.'[21] Wilkie, who called Mudie and W. H. Smith the twin tyrants of literature, wondered whether they might publish a cheap edition first, and the expensive one later, to give ordinary readers a chance to make up their minds about the book. Bentley was alarmed, and the idea came to nothing. But Wilkie continued to brood about changing English publishing methods, bringing them closer to the needs and pockets of his readers. He was a novelist with several kinds of purpose in the 1870s and '80s.

Wilkie's preference for the theatre was confirmed when *Man and Wife* was at last produced by Squire and Marie Bancroft at the Prince of Wales Theatre. Wilkie read the play to the company before they began rehearsals, and read it very well, 'giving a clear insight into his view of the characters . . . acting the old Scotch waiter with rare ability'. He attended many of the rehearsals, but always deferred to the Bancrofts' greater experience, readily agreeing to alter the second act.

It was the first new play the Bancrofts had put on for some years, and the first time they had broken away from their usual style of light comedy. Expectations were running high. Everyone in literary and artistic London wanted to be at the first night on 22 February 1873: stalls were changing hands on the black market at five guineas each, less good seats for two guineas. With so much riding on it, Wilkie was overcome by nervous terror, and spent the evening in Squire Bancroft's dressing-room, unable to watch what was happening on stage. When it was all over, he told Wybert Reeve of his reception at the end of the play:

> It was certainly an extraordinary success. The pit got on its legs and cheered with all its might the moment I showed myself in front of the curtain . . . I had only thirty friends in the house to match against a picked band of the 'lower orders' of literature and drama assembled at the back of the dress circle to hiss and laugh at the first chance . . . the public never gave the 'opposition' a chance.[22]

Wilkie modestly – and probably correctly – claimed the success was due to the superb acting and the up-to-date staging. The Bancrofts used electric lightning in a storm scene, for the first time on the London stage, and an effect of moving clouds. Wilkie was also delighted by the audience's appreciation. Ideas that many critics had found repellent in the novel pleased them on the stage, where the action seemed complete and coherent. Wilkie was praised as a dramatist of unusual ability whose dialogue was pointed and skilful.

Receipts were over £100 a night, and the play had royal patronage. The Prince of Wales saw it twice, the Princess three times: on one occasion they took the Tsarevich and Tsarina of Russia. The triumphant run was finally brought to an end by a heatwave, after 136 performances. It was rapidly followed by an equally successful tour.

In the middle of his brother's triumph Charley Collins finally turned his face to the wall and gave up his feeble hold on life. Wilkie had asked Wybert Reeve to go to the theatre with him on the night of

9 April, but when Reeve arrived at Gloucester Place he discovered that Charley had been gravely ill for the past four days, and Wilkie, after dining with Reeve, went back to his bedside. Charley was by now unconscious, and he died later that night, of cancer of the stomach.

Charley had suffered greatly, and no one, Georgina Hogarth thought, could have seen his death as anything but a merciful release. For Wilkie, lacking any belief in a future existence, Charley's death was the sad end of a life largely vitiated by self-doubt. He asked their lifelong friend Holman Hunt to make a deathbed drawing of Charley for him, and in the entry he wrote for the *Dictionary of National Biography* he could only say, '. . . it was in the modest and sensitive nature of the man to underrate his own success. His ideal was a high one; and he never succeeded in satisfying his own aspirations.'

The last years of Charley's life were miserable. As long ago as 1868, someone meeting him for the first time was struck by his thinness and pallor, and his friends already considered that he was a dying man.[23] He was constantly ill, and in increasing pain, though the cancer was only diagnosed *post mortem*. After Dickens' death Kate virtually deserted him for a while, spending all her time at Gad's Hill with Georgina and Mamie until the house was sold. At the time there was some doubt whether she would ever return to her husband, now that Dickens was no longer there to insist on it. 'I earnestly hope all will be right', Annie Fields wrote in her diary. 'Charles is a tender devoted husband and will be more to [her] now than ever before if she can only bring herself to go back to him.'[24] Charley took refuge with Leslie and Minnie Stephen, looking 'quite broken down and miserable – not that he is ever very cheerful'.[25]

Charley's habitual indecisiveness increased as his health deteriorated, until he was paralysed by conflicting emotions. He and Kate bought a new house in 1871, with part of her inheritance. It was large enough to provide a studio for Kate, who had discovered a talent for painting and was beginning to have her work exhibited. Charley, who had exhibited nothing since 1855, evidently found this too much to bear. At the last moment he refused to move, but refused to sell or let either house. Georgina found him infuriating. '[Katy] won't let us go and *shake* C.C.! which we would like to do – morally at all events – and I should like someone to do it bodily too!'[26] She retracted after his death, acknowledging his gentleness and patience, but 'It was a weary existence – both for him and for Katy – for at least *ten* years out of the thirteen . . . Katy feels his loss *very* sincerely.'[27] After the obligatory year's mourning, Kate was married again to another Charles, the painter Carlo Perugini. (Millais' nickname for Charles Collins had been 'Saint Carlo'.) Though their only son died at a few months old, it was a happy marriage.

The New Magdalen, dedicated to the memory of Charles Collins, was published by Bentley in two volumes on 20 May, the day after the play opened at the Olympic Theatre. Ada Cavendish, who played the lead, also produced the play. Wilkie had wanted Wybert Reeve to play the clergyman Julian Gray; as he was unavailable the part was taken by Frank Archer. The only changes made from the novel were some pruning of the narrative and a cut in Mercy Merrick's long account of her miserable childhood, and the details of her rape, 'fall' and subsequent reclaim. It was notable for being the first play ever presented on the English stage to include a clergyman as one of the principal characters – let alone a clergyman who married a reformed prostitute. The Examiner of Plays, having swallowed that camel, strained at the gnat of a biblical quotation in the advance publicity, 'Joy shall be in Heaven over one sinner that repenteth', calling it 'an unprecedented and unnecessary allusion'.[28] *The New Magdalen* also had successful productions in Paris, Vienna, Rome, Florence and Milan. In Italy Julian Gray had to be turned into an austere magistrate, as the Italian public, not bothered by the erstwhile prostitute, would not have a priest of any sort on the stage.[29]

Wilkie, after his troubles with George Vining, insisted on a carefully drawn-up contract with Ada Cavendish, who became one of his favourite actresses, and a close friend for the rest of his life. It made demands few authors would dare to insist on now.

> No alterations of any sort are to be made in the dialogue without my permission. The play is to be produced under my directions. The cast of characters, the scenery, and the dresses are to satisfy me – or failing that I am to have the right of withdrawing the play. If the continuous

> run of the play is interrupted it is to be left to my discretion to resume the performance of it at the Olympic theatre or not. Proofs of the posters play bills and of all other advertisements are to be submitted to me – and I am to have the right of altering adding to or cutting out any words or expressions to which I may object.[30]

But Wilkie on paper and Wilkie in person were two very different people. Reeve's account of his patience with Vining, and the Bancrofts' memory of him as a helpful and compliant author, are confirmed by Arthur Pinero's recollections of his behaviour with Ada Cavendish and the Olympic company. The future playwright, then a very young actor, took the minor part of the elderly solicitor in Wilkie's next play, the adaptation of *Armadale*, which took the stage as *Miss Gwilt*. Pinero remembered Wilkie's kindness to an unknown young man, and his unpretentious presence at rehearsals:

> He used to sit, his manuscript before him, at a small table near the footlights, and there he made such additions and alterations as Miss Ada Cavendish deemed necessary. He did this with the utmost readiness and amiability, influenced perhaps by her habit of calling him 'Wilkie' . . . which, I recollect, surprised and shocked me not a little.[31]

Between author, management and actors, another theatrical triumph was achieved with *The New Magdalen*. On the first night Wilkie had to take a curtain call between the acts, as well as at the end of the play. 'I don't think I ever saw such enthusiasm in a theatre before', he told George Bentley.[32] There was some condemnation of its immorality by the critics, and some criticism of the diffuse dialogue and of Julian Gray's sermonizing. But it was greatly admired by Matthew Arnold, of all people. It drew full houses, and played four months at the Olympic, before going on tour. It was repeatedly revived. Wilkie thought the performances at the smaller Charing Cross Theatre, in 1875, were even better than those in the original production. In 1877 Wilkie told Archer, 'Your old friend Julian Gray still strolls through the country theatres with Miss Cavendish,' and the play was produced again in London in 1884. It was a perfect starring vehicle for an actress: Shaw saw Janet Achurch play Mercy Merrick in 1895. According to Shaw she showed there was still interest to be wrung out of the old melodrama:

> Miss Achurch [has] taken this innocent old figment of Wilkie Collins's benevolent and chivalrous imagination, and played into it a grim truth that it was never meant to bear – played it against the audience . . . Miss Achurch disturbed and appalled us . . .[33]

With three such successes in the theatre in less than two years, it was not surprising that Wilkie found the drama more exciting and more rewarding than novel-writing. 'That fanatical old fool Mudie will be obliged to increase his order', he crowed after the success of the first night of *The New Magdalen*; but the sales were thoroughly discouraging. By September he doubted, in a moment of irritation, whether he would write any more stories for English readers 'as long as the Mudie system obtains'.[34] The contrast with America was instructive. The library system had never taken hold there, and the sales of *The New Magdalen* were enormous. Wilkie was already having the prospect of touring the United States and Canada dangled enticingly before him, and he was longing to go. In 1871 he had reluctantly refused an offer, on doctor's advice. The following year he was still not ready, feeling in need of a long rest. But he promised an American enquirer, 'All that rest and freedom from literary responsibility can do to fit me physically for a visit to America – they *shall* do.'[35]

In the spring of 1873, a firm offer was made by a 'Speculator who offers to buy me for the U.S.'.[36] It was 'a proposal . . . all but irresistible to a poor man. If I can get away this autumn, I *must*.'[37] Though he was hardly a poor man, the large sums that could be made by English writers touring America rapidly decided Wilkie, though he was careful not to commit himself at the outset to more than ten readings.

To compete in this way with Dickens, however inadequately, was to invite disapproval. Georgina Hogarth, jealous of Dickens' unique status, wrote scornfully to her friend Annie Fields, wife of the Boston publisher James T. Fields, when the idea was first mooted: 'I cannot imagine that he is fitted for the part in any way – nor can I conceive how his books could bear being cut up into *portions* for Readings – they seem to me to depend so entirely upon the interest and excitement of the *whole plot*.'[38] Wilkie seems to have agreed. Rather than condensing his novels, as Dickens had done, he expanded his short stories. On 28 June he had a 'try-out' as one of the turns at a charity matinée at the Olympic. Other items in this ill-assorted entertainment included Ada Cavendish reading 'The Charge of the Light Brigade' and Gounod playing the piano. Wilkie read a specially prepared version of 'A Terribly Strange Bed'. It was not a great success. Wilkie was now balding, grey-haired, overweight and bent by arthritis. He had never had Dickens' physical command of the stage, and his voice was inadequate for a large theatre. Percy Fitzgerald, one of the Dickens worshippers, thought the reading 'singularly tame ... clever man as he was, the impression he produced was that of all things in the world he had selected the one for which he was the least fitted'.[39] Frank Archer was kinder, but not over-enthusiastic: 'He lacked the physique and varied gifts for a public reader, but what he did I thought was earnest and impressive.'[40] A notice of his performance in the *Pall Mall Gazette* gave a warning which Wilkie seems to have heeded. 'We should counsel him to adopt the tone and method of a lecturer, which almost anyone can acquire, rather than those of an actor, which lie beyond his reach. Otherwise, he will expose himself to the ridicule of the unfeeling.'[41]

For Wilkie to follow in Dickens' footsteps as a 'reader' was *lèse-majesté* to Georgina Hogarth; to Forster it was a part of Dickens' success he would rather forget. Georgina was quite fond of Wilkie, so long as he did not succeed in emulating Dickens. But her opinion of him as not worthy of association with her hero was made quite clear when she was distributing mementoes of Dickens to his friends. Charles Reade, never so close a friend as Wilkie, was given a pen-tray from the office, Carlyle a walking-stick Dickens had used constantly. To Wilkie, no doubt with an ironic gleam in her eye, she sent a more ephemeral present: some of the special orange brandy she made for Dickens every year. Wilkie's thanks were warm and genuine:

> Thank you again and again for another proof of your affectionate remembrance of the old times ... I saw his kind face, and heard his friendly voice once more, when I looked into the open hamper ... and God knows my heart ached when I thought of you and the girls, and of the days that we shall never see again.[42]

Wilkie and Georgina continued to be friends, if not intimates, and she and Mamie were very grateful for his help and professional advice when they were preparing their edition of Dickens' letters in 1879. Once the American tour was unavoidable she wrote to Annie Fields, shutting her eyes firmly to Wilkie's unorthodox family situation:

> Poor Wilkie Collins is terriby cut up by his brother's death. They were very fond of each other . . . now Wilkie has no one left belonging to him . . . He told me the other day he was going to America in the autumn. If he does no doubt you will see him. I think you would like him. He is very agreeable and easy to get on with. I *cannot* conceive that he will be successful as a lecturer or Reader. However I suppose he knows best what he can do –[43]

Georgina had forgotten that the Fields had met Wilkie, at a dinner at Tavistock House in 1860, and again in 1869 at the Lehmanns'.[44]

Forster was less lenient. According to Wilkie, he was angry about his reading tour. He had been violently opposed to Dickens' readings in America in 1867, and he always became unreasonably annoyed when his friends ignored his advice. Furthermore, as far as Forster was concerned, Dickens' friendship with Wilkie was a blemish best forgotten as quickly as possible. Yet Wilkie and Forster, so different in temperament, had at one time been good friends – or so Wilkie had thought. 'John Forster is a very intimate and valued friend of mine', Wilkie told Émile Forgues in 1861.[45] While Dickens was alive, they saw each other often, and Wilkie genuinely admired Forster's writing. In 1864 he sent Forster a collection of his novels, inscribed 'with affectionate regard to my friend John Forster'. He dedicated *Armadale* to Forster in the warmest terms, 'in affectionate remembrance of a friendship which is associated with some of the happiest years of my life'. After Dickens' death he continued to see Forster and his wife, if less often. He sent them the advance proofs of his novels to read. He wrote enthusiastically about the first volume of Forster's *Life of Charles Dickens*: 'I am more interested than any words of mine can tell in your admirable narrative – to my mind, the most masterly biographical story you have ever told . . . I congratulate you with all my heart.' Three weeks later he wrote again. 'I have all sorts of things to say to you about the "Life" ', and signed himself 'With love. Ever yours affly [affectionately]'.[46]

Nevertheless Wilkie knew that Forster's insistence on a monopoly of the sacred memory was making trouble even before the first volume of his biography appeared. George Bentley wanted any letters from his father which referred to Dickens' quarrel of 1837–38 with Richard Bentley to be destroyed, and any mention of the disagreement omitted, 'because I . . . felt sure that nothing could be more opposed to the genial tempers of both parties than the public discussion of a disagreement that each party had long forgotten'.[47] He asked Wilkie to act as go-between. Wilkie had to tell him: 'Mr Forster's answer to my letter makes it, I am sorry to say, impossible for me to represent your views any farther. There is some soreness in his mind on this subject which I don't in the least understand. He has not answered my second letter.'[48] Forster, who had been behind Dickens' 'asking for more' at the time of the quarrel with Bentley, did include the quarrel in his first volume. George Bentley felt he misrepresented what had happened; he put his father's side of the case in a reasoned letter to *The Times*.[49] Later biographers have felt his point of view was justified.* Wilkie advised Georgina to omit a letter relating to the quarrel from her edition of Dickens' letters.[50]

Wilkie's private criticisms of the *Life of Charles Dickens* were severe. There had been suggestions at the time of Dickens' death that Wilkie might have written his biography. He did make some notes on Dickens for the use of one of his French translators, who published a book on him in 1889.[51] But he refused to contribute to Frederick Kitton's collection of reminiscences, *Charles Dickens by Pen and Pencil*, explaining, 'He more than once expressed to me his dislike of being presented to public curiosity by means of "pen-portraits", and his desire to be only known to the great world of readers after his death by his books'.[52]

A life of Dickens by Wilkie Collins would clearly have been quite different from that by John Forster, and would have permanently

* '[Dickens] characteristically transformed a situation in which he was morally culpable into an emotive thunderstorm whose main point was that he had been abused and that his abusers were immoral.' (Kaplan, p. 101)

altered our view of Dickens. Wilkie insisted in his memoir of Charles Fechter:

> One of the worst vices of the age we live in is the shameless disregard of truth prevalent among friends, writing or speaking in public, of celebrated persons whom they have survived. Unblushing exaggeration of the merits, position and influence of the dead man seems to be considered as sufficient warrant for a deliberate concealment of his failings and faults – which is nothing less than lying of the passive sort, artfully adapted to its purpose as a pedestal on which the writer or speaker can present himself to the public in a favorable light.[53]

This was obviously written with Forster in mind. 'Forster's own vanity and identity with all Dickens's works and actions are so persistently put before the reader that John Forster is as prominent as Charles Dickens throughout,' he told Wybert Reeve.[54] More pithily, he described the biography to Shirley Brooks as 'The Life of John Forster, with notices of Dickens'.[55]

His attitude seems clear and admirable. Yet his practice was rather different. He tidied up his own father's letters in his biography of him, making the perfectly innocuous originals more dignified. Forster suppressed facts and destroyed evidence about Dickens. But Wilkie, it emerges, would have done the same: several accounts of Wilkie's comments on Forster's biography are in direct contrast to his claim to be the enemy of censorship. The first is from the diary of the American diplomat, John Bigelow:

> [Forster's] Life of Dickens worries him because of the criticism it has provoked. He has presented the selfish aspects of Dickens' character. This seems to be in consequence of Forster's plan to give only his own letters. Collins has a great many which Forster proposed to use, if he could use them in the same way, but that did not suit Collins and he retained them. Collins says he has a letter from Dickens assigning his reasons for separating from his wife.* He thinks Forster very injudicious

* This letter, now lost, was in existence after Wilkie's death. It is listed among 'Letters of Charles Dickens to Wilkie Collins' as one of the 'letters I recommend should not be sold'. The list, in an unknown hand, is on the stationery of A. P. Watt. It describes the letter, dated 16 August 1859, as containing 'references to Messrs. Bradbury Evans & Co., and to Mrs. Dickens, about the time of the separation'. (Berg Collection, NYPL)

> in publishing what Dickens says about his mother, who after all, behaved quite sensibly in insisting that this boy should contribute towards the family support by sticking labels on blacking bottles so long as that was the best remunerated work he could do. Collins said he would not have published these letters.[56]

This was the conventional point of view at the time. A reviewer of Forster's second volume complained that his mention of Dickens' mother was contemptuous, and that Dickens' allusion to her was 'unjust and unfilial'.[57] J. W. T. Ley considered that 'There is nothing . . . that has so grated on its readers as Dickens's reference to his mother . . . It has threatened disillusionment to more people than anything else written by or about Dickens.'[58] Yet Wilkie's apparent siding with Elizabeth Dickens, and his failure to understand the significance of the blacking-warehouse episode to her son, his intimate friend for almost twenty years, seems strange to a modern reader. If Wilkie had been Dickens' biographer, the whole matter might have been suppressed.

Wilkie may have resented the discovery that Dickens had secrets to which he was not privy. In 1856 Dickens had sent him a carefully censored account of his early life, to be sent on to Émile Forgues. There was no mention of his father's imprisonment in the Marshalsea, and his own suffering in Warren's warehouse. Dickens told Wilkie: 'This is the first time I ever set down these particulars, and, glancing them over, I feel like a wild beast in a caravan, describing himself in the keeper's absence.'[59] Yet Forster's *Life* revealed that Dickens had told him the whole truth in 1847. The 'want of entire intimacy' that Charley Collins had always sensed was dramatically revealed as a fact.

The biography, while it revealed some things previously unknown, also avoided aspects of his life familiar to Dickens' close friends. Yet Wilkie told Wybert Reeve that 'He and other friends . . . were most desirous of suppressing many things Forster had written . . . we all have our weaknesses; and however great a man may be, he is not exempt. Why parade them?' The separation of Dickens and Catherine was one of the episodes Wilkie felt should have been even more sparingly handled for public consumption. 'Entering into so much detail was unwise, unnecessary, and a mistake . . . there were faults on both sides.'[60] In private he was more outspoken about the relationship. He spoke of Dickens' faults, but also said, '. . . there is little doubt [Mrs Dickens] was unsuited to a sensitive, quick-tempered nature. She was entirely wanting in tact'. By way of illustration Wilkie described to Wybert Reeve a dinner party at which Catherine Dickens interrupted praise of her husband's latest book to say 'she could not understand what people could see in his writings to talk so much about them', and went on to drive Dickens out of the room.

> A lady present said she wondered when and how many strange thoughts came into his head. 'Oh' replied Dickens, 'I don't know. They come at odd times, sometimes in the night, when I jump out of bed, and dot them down, for fear I should have lost them by the morning.' 'That is true,' said Mrs. Dickens. 'I have reason to know it, jumping out of bed, and getting in again, with his feet as cold as a stone.' Dickens left the table, and was afterwards found sitting alone in a small room off the hall – silent and angry. It was a long time before they could induce him to join the circle again.[61]

This, Wilkie said, took place at Judge Talfourd's. Talfourd died in 1854, so Wilkie was deliberately supporting Dickens' claim that the troubles in his marriage dated from long before the separation.

Wilkie was also justifiably angry at Forster's refusal to consult him in preparing the biography. He commented, in his copy of Forster's *Life*, 'The assertion (quite sincerely made) that no letters addressed by Dickens to other old friends revealed his character so frankly and completely as his letters to Forster, it is not necessary to contradict. Dickens's letters published by his sister-in-law and his eldest daughter may be left to settle that question.'[62] Wilkie was the only friend consulted when Georgina and Mamie were preparing Dickens' letters for the press in 1879. Forster was by then dead. Once more Wilkie had no compunction in suggesting cuts, and censorship of sensitive passages. Again, he withheld many of the letters Dickens had written him. The obligations of friendship, to the Dickens family as well as Dickens himself, in the end took precedence over biographical truth.

Wilkie's copy of Forster's life was annotated with pungent marginalia, attacking Forster's judgements on Dickens' novels and his estimate of his character, and adding his own views. *Oliver Twist* was not, as Forster wrote, well constructed; the construction was 'the one defect in that wonderful book ... That the same man who could create "Nancy" created the second Mrs. Dombey is the most incomprehensible anomaly that I know of in literature'; 'The latter half of "Dombey" no intelligent person can have read without astonishment at the badness of it'. Where Forster compares the description in *Edwin Drood* with the dialogue in *Oliver Twist*, Wilkie retorts, 'A novelist knows what Forster does not know – that dialogue is more easily written than description ... it was cruel to compare Dickens in the radiant prime of his genius with Dickens's last laboured effort, the melancholy work of a worn-out brain.' Forster's agreement with the prim verdict that all Dickens' work could be put into the hands of children annoyed him most of all:

> It is impossible to read such stuff as this without a word of protest. If it is true, which it is not, it would imply the condemnation of Dickens's books as works of art, it would declare him to be guilty of deliberately presenting to his readers a false reflection of human life. If this wretched English claptrap means anything it means that the novelist is forbidden to touch on the sexual relations which literally swarm about him, and influence the lives of millions of his fellow creatures [except] those relations are licensed by the ceremony called marriage. One expects this essentially immoral view of the functions of the novelist from a professor of claptrap like the late bishop of Manchester. But that Forster should quote it with approval is a sad discovery indeed.

On Forster's statement that 'unbroken continuity of kindly impulse' was one of Dickens' personal characteristics, Wilkie commented, 'More than once there were fierce quarrels between Dickens and Forster (sometimes at Forster's own table) which took place in my presence. Dickens' sense of what he owed to Forster's devotion ... was often subjected to severe trial by Forster himself.'[63] This is confirmed by other witnesses.

Though Wilkie's annotations are scattered through all three volumes, it was undoubtedly the third, covering the last twenty years of

Dickens' life, that annoyed him most. He was not the only member of the Dickens circle to dislike it. Charles Dickens Junior thought it 'singularly weak and loosely put together', adding, 'I am grateful for small mercies. It might have been so much worse!'[64] He was chiefly concerned about Forster's handling of his parents' separation. Wilkie objected as much to Forster's treatment of him as a casual acquaintance, briefly and uninformatively mentioned, at the time when Wilkie was not only an intimate friend of Dickens but a close friend of Forster himself. Twenty years of friendship, when they had acted together during the 'splendid strollings' of Dickens' amateur company, and been Dickens' guests together at Gad's Hill and in France, years in which Forster had been a frequent and welcome visitor to Wilkie's home, went for nothing. All that mattered to Forster now was that his view of Dickens should be the one enshrined in literary history. To a remarkable extent, that was exactly what he achieved.

There was no open quarrel; that was never Wilkie's style. The two men simply ceased to see each other except at public gatherings. But Wilkie, universally known as the kindest of men, did on occasion carry on the Dickens tradition of presenting Forster as a pompous fool. On his return from America he wrote to Mrs Bigelow:

> I cannot even tell you about Forster's health, having seen nothing of him, and heard nothing from him, for months past. Did I tell you how he once distinguished himself on landing at Boulogne-sur-mer . . .? . . . Dickens and I went to the Port to 'clear' Forster (in the custom-house phrase) . . . He could neither speak nor understand French at that time – whatever he may be able to do now. In due time, he landed, walking in his most majestic manner between the custom house lines of rope . . . he was . . . accosted by a very small French military official, in these customary terms: – 'Avez vous rien à déclarer, Monsieur?' Forster paused, smiled his sweetest smile, bowed his grandest bow, and answered in his most mellifluous tones: – '*Bon jour*!' . . . he was instantly seized, and Dickens had to become answerable for him. To see F.'s astonishment and the little Frenchman's indignation – is to have lived to some advantage and to have made the most of life.[65]

After Forster's death in 1876 Wilkie wrote, 'Another old friend gone – in Forster! He was angry with me because I did not "consult him" before I went to America! I am glad to think now I was never angry with *him*.'[66] He did not show his anger to Forster, no doubt. But there can also be no doubt that he felt it. In 1888, in his article 'Reminiscences of a Story-Teller', he was still associating Forster with the 'British clap-trap' that tried to censor what he wrote, and that praised Dickens for the wrong reasons:

> She dropped the book, and I picked it up for her. It was a cheap edition of 'The New Magdalen'. She reddened a little as she thanked me. I observed with interest the soft round object, sacred to British clap-trap – the cheek of the young person – and I thought of a dear old friend, praised after his death by innumerable humbugs, who discovered the greatness of his art in its incapacity of disturbing the complexion of young Miss . . . Her sister . . . put a question: 'Is it interesting?' The fair reader answered 'It's perfectly dreadful.' . . . Alas for my art! It was worse than 'poor stoof' . . . it was stuff concealed from Papa, stuff which raised the famous Blush, stuff registered on the Expurgatory Index of the national cant.[67]

TWENTY

America

(1873–1874)

Wilkie seems to have felt that he might not survive the six-month absence in America. It was generally believed that the strain of Dickens' last American tour had hastened his death, and Wilkie had been told in 1871 that his heart was weak.[1] In addition there was the chronic 'rheumatic gout' which often crippled him for weeks or months at a time. He could not, of course, take Caroline to look after him, as he did when he travelled privately on the Continent. As Dickens rapidly realized in 1867, a female companion who was not a wife would have scandalized the American public and seriously jeopardized the success of the readings. Rather than taking his manservant with him, Wilkie thriftily dismissed him with a written reference.[2] He had hoped to sail with Wybert Reeve, who was booked to open in a New York production of *The Woman in White* in December. But Reeve could not get away in time; Wilkie left alone.

He tidied up his affairs before he left, signing a new will which clearly expressed his attitude to the women and children this most unpatriarchal man had, in patriarchal fashion, gathered around him. It divided his estate equally. Half was to go to Caroline and Carrie, and half to Martha and the two children. Martha and her daughters were to be the surviving legatees if Caroline and Carrie died first.[3] He also arranged for the insurance of Martha's furniture at her new address, 55 Marylebone Road. He asked Tindell to keep an eye on his families while he was in America: 'I know you will, like a good fellow, give personal as well as professional advice to those whom I leave to the care of old friends like you . . . Help them here, and at Marylebone Road when they want help.'[4] Charles Ward, Fred Lehmann and other old friends were asked to call at 90 Gloucester Place, to keep in touch with Caroline and Carrie. 'Mrs. Dawson' was kept more closely under wraps.

Wilkie also made an uncharacteristic mistake, perhaps in the hurry of leaving, in appointing a dubious agent, Stefan Poles, to act as his representative in productions of *The New Magdalen* on the Continent, an authorization he later had difficulty in rescinding. Poles, who was one of the first people to be listed as a literary agent in the Post Office Directory for 1874, turned out to be thoroughly untrustworthy. There was a rumour that he was a Russian spy. More to the point, for Wilkie, he was financially unscrupulous. When he died, penniless, in 1875, a subscription was got up by a friend to pay for his burial: Wilkie grumblingly contributed £2. The theatre might be a more rewarding marketplace for his work than the world of publishing, but it was even more likely to attract slippery characters.

Wilkie sailed from Liverpool – he had last been there to see Dickens off on his final journey to America – on the *Algeria*, on 13 September. The crossing, with a stop at Queenstown, took twelve days, and was uneventful. The familiar face of Charles Fechter greeted him on the quay in New York. Fechter took him to the Westminster Hotel, and they dined together. 'You will find friends here wherever you go,' Fechter promised. 'Don't forget that I was the friend who introduced you to soft-shell crab.'[5] Wilkie had the suite previously occupied by Dickens at the Westminster Hotel, which had a convenient private staircase leading to an outside door.[6] He was watched for suitable signs of emotion – the reporters would not leave him alone – and seems to have reacted satisfactorily to the sight of the desk at which Dickens had worked.

Wilkie was already well known in America as a novelist and playwright, and his friendship with Dickens added to his interest for the American public. Since the United States had still not signed an international copyright agreement, and was not to do so until after Wilkie's death, his novels were widely circulated in pirated editions as well as authorized ones. Wilkie was told that one American publisher (not Harper) boasted of having sold 120,000 copies of *The Woman in White*. 'He never sent me sixpence', Wilkie recalled.[7] His plays had also been performed, legitimately and illegitimately. *The Lighthouse* was given its first professional production in New York, in 1855, two years before it was seen on the professional stage in London. *Man and Wife* had a ten-week run at the Fifth Avenue Theatre in 1870, and *Black and White*, with Fechter, was performed in Boston in the same year. *No Name*, never acted in England, was given a not very successful production at the Fifth Avenue Theatre in 1871. Productions of *The New Magdalen* and *The Woman in White* were already being planned. Americans greeted Wilkie's arrival with curiosity and enthusiasm, both as the friend and collaborator of Dickens and on his own account.

Harper's marked the occasion by immediately issuing a 'Library Edition' of his works, $1.25 per volume, cloth-bound, with a dedication in a facsimile of Wilkie's handwriting, 'to The American People'. The insatiable curiosity of the Americans about every detail of the lives and habits of English writers was soon apparent in the newspaper reports of his activities, even before the readings started. The lionizing began at once. Wilkie was guest of honour at a dinner at the Lotos Club on 27 September. Also present were Charles Bradlaugh, whose notoriety as a professional free-thinker outweighed any rumours about Wilkie; the Italian actor Salvini, famous for his Othello; and the writer Bret Harte. Harte was by no means an uncritical fan. He had written a clever parody of Wilkie's earlier novels in 1867, and had more recently sharply criticized *Man and Wife* for its 'fell moral purpose . . . Mr. Reade's Trade Union outrages, Mr. Disraeli's Catholic tempest in a Protestant teapot are as nothing to this.' He complained too of 'that slight suspicion of insanity without which Mr. Collins seems to find it impossible to express originality'.[8] But he turned up at the dinner, where Wilkie was introduced by Whitelaw Reid, editor of the influential and respected *New York Herald Tribune*. Wilkie made a graceful speech, dating his friendly feelings for America and the Americans back to his first boyhood acquaintance with one in Sorrento, and taking his welcome as an expression of 'a recognition of English literature, liberal, spontaneous, and sincere'.[9]

Similar occasions followed throughout the tour. A 'breakfast' for twenty-four guests at the Union Club in New York, given by William Seaver, was less a breakfast than a banquet, with a good deal to drink and a menu that included oysters, fillet of bass, lamb chops, canvas-back duck, woodcock and ice-cream. At a dinner in Boston in February, many of the great names of American literature were present. Wilkie met Longfellow, Whittier, Mark Twain, Oliver Wendell Holmes. Wilkie took to Holmes, who read a 'verse tribute' to him. Wilkie reciprocated by dedicating *Readings and Writings in America*, published the following year, to Holmes. Each guest at this dinner was presented with a bon-bon box, designed to look like a volume from the 'cabinet edition' of Wilkie's works, covered in Turkey morocco and containing his photograph and autograph. There was a band playing in the next room throughout the meal, and 'a dove with a pen in her mouth, hanging from the chandelier'.[10] Wilkie was fully aware of the absurdity of it all, but joined in with his usual good humour. The meals were of innumerable courses, sometimes served 'on the American plan, in (say) forty soap-dishes, all round you, with a servant at the back of your chair to see that you eat out of every one of them'.[11]

It was horribly exhausting. The curiosity of the Americans about the great English writer and friend of Dickens grew daily: he was interviewed by all the newspapers and the demands for autographs and signed photographs were insatiable. He was recognized everywhere. In New York he was stopped in the street by an autograph hunter; at Boston he had to change hotels to get away from them. To keep up with the requests, Wilkie sat for the fashionable photographer Baron Sarony, who took, Wilkie considered, the best likenesses of him ever produced. Sarony became a personal friend. One of his portraits shows Wilkie full-length, wearing an opulent fur-lined overcoat and contemplating a moody-looking seascape, perhaps one of his father's, on an easel. In others Wilkie is seated, and there is a glimpse, under the fur coat and respectable dark jacket, of a loud checked shirt.

To cut down on the interviews, he tried to arrange for the journalists to come in batches. On one occasion he found twelve women, several of them editors, waiting in his sitting-room at the hotel. 'They seemed to have formed a sort of alliance, for no sooner had I made my bow than the oldest and ugliest of them stood forth and solemnly observing, 'Let me embrace you for the company' offered me a chaste salute . . . I suppose I did look grim, for I felt it. Really, they were not attractive.'[12]

America was still as unfamiliar and exotic as China to most English people. Wilkie found that it was, in many ways, what he had been looking for all his life. The people were enthusiastic, cordial and sincere. 'When an American says, "Come and see me," he *means* it. This is wonderful to an Englishman.' But there were minor drawbacks. He found that Americans never hummed or whistled; that not one in five hundred kept a dog and not one in a thousand carried a walking-stick. 'I who hum perpetually, who love dogs, who cannot live without a walking stick, am greatly distressed at finding my dear Americans deficient in the three social virtues just enumerated.'[13] Americans, he discovered, did not carry walking-sticks for the good reason that they did not walk. 'I . . . thought nothing of a daily constitutional from my hotel in Union-square to Central Park and back. Half a dozen times on my way, friends in carriages would stop and beg me to jump in. I always declined, and I really believe that they regarded my walking exploits as a piece of English eccentricity.'[14] Wilkie, with his bent little figure leaning on his stick, 'toddling' along on his tiny feet, might well have looked in need of a lift.

His travels provided him with plenty of new material for his fund of good stories. He insisted the dry, cold climate of the New England winter suited him perfectly; the atmosphere of democratic informality invigorated him at least as much. 'A kinder, warmer-hearted set of people surely does not exist – only their ways *are* queer', Wilkie said.[15] Asked out to dinner one Sunday, he found, to his amusement, his hosts had to open the door to him themselves. They were greatly embarrassed because they could only give him a cold meal: the servants had walked out in a body when they were asked to work on their day off. More aggressively egalitarian was the servant at a hotel in a small town, who opened the door without knocking and stayed without invitation, idly spitting out of the window.[16] A rough suit of clothes, bought at 'Mr. Moses' emporium' in the City, for travelling, was described in a newspaper report as a stylish West End tailor's suit, and Wilkie, the most idiosyncratic of dressers, as 'a connoisseur in dress'. On occasion he could not resist improving this story, claiming that his original suit had been eaten by rats during the voyage, and was replaced by the 'slops' in New York.[17]

After his first few days in New York Wilkie escaped the reporters, the autograph hunters and the indigestible dinners, going to stay with Fechter at his farm near Quakertown, Pennsylvania. He needed to rehearse, and get some much-needed reassurance and professional advice. He planned, perhaps at Fechter's suggestion, to begin the readings in the smaller towns, waiting to tackle New York and Boston when he had gained some confidence.

To see how Fechter had deteriorated since his London triumphs was a shock. His drinking, his eccentricity and his bouts of paranoia had isolated him, and his great days as an actor were virtually over. He had become gross and bloated. With his habitual instinct for self-destruction, he had quarrelled with his theatrical partners in Boston, killing his chances of success there. Worse, he had quarrelled with his leading lady, Carlotta Leclercq, and become estranged from her. He tried, and failed, to become a theatrical manager in New York. When he returned briefly to London in December 1873, to play in a revival of his production of Bulwer-Lytton's *The Lady of Lyons*, he was a pathetic wreck. Perhaps it was fortunate that Wilkie, incapable though he was of quarrelling with anyone, could not spend very long with him: what he saw in Pennsylvania was profoundly depressing. Fechter had formed a relationship with Lizzie Price, 'a handsome and capable Philadelphia actress, who became and remained his devoted slave'.[18] He married her that winter, bigamously: Fechter already had a wife and two children in Europe. When this became widely known, it was the last straw for the American public who had greeted him rapturously a few years before. He died of cirrhosis of the liver in 1879, penniless, despised and isolated.* Wilkie seems to

* Though Kate Field in her biography of Fechter denied he died of drink, the account in the *Dictionary of American Biography* cites the autopsy.

have liked and pitied Lizzie Price, for he wrote later, 'When Fechter died in poverty . . . it is not true – I assert it from what I myself had opportunities of knowing – . . . that the miserable end was due to connections which he formed in the United States. The one enemy to his prosperity was the enemy in himself.'[19]

Wilkie began his reading tour at Albany, New York, in early October, going on to read at Troy and Syracuse. It began well. He prefaced the reading with an introduction, to set the scene he hoped to create in the audience's imagination. 'I am in a very large parlour, surrounded, I hope I may say, by friends, and it is my duty to keep myself in the background, and to let my story find its way to your favor . . .'[20] Remembering the criticisms of his reading in London, he emphasized that he was not an actor, and was not trying to act: '. . . my way of reading surprises them . . . because I don't flourish a paper knife and stamp about the platform, and thump the reading desk . . .';[21] 'the story so arrested the audience that not a soul stirred – even when there was an alarm of fire in the neighbourhood'.[22] Wilkie had only prepared one story for reading, a much expanded version of 'The Dream Woman', which took two hours to deliver. He must have been dissatisfied with his try-out of 'A Terribly Strange Bed', for he never used it again. The alterations to 'The Dream Woman' spoil the economy and mystery of the story, replacing the effectively inconclusive ending with a 'closed' one in which the woman does murder her husband. There is far more circumstantial detail than in the original; a story in which the uncanny and irrational predominate is turned into a piece of low-grade sensation. It was probably the realism of the reading version that aroused considerable antagonism in some places. Though Wilkie insisted to friends that audiences were always complimentary, there were complaints at Philadelphia, where he read on 17 October, that his voice was low and monotonous, and the morality of the story was attacked in the press: 'It was not pleasant to hear a famous Englishman describing, before several hundred pure girls, how one wretched, fallen woman, after mysteriously killing her man, had captivated two more, and stabbed another to death in a drunken frenzy.'[23]

In Boston, where Wilkie read for the first time on 30 October, the press was kinder, though he was rapped over the knuckles by the Boston *Evening Transcript*, surprised that 'an Englishman with the reputation and favor enjoyed by Wilkie Collins should be willing to create such an impression as the reading of "The Dream Woman" creates'.[24] But the Boston Brahmins competed to entertain him. James T. Fields and his wife dined him and took him to the opera; but Annie Fields, who had been infatuated with Dickens, did not think much of Wilkie on closer acquaintance: 'A small man with an odd figure and forehead and shoulders much too large for the rest of him. His talk was rapid and pleasant but not at all inspiring . . . A man who has been fêted and petted in London society, who has overeaten and overdrunk, has been ill, is gouty, and in short is no very wonderful specimen of a human being.'[25] Wilkie got on better with Fred Lehmann's friend and business partner, Sebastian Schlesinger, and spent all his spare time at Schlesinger's house. '. . . He is the brightest, nicest kindest little fellow I have met with for many a long day . . . he also makes the best cocktail in America', he told Fred.[26]

Wilkie returned to New York in November to oversee the authorized production of *The New Magdalen* – the play had already been pirated more than once – with Carlotta Leclercq playing Mercy Merrick. He was joined by his young godson, Frank Ward, who was working for Sebastian Schlesinger in Boston. Wilkie originally asked for a few days' leave for Frank, to attend the first night and his first reading. Finding Frank invaluable to him as secretary and general assistant, he asked if this might be extended, to allow Frank to accompany him on his next tour. Schlesinger generously allowed him to stay as long as Wilkie needed him.

The New Magdalen opened at the Broadway Theatre on 10 November. Wilkie's first reading in New York was timed for the following day. Leclercq's performance was rated a triumph, but the American critics were more shocked by the play than the London ones, reacting automatically to the idea of presenting a reformed prostitute on stage, more than to anything actually seen or heard. 'The theatre is not a dissecting room, nor a place for the examination of social problems,' one reviewer complained, while a correspondent to the *Daily Graphic* protested, 'The author . . . has opened a recruiting office for prostitutes ... a play so utterly vicious, so shamefully profligate in its teaching, has never before been produced at a New York theatre.'[27] The play ran for three weeks, before going on tour. Despite the initial disapproval it proved as hardy a perennial in the States as it did in England, and was toured for years. Oscar Wilde saw Clara Morris, who had played Anne Silvester in the first American production of *Man and Wife*, play Mercy Merrick in New York in 1882. He was bowled over by her: 'the greatest actress I ever saw'.[28]

Wilkie's New York reading at the Association Hall on 11 November had a mixed reception. The sophisticated audience seems to have been as much bored as shocked, if the report in the *Herald* that some went to sleep and some left before the end is to be believed. Wilkie went on to Washington, to read there, but returned to New York in time for the first night of *The Woman in White*, which followed *The New Magdalen* at the Broadway Theatre in the middle of December. Wybert Reeve, who had joined Wilkie in New York, played Fosco. It did less well, perhaps because there had been several unsuccessful plagiarized productions in the 1860s, perhaps because Wybert Reeve lacked the magnetism needed for Fosco. It ran for only two weeks.

Wilkie left for a reading tour of Canada. With Frank Ward's help, and fortified by a sumptuous picnic of dry champagne and a cold turkey, he survived a fifteen-hour train journey from Montreal to Toronto. 'Ward becomes more and more indispensible to my existence every day', Wilkie wrote to Sebastian Schlesinger on Christmas Day.[29] His Canadian publishers, Hunter, Rose, took care of him in Toronto, and Wilkie throve in the dry, cold air. Well wrapped up, he was even taken for a drive in a sledge. He took in Niagara on his way back to the States, and though he commented politely and conventionally to Mr Rose that it was worth the voyage from England to see the Falls, he had been looking forward to the sight with some dismay: 'My next duty is a severe one – Niagara. The lake here [at Toronto] makes me feel rheumatic. What will the waterfall do? Besides I don't like waterfalls – they are noisy. I prefer mountains – and other silent works of Nature.'[30]

At the end of the year Wilkie had to sever his connection with the agents who had been (mis)managing his readings and cheating him, and find new ones. It was an annoying problem which may explain why he did not, in the end, make as much as he had hoped from the tour. He said that he met with kindness and enthusiasm wherever he went: '. . . my reception in America . . . is not only more than I have deserved – it is more than any man could have deserved'.[31] He could have made $350 a week if he had been willing to read every night. But though he remained remarkably free from gout, he was unwilling to overtax himself.

At the beginning of January he was still hoping to go west – 'perhaps as far as Salt Lake City itself'.[32] It is intriguing to imagine Wilkie among the Mormons. As an unofficial polygamist he might have appreciated the marriage customs; as a confirmed drinker (his favourite tipple, dry champagne, was hard to come by in the United States) he would have found the strict teetotalism hard to bear. He celebrated his fiftieth birthday by reading in Cleveland, Ohio, but in the event he got no farther west than Chicago. The experience of travelling long distances by train was exhausting; the overnight journeys by sleeping car were shattering. He could get no sleep, and 'I feel the "sleeping car" in the "small of my back", and in the drums of my ears at this moment', he complained.[33] Instead he turned east, breaking the journey back to Boston at Detroit and Rochester, and read in towns in New England through January and February.

Wilkie's readings were certainly helped by the slightly scandalous fame attached to the author of *The New Magdalen*. In spite of the mixed reviews and the trouble with his agents, he was making good sums of money, though the amounts varied from place to place. 'Providence (the city not the Deity) paid me 400 dollars', he reported.[34] He even found time to write a story, 'The Dead Alive', based on a true American case, 'The Trial of Jesse and Stephen Boone', in which a man supposedly murdered and buried in a lime pit turns up safe and well. The story, first published in the *New York Fireside Companion*, was renamed 'John Jago's Ghost' when it appeared in England. The plot, though it has a quite different origin, has a curious similarity to that of *Edwin Drood*. Wilkie was furious when a French forger published a conclusion to *Drood* supposed to be by Wilkie Collins and Charles Dickens Junior, in 1879. They went to law to get the publication stopped.

Wilkie was urged not to repeat his reading of 'The Dream Woman' in Boston, and instead made an adaptation of *The Frozen Deep* for his farewell reading there. The original play had inspired *A Tale of Two Cities*. Now the newly written ending of the much-altered 'reading' version drew heavily on Dickens' novel. '"The loss is ours," he said. "The gain is his. He has won the greatest of all conquests – the conquest of himself. And he has died in the moment of victory. Not one of us here but may live to envy *his* glorious death."'[35] The story took two hours to deliver, but, according to Wilkie, 'kept its hold from first to last on the interest and sympathies of the audience'.

Wilkie had originally intended to stay until the end of March, but, as he told the publisher George Childs, who had entertained him in Philadelphia and was expecting him to return there, 'letters from home have obliged me to hasten my departure . . . to attend to some business which was all going wrong in my absence'.[36] The business was to do with Martha. He heard in January that her landlord was selling the house, and wanted her to move, unless 'Mr Dawson' would buy the lease, 'which I cannot and will not do . . . I had hoped we were settled – but there is no such luck for me.'[37] Martha was entitled to three months' notice; but now he had to return to sort out the problem of where his family was to live. He left with reluctance. 'If all goes well with me, I shall return to my good American friends at the first opportunity . . . I leave you with a grateful heart – with recollections of American kindness and American hospitality which will be, as long as I live, among the happiest recollections to which I can look back.'[38]

Wilkie had made about £2,500 from the trip. It was nothing compared with the £20,000 Dickens had scooped up in 1867, but it enabled him to put by something for both his families. Just before he left, he took out two insurance policies on his life for $5,000 (£1,000) each, paying the first year's premiums and leaving the policies in the care of Sebastian Schlesinger.[39] After a farewell dinner with Fechter in New York – the last time Wilkie ever saw him – he left from Boston on the Cunarder *Parthia*, on 7 March. He had a good journey: 'Travel by Cunard,' he advised an American friend, 'he takes soundings in a fog and is not in such a damned hurry that he has no time to think of the lives of his passengers'.[40]

Wilkie had enjoyed the country, the climate and the people: America invigorated and liberated him. Where Dickens had found that the dry air of a New England winter gave him 'American catarrh', Wilkie, who hated damp weather, enjoyed it. 'In *your* country, I felt five and twenty years old. In *my* country, I (not infrequently) feel five and ninety', he wrote to Mrs Bigelow ten months later.[41] He made many friends, chief among them Sebastian Schlesinger, and he was often urged to return. But it was his only visit. The readings, though not a failure, were successful chiefly because of his reputation, not his performance, and as a financial venture they had proved disappointing. He hoped to repeat the readings in England; but in this, too, he was to be disappointed.

TWENTY-ONE

The Law and the Lady

(1874–1879)

Wilkie was back in London at the end of March. He quickly found a new home for Martha and the children, at 10 Taunton Place, then a row of semi-rural cottages off Park Road, Regent's Park. He had only to walk the short distance to the north end of Gloucester Place to see her. He located the idealized love-nest of Amelius Goldenheart and Simple Sally in his 1879 novel, *The Fallen Leaves*, in the same spot.

> He turned northward towards the Regent's Park.
>
> The cottage was in a by-road, just outside the park: a cottage in the strictest sense of the word. A sitting-room, a library, and a bedroom – all of small proportions – and, under them, a kitchen and two more rooms, represented the whole of the little dwelling . . . It was simply and prettily furnished; and it was completely surrounded by its own tiny plot of garden-ground. The library especially was a perfect little retreat, looking out on the back garden; peaceful and shady, and adorned with book-cases of old carved oak. (*The Fallen Leaves*, Vol. 3, p. 256)

One hopes that Martha had a little more space. With two (soon to be three) children, she might have appreciated an extra bedroom rather more than Amelius' library. It was, at any rate, a pleasant place to bring up children, close to the lake and the open spaces of the park.

Wilkie seems to have run into some difficulty with the landlord, which recalls his early problems with Caroline, and would not be out of place in one of his later novels, where troubles with straitlaced landladies play an increasing part. This was either to do with the legality of taking a house in a false name or the morality of installing an unmarried mother and two children in it. Wilkie wrote to Tindell, 'Talk of the Devil – here he is [down on] me in a fury! Will the enclosed answer do? . . . If no – what had I better do? Let the house instantly to Caroline? – eh?'[1] Caroline Graves appears in the rates books as the rate payer for 10 Taunton Place, from 1874 to 1877: a curious knot in the tangled web of Wilkie's private affairs.

Wilkie and Martha's third and last child, William Charles Collins Dawson, known as Charley, was born in this house on Christmas Day 1874, nine months almost to the day after Wilkie got back to London. Wilkie loathed the 'filthy "Christmas festivities"' which prevented 'any proceeding that is not directly connected with the filling of fat bellies, and the exchange of vapid good wishes'. He mentioned his 'Christmas Box, in the shape of a big boy' only in a postscript to a letter to Tindell, but he did instantly take steps to have him added to his latest will.[2] His birth was registered, which was now required by law; but it was left to Martha to do so: she signed the certificate on 1 February 1875. Martha's older sister Alice Rudd, who had been a servant with her in Yarmouth in the 1860s, came to Taunton Place to help her with the family.[3]

Wilkie's publishing arrangements, which always gave him so much trouble, were almost as complicated as his family affairs. He had been trying for some time to simplify them. But he seems to have been unable to decide whether it was better to make his books cheaper, to increase the volume of sales, or more expensive, to increase the profit on each unit sale. In 1870 he had seriously considered a proposal from Cassell to buy up his copyrights and issue a cheap, uniform edition, but eventually turned it down because they were not offering him enough to justify tying up his copyrights for the ten-year term they requested. In 1871 he once more meditated a scheme to reach 'the unknown public' by publishing *The Woman in White*, and possibly other novels, in weekly 'penny numbers'. After asking George Smith's advice, he once more dropped the idea, though he felt that 'a *very few* years more will see a revolution in the publishing trade for which most of the publishers are unprepared . . . I don't believe in the gigantic monopolies, which cripple *free* trade, lasting much longer. The Mudie monopoly and the W. H. Smith monopoly are anomalies in a commercial country.'[4] 'Capital and courage are all that are wanted to break down the Library system . . . the market is immense – but nobody here seems to know how to get at it', he explained to Harper.[5] But he was unwilling to go the whole distance, and drop down to 'that miserable 2/- which leaves us such a small margin of profit' on the new edition of *Man and Wife*. 'I may certainly, without undue arrogance, consider myself to be a rather better novelist, with a rather wider reputation, than Mrs. Henry Wood', he boasted, claiming that he knew she averaged £1,000 a year by the sale of her novels in 6s. editions.[6] In May 1874, having had heavy payments to make to resettle Martha, and with '"outgoings" looming on the horizon' in the shape of the new baby, he induced Bentley to agree to issue all his old novels in a 6s. edition, though he had to concede that the contrast between his sales and those of Mrs Henry Wood was not encouraging 'and does not *add* to my faith in the British Public!'.[7] But before Bentley could put the scheme into operation, Wilkie had had a better proposal. Andrew Chatto, who had taken over the firm of John Camden Hotten in 1873, renaming it Chatto & Windus (Windus was a sleeping partner), made an offer of £2,000 for the exclusive right to publish Wilkie's earlier novels in Great Britain, Ireland and the English Colonies except Canada (where the arrangement with Hunter, Rose precluded it). Initially he asked for a seven-year licence to publish, with Wilkie retaining the copyright.[8] Wilkie was glad to agree. It relieved him of anxiety, and gave him the advantage of a uniform edition and 'a pecuniary interest of unusual importance'.[9] He persuaded Bentley to relinquish his rights, and Chatto also tried to buy back *No Name*, *After Dark* and *Armadale* from Smith, Elder, who still had the rights to these titles. Smith refused to give them up, and they were not published by Chatto & Windus until 1890, after Wilkie's death. All Wilkie's subsequent novels appeared with the Chatto & Windus imprint.

Andrew Chatto had worked from the age of fifteen in the firm he bought. Unlike John Camden Hotten, who was something of a rogue, Chatto was not only an active and successful publisher, but an honest one. 'I should like to see my friend Chatto driving in a gilded coach!' Walter Besant said once.[10] He published many of the best authors of his time, and was one of the few publishers to approve of the rise of the literary agent. He read everything that came to the firm himself, and personally negotiated the sales to the circulating libraries.

However, Chatto was unable to bypass the three-volume first-edition format, and Wilkie's new novels still appeared, in the first instance, at a guinea and a half. The 6s. one-volume edition, a price Wilkie had been rather attached to, was omitted. Cheaper one-volume editions at 3s. 6d. (illustrated), 2s. 6d. (cloth, limp), and 2s. (illustrated boards) followed within a year or two, rather more rapidly than was customary. Wilkie had achieved no more, in effect, than a comfortable sum of ready money, at a time when he needed it, and a tidy arrangement with an efficient publisher. The power of the circulating libraries, and the serial system of publication, were as entrenched as ever.

Chatto's monopoly on Wilkie's earlier works seems to have taken some time to implement, for Smith, Elder were still advertising their cheap 'yellowback' edition of nine of his books in 1876, as well as the more expensive editions of *Armadale*, *After Dark* and *No Name*. Chatto's handsome illustrated 'New Library Edition' of twenty-nine Wilkie Collins titles, published from the 1890s, sold at the old 6s. price. The vast sums that Wilkie believed could be made from the 'unknown public' he longed to reach were still elusive. Not until the 1890s, when he was no longer there to appreciate it, was a 6d. edition in paper wrappers published by Chatto & Windus.[11] It would have delighted him.

Wilkie's next novel, *The Law and the Lady*, was the first new work of his to be published under the Chatto & Windus imprint. It explores, with considerable candour, the question: Why do admirable women devote themselves to such awful men? Wilkie's seven months away from England was the longest time in his whole life he had been without the support of a woman. His welcome back had produced another child to be acknowledged, concealed and paid for. The mixed responsibilities and compensations of his intricate family life seem to have prompted him to consider what he might mean to the women who relied on him; also the nature and degree of his reliance on them.

The Law and the Lady was serialized from September 1874 to March 1875 in the *Graphic*, an illustrated weekly newspaper of no literary pretensions. It was an unhappy choice. Wilkie had an acrimonious exchange of letters with the paper over a passage which was deleted, in spite of a clause in the contract forbidding any alterations without his permission. The passage, objected to by the editor as 'an attempted violation of the heroine' and 'unfit to appear in the pages of a family newspaper', described the married heroine's annoyance when a lustful cripple put his arm round her waist and tried to kiss her. 'You distinctly told me before the story began', the editor complained, 'that as it was the autobiography of a young lady there would certainly be nothing coarse or improper in it; whereas, in my opinion, and in the opinion of a good many other people too, there is a disagreeable flavour pervading the story generally.'[12] Wilkie was furious. He successfully insisted through his lawyers that the disputed passage be reinstated in the next issue. The *Graphic* retaliated by publicly disavowing the novel – 'the story is not one which we should have voluntarily selected to place before our readers' – a piece of spite which Wilkie arranged for *The World*, edited by his friend Edmund Yates, to attack as 'a gross violation of the rules by which literary courtesy and good feeling are governed . . . conduct as ungenerous as it is ill-judged'.[13]

The novel appeared in the usual three-volume format on 12 February 1875. It was not written with dramatization in mind; nor was it in the accepted sense 'a novel with a purpose'. The Scottish verdict of 'not proven', given in a murder case, is used as a psychological, rather than a legal question mark: though the accused man is finally cleared of murder, he is not cleared of responsibility for a death. Wilkie made a gesture towards the necessity for reform, in a couple of sentences, and then got on with his story.

The Law and the Lady is one of the strangest, and in some ways one of the most interesting, novels he ever wrote. Its inferiority to the novels of his vintage years lies chiefly in the careless handling of the plot. Either Wilkie lost interest in the detective element of the story, or he wanted to focus the reader's attention on something else. The novel has, until recently, been dismissed as a mixture of low-key detective story and absurd sensationalism; but it also contains an exploration of irrational behaviour and the psychological motivation behind it which is in some ways an advance on anything he had done before.[14] Wilkie's prefatory 'Note' to the reader puts the emphasis on the real point of the novel.

> . . . The actions of human beings are not invariably governed by the laws of pure reason . . . we are by no means always in the habit of bestowing our love on the objects which are the most deserving of it, in the opinions of our friends . . . Characters which may not have appeared, and Events which may not have taken place, within the limits of our own individual experience, may nevertheless be perfectly natural Characters and perfectly probable Events, for all that. (*The Law and the Lady*, Vol. I, p. v)

The story is told by a young woman, Valeria Macallan, who marries, in defiance of her family, a man who is extremely secretive about his past. Wilkie's impersonation of an infatuated young woman is sometimes awkward, but as the reader gradually perceives the irony of the gap between her perceptions of her husband and the reality, and Valeria struggles to maintain the impossible posture of an admiring and submissive wife, the narrative becomes increasingly convincing. Eustace Macallan has concealed his true identity, and married Valeria under a false name, because he is ashamed to admit that he was tried for the murder of his first wife and only got off on a verdict of 'not proven'. When Valeria finds this out, Eustace runs away, unable to face her. She sets out, single-handed, to exonerate him by discovering the true murderer. Discouraged and hampered on all sides, she persists in her investigation. The truth, as so often in a Wilkie Collins story, is that there has been no murder, and hence no murderer. The first wife committed suicide, poisoning herself by taking arsenic. But the question of guilt remains. Eustace Macallan had been pursued by a woman who was infatuated with him. When she was found in a compromising position in his lodgings he married her out of kindness, not love. He came to long for her death; she came to know this from reading his diary, and did the deed for him. Curiously, some elements of the plot are borrowed, consciously or unconsciously, from Charles Collins' novel of 1866, *At the Bar*, in which an innocent person stands trial for murder by arsenical poisoning of a woman who has in fact killed herself.

There are three proto-Wilkie Collinses in *The Law and the Lady*. Each is seen from a very different point of view, and embodies a part only of their creator, but each is concerned with the relationship of that part to a woman. Eustace Macallan, whose very kindness and incapacity to face hard fact make him unintentionally brutal to both his wives, is the closest, physically as well as psychologically, to a candid naturalistic portrait of Wilkie. He is much older than Valeria, and not quite as tall as she. He has a beard and moustache streaked with grey, and walks with a limp, using a 'thick bamboo cane, with a curious crutch handle'. Valeria describes him as having 'the tenderest and gentlest eyes (of a light brown) . . . smile rare and sweet; his manner . . . has . . . a latent persuasiveness in it, which is (to women) irresistibly winning'.[15] He is also a coward, despised by his mother for running away from any unpleasantness, and a modern Bluebeard, who keeps saying, 'Don't ask! Don't look!' to his unfortunate bride. She, with dawning self-awareness, refuses to accept his false identity, and in the end discovers more than she really wants to know about him – more, indeed, than he knows about himself. In the process, she also discovers much about herself. The Roman courage suggested by her name persists to the end: she conceals from her husband the truth of his responsibility for his first wife's death.

The second appearance of the author in his novel is a parodic version of Wilkie-and-Martha as seen by the outside world: the stereotype of a womanizer finally brought low by a tart. The ancient Don Juan, Major Fitz-David, to whom Valeria goes to discover more about her husband, lives in a house in 'Vivian Place' near Portman Square, clearly modelled on 90 Gloucester Place. He surrounds himself with mementoes of earlier loves, and with reproductions of Wilkie's favourite erotic works of art, 'the Venus Milo and the Venus Callipyge'. The major is in the tradition of the superannuated military roué of early Victorian fiction, a clone of Major Pendennis. He is clearly meant as a parody. 'All the misfortunes of my youth and my manhood have come to me through women', he boasts. 'I am not a bit better in my age – I am just as fond of the women, and just as ready to be misled by them as ever, with one foot in the grave.' He meets his nemesis, as such characters traditionally do, in the form of a common little gold digger, again conventionally characterized. But it is worth noting that the major encountered her at a railway-station refreshment-room: 'She was behind her counter . . . rinsing wine-glasses, and singing over her work.' She submits him to 'the ordeal of marriage', and bullies him at last into becoming an old man.

The third aspect, Wilkie as a writer, and the dangers of the imaginative and creative inner life, is embodied in the fantastic figure of the legless Miserrimus Dexter. He is only an author-surrogate in a generalized sense. The extraordinary portraits of Dexter and his willing slave Ariel, on whom he plays like a musical instrument, may come as much from opium visions as from an imaginative extension of reality. If so, opium has this time served Wilkie well. At all events, Dexter has, as Sue Lonoff has noted, several points of resemblance with Wilkie Collins.[16] As Wilkie's illness seized hold of him with increasing ferocity after the remission of the American tour, there were times when he must have felt, as he was carried out to be 'aired' in a carriage, that the slide from Eustace Macallan's limp and walking-stick to the state of Miserrimus Dexter as the 'new Centaur – half man, half chair' could not be long postponed. Dexter's wild, misdirected energy, the cruelty of his fantastic imaginings, his libidinous desires, so sharply and pathetically contrasting with his crippled body – all suggest aspects of Wilkie hidden from those who could only see the weak Eustace Macallan, or the ridiculous Major Fitz-David. Dexter is a story teller and a weaver of plots, which he tries out on his servant: 'Her great delight is to hear me tell a story. I puzzle her to the verge of distraction; and the more I confuse her, the better she likes the story.' His mischievous creation of a conventional 'maid and mistress' sensation plot to mislead Valeria and direct her attention away from the true solution takes the form of a play, Wilkie's favourite genre. 'I excel in dramatic narrative,' Dexter tells her.

Dexter is unbalanced, mentally and physically (he was born without legs), but not, for most of the novel, actually mad. But his eccentricity, his abrupt changes of mood and his appearance and habits, described in great detail, make him frightening enough, as he swings his legless body about, performing a grotesque leap-frog over a row of chairs, or speeds through the rooms of his tumbledown mansion in a wheelchair, imagining himself Napoleon or Shakespeare.

Dexter, immured in a circular study in his crumbling manor house, which he refuses to sell to the developers who are building a suburb around it, dominates more than half the novel. He floats free of nineteenth-century realism, coming closer to Samuel Beckett's Murphy and Malone than to 'a legless Quilp'.[17] Valeria feels a secret sympathy with him: 'It seems to me that he openly expresses . . . thoughts and feelings which most of us are ashamed of as weaknesses, and which we keep to ourselves accordingly.' Of his acting-out of his fantasies she says, 'I have often fancied myself transformed into some other person . . . One of our first amusements as children (if we have any imagination at all) is to get out of our own characters, and to try the characters of other personages as a change – to be fairies, to be queens, to be anything in short, but what we really are. Mr. Dexter lets out the secret, just as the children do'.[18]

The novel was dedicated to an actor, Wilkie's old friend and collaborator François-Joseph Régnier of the Comédie Française, and in Miserrimus Dexter Wilkie explored the personality of an actor as searchingly as that of a writer. 'I have an immense imagination,' Dexter tells Valeria:

> It runs riot at times. It makes an actor of me. I play the parts of all the heroes who ever lived. I feel their characters. I merge myself in their individualities. For the time being I *am* the man I fancy myself to be. I can't help it. I am obliged to do it . . . (*The Law and the Lady*, Vol. 2, p. 200)

Though Dexter has an obvious if tangential relationship to his creator, he is also a bizarre portrait of Charles Fechter. Fechter's mental instability, his notorious temper and bitter grudge-holding, his immersion in the parts he played, his heavy drinking, even his gourmet's interest in food, are all mirrored in Dexter. Fechter studied music, painting and literature before becoming an actor. Dexter paints nightmarish pictures, illustrations of such themes as 'Revenge' and 'Cruelty'. He plays a Welsh harp, wears a stage wardrobe of rich and fantastical clothes, and cooks elaborate and exquisite dishes, preparing for Valeria (who doesn't appreciate it) a single truffle stewed in Clos Vougeot. He considers (as Wilkie and Fechter did) that 'A man who eats a plain joint is only one remove from a cannibal – or a butcher.'[19]

Wilkie knew, too, the dangers of Fechter's temperament and habits. The doctor's opinion of Dexter's 'latent insanity' expresses the fears of the few friends Fechter still had. 'His nervous system is highly sensitive; and there are signs that his way of life has already damaged it . . . If he persists in his present way of life . . . his lapse into insanity must infallibly take place.'[20] Dexter's mind gives way, and he dies in an asylum. Wilkie may have seen Fechter at his Pennsylvania farm, carried 'legless' to bed by a faithful servant after a drinking bout, and wondered, as Valeria does in the novel, at his ability to arouse love and fidelity in those who served him.

> The rough man lifted his master with a gentleness that surprised me. 'Hide my face,' I heard Dexter say to him, in broken tones. He opened his coarse pilot jacket, and hid his master's head under it, and so went silently out – with the deformed creature held to his bosom, like a woman sheltering her child . . . (*The Law and the Lady*, Vol. 3, p. 104)

'Could a man who was hopelessly and entirely wicked', Valeria wonders, 'have inspired such devoted attachment to him as Dexter had inspired in the faithful woman who had just left me – in the rough gardener who had carried him out so gently on the previous night? Who can decide? The greatest scoundrel living always has a friend – in a woman, or a dog.' Lizzie Price, bigamously married to Fechter, remained his devoted slave. Wilkie, more fortunate and less disturbed, was surrounded by his loving women. Whether this was the proper role for women is at least considered in the novel. Miserrimus Dexter dismissively tells Valeria:

> The one obstacle . . . to your rising equal to the men in the various industrial processes of life is not raised, as the women vainly suppose, by the defective institutions of the age they live in . . . No institutions that can be devised to encourage them, will ever be strong enough to contend successfully with the sweetheart and the new bonnet . . . What does it matter? Women are infinitely superior to men in the moral qualities which are the true adornments of humanity.[21]

Dexter is hardly a reliable spokesman for society. By putting the usual platitudes into the mouth of so weird a character, addressed to a woman who has shown heroic qualities of single-minded fortitude and initiative as well as of self-sacrifice, Wilkie has at least put a question mark over complacent male acceptance of women's abnegation.

The Law and the Lady was not popular with the critics. The *Athenaeum* called it, in comparison with his earlier work, 'an outrageous burlesque upon himself'. The reviewer in *The Academy*, in a phrase which may not wholly have displeased Wilkie, wrote, 'he has played such fantastic tricks with his former works as must have made Mr. Mudie weep'.[22] A kinder review in *The World* identified the problem. This reviewer also thought it 'a parody on his previous writings', but went on:

> To him life is in the most literal sense of the word a riddle and an enigma. The causes of human action must be sought in dark corners and in crooked ways, and the apparent causes are scarcely ever the real . . . The contrast between Mr Wilkie Collins and most of his contemporaries is striking . . . the novels of the day . . . dwell . . . with a new emphasis on the beauties and the phenomena of the natural world . . . Mr. Wilkie Collins is wholly unaffected by the influence. He dwells in a world of strange and lurid imaginings, which is entirely his own.[23]

Wilkie gave his verdict on naturalism in a later novel: nursery stuff suitable for second childhoods. '"These new writers are so good to old women. No story to excite our poor nerves; no improper characters to cheat us out of our sympathies; no dramatic situations to frighten us; exquisite management of details (as the reviewers say), and a masterly anatomy of human motives which – I know what I mean, my dear, but I can't explain it."'[24] He felt he was living in a 'period of "decline and fall" in the art of writing fiction . . . It may be hundreds of years before another Fenimore Cooper appears in America, or another Walter Scott in England.' These, with Balzac, were his three 'Kings of Fiction'.[25] He cared no more for Zolaesque French naturalism than for the English variety, describing it as 'dull and dirty. The "Nabab" by Daudet . . . proved to be such realistic rubbish, that I rushed out . . . to get something "to take the taste out of my mouth" as the children say. Prosper Merimée's delicious "Columba" appeared providentially in a shop-window . . .'[26]

The unpalatable truth was that he was becoming old-fashioned. Julian Hawthorne, who met him at this time, and gave a cruel and distorted picture of him, summed it up: 'Wilkie Collins . . . still lingered, not superfluous, but not indispensable; like an historic edifice, respected but unoccupied.'[27] He came increasingly to pin his hopes on finally reaching a public that didn't read reviews or subscribe to Mudie.

Meanwhile another theatrical triumph was waiting in the wings. *Miss Gwilt*, the final version of the long-postponed dramatic *Armadale*, was at last pulled into shape and staged by Ada Cavendish and her company at the Alexandra Theatre, Liverpool, on 9 December 1875. 'We had great luck', Wilkie reported. 'The audience received the piece with open arms.'[28] The play, as the title suggests, concentrates on the character of Lydia Gwilt, played by Ada Cavendish. Dickens' original criticism, that there was no female character for the audience to feel sympathy with, was overcome by softening the villainess of the original novel so much that she becomes a flawed heroine, the victim of the wickedness of others rather than the mainspring of crime. She is not bigamously married, does not commit a murder, and is a pawn in the hands of the sinister Dr Downward, who becomes the central villain of the play. With her character made so much more sympathetic, her husband, Ozias Midwinter, is allowed to remain in love with her to the end. The uncanny elements that are so strong in the novel, the coincidences, the dream, the paired characters, the 'shadow' aspect of Midwinter suggested by his appearance and his black ancestry, are all eliminated. On the page the play seems, compared with the novel, thin and uninteresting. Even so, some critics thought it 'unwholesome', with more than a whiff of the boulevards: 'The supply of poisoned air is not confined to the last scene; the atmosphere throughout is oppressively miasmic.'[29] Wilkie and Ada Cavendish clearly knew what they were about in toning it down so vigorously.

The play was scheduled to open in London in April. Wilkie, blinded in one eye by a sharp attack of 'rheumatic gout', struggled to rehearsals when he could, and was so horrified at the confusion at the Globe Theatre that he predicted a disaster. 'I have but one excuse for not having sent you the best places in the theatre – I was *afraid* to ask any of my friends to go to the first night', he told Charles Reade.[30] To his astonishment his 'good and dear public' liked the play, and the critics admired its power. Ada Cavendish triumphed, giving one of her best performances as Lydia Gwilt, and, though it did not create quite the sensation enjoyed by *The New Magdalen*, *Miss Gwilt* had a respectable twelve-week run. Ada Cavendish took *Miss Gwilt* to New York in 1879, but it ran for only three weeks, and was not revived. It was the last of his plays to be staged in the United States.

There was also a revival of *Man and Wife*, which ran concurrently with *Miss Gwilt*. Encouraged by his continued popularity with theatre audiences, he drew up, at some time in the late 1870s, an outline and notes for a projected comedy called 'The Widowed Wives' or 'The Divorced Women'. The action concerns three married couples who divorce and then marry each other's spouses.

> In the case of the husband and wife who represent the serious and pathetic interest, the marriage has been consented to by the man from a sense of duty – his honour as a gentleman is involved in his making the woman whom he has innocently led to suppose that he loves her his wife. (See Lewes' Life of Goethe, p. 103.)[31]

This situation is that of Eustace Macallan and his first wife in *The Law and the Lady*. The play must have been conceived after the novel, for the page reference is to the 1875 edition of Lewes' *Life of Goethe*. The young Goethe's failure to marry Frederike Brion is defended by Lewes:

> he was perfectly right to draw back from an engagement which he felt his love was not strong enough properly to fulfil . . . he acted a more moral part in relinquishing her, than if he had swamped this lesser in a greater wrong . . . the *formal* morality of the world, more careful of the externals than of the soul, declares it to be nobler for such rash engagements to be kept . . . than a man's honour should be stained by a withdrawal. The letter thus takes precedence of the spirit. To satisfy this prejudice a life is sacrificed. A miserable marriage rescues the honour . . . an unholy marriage, which cannot come to good.

It is a typically Collinsian situation, with the potential for an interesting play. Perhaps three divorces in a single play were too many for theatrical managements to stomach, for the play was never completed or produced.

It was not yet obvious, but Wilkie's few years of theatrical success were already behind him. When his adaptation of *The Moonstone* was staged in September 1877, it was not well received. Wilkie's alterations to the story were perhaps made in response to the reviewers' objections to his strange and lurid fictional imaginings, and in line with the more naturalistic theatre becoming popular. It did not suit his style. He removed the Indians, and with them the mystical significance of the diamond. All mention of opium was deleted, and Franklin Blake's sleep-walking was made the consequence of indigestion, not laudanum. The characters were ruthlessly pruned, entailing the loss of the two most interesting, Rosanna Spearman and Ezra Jennings. Godfrey Ablewhite was not murdered, but exited pursued by the police. What was left, disastrously, was Wilkie's determination to leave nothing to the imagination of the audience, who were subjected to long descriptions of somnambulism and extracts from Elliotson's *Human Physiology*.

The part of Miss Clack was played by Wilkie's old friend Laura Seymour. Wilkie was delighted when she agreed, and asked her advice about casting the other parts. 'I am quite confident about Miss Clack and the public with *you* to make them known to each other', he told her.[32] He was wrong: she was not a success in what turned out to be her last role. The character 'wearies far more than she amuses', Dutton Cook thought, and Seymour overacted.[33]

It seemed that Wilkie was losing his touch. The short novel that followed *The Law and the Lady*, *The Two Destinies*, was written under severe difficulties. Gout in *both* eyes in the spring of 1876 meant that he got badly behind with his work. He gave an account of his state to Fred Lehmann, laden with Swiftian disgust: 'I am still forbidden Dinners, Theatres, and all assemblies in which part of the pleasure consists of breathing vitiated air and swallowing superfluous particles of flesh given off by our fellow-creatures and ourselves in the act of respiration. Work, walk, visit to my morganatic family – such is life . . .'[34]

At one point in *The Two Destinies* the hero, who is shuttled between three women – his mother, his 'destiny' (who has married someone else – bigamously – and has a daughter) and a mysterious veiled woman suffering from a hideously disfiguring disease – thinks impatiently, '. . . the disturbing influence of women seems the only influence that I am fated to feel'. A feeling of physical and emotional claustrophobia seems to have been growing on Wilkie. His horror of gas lighting led him to write a curious article, 'The Air and the Audience', about the effect of overheated, gas-lit theatres, where the audience are perpetually 'inhaling each other's particles'. Lack of oxygen, Wilkie claims, leads to lapses of memory, so that the audience can't remember what good plays they have seen. 'It is impossible to imagine that men . . . can have wilfully suppressed notorious examples of good dramatic writing . . . The . . . alternative is to suppose a remarkable failure of memory, and to hold the absence of oxygen accountable'.[35] He is only half joking. He was now consulting George Critchett of the Middlesex Hospital, probably the best eye surgeon in England, who would not allow him to go to the revival of *Man and Wife* or to receive visitors.

It was a dreary life, and, not surprisingly, *The Two Destinies* is a dreary and badly constructed book. It is a ghost story – or rather a 'fetch' story, for the apparitions are not dead – in which a man and a woman 'destined' for each other from childhood keep on meeting without recognizing each other. It would have been adequate as a short story, a form that Wilkie used increasingly often after his return from America. Stretched on the procrustean bed of the library novel, with the anagnorisis repeatedly postponed, it becomes absurd. Apart from some background description of Shetland, taken from Wilkie's memories of his boyhood journey with his father and from Scott's *The Pirate*, the only interest of the book is a curious emphasis on dictation in the ghostly incidents, which suggests that Wilkie feels he is not, physically or imaginatively, in control of his own pen.

Nevertheless the novel, serialized in *Temple Bar* from January to September 1876 and published by Chatto in two volumes, sold well in England. In the United States there was a problem when booksellers imported the Canadian edition, undercutting Harper's edition, which initiated a diminution in Wilkie's hitherto excellent relationship with Harper. Wilkie dedicated the novel to Charles Reade, 'My old friend and brother in the Art', who had written enthusiastically to Wilkie while it was being serialized, saying that 'there is a pace of language, and a vein of sweet tenderness running through the whole, which reveal maturing genius'.[36] It was kind; perhaps it was genuine; but it is not true.

Perhaps because of perpetual illness, Wilkie seemed at this time unable to sustain the long, involved stories, with their intricate plots, that he had earlier excelled in. Short stories were easier to manage. He wrote an effective ghost story, 'The Clergyman's Confession', in 1875. In 1876 'The Captain's Last Love', probably a chastened and condensed version of his first, unpublished, Tahitian novel, was published in *Belgravia*. He produced three more stories in 1877. 'Percy and the Prophet' was written for *All the Year Round* in response to a request from Charles Dickens Junior. 'My Lady's Money' appeared in the *Illustrated London News* Christmas number; it is a trivial social comedy that seems a sketch for a play. The third, 'The Duel in Herne Wood', is so similar in its central ideas to 'Percy and the Prophet' that it almost seems a self-plagiarism. In each there is a triangle of a woman and two rival suitors, a duel, and elements of the ghostly and uncanny that are not an integral part of the structure, but Gothic ornamentation.

By the autumn of 1877 it was clear that Wilkie, who had been ill all summer, was badly in need of a long rest. He was in the habit of fleeing to the sea breezes of Ramsgate as often as he could, not only in the summer, but all the year round; now he took a more extended holiday. He and Caroline left for a three-month tour of the Tyrol and North Italy at the end of September, after the fiasco of the dramatic *Moonstone*, leaving Carrie to deal with his correspondence and take charge of the house. Wilkie was in such poor health that they had to stop to rest at Brussels. But he improved steadily, and by the end of November, when they had reached Venice, Carrie could report to his publishers that he was quite well again. He got back in time for 'the season of cant and Christmas', looking twenty years younger and feeling much stronger. 'There are all sorts of impediments, literary and personal – which keep me in England at the most hateful of all seasons', he told Nina Lehmann as an excuse for not joining her and Fred in their villa at Cannes.[37] One of them was his son's third birthday on Christmas Day.

Wilkie, in spite of the hinted self-criticisms of *The Law and the Lady*, and his apparent cynicism about family festivals, was a loving and generous provider to his families. He surrounded Caroline and Martha with all the material comforts he uninhibitedly enjoyed himself. A man who likes comfort, he would have been the first to point out, is a more comfortable person to be with than an ascetic. The atmosphere at Gloucester Place was relaxed and sybaritic. Martha's allowance was generous and was increased whenever necessary, and his wine merchants, Beechens and Yaxley, received orders for delivery to both his addresses. No doubt much of it was for his consumption, but the shepherd's daughter, too, was introduced to the pleasures of dry champagne and Ribera sherry.

Wilkie also hugely enjoyed spoiling his children, and glimpsing the richness of their imaginative lives. Elderly parents are inclined to be over-strict, or over-indulgent. The reports by Martha's grandchildren of her stern Victorian attitudes suggest she felt the need to compensate for Wilkie's permissiveness.[38] 'Spoilt children (whatever moralists may say to the contrary) are companionable and affectionate children', he knew from the responses he always got from them, and he was constitutionally incapable of inducing guilt or imposing punishment.[39] His pleasure and interest resulted in the many truthful and unsentimental portraits of children in his later novels.

As soon as Christmas was out of the way, he started thinking about a new novel, more controversial than anything he had so far written. It would require cautious introduction to the public. Wilkie tentatively put his ideas to Andrew Chatto. He proposed to divide it into three parts, each separately published: 'I should propose to be guided by the public reception of the first Part in the matter of continuing the work in the same form through the two other Parts.'[40] He did not disclose at this stage why the novel would require such careful handling, and so much thought and preliminary planning.

In the mean time he kept the pot boiling with a short novel, *The Haunted Hotel*, which had a Venetian setting inspired by his recent visit. It is a ghost and murder mystery, more Gothic than sensation, with a good deal of energy and popular appeal. ' "Sad stuff, if you look at it reasonably" ', one of the characters remarks, after telling the villainess about the ghostly manifestations of her crime. ' "But there is something dramatic in the notion of the ghostly influence making itself felt by the relations in succession, as they one after another enter the fatal room – until the one chosen relative comes who will see the Unearthly Creature, and know the terrible truth. Material for a play, Countess – first-rate material for a play!" '[41]

Narrative subversion of this kind is tricky to handle without destroying the reader's complicity and turning the *frisson* to a giggle. There is an emphasis on physical horrors in *The Haunted Hotel* quite unlike Wilkie's avoidance, in his greatest novels, of blood and violence. The visible and olfactory presences are described in grisly detail. A substitution-plot, though largely lifted from *The Woman in White*, is effectively and excitingly handled. Though there is little scene-setting, the story is also full of hints and unresolved mysteries that seem appropriate to Venice, a city of corners and shadows. The wicked brother and sister may or may not be lovers, and perhaps are not siblings. The victim may be thoroughly deserving of his fate. The manifestations, seen only by the relations of the murdered man, may be hysterical symptoms. The villainess invites discovery and retribution, by writing the truth in the form of a play which trails off into incoherence as she becomes increasingly demented.

The Haunted Hotel was serialized in *Belgravia* in six monthly parts, from June to November 1878, before being rather inappropriately shoehorned into a couple of volumes together with 'My Lady's Money'. Though the story was very popular, Wilkie was paid only £50 for each part. It was adequate but not princely, and he needed every penny he could get, from translations, American publication and republication in every available form, to keep up with his very heavy expenses. New versions of old stories were produced, often expanded, to their detriment, or altered in minor ways and issued with new titles. He was increasingly involved in arguments over the clashing interests of various magazines and publishers to whom he had granted publication rights that were not really his to give. 'A Shocking Story', written in 1878, was sold to the American *International Review* and also to the *Belgravia Annual*. The *International Review* also circulated in England, and Chatto & Windus, the proprietors of *Belgravia*, protested. Wilkie claimed he had no reason to suppose there would be a clash of interest, and reminded Chatto that, at £31. 10s., they had got the story cheap. There was worse trouble ahead. His planned tripartite novel, finally begun late in 1878 and serialized in *The World*, turned out to be a disaster.

TWENTY-TWO

The Unknown Public

(1878–1885)

Wilkie's original intention of writing a series of novels illustrating the theme of 'those who have drawn blanks in the lottery of life – the people who have toiled hard after happiness, and have gathered nothing but disappointment and sorrow; the friendless and the lonely, the wounded and the lost' survived in his next novel only in the title, *The Fallen Leaves*.[1] The histories of the unfortunate, in the only part he completed, are looked at from two perspectives: that of the ruthless capitalist society in which they live, which has nothing to give them, and the Utopian Christian socialism of the hero, idealistic but in its way equally rigid. The book was dedicated to Caroline.

The venture was potentially significant and important. In the hands of Zola, whose Rougon-Macquart cycle had begun to appear in 1871, the same impetus produced naturalistic masterpieces. Wilkie himself could have done something remarkable with the theme twenty years earlier. Now a heavily didactic and moralistic strain, dangerously sentimental at times, took over his pen. It was the same *alter ego* who had been at odds with the imaginative writer in *Man and Wife* and *The New Magdalen*. *The Fallen Leaves*, more ambitious in scope, is arguably the worst book Wilkie ever wrote.

It is certainly the worst-constructed. It is usually described as a book about a prostitute, but the story of 'Simple Sally', half-witted as a result of harsh treatment, is only one part of the novel. The stories of three other women, all in one way or another 'Fallen Leaves', are also examined, and the narrative becomes fatally disjointed. Perhaps, if Wilkie had carried out his original plan, the disparate threads of these stories could all have been gathered up and woven into a convincing narrative to illustrate the effects of hypocrisy and repression. As it stands, the novel jumps bewilderingly from one story to another, and the women are only tenuously linked by the figure of Amelius Goldenheart, the deeply embarrassing hero.

He is a latter-day Candide, coming from the innocence of the New World to the corruption of the Old. His name signals that he must be interpreted as an archetypal figure: there is neither Jamesian irony nor Voltairean satire in the way he is viewed; instead Dante becomes the model. Wilkie meant his hero to be taken seriously, which is not easy.

Amelius has been brought up in a Utopian community in America, practising the kind of Christian socialism expounded by Julian Gray in *The New Magdalen*. Wilkie took the details of the community from a description of the Oneida communities in a book he owned, *The Communistic Societies of the United States* by Charles Nordhoff. He glossed over the most controversial feature of the community, and the one which might have appealed to him most, the 'complex marriage' by which 'the exclusive and idolatrous attachment of two persons for each other' was replaced by cohabitation of any man with any woman, so long as the community's approval had first been obtained.[2] Wilkie kept the need for the community's sanction, which leads to his hero's temporary suspension from the community, but he must have thought that the loose serial cohabitation of the Oneidans was too much for English readers to accept. His hero does, however, expound a Christian socialism which was close to Wilkie's own philosophy. He loathed all forms of organized religion, and had no belief in an afterlife. But he did quite sincerely believe, as did the Oneidans, that the life of Christ, as described in the Gospels, was the best guide to human behaviour.

Amelius has an innocent relationship with a much older woman who falls in love with him, and both are forced to leave the community.

Turned out of his Eden, Amelius arrives in the inferno of London, where he plumbs the depths with a bluff and practical American as his Virgil. Then he is gradually led to an earthly Paradise by his Beatrice, a young prostitute whom he rescues from degradation, violence and starvation. Along the way he meets a middle-aged woman who 'lives in some secret hell of her own making, and longs for the release of death', and falls in love with two young women, first her respectable niece and then the prostitute. The women are all related, for the prostitute, Simple Sally, is the older woman's lost illegitimate daughter. In the closing pages of the book Amelius and Sally marry, and Wilkie promised that the next 'Series' would deal with their married life. There are hints that they would have rejoined the American community, and that a conflict between exclusive, 'selfish love' and the social organization of the community would have arisen.

The second part was planned out but never written, partly because of the adverse public reaction to the book, which attracted the expected attacks from reviewers. Wilkie continued to insist, defiantly, that it was the best book he had written since *Man and Wife*, and gave another reason for not writing the sequel: the difficulty of portraying a married life which was, because of society's prejudices, bound to go wrong. He told one correspondent that it would have been necessary to kill Sally, and he could not bring himself to do it.

It may also be that the home life of Sally and Amelius, as planned out in his notes, was coming rather too close to his own, and that Martha and Caroline begged him to stop. Much of *The Fallen Leaves* is ruined by an unusual lack of literary imagination. For once Wilkie's invention fails, and the few scenes that feel authentic are those where he seems to be describing something he has actually experienced. This is particularly striking at the moment when Amelius is accosted by the sixteen-year-old girl in the street, and she asks him, '"Are you good-natured, sir?"' The curious phrase rings true, though the idealized description of her as a potential Raphael angel which follows rather spoils it.[3] When Amelius takes Sally home to his lodgings and leaves her to sleep alone in his bed, she is distressed, thinking she has offended him. When she is discovered in his bed by the landlady in the morning, there is an unusual precision of detail in the narrative which suggests that Wilkie, perhaps in his early days with Caroline, had known something similar. For example, the maid of all work who unwittingly betrays them to the landlady is deaf. In any other novel by Wilkie Collins, such a detail would be vital to the plot; here it has no particular significance. Sally is measured for new clothes, for which the inexperienced Amelius goes shopping with two pieces of string; again, this has no relevance to the situation but feels like an authentic event.[4] The rest of the novel, in strong contrast, is a mixture of melodrama and sentimentality: the narrative is coarse, over-emphatic and forced. In spite of his affection for *The Fallen Leaves*, it seemed to many of his readers that his powers were failing. He was becoming a crippled Sisyphus trundling the products of his tired brain up an increasingly steep hill.

The needs of his families, whose bourgeois comfort was increasingly costly, were part of the problem. Wilkie habitually lived up to his income, and there was surprise, when he died, that so successful a writer did not have more to leave. One burden was removed in 1877, when old Mrs Graves died.

Caroline's mother-in-law was her last link with her true origins. The following year her daughter Carrie married into the respectable middle class: her husband, Henry Bartley, was a young solicitor in practice in Somerset Street, Portman Square. Wilkie had already transferred his legal affairs to Bartley from his friend William Tindell, whose firm had handled them since the 1860s. It was convenient to have his lawyer on the doorstep as he became feebler, but Tindell was a trusted friend, and Wilkie can only have done this in order to help Carrie. It was unfortunate that Bartley turned out to be financially incompetent, if not worse. In his hands, much of Wilkie's estate was to vanish without trace.[5]

Carrie was older than her husband by more than three years: she followed her mother's example in reducing her age on the marriage certificate. She also continued her mother's gentrification of her dead father, describing him as a 'Captain in the Army', though she must have known the truth from her grandmother, even if Caroline had wanted to keep it from her.[6] She also added another Christian name, associating herself with her dear Wilkie's *The Woman in White* by signing herself 'Harriette Elizabeth Laura'. She continued to falsify her age, giving it as twenty-seven rather than thirty in the 1881 census.

Carrie went on acting as Wilkie's secretary and copyist after her marriage. Though Wilkie does not seem to have given her a regular salary, he may have paid her in cash. At any rate, she and her husband clearly gained financially from Wilkie's generosity. Carrie gave birth to three daughters in rapid succession, and Wilkie sometimes had to use other copyists when she was unable to keep up with the work: he employed Alfred Ward, a son of Charles and Jane, as his secretary for over a year. In the last few years of his life, his elder daughter Marian sometimes wrote letters for him. But it was Carrie who continued to be most closely associated with his books, and Wilkie found it impossible to dictate to anyone else when his eyes were so bad that he could not write his first draft himself.[7] Wilkie was godfather to Carrie's eldest daughter Doris, born in 1879, and the Bartley babies were happily absorbed into his peculiar family structure. 'Come – the sooner the better – and bring *all* the children', he wrote from Ramsgate. 'Good heavens! don't I like Dah [Doris] and the quiet little curlyhead. I wish *I* was a baby again – with nothing to do but suck and sleep.'[8]

Wilkie was spending more and more of his time at Ramsgate: weeks and months at a time. He and Frank Beard both thought the sea air did him good; he told Pigott, 'Beard seems to think that my destiny is to *live* at Ramsgate. With two houses to keep going in London, I don't quite see how I am to accommodate myself to this future.'[9] The town had many advantages: it was not too far from London, and could be reached by steamer, or by the direct railway line from London. Wilkie was more or less reconciled to travelling by rail, going first-class and urging his friends to do the same, because the carriages were better made and less draughty.

At Ramsgate he could sail. Sometimes, in his later years, he hired a steam yacht, the *Phyllis*: 'A lovely little steam-launch . . . the admiration of nautical mankind. The Engineer is bigger than the funnel, and can only just squeeze himself into the Engine Room.'[10] Memories of his own happy childhood were relived in the holidays his own children and Carrie's spent there with him.

Ramsgate, which is used as a setting for scenes in several of his late novels and his play *Rank and Riches*, was known, according to a reviewer of that play, for 'the freedom of its manners', which suited Wilkie.[11] *Ramsgate Sands*, painted by his friend William Frith in 1853, gives a good idea of the atmosphere of the resort: in thirty years it had grown considerably, but it was still cheerful, crowded and slightly vulgar. The sea-front crescents where he housed his families overlooked the busy harbour. There was always something going on. Wilkie preferred it out of season: in the summer of 1885 the town was made a 'hell on earth' by 'Organs – brass bands – howling costermongers selling fish . . . nobody complains but me.'[12]

But Ramsgate was free of associations with dead friends. Broadstairs, only a few miles away, was haunted by the ghosts of Charley, Dickens, Augustus Egg and other old friends. He told Fred Lehmann that it was years since he had been into the Athenaeum, because of its associations.[13] Ghosts and revenants of one kind and another increasingly haunt his later fiction, as though the world of shadows closed in on him when he was writing. Shut in his first-floor work-room, with a black patch over one inflamed eye, barely able to see out of the other, he often had to excuse himself from evening engagements. 'I am forbidden night air – like old Rogers.* But *he* was only eighty – I am a hundred'.[14]

Wilkie seemed to his remaining friends to be disintegrating rapidly. Perhaps feeling they might soon need a memento of their old friend, Fred Lehmann commissioned a portrait of Wilkie from his brother Rudolf, as a present for Nina. Rudolf Lehmann had known Wilkie for many years – he made a pen-and-ink sketch of him in 1862 – and his portrait, though not a great work of art, captures something of the humour and energy that Wilkie still possessed. He remained as unconventional in outward appearance as ever. 'Yesterday, being out for a little walk, and wearing a *paletot with a hood* . . . I heard a woman

* Samuel Rogers, famous for his literary 'breakfasts', died in 1855, aged ninety-two.

remark . . . "To think of a man wearing such a coat as that – at *his* time of life!" The question that arises is – shall I dye my beard?'[15]

Not everyone interpreted him correctly. At some time in the 1870s or early 1880s Julian Hawthorne, the son of the novelist, came to Gloucester Place.* He later recorded his unflattering impressions of a man who seemed to him to have outlived his era and to be on the verge of senility:

> I found him sitting in his plethoric, disorderly writing-room: there are two kinds of bachelors, the raspingly tidy sort, and the hopelessly ramshackle; Wilkie was of the latter . . . He was soft, plump, and pale, suffered from various ailments, his liver was wrong, his heart weak, his lungs faint, his stomach incompetent, he ate too much and the wrong things. He had a big head, a dingy complexion, was somewhat bald, and his full beard was of a light brown colour. His air was of mild discomfort and fractiousness; he had a queer way of holding his hand, which was small, plump, and unclean, hanging up by the wrist, like a rabbit on its hind legs . . . One felt that he was unfortunate and needed succour. To his visitor he was very gracious, in a distressful way.
>
> '"The Scarlet Letter" is one of the great novels. Even the second volume, where most novelists weaken, is fine; and the third fulfils the splendid promise of the first.'
>
> A noble tribute! 'But three volumes? It is all in one.'
>
> 'Pardon me! Three volumes, and long ones!'
>
> And to prove it he toddled to a bookshelf and reached it down. He was much perplexed.
>
> 'You are right: one volume, not over 70,000 words in all! It is incomprehensible! Such a powerful impression in so small a space!'
>
> 'When I read "The Moonstone" I wished it were longer,' was all I could say. But he would not be comforted.[16]

The picture of Wilkie as disorderly and ramshackle was only partly true. As far as business was concerned, he was meticulous to the day of his death. The two diaries which survive, for 1868 and 1889, show that he noted down the dates on which manuscripts had to be dispatched, and corrected proofs and 'revises' returned, both for English publishers and for America and Australia. He kept a 'letter-book', in which his manservant had to write down the time

* Julian Hawthorne lived in London 1871–82.

and date he posted letters and parcels.[17] His work was corrected and recorrected, in meticulous and sometimes excessive detail. It was fortunate that he still had Carrie to act as his willing slave: many secretaries would have cracked under the strain. But the legend that Wilkie was 'hopeless' somehow persisted. Any of the publishers with whom he fought fierce battles could have contradicted it.

Perhaps Wilkie encouraged the idea himself. When Anthony Trollope, a good friend though not a close one, died in 1882, Wilkie wrote to his American friend William Winter:

> You knew Anthony Trollope of course. His immeasurable energies had a bewildering effect on my invalid constitution. To me, he was an incarnate gale of wind. He blew off my hat; he turned my umbrella inside out. Joking apart, as good and staunch a friend as ever lived – and . . . a great loss to novel-readers. Call his standard as a workman what you will, he was always equal to it. Never in any marked degree either above or below his own level. In that respect alone, a remarkable writer, surely? If he had lived five years longer, he would have written fifteen more thoroughly readable works of fiction.[18]

When Trollope's *Autobiography* was published in 1883 Wilkie could read his equally qualified opinion of Wilkie's own work:

> Of Wilkie Collins it is impossible for a true critic not to speak with admiration, because he has excelled all his contemporaries in a certain most difficult branch of his art; but as it is a branch which I have not myself at all cultivated, it is not unnatural that his work should be very much lost upon me . . . When I sit down to write a novel I do not at all know, and I do not very much care, how it is to end. Wilkie Collins seems so to construct his that he not only, before writing, plans everything on, down to the minutest detail, from the beginning to the end; but then plots it all back again, to see that there is no piece of necessary dove-tailing which does not dove-tail with absolute accuracy. The construction is most minute and most wonderful. But I can never lose the taste of the construction. The author seems always to be warning me to remember that something happened at exactly half-past two o'clock on Tuesday morning; or that a woman disappeared from the road just fifteen yards beyond the fourth milestone. One is constrained by mysteries and hemmed in by difficulties, knowing, however, that the mysteries will be made clear, and the difficulties overcome at the end of the third volume. Such work gives me no pleasure. (Anthony Trollope, *Autobiography*, Chap. 13)

It was the old complaint; over-elaboration and over-plotting. Wilkie retaliated by claiming he could not read the *Autobiography* through: 'The first part I thought very interesting – but when he sits in judgement on his own novels and on other people's novels he tells me what I don't want to know'.[19]

Charles Reade's death in 1884 – he had been in decline since Laura Seymour's death – was the latest in a long series. Wilkie stood at his graveside, recalling Dickens' funeral when he and Reade had stood together. Even more tragic was E. M. Ward's suicide. Ward, who had a long history of serious depression – he had severe episodes in 1875 and 1878 – cut his throat in January 1879. He made a mess of it, not dying instantly but lingering for five days. It was a horrific method of suicide, and one that Wilkie brooded over. He used it several times in his fiction, and in his last novel, *Blind Love*, the Byronic Lord Harry cuts his throat on Hampstead Heath and survives, saved by the woman who loves him and a quick-thinking surgeon. The episode is described in sanguinary detail, as if to live through and exorcize Ward's death.

The death of Charles Ward some years later was not only a personal grief. As Wilkie's financial adviser, one of the executors named in his final will, made in 1882, and the husband of his cousin, Charles knew more about his private life and finances than anyone else. His death, coupled with the substitution of the inexperienced Henry Bartley for William Tindell as Wilkie's legal adviser, left a gap that was to some extent filled by Wilkie's relationship, from 1881 until his death, with the literary agent A. P. Watt.

Watt, ten years younger than Wilkie, was not the first literary agent in England; but he was the first to be generally accepted as a professional, and to begin improving the status of the trade. He rapidly became successful. He was a Scot, born in Glasgow but brought up in Edinburgh. He married the sister of the Scottish publisher Alexander Strahan, and came to London as assistant, and then partner, to his brother-in-law. In the late 1870s he began to act as an author's agent, negotiating with publishers on their behalf and vigorously selling their work for them. He sent round a prospectus to the leading authors of the day, and in December 1881 Wilkie responded, asking him to represent him in the negotiations for his next novel, *Heart and Science.* He had been approached by a newspaper syndicate, and wanted Watt's advice.

At last Wilkie had found someone to pursue energetically and efficiently his idea of selling his fiction cheaply in large numbers, rather than relying on high prices for library editions. Watt took over the arrangements for syndicating his work in provincial newspapers, sometimes simultaneously with serialization in a London magazine. Wilkie had begun this in 1879, when Tillotsons, proprietors of the *Bolton Weekly Journal*, took on *Jezebel's Daughter.* The correspondence of Wilkie with Watt, and of the various 'curious savages' (Wilkie's description of the provincial newspaper proprietors) with Watt and Wilkie, gives a detailed picture of some of the negotiations for later novels, and their effect on Wilkie's fiction.[20]

Though Wilkie was always highly complimentary to Watt about his handling of the arrangements, expressing his gratitude in letter after letter, and was emphatic that Watt was in no way to blame when things went wrong, it is not an altogether happy picture. London publishers varied from the gentlemanly to the dubious – some were scholarly and others virtually illiterate – but they did have some idea of Wilkie's literary standing. Now, with the 'unknown public' at last within his grasp, Wilkie and the newspaper proprietors were at cross purposes. He imagined he was about to educate the masses to new standards of literary appreciation. They thought he would supply them with the kind of fiction they were accustomed to buy, very cheaply, from authors unknown to the circulating libraries and London bookshops. 'It is principally for the masses', wrote one, inviting him to supply a story, '& therefore the more sensational the more effective.'[21] 'Will you please suggest to Mr. Collins', the same man insisted to Watt, 'that the first chapter should be if possible a specially startling one. I mean rather sensational in order to attract the masses.'[22]

Nothing had changed since 1858, when Wilkie had investigated the serial stories in the 'penny journals' and found them all 'a combination of fierce melodrama and meek domestic sentiment . . . incidents and characters taken from the old exhausted mines of the circulating library'.[23] He reacted furiously in 1882 to a demand that he should supply a title and a description of the characters before the northern proprietors would decide whether to buy the rights to *Heart and Science*. Neither Charles Dickens himself, he insisted, nor any of the reputable London publishers who had published his novels, had made such a demand: 'Every one of these gentlemen remembered that my works were circulated by hundreds of thousands wherever the English language was read, and were translated into all the languages of Europe. *They* understood that a man with this reputation . . . was to be implicitly trusted as a writer.'[24]

Wilkie found, too, that mass circulation would not bring higher prices. Letters came in from all over the British Isles, from Wales, from Glasgow, from Bristol, Liverpool and Manchester, protesting that the sums Watt was demanding were too high, though they were very reasonable by London standards. Fifty pounds was 'much in excess of what can be paid for fiction in this district'; 'We are in want of a story but are not prepared to give more than £50'; 'I should not dream of giving more than £200 and even then it would depend on the scene and subject.'[25] There were also problems over competing spheres of influence. Watt seems often to have sold the same work to newspapers whose circulations overlapped. Wilkie's stories began to meet with as many rejections as acceptances.

Wilkie was, as the proprietors candidly admitted, too highbrow for their readers. *Heart and Science*, his passionate anti-vivisection thesis-novel, was not a success in the provincial papers, and one after another they turned down the offer of his next book. '. . . For our purposes his stories are too high-class', wrote the *Western Daily Mercury*. A 'far inferior tale' was more telling – and cheaper. It was folly, from their point of view, to spend the extra money.[26]

Wilkie was being attacked by the literary critics for being out of touch with contemporary taste, and by the suppliers to the masses for being too literary. Widening literacy, far from creating a larger public for established writers, was beginning to open up a rift between 'serious' and 'popular' writing. Wilkie, who had always believed passionately that the two could and should be combined, found himself caught in the middle.

In spite of these disappointments he found Watt's help invaluable.

By dealing with such 'savages' as Tillotson, the proprietor of a chain of northern newspapers and agent for a number of others, Watt saved Wilkie time and annoyance, and ensured that, if his income did not rise in the first half of the decade, it did not actually fall. As always with Wilkie, the business association soon became a friendship. Watt, who called regularly at Gloucester Place to discuss Wilkie's literary affairs, was let into the open secret of his double family, and Wilkie confided in him about personal as well as literary matters. 'It is high time we left off "Mistering" each other,' Wilkie wrote, thanking Watt warmly for the gift of a stick cut from Walter Scott's own plantation.[27]

Whether the demands from the newspapers for more and more sensationalism, and the insistence of the reviewers on more and more naturalism, had any effect on what Wilkie actually wrote is hard to judge: the quality of his work in these years is extremely variable. In 1881 he was still, rather touchingly, waiting to write the second part of *The Fallen Leaves* until the cheapest edition of the 'First Series' had been circulated 'among a far wider circle of readers . . . You can hardly form an idea of the astonishment and indignation with which the character of "Simple Sally" has been received in certain prudish and prejudiced quarters. I am waiting (with some confidence, inspired by previous experience) for the Verdict of the People.'[28] The People were not encouraging.

The more familiar territory of the London literary establishment was being severely pruned by death and altered by changing fashion: younger writers were pushing their way to the front. Wilkie said he disliked most of their work, though it is not clear how much of it he read. 'We are living in a period of "decline and fall"', he considered.[29] He may have recognized that he was in danger of becoming an old fogey, for in *The Black Robe* (1881) it is a tiresome old woman who praises a novel for being 'A very remarkable work . . . in the present state of light literature in England – a novel that actually tells a story . . . [and] isn't written by a woman.'[30] Wilkie's championing of women, forceful and indignant while they were oppressed outcasts, did not extend to hailing their achievements when they began to take their places with men in the professions. He admired actresses, whose status continued to be ambiguous, but a short story he published in the United States in 1882, 'Fie! Fie! Or the Fair Physician', makes heavy-handed jokes at the expense of a woman doctor who falls in love with a patient and tries to break up his romance with another woman.[31] To his credit he included this story, never published in England, in a short list of works he did not wish to have republished after his death.

He continued to hail each novel he wrote as a new and exciting departure. *The Black Robe* was 'thought the best thing I have written for some time past'.[32] Once he had written *Heart and Science*, however, he thought that a great advance on *The Black Robe*: a new departure in character and humour.

Wilkie's irrepressible spirits kept him optimistic, though he was incensed at the £10,000 paid for *Endymion*, Disraeli's last novel, calling him 'the very worst novelist that has ever appeared in print'.[33] But *Jezebel's Daughter*, his own 1880 novel adapted from *The Red Vial*, was a miserably inadequate stopgap. Wilkie made an attempt to bring the old play up to date by incorporating a business*woman*, a widow who takes over when her husband dies and insists on employing women in the office, but it was hardly a daring innovation by then. The novel gave him more space than the play to explore the psychology of a madman cured by substituting kindness for restraint and harsh treatment, and these episodes are the best part of a poor book. It was the first of his novels to be syndicated by Tillotson, and the sensation elements – a madman cured by kindness, obscure poisons and antidotes unknown to science; a murdering woman whose only positive emotion is her love for her daughter; the dramatic revival of a supposed corpse in the 'dead house' at Frankfurt – suited Tillotson's market.

The Black Robe, his anti-Catholic, or more accurately anti-Jesuit, novel of 1881, was considerably better. The thesis – that the Jesuits, given half a chance, would infiltrate British life and convert the leading figures in the nation – was a popular one; the novel sold well, though few of the characters are memorable. The Machiavellian Father Benwell is a sketchy villain compared with Fosco, and the worldly, raddled mother of the heroine, Mrs Eyrecourt, is, in spite of Wilkie's withering opinion of the second half of *Dombey and Son*, a poor imitation of Ethel Dombey's mother Mrs Skewton. But the complexity of relationships between a wife, her husband and the young Jesuit who is trying to convert him, and the understated suggestion of the husband's repressed homosexual feelings, are well handled. The aural hallucinations of the husband, who feels terrible guilt at killing a man in a duel, are given the ambiguity of the uncanny happenings in *Armadale*. Wilkie showed, too, that he had not lost his interest in scientific research. A mad boy becomes sane when he contracts a physical illness with a high fever: a well-documented effect in cases of schizophrenia.

But *The Black Robe* contains too many 'vamp till ready' passages, designed to fill space rather than advance the narrative: an elderly habit of discursiveness was growing on him, more Trollopian than he realized. There are paragraphs on the deficiency of the modern novel; the mental incapacities of women, in particular to appreciate 'the hard brain-work of a man devoted to an absorbing intellectual pursuit'; the failure of the public to appreciate the extent of an author's ruthless self-criticism; the drawbacks of parliamentary democracy; and the compensations of family life: prosy stuff which would once have been used, with more wit, in Wilkie's journalism. Even with this padding, rather large print was needed to fill the obligatory three volumes. Nevertheless *The Black Robe* was successful with the readers of the *Sheffield Independent*, which serialized the novel in England, and with those of *Frank Leslie's Magazine* in the States and the *Canadian Monthly*. Chatto sold the library edition satisfactorily, reprinting at least once in 1881, and the translations also sold well: Wilkie claimed it was as popular in Roman Catholic countries as in Protestant ones.

He finished the novel early in 1881, and Chatto published the three-volume edition in April. But Wilkie discovered he had made some legal errors, to do with the 'Statute of Mortmain' of 1729, which provided that land could not be given to the Church without royal licence. These had to be corrected for the later editions. Harried by such complications, his health deteriorated abruptly. A severe attack of 'rheumatic gout' left him so weak that his knees trembled on the stairs, though he still insisted on tottering along the sunny side of the street for exercise, rather than driving in a carriage. The attack lasted all summer: in September he could still only read or write for a minute or two at a time. He managed to write two lively short stories for *Belgravia*, did some work on arranging and rewriting a collection of his stories Chatto had asked for, and was already thinking about his next novel, *Heart and Science*, promised for publication in *Belgravia* the following summer, simultaneously with syndication in the provincial papers.

It proved to be one of the best and liveliest of his later novels. It was written out of personal indignation and enthusiasm, and Wilkie, in spite of a further attack of illness in early 1882, plunged into it with all his old energy. Sending Andrew Chatto the first six chapters in June, he wrote, 'My own vainglorious idea is that I have never written such a first number since "The Woman in White." '[34] He continued to compare it with his most famous novel, claiming that if, as a critic had said, *The Woman in White* was written in blood and vitriol, *Heart and Science* was written in 'blood and dynamite'.[35]

A famous case of 1882, in which David Ferrier, the Professor of Forensic Medicine at King's College, London, was charged under the Vivisection Act and acquitted, was probably the spark that ignited him. As usual, he did his homework. He read Ferrier himself on brain disease, and corresponded with Frances Power Cobbe, who headed the anti-vivisection movement. He found himself having to tone down the material she supplied. 'I shall leave the detestable cruelties of the laboratory to be merely inferred', he told her, 'and, in tracing the moral influence of those cruelties on the nature of the man who practises them, and the result as to his social relations with the persons about him, I shall be careful to present him . . . as a man *not* infinitely wicked and cruel, and to show the efforts made by his better instincts to resist the inevitable hardening of the heart . . . produced by the deliberately merciless occupations of his life.'[36]

The sinister Dr Benjulia's better instincts are shown chiefly in his relationship with a little girl, Zo (short for Zoe). She is one of the best child-portraits in Wilkie's work, and her name at once reveals her central place in the story. Zo is a ten-year-old dyslexic, bright but hopeless at lessons. She is despised by her fashionably intellectual mother and her superior elder sister Maria, who is 'one of the successful new products of the age . . . – the conventionally-charming child (who has never been smacked); possessed of the large round eyes that we see in pictures, and the sweet manners and perfect principles that we read of in books . . . alas, poor wretch! she had never wetted her shoes or dirtied her face since the day she was born.'[37] Tottie and Hetty Dawson were the approximate ages of Maria and Zoe when Wilkie began the book. Perhaps he was signalling his affection for his less clever and less good-looking younger daughter: if Hetty was as much fun to be with as Zo, she was clearly a child after Wilkie's own heart. The only person who appreciates Zo is her father, 'a little, rosy, elderly gentleman, with a round face, a sweet smile, and a curly grey head'.[38] The irrepressible Zo, singled out for praise by Swinburne, is both original and totally believable. In the following passage she describes her friend Donald, a Highland piper:

> 'He takes snuff out of a cow's horn. He shovels it up his fat nose with a spoon, like this. His nose wags. He says, "Try my sneeshin." Sneeshin's Scotch for snuff. He boos till he's nearly double when uncle Northlake speaks to him. Boos is Scotch for bows. He skirls on the pipes – skirls means screeches. When you first hear him, he'll make your stomach ache. You'll get used to that – and you'll find you like him. He wears a purse and a petticoat; he never had a pair of trousers on in his life; there's no pride about him. Say you're my friend and he'll let you smack his legs –'
>
> Here, Ovid was obliged to bring the biography of Donald to a close. Carmina's enjoyment of Zo was becoming too keen for her strength; her bursts of laughter grew louder and louder – the wholesome limit of excitement was being rapidly passed. 'Tell us about your cousins,' he said, by way of effecting a diversion.
>
> 'The big ones?' Zo asked.
>
> 'No; the little ones, like you.'
>
> 'Nice girls – they play at everything I tell 'em. Jolly boys – when they knock a girl down, they pick her up again, and clean her.' (*Heart and Science*, p. 333)

As Wilkie suggested, *Heart and Science* does have some similarities, mostly superficial, with *The Woman in White*. The plot involves a helpless girl, Carmina, and an attempt to deprive her of her inheritance. (Probably to counteract accusations of anti-Catholic bias, raised after *The Black Robe*, Carmina is a Catholic, and half-Italian.) Though Carmina's identity is not taken from her, she is so brutally treated that she suffers a serious nervous illness, a 'complicated hysterical disturbance' with 'simulated paralysis', and loses her memory for a while. The young man who is in love with her is absent for a crucial period, coming back to save her in the nick of time. There is a bizarre and brilliant villain, the vivisectionist Dr Benjulia. He is less convincing than Fosco, but cast in the same mould. The ugly and strong-minded governess, Miss Minerva, shares some of the functions of Marian Halcombe with the heroine's Italian nurse, Theresa. Miss Minerva begins promisingly, as a study in jealousy, in whom instincts of humanity and self-interest fight a fierce war: once she gains control of her feelings, however, she fades into insignificance. The feeble ineffectiveness of Mr Fairlie is shared out between a trio of weak men: a doctor, a lawyer and the husband of the villainess.

Swinburne's dismissal of the didactic message of *Heart and Science* as a 'childish and harmless onslaught on scientific research attempted if not achieved by the simple-minded and innocent author' needs some qualification.[39] By using brain disease as his example, Wilkie strengthened his case against vivisection as not only cruel but scientifically useless. The cure for Carmina's hysterical catalepsy is found not in Dr Benjulia's sinister laboratory but by observation and the comparison with other case histories. The explanations Wilkie gives may be scientifically naïve, but his conclusion was correct. The secrets of mental processes were not being unlocked in the laboratory, but in the observations of Charcot and his followers. Freud published his first paper on hysteria in 1888, the year before Wilkie died. Wilkie's adviser Frances Power Cobbe, as well as being in the forefront of the anti-vivisection movement, was also well informed on the latest research into mental process: a review-article by her on 'Unconscious Cerebration' appeared in *Macmillan's Magazine* as early as 1870.[40]

The writing of *Heart and Science*, Wilkie told William Winter, 'so mercilessly excited me that I went on writing week after week without a day's interval of rest'.[41] A visit to Ramsgate, intended to be a break from work, did him no good at all: he was writing his book in his head all the while. He paid the expected price in exhaustion and threatened gout when he finished in January; in April, a month before the novel was published, he wrote confidentially to Sebastian Schlesinger that he also had angina. His anxiety that *Heart and Science* should be a success – he cared more about it than about any novel for years past, he told Andrew Chatto – was to be disappointed, as far as sales were concerned. Wilkie received the moderate sum of £600 for the first edition from Chatto. In America a piracy issued at 20c. stopped Harper from publishing the book; the pirate graciously sent Wilkie £40. In England the reviews were mostly positive and friendly; some were enthusiastic.

Heart and Science might be counted a reasonable success. *Rank and Riches*, produced at the Adelphi on 9 June 1882, was an unmitigated disaster. It was not for want of effort: there are at least three versions of the manuscript, variously titled, in existence, and Wilkie wrote and rewrote with as much care as usual.[42] He took enormous trouble with the casting of the play, engaging an Australian actress, Miss Lingard, who had taken London by storm in a production of *La Dame aux Camélias*, to play the heroine. George Alexander was her leading man, and the stage manager, G. W. Anson, played an Italian vet or 'bird-doctor'.

Both Wilkie and the producer, Edgar Bruce, were confident of success. Bruce told Charles Hawtrey several times that Wilkie had never had a failure with a play.[43] On the first night Wilkie, less nervous than usual, stood at the back of the dress circle next to Arthur Pinero, a large camellia in his buttonhole, perhaps in compliment to Miss Lingard's previous triumph. He was clearly expecting to take a curtain-call with her at the end of the play. Instead there was a near-riot. The audience found the complicated plot impossible to follow (as it is virtually impossible to summarize). The *Saturday Review* called it a 'curious compound of improbability and commonplace'. Action and dialogue seemed ludicrous, characters capricious to the point of insanity. One character – the heroine's maid – is intended to be revealed as mad, but, in the opinion of the *Saturday Review* critic, 'the author has made a somewhat invidious distinction'.[44] The actors' voices were drowned by catcalls and laughter, Miss Lingard was reduced to tears, and eventually Anson, in a fury, addressed the audience directly at the end of the third act, attacking them for their want of courtesy to the work of 'a great master' and to the actors, in particular Miss Lingard. When the howls became even louder, he shook his fist at the audience, and shouted that they were 'a lot of damned cads'. British audiences never forgave him: Anson emigrated and ended his acting career in Australia.

Wilkie, more deeply and publicly humiliated than he had ever been – even the reception of *The Red Vial* was not as bad as this – quickly had the play taken off. Though not the last play he wrote, it was the last ever to be produced. Offering it for publication, he insisted that *Rank and Riches* was not a failure. He felt that he and the cast had been 'brutally treated by persons interested in opposing the return of an original writer to the theatre . . . I offer my play to speak for itself. I will submit to be judged by my own work – provided it be read by critics who have *not* attempted to write novels, and failed – and who have no pecuniary interest in importing their own stage-work (with or without acknowledgement) from France.'[45]

The play was never published, and there is no evidence that there was any basis for his paranoia. It is difficult to see, in retrospect, how anyone can have thought *Rank and Riches* (which instantly became known as 'Rant and Rubbish') was worth staging. Yet Wilkie read the piece on three separate occasions to theatrical experts, all of whom predicted success. Whatever Wilkie's intentions in this extraordinarily convoluted melodrama, they singularly failed to take effect. The *Athenaeum* reviewer put the failure down to over-elaboration, 'sufficiently hazardous in ordinary fiction . . . impossible in drama'.[46] But a reading of the play is almost as bewildering as seeing it must have been. Hidden somewhere in it there seems to be an appeal for a more democratic structuring of society, and greater freedom of action for women. One has to dig hard to disinter any coherent intention at all.*

Wilkie's inventive powers seem, in his last years, not to have dwindled in an orderly and comprehensible, if distressing fashion, but to have flashed on and off like the North Foreland light. No one who had read *Heart and Science* can have felt that his ability to create

* According to the *Times* obituarist, *Rank and Riches* 'succeeded well in America'; I have found no evidence that it was ever produced there.

incident and handle plot had disappeared; yet the evidence of *Rank and Riches*, taken on its own, would suggest a sharp deterioration, which illness alone cannot account for. He complained from time to time of being 'stupefied' by gout; it was more likely the remedies (especially laudanum) that stupefied him. Most of the time he was as sharp and as enthusiastic as ever. 'Don't tell anybody,' he confided to Carrie a month after the *Rank and Riches* débâcle, 'I *am quite mad* over my new book. It is at the present writing half-a-dozen books, with four or five hundred characters – and full of immoral situations.'[47]

By the time *I Say No* was published, he had reduced it to manageable proportions, in spite of the usual bouts of illness. 'Gout and work and age . . . try to persuade me to lay down my pen, after each new book – but, well or ill, I go on'.[48] Even with only one eye functioning, he remained hard at work, 'living in a new world of my own', only taking breaks for rest and sleep. He even refused to write an obituary of Charles Reade, which would have taken precious working time, or still more precious hours of rest. There was no one left to read it that he cared about, perhaps. He was cheered at the end of the year by the news that his novels were to be translated into Bengali by an Indian novelist, beginning with *The Woman in White*.

I Say No, not wanted by the newspaper syndicates, was written as a commission for Kelly's, the publisher, among other things, of the Post Office Directories. Wilkie and Watt had the usual trouble over payment, over getting proofs in time to send them overseas, and over Mr Kelly's transfer of the story, without notice, from a magazine called *Time* to another called *London Society*. 'If we live to get rid of the Kellys', Wilkie promised Watt, 'we will celebrate that happy day, here, with a bottle of champagne.'[49] Kelly finally paid out a total of £900, and Wilkie was paid a further £500 for the Chatto three-volume edition, £100 less than for *Heart and Science*.

I Say No is a mystery story, with no message beyond a practical warning that it is best to tell children the truth about their parents. The heroine, an orphaned girl, gradually unravels the secret of her father's death, in spite of 'the immovable obstacles set in her way by her sex and her age . . . the most helpless hopeless creature on the wide surface of the earth – a girl self-devoted to the task of a man'.[50] Those who love her all try to keep the truth from her: that he was apparently murdered, found with his throat cut. It eventually comes out that his death was suicide, not murder. As one reviewer wrote, the revelation is 'a very ridiculous mouse creeping timid and ashamed from one of the innumerable crannies of the labouring mountain'.[51] The suicide was in love with a fallen woman who refused to marry him. 'Have I any right to love? Could I disgrace an honourable man by allowing him to marry me?' she cries, in chorus with all the unfortunates of Wilkie's later novels.[52]

Again, the American pirates swooped, publishing a serial edition which appeared only one day after the instalments in *Harper's*. Wilkie suspected that there was a rogue among the British printers who was sending proofs to an accomplice, but nothing could be proved. When the Society of Authors was founded that year by Walter Besant, with its first objective 'The maintenance, definition, and defence of Literary Property', Wilkie was an enthusiastic founder-member. He readily agreed to be a vice-president, and in spite of illness he attended the society's annual dinners, and was a steward at one held in July 1888 to entertain American writers in England. Edmund Yates encountered him there, 'very bent, and gnarled and gnome-like . . . dreadfully crippled . . . but in fair spirits, and anxious for me to point out such celebrities as had risen since his time'.[53] At last, as Dickens, Reade and Wilkie had always wished, the profession was banding together to protect itself. It was too late for Dickens and Reade, and almost too late for Wilkie.

TWENTY-THREE

The Final Years

(1885–1889)

Though Wilkie continued to work as hard as ever, he was perceptibly failing. The painful and increasingly frequent attacks of angina which clawed at his chest seemed worse when he was at rest than when he was working. He had what he called 'neuralgia', some of it certainly ascribable to the heart condition. The 'rheumatic gout' attacked his eyes as often as his joints; he suffered from bronchitis in wet weather, weakness in hot weather, 'nervous exhaustion' when he stopped work. He vividly described his state after finishing a book in a letter to Nina Lehmann:

> Fidgets, aching legs, gloom, vile tempers, neuralgic trouble in the chest . . . 'The Guilty River' (I am so glad you like it) has I am afraid had something to do with the sort of constitutional collapse which I have endeavoured to describe. You know well what a fool I am – or shall I put it mildly and say how indiscreet? For the last week, while I was finishing the story, I worked for twelve hours a day – and galloped along without feeling it, like the old post-horses, while I was hot. Do you remember how the forelegs of those post-horses quivered, and how their heads drooped, when they came to the journey's end? That's me, Padrona – that's me.[1]

He loathed the quinine and colchicum he took for gout, and the amyl nitrite, which relieved the pain of angina, but also had unpleasant side effects. In his interludes of reasonable health he could enjoy very dry champagne, but too often he was forbidden all the food and drink he liked best, and confined to weak brandy and water and bread soaked in gravy. The latest of his gadgets was a patent French machine for making strong meat jelly, with which Caroline also supplied their invalid friends.* His eating habits became ever more eccentric: sometimes he would eat cold soup and champagne in the middle of the night. In letter after letter he regretfully refuses invitations to lunch and dinner.

He continued to enjoy the idea of food and drink, even when he was forbidden his favourite things. He wrote with appreciation to Pigott's nephew Henry, who kept him supplied with country produce, about his asparagus – the small green kind was the only kind worth eating, cold, with salad oil.[2] He told Pigott, 'There is some damnable perversity in me that won't *feel* old, after years of ill-health. I have not even learnt to be discreet.'[3] He sent his rules for health to his old friend Holman Hunt, also ailing: as much fresh air as possible, light and nourishing food, the wine that agrees with you, and no dwelling on work during the night.[4] He continued to smoke, in moderation, finding that tobacco helped to soothe his irritable nerves when he had an attack of gout.

Even the medicines Wilkie was prescribed sometimes seemed to spark off new ideas: 'My heart has been running down like a clock that is out of repair. For the last fortnight the doctor has been winding me up again . . . I have been (medically) intoxicated with sal volatile and spirits of chloroform; the result has been a *new* idea of a ghost story. I am hard at work, frightening myself, and trying to frighten the British reader.'[5] Though Beard insisted he should not see visitors when the attacks were severe, he was always making exceptions for friends. He used his illnesses as an excuse when it suited him, and described himself as a 'hermit' when refusing invitations; but he would still make enormous efforts to see old friends, such as the Lehmanns, and also new ones, of whom there were a great many in spite of his carefully nurtured reputation as a recluse.

They included several actresses. Ada Cavendish remained a great

* Probably a 'digester', a primitive form of pressure cooker.

favourite. Wilkie wrote to tell William Seaver his 'nice little "New Magdalen"' was coming to New York: '... if you *can* do her a kindness, don't forget that it is another kindness shown to *me*'.[6] Others were Fanny Davenport, Lillian Neilson, Blanche Roosevelt, who dedicated a book to him in 1887, and the amazingly beautiful American actress Mary Anderson. He met her in 1883 when she was twenty-four and became devoted to her. More remarkable for her looks than her histrionic ability, she inspired Mrs Humphry Ward's first novel, *Miss Bretherton*, based on her career, and a play by Oscar Wilde, *The Duchess of Padua*, written as a starring vehicle for her in 1883. To his chagrin she turned it down. She also asked Wilkie to write a play for her. He never found a suitable subject, but they continued to see each other. Looking at photographs of her, it is not hard to see why she had the effect she did on Wilkie. When she was playing Juliet he wrote to her, a year before his death:

> Mr Terris, dear Mary Anderson, is not Romeo. I am Romeo – because I am in sympathy with you ... When may I climb the area railings, with my umbrella in one hand and my guitar in the other, and hope to see Juliet in the balcony (well wrapped up)?[7]

She responded to his affectionate banter, encouraging him to tell stories of his life and friendships, taking as gospel his frequent heightening of the facts. She once praised one of his books: '"Ah" he answered, "I am only an old fellow who has a liking for story-telling, nothing more."'[8]

In 1886 Pigott asked him to advise Lillie Langtry on her career, and Wilkie responded with enthusiasm. He went to see her play Margaret in *Enemies* and congratulated her on her performance. Later he called on her, and reported to Pigott:

> The one obstacle in her way – with such intelligence and such resolution as she possesses – is ... the want of a master in the art to act with her. Coghlan does his best – but *he* can teach her nothing – and who *can*, in the present state of the stage? I took Caroline and Carrie to my box. They had never seen or read 'The Lady of Lyons' – were breathlessly interested in the piece ... but did not know that 'Claude

> Melnotte' was speaking blank verse, in the great love scene of the 2nd act!!!*[9]

He was also asked to advise the young Rosa Kenney, and consider her for his play *The Evil Genius*. Rosa was the daughter of his friend Charles Kenney, and the granddaughter of James Kenney, the author of *Raising the Wind*, in which Wilkie made one of his first stage appearances, forty years earlier. Wilkie was kind but honest about the deficiencies in her acting. 'It seemed to me that you were still under the influence of a system of Dramatic instruction which has directed your efforts a little *too* exclusively to the artifices and conventions of the stage,' he told her.[10] But he was no believer in amateurism on the stage. He had been a supporter of a proposal, in 1882, to set up a School of Dramatic Art. The expressionless acting of the young Charles Hawtrey in the death scene in *La Dame aux Camélias* prompted him to send a message backstage: 'For God's sake tell the boy with the wooden face to turn his back to the audience!'[11]

Wilkie Collins never settled into old age, though his crippled body made him look twenty years older than he really was. 'Who could suppose he was ten years younger than I?' said Frank Beard, seeing him walk painfully away down Wigmore Street, bent double and leaning on a heavy stick.[12] He was desperately overworked, still responsible for the support of two women, and three children at the most expensive stage of their education. Yet his face remained unlined, and he still had an extraordinary inner vitality. It showed itself in his letters, his conversation, his ability to strike up friendships with much younger men, and in the many relationships with women. These are more fully documented by the women themselves in his later years, because, even with a reputation such as Wilkie's, they could now be assumed to be platonic.

One of the strangest relationships of his life began in 1885 and lasted until the year before his death. The man who had so obstinately refused to be tied down by marriage started to play marriage-games with, of all people, a twelve-year-old girl, Anne le Poer Wynne, known

* Charles F. Coghlan, who acted chiefly in romantic comedy, had played Claude Melnotte in a revival of *The Lady of Lyons* with Ellen Terry in 1875.

as 'Nannie'. She was the posthumous only child of a promising member of the Indian Civil Service who died of cholera at the age of thirty-five. She and her widowed mother lived in Delamere Gardens, in the area now called Little Venice. They probably met Wilkie through Frank Beard, who was their doctor too. Wilkie's friendship with Nannie was conducted partly at luncheons and afternoon visits at Gloucester Place and Mrs Wynne's house, more often by correspondence.

Wilkie wrote to her regularly, once or twice a month, over a period of four years. His first letter is dated 12 May 1885. By 5 November he was addressing her as 'Dear and admirable Mrs. Collins', and the joke that they are married is carried on and elaborated throughout the rest of the correspondence, with references to their children and to Wilkie's jealousy of her other admirers. They exchanged photographs – Wilkie disliked Nannie's, thinking none of them did her justice; she sent him flowers and Christmas cards; and he wrote a story, 'The Ghost's Touch', with a little girl in it, which he told her was written for her.

There is nothing in the letters to suggest that Wilkie had suddenly become a paedophile. He had always found women – adult women – irresistible, and pursued them in a straightforward and uninhibited way. While he was writing his letters to 'dearest Mrs. Wilkie' he was also writing ecstatic praise to the photographer Baron Sarony, of his drawings of nude women:

> In your artistic handling of the Nude there is now more firmness, more knowledge, more power . . . Wonderful, and I add, sympathetic man. For I too think the back view of a finely-formed woman the loveliest view – and her hips the most precious parts of that view. The line of beauty in those quarters enchants me, when it is not overladen by fat.[13]

This long and enthusiastic letter, which goes into considerable detail about the delights of the mature female figure, ends 'Ever yours (in the Blessed Bands of Bohemia)'.

Though Wilkie did suggest to Nannie Wynne, sweltering in the heat of Monaco, that she might do well to adopt 'the costume of a late Queen of the Sandwich Islands – a hat and feathers and nothing else', the tone of the letters to her is not at all suggestive.[14] The innocence of the relationship was carefully guarded. Wilkie also wrote to Mrs Wynne, who was fully aware of the game he was playing with her daughter, and he seems never to have seen Nannie except in the presence of her mother. The sixty-one-year-old Wilkie seemed, to those who did not know him well, a gentle, decrepit old bachelor. I would guess that Mrs Wynne took at face value the description of Caroline as the housekeeper at Gloucester Place, and had no knowledge of the other household in Taunton Place. Wilkie wrote to her that he was at work at his desk, 'living in a "family circle" of my own creating', as though he had none in the real world.[15] The meetings with Nannie were always pre-arranged, always with reference to her mother. As for the marriage joke, the child, with the directness that delighted him in the young, probably asked Wilkie why he wasn't married and was offered the vacant post.

Wilkie was undoubtedly extremely fond of Nannie. He wrote to her as 'his dearest little wife', 'darling', 'Mia sposa adorata'. We, in our more anxious sexual climate, may wonder about his underlying feelings. But Nannie was no Rose la Touche. Wilkie never put any burden of responsibility for his happiness and well-being on her, though he wrote without reservation about his state of health and temper and his worries about his writing, as he would have done to an adult. Nannie's need for a father who would make a fuss of her was being met; if Mrs Wynne regretted that Wilkie chose to make his approach uxorious rather than paternal, she had the good sense not to make any objection that might have disturbed the child.

Many of Wilkie's lifelong preoccupations come through in his letters to Nannie, which are written with the unconventionality that marks the best of his letters to adults. 'Mrs. Wilkie Collins', she is told:

> if this weather goes on . . . you will be a *widow*. I don't object to your marrying again, but when you order your mourning cap I have to request that you will shorten those long floating streamers . . . I don't like a widow who expresses grief by long streamers and by tight-lacing . . .
>
> On Sunday . . . I have arranged to pass the day in bed – the agravation [*sic*] of the church bells being unendurable to me in any other than a

> horizontal position . . . I am steeped in devilish drugs – arsenic among them. Never, in all your experience of me, has my temper been so vile as it is now. Je reste, Madame, votre atroce epoux, Vilkie. P.S. How are the children?[16]

In another letter, he asked Nannie's advice. Everyone tells him he should take care of himself if he wants to get well.

> My misfortune is that I don't know how to take care of myself. I should like to hear . . . whether *you* have ever been in the habit of taking care of yourself, and (if yes) how you did it, and whether after all you found it worth your while? I am – as I take it – not more than fifty two (or three) years older than you are – and your example would therefore be of the utmost value to your faithful Old Man.[17]

In other letters the fantasies proliferate. They will end in the workhouse: '. . . we have a very nice workhouse in this neighbourhood and we will dine there. The gruel is said to be strong, and the master won't be hard on us when we are set to breaking stones if we do it badly.'[18] The nitro-glycerine he is prescribed for his heart condition is linked to a Guy Fawkes party she has been to: 'To know that I burnt beautifully without popping is a great consolation to me . . . As yet . . . we are keeping the Nitro-Glycerine in reserve. When I *am* blown up, rely on my bursting in your direction – just at lesson-time.'[19] Nannie asks him if he has written a story about a murder in a hansom-cab (she seems to have had advance knowledge of Fergus Hume's *The Mystery of a Hansom Cab*, eventually to outsell even *The Woman in White*). Wilkie disclaims the story but adds, 'But if one of your young men (of whom I am jealous) should get murdered in the cab, I shall be interested in hearing of it.'[20]

We may be certain that Nannie Wynne, on her lunch- and tea-time visits to Gloucester Place, was not introduced to Marian, Harriet and Charley Dawson. As Wilkie Collins' children grew up, they had to come to terms with their double identity. At Taunton Place they were Dawsons, and their intermittently present father was William Dawson, a barrister-at-law. As the Post Office Directory listed several William Dawsons, one of whom was a barrister, there must have been some awkward explanations at times, and rumours of their true parentage probably haunted their lives at school and outside it. At Gloucester

Place they were the illegitimate children of the famous author Wilkie Collins, and as such had to be hidden from anyone who did not know of Wilkie's family arrangements.

Sometimes his children would stay with Wilkie and Caroline in Ramsgate. 'Nobody with us but little Charley', he wrote to Pigott, inviting him to stay for a day or two.[21] He gave Carrie's six-year-old daughter Doris Bartley a more detailed account of Charley's adventures, in a letter typical of his unsentimental approach to children:

> He rowed in a boat in the harbour – and he went to a place called Sandwich on a tricycle – and he eat good dinners – and he enjoyed himself very much. We came home yesterday – and a man ran after our omnibus all the way from the railway station to this house. He was poor, and he wanted to get a little money by carrying our luggage upstairs, and he did it very well, being a strong young man. He was pleased when I paid him, and I think he went away and got some beer.[22]

Carrie and her husband often came too with their children, staying a couple of doors away. 'The children are in and out a dozen times a day', Wilkie told Frank Beard.[23]

Sometimes he would undergo a swift sea-change, becoming 'William Dawson' at Wellington Crescent, a short walk away on the other side of the bay. He wrote many letters from Nelson Crescent; only one survives from Wellington Crescent. But he may have spent quite as much time at one address as at the other, though only his closest friends knew of the alias and the second address. *The Fallen Leaves* opens with the unmasking of a secret of this kind, at Ramsgate. Wilkie wrote to Sebastian Schlesinger, in the last year of his life:

> Wilkie Collins, of 82 Wimpole Street has disappeared from this mortal sphere of action, and is replaced by
>
> William Dawson,
27 Wellington Crescent,
Ramsgate
>
> In plain English, I am here with my 'morganatic family' – and must travel (like the Royal Personages) under an alias – or not be admitted into this respectable house now occupied by my children and their mother. So – if there is any more news from America – address W. Dawson Esq. for the next fortnight.[24]

The risk of discovery in a small town like Ramsgate is obvious. For Wilkie was not merely a casual summer visitor: he often stayed out of season, and he came regularly to the same address for nearly twenty years. He continued his writing there. He was well known to the boat hirers and sailors; his friends joined him for trips along the coast. It was all characteristically open and shameless, quite unlike Dickens' 'disappearances'. Any investigative journalist could have unmasked him in a moment.

The children may have considered it a game while they were small. As they grew up their involvement in his double identity and the prevarication it entailed became a source of shame and embarrassment, particularly to the girls. (Charley, who was only fourteen when his father died, was less affected.) On the one hand they were known, and known as Wilkie's, not only to Carrie and her husband and daughters, but also to Wilkie's closest circle of friends. His daughters were given tickets by Holman Hunt to an exhibition of his paintings; Wilkie wrote of them frequently in his letters; they were encouraged to treat Gloucester Place as a second home. But they also had 'no name' and were 'nobody's children'. Marian, aged eleven, was at Gloucester Place on census night 1881, and was listed in the return as 'Marian Collins', not Marian Dawson. Her father was originally listed as 'unmarried'; this has been crossed out and 'widower' substituted, presumably by a bewildered or tactful enumerator.[25]

Yet Wilkie loved his children dearly. He postponed a holiday in order to be in London for Hetty's fourteenth birthday.[26] He took care to give them a good education that would equip them, the girls as well as the boy, to make their own way in the world. The girls were sent to one of the excellent new schools for girls, the preparatory department of the Maria Grey Teacher Training College. The principal, Agnes Ward, was the sister-in-law of the best-selling author and pioneer of female education, Mrs Humphry Ward.[27] At the beginning of the century Harriet Geddes had earned her living as an inadequately trained and much-exploited teacher; at its end, her granddaughters were being better equipped, in case they remained single, to fend for themselves. Even if they did marry, Wilkie was determined they should remain independent. A clause in his will stipulated that anything left to any female named in it 'shall be In Trust for her sole and separate use free and independently of any husband to whom she may be married at the time of my death or shall thereafter marry'.[28] But his good intentions were not enough to prevent Carrie from being financially exploited by her solicitor husband. And his own children, for all his loving care, bore the burden of a double identity, a secret they had to carry all their lives. They did not inherit his fascination with the double, and they hid their parentage to the end. Neither Marian nor Harriet ever married, and they never admitted their relationship to the famous author. When they died in 1955, within three months of each other, their death certificates recorded them as the daughters of '— Dawson, Occupation unknown'.[29]

Wilkie never expressed any regrets over his children's illegitimacy. As the law stood then, a deathbed marriage would not have altered their status – indeed it might have disinherited them, as happens to the Vanstone daughters in *No Name*. It would also have upset the equilibrium he had so carefully engineered between Caroline and Martha. But it seems a failure of imagination in the author of *No Name* not to see that, society being as it was, the effect on them was bound to be traumatic.

During the first year of his friendship with Nannie Wynne and her mother, Wilkie was writing *The Evil Genius*, a novel with a purpose often referred to in his letters to them. He does not say so directly, but the lively little girl Kitty in that novel, with her closely observed conversation and affectionate behaviour to her governess, suggests that Nannie's letters and chatter have contributed to the character. 'I am only fit to sulk in my chair – and smoke – and wish I was *you* with a lovely velvet dress, and a broad sash, and a charming governess to teach me', he told her, exhausted from writing the last chapters of the novel.[30]

The Evil Genius was bought by Tillotson, who paid £1,000 for the newspaper-syndication rights, more than Wilkie had received for previous novels. But Tillotson complained that Wilkie was giving short measure: 'Of the quality of the Story, I must express myself highly satisfied; but the interest created by the admirable – shall I say hysterical – divisions will only heighten the reader's aggravation of what he will justly term the scant supply.'[31] Wilkie reacted first with fury to the complaints of 'that impudent little cad', and then evasion, sending on Tillotson's frequent letters unopened to Watt. 'I am a hunted man', he wrote from Ramsgate. 'I look at the boatmen here, eternally idling with their hands in their pockets, with feelings of ferocious envy.'[32] There was trouble, too, over the title. There was confusion with another novel, *Her Evil Genius*; Wilkie found there was no way to stop this 'theft'.

The central idea of *The Evil Genius* – a couple who divorce and finally remarry – came to Wilkie while he was cruising off the Kent coast. The friends he was with were struck by the novelty of it, he told a woman who wrote to him complaining gently that she had written a novel with the same theme, published earlier.[33] It seems obvious enough now. Two women, a charming governess and the equally attractive wife she supplants, are in conflict over the same man, in spite of their liking for one another. The topical and scandalous theme, the rights and wrongs of divorce, is unconventionally handled, and Wilkie managed the difficult feat of maintaining sympathy for both the injured wife and the governess, abused and abandoned as a child by her brutal mother. The child Kitty, who loves them both and nearly dies of grief when she is parted from her governess, is the catalyst, and it is the women, from Kitty to her tiresome old grandmother Mrs Presty, who matter. The men, as so often in Wilkie's novels, come off badly. The weak husband, torn between two women, and the rigid captain, who cannot bring himself to accept the woman he loves when he finds that she is divorced, are less sympathetic and less interesting.

A long interpolation, added to the manuscript as an afterthought, gives what seem to be Wilkie's own opinions, based on his own experiences, in the mouth of a character seen throughout the book as balanced and moderate:

> 'Where there is absolute cruelty, or where there is deliberate desertion, on the husband's part, I see the use and the reason for Divorce. If the unhappy woman can find an honourable man who will offer her a home, Law and Society which are responsible for the institution of

> marriage, are bound to allow the woman outraged under the shelter of their institution, to marry again. But where the husband's fault is sexual frailty, I say the English law is right in refusing divorce on that ground alone, and the Scotch law wrong in granting it . . . Why are the lives of a father a mother and a child to be wrecked, when those lives might be saved by the exercise of the first of the Christian virtues – forgiveness of injuries.'[34]

The situation of *The Evil Genius* also owed something to the early experience of his old friend Frances Elliot. The difficulty for a mother of gaining custody of her own child, even when she was the innocent party; the cold-shouldering of a divorced woman, and even of her child; the need to take refuge abroad: Frances Elliot had experienced them all after the collapse of her first marriage. Like the wife in the novel, she lived in Scotland throughout her first marriage, and resumed her maiden name, calling herself 'Mrs. Dickinson' after the separation. Her daughters experienced the struggle for possession of them by their parents, the bewilderment of a new name, and the final disappearance of their father.

Wilkie wrote *The Evil Genius* simultaneously as a play and a novel, nearly killing himself with the double load. 'It *is* a good play "though I say it that shouldn't",' he told Watt.[35] The play is lively and intelligent, in some ways better than the novel, and infinitely better than *Rank and Riches*, but it was never produced. One bogus 'performance' was given, to secure copyright. Watt opened negotiations with Carl Rosa which dragged on for nearly a year. Wilkie was not surprised when Rosa finally turned it down: it had already been refused by three managements in the States. The subject of divorce was still a tricky one, and managements were wary of his plays after the *Rank and Riches* débâcle.

In 1886 Wilkie wrote a 'one shilling novel' in great haste, for a Bristol publisher, Arrowsmith, issued in cheap and flimsy paper covers. He had great problems while he was writing this 133-page story; though he worked twelve hours a day, the first half had to be printed before he had written the second, to save time. He later said it was 'spoiled for want of room'; certainly the conclusion is hurried and unconvincing.[36] *The Guilty River* sold very badly: Arrowsmith printed a large edition and complained to Watt after Wilkie's death that he still had twenty-five thousand copies left on his hands.[37] But it begins well, with a carefully researched study of a deaf man, which fascinated and absorbed him. This tragic figure, who has 'the most beautiful face that I had ever seen', was given Wilkie's dead brother's auburn hair and deep blue eyes. In his depression and monomania there was also something of Charley's character.

The story is self-revelatory. It has a strange, dreamlike atmosphere, as though Wilkie, in reverie, is summing up much about himself. The narrator falls in love with and finally marries a simple country girl who, in her courage and forthrightness as well as her dark good looks, seems to be modelled on Martha Rudd. He is half intrigued, half repelled by the deaf man, who becomes his *doppelgänger* and rival. Though the deaf man is pale-complexioned, he is, like Ozias Midwinter in *Armadale*, the grandchild of slaves from the southern States of America – another of Wilkie's dark twins. He also has an ancestral history of crime and cruelty in his father's family, which he struggles to escape.

The deaf man has no name: he calls himself 'The Lodger' or 'The Cur'. He retreats from action into art, perhaps as Wilkie felt he did in writing his 'missionary' novels. He knows that he should interfere when he sees a carter beating his horse, but instead makes a drawing of the incident: '. . . this representation of what I ought to have done, relieved my mind as if I had actually done it. I looked at the pre-eminent figure of myself, and felt good'. He moves from drawing to writing, becomes obsessed with reading French trials, and then with constructing mystery stories. 'I cannot remember having read any novel with a tenth part of the interest that absorbed me, in constructing my imaginary train of circumstances . . . I felt as if the murder I was relating had been a crime committed by myself.' So far the story develops promisingly, but when he moves back from art to action, making a complicated attempt to poison his rival, foiled by the girl, the story descends into crude sensationalism and loses its force. A weak and confused ending compounds the disappointment.

That Christmas A. P. Watt sent Wilkie a novel by a newly fashionable writer. Wilkie, as he frankly confessed to Watt, was not hopeful that Rider Haggard's *King Solomon's Mines* would live up to its excellent reviews. But, as he wrote a fortnight later:

> To my wonder and delight the book seized me at once . . . I found myself reading the work of a man, possessing imagination, invention, sense of dramatic effect, respect for truth to nature, and – in an inferior degree as yet – an eye for character. Here I find room for improvement in Mr. Haggard . . .

Wilkie's one reservation was that Allan Quartermaine, an 'uncultivated elephant hunter', often uses language that is unsuitably literary and eloquent: 'Mr. Haggard's poetical feeling, and Mr. Haggard's skilled handling of English pouring miraculously from Mr. Quartermaine's pen'.[38] Watt continued to send him Haggard's novels as they appeared, and Wilkie read them and kept them on his shelves, but he thought *She* inferior to *King Solomon's Mines*: '. . . it has not got the movement in the story and the variety of situations . . . And I doubt the effect on the stupid reader (a most important person, unhappily, to please) of the lady who is 2000 years old.'[39]

In 1886–87 *Macmillan's Magazine* serialized Thomas Hardy's *The Woodlanders*, and Henry James' *The Reverberator*. Wilkie read and admired *Macmillan's*, and told Watt he would be prepared to take lower terms to be published in it. (He never succeeded.) But he never mentions Hardy or James by name in his letters, though he disliked 'the new American school of fiction' which he thought was responsible for the increasing difficulty in placing his stories in American magazines.[40] His view of 'the art of fiction' was closer to Besant's than to James'. When Watt sent him Stevenson's *Kidnapped*, also published in 1886, Wilkie liked the first half of the story, but thought, '"The Flight in the Heather" is prolonged to the utmost limits of (my) human endurance . . .'[41] He returned Mrs Oliphant's *Chronicles of Carlingford* to Watt with excuses for keeping them so long, but without comment: 'I found them this morning buried under heaps of other books' – obviously unread. At Andrew Chatto's instigation he did read *Little Lord Fauntleroy*: 'I wonder whether Mrs Burnett knows that she has given to her charming little boy the name of the last man hanged for forgery in England?'[42] Mostly he avoided new fiction, preferring to reread his beloved Scott, and wishing *Redgauntlet* was three times as long. 'What a set of pigmies we are, by comparison with Scott!' he wrote, recalling that *Guy Mannering* was written in six weeks.

Wilkie was now outside the main current of literary life, the cross-fertilization of the Dickens days long behind him. Invited to write an article on 'Books Necessary for a Liberal Education', he confessed, 'I pick up the literature that happens to fall in my way, and live upon it as well as I can . . . I have never got any good out of a book unless the book interested me in the first instance . . .'[43] His favourite authors remained those of his youth, Scott and Byron. 'I am so completely out of the "literary world" ', he joked to Chatto, 'that I have only the other day . . . seen your announcement of "Marino Faliero", a tragedy by Lord Byron [crossed through] – I beg your pardon – by Mr. Swinburne. When do you publish "Marmion", "Prometheus Unbound" and "The Ancient Mariner" by the same author?'[44]

Wilkie's new friends were minor figures. Harry Quilter, the editor of the *Universal Review*, was, according to Oscar Wilde, 'the apostle of the middle-classes . . . [who] raises literature to the position of upholstery, and puts thought on a level with the anti-macassar!'.[45] The novelist Hall Caine, a literary groupie who had already attached himself to Rossetti, wrote melodramatic stories, best-sellers in their time but soon outmoded. Wilkie was now grateful for the admiration of these younger men, in particular for Harry Quilter's enthusiastic endorsements of his work. Quilter pestered him for an article for the *Universal Review*, and Wilkie at last responded with the amusing, elderly, 'Reminiscences of a Story-Teller', defending himself for the last time against the Grundys and Podsnaps. 'In the thousands of pages that I have written, I never remember to have asked myself: Will this passage be favourably received if the prying eyes of prudery discover my book?'[46] But he found himself old-fashioned enough to gasp and stretch his eyes when Watt sent him a copy of the magazine *Good Words*, published by his brother-in-law Strahan: ' "Good Words" staggered me . . . A frontispiece illustration represents two gentlemen in top boots, talking – and under it is this extract from the book . . . "*I want her, and I mean to have her.*" And this is a virtuous publication! What can I write that will be vicious enough for "Good Words"?'[47]

The political world as well as the literary one had moved on without him. The violent turmoil of the 1880s was throwing up a working-class movement very different from the romantic Christian socialism of *The New Magdalen* and *The Fallen Leaves*. Henry James, newly settled in London, saw that England was 'heaving . . . cracking and fermenting'.[48] The return of a Tory government in 1886 increased Fenian terrorism, reflected in Wilkie's last, unfinished novel; there was unrest everywhere among the unemployed and destitute. There were riots in London: shop-fronts were smashed and traffic brought to a standstill. In 1887, the year of the Queen's golden jubilee, Wilkie wrote to his American friend William Winter, 'Has anybody told you that "the Jubilee" was an outburst of loyalty? I tell you that it was an outburst of Fear and Cant. In my neighbourhood, there was a report that we should have our windows broken if we did not illuminate.' Wilkie recalled his childhood, and the Reform Bill mobs of 1832, and illuminated, 'on a cheap scale which accurately represented the shabby nature of my loyalty'.[49] The working classes were no more loyal than he was; they had other reasons for smashing windows. The violence culminated in 'Bloody Sunday', 13 November 1887, when a demonstration in Trafalgar Square was met by a 1,500-strong police force, backed up by the army, after which, in the usual British way, things subsided rather than developing into revolution.

Wilkie spent most of 1887 on the humdrum task of revising his unpublished short stories for a three-volume collection, *Little Novels*. He also wrote some new short stories and minor journalism, and planned the last novel that he completed, *The Legacy of Cain*. He was often unable to work at all, and to make matters worse he was unexpectedly faced with a complete disruption of his life.

Wilkie had lived for twenty years at 90 Gloucester Place. He had expected to die there. But his twenty-one-year lease was about to run out, and he discovered that his landlord, the 'enormously rich Lord Portman', was demanding an outrageous sum to renew it. He solemnly vowed never to take another house, and looked around for a flat where he and Caroline could live in more modest comfort. Finding nothing he liked in the immediate neighbourhood, he finally settled for the upper floors of 82 Wimpole Street, round the corner from his doctor, Frank Beard. He would have, he told Mrs Wynne, 'the whole place to myself excepting only the dining rooms'.[50]

He insisted that the Wimpole Street house was a much better one than Gloucester Place, as well as being cheaper. It was a good deal further from Taunton Place, and though his children came to visit him he must, in his invalid state, have seen less of Martha. The upheaval of moving, keeping his writing going and struggling with illness were almost too much for him. Even his bath was taken away, to be set up in the new house, with a new cistern and pipes. He skulked in his dressing-room: 'I have got two chairs and a table – and a desk and pen and ink – and cigars and brandy and water – and plenty of physic – and that is all.'[51] He described the chaos to Harry Quilter:

82 Wimpole Street
11 April 1888

'If you please, sir, I don't think the looking-glass will fit in above the book-case in this house.' 'Your father's lovely little picture can't go above the chimney-piece. The heat will spoil it.' 'Take down the picture in the next room, and try it there.' 'But that is the portrait of your grandmother.' 'Damn my grandmother.' 'If the side-board is put in the front dining-room, we don't know where the cabinets are to go.' 'I am sorry to trouble you, but I miss three books out of the library catalogue – Forster's Life of Goldsmith, and Lamb's Essays and Leigh Hunt's Essays. Do you think they have been stolen?' 'Here is the man, sir, with the patterns of wall-paper.' 'What on earth is to be done with the Story of Cupid and Psyche – ten big photographs and no place to hang them in.' 'How will you have your bed put? against the side of the wall, or standing out from the wall?' 'I say, Wilkie! When you told Marian and Harriet that they might help to put the books in their places, did you know that Faublas and Casanova's Memoirs were left out on the drawing-room table?' 'I beg your pardon, sir, did I understand that you wanted a lamp in the water-closet?' 'Do take some notice of the cat, he's fond of you, and the workmen are frightening him out of his senses.' 'When will you see Mr. Bartley about the dilapidations at Gloucester Place?' 'Dear Sir, we are sorry to notice irregularity in the supply of copy lately . . . We must not keep the colonial newspapers waiting for their proofs.'[52]

This letter summarizes much about Wilkie in his last years. The conflicting demands of work and domesticity are alleviated by the support of his family (Caroline, Marian and Hettie are all present in the scene, as well as his servants and the workmen). It is a picture of a busy, loving bourgeois family, bothered by the upheaval but not overwhelmed by it, and all determined to rally round Papa. In its concern for, even delight in, domestic detail, it is extraordinarily reminiscent of William Collins. In its insistence on the uncensored pictures hung on the walls and books left on the drawing-room table, it is all Wilkie. (He was delighted to hear in 1887 that a famous trotting stallion in the United States had been named 'Wilkie Collins'. 'A printed pamphlet . . . records his virtues, and says "Wilkie Collins covers mares at $75 each"!!!'[53])

By sheer persistence, Wilkie had combined the best aspects of his secure childhood with an unconventional family structure, and forced the world to accept him as he was. He was now wrapped in a protective cocoon of female concern. Caroline had developed many of the traits of her implacable opponent, Harriet Collins. When a present of game from Sebastian Schlesinger went missing, Wilkie promised to make enquiries at the railway station 'not by means of a man, who may be trifled with – but by means of a woman who is *not* to be trifled with – who will insist and persevere – and take advantage of the "privilege of her sex" and bother the authorities till they will wish they had never been born'.[54] His fussiness about the exact arrangements for his comfort was unashamed. A wallpaper in the dining-room had to be replaced because 'it inflames my eyes every time I look at it'; but the alternatives presented 'every variety of hideous ugliness'.[55]

He was to have eighteen happy months at Wimpole Street, his '*elastic* nature' reasserting itself. Feeling he might never write another novel, he dedicated *The Legacy of Cain* to Carrie, very formally using her respectable married name, 'Mrs Henry Powell Bartley'. 'Permit me to add your name to my name, in publishing this novel', he wrote, acknowledging her help over the past twenty years.

Carrie was totally uncritical in her adoration of Wilkie and everything he wrote, or she might have preferred a better novel. Wilkie thought well of it, and was only afraid that he might have 'aimed over the heads of the present generation of novel-readers'.[56] Wilkie the missionary is once more in the ascendant, in a story designed to explode the theory of hereditary wickedness, and show that the nature/nurture debate is more complicated than it was thought to be. Two girls are brought up together from infancy, as sisters. But one is adopted, the daughter of a murderess. The reader is expected to swallow the absurd idea that though one of the girls is two years older than the other, they do not themselves know which is the elder, and consequently which one is adopted. Nor, until half-way through, does the reader, who may nevertheless suspect that it is the daughter of the Nonconformist clergyman, not the daughter of the murderess, who is going to the bad. She ends as an American feminist. In his last years Wilkie could imagine nothing worse. One of his last letters to Andrew Chatto complained of 'a German *Female* Doctor' who wanted to translate *Heart and Science*: 'I felt inclined to . . . tell her to "go to hell". But even when a woman is a doctor, she is a woman still.'[57]

In spite of Wilkie's running battles with Tillotson, *The Legacy of Cain* was sold to him, and though Wilkie was sometimes, very uncharacteristically, behindhand with copy, Tillotson was eventually pleased with the book. But his former good relations with Harper had by this time collapsed. The trouble with the pirates slashed Harper's profits, and Wilkie's new novels were in any case no longer so saleable in America.

There was no prospect that he might be able to take things easily: it did not come naturally to him to do so, even now. As he wrote his last, unfinished, book, he was enthusiastically thinking of another. 'I have got a really admirable idea', he told Watt in March 1889. 'It is another "Moonstone" – and yet as different . . . as one book can well be to another. But the regular application to carrying out my invention is what I cannot do'.[58]

Death nearly caught up with him at the end of 1887, when he was going for his usual walk and suddenly found himself unable to breathe, and only just able to stagger home. He had to push himself to the labour of writing even a short article: 'I must spur the jaded horse – and the horse doesn't like it'.[59] When Carrie's youngest daughter died, only a few months old, in the spring of 1888, Wilkie was distressed, but honest. Though he wrote Carrie a loving letter, he was incapable of the conventional pieties she expected. 'With my way of thinking, I cannot honestly suggest copies of "religious consolation". And no *man*, let him feel for you as he may – (and I have felt for you with all my heart) – is capable of understanding what a woman must suffer who is tried as you have been tried. The fate of that poor little child – after making such a gallant fight for its life – is something that I must not trust myself to write about.'[60]

TWENTY-FOUR

The Journey's End

(1889)

Rather to his surprise, Wilkie was still alive to celebrate his sixty-fifth birthday on 8 January 1889. Ten days later he survived a potentially serious accident. As he was coming home in a four-wheeler from a dinner with Sebastian Schlesinger on 19 January, there was a collision as the cab turned from Wilton Place into Knightsbridge. He gave a graphic account to Watt:

> Smashed glass flying all over me – the cab tipping over – and I flying out of the uppermost door like a young man of 20. Not a morsel of the glass touched my face or my hands – and I landed on the pavement without a bruise. But next day's work went badly.[1]

An attack of bronchitis followed, triggered by the winter fogs, and his ills were complicated by biliousness, neuralgia and a tooth abscess, eased by a mouthful of laudanum. He had to ask for an extension of time for his new novel, due to begin serialization in the *Illustrated London News*.

Wilkie had prepared the groundwork of the novel with his usual care. It was originally two stories, which he eventually amalgamated. The draft of the first, called 'Iris', reuses some episodes from *Rank and Riches*. It is the love story of a woman who remains infatuated with a scoundrel who treats her appallingly. Mostly in Wilkie's own handwriting, the manuscript shows signs of forced and weary labour.

As usual, there are innumerable alterations, additions and deletions. A note in Wilkie's hand on Carrie's fair copy states that it has been given up as unsatisfactory. Another note dated '1st August /88' is a reminder that the draft should be destroyed 'when it has served as hints for the "The Lord Harry" '.[2] 'The Lord Harry' is the draft of the second story, based on '*such* a true story – confided to me alone – and with the material in it for a grand book'.[3] A friend, Horace Pym, had told him of an insurance fraud perpetrated in Germany. A dying man, bearing a sufficient likeness to the perpetrator of the fraud, was substituted for him so that he could collect on a large life-insurance policy. Though the outline of the story had been in the newspapers, only Wilkie had been told the details. It was a story of doubling bound to appeal to him.

Wilkie added murder to the fraud, injected a topical touch by making Lord Harry a Fenian conspirator, and added a love story, emphasized by choosing *Blind Love* as his final title.[4] Lord Harry (the name was a colloquial euphemism for the Devil) is volatile, manic-depressive and amoral, throwing himself into politics, love and crime with equal recklessness. Both self-destructive and murderous, he is one of the better male characters in Wilkie's later fiction. The maid, Fanny Mere, taken on by Iris in spite of having 'fallen', is the other point of interest in the story. Like the 'hybrid' housemaid once part of Wilkie's household, she is 'one of the whitest of fair female human beings'. She is introduced by a description which shows that Wilkie's fascination with certain aspects of women's appearance had not changed since the creation of Marian Halcombe:

> Slim and well balanced, firmly and neatly made, she interested men who met her by accident (and sometimes even women), if they happened to be walking behind her. When they quickened their steps, and, passing on, looked back at her face, they lost all interest in Fanny from that moment.[5]

The two women, maid and mistress, become close friends, more sisters than employer and employee.

By the time serialization began in June, enough instalments were written to take Wilkie through to October. The rest of the novel was 'set forth in careful outline' in a black hard-cover notebook, with a label identifying it in Wilkie's own, now very shaky handwriting. He carefully noted in his diary the dates on which the instalments were due to be serialized, and the dates on which he posted proofs to the *Illustrated London News*.

After a wet and foggy winter and spring, the early summer was hot and humid: Wilkie was driven out of London to the sea breezes of Ramsgate. He was back by 21 June, when he noted on his manuscript that 'the story, so far, has been written for press to the end of Part 18'. He seemed well on the way to the successful completion of another novel. Nine days later, on Sunday 30 June, he had a stroke. His left side was paralysed, and at first it seemed his mind might be affected. Beard came, and stayed the night. Carrie, at once summoned by her mother, wrote to Watt, 'He is light headed at times, and does not know how ill he is.'[6] Wilkie, agitated by anxiety over his work, was 'hyper-excited': Mary Braddon wrote comfortingly that 'silence and apathy' would be far more alarming, and so it proved.[7] Though Wilkie remained gravely ill, the agitation passed off to some extent and the paralysis improved. There was a crisis on 4 August, when Wilkie seemed to be dying, and neither ate nor drank anything for twenty-six hours, but he rallied the following day. By the middle of August the entries in his diary, made by Caroline during the worst of his illness, are again in his own hand: he touchingly notes when 'Keates' (Caroline) breakfasts with him. Carrie felt sanguine enough about his condition to take her children to Brighton, Marian taking her place as Wilkie's letter writer. There was still a hired nurse in the house, to help Caroline look after him, but on 3 September he was well enough to write to Fred Lehmann himself.

> Sleep is my cure [the doctor] says – and he is really hopeful of me. Don't notice the blots – my dressing-gown sleeve is too large – but my hand is still steady. Goodbye for the present dear old friend – we may really hope for healthier days.
>
> My grateful love to the dearest and best of Padronas.[8]

It was clear, though, that he would never be well enough to continue his work. He thought about asking Hall Caine to finish the book for him, but decided that he was not up to the job. Carrie, who didn't care for Caine, told Watt of Wilkie's 'cruel qualifications as to his capabilities'.[9] Instead Wilkie asked Watt to enquire whether Walter Besant, whose ideas on fiction were close to his own and who had taken up so vigorously the defence of the rights of authors, would do it for him. Besant undertook to do so, and made a workmanlike, if uninspired job of it. He was amazed to discover how detailed Wilkie's notes for the rest of the novel were. Not only was the plot clearly laid out, and incidents sketched in, but fragments of dialogue were inserted at key moments. 'I was much struck', Besant wrote, 'with the writer's perception of the vast importance of dialogue in making the reader seize the scene.'*[10]

Many friends and acquaintances came to call, and were listed by Caroline in the diary. Most left without seeing him – he was too weak to bear much company. Among those admitted was George Redford, an old friend from the *Leader* days, who used to play his cello at George Eliot's musical evenings. Redford was touched to discover that the dying man was still so much his old self, physically weak and wasted but mentally alert. 'He said as he grasped my hand with all his old warmth "you see I'm all right – feel my arm" – but I had hard work to hide my eyes lest he should see what I really dreaded.'[11] Wilkie smoked little in his last years, but on this occasion he asked Caroline to bring the cigar-box, and he and Redford had a last smoke together. On 26 August he dictated a letter to Marian, thanking Watt for arranging for Besant to take over the serial. He wrote cheerfully, 'My good friends encourage me to get better, and the doctor is content with my progress'. At the beginning of September he sounded optimistic in an account of himself to Sebastian Schlesinger: 'Here is my report declaring myself with my own hand on the way to recovery . . . I am well looked after. Two good nurses the Doctor who is curing me – and my two daughters to see it and help. I want you to see my children – *why* you will easily guess.' But he ended the letter 'Goodbye old friend'.[12] He was more realistic in his last illness than his father had been.

Two weeks later he was dying. A further attack of bronchitis, so

* Besant did alter the final sentence of the novel. Wilkie's manuscript reads, 'Blind love to the last! How like a woman!' The published version has, 'Blind Love doth never wholly die.'

severe that he could not lie in bed but sat up in an armchair by the fire, wrapped in blankets, clearly signalled the end. Harried by the well-meaning nurse, he pencilled a note to Frank Beard, faint and almost indecipherable: 'I am *dying*, old friend'. And on a separate scrap of paper, 'I am too wretched to write. They are driving me mad by forbidding the [ ]*. Come for God's sake.'[13]

Beard came at once. Wilkie sank slowly, and without pain, lasting until the morning of Monday, 23 September, when Caroline wrote in his diary, 'Wilkie died at 10 a.m.' She and Beard were with him. One obituary suggests that his children may have been called in time.[14] Whether Caroline summoned Martha, as Queen Alexandra called Alice Keppel to the deathbed of Edward VII, we cannot tell. After his death Caroline was treated as the widow and received the letters of condolence, Carrie as an adopted daughter. Martha remained silent and invisible.

Wilkie's will had stipulated a simple funeral, that should not cost more than £25. It seems he would have preferred cremation: there are several references to the Cremation Society in the letters of his last years. But he bought a burial plot at Kensal Green, perhaps because Caroline wished it, and wanted to be buried with him, as she eventually was. In *The Fallen Leaves*, the novel dedicated to her, the hero wants to be cremated, but the girl he saves from the streets begs that they may both be buried near each other.

Like Dickens and Thackeray, Wilkie hated the elaborate paraphernalia of Victorian mourning rituals: he ordered that there were to be no funeral scarves, hatbands or feathers. On the wet Friday morning after his death a small funeral procession – a hearse, covered with flowers instead of a pall, and three carriages – left Wimpole Street at eleven-thirty for Kensal Green Cemetery. A small crowd gathered in the street outside; a larger one was waiting at the cemetery. There were a few from the thinned ranks of his oldest friends round the grave. His cousin Jane Ward, Holman Hunt, Pigott and George Redford went back to his earliest days. From the Dickens years there

* The first letter of this word is clearly 'h', the second probably 'y'. The remainder is indecipherable. Wilkie had been taking hypophosphates. 'Hypodermic' is another possibility, or the powerful sedative hyoscine.

were Edmund Yates, Charles Dickens Junior and Frank Beard. The representatives of his 'family' consisted of Caroline, Carrie and her husband. They could be discreetly described as his housekeeper, his solicitor and his solicitor's wife; Martha and the children were represented only by a wreath. The theatrical days produced many friends: Ada Cavendish was there, Arthur Pinero, who had seen him last at the disastrous first night of *Rank and Riches*, and Squire Bancroft. So was Sebastian Schlesinger, who first met Wilkie in the United States. Wilkie's business associates, Andrew Chatto and A.P. Watt, who were also good friends, naturally attended, as did the young disciples, among them Hall Caine; Edmund Gosse represented the Society of Authors. Those who did not come sent wreaths. Mamie Dickens sent two: one on her own behalf, another, of red geraniums, 'From Mamie Dickens in Memory of Charles Dickens' – an oddly ambiguous way of phrasing it.

But beyond the mourners there was an outer circle. A press report was indignant.

> There must have been at least a hundred of those unwholesome creatures who call themselves women, who seem to live in graveyards. When the coffin had been lowered into the bricked grave there was a general rush of these people who craned over into space, and clawed the wreaths of flowers, and pulled about the cards . . . and laughed and cried and chattered until they were moved on by the graveyard police.[15]

These representatives of his longed-for unknown public might have seemed less offensive to Wilkie than they did to the outraged mourners. Their tears and laughter were more likely to have been for the writer than the man, and the inscription he chose for his memorial, 'Author of *The Woman in White* and other works of fiction' – forbidding anything to be added to it – acknowledged where he felt the final significance of his life to lie. He wanted no religious or sentimental effusions, no mention of heaven or family. When the grave was opened again in 1895, for Caroline's coffin, no word was added to mark it as her resting place.

Not that he was in any way secretive. Wilkie's will was entirely open, so open that Henry Bartley pointed out to A. P. Watt the caution needed in explaining it to the editor of the *Illustrated London News*: 'he will at once see what is unhealthy and undesirable to publish'.[16] It was also scrupulously even-handed. After minor bequests to his servants, to Jane Ward and his mother's sisters, he divided his estate between Caroline and Carrie, and Martha and his children, whom he took care to acknowledge. His copyrights were left in trust to his executors, to manage for their benefit, and he made careful arrangements for the valuation and sale of his books, pictures and manuscripts.[17]

Wilkie's estate turned out to be worth less than expected, being sworn at £10,831. 11s. 3d. The earlier depredations of Henry Bartley (who wrote to A. P. Watt the day after Wilkie died demanding, as executor, immediate payment of the money due for *Blind Love*), may have had some effect. Nor was his literary property to produce much for his heirs. 'I cannot . . . conceal from you', the son of his old friend Baron Tauchnitz wrote to Watt in October 1889, 'that the sale of his latest novels remained extraordinarily behind that of his former ones and that it was chiefly out of regard for our long personal friendly relations that we did not propose to himself to lessen the price.'[18]

The coinage of his reputation was also debased. Harry Quilter started an energetic campaign to raise a subscription for a memorial to Wilkie, in Westminster Abbey or St Paul's. Meredith and Hardy were on the committee, but the *Daily Telegraph* denounced the idea in a leader, and less than £400 was subscribed. The Dean and Chapter of St Paul's refused, on grounds of morality as well as literary merit, to allow any memorial to be erected. Wilkie would have had no interest in such a memorial, but he might have been ironically amused at the different treatment accorded to himself and to Dickens, now virtually canonized as a secular saint. Hardy was astonished and angry at the news, but the general public was indifferent. The money was finally used to create a 'Wilkie Collins Memorial Library of Fiction' at the People's Palace in the East End, later Queen Mary's College. It was an outcome Wilkie himself would surely have approved.

His immediate memorial was in the recollections of those who loved him, his family and friends. Many of them wrote of him, all with affection and gratitude for his friendship. 'And so our poor dear genial delightful *matchless* old Wilkie is gone,' Nina Lehmann wrote to her son Rudie. 'Wilkie was almost the very last link left that bound us to the glory of departed days . . . it seems like a former life, not on this earth at all.'[19]

The friends who valued the man would have been surprised, perhaps, to know that his books are once more being taken seriously. Though his novels continued to sell steadily after his death – the 6d. edition of *The Woman in White* was said to have sold three hundred thousand copies – much of his work seemed old-fashioned and unimportant. For many years afterwards he was known chiefly as the author of *The Moonstone* and *The Woman in White* (in that order), a supreme spinner of ingenious plots, the father of the detective story. A hundred years later the novels have an added value: they give us access to the oddity and passion that lay beneath the surface of Victorian life. These glimpses into the secret places of his time, revealed by a man whose own refusal to conform was open and unashamed, are as strange and fascinating as anything the age produced. There are greater Victorian writers; but none who is quite like Wilkie Collins.

APPENDIX A

Charles Collins' 'Secret Connection'

The Huntington Library possesses, in its Holman Hunt collection, a long letter from John Everett Millais to William Holman Hunt. The letter is undated, but internal evidence proves that it was written in the summer of 1856.[1] It contains a lengthy passage referring to the plight of an old friend of Millais and Hunt. The name of the friend has been overscored, presumably by Hunt, and was endorsed, in his handwriting, 'private and valuable letter illustrating J.M's rightmindedness'. At some time subsequently, '?Wilkie Collins' has been pencilled on the letter, not in Holman Hunt's hand. The relevant passage in Millais' letter reads:

> I had a long letter from [two words heavily overscored] the other day in answer to some advice I ventured to give him respecting a certain lady in his possession. I expressed an opinion once for all, which appeared to me clearly for his benefit, but he has the art of making faults nearly into virtues, and of quietly submitting to his indiscretion. I have known him so long that I did not hesitate to write on the subject, more particularly as I was certain I was advising him according to his best interests, and as his Mother, or Father (if he were alive) would have wished – But in writing I felt it hopeless, for the few words I had with him in London about this affair, admitted such complete consenting to the mistake that at the time I scarcely made an observation upon it. I see *nothing* to prevent him getting quit of this disreputable kind of secret connection, and finding a wife, except that his taste is so unhealthy that I am not sure that he wd. prefer the latter, in which case perhaps it had better stand as it does. I write to you about this, as you are the only person with whom I cd. speak, and I think you wd. have now the most influence over him – I am married now, & I am inclined to think from his manner at times, that he imagines I have in consequence a little degenerated. You will probably see more of him since I am away, and I think may greatly forward a separation

between him & this woman. Every day will make it more difficult, and will certainly accustom himself [*sic*] to the circumstances and to look upon it with less hope of escape – If a man requires a woman for a companion & for his pleasure, what in the name of fortune, is there to prevent his honourably living with one, lawfully, & in the sights of his fellow men, and why shd. this stupid fellow go and tie himself to such a woman? but there is little need for me to say this to you as you must clearly see the folly of such a liason [*sic*] as this of [one word overscored]. I know his answer to all you will say, 'that he is a blighted creature, & incapable of the effort of contracting marriage' &c &c but this is all bosh, and a kind of basking in melancholy reflection (there is a happy misery which is most dangerous) and this I fear will stop him taking steps towards a change of life altho' independently of the sin it will prove such an awful drag, & inconvenience. Anyhow I think you shd. *once seriously* advise him as you really regard it, with all the tolerance your notion of justice permits, as it is only a friendly action, and he may be thankful someday in having followed your counsel.

Sara S. Hodson, the Assistant Curator of Literary Manuscripts at the Huntington Library, kindly examined this letter for me. She writes:

I have examined the crossed-out name under the ultra-violet light, which is only of minimal help in deciphering the name. However, I do not believe the name is Wilkie Collins . . . The obliterated surname is probably Collins; I cannot be absolutely certain, but the length of the name, the number and position of the ascenders, the visible appearance of the initial letter, all are consistent with the name Collins. The first name, I am sure, is not Wilkie. The most telling evidence is in the last two letters of the name, which strongly look like 'ey' not 'ie'. The descender is unmistakable and matches other terminal 'y's' in Millais' hand. Also, the first letter is absolutely not a 'W'; rather, it is rounded and might therefore be a 'C' or an 'O'.

One possibility is that the obliterated name is Charles Collins and the reference might be to Charles Allston Collins . . . strictly from the graphology, it is quite possible that Charles Collins is the one referred to in the letter. My evidence comes from one other letter in the Huntington's collections, written from Millais to Charles Collins. This letter is addressed to 'My dear Charley'. This confirmed that Millais not only refers to Collins as Charley but also he spells it with the 'ey' ending rather than 'ie'. The salutation on this letter also shows resemblance to the obliterated first name in HH 389. This is not to say that I am absolutely certain that the name in question is Charley Collins, but I do feel it is a possibility with some strength.

The letter, therefore, referred to a man who was an old and close friend of both Millais and Holman Hunt, whose father was dead and whose mother was still alive. His Christian name began either with 'C' or 'O' and ended 'ey', and his surname was similar in outline and length to 'Collins'. I have been unable to identify anyone (other than Charles Allston Collins) who would satisfy all these criteria. It would have been typical of Charles Collins to consider himself a 'blighted creature, & incapable of the effort of contracting marriage'; the 'basking in melancholy reflection' and 'happy misery' also fit with everything that is known of his character.

A mysterious liaison of this kind might also account for the rumours of his alleged impotence when married to Kate Dickens. Charles Collins, who suffered intermittently from religious melancholia and was at all times inclined to feel a strong sense of sin, might well have found it impossible to have a physical relationship with a virtuous woman after his earlier escapade. Fred Lehmann, perhaps with some knowledge of this, thought he had been 'guilty of an infamy' in marrying Kate.

APPENDIX B

Wilkie Collins' Travelling Desk

Wilkie much admired Dickens' travelling desk, and had an exact copy made for himself by Messrs Fisher, 188 Strand. It is a sturdy box covered in black leather and brass-bound, with a brass carrying-handle and Bramah lock. It opens to form a writing slope, and there are various compartments for papers, ink, pens, etc. He took it with him whenever he travelled abroad, and it went to America with him in 1873.

The subsequent history of this box is closely bound up with the sad decline of his family after his death. It passed into Harriet Bartley's keeping – as 'the amanuensis' it seems appropriate that she should have had it. But in 1901 Carrie wrote to A. P. Watt explaining that she must now try to sell it.

> I grieve to tell you that we know what it is, to want for food, & seeing that Dickens' desk was worth money, I hoped I could sell dear Wilkie's. I know I could send it to Sotheby's – but I dont think Mr. Hodge would sell it for me. You may have heard, that I offered for sale 48 letters of Sir John Millais, which I found among my poor Mother's papers when she died & which she told me were *given* her by dear Wilkie. I did not read them – but sent them to Mr. Hodge & then I understood I had no right to them. You must please remember that I had no one to advise me that *I had no right* or I should have sent them at once to *you* – I did send you papers to which I saw I had no claim, didn't I? Well to spare your valuable time I must hurry. I want to sell dear Wilkie's dispatch-box, do you not think the Americans love his works & memory now more than the English. I am so poor, & know what it is to do without a meal & not only me but my little Iris [her youngest daughter, aged ten]. My 2 daughters have been out of engagements since January [Doris and Cecile Bartley were both on the stage] – and they are cruelly trying. I have to keep applying to Mr. Low for money 'in advance' of the legacy dear Wilkie

> left my mother & which I inherit – that is to say what Mr. Bartley left, after he had helped himself to the whole of it nearly – and so I should be so very very grateful, even for your advice.[1]

A. P. Watt bought the desk himself, paying Carrie £10 for it. He noted on another letter from her that she was 'greatly pleased'. Four years later she died, at the age of fifty-four.

Ten pounds may not sound much in these days of wildly inflated prices for memorabilia, but Watt was being generous. Twelve years after his death, Wilkie Collins' literary reputation was in decline, his books, apart from *The Woman in White* and *The Moonstone*, largely forgotten. Watt had always done his best for Wilkie in his last years, and as literary executor he remained a friend to the family, doing his best to sell Wilkie's literary property as and when he could. Wilkie would have been grateful for his kindness to Carrie.

APPENDIX C

Wilkie Collins' First, Unpublished Novel

The manuscript of Wilkie Collins' 'Tahitian' novel, written when he was twenty, was thought to have disappeared. But the complete holograph of 'Ioláni; or, Tahiti as it was. A Romance' has recently come on to the market in New York. Glenn Horowitz, a New York antiquarian bookseller, acquired the manuscript in October 1991. It has since been sold to a private collector. I am indebted to Mr. Horowitz for a description of the manuscript and information about its provenance.

The manuscript consists of 160 quarto pages, on laid paper watermarked '1844'. It is written in ink, with some pencil emendations, entirely in Collins' hand. It seems to be a fair copy. Though there are corrections and deletions throughout, these are fewer than he habitually made: 'Ioláni' is considerably tidier than the surviving manuscripts of his second and third novels, *Antonina* and *Basil.*

I have no doubt the manuscript of 'Ioláni' is genuine. The handwriting matches that of Wilkie Collins' early letters, and differs somewhat from his later hand. The provenance, too, is complete and convincing. The manuscript was first put on the market in 1899, when the library of Augustin Daly was sold after his death. Daly, a New York theatrical impresario, playwright and theatre proprietor, had, after their initial falling-out over an adaptation of *Man and Wife*, become a friend of Collins', and the 1873 production of *The New Magdalen* was put on at Daly's Broadway Theatre. It seems probable that Wilkie gave the manuscript of 'Ioláni' to Daly, who was well known as a collector of pictures, books, manuscripts and autograph letters. The manuscript was bought at the 1899 sale by George Smith, a young New York bookseller who later became well known among American rare book dealers and collectors. Smith sold the manuscript to a Philadelphia collector, Howard T. Goodwin, who had it splendidly bound by Pfister. It was sold again after Goodwin's death in 1903 to a Philadelphia lawyer, Joseph M. Fox, and remained with the Fox family until 1991.

Wilkie Collins seems to have been at work on his first novel during the last months of 1844, after his return from his holiday in France. As with *Antonina* he clearly did a good deal of background research, and this may have begun much earlier. The 1831 edition of the missionary William Ellis's *Polynesian Researches*, a detailed account in four volumes of the civilisations of the South Seas, was among the books in Collins' library sold at his death. Ellis dwells, with fascinated horror, on the practice of infanticide, which Collins uses as the mainspring of his plot. He also relied on Ellis for descriptions of the Tahitian landscape, instructions on pronunciation of the language and an account of the fanatical religious sect, the Areoi, that was responsible for the instigation of infanticide.

Another source seems to have been a narrative poem by Mary Russell Mitford, from which he borrowed the name of his heroine. *Christina, the Maid of the South Seas* (1811), tells the tale of the romance of the Bounty mutineer Fletcher Christian with a native woman, 'Iddeah', who is terrified of losing their baby to ritual sacrifice.

Though the setting, Tahiti before the coming of the Europeans, is even more exotic than that of *Antonina*, both the long-winded style and the violent plot are reminiscent of his second novel. Ioláni is a cruel and fanatical high priest who resembles the pagan high priest Ulpius. Idea, the persecuted woman who has borne his child and has to flee into hiding with the child and her loyal friend Aimata, lest her first-born be taken as a human sacrifice, has to hide from male persecution as Antonina does. She is also, though crude in conception, a forerunner of the many courageous and wronged women who recur throughout Collins' fiction.

The style of the novel betrays the author's youth and dependence on his reading. The opening is like that of a novel by G. P. R. James – or Thackeray's *Punch* parody of one – two lone figures in a landscape which is minutely and repetitiously described.

> The last days of summer were near at hand, as one night, (while Tahiti was yet undiscovered by the voyagers of the North) the desolation of the great

> lake Vahinia was brightened by the presence of two human beings – a man and woman – who were listlessly wandering along its rugged and deserted shores.
>
> It was a strange and, to most hearts, an unalluring place. Looking upward from the spot occupied on this particular occasion by the woman and her companion, the eye encountered a long and almost unbroken range of mountains, whose jagged sides, though occasionally checquered by a clump of dwarf trees, or a patch of parched, scanty verdure, were for the most part bare and precipitous in the extreme. ('Ioláni', p. 1)

Collins' interest in landscape is already apparent, but there is nothing of his later easiness of style and heart-stopping immediacy of impact. That began with *Basil*, his 'Story of Modern Life', eight years later, and was to be perfected in *The Woman in White*. But the discipline of constructing a full-length novel involving a combination of careful research with wild imaginative flights of fancy was a fitting beginning to the writing career of the king of inventors.

References

First references are given in full. The following abbreviations and short titles are used in subsequent references.

Names

Charles Allston Collins	C. A. Collins
Harriet Collins	H. Collins
Wilkie Collins	W.C.
William Collins	Wm Collins
Charles Dickens	C.D.

Manuscript Sources

Arents Collections, The New York Public Library, Astor, Lenox and Tilden Foundations	Arents
Armstrong Browning Library, Baylor University, Waco, Texas	Armstrong Browning
Henry W. & Albert A. Berg Collection, The New York Public Library, Astor, Lenox and Tilden Foundations	Berg
Bodleian Library, Oxford	Bodleian
British Library	BL
Dickens House Museum	DHM
Folger Shakespeare Library, Washington, DC	Folger
Humanities Research Center, University of Texas at Austin	HRC
Houghton Library, Harvard University	Houghton
Henry E. Huntington Library, San Marino, California	Huntington
University of Illinois at Urbana	Urbana
University of Iowa Libraries	Iowa
Mitchell Library, Glasgow	Mitchell
National Art Library, Forster Collection, Victoria & Albert Museum	V&A
Pierpont Morgan Library, New York	Morgan

Morris L. Parrish Collection, Princeton University	Parrish
Robert Taylor Collection, Princeton University	Taylor

Books

William M. Clarke, *The Secret Life of Wilkie Collins*	Clarke
Wilkie Collins, *Memoirs of the Life of William Collins Esq., R.A.*	*Memoirs*
The Letters of Charles Dickens, Vols. 1–3, ed. Walter Dexter	Nonesuch
The Letters of Charles Dickens, Vols. 1–6, ed. Madeline House, Graham Storey, Kathleen Tillotson and K. J. Fielding	Pilgrim
Wilkie Collins: the Critical Heritage, ed. Norman Page	Page
Kenneth Robinson, *Wilkie Collins*	Robinson

Periodicals

All the Year Round	*AYR*
Household Words	*HW*
Wilkie Collins Society Journal	*WCSJ*

Page references to Wilkie Collins' full-length works are to the first edition where a work is out of print. For works currently in print, the following editions are used, unless otherwise indicated.

Armadale: World's Classics, Oxford 1989, ed. Catherine Peters
Basil: World's Classics, Oxford 1990, ed. Dorothy Goldman
Blind Love: Dover Books, New York & London 1986
The Dead Secret: Dover Books, New York & London 1979
The Haunted Hotel: Dover Books, New York & London 1982
Heart and Science: Alan Sutton Pocket Classics, Gloucester 1990
Hide and Seek: Dover Books, New York & London 1981
Little Novels: Dover Books, New York & London 1977
Man and Wife: Dover Books, New York & London 1983
The Moonstone: World's Classics, Oxford 1982, ed. Anthea Trodd
No Name: World's Classics, Oxford 1986, ed. Virginia Blain
Rambles Beyond Railways: The Cornish Library, London 1982
A Rogue's Life: Alan Sutton Pocket Classics, Gloucester 1984
The Woman in White: World's Classics, Oxford 1984, ed. Harvey Peter Sucksmith

Chapter One: Families (1788–1822)

1. Percy Fitzgerald, *Memoirs of an Author*, London 1894, Vol. I, p. 86
2. Unidentified newspaper article, quoted in William M. Clarke, *The Secret Life of Wilkie Collins*, London 1988, p. 165

3. Thomas De Quincey, *Confessions of an English Opium-Eater*, Oxford 1985, p. 5
4. Nathaniel Beard, 'Some Recollections of Yesterday', *Temple Bar* 102 (July 1894), p. 320
5. Letter from Ann Procter to Nina Lehmann, 2.8.1870, quoted in N. P. Davis, *The Life of Wilkie Collins*, Urbana, Illinois, 1956, p. 266
6. TSs reminiscences of Mary Cunliffe, Armstrong Browning Library, Baylor University, Waco, Texas
7. MS in Harriet Collins' hand, dated 25.4.1853, with MS alterations and deletions in the hand of Wilkie Collins, Humanities Research Center, University of Texas at Austin. This MS, which has never been published or identified as by Harriet Collins, has been checked against other sources for the facts contained in it, wherever these exist
8. ALS to H. Collins, 1.10.1867, Pierpont Morgan Library, New York, MA3150 113
9. Army Lists. The statement in the DNB, repeated by Robinson and others, that Harriet Collins was the daughter of Andrew Geddes, ARA, is incorrect. Andrew Geddes, born in 1783, was only seven years older than Harriet
10. He published, among other things, a *Guide to Salisbury*, which went into twenty editions
11. *Gentleman's Magazine* 59 (July–Dec 1789), p. 954
12. Allan Cunningham, *Life of Sir David Wilkie*, London 1843, Vol. 2, p. 94
13. There was a new incumbent at Alderbury in 1811, the Rev. H. Stephens, who may have been Harriet's spiritual guide. In her narrative he is called 'Marsden'.
14. *The Selected Letters of Jane Austen*, ed. R. W. Chapman, Oxford 1986, p. 174
15. H. Collins' MS, HRC
16. Ibid.
17. Wilkie Collins, *Memoirs of the Life of William Collins Esq., R.A.*, London 1848, Vol. 1, p. 5
18. Ibid., p. 7
19. *The Slave Trade: A Poem* (no author given), London 1793
20. William Collins [Senior], *Memoirs of a Picture*, London 1805, Vol. 2, p. 74
21. Ibid., Vol. 1, pp. iv–v
22. *Memoirs*, Vol. 1, p. 97
23. Ibid., p. 8
24. Cunningham, op. cit., Vol. 2, p. 99
25. *Memoirs*, Vol. 1, p. 186
26. Thomas Gainsborough, 'Portrait of Miss Isabelle Bell Franks', *c.* 1775, Birmingham Art Gallery
27. Two MS notebooks, National Art Library, V&A
28. Thomas De Quincy, *Recollections of the Lakes and the Lake Poets*, London 1970, p. 403

29. Alfred J. Story, *Life of John Linnell*, London 1892, Vol. 1, p. 278
30. *Memoirs*, Vol. 1, p. 83
31. Quoted in Rupert Christiansen, *Romantic Affinities: Portraits from an Age 1780–1830*, London 1988, p. 187
32. W. Holman Hunt, *PreRaphaelitism and the PreRaphaelite Brotherhood*, London 1913, Vol. 1, p. 224
33. William Macready, *Reminiscences and Diaries*, ed. Frederick Pollock, London 1875, Vol. 2, p. 142
34. The family, called 'Archer' in the manuscript, may have been the Otters of Southsea, who were her lifelong friends
35. H. Collins' MS, p. 131, HRC
36. ALS Wm Collins to H. Collins, 27.3.1822, Morgan, MA3154 1
37. Now in the Clore Gallery, Tate Gallery, London
38. Cunningham, op. cit., Vol. 2, p. 94

Chapter Two: A Happy Family (1823–1835)

1. *Memoirs*, Vol. 1, p. 230
2. ALS to W.C. and C. A. Collins, 31.8.1832, in private hands
3. Beard, op. cit., p. 324
4. Obituary in the *Daily Telegraph*, 24.9.1889
5. AMS of *The Woman in White*, Morgan, MA 79
6. ALS to H. Collins, 11.3.[1867], Morgan, MA 3150 100
7. Beard, op. cit., p. 324
8. Nina Lehmann, *Familiar Letters 1864–1867*, privately printed 1892, p. 45
9. *Memoirs*, Vol. 1, p. 227
10. Ibid., pp. 235, 292
11. Ibid., p. 192
12. Ibid., p. 264
13. Ibid., p. 299
14. ALS to W. Phillips, 26.6.1874, Parrish Collection, University of Princeton Libraries
15. *Memoirs*, Vol. 1, p. 297
16. Ibid., p. 125
17. ALS to E. M. Ward, 3.8.1860, HRC
18. W. H. Hunt, op. cit., Vol. 1, p. 146
19. Quoted in E. D. H. Johnson, *Paintings of the British Social Scene: from Hogarth to Sickert*, London 1986, p. 179
20. William Winter, *Old Friends*, New York 1909, p. 214
21. Transcript at HRC
22. ALS Wm Collins to H. Collins, 28.9.1833, Morgan, MA 3154 37
23. An engraving of the painting appeared in *The Cabinet of Modern Art*, ed. Alaric Watts, London 1837. ALS H. Collins to Francis Collins, 13.9.1829, Morgan, MA 3156 2

24. ALS to William Winter, 30.7.1887, Parrish
25. ALSs Wm Collins to H. Collins, 17.10.1831, Morgan, MA3154 22
26. ALSs Wm Collins to H. Collins, 2.9.1828, 28.8.1835, Morgan, MA 3154 19, 43
27. ALS C. A. Collins to Wm Collins, [n.d.]1835, Morgan, MA3152 6
28. ALS Wm Collins to H. Collins, 29–30.8.1827, Morgan, MA3154 15
29. *Memoirs*, Vol. 2, p. 57
30. ALS Wm Collins to H. Collins, 15.9.1833, Morgan, MA3154 35
31. *Memoirs*, Vol. 1, pp. 274–75
32. ALS Wm Collins to H. Collins, 10.8.1841, Morgan, MA3154 52
33. H. Collins' MS journal, entries for 5 & 6.10.1837, V&A
34. Alfred J. Story, op. cit., Vol. 1, p. 287
35. *Memoirs*, Vol. 1, p. 209
36. ALSs Wm Collins to H. Collins, 20.9.1830, 11.8.1832, 2.9.1833, 28.9.1833, 24.8.1841, 17.9.1841, Morgan, MA3154 21, 23, 34, 54, 58
37. *Men and Women*, Vol. III, 36 (5.2.1887), p. 281
38. *Memoirs*, Vol. 1, p. 269
39. C. A. Collins, *The Eyewitness and his Evidence about Many Wonderful Things*, London 1860, p. 319
40. ALS to William Winter, 14.1.1883, Parrish
41. *Catalogue of the Library of the late Wilkie Collins, Esq.*, Puttick and Simpson, 1890
42. ALS Wm Collins to H. Collins, 23.8.1833, Morgan, MA 3154 33
43. *Memoirs*, Vol. 2, p. 33
44. ALSs, 23.9.1833, Morgan
45. *Memoirs*, Vol. 2, p. 34
46. Ibid., p. 33
47. Ibid., p. 38
48. Alfred J. Story, op. cit., Vol. 1, p. 282
49. H. Collins' MS journal, 8.1.1835, V&A
50. *The Lazy Tour of Two Idle Apprentices, Household Words* 16, p. 363
51. H. Collins' MS journal, 6–20.7.1835, V&A

Chapter Three: Educations (1839–1840)

1. 'Memorandum, relating to the life and writings of Wilkie Collins 1862', MS, HRC. Published *Bentley's Miscellany*, 21.3.1862
2. Beard, op. cit., p. 322
3. H. Collins' MS journal, 27.9.1836, V&A
4. Ibid., 25–30.9.1836
5. ALS H. Collins to Francis Collins, 13.9.1829, Morgan, MA3156 2
6. 'The Dead Lock in Italy', *AYR* 16 (8.12.1866), p. 511
7. ALS Berg Collection, New York Public Library, Charles Dickens to Georgina Hogarth, 25.11.1853, quoted Arthur Adrian, *Georgina Hogarth and the Dickens Circle*, Oxford 1957, p. 216

8. Ernst von Wolzogen, *Wilkie Collins: Ein Biographisch-Kritischer Versuch*, Leipzig 1885, p. 11
9. Some biographers have assumed that Wolzogen (who does not name the setting) and Dickens are referring to two separate episodes. This is possible, but seems to me unlikely
10. *No Name*, p. 200
11. James Dafforne, *The Life and Works of Edward Matthew Ward, RA*, London [1879], p. 9
12. H. Collins' MS journal, 31.3.1837, V&A
13. Henry Crabb Robinson, *On Books and their Writers*, ed. Edith Morley, London 1938, Vol. 2, p. 682
14. *Memoirs*, Vol. 2, p. 97
15. ALS Charles Russell to Wm Collins, 9.9.1836, Morgan
16. Letter to R. H. Dana, 17.6.1850, published in Robert L. Wolff, *Nineteenth Century Fiction, a Bibliographical Catalogue*, New York & London, 1981–86, Vol. I, p. 256
17. Clyde K. Hyder, 'Wilkie Collins in America', *Studies in English VI* 4, Lawrence, Kansas, 1940, p. 51
18. *Memoirs*, Vol. 2, pp. 106–7
19. H. Collins' MS journal, 29.6., 24.7., 25.7.1837., V&A
20. Ibid., 31.12.1837
21. *Memoirs*, Vol. 2, p. 121
22. Ibid., p. 131
23. Ibid., p. 127
24. Ibid., p. 148
25. ALS to William Winter, 3.9.1881, Berg
26. Edmund Yates, *Celebrities at Home*, 3rd series, London 1879, p. 146
27. 'Reminiscences of a Story-Teller', MS, HRC. Published (with some omissions) in *Universal Review*, 1888
28. L. B. Walford, *Memories of Victorian London*, London 1912, p. 62
29. Beard, op. cit., p. 325
30. Yates, op. cit., p. 146
31. ALS, 2.2.1887, Parrish
32. ALS, 18.9.39, Morgan, MA3150 3
33. Mary Cunliffe, TS reminiscences, Armstrong Browning; Walford, op. cit., p. 62
34. ALS to H. Collins, 6.12.1839, Morgan, MA3150 7
35. ALS to W. H. Hunt, 2.2.1861, Huntington, HH 100
36. Note in H. Collins' hand, 12.9.1840, V&A

Chapter Four: The Prison at the Strand (1841–1847)

1. ALS Wm Collins to Sir Robert Peel, 18.5.1842, BL adds., MS 40509 ff. 3–7
2. ALS Wm Collins to H. Collins, 9.6.1843, Morgan, MA31254 65
3. *Appleton's Journal of Popular Literature, Science and Art*, New York, 3.9.1870

4. ALS Wm Collins to H. Collins, 19.4.1844, Morgan, MA3154 73
5. *Hide and Seek*, p. 110
6. ALS Wm Collins to H. Collins, 13.9.1841, Morgan, MA 3154 57
7. ALS to Wm Collins, 24.8.1842, Morgan, MA 3155
8. ALS Wm Collins to H. Collins, 24.7.1841, Morgan, MA3154 50
9. ALS Wm Collins to H. Collins, [22.8.1841], Morgan, MA3154 53
10. ALS to H. Collins, 13.6.1842, in private hands
11. *Memoirs*, Vol. 2, pp. 215, 216, 221
12. *Appleton's Journal*, 3.9.1870
13. *Memoirs*, Vol. 2, p. 247
14. ALS Wm Collins to H. Collins, 20.5.1840, Morgan, MA3154 48
15. ALS Wm Collins to H. Collins, 7.1.1844, Morgan, MA3154 68
16. ALS to H. Collins, 13.1.1844, in private hands
17. ALS to H. Collins, 30.9.45, Morgan, MA3150 19
18. ALS to H. Collins, 30.7.1844, Morgan, MA3150 11
19. ALS to H. Collins, [n.d. July 1844], Morgan, MA3150 10
20. ALS to H. Collins, 30.7.1844, Morgan, MA3150 11
21. ALS to H. Collins, 8.8.1844, in private hands
22. ALSs to H. Collins, 4.9.1844, 21.9.1844, Morgan, MA3150 13, 14
23. ALS Wm Collins to H. Collins, 24.9.1844, Morgan, MA3154 74
24. *Appleton's Journal*
25. Draft letter, Wm Collins to unnamed addressee (? Longmans), 8.3.1845, BL adds., MS 42575, f. 158
26. *Men and Women*, 5.2.1887, p. 281
27. First published in 1876 and reissued as 'Mr Captain and the Nymph' in *Little Novels*, 1887
28. Marriage certificate of Charles James Ward and Jane Carpenter, 4.2.1845
29. ALS to H. Collins, [9.9.1845], Morgan, MA3150 15
30. Oliver Goldsmith, *She Stoops to Conquer*, Act II
31. ALS to H. Collins, 16.9.1845, Morgan, MA3150 17
32. ALS to H. Collins, 13.9.1845, Morgan, MA 3150 16
33. ALS to H. Collins, 16.9.1845, Morgan, MA3150 17
34. ALS to H. Collins, 6.10.1845, Morgan, MA3150 19
35. ALS to H. Collins, 23.9.1845, Morgan, MA3150 18
36. ALS to H. Collins, 30.9.1845, Morgan, MA3150 19
37. ALS to H. Collins, 6.10.1845, Morgan, MA 3150 20
38. *Memoirs*, Vol. 2, p. 282
39. 'Miss Jeromette and the Clergyman', *Little Novels*, 1887, p. 84
40. *Heart and Science*, p. 17
41. A note on the manuscript of *Antonina* gives the date the novel was begun, 23.4.1846
42. Edmund Yates, *Celebrities at Home*, 1879, p. 145
43. The MS of *Antonina*, HRC
44. ALS to H. Collins, 6.8.1846, Morgan, MA3150 22
45. Will of William John Thomas Collins, proved 26.4.1847

Chapter Five: Publication (1847–1851)

1. *Memoirs*, Vol. 1, pp. 111, 131
2. ALS to J. Richmond, 20.5.1847, Parrish
3. MS of *Antonina*, HRC
4. Alfred J. Story, op. cit., London 1892, Vol. 2, pp. 285–86
5. *The Illuminated Magazine* 1 (June 1843), p. 123
6. ALS to R. H. Dana, 15.11.1848, Parrish
7. ALS Maria Edgeworth to W.C., 22.4.1849, Morgan, R-V Autogrs. Misc. English
8. ALS to R. H. Dana, 15.11.1848, Parrish
9. ALS John Wilson Croker to W.C., 21.5.1848, Parrish
10. *The Observer*, 31.12.1848
11. ALS to R. H. Dana, 12.1.1849, Parrish
12. MS draft, with corrections in W.C.'s hand, BL adds., MS 28509 f. 345. ALS to Richard Bentley, 12.7.1854, Urbana
13. 'A Pictorial Tour to St. George Bosherville', *Bentley's Miscellany* 29 (1851), p. 496
14. ALS to H. Collins, 2.8.1847, Morgan, MA3150 23
15. ALS to H. Collins, 2.8.1847, Morgan, MA3150 23
16. Ibid.; ALS to Charles Ward, 10.8.1847, Morgan, MA3151 1
17. Henrietta Ward, *Memories of Ninety Years*, London 1924, p. 38
18. Marriage certificate of Edward Matthew Ward and Henrietta Mary Ada Ward, 4.5.1848
19. Henrietta Ward, *Reminiscences*, London 1911, p. 262
20. ALS to [Alaric?] Watts, 38 Blandford Square, [n.d. n.y.], Fales
21. W. H. Hunt, op. cit., Vol. 1, p. 293
22. Gladys Storey, *Dickens and Daughter*, London 1939, p. 214
23. ALS to Richard Bentley, 28.7.1850, University of Illinois, Urbana
24. Printed 'Prologue Written by Wilkie Collins, June 1849 on the Occasion of an amateur performance (at 38 Blandford Square,) of Goldsmith's comedy "The Good-Natured Man"', Morgan, R-V Autogrs. Misc. English, 25
25. ALS to Miss Clarkson, 38 Blandford Square, 'Tuesday evening', [n.d. n.y.], Morgan, R-V Autogrs. Misc. English, 24
26. ALS to E. M. Ward, 1.4.1862, HRC
27. *Lord Chamberlain's Plays*, Vol. 160 (ff. 1000–25), British Library MSs. Each act is in a different hand, the third act Wilkie Collins' holograph; the translation may have been a collaborative effort
28. AMS draft of Preface to *After Dark* (passage omitted from published version), January 1856, Wolff, op. cit., p. 255
29. ALS to Kate Field, 19.6.1877, Parrish
30. ALS to R. H. Dana, 12.1.1849, Parrish
31. ALS to H. Collins, 8.9.1849, in private hands
32. ALS to Richard Bentley, 22.11.1849, Urbana
33. ALS to Richard Bentley, 6.12.1849, Berg

34. ALS to Richard Bentley, [n.d. ?1850], Parrish
35. *Antonina*, Vol. 1, p. xii
36. *Wilkie Collins: The Critical Heritage*, ed. Norman Page, London 1974, p. 6
37. ALS to E. M. Ward, 28.6.[1851], HRC
38. ALS to H. Collins, 29.7.1850, Morgan, MA3150 25
39. ALS to H. Collins, 14.8.1850, Morgan, MA3150 27
40. ALS to Charles Ward, August 1850, in private hands
41. ALS to H. Collins, 14.8.1850, Morgan, MA3150 27
42. Ibid.
43. Ashmolean Museum, Oxford
44. Diana Holman-Hunt, *My Grandfather, His Wives and Loves*, London 1969, p. 74
45. Ashmolean Museum, Oxford
46. W. M. Thackeray, *The Book of Snobs*, Oxford 1908, p. 286
47. ALS to H. Collins, 14.8.1850, Morgan, MA 3150 27
48. ALS to H. Collins, 3.8.1850, 14.8.1850, Morgan, 3150 26, 27
49. Quoted in S. M. Ellis, *Wilkie Collins, le Fanu and others*, London 1951, p. 22
50. Edmund Yates, *Recollections and Experiences*, London 1883, Vol. 2, p. 173
51. The Pilgrim Edition of *The Letters of Charles Dickens*, Vol. 6, Oxford 1988, p. 310

Chapter Six: 'The Fire of Artistic Ambition' (1851–1852)

1. Pilgrim 6, p. 310
2. Wm Collins' notebooks, V&A. The picture was not among those sold after Dickens' death
3. Pilgrim 6, p. 310
4. Nigel Cross, *The Common Writer: Life in Nineteenth Century Grub Street*, London 1985, p. 71; Pilgrim 6, p. 614*n*
5. Pilgrim 6, p. 351
6. Ibid., pp. 330, 331, 332
7. G. A. Sala, *Things I have seen and people I have known*, London 1894, Vol. 1, p. 115
8. Pilgrim 6, p. 824
9. Ibid., p. 83
10. ALS, 11.8.1858, Morgan, MA93; differs slightly from Nonesuch 3, p. 38
11. Leslie Ward, *Forty Years of 'Spy'*, London 1915. (No one else ever commented on this)
12. Edmund Yates, *The World*, 25.9.1889, p. 12
13. In the Fitzwilliam Museum, Cambridge
14. *The Woman in White*, p. 539
15. Beard, op. cit., p. 321
16. ALS Kate Collins to H. Collins, 3.12.1860, Morgan, MA 3153 25

17. Beard, op. cit., p. 321
18. Quoted in Hesketh Pearson, *Charles Dickens*, London 1949, p. 175
19. Nonesuch 3, p. 58
20. 'A Pictorial Tour to St. George Bosherville', *Bentley's Miscellany* 29 (May 1851), p. 503
21. John Ruskin, *Works*, Vol. XII, pp. 319, 327
22. 'The Exhibition of the Royal Academy', *Bentley's Miscellany* 29 (June 1851), p. 617. Unsigned, but attributed by Bentley's accounts, BL
23. W. H. Hunt, op. cit., Vol. 1, p. 304
24. Ibid., p. 268
25. Ibid., p. 271
26. Leslie Ward, op. cit., p. 7
27. Diana Holman-Hunt, op. cit., p. 100
28. *Bentley's Miscellany* 31, pp. 153, 154
29. See Beetz, K., 'Wilkie Collins and *The Leader*', *Victorian Periodicals Review* 15, pp. 20–29 for a more detailed account of Wilkie Collins' contributions
30. Michael Holroyd, *Bernard Shaw: The Search for Love*, London 1988, p. 334
31. ALS to E. S. Pigott, Huntington Pigott Coll., Box 3
32. ALS to E. S. Pigott, 'Monday evening', [16.2.1852], 'Friday', [20.2.1852], Huntington Pigott Coll., Box 3
33. *The Autobiography and Letters of Mrs O. W. Oliphant*, ed. Mrs Harry Coghill, Edinburgh & London 1899, pp. 135–36
34. He acquired a presentation copy of Reichenbach's *Researches on Magnetism* in 1850 (Puttick & Simpson's *Catalogue of the Library of the Late Wilkie Collins, Esq.*, 1890)
35. ALS to Richard Bentley, 6.8.1853, Berg
36. *The Leader*, 21 February, p. 184
37. 'My Black Mirror', *HW* 14 (6.9.1856), pp. 169–75
38. *Foster's Hand-List of Men at the Bar*, 1885, pp. 95, 366
39. ALS to E. S. Pigott, 'Saturday morning', [22.11.1851], Huntington Pigott Coll., Box 3
40. ALS John Millais to W. H. Hunt, 25.10.[1852], Huntington, HH 349
41. Though the book is dated 1852, the Bentley Private Catalogue gives the publication date as 17.12.1851
42. *Ruskin's Letters from Venice*, ed. John Lewis Bradley, New Haven 1955, p. 270
43. ALS to George Bentley, [December 1851], Berg
44. Nuel Pharr Davis' suggestion that *Basil* – the hero was originally called 'Philip' – is based on the relationship of Lord Chesterfield and his illegitimate son would indicate that the historical researches were perhaps put to use in the 'story of modern life'
45. Pilgrim 6, p. 590
46. ALS to H. Collins, [13.]2.1852, in private hands
47. ALS to H. Collins, 1.9.1852, Morgan, MA3150 31

48. Pilgrim 6, p. 720*n*
49. ALS to E. S. Pigott, 16.9.1852, Huntington Pigott Coll., Box 3
50. ALS to H. Collins, 9.9.1852, Morgan, MA 315032
51. ALS to H. Collins, 16.9.1852, Morgan, MA3150 33

Chapter Seven: The Sorcerer and the Apprentice (1852–1853)

1. AMS, BL adds., MS 41060, f. 40, recto
2. ALS to Richard Bentley, [October/November 1852], Urbana
3. Wolzogen, op. cit., p. 16
4. Ford Madox Brown, *Diaries*, ed. Virginia Surtees, New Haven & London 1981, p. 172
5. The similarity between *Basil* and *The Awakening Conscience* has been pointed out by Kate Flint, 'Reading *The Awakening Conscience* rightly' in *Pre-Raphaelites Re-viewed*, ed. Marcia Pointon, Manchester 1989, pp. 51–52
6. ALS to Richard Bentley, [November 1851], Urbana
7. *The Leader*, 27.11.1852, p. 1141
8. *Basil*, p. xxxvii
9. Page, p. 46
10. Extract in *Mounts of Venus*, ed. Alan Bold, London 1980, pp. 210–11
11. ALS to Baron Sarony, 19.3.1887, Folger. The reference is to the 'Callipygean Venus' in the Museo Nazionale, Naples
12. *Basil*, p. 108
13. Page, p. 48
14. Page, p. 50
15. ALS to E. S. Pigott, [n.d.], Huntington Pigott Coll., Box 3
16. Pilgrim 6, p. 720*n*; ALS Catherine Horne to R. H. Horne, 5.2.1853, Huntington, HM 37774
17. Lady Priestley [Eliza Chambers], *The Story of a Lifetime*, London 1904, p. 78
18. John Lehmann, *Ancestors and Friends*, London 1962, p. 136
19. Pilgrim 6, p. 100
20. For details of the contributions to *Household Words*, see Ann Lohrli, *Household Words: A Weekly Journal 1850–1859 Conducted by Charles Dickens*, 1973, *passim*
21. ALS to C. A. Collins, 13.11.1853, Morgan, MA3152 2
22. ALS to H. Collins, 8.8.1844, in private hands
23. ALS to Charles Ward, August 1850, in private hands
24. ALS to E. M. Ward, [28.3.1855], HRC; ALS to E. S. Pigott, [1.2.1853], Huntington Pigott Coll., Box 3
25. ALS C. A. Collins to W. H. Hunt, 7.2.1855, Huntington, HH 68
26. Mary Lutyens, *Millais and the Ruskins*, London 1967, p. 261
27. ALS to E. S. Pigott, [July 1855], Huntington Pigott Coll., Box 3
28. Geoffroy Millais, *Millais*, London 1979, p. 67
29. Unsigned notice, *The Leader*, 17.2.1855, pp. 164–65
30. Nonesuch 2, p. 447

31. 'Douglas Jerrold', *HW* 19, p. 220
32. H. Wreford and Henry Morley, *HW* 4 (29.11.1851), pp. 235–37
33. Note on the MS, 'Begun April 1853', Morgan, MA 724
34. ALS, 17.8.1853, Berg
35. Nonesuch 2, p. 467
36. ALS to E. S. Pigott, 25.6.[53], Huntington Pigott Coll., Box 3
37. W. Teignmouth Shore, *Charles Dickens and his Friends*, London 1909, p. 196

Chapter Eight: In the Sorcerer's Footsteps (1853–1854)

1. William Powell Frith, *My Autobiography & Reminiscences*, London 1887–88, Vol. 3, p. 216
2. [W. H. Hunt], 'Notes of the Life of Augustus L. Egg', the *Reader* 1 (16.5.1863), p. 486
3. The *Reader* 2 (31.10.1863), p. 516
4. Richard Hengist Horne, 'Bygone Celebrities: The Guild of Literature and Art', *Gentleman's Magazine* 6 (May 1871), pp. 665–66
5. *Mr & Mrs. Charles Dickens: His Letters to Her*, ed. Walter Dexter, London 1935, p. 188
6. Nonesuch 2, p. 500
7. Ibid., p. 498
8. ALS to H. Collins, 16.10.1853, Morgan, MA3150 38
9. ALS to H. Collins, 28.10.1853, Morgan, MA3150 39
10. Ibid.
11. ALS to Charles Ward, 31.10.1853, Morgan, MA 3151 3
12. *Mr. & Mrs. Charles Dickens*, p. 216
13. Ibid., p. 179
14. Ibid., p. 216
15. Ibid., p. 182
16. Nonesuch 2, p. 499
17. ALS to E. S. Pigott, 4.11.1853, Huntington
18. Nonesuch 2, p. 508
19. ALS to C. A. Collins, 13.11.1853, Morgan, MA3152 2
20. Ibid.
21. *Mr. & Mrs. Charles Dickens*, p. 209
22. Ibid., p. 216
23. ALS to C. A. Collins, 13.11.1853, Morgan, MA3152 2
24. ALS to H. Collins, 25.11.1853, Morgan, MA3150 40
25. *Mr. & Mrs. Charles Dickens*, p. 220
26. ALS to Richard Bentley, 14.1.1854, Berg. A manuscript draft of one article, 'The Marriage in Cana', is in the Beinecke Library, Yale University
27. ALS to S. C. Hall, 3.5.1854, HRC
28. These articles have been mistakenly attributed to Wilkie Collins by Jeremy Maas, *The Victorian Art World in Photographs*, London 1984, and, more tentatively, in Clarke, pp.75–76

29. ALS to H. Collins, [early June 1854], in private hands
30. Bentley Papers, BL adds., MS 46616, f. 309
31. ALS to Messrs Bentley, [n.d.], Urbana
32. ALS to George Bentley, 24.1.1855, BL, 46652, f. 247
33. *Hide and Seek*, Chap. 1, p. 19
34. John Kitto, *The Lost Senses*, 1845
35. Gordon Haight suggests George Eliot may have been the reviewer. *George Eliot*, Oxford 1968, p. 144
36. Page, pp. 55–56
37. Nonesuch 2, p. 570
38. Ibid., p. 565
39. ALS to H. Collins, 27.7.1854, Morgan, MA 3150 41
40. ALS to Charles Ward, 10.9.1854, Morgan, MA3151 4
41. ALS to Richard Bentley, 12.7.1854, Urbana
42. *The Seven Poor Travellers*, *HW Christmas Extra Number*, 1854, p. 19
43. Nonesuch 2, p. 610

Chapter Nine: The Setting-up of a Balloon (1855–1856)

1. Nonesuch 2, [March 1856], p. 754
2. *Appleton's Journal*, New York, 3.9.1870
3. Nonesuch 2 (30.4.1856), p. 768
4. Nonesuch 2, p. 623
5. Nonesuch 2, p. 630
6. ALSs to H. Collins, 14.2.1855, 19.2.1855, Morgan, MA3150 43, 44
7. ALS to E. M. Ward, 20.3.1855, HRC
8. Nonesuch 2, pp. 638, 650, 654
9. ALS to E. M. Ward, 'Tuesday', [20.3.1855], HRC
10. Nonesuch 2, p. 643
11. Nonesuch 2, p. 660
12. John Lehmann, op. cit., p. 173
13. Henry Morley, *The Journal of a London Playgoer*, Leicester 1979, pp. 103–5
14. ALS to Charles Ward, 20.8.1855, Morgan, MA 3151 5
15. ALS to E. S. Pigott, [9.8.1855], Huntington Pigott Coll., Box 3
16. ALS to H. Collins, 2.9.1855, Morgan, MA3150 45
17. *After Dark*, 1856, Preface, pp. v–vi
18. ALS to H. Collins, 2.9.1855, Morgan, MA3150 45
19. 'My Black Mirror', *HW* 14 (6.9.1856), p. 174
20. ALS to E. S. Pigott, [4.9.1855], Huntington Pigott Coll., Box 3
21. Included in the 1861 reprint of *Rambles Beyond Railways*
22. Nonesuch 2, p. 714
23. ALS to H. Collins, 2.9.1855, Morgan, MA3150 45
24. Nonesuch 2, p. 660
25. É.-D. Forgues, 'Études sur le Roman Anglais; William Wilkie Collins', *Revue des Deux Mondes*, 2ᵉ série 12 (October–December 1855)
26. Preface to *The Moonstone*, 1871 edition

27. ALS to H. Collins, 19.3.1856, Morgan, MA 3150 49
28. ALS C. A. Collins to W. H. Hunt, 7.2.1855, Huntington, HH 68
29. MS at Huntington. Reproduced in full by Martin Meisel, 'Fraternity and Anxiety: Charles Allston Collins and the Electric Telegraph', *Notebooks in Cultural Analysis*, Vol. 2, ed. Norman F. Cantor and Nathalia King, Duke University Press, Durham 1985
30. ALS C. A. Collins to W. H. Hunt, 20.6.1860, Huntington, HH 74
31. 'Biography at a Discount', *Macmillan's Magazine* 10 (1864), p. 163
32. Nonesuch 2, p. 732
33. Nonesuch 2, p. 744
34. ALS to H. Collins, 28.2.1856, Morgan, MA3150 46
35. 'Laid up in Two Lodgings', *HW* 13 (7.6.1856), pp. 481–86
36. ALS to H. Collins, 11.3.1856, Morgan, MA 3150 47; to C. Ward, 19.3.1856, Morgan, MA 3151 6
37. *HW* 13, p. 482
38. ALS to H. Collins, 5.4.1856, Morgan, MA 3150 50
39. Nonesuch 2, p. 754
40. ALS to H. Collins, 19.3.1856, Morgan, MA 3150 49
41. ALS to Charles Ward, 19.3.1856, Morgan, MA3151 6
42. Nonesuch 2, p. 765
43. Frank Archer, *An Actor's Notebooks*, London 1912, p. 303
44. Nonesuch 2, p. 757
45. Nonesuch 2, p. 762

Chapter Ten: The Frozen Deep (1856–1858)

1. ALS to H. Collins, 19.3.1856, Morgan, MA 3150 49
2. The Collins' family doctor William Thomson had for many years lived and practised at 51 Charlotte Street, but from 1853 he was no longer listed as the rate payer
3. Nonesuch 2, p. 761
4. 'Laid up in Two Lodgings', *HW* 13 (14.6.1856), pp. 517–23
5. ALS to H. Collins, 2.7.1856, in private hands
6. ALS to C. A. Collins, 26.6.1856, in private hands
7. Ibid.
8. ALS to H. Collins, 2.7.1856, in private hands
9. ALS to H. Collins, [8.9.1856], Morgan, MA3150 52
10. Nonesuch 2, p. 792
11. Ibid., p. 800
12. Ibid., p. 801
13. Ibid., p. 814
14. Ibid., p. 807
15. Ibid., p. 834
16. ALS to W. R. Sims, 31.1.1857, Huntington, HM 16010
17. Nonesuch 2, p. 859
18. Ibid., p. 838

19. Ibid., p. 848
20. Page, pp. 70–71
21. *The Dead Secret*, 1861, pp. vii, viii
22. *The Train*, June 1857, p. 354
23. ALS to Smith, 8.6.1857, in private hands
24. Nonesuch 2, p. 857
25. 'A New Mind', *HW* 19 (1.1.1859), pp. 112–13
26. Charles Beaumont Phipps to Charles Dickens, 5.7.1857, Morgan, MA81 1
27. Elias Bredsdorff, *Hans Andersen and Charles Dickens: A Friendship and its Dissolution*, Copenhagen 1956, p. 79
28. *AYR* I, 15, pp. 355–60
29. Frederick Kitton, *Charles Dickens by Pen and Pencil*, London 1889, p. 19
30. ALS to H. Collins, 10.8.1857, in private hands
31. ALS to H. Collins, 5.10.1857, in private hands
32. Bredsdorff, op. cit., p. 100. Contract with Lahure, Princeton
33. ALS to James Lowe, 13.4.1858, HRC
34. Nonesuch 2, p. 873
35. Ibid., p. 880
36. Ibid., p. 881
37. Ibid., p. 883
38. Ibid., pp. 883, 884
39. Ibid., p. 883
40. Fred Kaplan, *Dickens: A Biography*, London 1988, p. 374
41. ALS to Mrs Bullar, 23.2.1859, HRC
42. ALS to H. Collins, 5.10.1857 (note inside envelope flap), in private hands
43. Henry Morley, 'Our Phantom Ship. Central America', *HW* 17 (22.2.1851), pp. 516–22. The connection with *The Woman in White* is made by Sucksmith, World's Classics edition
44. 'Dramatic Grub Street', *HW* 17 (6.3.1858), pp. 265–70
45. Marie and Squire Bancroft, *The Bancrofts*, London 1909, p. 38
46. John Hollingshead, *My Lifetime*, London 1895, p. 128
47. Henry Morley, *The Journal of a London Playgoer*, Leicester 1979, pp. 189–90
48. 24.2.1859, probably to Emden, manager of the Olympic Theatre. Wolff, op. cit., p. 270
49. 'The Unknown Public', *HW* 18 (21.8.1858), pp. 217–22
50. Nonesuch 3, p. 58
51. Ibid., p. 38
52. 'Dr. Dulcamara, M.P.', *HW* 19 (18.12.1858), pp. 49–52

Chapter Eleven: Secret Connections (1856–1859)

1. Nonesuch 3, p. 14
2. John Bigelow's Diary, quoted in Adrian, op. cit., p. 185
3. Nonesuch 3, p. 24

4. Diana Holman-Hunt, op. cit., p.167. Her natural assumption that this refers to *Wilkie* Collins would seem to be mistaken
5. The Charles A. Collins who occupied 63 Albany Street from September 1857 to February 1858 (Clarke, p. 96) was Charles Augustus Collins, surgeon. Post Office London Directory
6. 'Her Face', *HW* 18 (28.8.1858), pp. 258–64
7. John G. Millais, *Life and Letters of Sir John Everett Millais*, London 1899, Vol. 1, pp. 278–79
8. Gladys Storey, op. cit., p. 213. The connection between the two stories was first made by Clyde K. Hyder, 'Wilkie Collins and *The Woman in White*', *PMLA* 54 (1939), pp. 298–29
9. Post Office London Directory, 1853, Commercial Section. There is only one Mrs Elizabeth Graves in the Directory, and no Caroline Graves
10. Death certificate of Caroline Elizabeth Graves, 8.6.1895; marriage certificate of Harriette Elizabeth Laura (*sic*) Graves, 12.3.1878; marriage certificate of Caroline Elizabeth Graves to Joseph Charles Clow, 29.10.1868; census return, 12 Harley Street [7.4.]1861, 90 Gloucester Place, [2.4.]1871, [3.4.]1881. No birth certificate has been found for her, but on census day 1841, [6.6.1841], she was living with her parents at Toddington, near Cheltenham. Her age is given as eleven
11. Marriage certificate of George Robert Graves and Elizabeth Compton, 30.3.1850. Both are described as 'of full age'
12. His baptism record, East Greenwich, Kent, 17.2.1829, shows that he was born in Thames Street, Greenwich, on 6.11.1828. Marriage certificate of George Robert Graves and Elizabeth Compton. Census return for 11 Cumming Street, Pentonville, 1851
13. Birth certificate of Elizabeth Harriet Graves
14. Death certificate of George Robert Graves
15. Elizabeth Graves was not the rate payer at 5 Charlton Street, and must therefore have been a sub-tenant
16. C. A. Collins, *The Eye-witness*, p. 259
17. ALSs C. A. Collins to H. Collins, 19.11.1858, 20.11.1858, Morgan, MA3153 1, 2
18. ALS to Jane Ward, 1.12.1858, in private hands
19. ALS to E. M. Ward, 13.1.1859, HRC; ALS to Richard Bentley, 10.2.1859, Urbana; ALS to Mr Marsh (of Messrs Bentley), 21.2.59
20. 'New View of Society', *AYR* 1, p. 396
21. W. H. Hunt, op. cit., Vol. 2, p. 143
22. ALS to James Lowe, 13.4.1858, HRC
23. Nonesuch 3, p. 34
24. *The Woman in White*, pp. 380, 526
25. ALS to Mrs Henry Bullar, 23.2.1859, HRC. ALS to ?, 16.2.1859, Parrish
26. Census return for 12 Harley Street, 1861
27. John Lehmann, op. cit., p. 175. The Lehmanns' son Rudolph ('Rudy') was at Pau with his mother

28. R. C. Lehmann, op. cit., p. 30
29. Beard, op. cit., p. 321
30. ALSs to E. M. Ward, 3.8.1860, to Henrietta Ward, 8.3.1862, HRC
31. ALS to Alice Ward, 14.6.1865, in private hands
32. Beard, op. cit., p. 324, ALS to Nina Lehmann, 20.12.1878, Parrish
33. ALS George Redford to Harriet Bartley, 25.09.1889, Parrish
34. Nonesuch 3, p. 123

Chapter Twelve: The Woman in White (1859–1860)

1. ALS C. D. to W.C., 6.2.1859, Dickens House Museum
2. Robert L. Patten, *Dickens and his Publishers*, Oxford 1978, p. 275
3. ALS to H. Collins, 2.9.1859, Morgan, MA3150 55
4. ALS to Charles Ward, 18.8.1859, Morgan, MA3151 13
5. ALS to Dr Deeming, 5.10.1865, Fales
6. Edmund Yate, *Celebrities at Home*, 3rd series, 1879, p. 150
7. 'How I Write My Books', *The Globe* (26.11.1887)
8. Wybert Reeve, 'Recollections of Wilkie Collins', *Chamber's Journal* ix (June 1906), p. 458
9. Clyde K. Hyder, 'Wilkie Collins and the Woman in White', *PMLA liv.*, 1939, pp. 297–303. For a summary of the Douhault case, see the World's Classics edition
10. 'How I write my books'
11. Ibid.
12. *The Woman in White*, p. 15
13. 'How I write my books'
14. R. C. Lehmann, op. cit., p. 35
15. Yates, op. cit., p. 154
16. ALS to Charles Ward, [October 1859], Morgan, MA3151 16
17. R. C. Lehmann, op. cit., p. 35
18. *The Queen of Hearts*, Vol. 1, pp. 148–49
19. Page, p. 77
20. John Cordy Jeaffreson, *Novels and Novelists from Elizabeth to Victoria*, London 1858, Vol. 2, p. 345
21. Peter Caracciolo, 'Wilkie Collins's "Divine Comedy": the use of Dante in *The Woman in White*', *Nineteenth Century Fiction* 25, 4 (March 1971), p. 402. Caracciolo's discussion of the novel's imagery is exceptionally stimulating and thought-provoking
22. H. Mansel, 'Sensation Novels', *Quarterly Review* 113 (April 1863), p. 482
23. Margaret Oliphant, 'Sensation Novels', *Blackwood's Magazine* 91 (May 1862), p. 566
24. Charles Knight, *Passages of a Working Life*, London 1858, Vol. 3, p. 185
25. Nonesuch 3, p. 145
26. Ibid., p. 124
27. Page, p. 122
28. Margaret Oliphant, *Autobiography*, p. 186

29. *The Woman in White*, p. 1
30. ALS to H. Collins, 12.9.1860, Morgan, MA3150 58
31. Page, p. 123
32. ALS to E. S. Pigott, 11.12.1859, Huntington Pigott Coll., Box 3
33. Yates, *Celebrities at Home*, p. 151
34. *The Woman in White*, p. 213
35. Ibid., p. 232
36. ALS to Charles Ward, 19.7.59, Morgan, MA3151 10
37. 'Portrait of an author, painted by his publisher', *AYR* I (18.6.1859), pp. 184–89
38. ALS to Nugent Robinson, 28.8.1860, Taylor
39. Henry James to his father, 10.5.1869, quoted Gordon Haight, *George Eliot*, p. 417
40. Haight, op. cit., p. 103
41. Nonesuch 3, p. 91
42. Nonesuch 2, p. 796
43. *The Woman in White*, p. 193
44. Henry Catherick, cabinet maker, Charlotte Street; William Catherick, lodging-house keeper, Percy Street (the street in which Charles Collins lodged in 1856)
45. *The Woman in White* AMS, Morgan, MA 79. The passage follows, 'Our words are giants when they do us an injury, and dwarfs when they do us a service.' *The Woman in White*, p. 53
46. *The Woman in White*, p. 286
47. ALSs to F. C. Beard, [5.2.1863], [8.2.1863], Parrish
48. Florence E. Hardy, *The Early Life of Thomas Hardy*, London 1928, p. 268
49. *The Woman in White*, p. 42
50. Ibid., p. 167
51. Ibid., p. 180
52. Ibid., p. 584
53. Ibid., p. 403
54. Ibid., p. 166
55. Ibid., pp. 191, 197
56. Ibid., pp. 61, 374
57. Ibid., p. 32
58. Page, p. 120

Chapter Thirteen: At the Top of the Tree (1860–1862)

1. ALS to Sampson Low, 11.1.1860, Taylor
2. ALS to Mrs Procter, 26.3.1860, Parrish
3. ALS to Edward Marston, 31.10.1860, Parrish
4. ALS to Charles Ward, 14.8.1860, in private hands
5. ALS to Charles Ward, 19.7.1859, Morgan, MA3151 10
6. ALS to Mrs Procter, 23.7.1860, Parrish

7. Gladys Storey, op. cit., p. 106
8. Ibid., p. 153
9. John Lehmann, op. cit., p. 211
10. Nonesuch 3, p. 159
11. Letter to Esther Elton, Clarke, p. 97
12. Ibid.
13. ALS to H. Collins, 3.10.1860, in private hands
14. Kate Collins to H. Collins, 20.12.1860, Morgan, MA 33153 27
15. C. A. Collins, *At the Bar*, London 1866, p. 24
16. Nonesuch 3, p. 172
17. ALS to Charles Ward, 14.8.1860, in private hands
18. ALS to H. Collins, 12.9.1860, Morgan, MA3150 58
19. ALS to Charles Ward, 5.10.1860, Morgan, MA3151 23
20. ALS to H. Collins, 3.10.1860, in private hands
21. ALS to Charles Ward, 12.10.1860, Morgan, MA3151 24
22. ALS to Edward Marston, 31.10.1860, Parrish, quoted in Marston, *After Work*, London 1904, p. 85
23. ALS C.D. to W.C., 24.10.1860, Morgan, MA93
24. Nonesuch 3, p. 190
25. Ibid., p. 192
26. Ibid., p. 193
27. ALS to Charles Ward, 16.4.1861, Morgan, MA 3151 25
28. Ibid.
29. Nonesuch 3, p. 221
30. ALS to H. Collins, 24.5.1861, Morgan, MA3150 59
31. ALS to H. Collins, 11.7.1861, Morgan, MA3150 60
32. ALS to H. Collins, 31.7.1861, Morgan, MA 3150 61
33. Clarke, p. 228
34. Ibid., p. 99
35. ALS to E. M. Ward, 9.1.1861, HRC
36. ALS to H. Collins, 12.12.1861, Morgan, MA3150 63
37. Advertised in the end pages of the 1861 edition of *The Woman in White*, and also in *My Miscellanies*, 1863
38. ALS to H. Collins, 22.8.1861, in private hands
39. ALS to Charles Ward, 26.8.1861, Morgan, MA3151 28
40. ALS to H. Collins, 12.12. 1861, Morgan, MA 3150 63
41. In *Miss or Mrs? and Other Stories in Outline*, 1873
42. ALS to H. Collins, 12.12.1861, Morgan, MA3150 63
43. Autograph 'Memorandum, relating to the life and writings of Wilkie Collins, 1862', Parrish
44. ALS to ?, 16.2.1859, Parrish
45. Nonesuch 3, p. 275
46. Nonesuch 3, pp. 282, 284
47. The published text of C.D.'s letter lists twenty-seven, but the original reveals that one of these has been added in W.C.'s hand
48. Virginia Blain, 'The Naming of *No Name*', *WCSJ* 4 (1984), p. 26

49. ALS to H. Collins, 4.2.1862, in private hands
50. ALS to F. C. Beard, 30.6.1862, Parrish
51. ALS C.D. to W.C., 27.7.1862, Morgan, MA93 108
52. ALS to J. E. Millais, 22.7.1862, Parrish
53. ALSs to Charles Ward, 17.3., 9.7., 6.10.1862, Morgan, MA3151 33, 37, 40
54. ALS to H. Collins, 12.8.1862, Morgan, MA 3150 64
55. Nonesuch 3, pp. 304–5
56. ALS to H. Collins, 1.10.1862, Morgan, MA3150 65
57. ALS to F. C. Beard, 10.10.1862, Parrish
58. Ibid.
59. Nonesuch 3, p. 310
60. ALS to H. Collins, 18.11.1862, Morgan, MA 3150 67
61. ALS to Nina Lehmann, 13.11.1862, Parrish
62. ALS to F. C. Beard, 24.12.1862, Parrish

Chapter Fourteen: No Name (1862–1864)

1. Page, p. 132
2. Page, p. 143
3. Page, p. 142
4. MS 'A Story told me (Dec 20/60) by Mr. Lutwych', HRC
5. H. Collins' MS journal, HRC
6. *No Name*, p. 3
7. Ibid., p. 116
8. Ibid., p. 105
9. Ibid., p. 434
10. H. Collins' MS journal, HRC
11. *No Name*, p. 56
12. ALSs C.D. to Frederick and Nina Lehmann, 3.2.1863, 23.2.1863, 8.3.1865, HRC. Quoted in part in John Lehmann, *Ancestors and Friends*, p. 165
13. Page, p. 135
14. *No Name*, p. 436
15. Ibid., p. 453
16. *No Name: a Drama in Four Acts*, Author's corrected proof copy, Berg
17. *No Name*, p. 547
18. *Armadale*, p. 414
19. ALS to John Hollingshead, 15.1.1863, Fales
20. ALS to F. C. Beard, 30.1.1863, Parrish
21. ALS to F. C. Beard, 5.2.1863, Parrish
22. ALS to Charles Benham, 25.9.1868, Mitchell
23. ALS to Charles Ward, [n.d.], Morgan, MA 3151 79
24. ALS to H. Collins, 19.7.1864, Morgan, MA3150 83
25. Nonesuch 3, p. 333
26. Nonesuch 3, p. 337

27. ALS to F. C. Beard, [8.2.1863], Parrish
28. Nonesuch 3, p. 348
29. Marriage certificate of Augustus Leopold Egg and Esther Mary Brown, St Anne's, Limehouse, 11.4.1860
30. Will of Augustus Leopold Egg, drawn up 6.2.1861, proved 28.4.1863
31. The *Reader* 2 (31.10.1863), p. 516
32. ALS to F. C. Beard, 7.2.1863, Parrish
33. ALS to H. Collins, 21.4.1863, Morgan, MA 3150 70
34. ALS to C. A. Collins, 22.4.1863, Morgan, MA3152 5
35. Ibid.
36. ALS to H. Collins, 21.5.1863, Morgan, MA 3150 71
37. ALS to Charles Ward, 29.8.1863, Morgan, MA3151 45
38. ALS to H. Collins, 1.9.1863, Morgan, MA 3150 76
39. *My Miscellanies*, Vol. 1, p. vi

Chapter Fifteen: Armadale: The Self and the Shadow (1863–1866)

1. ALS to H. Collins, 24.10.1863, in private hands
2. ALS to Charles Ward, 4.11.1863, Morgan, MA3151 47
3. ALS to H. Collins, 13.11., 22.11.1863, Morgan, MA3150 77, 78
4. ALS to H. Collins, 8.1.1864, Morgan, MA3150 80
5. ALS, 17.2.1864, Berg, quoted in Gordon Ray, *The Letters and Private Papers of W. M. Thackeray*, Vol. 4, p. 296
6. ALS to Charles Ward, 14.1.1864, Morgan, MA3151 48
7. ALS to H. Collins, 4.12.1863, Morgan, MA3150 79
8. ALSs to Frederic Ouvry, 4.4., 5.4.1864, HRC
9. ALS to H. Collins, 20.4.1864, in private hands
10. ALS to E. S. Pigott, 24.9.1864, Huntington Pigott Coll., Box 3
11. ALS to H. Collins, 3.11.1864, Morgan, MA 3150 87
12. ALS to H. Collins, 19.10.1864, Morgan, MA 3150 86
13. Robinson, p. 172
14. ALS to H. Collins, 6.2.[1865], in private hands
15. ALS to C. A. Collins to W.C., 16.1.1865, Morgan, MA3152 5
16. ALS C. A. Collins to H. Collins, 29.1.1865, Morgan, MA3152 39
17. ALS to H. Collins, 8.7.1866, Morgan, MA3150 97
18. ALS to H. Collins, 24.7.1866, Morgan, MA3150 98
19. ALS to the Rev. Dr Deeming, 5.10.1865, Fales
20. ALS to H. Collins, 1.4.1866, Morgan, MA 3150 92
21. ALS to H. Collins, 22.4.1866, in private hands
22. R. C. Lehmann, op. cit., pp. 53–54
23. Nina Lehmann, op. cit., p. 45
24. Quoted in ALS to H. Collins, 4.6.1866, Morgan, MA3150 95
25. Page, p. 149
26. The *Reader* 7, 179 (2.6.1866), pp. 538–39
27. *The Law and the Lady*, Vol. 1, p. 106

28. William Roughhead, *Bad Companions*, Edinburgh 1930, p. 36
29. *Armadale*, p. 575
30. Ibid., p. 506
31. T. S. Eliot, *Selected Essays*, London 1932, p. 468
32. *Jung: Selected Writings*, ed. A. Storr, London 1983, p. 91
33. ALS to H. Collins, 22.4.1866, in private hands
34. Nonesuch 3, p. 477
35. ALS to Nina Lehmann, 26.10.1866, Parrish
36. ALS to Nina Lehmann, 9.12.1866, Parrish, quoted in R. C. Lehmann, op. cit., pp. 52–53
37. ALS to H. Collins, 26.2.1867, Morgan, MA 3150 99
38. ALS to H. Collins, 6.1., 8.1.1867, in private hands
39. Nonesuch 3, p. 511
40. John Coleman, *Charles Reade as I Knew Him*, London 1904, p. 378
41. For further details of the friendship see Thomas D. Clareson, 'Wilkie Collins to Charles Reade: some Unpublished Letters', *Victorian Essays*, 1967, pp. 107–24
42. A dramatization of Anthony Trollope's *Ralph the Heir, Shilly-Shally*, staged in 1872, and *Joan*, a dramatization of Frances Hodgson Burnett's *That Lass o' Lowrie's*, in 1878
43. In Charles Reade's Letter Book, Taylor
44. Clareson, pp. 118–20
45. ALS to C. Reade, 30.11.[1869], Parrish
46. ALS to W. D. Booth, 15.4.1867, Parrish
47. ALS to W. H. Wills, 13.5.1867, Morgan, R-V Autogrs. Misc. English, 13

Chapter Sixteen: 'Wild yet domestic': Wilkie's family mysteries (1867–1868)

1. ALS to H. Collins, 12.12.1867, in private hands. He was shocked to discover in July 1868 that Benham and Tindell had placed a distrainer on the £5,000 worth of stocks he and Charley had inherited from their mother, as additional security for the loan. ALS to W. F. Tindell, 19.7.1868. By September he had repaid the £800, partly funded by selling some stock. Clarke, p. 116, identifies this payment, to 'Benham & Co.', as being for household equipment. The coincidence of name and amount suggests to me this is repayment of the loan
2. ALS to H. Collins, 12.9.1867, Morgan, MA3150 110
3. ALS to James Payn, 22.6.1882, HRC
4. ALS to A. P. Watt, 7.9.1885, in private hands
5. ALS to H. Collins, 12.9.1867, Morgan, MA3150 110
6. On census night 1871 there were three servants in the house, Lydia Bradford, aged thirty-four, Emily Bradford, fifteen, and Joseph Humphries, fifteen. In 1881 (apart from Caroline, for the first time described as a servant, as well as 'housekeeper') there were two, Sarah Masey,

thirty-three, 'cook', and George Wells, twenty-four, 'manservant'
7. ALSs to Charles Kent, 24.10., 26.10.1867, Huntington
8. ALS to H. Collins, 26.11.1867, in private hands
9. ALS to Frederick Lehmann, 25.10.1869, Parrish
10. Wilkie Collins, 'Recollections of Charles Fechter' in Kate Field, *Charles Albert Fechter*, Boston 1882, p. 163
11. Kaplan, op. cit., p. 493
12. John A. Mills, 'The Modesty of Nature: Charles Fechter's *Hamlet*', *Theatre Survey* 15, 1 (1974), p. 65
13. ALS to Nina Lehmann, 4.1.1869, Parrish
14. 'Recollections of Charles Fechter', p. 170
15. John Coleman, *Players and Playwrights*, London 1888, p. 312
16. 'Recollections of Charles Fechter', p. 164
17. ALS to Henry Pigott, 10.5.1883, Huntington Pigott Coll., Box 3
18. Louis Dépret, *Chez les Anglais*, Paris 1879, p. 80
19. A collection of notes and related material for *The Moonstone*, now in Parrish
20. ALS to W. H. Hunt, 21.3.1868, Huntington, HH 87
21. ALS to ?, 10.3.1883, Fales
22. Preface to 1871 edition of *The Moonstone*
23. 1851 census return for 10 Black Street, Winterton, Norfolk; Rudd family gravestone in Winterton churchyard
24. 1861 census return, 15 New Toll Gate, Runham, Norfolk. The enumerator has given Martha's Christian name as 'Maria', but all the other details – age, place of birth, sister's name, age, and place of birth – are correct. The enumerator's schedule describes the district as 'That part of the Parish of Runham lying on the West side of the Suspension bridge at Great Yarmouth, including the terminus of the Eastern Counties Railway, Vauxhall Gardens, the old and new Toll Houses . . .'
25. ALS to Lord Houghton, 6.8.1864, Houghton
26. ALS to H. Collins, 1.7.1865, Morgan, MA3150 90; ALS to Frederick Enoch, 5.8.1865, HRC
27. Marriage certificate of Caroline Graves and Joseph Charles Clow; Storey, p. 214
28. Nonesuch 3, p. 676
29. Gladys Storey, op. cit., p. 214
30. Mary Anderson, *A Few Memories*, London 1896, p. 143; William Winter, *Old Friends*, New York 1909, p. 211
31. ALS to Harper's, 22.2.1868, HRC; MS of *The Moonstone*, Morgan, MA78
32. Harriet Graves' hand: 'Living in my present isolation . . . a valuable of great price which Mr. Luker had that day left in the care of his bankers.' Unknown hand: 'This document would be useless . . . she not only disappointed – she really shocked me.' Pp. 217–24 in World's Classics edition
33. She was at 90 Gloucester Place on census night, 2.4.1871, but died

nearby at 21 Molyneux Street in 1877. Her death was registered by Wilkie Collins' servant, Sarah Masey

34. *Man and Wife*, p. 11
35. Clarke, p. 131
36. *The New Magdalen*, Vol. 2, p. 249
37. Caroline Graves appears in the 1871 census return for 90 Gloucester Place. Census night was 2 April
38. Wolff collection, HRC. This copy may have been presented to Caroline Graves' mother-in-law, rather than to Caroline. Her husband's name was erroneously given as 'George' on her death certificate, from information supplied by Wilkie Collins' servant Sarah Masey
39. She went (e.g.) with W.C. to a performance of *The Lady of Lyons*, ALS to E. S. Pigott, 3.4.1886, Huntington; and to see Holman Hunt's pictures, ALS to W. H. Hunt, 24.7.1886, Huntington. She refused an invitation to dine with Andrew Chatto, 19.5.1880, Parrish
40. ALS to Caroline Graves to Andrew Chatto, 9.1.1883, Parrish
41. ALS to Mrs Clunes, 26.11.1884, HRC
42. Clarke, p. 135
43. Their births are recorded with these nicknames in W.C.'s memorandum of anniversaries
44. ALS to W. F. Tindell, 18.6.[1872], Mitchell; ALS to G. M. Rose, 27.7.1882, Parrish
45. Clarke, p. 178

Chapter Seventeen: The Moonstone (1868–1870)

1. Anderson, op. cit., p. 143
2. Squire Bancroft, *Empty Chairs*, London 1925, pp. 103–4
3. Leslie Stephen, 'The Decay of Murder', *Cornhill Magazine* 20 (December 1869), p. 722
4. Introduction to the World's Classics edition of *The Moonstone*, Oxford 1982, p. xiii
5. *Pall Mall Gazette* 50 (20.1.1890)
6. ALS to H. Collins, 26.10.1867, Morgan, MA3150 115
7. ALS to Harper's, 20.1.[1868], HRC
8. *The Moonstone*, First Period, Chap. 12, p. 105
9. Page, pp. 170–71
10. Page, p. 123
11. George Moore, *Confessions of a Young Man*, London 1941, pp. 130, 160
12. Edmund Downey, *Thirty Years Ago*, London 1905, p. 25
13. The contract for *The Moonstone*, 10.6.1868, gave Tinsley the exclusive right to publish for twelve months. After 1,500 copies had been sold, Tinsley only had to pay £250 for the next five hundred. Huntington
14. ALS to Charles Benham, 9.9.1868, Mitchell
15. William Tinsley, *Random Recollections of an Old Publisher*, London 1900, Vol. 1, pp. 114–15

16. ALS to W. Tinsley, 11.7.1868, Morgan, R-V Autogrs. Misc. English, 14
17. 'The Moonstone and Moonshine', *The Mask*, August 1868, p. 212
18. *The Moonstone* MS, p. 280, Morgan, MA78
19. Nonesuch 3, p. 659
20. Adrian, op. cit., p. 130
21. ALS C. A. Collins to W. H. Hunt, 23.11.1871, Huntington, HH 78
22. Nonesuch 3, p. 681
23. Ibid., p. 715
24. Ibid., p. 762
25. See Alethea Hayter, *Opium and the Romantic Imagination*, London 1968, Chap. 11
26. A. C. Swinburne, 'Wilkie Collins', *Fortnightly Review*, November 1889
27. Robinson, pp. 218, 237
28. ALS to C. Benham, 25.9.1868, Mitchell
29. ALS to John Hollingshead, 24.5.1869, Parrish
30. ALS to John Hollingshead, 1.6.1869, HRC
31. John Coleman, *Players and Playwrights*, Vol. II, p. 315
32. 'Charles Albert Fechter', *Dictionary of American Biography*
33. ALS to Frederick Lehmann, 24.4.[1869], HRC
34. ALS to Elizabeth Benzon, 26.2.1869, in private hands
35. ALS to Messrs Cassell, 25.9.1869, HRC
36. ALS to Frederick Lehmann, 25.10.1869, Parrish
37. ALS to Messrs Hunter, Rose, 4.6.1870, Parrish
38. ALS to Thomas Galpin, 22.8.1870, HRC
39. ALS to W. F. Tindell, 8.5.1870, Mitchell
40. For a fuller account of the publishing history of *Man and Wife* see Andrew Gasson, 'Wilkie Collins, A collector's and bibliographer's challenge', *The Private Library*, 3rd series 32 (Summer 1980)
41. ALS to W. F. Tindell, 26.6.1870, Mitchell

Chapter Eighteen: After Dickens (1870–1871)

1. *Suzannet Dickens Collection Catalogue*, ed. Michael Slater, London 1975, p. 144
2. ALS to W. F. Tindell, 1.6.1870, Mitchell
3. ALS to W. F. Tindell, 10.6.1870, Mitchell
4. ALS to W. F. Tindell, 16.6.1870, Mitchell
5. ALS to Frederick Lehmann, 20.6.1870, Parrish
6. ALS to Dr Emil Lehmann, 7.8.1870, Parrish
7. ALS to W. F. Tindell, 23.7.[1870], Mitchell
8. ALS to G. A. Sala, 23.2.1871, Princeton
9. One at least of these interventions was an afterthought. 'Additional copy' for the thirty-fourth weekly part is a long discussion of Geoffrey Delamayn's moral degeneration. Holograph MS, Parrish
10. ALS to J. C. Parkinson, 30.9.1869, in private hands
11. Beard, op. cit., p. 322

12. Lilian Whiting, *Kate Field: A Record*, London 1899, p. 346
13. Yates, *Celebrities at Home*, 1879, p. 146
14. R. C. Lehmann, op. cit., p. 30
15. *Man and Wife*, p. 161
16. John Lehmann, *Ancestors and Friends*, pp. 161, 204
17. George Curry, 'Charles Dickens and Annie Fields', Huntington Library Quarterly 51, 1 (Winter 1988), p. 38
18. Mary Cunliffe, TSs reminiscences, p. 52, pp. 40–41, Armstrong-Browning
19. ALS to Nina Lehmann, 12.6.[1860–62], Parrish
20. ALS to Elizabeth Benzon, 26.2.1869, in private hands
21. *Harper's Magazine*, November 1869 (proof copy, Morgan)
22. ALS to Messrs Cassell, Petter & Galpin, 14.7.1871, HRC. ALS to Charles Ward, 14.4.1871, Morgan, MA3151 65
23. ALS to Cassell, Petter & Galpin, 2.8.1871, HRC
24. ALS to John Hollingshead, 25.2.1873, Huntington, HD 3
25. Ibid.
26. ALS to William D. Booth, 20.9.1870, HRC
27. Page, p. 191
28. *Poor Miss Finch*, Vol. 1, p. vi
29. ALS to Arthur Locker, 18.6.1872, Parrish
30. *Poor Miss Finch*, Vol. 1, p. 127
31. *Poor Miss Finch*, Vol. 1, p. 151
32. Page, p. 21
33. ALS to George Bentley, 22.3.1872, Berg
34. Royal Gettmann, *A Victorian Publisher: a Study of the Bentley Papers*, Cambridge 1960, p. 140
35. *Poor Miss Finch*, Vol. 1, p. v
36. Nonesuch 3, p. 359
37. ALS H. Collins to W. H. Hunt, 24.7.[1865], Parrish

Chapter Nineteen: Wilkie and the Theatre (1871–1873)

1. Mary Cunliffe, TSs reminiscences, pp. 71–72. Armstrong Baylor
2. Wybert Reeve, 'Recollections of Wilkie Collins', p. 458
3. ALS (incomplete) to unknown addressee, 7.8.1871, Parrish
4. The holograph manuscript of the play is in the Houghton Library. There is a copy in the hand of Harriet Graves in the Huntington Library
5. *The Times*, 12.10.1871
6. ALS to ?, 7.8.71, Parrish
7. Percy Fitzgerald, *Some Memories of Charles Dickens and 'Household Words'*, London 1913, p. 262
8. 'How I write my Books'
9. Squire Bancroft, *Empty Chairs*, London 1925, p. 104
10. W.C.'s diary for 1889, in private hands
11. Mary Anderson, op. cit., p. 143; Robert Ashley, *Wilkie Collins*, London 1952, p. 110

12. William Winter, op. cit., p. 213
13. ALS to E. S. Pigott, 20.11.1888, Huntington Pigott Coll., Box 3
14. ALSs to Charles Kent, [n.d.], Fales; 17.8.1884, Parrish
15. Eric Trudgill, *Madonnas and Magdalens: the Origins and Development of Victorian Sexual Attitudes*, London 1976, p. 297
16. Anthony Trollope, *The Vicar of Bullhampton*, London 1870, Chap. 25, pp. 156–62
17. *The New Magdalen*, Vol. 2, p. 252
18. Ibid., p. 221
19. Dutton Cook, *Nights at the Play*, London 1883. Vol. I, p. 281
20. Gettmann, op. cit., p. 140
21. ALS to George Bentley, 18.3.1873, Berg
22. Marie and Squire Bancroft, *The Bancrofts: Recollections of Sixty Years*, London 1909, p. 169
23. Mary Cunliffe, TSs reminiscences, p. 51, Armstrong Baylor. George Curry, 'Charles Dickens and Annie Fields', *Huntington Library Quarterly* 51, 1 (Winter 1988), p. 32
24. Arthur Adrian, op. cit., p. 146
25. ALS Leslie Stephen to James T. Fields, 31.7.1870, Huntington, FI 4280
26. ALS Georgina Hogarth to Annie Fields, 5.8.1871, Huntington, FI 2701
27. ALS Georgina Hogarth to Annie Fields, 12.5.1873, Huntington, FI 2713
28. John Russell Stephens, *The Censorship of English Drama, 1824–1901*, London 1980, p. 107
29. Frank Archer, op. cit., London 1912, p. 185
30. Autograph 'Heads of Agreement', Mitchell
31. Quoted Walter de la Mare, 'The Early Novels of Wilkie Collins', in *The Eighteen Sixties*, ed. John Drinkwater, Cambridge 1932, p. 68
32. ALS to George Bentley, 21.5.1873, Berg
33. Michael Holroyd, *Bernard Shaw: The Search for Love*, London 1988, p. 370
34. ALSs to George Bentley, 21.5., 10.9.1873, Berg
35. ALS to C. S. Carter, 27.2.1872, in private hands
36. ALS to W. F. Tindell, 21.7.1873, Mitchell
37. ALS to Mary Cunliffe, 13.3.1873, HRC
38. ALS Georgina Hogarth to Annie Fields, 10.10.1871, Huntington, FI 2702
39. Percy Fitzgerald, *Memoirs of an Author*, London 1894, Vol. 1, p. 88
40. Archer, op. cit., p. 152
41. *Pall Mall Gazette*, 30.6.1873
42. ALS to Georgina Hogarth, 20.7.1870, DHM
43. ALS Georgina Hogarth to Annie Fields, 30.8.1873, Huntington, FI 2715
44. Curry, op. cit., pp. 5, 38

45. ALS to Émile Forgues, 13.4.1861, Parrish
46. ALSs to John Forster, 16.11.1872, Parrish; 9.12.[1872], V&A
47. *The Times*, 8.12.1871
48. ALS to George Bentley, 30.11.1871, Berg
49. *The Times*, 8.12.1871
50. ALS to Georgina Hogarth, 18.3.1879, Urbana
51. ALS to Vicomte Robert du Pontavice de Heussey, 19.9.1885, Parrish; Robert Du Pontavice de Heussey, *L'Inimitable Boz*, Paris 1889, copy inscribed by the author to Wilkie Collins. In collection of Alexander D. Wainwright, Princeton
52. ALS to Frederick Kitton, 2.8.1886, Parrish
53. 'Recollections of Charles Fechter', p. 159
54. Wybert Reeve, *From Life*, London 1892, p. 109
55. J. W. T. Ley, *The Dickens Circle: a Narrative of the Novelist's Friendships*, London 1919, p. 349
56. Adrian, op. cit., p. 185
57. J. W. T. Ley, Introduction to Forster's *Life of Charles Dickens*, 1928 edition, p. xix
58. Ibid.
59. Nonesuch 2, p. 777
60. Wybert Reeve, 'Recollections of Wilkie Collins', p. 458
61. Wybert Reeve, *From Life*, p. 110
62. *Pall Mall Gazette* 50 (20.1.1890)
63. Ibid.
64. ALS to G. A. Sala, 2.2.1874, Princeton
65. ALS to Mrs Bigelow, 31.12.1874, Berg
66. Clareson, op. cit., p. 116
67. 'Reminiscences of a Story-Teller', *Universal Review*, 15.6.1888, p. 191

Chapter Twenty: America (1873–1874)

1. ALS to Charles Ward, 6.12.1871, Morgan, MA3151 71
2. ALS to W. F. Tindell, 12.9.1873, Mitchell
3. Ibid.
4. Ibid.
5. 'Recollections of Charles Fechter', p. 172
6. Nonesuch 3, p. 581
7. Wilkie Collins, *Considerations on the Copyright Question addressed to an American Friend*, London 1880, p. 12
8. Bret Harte, *Condensed Novels*, 1867, in Page, pp. 161–67; MS draft of review in *Overland Monthly*, Huntington
9. Clyde K. Hyder, 'Wilkie Collins in America', *Humanistic Studies of the University of Kansas* VI, 4, Kansas 1940, p. 51
10. ALS to Sebastian Schlesinger, 17.2.1874, Houghton
11. ALS to Sebastian Schlesinger, 25.12.1873, Houghton
12. Walford, op. cit., pp. 208–9

13. R. C. Lehmann, op. cit., p. 66
14. *Men and Women*, Vol. III, 36 (5.2.1887), p. 282
15. L. B. Walford, op. cit., p. 206
16. Wybert Reeve, *From Life*, p. 116
17. Wybert Reeve, 'Recollections', p. 460. L. B. Walford, op. cit., p. 207
18. *Dictionary of American Biography*
19. 'Recollections of Charles Fechter', p. 162
20. Hyder, op. cit., p. 53
21. R. C. Lehmann, op. cit., p. 66
22. ALS to Dion Boucicault, 8.10.1873, Parrish
23. Hyder, op. cit., p. 52
24. Hyder, op. cit., p. 56
25. Adrian, op. cit., p. 198
26. R. C. Lehmann, op. cit., p. 67
27. Robert Ashley, 'Wilkie Collins and the American Theater', *Nineteenth Century Fiction* 8 (March 1954), p. 250
28. Richard Ellmann, *Oscar Wilde*, London 1987, p. 156
29. ALS to Sebastian Schlesinger, 25.12.1873, Houghton
30. Ibid.
31. ALS to George Harper, 2.1.1874, Morgan, MA1950 24
32. Ibid.
33. ALS to Sebastian Schlesinger, 17.1.1874, Houghton
34. R. C. Lehmann, op. cit., p. 68
35. *The Frozen Deep and Other Stories*, London 1874, p. 220
36. ALS to George W. Childs, 16.3.1874, Professor Norman Page
37. ALS to W. F. Tindell, 27.1.1874, Mitchell
38. ALS to G. W. Childs, 16.3.1874, Professor Norman Page
39. ALS to W. F. Tindell, 3.3.1874, Mitchell
40. ALS to William Seaver, 7.6.1875, Parrish
41. ALS to Mrs Bigelow, 31.12.1874, Berg

Chapter Twenty-one: The Law and the Lady (1874–1878)

1. ALS to W. F. Tindell, 10.4.[n.y.], Mitchell
2. ALS to W. F. Tindell, 29.12.1874, Mitchell
3. 1881 census for 10 Taunton Place. Alice Rudd is described as 'housekeeper'
4. ALS to George Smith, 23.10.1871, Berg
5. ALS to Messrs Harper, 28.5.1872, Morgan, MA1950 20
6. ALS to George Smith, 5.12.1872, Berg
7. ALS to George Bentley, 12.5., 3.7.1874, Berg
8. ALS to W. F. Tindell, 6.11.1874, Mitchell; holograph memorandum, Berg
9. ALS to George Bentley, 27.10.1874, Berg
10. Oliver Warner, *Chatto and Windus: a brief account of the firm's origin, history and development*, London 1973, p. 14

11. Andrew Gasson, op. cit., p. 59
12. Copy of letter from Arthur Locker to W.C., 25.1.1875, Mitchell
13. *The World* IV (January–June 1876), p. 243
14. Sue Lonoff and Jenny Bourne Taylor both give serious critical accounts of *The Law and the Lady*
15. *The Law and the Lady*, Vol. I, p. 10
16. Sue Lonoff, *Wilkie Collins and His Victim Readers*, New York 1982, p. 166
17. Julian Symons, *Bloody Murder*, London 1985, p. 53
18. *The Law and the Lady*, Vol. II, p. 207
19. Ibid., p. 257
20. *The Law and the Lady*, Vol. III, p. 66
21. *The Law and the Lady*, Vol. II, pp. 260–61
22. Page, pp. 26–27
23. *The World* II (January–June 1875), p. 176
24. *The Evil Genius*, Vol. I, pp. 117–18
25. ALS to Paul Hamilton Hayne, 3.5.1884, HRC
26. ALS to Nina Lehmann, 28.12.1877, Parrish
27. Julian Hawthorne, *Shapes that Pass*, London 1928, p. 227
28. Clareson, p. 112
29. Dutton Cook, op. cit., Vol. II, p. 118
30. Clareson, p. 111
31. MS notes, HRC
32. Clareson, pp. 115–16
33. Dutton Cook, op. cit., Vol. II, p. 156
34. ALS to Frederick Lehmann, 26.4.1876, HRC
35. 'The Use of Gas in Theatres', *The Mask* X, 4 (October 1924)
36. ALS from Charles Reade, [n.d.1876], Parrish
37. ALS to Nina Lehmann, 28.12.1877, Parrish
38. Clarke, p. 203
39. *The Evil Genius*, Vol. I, p. 165
40. ALS to Andrew Chatto, 7.1.1878, Parrish
41. *The Haunted Hotel*, Chap. 20, p. 83

Chapter Twenty-two: The Unknown Public (1878–1884)

1. *The Fallen Leaves*, Vol. I, p. 87
2. Charles Nordhoff, *The Communistic Societies of the United States*, London 1875, p. 276
3. *The Fallen Leaves*, Vol. II, p. 163
4. Ibid., pp. 181–87
5. See Appendix B, and Clarke, pp. 192–93
6. Marriage certificate of Harriet Graves and Henry Bartley, 12.3.1878
7. ALS to A. P. Watt, 12.11.1884, in private hands
8. ALS to Harriet Bartley, 11.7.[1882], Parrish
9. ALS to E. S. Pigott, 20.10.1888, Huntington Pigott Coll., Box 3

10. ALS to F. C. Beard, 21.10.1872, Parrish
11. The *Saturday Review*, 16.6.1883
12. ALS to A. P. Watt, 24.6.1885, in private hands
13. ALS to F. Lehmann, 7.12.1886, HRC
14. ALS to Nina Lehmann, 25.2.1883, HRC
15. ALS to Nina Lehmann, 1.3.1883, HRC
16. Julian Hawthorne, op. cit., pp.169–70
17. ALS to A. P. Watt, 1.4.1884, in private hands
18. ALS to William Winter, 14.1.1883, Parrish
19. ALS to A. P. Watt 30.1.1884, in private hands
20. Some letters from the newspaper proprietors are in the A. P. Watt files in the Berg Collection; others are in private hands
21. ALS to W.C. from E. S. Bartlett, 20.12.1881, Berg
22. ALS from E. S. Bartlett to A. P. Watt, 24.5.1882, Berg
23. 'The Unknown Public', *HW* 18 (21.8.1858), p. 220
24. ALS to E. S. Bartlett, 8.2.1882, in private hands
25. ALSs to A. P. Watt from D. Duncan & Sons, *South Wales Daily News*; *Western Daily Press*; J. R. Manners, *North British Daily Mail*. Berg
26. ALS to A. P. Watt, 12.10.1883, Berg
27. ALS to A. P. Watt, 23.10.1885, in private hands
28. ALS to Charles H. Willis, 8.8.1881, Parrish
29. ALS to Paul Hamilton Hayne, 3.5.1884, HRC
30. *The Black Robe*, Vol. 3, p. 32
31. *Pictorial World* Special Supplement, 23.12.1882. MS at HRC
32. ALS to William Winter, 3.9.1881, Berg
33. ALS to G. M. Rose, 29.1.1881, Parrish
34. ALS to Andrew Chatto, 5.6.1882, Parrish
35. ALS to Frederick Lehmann, 5.7.1882, HRC
36. Frances Power Cobbe, *The Life of Frances Power Cobbe*, London 1904, Vol. II, p. 184
37. *Heart and Science*, p. 25
38. Ibid., p. 24
39. Swinburne, op. cit., p. 217
40. Lancelot Law Whyte, *The Unconscious before Freud*, London 1962, p. 171
41. ALS to William Winter, 14.1.1883, Parrish
42. 'The Bird Doctor', HRC; 'Lady Calista', Huntington; *Rank and Riches*, Phillips Exeter Academy
43. Charles Hawtrey, *The Truth at Last*, London 1924, p. 109
44. *The Saturday Review*, 16.6.1883, p. 766
45. ALS to E. A. Buck, 1.7.1883, HRC
46. The *Athenaeum*, 16.6.1883, p. 774
47. ALS to Harriet Bartley, 11.7.[1883], Parrish
48. ALS to Paul Hamilton Hayne, 3.5.1884, HRC
49. ALS to A. P. Watt, 28.3.1884, in private hands
50. *I Say No*, Vol. 3, Chap. 52, pp. 143–44
51. Page, p. 218

52. *I Say No*, Vol. 3, Chap 66, p. 305
53. *The World*, 25.9.1889, p. 12

Chapter Twenty-three: The Final Years (1885–1889)

1. ALS to Nina Lehmann, 2.2.1887, Parrish
2. ALS to Henry Pigott, 21.2.1886, Huntington Pigott Coll., Box 3
3. ALS to E. S. Pigott, 10.12.1886, Huntington Pigott Coll., Box 3
4. ALS to W. H. Hunt, 8.10.1885, Huntington, HH 98
5. Anderson, op. cit., p. 146
6. ALS to William Seaver, 6.8.1878, Parrish
7. Anderson, op. cit., p. 146
8. Ibid., p. 144
9. ALS to E. S. Pigott, 3.4.1886, Huntington Pigott Coll., Box 3
10. ALS to Rosa Kenney, 17.5.1882, Houghton
11. Charles Hawtrey, op. cit., p. 111
12. Beard, op. cit., p. 326
13. ALS to Baron Sarony, 19.3.1887, Folger
14. ALS to Nannie Wynne, 10.3.1887, in private hands
15. ALS to Mrs Wynne, 22.8.1885, in private hands
16. ALS to Nannie Wynne, 27.11.1885, in private hands
17. ALS to Nannie Wynne, 12.6.1885, in private hands
18. ALS to Nannie Wynne, 1.2.1886, in private hands
19. ALS to Nannie Wynne, 5.11.1885, in private hands
20. ALS to Nannie Wynne, 12.6.1885, in private hands. Hume's novel had appeared in Australia, but was not published in England until the following year
21. ALS to E. S. Pigott, 23.10.1885, Huntington Pigott Coll., Box 3
22. Letter in hand of Caroline Graves, signed by W.C., to Doris Bartley, 13.11.1885, Parrish
23. ALS to F. C. Beard, 16.7.1886, Parrish
24. ALS to Sebastian Schlesinger, 26.8.1888, Houghton
25. 1881 census return for 90 Gloucester Place
26. ALS to A. P. Watt, 10.5.1885, in private hands
27. John Sutherland, *Mrs. Humphry Ward*, Oxford 1990, p. 44
28. Will of William Wilkie Collins, dated 22.3.1882
29. Death certificates of Marian Dawson, Rochford, Essex, 6.4.1955 and Harriet Constance Dawson, Southend-on-Sea, 6.7.1955
30. ALS to Nannie Wynne, 15.1.1886, in private hands
31. ALS Tillotson to W.C., 20.11.1885, in private hands
32. ALS to A. P. Watt, 29.10.1885, in private hands
33. ALS addressed 'Dear Madam', 24.9.1886, Parrish
34. *The Evil Genius*, MSs, p. 290, verso, Arents Collection, NYPL. This differs slightly from the published version
35. ALS to A. P. Watt, 18.6.1886, in private hands
36. ALS to William Winter, 30.7.1887, Parrish

37. ALS to A. P. Watt, 5.10.1889, Berg
38. ALS to A. P. Watt, 4.1.1887, in private hands
39. ALS to A. P. Watt, 25.1.1887, in private hands
40. ALS to A. P. Watt, 28.6.1887, in private hands
41. ALS to A. P. Watt, 29.7.1887, in private hands
42. ALS to Andrew Chatto, 26.4.1888, Parrish
43. 'Books Necessary for a Liberal Education', *Pall Mall Gazette*, 11.2.1886
44. ALS to Andrew Chatto, 19.6.1885, Parrish
45. *Pall Mall Gazette*, 18.11.1886
46. The *Universal Review*, 15.6.1888, p. 183
47. ALS to A. P. Watt, 17.10.1885, in private hands
48. Quoted in Leon Edel, *The Life of Henry James* (two-volume edition), Harmondsworth 1977, Vol. I, p. 761
49. ALS to William Winter, 30.7.1887, Parrish
50. ALS to Mrs Wynne, 22.12.1887, in private hands
51. ALS to Nannie Wynne, 8.2.1888, in private hands
52. ALS to Harry Quilter, 11.4.1888, Huntington, HM 32314
53. ALS to A. P. Watt, 4.1.1887, in private hands
54. ALS to Sebastian Schlesinger, 9.1.1889, Houghton
55. ALS to Mrs Wynne, 27.4.1888, in private hands
56. ALS to Andrew Chatto, 7.12.1888, Parrish
57. ALS to Andrew Chatto, 2.5.1889, Parrish
58. ALS to A. P. Watt, 3.3.1889, in private hands
59. ALS to A. P. Watt, 30.5.1888, in private hands
60. ALS to Harriet Bartley, 14.3.1888, Parrish

Chapter Twenty-four: The Journey's End (1889)

1. ALS to A. P. Watt, 23.1.1889, in private hands
2. MSs, Berg
3. ALS to A. P. Watt, 2.12.1887, in private hands
4. MSs of 'The Lord Harry' and *Blind Love*, HRC
5. *Blind Love*, Chap. 14, p. 95
6. ALS from Harriet Bartley to A. P. Watt, 30.6.1889, in private hands
7. ALS from Mrs Maxwell to Harriet Bartley, 'Tuesday evg.', [n.d.], HRC
8. ALS to Frederick Lehmann, 3.9.1889, Parrish
9. ALS Harriet Bartley to A. P. Watt, 4.10.1889, Berg
10. Walter Besant, Preface to *Blind Love*
11. ALS from George Redford to Harriet Bartley, 25.9.1889, Parrish
12. ALS to Sebastian Schlesinger, 7.9.1889, Houghton
13. Pencil note to F. C. Beard, Parrish
14. The *Daily Telegraph*, 24.9.1889, 'Summonses were then hurriedly despatched to relatives, and some of them were able to be present before the end came'
15. *Pall Mall Budget*, 3.10.1889, p. 5

16. ALS Henry Bartley to A. P. Watt, 11.10.1889, Berg. The report in the paper did not mention any specific bequests
17. For a detailed analysis of this will and its outcome, see Clarke, pp. 4–8, and Chap. 15, *passim*
18. ALS from Tauchnitz Junior to A. P. Watt, 9.10.1889, Berg
19. John Lehmann, op. cit., p. 184

Appendix A: Charles Collins' 'Secret Connection'

1. ALS 'Annat Lodge, Perth, Sunday Evening', [n.d. n.y.]. References to Millais' infant son in another section of the letter date it to the summer of 1856. Huntington Library, HH 389

Appendix B: Wilkie Collins' Travelling Desk

1. ALS Harriet Bartley to A. P. Watt, 8.7.1901, in private hands

Bibliography

Manuscript Sources

The original manuscripts of many of Wilkie Collins' works have survived. Most are now held in libraries in the United States, though the manuscript of *Basil* is in the British Library, and that of *No Name* is owned by the King's School, Canterbury. Many of Collins' letters are also in existence. An unknown number are still in private hands, and surface at auction from time to time; the important collection of letters to Anne le Poer Wynne and her mother, previously unknown, was sold at Sotheby's in 1989. The following libraries have significant collections of material by, and/or relating to, Wilkie Collins.

Bodleian Library, Oxford
Boston Public Library, Boston, Mass.
The British Library, London
University of Durham Library
Dickens House Museum
Folger Shakespeare Library, Washington, DC
City of Glasgow, Mitchell Library
Houghton Library, Harvard University, Cambridge, Mass.
Henry E. Huntington Library, San Marino, California
University of Illinois, Rare Book Room, Urbana, Ill.
University of Iowa Libraries, Iowa
King's School, Canterbury, Kent
New York Public Library, Arents and Berg Collections
The Pierpont Morgan Library, New York
Phillips Exeter Academy, New Hampshire
Princeton University Libraries, Morris L. Parrish and Robert H. Taylor Collections
The Free Library of Philadelphia Rare Book Department
The Harry Ransom Humanities Research Center, University of Texas at Austin
Victoria & Albert Museum, London, National Art Library

Wilkie Collins' Works

The Major Works: first English editions in order of publication in volume form

Memoirs of the Life of William Collins, Esq., R.A. (2 vols.), Longmans, London 1848
Antonina: or the Fall of Rome (3 vols.), Bentley, London 1850
Rambles Beyond Railways: or, Notes in Cornwall Taken A-Foot, Bentley, London 1851
Mr. Wray's Cash Box: or The Mask and the Mystery, Bentley, London 1852
Basil: A Story of Modern Life (3 vols.), Bentley, London 1852
Hide and Seek (3 vols.), Bentley, London 1854
After Dark (2 vols.), Smith, Elder, London 1856
The Dead Secret (2 vols.), Bradbury & Evans, London 1857
The Queen of Hearts (3 vols.), Hurst & Blackett, London 1859
The Woman in White (3 vols.), Sampson Low, London 1860
No Name (3 vols.), Sampson Low, London 1862
My Miscellanies (2 vols.), Sampson Low, London 1863
Armadale (2 vols), Smith, Elder, London 1866
The Moonstone (3 vols.), Tinsley, London 1868
Man and Wife (3 vols.), F. S. Ellis, London 1870
Poor Miss Finch (3 vols.), Bentley, London 1872
The New Magdalen (2 vols.), Bentley, London 1873
Miss or Mrs? And Other Stories in Outline, Bentley, London 1873
The Frozen Deep and Other Tales (2 vols.), Bentley, London 1874
The Law and The Lady (3 vols.), Chatto & Windus, London 1875
The Two Destinies (2 vols.), Chatto & Windus, London 1876
The Haunted Hotel (2 vols.), Chatto & Windus, London 1879
A Rogue's Life, Bentley, London 1879
The Fallen Leaves, First Series (3 vols.), Chatto & Windus, London 1879
Jezebel's Daughter (3 vols.), Chatto & Windus, London 1880
The Black Robe (3 vols.), Chatto & Windus, London 1881
Heart and Science (3 vols.), Chatto & Windus, London 1883
'I Say No': or The Love Letter Answered (3 vols.), Chatto & Windus, London 1884
The Evil Genius (3 vols.), Chatto & Windus, London 1886
The Guilty River, Arrowsmith, Bristol 1886
Little Novels (3 vols.), Chatto & Windus, London 1887
The Legacy of Cain (3 vols.), Chatto & Windus, London 1889
Blind Love (3 vols.) (completed by Walter Besant), Chatto & Windus, London 1890

Biographical Articles

'How I write my books: Related in a Letter to a Friend', *The Globe*, 26.11.1887, pp. 511–14

'Reminiscences of a Story-Teller', *Universal Review* 1 (May–August 1888), pp. 182–92

Collaborations with Charles Dickens

The Wreck of The Golden Mary, Household Words Christmas Extra Number, 1856

The Lazy Tour of Two Idle Apprentices, Household Words, 1857

The Perils of Certain English Prisoners, Household Words Christmas Extra Number, 1857

A Message from the Sea, All the Year Round Christmas Extra Number, 1860 (four sections of one of the five chapters are not by either Charles Dickens or Wilkie Collins)

No Thoroughfare, All the Year Round Christmas Extra Number, 1867

The Lazy Tour of Two Idle Apprentices, No Thoroughfare, The Perils of Certain English Prisoners, London 1890

Wilkie Collins also contributed to the following Christmas extra numbers of *Household Words* and *All the Year Round*, collaborations by several hands:

Seven Poor Travellers, Household Words (Christmas 1854), 'The Fourth Poor Traveller'

The Holly Tree Inn, Household Words (Christmas 1855), 'The Ostler'

A House to Let, Household Words (Christmas 1858), 'Over the Way', 'Trottle's Report' (and, with Charles Dickens, 'Let at Last')

The Haunted House, All the Year Round (Christmas 1859), 'The Ghost in the Cupboard Room'

Tom Tiddler's Ground, All the Year Round (Christmas 1861), 'Picking Up Waifs at Sea'

Collected Editions

There is no comprehensive standard edition of the works of Wilkie Collins. *Wilkie Collins's Novels: A New Edition* (also called the Library Edition, and in the 6s. version with a superior binding The Piccadilly Novels) was published by Chatto & Windus (29 vols.), London 1889–1908. *Wilkie Collins's Novels: Harper's Illustrated Library Edition* (17 vols.), New York and London 1873–1902, does not include all the novels. *The Works of Wilkie Collins* (30 vols.), published by Peter Fenelon Collier, New York 1900, has been reprinted by the AMS Press, New York 1970. None of these editions includes *Memoirs of the Life of William Collins* or *Mr. Wray's Cash Box*, and none includes all the short stories. Wilkie Collins' plays have not so far been collected. Though they were, with the exception of *The Red Vial*, printed during his lifetime, they were not put on sale to the general public, and copies are extremely rare. Robert Louis Brannan has published an annotated edition of the original version of *The Frozen Deep* (see *infra*).

Individual Works

Many editions of individual works by Wilkie Collins have been published, though until recently few have had authoritative texts or scholarly apparatus. Of those now out of print the following are notable.

The Moonstone, Oxford University Press, London 1928, Introduction by T. S. Eliot (original World's Classics edition)
J. M. Dent & Sons, London 1944. Introduction by Dorothy L. Sayers (Everyman's Library)
The Woman in White, Houghton Mifflin Co., Boston 1969. Introduction by Kathleen Tillotson, Preface by Gordon N. Ray, ed. Anthea Trodd (Riverside edition)

The following editions of works by Wilkie Collins are currently in print.

Armadale, Dover Publications, Inc., New York 1977. With original illustrations
World's Classics, ed. Catherine Peters, Oxford & New York 1989
Basil, Dover Publications, Inc., New York 1980
World's Classics, ed. Dorothy Goldman, Oxford & New York 1990
The Best Supernatural Stories of Wilkie Collins, ed. Peter Haining, Robert Hale, London 1990
The Biter Bit & Other Stories, Alan Sutton Publishing Ltd, 1982
Blind Love, Dover Publications Inc., New York 1986. With original illustrations
The Dead Secret, Dover Publications Inc., New York 1979
Alan Sutton Publishing Ltd, Gloucester 1986
The Guilty River, Alan Sutton Publishing Ltd, Gloucester 1991
The Haunted Hotel, Dover Publications Inc., New York, 1982
Alan Sutton Publishing Ltd, Gloucester 1990
Heart and Science, Alan Sutton Publishing Ltd, Gloucester 1990
Hide and Seek, Dover Publications Inc., New York 1981
World's Classics, ed. Catherine Peters, Oxford & New York 1993
The Law and the Lady, World's Classics, ed. Jenny Bourne Taylor, Oxford & New York 1992
Little Novels, Dover Publications Inc., New York 1977
Man and Wife, Dover Publications Inc., New York 1983
Alan Sutton Publishing Ltd, Gloucester 1990
The Moonstone, ed. J. I. M. Stewart, Penguin Books, Harmondsworth 1966
Pan Books, London 1967. Introduction by Anthony Burgess, notes by David Williams
World's Classics, ed. Anthea Trodd, Oxford & New York 1982
Everyman's Library, J. M. Dent, London 1985
Alan Sutton Publishing Ltd, Gloucester 1991
Alfred A. Knopf, ed. Catherine Peters, New York 1992
My Lady's Money, Alan Sutton Publishing Ltd, Gloucester 1990
My Miscellanies, Gregg International, London 1971

No Name, Dover Publications Inc., New York 1978
World's Classics, ed. Virginia Blain, Oxford & New York 1986
No Thoroughfare and Other Stories (with Charles Dickens), Alan Sutton Publishing, Gloucester 1990
Rambles Beyond Railways, Anthony Mott Ltd, London 1982. Introduced by J. C. Trewin
A Rogue's Life, Dover Publications Inc., New York 1986
Alan Sutton Publishing Ltd, Gloucester 1984
Tales of Terror and the Supernatural, Dover Publications Inc., New York 1972. Selected and introduced by Herbert Van Thal
The Woman in White, Everyman Library, J. M. Dent, London 1963
Alfred A. Knopf, ed. Nicholas Rance, New York 1991
World's Classics, ed. Harvey Peter Sucksmith, Oxford 1980
Penguin Books, ed. Julian Symons, Harmondsworth 1984
Isis Large Print Books, 1990
The Yellow Mask and Other Stories, Alan Sutton Publishing Ltd, Gloucester 1987

Bibliographies, Indices and Catalogues

Andrew, R. V., 'A Wilkie Collins Check-list', *English Studies in Africa* 3 (1960), pp. 79–98
Wilkie Collins: A Critical Survey of his Prose Fiction, with a bibliography, New York 1979
Ashley, R., 'Wilkie Collins', *Victorian Fiction: a Guide to Research*, ed. Lionel Stevenson, Cambridge, Mass., 1964
'Wilkie Collins' in *Victorian Fiction: A Second Guide to Research*, ed. George H. Ford, New York 1978
'The Wilkie Collins Collection', *Princeton University Library Chronicle* 18 (Winter 1956), pp. 81–84
Beetz, K., *Wilkie Collins: An Annotated Bibliography, 1889–1976*, New Jersey & London 1978
'Wilkie Collins Studies, 1972–1983', *Dickens Studies Annual* 13, 1984, pp. 333–55
Bennett, M. L., *Caxton Head Catalogue 198: Books from the Library of the late Wilkie Collins*, London February 1890
Brussel, I. R., 'Wilkie Collins' in *Anglo-American First Editions, 1826–1900* 1, London 1935
Cordasco, F. and Scott, K. W., *Wilkie Collins and Charles Reade: A Bibliography of Critical Notices and Studies*, Brooklyn 1949
Gasson, A., 'Wilkie Collins: A collector's and bibliographer's challenge', *The Private Library*, 3rd series 3:2 (Summer 1980), pp. 51–77
Lohrli, A., *Household Words: 1850–1859. Table of Contents, List of Contributors, and their Contributions*, Toronto 1973
Oppenlander, E. A., *Dickens' 'All the Year Round': Descriptive Index and Contributors List*, New York 1984
Parrish, M. R. with Miller, E. V., *Wilkie Collins and Charles Reade: First Editions Described with Notes*, London 1940, reprinted 1968
Puttick & Simpson, *Library of the Late Wilkie Collins Esq.*, London January 1890

Quayle, E., 'Charles Dickens and Wilkie Collins', *The Collector's Book of Victorian Fiction*, London 1940, pp. 42–50
Rosenbaum, B., and White, P., *Index of English Literary Manuscripts* 4 (1800–1900), London & New York 1982
Sadleir, M., 'Wilkie Collins, 1824–1889', *Excursions in Victorian Bibliography*, London 1922, reprinted 1974
XIX Century Fiction: A Bibliographical Record Based on His Own Collection (2 vols.), London 1951
Slater, M., *Catalogue of the Suzannet Charles Dickens Collection*, London 1975
Wolff, R. L., 'Wilkie Collins', *Nineteenth Century Fiction, a Bibliographical Catalogue* 1, New York & London 1981–86

Biographies

Ashley, R., *Wilkie Collins*, London 1952
Clarke, W. M., *The Secret Life of Wilkie Collins*, London 1988
Davis, N. P., *The Life of Wilkie Collins*, Urbana, Illinois, 1956
Ellis, S. M., *Wilkie Collins, Le Fanu, and Others*, London 1931
Robinson, K., *Wilkie Collins*, London 1951, 1974
Sayers, D. L., *Wilkie Collins: a Biographical and Critical Study* (unfinished), ed. E. R. Gregory, Toledo, Ohio, 1977
Wolzogen, E. von, *Wilkie Collins: Ein Biographisch-Kritischer Versuch*, Leipzig 1885

Memoirs and Reminiscences, etc.; criticism before 1900

Ainger, A., 'Mr. Dickens's Amateur Theatricals. A Reminiscence', *Macmillan's Magazine* 23 (January 1871), pp. 72–82
Anderson, M., *A Few Memories*, London 1896
Anon., 'Sensation Novels', *Westminster Review* 25 (July 1866), pp. 269–70
'Mr. Wilkie Collins', *Men and Women* 3:36 (5.2.1887), pp. 281–82
'Wilkie Collins', *Appleton's Journal of Popular Literature, Science and Art* (3.9.1870), pp. 278–81
Archer, F., *An Actor's Notebooks*, London 1912
Bancroft, S., *Empty Chairs*, London 1925
Bancroft, S. and M., *Mr. And Mrs. Bancroft on and off the Stage*, London 1888
The Bancrofts: Recollections of Sixty Years, London 1909
Beard, N., 'Some Recollections of Yesterday', *Temple Bar* 102 (July 1894), pp. 315–39
Berger, F., *97*, London 1931
Blanchard, E. L., *The Life and Reminiscences of E. L. Blanchard*, ed. Cecil Howard and Clement Scott, London 1891
Caine, H., 'Wilkie Collins. Personal Recollections', *The Globe*, 4.10.1889
My Story, London 1908
Coleman, J., *Players and Playwrights*, London 1888
Charles Reade as I knew Him, London 1904
Collins, P. (ed.), *Dickens: Interviews and Recollections* (2 vols.), London 1981

Compton-Rickett, A., 'Wilkie Collins', *The Bookman* (June 1912)
Cook, E. D., *Nights at the Play*, London 1883
Dépret, L., *Chez les Anglais*, Paris 1879
Dickens, C., *Letters of Charles Dickens to Wilkie Collins, 1851–1870, Selected by Georgina Hogarth*, ed. Laurence Hutton, London 1892
Mr. and Mrs. Charles Dickens: His Letters to Her, ed. Walter Dexter, London 1935
The Letters of Charles Dickens, ed. Walter Dexter (3 vols.), London 1938
The Letters of Charles Dickens, Vol. 6 (1849–52), ed. Graham Storey and K. J. Fielding, Oxford 1988
Dickens, C. Jr, 'Glimpses of Charles Dickens', *North American Review* 160 (1895)
Dickens, H. F., *The Recollections of Sir Henry Dickens, K.C.*, London 1934
Dolby, G., *Charles Dickens as I Knew Him*, London 1885
Downey, E., *Twenty Years Ago*, London 1905
Field, K., *Charles Albert Fechter*, Boston 1882
Fields, J. T., *Yesterdays with Authors*, Boston 1900
Fitzgerald, P., *Memoirs of an Author* (2 vols.), Guildford 1894
Some Memories of Charles Dickens and 'Household Words', London 1913
Forgues, E.-D., 'William Wilkie Collins', *Revue des Deux Mondes, 2e série* 12 (October–December 1855)
Forster, J., *The Life of Charles Dickens*, London 1873
Frith, W. P., *My Autobiography and Reminiscences* (3 vols.), London 1887–88
Hawthorne, J., *Shapes that Pass*, London 1928
Hodder, G., *Memories of my Time*, London 1870
Hollingshead, J., *My Lifetime*, London 1895
Holmes, O. W., 'A Toast to Wilkie Collins', *Poetical Works*, Cambridge, Mass., 1891
Horne, R. H., 'Bygone Celebrities: 1. The Guild of Literature and Art', *Gentleman's Magazine* 6 (1871), pp. 247–62
'Bygone Celebrities: 2. Mr. Nightingale's Diary', ibid., pp. 660–72
Hunt, W. H. (unsigned), 'Notes of the Life of Augustus L. Egg', The *Reader* 1 (1863), 2 (1863), 3 (1864)
PreRaphaelitism and the PreRaphaelite Brotherhood (2 vols.), London 1913
James, H., 'Mrs. Braddon', *Notes and Reviews*, Cambridge, Mass., 1921
Kitton, F. G., *Charles Dickens by Pen and Pencil*, London 1889
Knight, C., *Passages of a Working Life during half a century*, London 1864
Lang, A., 'Mr. Wilkie Collins's Novels', *Contemporary Review* 57 (January 1890), pp. 20–28
Lehmann, N., *Familiar Letters 1864–1867* (privately printed), 1892
Lehmann, R. C., *Memories of Half a Century*, London 1908
Charles Dickens as Editor, London 1912
Lehmann, R., *An Artist's Reminiscences*, London 1894
Men and Women of the Century, London 1896
MacCarthy, J., 'Novels with a Purpose', *Westminster Review* 26 (July 1864), p. 27

Macready, W. C., *Diaries*, ed. W. Toynbee (2 vols.), London 1912
Mansel, H., 'Sensation Novels', *Quarterly Review* 113 (1863) pp. 481–514
Marston, E., *After Work*, London 1904
Masson, D., 'Pre-Raphaelitism in Art and Literature', *British Quarterly Review* 16 (August 1852), pp. 197–220
Millais, J. G., *The Life and Letters of Sir John Everett Millais*, London 1899
Morley, H., *The Journal of a London Playgoer*, Leicester 1974. Introduced by Michael Booth
Nordhoff, C., *The Communistic Societies of the United States*, London 1875
Oliphant, M., 'Sensation Novels', *Blackwood's Magazine* 91 (May 1862), pp. 564–84
'Novels', *Blackwood's Magazine* 94 (August 1863), pp. 168–83
'Novels', *Blackwood's Magazine* 102 (September 1867), pp. 257–80
The Autobiography and Letters of Mrs. O. W. Oliphant, ed. Mrs H. Coghill, Edinburgh & London 1899
Payn, J., *Some Literary Recollections*, London 1884
The Backwater of Life: or Essays of a Literary Veteran, London 1899
Pemberton, T. E., *Charles Dickens and the Stage*, London 1888
Pollock, F., *Personal Remembrances of Sir Frederick Pollock*, London 1887
Priestley, E., Lady, *The Story of a Lifetime*, London 1904
Quilter, H., 'In Memoriam Amici', *Universal Review* 5 (October 1889), pp. 205–55
Preferences in Life, Literature and Art, London 1892
Reade, C. L. and Reade, C., *Charles Reade: a Memoir*, London 1887
Reeve, W., *From Life*, London 1892
'Recollections of Wilkie Collins', *Chamber's Journal* 9 (June 1906), pp. 458–61
Robinson, H. Crabb, *Diary*, ed. Thomas Sadler (2 vols.), London 1872
Sala, G. A., *Robson: a Sketch*, London 1864
Living London, London 1883
Things I have seen and People I have known, London 1894
Stirling, E., *Old Drury Lane* (2 vols.), London 1881
Story, A. T., *The Life of John Linnell*, London 1892
Swinburne, A. C., *Studies in Prose and Poetry*, London 1894
Tinsley, W., *Random Recollections of an Old Publisher* (2 vols.), London 1900
Trollope, A., *Autobiography*, London 1883
Walford, L. B., *Memories of Victorian London*, London 1912
Ward, H. M., *Mrs. E. M. Ward's Reminiscences*, ed. Elliott O'Donnell, London 1911
Memories of Ninety Years, ed. Isabel G. McAllister, London 1924
Ward, L., *Forty Years of 'Spy'*, London 1915
Watt, A. P. (ed.), *Letters to A. P. Watt*, London 1899
Whiting, L., *Kate Field, a Record*, London 1899
Williams, M., *Some London Theatres Past and Present*, London 1883
Winter, W., *Old Friends*, New York 1909

Yates, E., 'W. Wilkie Collins', *The Train* 3 (June 1857), pp. 352–57
Celebrities at Home, 3rd series, London 1879

Criticism and Background Studies after 1900

Adrian, A., *Georgina Hogarth and the Dickens Circle*, Oxford 1957
'A Note on the Dickens–Collins Friendship', *Huntington Library Quarterly* 16 (February 1953), pp. 211–13
Altick, R., *Victorian Studies in Scarlet*, London 1970
The English Common Reader: A Social History of the Mass Reading-Public, Chicago & London 1957
Ashley, R. P., 'Wilkie Collins' First Short Story', *More Books* 23 (March 1948), pp. 105–6
'Wilkie Collins and a Vermont Murder Trial', *New England Quarterly* 21 (September 1948), pp. 368–73
'Wilkie Collins Reconsidered', *Nineteenth Century Fiction* 4 (1949–50), pp. 265–73
'Wilkie Collins and the Detective Story', *Nineteenth Century Fiction* 6 (June 1951), pp. 265–73
'Wilkie Collins and the Dickensians', *The Dickensian* 49 (March 1953), pp. 59–65
'Wilkie Collins and the American Theater', *Nineteenth Century Fiction* 8 (March 1954), pp. 241–55
'Within My Experience', *Wilkie Collins Society Journal* 1 (1981), pp. 13–17
Auerbach, N., *Woman and the Demon*, Cambridge, Mass., 1982
Baker, W., 'Wilkie Collins, Dickens and *No Name*', *Dickens Studies Newsletter* 11:2 (June 1980), pp. 49–52
Barickman, R. S., MacDonald, and Stark, M., *Corrupt Relations: Dickens, Thackeray, Trollope, Wilkie Collins and the Victorian Sexual System*, New York 1982
Basch, F., *Relative Creatures: Victorian Women in Society and the Novel*, London 1974
Bedell, J. M., 'Wilkie Collins', *Twelve Englishmen of Mystery*, ed. Earl F. Bargainnier, Ohio 1984
Beetz, K., 'Wilkie Collins and *The Leader*', *Victorian Periodicals Review* 15:1 (Spring 1982), pp. 20–29
'Plots within Plots: Wilkie Collins's *After Dark*', *WCSJ* 4 (1984), pp. 31–34
Berridge, V., and Edwards, G., *Opium and the People: Opiate Use in Nineteenth Century England*, London 1981
Blain, V., 'The Naming of *No Name*', *WCSJ* 4 (1984), pp. 25–29
Blair, D., 'Wilkie Collins and the Crisis of Suspense', *Reading the Victorian Novel*, ed. Ian Gregor, London 1980
Boyle, T., *Black Swine in the Sewers of Hampstead*, London 1990
Brannan, R. L., *Under the Management of Mr. Charles Dickens: His Production of 'The Frozen Deep'*, Ithaca, NY, 1966

Brashear, B. A., 'Wilkie Collins: from novel to play', unpublished doctoral thesis, Case Western Reserve University, 1972
Bredsdorff, E., *Hans Andersen and Charles Dickens. A Friendship and its Dissolution, Anglistica* 7, Copenhagen 1956
Burgan, W. M., 'Masonic Symbolism in *The Moonstone* and *The Mystery of Edwin Drood*', *Dickens Studies Annual* 16 (1987), pp. 217–303
Burns, W., *Charles Reade: a Study in Victorian Authorship*, New York 1962
Calder, J., *Women and Marriage in Victorian Fiction*, London 1976
Caracciolo, P., 'Wilkie Collins's "Divine Comedy": the use of Dante in *The Woman in White*', *Nineteenth Century Fiction* 25, 4 (March 1971), pp. 383–404
Chesterton, G. K., *The Victorian Age in Literature*, New York 1913
Clareson, T. D., 'Wilkie Collins to Charles Reade: Some Unpublished Letters', *Victorian Essays, A Symposium*, ed. T. D. Clareson and W. D. Anderson, Ohio 1967
Clarke, W. M., 'The Mystery of Collins's Articles on Italian Art', *WCSJ* 4 (1984), pp. 19–24
'The Eternal Bachelor and his Schoolgirl in White', *The Sunday Times*, 19.11.1989
Coates, P., *The Double and the Other: Identity as Ideology in Post-Romantic Fiction*, London 1988
Colby, R., 'Harnessing Pegasus: Walter Besant, *The Author* and the Profession of Letters', *Victorian Periodicals Review* 23:3 (Fall 1990), pp. 111–20
Coleman, W. R., 'The University of Texas Collection of the Letters of Wilkie Collins, Victorian Novelist', unpublished doctoral dissertation, University of Texas at Austin, 1975
Collins, P., *Dickens and Crime*, London 1962
'The *All the Year Round* Letter Book', *Victorian Periodicals Newsletter* 10 (November 1970), pp. 23–29
Cross, N., *The Common Writer: Life in Nineteenth Century Grub Street*, Cambridge 1985
Curry, G., 'Charles Dickens and Annie Fields', *Huntington Library Quarterly* 51:1 (Winter 1988)
Daly, G., *The Pre-Raphaelites in Love*, London 1989
Davies, J. A., *John Forster: A Literary Life*, London 1983
Davis, E., *The Flint and the Flame: The Artistry of Charles Dickens*, London 1964
de la Mare, W., 'The Early Novels of Wilkie Collins', *The Eighteen Sixties*, ed. John Drinkwater, Cambridge 1932
Eliot, T. S., 'Wilkie Collins and Dickens', *Selected Essays*, London 1932
Elwin, M., *Charles Reade, A Biography*, London 1931
Victorian Wallflowers, London 1937
Exman, E., *The House of Harper: One Hundred and Fifty Years of Publishing*, New York & London 1967
Feltes, N. N., *Modes of Production of Victorian Novels*, Chicago 1986
Flower, D., 'Authors and Copyright in the Nineteenth Century, with Unpublished Letters from Wilkie Collins', *Book-Collector's Quarterly* 7 (July–September 1932), pp. 1–35

Gasson, A., '*The Woman in White*: a Chronological Study', *WCSJ* 2 (1982), pp. 5–14

'Wilkie Collins, Edmund Yates, and *The World*', *WCSJ* 4 (1984), pp. 5–17

Gettmann, R. A., *A Victorian Publisher: A Study of the Bentley Papers*, Cambridge 1960

Glynn, J., *Prince of Publishers: a Biography of George Smith*, London 1987

Griest, G. L., *Mudie's Circulating Library and the Victorian Novel*, Newton Abbot 1970

Hart, F. R., 'Wilkie Collins and the problem of Biographical Evidence', *Victorian Newsletter* 12 (Autumn 1957), pp. 18–21

Hartman, M., *Victorian Murderesses*, London 1977

Harvey, J. R., *Victorian Novelists and their Illustrators*, London 1970

Haworth-Booth, M., 'The Dawning of an Age, Chauncy Hare Townsend: Eyewitness', *The Golden Age of British Photography*, London 1984, pp. 11–21

Hawthorn, J., *Multiple Personality and the Disintegration of Literary Character*, London 1983

Hayter, A., *Opium and the Romantic Imagination*, London 1968

Hennelly, M. M., 'Twice-told Tales of Two Counts: *The Woman in White* and *Dracula*', *WCSJ* 2 (1982), pp. 15–31

Hepburn, J., *The Author's Empty Purse and the rise of the Literary Agent*, London 1968

Hill, T. W., 'The Enigma of Wilkie Collins', *Dickensian* 48 (March 1952), pp. 54–57

'The Late Wilkie Collins', ibid., pp. 114–16

Holman-Hunt, D., *My Grandfather, his Wives and Loves*, London 1969

Hopkins, T., 'The "Tauchnitz" Edition: The Story of a Popular Publisher', *Pall Mall Gazette* 25 (October 1901), pp. 197–208

House, H., *The Dickens World*, London 1961

Hughes, W., *The Maniac in the Cellar: Sensation Novels of the 1860s*, Princeton 1980

Huxley, L., *The House of Smith, Elder*, London 1923

Hyder, C. K., 'Wilkie Collins and The Woman in White', *PMLA* 54 (1939), pp. 297–303

'Wilkie Collins in America', *Studies in English* 6:4, Lawrence, Kansas, 1940

James, L., 'The Trouble with Betsy: periodicals and the common reader in nineteenth-century England', *The Victorian Periodical Press: Samplings and Soundings*, ed. J. Shattock and M. Wolff, Leicester 1982

Jenkins, E., *Six Criminal Women*, London 1949

Johnson, E., *Charles Dickens: His Tragedy and Triumph* (2 vols.), London 1953

Kaplan, F., *Dickens: A Biography*, London 1988

Keating, P., *The Haunted Study: A Social History of the English Novel 1875–1914*, London 1989

Keppler, C. F., *The Literature of the Second Self*, Tucson 1972

Knoepflmacher, U. C., 'The Counterworld of Victorian fiction and *The Woman in White*', *The Worlds of Victorian Fiction*, ed. J. Buckley, Cambridge, Mass., 1975

Lambert, G., *The Dangerous Edge*, London 1975

Lawrence, K., 'The Religion of Wilkie Collins: Three Unpublished Letters', *Huntington Library Quarterly* 52:3 (Summer 1989), pp. 389–402

Lawson, L. A., 'Wilkie Collins and *The Moonstone*', *American Imago* 20:1 (Spring 1963), pp. 61–79

Leavy, B. F., 'The Woman in White', *Dickens Studies Annual* 10 (1982), pp. 90–141

Lehmann, J., *Ancestors and Friends*, London 1962

Ley, J. W. T., 'The "Harbitrary Gent": John Forster's friendships', *Dickensian* 9 (1913), pp. 12–15

The Dickens Circle: A Narrative of the Novelist's Friendships, London 1919

'Wilkie Collins's Influence upon Dickens', *Dickensian* 20 (1924), pp. 65–69

Lohrli, A., 'Wilkie Collins and *Household Words*', *Victorian Periodicals Review* 15:3 (Fall 1982), pp. 118–19

'Andersen, Dickens, and Herr Von Muffe', *Dickensian* 62 (January 1966), p. 348

Lonoff, S., 'Charles Dickens and Wilkie Collins', *Nineteenth Century Fiction* 35 (September 1980), pp. 150–70

Wilkie Collins and his Victorian Readers: a Study in the Rhetoric of Authorship, New York 1982

Lottes, W., 'The Lure of Romish Art: Reflections of Religious Controversy in Nineteenth Century Art', *Journal of Pre-Raphaelite and Aesthetic Studies* 1:1 (Part 2) (Spring 1988), pp. 45–61

Lutyens, M., *Millais and the Ruskins*, London 1967

MacEachen, D. B., 'Wilkie Collins and British Law', *Nineteenth Century Fiction* 5 (September 1950), pp. 121–39

'Wilkie Collins' *Heart and Science* and the Vivisection controversy', *Victorian Newsletter* 29 (Spring 1966), pp. 22–25

McGregor, O. R., *Divorce in England*, London 1957

Marcus, S., *The Other Victorians*, London 1966

Marshall, W. H., *Wilkie Collins*, New York 1970

Meckier, J., *Hidden Rivalries in Victorian Fiction: Dickens, Realism, and Revaluation*, Lexington 1987

'Wilkie Collins' *The Woman in White:* Providence against the evils of propriety', *Journal of British Studies* 22:1 (Fall 1982), pp. 104–26

Meisel, M., 'Fraternity and anxiety: Charles Allston Collins and the Electric Telegraph', *Notebooks in Cultural Analysis* 2 (1985), pp. 112–65

Miller, D. A., 'Cage aux folles: Sensation and Gender in Wilkie Collins's *The Woman in White*', *The Nineteenth Century British Novel*, ed. Jeremy Hawthorn, London 1986

'From "roman policier" to "roman-police": Wilkie Collins's *The Moonstone*', *Novel* 13 (Winter 1980), pp. 153–70

Milley, H. J. W., 'Wilkie Collins', *Times Literary Supplement*, 20.3.1937, p. 222

'*The Eustace Diamonds* and *The Moonstone*', *Studies in Philology* 36 (October 1939), pp. 651–63
'Wilkie Collins and *A Tale of Two Cities*', *Modern Language Review* 34 (1939), pp. 525–34
Monod, S., 'Charles Dickens et Philoclès Régnier', *Études Anglaises* 11:3 (July–September 1958), pp. 210–25
Munby, F. A., and Norrie, I., *Publishing and Bookselling*, London 1974
Nadel, I. B., 'Science and *The Moonstone*', *Dickens Studies Annual* 11 (1983), pp. 239–59
Nelson, H. S., 'Dickens' Plots: The Ways of Providence or the influence of Collins?', *Victorian Newsletter* 19 (Spring 1961), pp. 11–14
Nichol, A., *A History of English Drama*, Vols. 4 & 5, Cambridge 1955, 1959
Nisbet, A., *Dickens and Ellen Ternan*, Berkeley 1952
Nowell-Smith, S., *The House of Cassell 1848–1958*, London 1958
' "Firma Tauchnitz", 1837–1900', *Book Collector* 15 (1966), p. 434
International Copyright Law and the Publisher in the Age of Victoria, London 1968
Nunn, P. G., *Victorian Women Artists*, London 1987
Olsen, D. J., *The Growth of Victorian London*, London 1976
O'Neill, P., *Wilkie Collins: Women, Property and Propriety*, London 1988
Oppé, A. P., *Early Victorian England: Vol. 2, Art*, Oxford 1934
Ousby, I., 'Wilkie Collins, *The Moonstone* and the Constance Kent case', *Notes and Queries* 21:1 (January 1974), p. 25
'Wilkie Collins and other Sensation Novelists', *Bloodhounds of Heaven*, Cambridge, Mass., 1976
Page, N. (ed.), *Wilkie Collins: The Critical Heritage*, London 1974
Patten, R. L., *Charles Dickens and his Publishers*, Oxford 1978
Pearson, H., *Dickens: His Character, Comedy and Career*, London 1949
Peters, C., 'Frances Elliot née Dickinson: Entries in the *Wellesley Index*', *Victorian Periodicals Review* 23:2 (Summer 1990), pp. 65–66
Phillips, W., *Dickens, Reade, and Collins, Sensation Novelists*, New York 1919
Plant, M., *The English Book Trade: An Economic History of the making and sale of Books*, New York 1939
Purton, V., 'Dickens and Bulwer Lytton: the Dandy Reclaimed?', *Dickensian* 74:1 (January 1978), pp. 25–29
'Dickens and Collins: the Rape of the Sentimental Heroine', *Ariel* 16:1 (1985), pp. 77–89
Quayle, E., *The Collector's Book of Detective Fiction*, London 1972
Rance, N., ' "A Terribly Strange Bed": Self-Subverting Gothic', *WCSJ* 7 (1987), pp. 5–12
Reed, J. R., 'English Imperialism and the Unacknowledged Crime of *The Moonstone*', *Clio* 2 (1973), pp. 281–90
Renton, R., *John Forster and His Friendships*, London 1912
Roughead, W., *Bad Companions*, Edinburgh 1930
Rubinstein, H., 'A. P. Watt: the First Hundred Years', *The Bookseller*, 3.5.1975, pp. 2354–358

Rycroft, C., 'The Analysis of a Detective Story', *Imagination and Reality: Psychoanalytical Essays 1951–1961*, London 1968, pp. 114–28
Sayers, D. L., Introduction to *The Omnibus of Crime*, London 1929
Sehlbach, H., *Untersuchungen über die Romanskünst von Wilkie Collins*, Jena 1931
Schmidt, B. Q., 'Novelists, Publishers and Fiction in Middle-class Magazines: 1860–1880', *Victorian Periodicals Review* 17:4 (Winter 1984), pp. 142–53
Schroeder, N., '*Armadale*: "A Book that is Daring Enough to Tell the Truth" ', *WCSJ* 3 (1983), pp. 5–19
Scull, A., *Museums of Madness: The Social Organization of Insanity in Nineteenth Century England*, London 1979
Shore, W. T., *Charles Dickens and his Friends*, London 1909
Showalter, E., 'Family Secrets and Domestic Subversion: Rebellion in the Novels of the 1860s', *The Victorian Family: Structures and Stresses*, ed. A. Wohl, London 1978, pp. 103–12
Slater, M., *Dickens and Women*, London 1983
Smith, M., ' "Everything to My Wife": The Inheritance Theme in *The Moonstone* and *Sense and Sensibility*', *WCSJ* 7 (1987), pp. 13–18
Storey, G., *Dickens and Daughter*, London 1939
Stephens, J. R., *The Censorship of English Drama 1824–1901*, Cambridge & London 1980
Sutherland, J., *Victorian Novelists and Publishers*, London & Chicago 1976
Symons, J., *Bloody Murder: from the Detective Story to the Crime Novel*, London 1972
Taylor, J. B., *In the Secret Theatre of Home: Wilkie Collins, Sensation Narrative, & Nineteenth Century Psychology*, London & New York 1988
Terry, R. C., *Victorian Popular Fiction 1860–1880*, London 1983
Trodd, A., *Domestic Crime in the Victorian Novel*, London 1989
Tomalin, C., *The Invisible Woman: the story of Nelly Ternan and Charles Dickens*, London 1990
Trudgill, E., *Madonnas and Magdalens: The Origins and Development of Victorian Sexual Attitudes*, London 1976
Tymms, R., *Doubles in Literary Psychology*, Cambridge 1949
Tyrrell, T. W., 'The Play which suggested *A Tale of Two Cities*', *Notes and Queries* 152 (January 1927), p. 12
Tytler, G., *Physiognomy in the European Novel*, Princeton 1982
Vann, J. D., *Victorian Novels in Serial*, New York 1985
Warner, O., *Chatto and Windus*, London 1973
Watt, G., *The Fallen Woman in the Nineteenth-Century English Novel*, London 1984

INDEX

Note: Works by Wilkie Collins appear directly under title; works by others appear under author's name